THE NEW TESTAMENT
IN MODERN ENGLISH

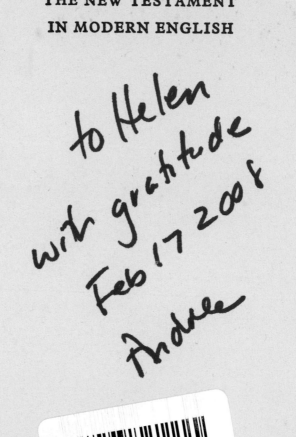

to Helen
with gratitude
Feb 17 2008
Andrew

to Helen
with gratitude
Feb 17 2001
[illegible]

THE NEW TESTAMENT in Modern English

J. B. PHILLIPS

Revised Edition

A TOUCHSTONE BOOK
Published by Simon & Schuster
New York London Toronto Sydney

TOUCHSTONE
Rockefeller Center
1230 Avenue of the Americas
New York, NY 10020

First Paperback Edition 1972
First Touchstone Edition 1995

Manufactured in the United States of America

11 13 15 17 19 20 18 16 14 12

Library of Congress catalog card number: 72-93470
ISBN-13: 978-0-684-82633-2
ISBN-10: 0-684-82633-X

I DEDICATE
THIS TRANSLATION TO
VERA
MY WIFE AND
FINEST CRITIC

INTRODUCTION TO THIS NEW EDITION

I would like to make it clear to my readers that this new edition is in fact a new translation from the latest and best Greek text published by the United Bible Societies in 1966 and recognised by scholars of all denominations as the best source available. Naturally some considerable parts of the former translation reappear, but that is only because after considerable thought I did not think I could improve upon their wording. However, the reader may rest assured that every single Greek word was read and considered. This rather exacting task took me more than two years.

I fear that a little personal history must be part of the explanation of why I have now been able to start completely afresh. I began the work of translation as long ago as 1941, and the work was undertaken primarily for the benefit of my Youth Club, and members of my congregation, in a much-bombed parish in S.E. London. I had almost no tools to work with apart from my own Greek Testament and no friends who could help me in this particular field. I felt then that since much of the New Testament was written to Christians in danger, it should be particularly appropriate for us who, for many months, lived in a different, but no less real, danger. I began with the Epistles since most of my Christian members had at least a nodding acquaintance with the Gospels, but regarded the Epistles as obscure and difficult and therefore largely unread. In those days of danger and emergency I was not over-concerned with minute accuracy, I wanted above all to convey the vitality and radiant faith as well as the courage of the early Church. The attempt succeeded and, as I have mentioned in the Translator's Preface to earlier editions, the strong encouragement of C. S. Lewis led me to continue the task. The war was over and I had been moved to a large and scattered country parish in Surrey before the translation of the Epistles was completed. I revised the typescript as well as I could with many other demands on my hands, and after many rejections succeeded in finding a publisher in the late Mr. Geoffrey Bles. The work, under the title *Letters to Young Churches*, appeared in 1947.

Within five years and not without trepidation I had completed *The Gospels in Modern English,* and this was similarly well received. I then began the Acts, which I renamed *The Young Church in Action.* But before I could complete this I realised that the work of translation plus the many duties of a large parish were proving too formidable a task for me. I therefore purchased a small house in a quiet part of Dorset where I could continue my translation and other writing, and attend properly to the huge volume of correspondence that was beginning to arrive from all over the English-speaking world. Thus it happened that *The Young Church in Action* and *The Book of Revelation* were both published after I had left parish work.

In 1958 the books were collected together in one volume and published under the title of *The New Testament in Modern English.* During the years from 1947 to 1958 I had been able to make some minor alterations and to correct some errors, many of which were pointed out to me by kind friends. The edition of my complete translation issued in 1960 incorporated a large number of small but significant emendations.

Now, more than ten years later, I offer this translation as a wholly new book. Having by this time done much collateral reading and learned more of the usages of the N.T. Greek, I felt that now, faced with a completely clean sheet, as it were, I could do a better job. Quite apart from my own feelings there were good reasons for tackling this rather daunting task. The most important by far was the fact, which perhaps I had been slow to grasp, that "Phillips" was being used as an authoritative version by Bible Study Groups in various parts of the world. I still feel that the most important "object of the exercise" is communication. I see it as my job as one who knows Greek pretty well and ordinary English very well to convey the living quality of the N.T. documents. I want above all to create in my readers the same emotions as the original writings evoked nearly 2,000 years ago. This passion of mine for communication, for I can hardly call it less, has led me sometimes into paraphrase and sometimes to interpolate clarifying remarks which are certainly not in the Greek. But being now regarded as "an authority", I felt I must curb my youthful enthusiasms and keep as close as I possibly could to the Greek text. Thus most of my conversationally-worded additions in the Letters of Paul had to go. Carried away sometimes by the intensity of his argument or by his passion for the welfare of his new converts I found I had inserted things like, "as I am sure you realise" or "you must know by now" and many extra words which do not occur in the Greek text at all. I must say that it was not without some pangs of regret that I deleted nearly all of them!

There was a further reason for making the translation not merely readable but as accurate as I could make it. It has been proposed that a Commentary on the Phillips translation should be undertaken. I felt it essential that the scholars who would contribute to such work should have before them the best translation of which I am capable. I certainly did not want them to waste time in pointing out errors which I had in fact by now corrected!

The last, but not least important, reason for making a fresh translation was to check the English itself. It must be current and easily understood, and I must confess that I thought that the twenty-five years since the publication of *Letters to Young Churches* might have seriously "dated" the English I used then. With the help of my wife, several friends, including some critical young people, we scrutinised the English very carefully. Rather to my surprise only a few alterations were necessary, and this showed me that the ordinary English which we use in communication changes far more slowly than I had imagined. I knew, however, that slang and colloquialisms change rapidly, but since I had used few of these there was not much to alter. A couple of examples may illustrate my meaning. The "little tin gods" of I Peter 5, *3* (an expression no longer current) have become "dictators". The colloquial use of the word "plutocrats" of James 5, *1* has been changed to "men of affluence".

The essential principles of translation

There seem to be three necessary tests which any work of transference from one language to another must pass before it can be classed as good translation. The first is simply that it must not sound like a translation at all. If it is skilfully done, and we are not previously informed, we should be quite unaware that it *is* a translation, even though the work we are reading is far distant from us in both time and place. That is a first, and indeed fundamental test, but it is not by itself sufficient. For the translator himself may be a skilful writer, and although he may have conveyed the essential meaning, characterisation and plot of the original author, he may have so strong a style of his own that he completely changes that of the original author. The example of this kind of translation which springs most readily to my mind is Fitzgerald's *Rubáiyát of Omar Khayyám.* I would therefore make this the second test: that a translator does his work with the least possible obtrusion of his own personality. The third and final test which a good translator should be able to pass is that of being able to produce in the hearts and minds of his readers an effect equivalent to that produced by the author upon his original readers. Of course no translator living would claim that his work successfully achieved these three ideals. But he must bear them in mind constantly as principles for his guidance.

Translation as interpretation

As I have frequently said, a translator is not a commentator. He is usually well aware of the different connotations which a certain passage may bear, but unless his work is to be cluttered with footnotes he is bound, after careful consideration, to set down what is the most likely meaning. Occasionally one is driven into what appears to be a paraphrase, simply because a literal translation of the original Greek would prove unintelligible. But where this has proved necessary I have always been careful to avoid giving any slant or flavour which is purely of my own making. That is why I have been reluctant to accept the suggestion that my translation is "interpretation"! If the word interpretation is used in a bad sense, that is, if it means that a work is tendentious, or that there has been a manipulation of the words of New Testament Scripture to fit some private point of view, then I would still strongly repudiate the charge! But "interpretation" can also mean transmitting meaning from one language to another, and skilled interpreters in world affairs do not intentionally inject any meaning of their own. In this sense I gladly accept the word interpretation to describe my work. For, as I see it, the translator's function is to understand as fully and deeply as possible what the New Testament writers had to say and then, after a process of what might be called reflective digestion, to write it down in the language of the people today. And here I must say that it is essential for the interpreter to know the language of both parties. He may be a first-class scholar in New Testament Greek and know the significance of every traditional crux, and yet be abysmally ignorant of how his contemporaries outside his scholastic world are thinking and feeling.

Words and their context

After reading a large number of commentaries I have a feeling that some scholars, at least, have lived so close to the Greek Text that they have lost their sense of proportion. I doubt very much whether the New Testament writers were as subtle or as self-conscious as some commentators would make them appear. For the most part I am convinced that they had no idea that they were writing Holy Scripture. They would be, or indeed perhaps are, amazed to learn what meanings are sometimes read back into their simple utterances! Paul, for instance, writing in haste and urgency to some of his wayward and difficult Christians, was not tremendously concerned about dotting the "i's" and crossing the "t's" of his message. I doubt very much whether he was even concerned about being completely consistent with what he had already written. Consequently, it seems to me quite beside the point to study his writings microscopically, as it were, and deduce hidden meanings of which almost certainly he was unaware. His letters are alive, and they are moving—in both senses of that word—and their meaning can no more be appreciated by cold minute examination than can the beauty of a bird's flight be appreciated by dissection after its death. We have to take these living New Testament documents in their context, a context of supreme urgency and often of acute danger. But a word is modified very considerably by the context in which it appears, and where a translator fails to realise this, we are not far away from the use of a computer! The translators of the Authorised Version were certainly not unaware of this modification, even though they had an extreme reverence for the actual words of Holy Writ. Three hundred years ago they did not hesitate to translate the Greek word EKBALLO by such varying expressions as *put out*, *drive forth*, *bring forth*, *send out*, *tear out*, *take out*, *leave out*, *cast out*, etc., basing their decision on the context. And as a striking example of their translational freedom, in Matthew 27,*44* we read that the thieves who were crucified with Jesus "cast the same in his teeth", where the Greek words mean simply, "abused him".

The translator must be flexible

I feel strongly that a translator, although he must make himself as familiar as possible with New Testament Greek usage, must steadfastly refuse to be driven by the bogey of consistency. He must be guided both by the context in which a word appears, and by the sensibilities of modern English readers. In the story of the raising of Lazarus, for example, Martha's objection to opening the grave would be natural enough to an Eastern mind. But to put into her lips the words, "by this time he's stinking", would sound to Western ears unpleasantly out of key with the rest of that moving story. Similarly, we know that the early Christians greeted one another with "an holy kiss". Yet to introduce such an expression into a modern English translation immediately reveals the gulf between the early Christians and ourselves, the very thing which I as a translator am trying to bridge. Again, it is perfectly true, if we are to translate literally, that Jesus said, "Blessed are the beggars in spirit". In an Eastern land, where the disparity between rich and poor was very great, beggars were common. But it is to my mind extremely doubtful whether the word "beggar" in our Welfare State, or indeed in most English-speaking countries, conjures up the mental image which Jesus intended to convey to his hearers. It was not the social misfit or the work-shy, but the one who was spiritually speaking obviously and consciously in need whom Jesus describes as "blessed" or "happy".

The use of insight and sympathy

I have found imaginative sympathy, not so much with words as with people, to be essential. If it is not presumptuous to say so, I attempted, as far as I could, to think myself into the heart and mind of Paul, for example, or of Mark or of John the Divine. Then I tried further to imagine myself as each of the New Testament authors writing his particular message for the people of today. No one could succeed in doing this superlatively well, if only because of the scantiness of our knowledge of the first century A.D. But this has been my ideal, and that is why consistency and meticulous accuracy have sometimes both been sacrificed in the attempt to transmit freshness and life across the centuries. By the use of cross-headings, solid and rather forbidding slabs of continuous writing (such as appear in the Greek Text) are made more digestible to the modern reader, whose reading habits have already been "conditioned" by the comparatively recent usage of clear punctuation, intelligent paragraphing and good printer's type.

Acknowledgments

It would be ungracious to forget the very many people who have made the work possible. I think first of the textual critics, whose patient work gives us a text to work from which is as near as possible to that of the original writers. I am most grateful to them, as all translators must be, and I should also like to express my thanks to the numerous commentators whose works I have consulted. As will be gathered from what I have said above, I have not always agreed with them, but they have informed my mind and stimulated my thoughts many times. Again, although it would be impossible to supply a full list, I am extremely grateful to the many people—including first-rate scholars, hard-working parish priests, busy ministers, doctors, scientists, missionaries, educationists, elderly saints and lively young people—who have, over the years, written me hundreds of letters, the great majority of which were constructive and useful. Their help has been invaluable.

I find myself therefore indebted to all kinds of people of different denominations. The assurance has grown within me that here in the New Testament, at the very heart and core of our Faith, Christians are far more at one than their outward divisions would imply. From this unquestionable evidence of fundamental unity I derive not only great comfort but a great hope for the future.

J. B. PHILLIPS

SWANAGE, DORSET
1972

CONTENTS

MAPS

THE GOSPELS

The Gospel of Matthew

Early tradition ascribed this Gospel to the apostle Matthew, but scholars nowadays almost all reject this view.

The author, whom we still can conveniently call Matthew, has plainly drawn on the mysterious "Q", which may have been a collection of oral traditions. He has used Mark's Gospel freely, though he has rearranged the order of events and has in several instances used different words for what is plainly the same story. The style is lucid, calm and "tidy". Matthew writes with a certain judiciousness as though he himself had carefully digested his material and is convinced not only of its truth but of the divine pattern that lies behind the historic facts.

Matthew is quite plainly a Jew who has been convinced of Jesus' messianic claim. It is probable that he is writing primarily for fellow Jews. The frequent references to the Old Testament, the sense that Jesus' primary mission is to the "lost sheep" of the house of Israel and the implication that the Church, founded on the rock of Peter's faith, is the new Israel, all bear the marks of a converted Jew writing for fellow Jews. He attempts to convey a logical conviction that the new teaching was not only prophesied in the old but does in fact supersede it in the divine plan.

If Matthew wrote, as is now generally supposed, somewhere between the years 85 and 90, this Gospel's value as a Christian document is enormous. It is, so to speak, a second generation view of Jesus Christ the Son of God and the Son of Man. It is being written at that distance in time from the great event where sober reflection and sturdy conviction can perhaps give a better balanced portrait of God's unique revelation of himself than could be given by those who were so close to the light that they were partly dazzled by it.

CHAPTER 1

The ancestry of Jesus Christ

THIS is the record of the ancestry of Jesus Christ who was the descendant of both David and Abraham:

Abraham was the father of Isaac, who was the father of Jacob, who was the father of Judah and his brothers, who was the father of Perez and Zerah (whose mother was Tamar). Perez was the father of Hezron, who was the father of Ram, who was the father of Amminadab, who was the father of Nahshon, who was the father of Salmon, who was the father of Boaz (whose mother was Rahab). Boaz was the father of Obed (whose mother was Ruth), and Obed was the father of Jesse, who was the father of King David, who was the father of Solomon (whose mother had been Uriah's wife). Solomon was the father of Rehoboam, who was the father of Abijah, who was the father of Asa, who was the father of Jehoshaphat, who was the father of Joram, who was the father of Uzziah, who was the father of Jotham, who was the father of Ahaz, who was the father of Hezekiah, who was the father of Manasseh, who was the father of Amon, who was the father of Josiah, who was the father of Jechoniah and his brothers, at the time of the deportation to Babylon.

After the Babylonian exile Jechoniah was the father of Shealtiel, who was the father of Zerubbabel, who was the father of Abiud, who was the father of Eliakim, who was the father of Azor, who was the father of Sadoc, who was the father of Achim, who was the father of Eliud, who was the father of Eleazar, who was the father of Matthan, who was the father of Jacob, who was the father of Joseph, who was the husband of Mary, who gave birth to Jesus called Christ.

The genealogy of Jesus Christ may thus be traced for fourteen generations from Abraham to David, fourteen from David to the deportation to Babylon, and fourteen more from the deportation to Christ.

His birth in human history

The birth of Jesus Christ happened like this. When Mary was engaged to Joseph, before their marriage, she was discovered to be pregnant—by the Holy Spirit. Whereupon Joseph, her future husband, who was a good man and did not want to see her disgraced, planned to break off the engagement quietly. But while he was turning the matter over in his mind an angel of the Lord appeared to him in a dream and said, "Joseph, son of David, do not be afraid to take Mary as your wife! What she has conceived is conceived through the Holy Spirit, and she will give birth to a son, whom you will call Jesus ('the Saviour') for it is he who will save his people from their sins."

All this happened to fulfil what the Lord had said through the prophet—

> Behold, the virgin shall be with child, and shall bring forth a son, and they shall call his name Immanuel. ("Immanuel" means "God with us.")

When Joseph woke up he did what the angel had told him. He married Mary, but had no intercourse with her until she had given birth to a son. Then he gave him the name Jesus.

CHAPTER 2

Herod, suspicious of the new-born king, takes vindictive precautions

JESUS was born in Bethlehem, in Judaea, in the days when Herod was king of the province. After his birth there came from the east a party of astrologers making for Jerusalem and enquiring as they went, "Where is the child born to be king of the Jews? For we saw his star in the east and we have come to pay homage to him."

When King Herod heard about this he was deeply perturbed, as indeed were all the other people living in Jerusalem. So he summoned all the Jewish chief priests and scribes* together and asked them where "Christ" should be born. Their reply was: "In Bethlehem, in Judaea, for this is what the prophet wrote about the matter—

> And thou Bethlehem, land of Judah,
> Art in no wise least among the princes of Judah:
> For out of thee shall come forth a governor,
> Which shall be shepherd of my people Israel."

Then Herod invited the wise men to meet him privately and found out from them the exact time when the star appeared. Then he sent them off to Bethlehem saying, "When you get there, search for this little child with the utmost care. And when you have found him report back to me—so that I may go and worship him too."

* See note 1, page 551.

The wise men listened to the king and then went on their way, to Bethlehem. And now the star, which they had seen in the east, went in front of them until at last it shone immediately above the place where the little child lay. The sight of the star filled them with indescribable joy.

So they went into the house and saw the little child with his mother Mary. And they fell on their knees and worshipped him. Then they opened their treasures and presented him with gifts—gold, incense and myrrh.

Then, since they were warned in a dream not to return to Herod, they went back to their own country by a different route.

But after they had gone the angel of the Lord appeared to Joseph in a dream and said, "Get up now, take the little child and his mother and escape to Egypt. Stay there until I tell you. For Herod means to seek out the child and kill him."

So Joseph got up, and taking the child and his mother with him set off for Egypt that same night, where he remained until Herod's death.

This again is a fulfilment of the Lord's word spoken through the prophet—

Out of Egypt did I call my son.

When Herod saw that he had been fooled by the wise men he was furiously angry. He issued orders for the execution of all male children of two years and under in Bethlehem and the surrounding district—basing his calculation on his careful questioning of the wise men.

Then Jeremiah's prophecy was fulfilled:

A voice was heard in Ramah,
Weeping and great mourning,
Rachel weeping for her children;
And she would not be comforted, because they are not.

Jesus is brought to Nazareth

But after Herod's death an angel of the Lord appeared in a dream to Joseph in Egypt and said, "Now get up and take the infant and his mother with you and go into the land of Israel. For those who sought the child's life are dead."

So Joseph got up and took the little child and his mother with him and journeyed towards the land of Israel. But when he heard that Archelaus was now reigning as king of Judaea in the place of his father Herod, he was afraid to enter the country. Then he received warning in a dream to turn aside into the district of Galilee and came to live in a small town called Nazareth—thus fulfilling the old prophecy, that he should be called a Nazarene.

CHAPTER 3

The prophesied "Elijah": John the Baptist

In due course John the Baptist arrived, preaching in the Judaean desert: "You must change your hearts and minds—for the kingdom of Heaven has arrived!"

This was the man whom the prophet Isaiah spoke about in the words:

> The voice of one crying in the wilderness,
> Make ye ready the way of the Lord,
> Make his paths straight.

John wore clothes of camel-hair with a leather belt round his waist, and lived on locusts and wild honey. The people of Jerusalem and of all Judaea and the Jordan district flocked to him, and were baptised by him in the river Jordan, publicly confessing their sins.

But when he saw many Pharisees and Sadducees* coming for baptism he said: "Who warned you, you serpent's brood, to escape from the wrath to come? Go and do something to show that your hearts are really changed. Don't suppose that you can say to yourselves, 'We are Abraham's children', for I tell you that God could produce children of Abraham out of these stones!

"The axe already lies at the root of the tree, and the tree that fails to produce good fruit will be cut down and thrown into the fire. It is true that I baptise you with water as a sign of your repentance, but the one who follows me is far stronger than I am—indeed, I am not fit to carry his shoes. He will baptise you with the fire of the Holy Spirit. He comes all ready to separate the wheat from the chaff and very thoroughly will he clear his threshing-floor—the wheat he will collect into the granary and the chaff he will burn with a fire that can never be put out."

* See note 1, page 551.

John baptises Jesus

Then Jesus came from Galilee to the Jordan to be baptised by John. But John tried to prevent him. "I need you to baptise *me*", he said. "Surely *you* do not come to me?" But Jesus replied, "It is right for us to meet all the Law's demands—let it be so now."

Then John agreed to baptise him. Jesus came straight out of the water afterwards, and suddenly the heavens opened and he saw the Spirit of God coming down like a dove and resting upon him. And a voice came out of Heaven saying, "This is my dearly-loved Son, in whom I am well pleased."

CHAPTER 4

Jesus faces temptation alone in the desert

THEN Jesus was led by the Spirit up into the desert, to be tempted by the devil. After a fast of forty days and nights he was very hungry.

"If you are the Son of God," said the tempter, coming to him, "tell these stones to turn into loaves."

Jesus answered, "The scripture says 'Man shall not live by bread alone, but by every word that proceedeth out of the mouth of God'."

Then the devil took him to the holy city, and set him on the highest pinnacle of the Temple. "If you are the Son of God," he said, "throw yourself down. For the scripture says—

> He shall give his angels charge concerning thee:
> And on their hands they shall bear thee up,
> Lest haply thou dash thy foot against a stone."

"Yes," retorted Jesus, "and the scripture also says 'Thou shalt not tempt the Lord thy God'."

Once again the devil took him to a very high mountain, and from there showed him all the kingdoms of the world and their magnificence. "Everything there I will give you," he said to him, "if you will fall down and worship me."

"Away with you, Satan!" replied Jesus, "the scripture says,

> Thou shalt worship the Lord thy God, and him only shalt thou serve."

Then the devil let him alone, and angels came to him and took care of him.

Jesus begins his ministry, in Galilee, and calls his first disciples

Now when Jesus heard that John had been arrested he went back to Galilee. He left Nazareth and came to live in Capernaum, a lake-side town in the Zebulun-Naphtali territory. In this way Isaiah's prophecy came true:

The land of Zebulun and the land of Naphtali,
Toward the sea, beyond Jordan,
Galilee of the Gentiles,
The people which sat in darkness
Saw a great light,
And to them which sat in the region and shadow of death,
To them did light spring up.

From that time Jesus began to preach and to say, "You must change your hearts and minds—for the kingdom of Heaven has arrived."

While he was walking by the lake of Galilee he saw two brothers, Simon (Peter) and Andrew, casting their net into the water. They were fishermen, so Jesus said to them,

"Follow me and I will teach you to catch men!"

At once they left their nets and followed him.

Then he went further on and saw two more men, also brothers, James and John. They were aboard the boat with their father Zebedee repairing their nets, and he called them. At once they left the boat, and their father, and followed him.

Jesus teaches, preaches and heals

Jesus now moved about through the whole of Galilee, teaching in their synagogues and preaching the good news about the kingdom, and healing every disease and disability among the people. His reputation spread throughout Syria, and people brought to him all those who were ill, suffering from all kinds of diseases and pains—including the devil-possessed, the insane and the paralysed. He healed them, and was followed by enormous crowds from Galilee, the Ten Towns, Jerusalem, Judaea, and from beyond the river Jordan.

CHAPTER 5

Jesus proclaims the new values of the kingdom

WHEN Jesus saw the vast crowds he went up the hill-side and after he had sat down his disciples came to him.

Then he began his teaching by saying to them,

"How happy are those who know their need for God, for the kingdom of Heaven is theirs!

"How happy are those who know what sorrow means, for they will be given courage and comfort!

"Happy are those who claim nothing, for the whole earth will belong to them!

"Happy are those who are hungry and thirsty for true goodness, for they will be fully satisfied!

"Happy are the merciful, for they will have mercy shown to them!

"Happy are the utterly sincere, for they will see God!

"Happy are those who make peace, for they will be known as sons of God!

"Happy are those who have suffered persecution for the cause of goodness, for the kingdom of Heaven is theirs!

"And what happiness will be yours when people blame you and ill-treat you and say all kinds of slanderous things against you for my sake! Be glad then, yes, be tremendously glad—for your reward in Heaven is magnificent. They persecuted the prophets before your time in exactly the same way.

"You are the earth's salt. But if the salt should become tasteless, what can make it salt again? It is completely useless and can only be thrown out of doors and stamped under foot.

"You are the world's light—it is impossible to hide a town built on the top of a hill. Men do not light a lamp and put it under a bucket. They put it on a lamp-stand and it gives light for everybody in the house.

"Let your light shine like that in the sight of men. Let them see the good things you do and praise your Father in Heaven.

Christ's authority surpasses that of the Law

"You must not think that I have come to abolish the Law or the Prophets; I have not come to abolish them but to complete them. Indeed, I assure you that, while Heaven and earth last, the Law will not lose a single dot or comma until its purpose is complete. This means that whoever now relaxes one of the least of these commandments and teaches men to do the same will himself be called least in the kingdom of Heaven. But whoever teaches and practises them will be called great in the kingdom of Heaven. For I tell you that your goodness must be a far better thing than the goodness of the scribes and Pharisees before you can set foot in the kingdom of Heaven at all!

"You have heard that it was said to the people in the old days, 'Thou shalt not murder', and anyone who does so must stand his trial. But I say to you that anyone who is angry with his brother must stand his trial; anyone who contemptuously calls his brother a fool* must face the supreme court; and anyone who looks down on his brother as a lost soul is himself heading straight for the fire of destruction.

"So that if, while you are offering your gift at the altar, you should remember that your brother has something against you, you must leave your gift there before the altar and go away. Make your peace with your brother first, then come and offer your gift. Come to terms quickly with your opponent at law while you are on the way to court. Otherwise he may hand you over to the judge and the judge in turn hand you over to the officer of the court and you will be thrown into prison. Believe me, you will never get out again till you have paid your last farthing!

"You have heard that it was said to the people in the old days, 'Thou shalt not commit adultery.' But I say to you that every man who looks at a woman lustfully has already committed adultery with her—in his heart.

"Yes, if your right eye leads you astray pluck it out and throw it away; it is better for you to lose one of your members than that your whole body should be thrown on to the rubbish-heap.

"Yes, if your right hand leads you astray cut it off and throw it away; it is better for you to lose one of your members than that your whole body should go to the rubbish-heap.

"It also used to be said that whoever divorces his wife must give her a proper certificate of divorce. But I say to you that whoever divorces his wife except on the ground of unfaithfulness is making her an adulteress. And whoever marries the woman who has been divorced also commits adultery.

"Again, you have heard that the people in the old days were told—'Thou shalt not forswear thyself, but shalt perform unto the Lord thine oaths', but I say to you, don't use an oath at all. Don't swear by Heaven for it is God's throne, nor by the earth for it is his footstool, nor by Jerusalem for it is the city of the great King. No, and don't swear by your own head, for you cannot make a single hair white or black! Whatever you have to say let your

* See note 2, page 551.

'yes' be a plain 'yes' and your 'no' be a plain 'no'—anything more than this has a taint of evil.

"You have heard that it used to be said 'An eye for an eye and a tooth for a tooth', but I tell you, don't resist evil. If a man hits your right cheek, turn the other one to him as well. If a man wants to sue you for your coat, let him have it and your cloak as well. If anybody forces you to go a mile with him, do more—go two miles with him. Give to the man who asks anything from you, and don't turn away from the man who wants to borrow.

"You have heard that it used to be said 'Thou shalt love thy neighbour and hate thine enemy', but I tell you, 'Love your enemies, and pray for those who persecute you,' so that you may be sons of your Heavenly Father. For he makes his sun rise upon evil men as well as good, and he sends his rain upon honest and dishonest men alike.

"For if you love only those who love you, what credit is that to you? Even tax-collectors do that! And if you exchange greetings only with your own circle, are you doing anything exceptional? Even the pagans do that much. No, you will be perfect as your Heavenly Father is perfect.

CHAPTER 6

The new life is not a matter of outward show

"BEWARE of doing your good deeds conspicuously to catch men's eyes or you will miss the reward of your Heavenly Father.

"So, when you do good to other people, don't hire a trumpeter to go in front of you—like those play-actors in the synagogues and streets who make sure that men admire them. Believe me, they have had all the reward they are going to get! No, when you give to charity, don't even let your left hand know what your right hand is doing, so that your giving may be secret. Your Father who knows all secrets will reward you.

"And then, when you pray, don't be like the play-actors. They love to stand and pray in the synagogues and at street-corners so that people may see them at it. Believe me, they have had all the reward they are going to get. But when you pray, go into your own room, shut your door and pray to your Father privately. Your Father who sees all private things will reward you. And when you pray don't rattle off long prayers like the pagans who think they will be heard because they use so many words. Don't be like them. For your Father knows your needs before you ask him. Pray then like this—

Our Heavenly Father, may your name be honoured;
May your kingdom come, and your will be done on earth as it is in Heaven.
Give us each day the bread we need for the day,
Forgive us what we owe to you, as we have also forgiven those who owe anything to us.
Keep us clear of temptation, and save us from evil.

Forgiveness of fellow-man is essential

"For if you forgive other people their failures, your Heavenly Father will also forgive you. But if you will not forgive other people, neither will your Father forgive you your failures.

"Then, when you fast, don't look like those miserable play-actors! For they deliberately disfigure their faces so that people may see that they are fasting. Believe me, they have had all their reward. No, when you fast, anoint your head and wash your face so that nobody knows that you are fasting—let it be a secret between you and your Father. And your Father who knows all secrets will reward you.

Put your trust in God alone

"Don't pile up treasures on earth, where moth and rust can spoil them and thieves can break in and steal. But keep your treasure in Heaven where there is neither moth nor rust to spoil it and nobody can break in and steal. For wherever your treasure is, your heart will be there too!

"The lamp of the body is the eye. If your eye is sound, your whole body will be full of light. But if your eye is evil, your whole body will be full of darkness. If all the light you have is darkness, it is dark indeed!

"No one can fully serve two masters. He is bound to hate one and love the other, or be loyal to one and despise the other. You cannot serve both God and the power of money. That is why I say to you, don't worry about living—wondering what you are going to eat or drink, or what you are going to wear. Surely life is more important than food, and the body more important than the clothes you wear. Look at the birds in the sky. They never sow nor reap nor store away in barns, and yet your Heavenly Father feeds them. Aren't you much more valuable to him than they are? Can any of you, however much he worries, make himself even a few inches taller? And why do you worry about clothes? Consider how the wild flowers grow. They neither work nor weave, but I tell you that even Solomon in all his glory was not arrayed like one of these! Now if God so clothes the flowers of the field, which are alive today and burnt in the stove tomorrow, is he not much more likely to clothe you, you 'little-faiths'?

"So don't worry and don't keep saying, 'What shall we eat, what shall we drink or what shall we wear?' That is what pagans are always looking for; your Heavenly Father knows that you need them all. Set your heart first on his kingdom and his goodness, and all these things will come to you as a matter of course.

"Don't worry at all then about tomorrow. Tomorrow can worry about itself! One day's trouble is enough for one day.

CHAPTER 7

The common sense behind right behaviour

"DON'T criticise people, and you will not be criticised. For you will be judged by the way you criticise others, and the measure you give will be the measure you receive.

"Why do you look at the speck of sawdust in your brother's eye and fail to notice the plank in your own? How can you say to your brother, 'Let me get the speck out of your eye', when there is a plank in your own? You hypocrite! Take the plank out of your own eye first, and then you can see clearly enough to remove your brother's speck of dust.

"You must not give holy things to dogs, nor must you throw your pearls before pigs—or they may trample them underfoot and turn and attack you.

"Ask and it will be given to you. Search and you will find. Knock and the door will be opened for you. The one who asks will always receive; the one who is searching will always find, and the door is opened to the man who knocks.

"If any of you were asked by his son for bread would you give him a stone, or if he asks for a fish would you give him a snake? If you then, for all your evil, quite naturally give good things to your children, how much more likely is it that your Heavenly Father will give good things to those who ask him?

"Treat other people exactly as you would like to be treated by them—this is the meaning of the Law and the Prophets.

"Go in by the narrow gate. For the wide gate has a broad road which leads to disaster and there are many people going that way. The narrow gate and the hard road lead out into life and only a few are finding it.

Living, not professing, is what matters

"Be on your guard against false religious teachers, who come to you dressed up as sheep but are really greedy wolves. You can tell them by their fruits. Do you pick a bunch of grapes from a thorn-bush or figs from a clump of thistles? Every good tree produces sound fruit, but a rotten tree produces bad fruit. A good tree cannot produce bad fruit, and a rotten tree cannot produce good fruit. The tree that fails to produce good fruit is cut down and burnt. So you may know the quality of men by what they produce.

"It is not everyone who keeps saying to me 'Lord, Lord' who will enter the kingdom of Heaven, but the man who actually does my Heavenly Father's will.

"In 'that day' many will say to me, 'Lord, Lord, didn't we preach in your name, didn't we cast out devils in your name, and do many great things in your name?' Then I shall tell them plainly, 'I have never known you. Go away from me, you have worked on the side of evil!'

To follow Christ's teaching means the only real security

"Everyone then who hears these words of mine and puts them into practice is like a sensible man who builds his house on rock. Down came the rain and up came the floods, while the winds blew and roared upon that house—and it did not fall because its foundations were on rock.

"And everyone who hears these words of mine and does not follow them can be compared with a foolish man who built his house on sand. Down came the rain and up came the floods, while the winds blew and battered that house till it collapsed, and fell with a great crash."

When Jesus had finished these words the crowd were astonished at the power behind his teaching. For his words had the ring of authority, quite unlike those of their scribes.

CHAPTER 8

Jesus cures leprosy, and heals many other people

LARGE crowds followed him when he came down from the hill-side. There was a leper who came and knelt in front of him. "Sir," he said, "if you want to, you can make me clean." Jesus stretched out his hand and placed it on the leper saying, "Of course I want to. Be clean!" And at once he was clear of the leprosy.

"Mind you say nothing to anybody," Jesus told him. "Go straight off and show yourself to the priest and make the offering for your recovery that Moses prescribed, as evidence to the authorities."

Then as he was coming into Capernaum a centurion approached. "Sir," he implored him, "my servant is in bed at home paralysed and in dreadful pain."

"I will come and heal him," said Jesus to him.

"Sir," replied the centurion, "I'm not important enough for you to come under my roof. You have only to give the order and my servant will recover. I'm a man under authority myself, and I have soldiers under me. I can say to one man 'Go' and I know he'll go, or I can say 'Come here' to another and I know he'll come—or I can say to my slave 'Do this' and he'll do it."

When Jesus heard this, he was astonished. "Believe me," he said to those who were following him, "I have never found faith like this, even in Israel! I tell you that many people will come from east and west and be fellow-guests with Abraham, Isaac and Jacob in the kingdom of Heaven. But those who should have belonged to the kingdom will be banished to the darkness outside, where there will be tears and bitter regret."

Then he said to the centurion, "Go home now, and everything will happen as you have believed it will."

And his servant was healed at that actual moment.

Then, on coming into Peter's house Jesus saw that Peter's mother-in-law had been put to bed with a high fever. He touched her hand and the fever left her. And then she got up and began to see to his needs.

When evening came they brought to him many who were possessed by evil spirits, which he expelled with a word. Indeed, he healed all who were ill. Thus was fulfilled Isaiah's prophecy—

Himself took our infirmities and bare our diseases.

When Jesus had seen the great crowds around him he gave orders to cross over to the other side of the lake. But before they started, one of the scribes came up to Jesus and said to him, "Master, I will follow you wherever you go."

"Foxes have earths, birds in the sky have nests, but the Son of Man has nowhere that he can call his own," replied Jesus.

Another of his disciples said, "Lord, let me first go and bury my father."

But Jesus said to him, "Follow me, and leave the dead to bury their own dead."

Jesus shows his mastery over the forces of nature

Then he went aboard the boat, and his disciples followed him. Before long a terrific storm sprang up and the boat was awash with the waves. Jesus was sleeping soundly and the disciples went forward and woke him up.

"Lord, save us!" they cried. "We are drowning!"

"Why are you so frightened, you little-faiths?" he replied.

Then he got to his feet and rebuked the wind and the waters and there was a great calm. The men were filled with astonishment and kept saying, "Whatever sort of man is this—why, even the winds and the waters do what he tells them!"

When he arrived on the other side (which is the Gadarenes' country) he was met by two devil-possessed men who came out from among the tombs. They were so violent that nobody dared to use that road.

"What have you got to do with us, you Son of God?" they screamed at him. "Have you come here to torture us before our time?"

It happened that in the distance there was a large herd of pigs feeding. So the devils implored him, "If you throw us out, send us into the herd of pigs!"

"Then go!" said Jesus to them.

And the devils came out and went into the pigs. Then quite suddenly the whole herd stampeded down the steep cliff into the lake and were drowned.

The swineherds took to their heels, and ran to the town. There they poured out the whole story of what had happened to the two men who had been devil-possessed. Whereupon the whole town came out to meet Jesus, and as soon as they saw him implored him to leave their territory.

CHAPTER 9

Jesus heals in his own town

So Jesus re-embarked on the boat, crossed the lake, and came to his own town. Immediately some people arrived bringing him a paralytic lying flat on his bed. When Jesus saw the faith of those who brought him he said to the paralytic, "Cheer up, my son! Your sins are forgiven."

At once some of the scribes said to themselves, "This man is blaspheming." But Jesus realised what they were thinking, and said to them, "Why must you have such evil thoughts in your minds? Do you think it is easier to say, 'Your sins are forgiven' or 'Get up and walk'? But to make it quite plain that the Son of Man has full authority on earth to forgive sins"—and here he spoke to the paralytic—"Get up, pick up your bed and go home." And the man sprang to his feet and went home. When the crowds saw what had happened they were filled with awe and praised God for giving such power to men.

Jesus calls a "sinner" to be his disciple

Jesus left there and as he passed on he saw a man called Matthew sitting at his desk in the tax-collector's office.

"Follow me!" he said to him—and the man got to his feet and followed him.

Later, as Jesus was in a house sitting at the dinner-table, many tax-collectors and other disreputable people came and joined him and his disciples. The Pharisees noticed this and said to the disciples, "Why does your master have his meals with tax-collectors and sinners?" But Jesus heard this and replied,

"It is not the fit and flourishing who need the doctor, but those who are ill! You should go and learn what this text means: 'I desire mercy and not sacrifice.' In any case I did not come to invite the 'righteous' but the 'sinners'."

He explains the joy and strength of the new order

Then John's disciples approached him with the question, "Why is it that we and the Pharisees observe the fasts, but your disciples do not?"

"Can you expect wedding-guests to mourn while they have the bridegroom with them?" replied Jesus. "The day will come when the bridegroom will be taken away from them—they will certainly fast then!

"Nobody sews a patch of unshrunk cloth on to an old coat, for the patch will pull away from the coat and the hole will be worse than ever. Nor do people put new wine into old wineskins—otherwise the skins burst, the wine is spilt and the skins are ruined. But they put new wine into new skins and both are preserved."

Jesus heals a young girl, and several others in need

While he was saying these things to them an official came up to him and, bowing low before him, said,

"My daughter has just this moment died. Please come and lay your hand on her and she will come back to life!"

At this Jesus got to his feet and followed him, accompanied by his disciples. And on the way a woman who had had a haemorrhage for twelve years approached him from behind and touched the edge of his cloak.

"If I can only touch his cloak," she kept saying to herself, "I shall be all right."

But Jesus turned round and saw her.

"Cheer up, my daughter," he said, "your faith has made you well!" And the woman was completely cured from that moment.

Then when Jesus came into the official's house and noticed the flute-players and the noisy crowd he said, "You must all go outside; the little girl is not dead, she is fast asleep."

This was met with scornful laughter. But when the crowd had been turned out, he came right into the room, took hold of her hand, and the girl got up. And this became the talk of the whole district.

As Jesus passed on his way two blind men followed him with the cry, "Have pity on us, Son of David!" And when he had gone inside the house these two came up to him.

"Do you believe I can do it?" he said to them.

"Yes, Lord," they replied.

Then he touched their eyes, saying, "You have believed and so it shall be."

Then their sight returned, but Jesus sternly warned them,

"Don't let anyone know about this." Yet they went outside and spread the story throughout the whole district.

Later, when Jesus and his party were coming out, they brought to him a dumb man who was possessed by a devil. As soon as the devil had been ejected the dumb man began to talk. The crowds were simply amazed and said, "Nothing like this has ever been seen in Israel." But the Pharisees' comment was, "He throws out these devils because he is in league with the devil himself."

Jesus is touched by the people's need

Jesus now travelled through all the towns and villages, teaching in their synagogues, proclaiming the gospel of the kingdom, and healing all kinds of illness and disability. As he looked at the vast crowds he was deeply moved with pity for them, for they were as bewildered and miserable as a flock of sheep with no shepherd.

"The harvest is great enough," he remarked to his disciples, "but the reapers are few. So you must pray to the Lord of the harvest to send men out to bring it in."

CHAPTER 10

Jesus sends out the twelve with divine power

JESUS called his twelve disciples to him and gave them authority to expel evil spirits and heal all kinds of disease and infirmity. The names of the twelve apostles are:

First, Simon, called Peter, with his brother Andrew;
James and his brother John, sons of Zebedee;
Philip and Bartholomew,
Thomas, and Matthew the tax-collector,
James, the son of Alphaeus, and Thaddaeus,
Simon the Patriot, and Judas Iscariot, who later turned traitor.

These were the twelve whom Jesus sent out, with the instructions: "Don't turn off into any of the heathen roads, and don't go into any Samaritan town. Go rather to the lost sheep of the house of Israel. As you go proclaim that the kingdom of Heaven has arrived. Heal the sick, raise the dead, cure the lepers, drive out devils—give, as you have received, without any charge whatever.

"Don't take any gold or silver or even coppers to put in your purse; nor a knapsack for the journey, nor even a second coat, nor sandals nor staff—the workman deserves his keep!

"Wherever you go, whether it is into a town or a village, find out someone who is respected, and stay with him until you leave. As you enter his house give it your blessing. If the house deserves it, the peace of your blessing will come to it. But if it doesn't, your peace will return to you.

"And if no one will welcome you or even listen to what you have to say, leave that house or town, and once outside it shake off the dust of that place from your feet. Believe me, it will be easier for Sodom and Gomorrah in the day of judgment than for that town.

He warns them of troubles that lie ahead

"Here am I sending you out like sheep with wolves all round you; so be as wise as serpents and harmless as doves. But be on your guard against men. For they will take you to the courts and flog you in the synagogues. You will be brought into the presence of governors and kings because of me—to give your witness to them and to the heathen.

"But when they do arrest you, never worry about how you are to speak or what you are to say. You will be told at the time what you are to say. For it will not be really you who are speaking but the Spirit of your Father speaking through you.

"Brother will betray brother to death, and a father his children. Children will turn against their parents and have them executed. You yourselves will be universally hated because of my name. But the man who endures to the very end will be safe and sound.

"But when they persecute you in one town make your escape to the next. Believe me, you will not have covered the towns of Israel before the Son of Man arrives. The disciple is not superior to his teacher any more than the servant is superior to his master, for what is good enough for the teacher is good enough for the disciple, and the servant will not fare better than his master. If men call the master of the household the 'Prince of Evil', what sort of names will they give to his servants? But never let them frighten you, for there is nothing covered up which is not going to be exposed nor anything private which will not be made public. The things I tell you in the dark you must say in the daylight, and the things you hear in your private ear you must proclaim from the housetops.

They should reverence God but have no fear of man

"Never be afraid of those who can kill the body but are powerless to kill the soul! Far better to stand in awe of the one who has the power to destroy body and soul in the fires of destruction!

"Two sparrows are sold for a farthing, aren't they? Yet not a single sparrow falls to the ground without your father's knowledge. The very hairs of your head are all numbered. Never be afraid, then—you are far more valuable than sparrows.

"Every man who publicly acknowledges me I shall acknowledge in the presence of my Father in Heaven, but the man who disowns me before men I shall disown before my Father in Heaven.

The Prince of Peace comes to bring division

"Never think I have come to bring peace upon the earth. No, I have not come to bring peace but a sword! For I have come to set a man against his own father, a daughter against her own mother, and a daughter-in-law against her mother-in-law. A man's enemies will be those who live in his own house.

"Anyone who puts his love for father or mother above his love for me does not deserve to be mine, and he who loves son or daughter more than me is not worthy of me, and neither is the man who refuses to take up his cross and follow my way. The man who has found his own life will lose it, but the man who has lost it for my sake will find it.

"Whoever welcomes you, welcomes me; and whoever welcomes me is welcoming him who sent me.

"Whoever welcomes a prophet because he is a prophet will get a prophet's reward. And whoever welcomes a good man because he is a good man will get a good man's reward. Believe me, anyone who gives even a cup of cold water to one of these little ones, just because he is my disciple, will by no means lose his reward."

CHAPTER 11

WHEN Jesus had finished giving his twelve disciples these instructions he went on from there to teach and preach in the towns in which they lived.

John enquires about Christ: Christ speaks about John

John the Baptist was in prison when he heard what Christ was doing, and he sent a message through his own disciples asking the question, "Are you the one who was to come or are we to look for somebody else?"

Jesus gave them this reply, "Go and tell John what you hear and see—that blind men are recovering their sight, cripples are walking, lepers being healed, the deaf hearing, the dead being raised to life and the good news is being given to those in need. And happy is the man who never loses his faith in me."

As John's disciples were going away Jesus began talking to the crowd about John:

"What did you go out into the desert to look at? A reed waving in the breeze? No? Then *what* was it you went out to see?—a man dressed in fine clothes? But the men who wear fine clothes live in the courts of kings! But what did you really go to see—a prophet? Yes, I tell you, a prophet and far more than a prophet! This is the man of whom the scripture says—

Behold, I send my messenger before thy face,
Who shall prepare thy way before thee.

"Believe me, no one greater than John the Baptist has ever been born of all mankind, and yet a humble member of the kingdom of Heaven is greater than he.

"From the days of John the Baptist until now the kingdom of Heaven has been subject to force and violent men are trying to seize it. For the Law and all the Prophets foretold it till the time of John and—if you can believe it—John himself is the 'Elijah' who must come before the kingdom. The man who has ears to hear must use them!

"But how can I show what the people of this generation are like? They are like children sitting in the market-place calling out to their friends, 'We played at weddings for you but you wouldn't dance, and we played at funerals and you wouldn't cry!' For

John came in the strictest austerity and people say, 'He's crazy!' Then the Son of Man came, enjoying life, and people say, 'Look, a drunkard and a glutton—the bosom-friend of the tax-collector and the sinner.' Ah, well, wisdom stands or falls by her results."

Jesus denounces apathy—and thanks God that simple men understand his message

Then Jesus began reproaching the towns where most of his miracles had taken place because their hearts were unchanged.

"Alas for you, Chorazin! Alas for you, Bethsaida! For if Tyre and Sidon had seen the demonstrations of God's power which you have seen they would have repented long ago in sackcloth and ashes. Yet I tell you this, that it will be more bearable for Tyre and Sidon in the day of judgment than for you.

"And as for you, Capernaum, are you on your way up to heaven? I tell you you will go hurtling down among the dead! If Sodom had seen the miracles that you have seen, Sodom would be standing today. Yet I tell you now that it will be more bearable for the land of Sodom in the day of judgment than for you."

At this same time Jesus said, "O Father, Lord of Heaven and earth, I thank you for hiding these things from the clever and intelligent and for showing them to mere children. Yes, I thank you, Father, that this was your will."

Then he said: "Everything has been put into my hands by my Father, and nobody knows the Son except the Father. Nor does anyone know the Father except the Son—and the man to whom the Son chooses to reveal him.

"Come to me, all of you who are weary and over-burdened, and I will give you rest! Put on my yoke and learn from me. For I am gentle and humble in heart and you will find rest for your souls. For my yoke is easy and my burden is light."

CHAPTER 12

Jesus rebukes the sabbatarians

It happened then that Jesus passed through the cornfields on the Sabbath day. His disciples were hungry and began picking the ears of wheat and eating them. But the Pharisees saw them do it.

"There, you see," they remarked to Jesus, "your disciples are doing what the Law forbids them to do on the Sabbath."

"Haven't any of you read what David did when he and his companions were hungry?" replied Jesus, "—how he went into the house of God and ate the presentation loaves, which he and his followers were not allowed to eat since only priests can do so?

"Haven't any of you read in the Law that every Sabbath day priests in the Temple can break the Sabbath and yet remain blameless? I tell you that there is something more important than the Temple here. If you had grasped the meaning of the scripture 'I desire mercy and not sacrifice', you would not have been so quick to condemn the innocent! For the Son of Man is master even of the Sabbath."

Leaving there he went into their synagogue, where there happened to be a man with a shrivelled hand.

"Is it right to heal anyone on the Sabbath day?" they asked him—hoping to bring a charge against him.

"If any of you had a sheep which fell into a ditch on the Sabbath day, would he not take hold of it and pull it out?" replied Jesus. "How much more valuable is a man than a sheep? You see, it is right to do good on the Sabbath day."

Then Jesus said to the man, "Stretch out your hand!" He did stretch it out, and it was restored as sound as the other.

But the Pharisees went out and held a meeting against Jesus and discussed how they could get rid of him altogether.

Jesus retires to continue his work

But Jesus knew of this and he left the place.

Large crowds followed him and he healed them all, with the strict injunction that they should not make him conspicuous by their talk, thus fulfilling Isaiah's prophecy:

> Behold, my servant whom I have chosen;
> My beloved in whom my soul is well pleased:
> I will put my Spirit upon him,
> And he shall declare judgment to the gentiles.
> He shall not strive, nor cry aloud;
> Neither shall anyone hear his voice in the streets.
> A bruised reed shall he not break,
> And smoking flax shall he not quench,
> Till he send forth judgment unto victory.
> And in his name shall the gentiles hope.

Then a devil-possessed man who could neither see nor speak was brought to Jesus. He healed him, so that the dumb man could both speak and see. At this the whole crowd went wild with excitement, and people kept saying, "Can this be the Son of David?"

The Pharisees draw an evil conclusion, and Jesus rebukes them

But the Pharisees on hearing this remark said, "This man is only expelling devils because he is in league with Beelzebub, the prince of devils."

Jesus knew what they were thinking and said to them, "Any kingdom divided against itself is bound to collapse, and no town or household divided against itself can last for long. If it is Satan who is expelling Satan, then he is divided against himself—so how do you suppose that his kingdom can continue? And if I expel devils because I am an ally of Beelzebub, what alliance do your sons make when they do the same thing? They can settle that question for you. But if I am expelling devils by the Spirit of God, then the kingdom of God has already swept over you! How do you suppose anyone could get into a strong man's house and steal his property unless he first tied up the strong man? But if he did that, he could ransack his whole house.

"The man who is not on my side is against me, and the man who does not gather with me is really scattering. That is why I tell you that men may be forgiven for every sin and blasphemy, but blasphemy against the Spirit cannot be forgiven. A man may say a word against the Son of Man and be forgiven, but whoever speaks against the Holy Spirit cannot be forgiven either in this world or in the world to come.

"You must choose between having a good tree with good fruit and a rotten tree with rotten fruit. For you can tell a tree at once by its fruit.

"You serpent's brood, how can you say anything good out of your evil hearts? For a man's words flow out of what fills his heart. A good man gives out good—from the goodness stored in his heart; a bad man gives out evil—from his store of evil. I tell you that men will have to answer at the day of judgment for every careless word they utter—for it is your words that will acquit you, and your words that will condemn you."

Jesus refuses to give a sign

Then some of the scribes and Pharisees said, "Master, we want to see a sign from you." But Jesus told them,

"It is an evil and unfaithful generation that craves for a sign, and no sign will be given to it—except the sign of the prophet Jonah. For just as Jonah was in the belly of that great sea-monster for three days and nights, so will the Son of Man be in the heart of the earth for three days and nights. The men of Nineveh will stand up with this generation in the judgment and will condemn it. For they did repent when Jonah preached to them, and you have more than Jonah's preaching with you now! The Queen of the South will stand up in the judgment with this generation and will condemn it. For she came from the ends of the earth to listen to the wisdom of Solomon, and you have more than the wisdom of Solomon with you now!

The danger of spiritual emptiness

"When the evil spirit goes out of a man it wanders through waterless places looking for rest and never finding it. Then it says, 'I will go back to my house from which I came.' When it arrives it finds it unoccupied, but cleaned and all in order. Then it goes and collects seven other spirits more evil than itself to keep it company, and they all go in and make themselves at home. The last state of that man is worse than the first—and that is just what will happen to this evil generation."

Jesus and his relations

While he was still talking to the crowds, his mother and his brothers happened to be standing outside wanting to speak to him. Somebody said to him, "Look, your mother and your brothers are outside wanting to speak to you." But Jesus replied to the man who had told him, "Who is my mother, and who are my brothers?"; then with a gesture of his hand towards his disciples he went on, "There are my mother and brothers! For whoever does the will of my Heavenly Father is brother and sister and mother to me."

CHAPTER 13

Jesus tells the parable of the seed

It was on the same day that Jesus went out of the house and sat down by the lake-side. Such great crowds collected round him that he went aboard a small boat and sat down while all the people stood on the beach. He told them a great deal in parables, and began:

"There was once a man who went out to sow. In his sowing some of the seeds fell by the road-side and the birds swooped down and gobbled them up. Some fell on stony patches where they had very little soil. They sprang up quickly in the shallow soil, but when the sun came up they were scorched by the heat and withered away because they had no roots. Some seeds fell among thorn-bushes and the thorns grew up and choked the life out of them. But some fell on good soil and produced a crop—some a hundred times what had been sown, some sixty and some thirty times. The man who has ears to hear should use them!"

At this the disciples approached him and asked, "Why do you talk to them in parables?"

"Because you have been given the privilege of understanding the secrets of the kingdom of Heaven," replied Jesus, "but they have not. For when a man has something, more is given to him till he has plenty. But if he has nothing even his nothing will be taken away from him. This is why I speak to them in these parables; because they go through life with their eyes open, but see nothing, and with their ears open, but understand nothing of what they hear. They are the living fulfilment of Isaiah's prophecy which says:

By hearing ye shall hear, and shall in no wise understand;
And seeing ye shall see, and shall in no wise perceive:
For this people's heart is waxed gross,
And their ears are dull of hearing,
And their eyes they have closed;
Lest haply they should perceive with their eyes,
And hear with their ears,
And understand with their heart,
And should turn again,
And I should heal them.

"But how fortunate you are to have eyes that see and ears that hear! Believe me, a great many prophets and good men have longed to see what you are seeing and they never saw it. Yes, and they longed to hear what you are hearing and they never heard it.

"Now listen to the parable of the sower. When a man hears the message of the kingdom and does not grasp it, the evil one comes and snatches away what was sown in his heart. This is like the seed sown by the road-side. The seed sown on the stony patches represents the man who hears the message and eagerly accepts it. But it has not taken root in him and does not last long—the moment trouble or persecution arises through the message he gives up his faith at once. The seed sown among the thorns represents the man who hears the message, and then the worries of this life and the illusions of wealth choke it to death and so it produces no 'crop' in his life. But the seed sown on good soil is the man who both hears and understands the message. His life shows a good crop, a hundred, sixty or thirty times what was sown."

Good and evil grow side by side in this present world

Then he put another parable before them. "The kingdom of Heaven," he said, "is like a man who sowed good seed in his field. But while his men were asleep his enemy came and sowed weeds among the wheat, and went away. When the crop came up and began to ripen, the weeds appeared as well. Then the owner's servants came up to him and said, 'Sir, didn't you sow good seed in your field? Where did all these weeds come from?' 'Some enemy of mine has done this,' he replied. 'Do you want us then to go out and pull them all up?' said the servants. 'No,' he returned, 'if you pull up the weeds now, you would pull up the wheat with them. Let them both grow together till the harvest. And at harvest-time I shall tell the reapers, 'Collect all the weeds first and tie them up in bundles ready to burn, but collect the wheat and store it in my barn.' "

The kingdom's power of growth, and widespread influence

Then he put another parable before them. "The kingdom of Heaven is like a tiny grain of mustard-seed which a man took and sowed in his field. As a seed it is the smallest of them all, but it grows to be the biggest of all plants. It becomes a tree, big enough for birds to come and nest in its branches."

This is another of the parables he told them: "The kingdom of Heaven is like yeast, taken by a woman and put into three measures of flour until the whole had risen."

All these things Jesus spoke to the crowd in parables, and he did not speak to them at all without using parables—to fulfil the prophecy:

I will open my mouth in parables;
I will utter things hidden from the foundation of the world.

Jesus again explains a parable to his disciples

Later, he left the crowds and went indoors, where his disciples came and said, "Please explain to us the parable of the weeds in the field."

"The one who sows the good seed is the Son of Man," replied Jesus. "The field is the whole world. The good seed? That is the sons of the kingdom, while the weeds are the sons of the evil one. The enemy who sowed them is the devil. The harvest is the end of this world. The reapers are angels.

"Just as weeds are gathered up and burned in the fire so will it happen at the end of this world. The Son of Man will send out his angels and they will uproot from the kingdom everything that is spoiling it, and all those who live in defiance of its laws, and will throw them into the blazing furnace, where there will be tears and bitter regret. Then the good will shine out like the sun in their Father's kingdom. The man who has ears should use them!

More pictures of the kingdom of Heaven

"Again, the kingdom of Heaven is like some treasure which has been buried in a field. A man finds it and buries it again, and goes off overjoyed to sell all his possessions to buy himself that field.

"Or again, the kingdom of Heaven is like a merchant searching for fine pearls. When he has found a single pearl of great value, he goes and sells all his possessions and buys it.

"Or the kingdom of Heaven is like a big net thrown into the sea collecting all kinds of fish. When it is full, the fishermen haul it ashore and sit down and pick out the good ones for the barrels, but they throw away the bad. That is how it will be at the end of this world. The angels will go out and pick out the wicked from among the good and throw them into the blazing furnace, where there will be tears and bitter regret.

"Have you grasped all this?"

"Yes," they replied.

"You can see, then," returned Jesus, "how everyone who knows the Law and becomes a disciple of the kingdom of Heaven is like a householder who can produce from his store both the new and the old."

Jesus is not appreciated in his native town

When Jesus had finished these parables he left the place, and came into his own country. Here he taught the people in their own synagogue, till in their amazement they said, "Where does this man get this wisdom and these powers? He's only the carpenter's son. Isn't Mary his mother, and aren't James, Joseph, Simon and Judas his brothers? And aren't all his sisters living here with us? Where did he get all this?" And they were deeply offended with him.

But Jesus said to them, "No prophet goes unhonoured except in his own country and in his own home!"

And he performed very few miracles there because of their lack of faith.

CHAPTER 14

Herod's guilty conscience

ABOUT this time Herod, governor of the province, heard the reports about Jesus and said to his men, "This must be John the Baptist: he has risen from the dead. That is why miraculous powers are at work in him."

For previously Herod had arrested John and had him bound and put in prison, all on account of Herodias, the wife of his brother Philip. For John had said to him, "It is not right for you to have this woman." Herod wanted to kill him for this, but he was afraid of the people, since they all thought John was a prophet. But during Herod's birthday celebrations Herodias' daughter delighted him by dancing before his guests, so much so that he swore to give her anything she liked to ask. And she, prompted by her mother, said, "I want you to give me, here and now, on a dish, the head of John the Baptist!" Herod was appalled at this, but because he had sworn in front of his guests, he gave orders that she should be given what she had asked. So he sent men and had John beheaded in the prison. Then his head was carried in on a dish and presented to the young girl who handed it to her mother. Later, John's disciples came, took his body and buried it. Then they went and told the news to Jesus. When he heard it he went away by boat to a deserted place, quite alone.

Jesus feeds a tired and hungry crowd

Then the crowds heard of his departure and followed him out of the towns on foot. When Jesus emerged from his retreat he saw a vast crowd and was very deeply moved and healed the sick among them. As evening fell his disciples came to him and said, "We are right in the wilds here and it is very late. Send away these crowds now, so that they can go into the villages and buy themselves food."

"There's no need for them to go away," returned Jesus. "You give them something to eat!"

"But we haven't anything here," they told him, "except five loaves and two fish." To which Jesus replied, "Bring them here to me."

He told the crowd to sit down on the grass. Then he took the five loaves and the two fish in his hands, and, looking up to Heaven, he thanked God, broke the loaves and passed them to his disciples who handed them to the crowd. Everybody ate and was satisfied. Afterwards they collected twelve baskets full of the pieces which were left over. Those who ate numbered about five thousand men, apart from the women and children.

Jesus again shows his power over the forces of nature

Directly after this Jesus insisted on his disciples' getting aboard their boat and going on ahead to the other side, while he himself sent the crowds home. And when he had sent them away he went up the hill-side quite alone, to pray. When it grew late he was there by himself while the boat was by now a good way from the shore at the mercy of the waves, for the wind was dead against them. In the small hours Jesus went out to them, walking on the lake. When the disciples caught sight of him walking on the water they were terrified. "It's a ghost!" they said, and screamed with fear. But at once Jesus spoke to them. "It's all right! It's I myself, don't be afraid!"

"Lord, if it's really you," said Peter, "tell me to come to you on the water."

"Come on, then," replied Jesus.

Peter stepped down from the boat and began to walk on the water, making for Jesus. But when he saw the fury of the wind he panicked and began to sink, calling out, "Lord save me!" At once Jesus reached out his hand and caught him, saying, "You little-faith! What made you lose your nerve like that?" Then, when they were both aboard the boat, the wind dropped. The whole crew came and knelt down before Jesus, crying, "You are indeed the Son of God!"

When they had crossed over to the other side of the lake, they landed at Gennesaret, and when the men of that place had recognised him, they sent word to the whole surrounding country and brought all the diseased to him. They implored him to let them "touch just the edge of his cloak", and all those who did so were completely cured.

CHAPTER 15

The dangers of tradition

THEN some of the scribes and Pharisees from Jerusalem came and asked Jesus, "Why do your disciples break our ancient tradition and eat their food without washing their hands properly first?"

"Tell me," replied Jesus, "why do you break God's commandment through your tradition? For God said, 'Honour thy father and thy mother', and 'He that speaketh evil of father or mother, let him die the death.' But you say that if a man tells his father or his mother, 'Whatever duty I might have owed you is now given to God,' then he will never honour his father again. And so your tradition makes the commandment of God ineffectual. You hypocrites! Isaiah described you beautifully when he said:

This people honoureth me with their lips;
But their heart is far from me.
But in vain do they worship me,
Teaching as their doctrines the precepts of men."

Superficial and true cleanliness

Then he called the crowd to him and said, "Listen, and understand this thoroughly! It is not what goes *into* a man's mouth that makes him common or unclean. It is what comes *out* of a man's mouth that makes him unclean."

Later his disciples came to him and said, "Do you know that the Pharisees are deeply offended by what you said?"

"Every plant which my Heavenly Father did not plant will be pulled up by the roots," returned Jesus. "Let them alone. They are blind guides, and when one blind man leads another blind man they will both fall into the ditch!"

"Explain this parable to us," broke in Peter.

"Are you still as dull as the others?" asked Jesus. "Don't you see that whatever goes *into* the mouth passes into the stomach and then out of the body altogether? But the things that come *out* of a man's mouth come from his heart and mind, and it is they that really make a man unclean. For it is from a man's mind that evil thoughts arise—murder, adultery, lust, theft, perjury and slander. These are the things which make a man unclean, not eating without washing his hands properly!"

A gentile's faith in Jesus

Jesus then left that place and retired into the Tyre and Sidon district. There a Canaanite woman from those parts came to him crying at the top of her voice,

"Lord, son of David, have pity on me! My daughter is in a terrible state—a devil has got into her!"

Jesus made no answer, and the disciples came up to him and said, "Do send her away—she's still following us and calling out."

"I was only sent," replied Jesus, "to the lost sheep of the house of Israel."

Then the woman came and knelt at his feet. "Lord, help me," she said.

"It is not right, you know," Jesus replied, "to take the children's food and throw it to the dogs."

"Yes, Lord, I know, but even the dogs live on the scraps that fall from their master's table!"

"You certainly don't lack faith," returned Jesus, "it shall be as you wish."

And at that moment her daughter was healed.

Jesus heals and feeds vast crowds of people

Jesus left there, walked along the shore of the lake of Galilee, then climbed the hill and sat down. And great crowds came to him, bringing with them people who were lame, blind, crippled, dumb and many others. They simply laid them at his feet and he healed them. The result was that the people were astonished at seeing dumb men speak, crippled men healed, lame men walking about and blind men having recovered their sight. And they praised the God of Israel.

But Jesus quietly called his disciples to him. "My heart goes out to this crowd," he said. "They've stayed with me three days now and have no more food. I don't want to send them home without anything to eat or they will collapse on the way."

"Where could we find enough food to feed such a crowd in this deserted spot?" said the disciples.

"How many loaves have you?" asked Jesus.

"Seven, and a few small fish," they replied.

Then Jesus told the crowd to sit down comfortably on the ground. And when he had taken the seven loaves and the fish into his hands, he broke them with a prayer of thanksgiving and gave them to the disciples to pass on to the people. Everybody ate and was satisfied, and they picked up seven baskets full of the pieces left over. Those who ate numbered four thousand men, apart from women and children. Then Jesus sent the crowds home, boarded the boat and arrived at the district of Magadan.

CHAPTER 16

Jesus again refuses to give a sign

ONCE the Pharisees and the Sadducees arrived together to test him, and asked him to give them a sign from Heaven. But he replied, "When the evening comes you say, 'Ah, fine weather—the sky is red.' In the morning you say, 'There will be a storm today, the sky is red and threatening.' Yes, you know how to interpret the look of the sky but you have no idea how to interpret the signs of the times! A wicked and unfaithful age insists on a sign; and it will not be given any sign at all but that of the prophet Jonah." And he turned on his heel and left them.

He is misunderstood by the disciples

Then his disciples came to him on the other side of the lake, forgetting to bring any bread with them. "Keep your eyes open," said Jesus to them, "and be on your guard against the 'yeast' of the Pharisees and Sadducees!" But they were arguing with each other, and saying, "We forgot to bring the bread." When Jesus saw this he said to them, "Why all this argument among yourselves about not bringing any bread, you little-faiths? Don't you understand yet, or have you forgotten the five loaves and the five thousand, and how many baskets you took up afterwards; or the seven loaves and the four thousand and how many baskets you took up then? I wonder why you don't yet understand that I wasn't talking about bread at all—I told you to beware of the yeast of the Pharisees and Sadducees." Then they grasped the fact that he had not told them to beware of yeast in the ordinary sense but of the influence of the teaching of the Pharisees and Sadducees.

Peter's bold affirmation

When Jesus reached the Caesarea-Philippi district he asked his disciples a question. "Who do people say the Son of Man is?"

"Well, some say John the Baptist," they told him. "Some say Elijah, others Jeremiah or one of the prophets."

"But what about you?" he said to them. "Who do you say that I am?"

Simon Peter answered, "You? You are Christ, the Son of the living God!"

"Simon, son of Jonah, you are a fortunate man indeed!" said Jesus, "for it was not your own nature but my Heavenly Father who revealed this truth to you! Now I tell you that you are Peter the rock, and it is on this rock that I am going to found my Church, and the powers of death will never have the power to destroy it. I will give you the keys of the kingdom of Heaven; whatever you forbid on earth will be what is forbidden in Heaven and whatever you permit on earth will be what is permitted in Heaven!"* Then he impressed on his disciples that they should not tell anyone that he was Christ.

Jesus speaks about his passion, and the cost of following him

From that time onwards Jesus began to explain to his disciples that he would have to go to Jerusalem, and endure much suffering from the elders, chief priests and scribes, and finally be killed; and be raised to life again on the third day.

Then Peter took him on one side and started to remonstrate with him over this. "God bless you, Master! Nothing like this must happen to you!" Then Jesus turned round and said to Peter, "Out of my way, Satan! . . . you stand right in my path, Peter, when you think the thoughts of man and not those of God."

Then Jesus said to his disciples, "If anyone wants to follow in my footsteps he must give up all right to himself, take up his cross and follow me. For the man who wants to save his life will lose it;

* See note 3, page 552.

but the man who loses his life for my sake will find it. For what good is it for a man to gain the whole world at the price of his real life? What could a man offer to buy back that life once he has lost it?

"For the Son of Man will come in the glory of his Father and in the company of his angels and then he will repay every man for what he has done. Believe me, there are some standing here today who will know nothing of death till they have seen the Son of Man coming as king."

CHAPTER 17

Three disciples glimpse the glory of Christ

SIX days later Jesus chose Peter, James and his brother John, to accompany him high up on the hill-side where they were quite alone. There his whole appearance changed before their eyes, his face shining like the sun and his clothes as white as light. Then Moses and Elijah were seen talking to Jesus.

"Lord," exclaimed Peter, "it is wonderful for us to be here! If you like I could put up three shelters, one each for you and Moses and Elijah——"

But while he was still talking a bright cloud overshadowed them and a voice came out of the cloud:

"This is my dearly loved Son in whom I am well pleased. Listen to him!"

When they heard this voice the disciples fell on their faces, overcome with fear. Then Jesus came up to them and touched them.

"Get up and don't be frightened," he said. And as they raised their eyes there was no one to be seen but Jesus himself.

On their way down the hill-side Jesus warned them not to tell anyone about what they had seen until after the Son of Man had been raised from the dead. Then the disciples demanded, "Why is it, then, that the scribes always say Elijah must come first?"

"Yes, Elijah does come first," replied Jesus, "and begins the world's reformation. But I tell you that Elijah has come already and men did not recognise him. They did what they liked with him, and the Son of Man will also suffer at their hands."

Then the disciples realised that he had been referring to John the Baptist.

Jesus heals an epileptic boy

When they returned to the crowd again a man came and knelt in front of Jesus. "Lord, have pity on my son," he said, "for he is a lunatic and suffers terribly. He is always falling into the fire or into the water. I did bring him to your disciples but they couldn't cure him."

"You really are an unbelieving and difficult people," Jesus returned. "How long must I be with you, and how long must I put up with you? Bring him here to me!"

Then Jesus spoke sternly to the evil spirit and it went out of the boy, who was cured from that moment.

Afterwards the disciples approached Jesus privately and asked, "Why weren't we able to get rid of it?"

"Because you have so little faith," replied Jesus. "I assure you that if you have faith the size of a mustard-seed you can say to this hill, 'Up you get and move over there!' and it will move—you will find nothing is impossible."

As they went about together in Galilee, Jesus told them, "The Son of Man is going to be handed over to the power of men, and they will kill him. And on the third day he will be raised to life again." This greatly distressed the disciples.

Jesus pays the Temple-tax—in an unusual way

Then when they arrived at Capernaum the Temple tax-collectors came up and said to Peter, "Your master doesn't pay Temple-tax, we presume?"

"Oh, yes, he does!" replied Peter. Later when he went into the house Jesus anticipated what he was going to say. "What do *you* think, Simon?" he said. "Whom do the kings of this world get their tolls and taxes from—their own family or from others?"

"From others," replied Peter

"Then the family is exempt," Jesus told him. "Yet we don't want to give offence to these people, so go down to the lake and throw in your hook. Take the first fish that bites, open his mouth and you'll find a silver coin. Take that and give it to them, for both of us."

CHAPTER 18

Jesus commends the simplicity of children

It was at this time that the disciples came to Jesus with the question, "Who is really greatest in the kingdom of Heaven?" Jesus called a little child to his side and set him on his feet in the middle of them all. "Believe me," he said, "unless you change your whole outlook and become like little children you will never enter the kingdom of Heaven. It is the man who can be as humble as this little child who is greatest in the kingdom of Heaven.

"Anyone who welcomes one child like this for my sake is welcoming me. But if anyone leads astray one of these little children who believe in me he would be better off thrown into the depths of the sea with a mill-stone hung round his neck! Alas for the world with its pitfalls! In the nature of things there must be pitfalls, yet alas for the man who is responsible for them!

The right way may mean costly sacrifice

"If your hand or your foot leads you astray, cut it off and throw it away. It is a good thing to go into life maimed or crippled—rather than to have both hands and feet and be thrown on to the everlasting fire. Yes, and if your eye leads you astray, tear it out and throw it away. It is a good thing to go one-eyed into life—rather than to have both your eyes and be thrown on the fire of the rubbish-heap.

"Be careful that you never despise a single one of these little ones—for I tell you that they have angels who see my Father's face continually in Heaven.

"What do you think? If a man has a hundred sheep and one wanders away from the rest, won't he leave the ninety-nine on the hill-side and set out to look for the one who has wandered away? Yes, and if he should chance to find it I assure you he is more delighted over that one than he is over the ninety-nine who never wandered away. You can understand then that it is never the will of your Father in Heaven that a single one of these little ones should be lost.

Reconciliation must always be attempted

"But if your brother wrongs you, go and have it out with him at once—just between the two of you. If he will listen to you, you have won him back as your brother. But if he will not listen to you, take one or two others with you so that everything that is said may have the support of two or three witnesses. And if he still won't pay any attention, tell the matter to the church. And if he won't even listen to the church then he must be to you just like a pagan—or a tax-collector!

The connection between earthly conduct and spiritual reality

"Believe me, whatever you forbid upon earth will be what is forbidden in Heaven, and whatever you permit on earth will be what is permitted in Heaven.*

"And I tell you once more that if two of you on earth agree in asking for anything it will be granted to you by my Heavenly Father. For wherever two or three people have come together in my name, I am there, right among them!"

The necessity for forgiveness

Then Peter approached him with the question, "Master, if my brother goes on wronging me how often should I forgive him? Would seven times be enough?"

"No," replied Jesus, "not seven times, but seventy times seven! For the kingdom of Heaven is like a king who decided to settle his accounts with his servants. When he had started calling in his accounts, a man was brought to him who owed him millions of pounds. As he had no means of repaying the debt, his master gave orders for him to be sold as a slave, and his wife and children and all his possessions as well, and the money to be paid over. At this the servant fell on his knees before his master, 'Oh, be patient with me!' he cried, 'and I will pay you back every penny!' Then his master was moved with pity for him, set him free and cancelled his debt.

"But when this same servant had left his master's presence, he found one of his fellow-servants who owed him a few shillings. He grabbed him and seized him by the throat, crying, 'Pay up what you owe me!' At this his fellow-servant fell down at his feet, and implored him, 'Oh, be patient with me, and I will pay you back!' But he refused and went out and had him put in prison until he should repay the debt.

* See note 3, page 552.

"When the other fellow-servants saw what had happened, they were horrified and went and told their master the whole incident. Then his master called him in.

" 'You wicked servant!' he said. 'Didn't I cancel all that debt when you begged me to do so? Oughtn't you to have taken pity on your fellow-servant as I, your master, took pity on you?' And his master in anger handed him over to the jailers till he should repay the whole debt. This is how my Heavenly Father will treat you unless you each forgive your brother from your heart."

CHAPTER 19

The divine principle of marriage

WHEN Jesus had finished talking on these matters, he left Galilee and went on to the district of Judaea on the far side of the Jordan. Vast crowds followed him, and he healed them there.

Then the Pharisees arrived with a test-question.

"Is it right," they asked, "for a man to divorce his wife on any grounds whatever?"

"Haven't you read," he answered, "that the one who created them from the beginning made them male and female and said: 'For this cause shall a man leave his father and mother, and shall cleave to his wife; and the twain shall become one flesh'? So they are no longer two separate people but one. No man therefore must separate what God has joined together."

"Then why," they retorted, "did Moses command us to give a written divorce-notice and dismiss the woman?"

"It was because you knew so little of the meaning of love that Moses allowed you to divorce your wives! But that was not the original principle. I tell you that anyone who divorces his wife on any grounds except her unfaithfulness and marries some other woman commits adultery."

His disciples said to him, "If that is a man's position with his wife, it is not worth getting married!"

"It is not everybody who can accept this principle," replied Jesus, "—only those who have a special gift. For some are incapable of marriage from birth, some are made incapable by the action of men, and some have made themselves so for the sake of the kingdom of Heaven. Let the man who can accept what I have said accept it."

Jesus welcomes children

Then some little children were brought to him, so that he could put his hands on them and pray for them. The disciples strongly disapproved of this but Jesus said,

"You must let little children come to me, and you must never stop them. The kingdom of Heaven belongs to little children like these!" Then he laid his hands on them and walked away.

Jesus shows that keeping the commandments is not enough

Then it happened that a man came up to him and said, "Master what good thing must I do to secure eternal life?"

"I wonder why you ask me about what is good?" Jesus answered him. "Only One is good. But if you want to enter that life you must keep the commandments."

"Which ones?" he asked.

"Thou shalt do no murder, Thou shalt not commit adultery, Thou shalt not steal, Thou shalt not bear false witness, Honour thy father and thy mother; and Thou shalt love thy neighbour as thyself," replied Jesus.

"I have carefully kept all these," returned the young man. "What is still missing in my life?"

Then Jesus told him, "If you want to be perfect, go now and sell your possessions and give the money to the poor—you will have riches in Heaven. Then come and follow me!"

When the young man heard that he turned away crestfallen, for he was very wealthy.

Then Jesus remarked to his disciples, "Believe me, a rich man will find it very difficult to enter the kingdom of Heaven. Yes, I repeat, a camel could more easily squeeze through the eye of a needle than a rich man get into the kingdom of God!"

The disciples were simply amazed to hear this, and said, "Then who can possibly be saved?"

Jesus looked steadily at them and replied, "Humanly speaking it is impossible; but with God anything is possible!"

Jesus declares that sacrifice for the kingdom will be repaid

At this Peter exclaimed, "Look, we have left everything and followed you. What will that be worth to us?"

"Believe me," said Jesus, "when I tell you that in the new

world, when the Son of Man shall take his seat on his glorious throne, you who have followed me will also be seated on twelve thrones as judges of the twelve tribes of Israel. Every man who has left houses or brothers or sisters or father or mother or children or land for my sake will get them back many times over, and will inherit eternal life. But many who are first now will be last then —and the last first!

CHAPTER 20

But God's generosity may appear unfair

"For the kingdom of Heaven is like a householder going out early in the morning to hire labourers for his vineyard. He agreed with them on a wage of a silver coin a day and sent them to work. About nine o'clock he went and saw some others standing about in the market-place with nothing to do. 'You go to the vineyard too,' he said to them, 'and I will pay you a fair wage.' And off they went. At about mid-day and again at about three o'clock in the afternoon he went out and did the same thing. Then about five o'clock he went out and found some others standing about. 'Why are you standing about here all day doing nothing?' he asked them. 'Because no one has employed us,' they replied. 'You go off into the vineyard as well, then,' he said.

"When evening came the owner of the vineyard said to his foreman, 'Call the labourers and pay them their wages, beginning with the last and ending with the first.' So those who were engaged at five o'clock came up and each man received a silver coin. But when the first to be employed came they reckoned they would get more; yet they also received a silver coin each. As they took their money they grumbled at the householder and said, 'These last fellows have only put in one hour's work and you've treated them exactly the same as us who have gone through all the hard work and heat of the day!'

"But he replied to one of them, 'My friend, I'm not being unjust to you. Wasn't our agreement for a silver coin a day? Take your money and go home. It is my wish to give the late-comers as much as I give you. May I not do what I like with what belongs to me? Must you be jealous because I am generous?'

"So, many who are the last now will be first then and the first last."

Jesus' final journey to Jerusalem

Then, as he was on his way up to Jerusalem, Jesus took the twelve disciples aside and spoke to them as they walked along. "Listen, we are now going up to Jerusalem and the Son of Man will be handed over to the chief priests and the scribes—and they will condemn him to death. They will hand him over to the heathen to ridicule and flog and crucify. And on the third day he will be raised again!"

At this point the mother of the sons of Zebedee arrived with her sons and knelt in front of Jesus to ask him a favour.

"What is it you want?" he asked her.

"Please say that these two sons of mine may sit one on each side of you when you are king!" she said.

"You don't know what it is you are asking," replied Jesus. "Can you two drink what I have to drink?"

"Yes, we can," they answered.

"Ah, you will indeed 'drink my drink'," Jesus told them, "but as for sitting on either side of me, that is not for me to grant—that is reserved for those for whom it has been prepared by my Father."

When the other ten heard of this incident they were highly indignant with the two brothers.

But Jesus called them to him and said,

"You know that the rulers of the heathen lord it over them and that their great ones have absolute power? But it must not be so among you. No, whoever among you wants to be great must become your servant, and if he wants to be first among you he must be your slave—just as the Son of Man has not come to be served but to serve, and to give his life to set many others free."

He restores sight to two blind men

A great crowd followed them as they were leaving Jericho, and two blind men who were sitting by the roadside, hearing that it was Jesus who was passing, cried out, "Have pity on us, Lord, you Son of David!" The crowd told them sharply to be quiet, but this only made them cry out more loudly still, "Have pity on us, Lord, you Son of David!"

Jesus stood quite still and called out to them, "What do you want me to do for you?"

"Lord, let us see again!"

And Jesus, deeply moved with pity, touched their eyes. At once their sight was restored, and they followed him.

CHAPTER 21

Jesus' final entry into Jerusalem

As they approached Jerusalem and came to Bethphage and the Mount of Olives, Jesus sent two disciples ahead telling them, "Go into the village in front of you and you will at once find there a donkey tethered, and a colt with her. Untie them and bring them to me. Should anyone say anything to you, you are to say, 'The Lord needs them', and he will send them immediately."

All this happened to fulfil the prophet's saying—

Tell ye the daughter of Zion,
Behold, thy King cometh unto thee,
Meek, and riding upon an ass,
And upon a colt the foal of an ass.

So the disciples went off and followed Jesus' instructions. They brought the donkey and the colt, and put their cloaks on them, and Jesus took his seat upon them. Then a vast crowd spread their cloaks on the road, while others cut down branches from the trees and spread them in his path. The crowds who went in front of him and the crowds who followed behind him all shouted, "God save the Son of David! Blessed is the man who comes in the name of the Lord! God save him from on high!"

And as he entered Jerusalem a shock ran through the whole city. "Who *is* this?" men cried. "This is Jesus the prophet," replied the crowd, "the man from Nazareth in Galilee!"

Then Jesus went into the Temple-precincts and drove out all the buyers and sellers there. He overturned the tables of the money-changers and the benches of those who sold doves, crying—

"It is written, 'My house shall be called a house of prayer.' But you have turned it into a thieves' kitchen!"

And there in the Temple the blind and the lame came to him, and he healed them. But when the chief priests and the scribes saw the wonderful things he did, and that children were shouting in the Temple the words, "God save the Son of David", they were highly indignant. "Can't you hear what these children are saying?" they asked Jesus.

"Yes," he replied, "and haven't you ever read the words, 'Out of the mouth of babes and sucklings thou hast perfected praise'?" And he turned on his heel and went out of the city to Bethany, where he spent the night.

His strange words to the fig-tree

In the morning he came back early to the city and felt hungry. He saw a fig-tree growing by the side of the road, but when he got to it he discovered there was nothing on it but leaves.

"No more fruit shall ever grow on you!" he said to it, and all at once the fig-tree withered away. When the disciples saw this happen they were simply amazed. "How on earth did the fig-tree wither away as suddenly as that?" they asked.

"Believe me," replied Jesus, "if you have faith and have no doubts in your heart, you will not only do this to a fig-tree but even if you should say to this hill, 'Be uprooted and thrown into the sea', it will happen! Everything you ask for in prayer, if you have faith, you will receive."

Jesus meets a question with a counter-question

Then when he had entered the Temple and was in the act of teaching, the chief priests and Jewish elders came up to him and said, "What authority have you for what you're doing, and who gave you that authority?"

"I am also going to ask you one question," Jesus replied to them, "and if you answer it I will tell you what authority I have for what I do. John's baptism, now, did it come from Heaven or was it purely human?"

At this they began arguing among themselves, "If we say, 'It came from Heaven', he will say to us, 'Then why didn't you believe in him?' But if we should say, 'It was purely human'—well, we are afraid of the people—for all of them consider John was a prophet."

So they answered Jesus, "We do not know."

"Then I will not tell you by what authority I do these things!" returned Jesus. "But what is your opinion about this? There was a man with two sons. He went to the first and said, 'Go and work in my vineyard today, my son.' He said, 'I won't'. But afterwards he changed his mind and went. Then the father approached the second son with the same request. He said, 'All right, sir'—but he never went. Which of these two did what his father wanted?"

"The first one," they replied.

"Yes," retorted Jesus, "and I tell you that tax-collectors and prostitutes are going into the kingdom of God in front of you!"

"For John came to you as a truly good man, and you did not believe in him—yet the tax-collectors and the prostitutes did! And, even after seeing that, you would not change your minds and believe him."

Jesus tells a pointed story

"Now listen to another parable. There was once a man, a landowner, who planted a vineyard, fenced it round, dug out a hole for the wine-press and built a watch-tower. Then he let it out to farm-workers and went abroad. When the vintage-time approached he sent his servants to the farm-workers to receive his share of the crop. But they took his servants, beat up one, killed another, and stoned a third. Then he sent some more servants, a larger party than the first, but they treated them in just the same way. Finally he sent his own son, saying, 'They will respect my son.' Yet when the farm-workers saw the son they said to each other, 'This fellow is the future owner. Come on, let's kill him and we shall get everything that he would have had!' So they took him, threw him out of the vineyard and killed him. Now when the owner of the vineyard returns, what will he do to those farm-workers?"

"He will kill those scoundrels without mercy," they replied, "and will let the vineyard out to other tenants, who will give him the produce at the right season."

"And have you never read these words of scripture," said Jesus to them:

The stone which the builders rejected,
The same was made the head of the corner:
This was from the Lord,
And it is marvellous in our eyes?

"Here, I tell you, lies the reason why the kingdom of God is going to be taken away from you and given to a people who will produce its proper fruit.
(Any man who falls on this stone will be shattered, and any man upon whom it falls will be ground into dust)."

When the chief priests and the Pharisees heard his parables they realised that he was speaking about them. They longed to get their hands on him, but they were afraid of the crowds, who regarded him as a prophet.

CHAPTER 22

The kingdom is not to be lightly disregarded

THEN Jesus began to talk to them again in parables.

"The kingdom of Heaven," he said, "is like a king who arranged a wedding-feast for his son. He sent his servants to summon those who had been invited to the festivities, but they refused to come. Then he tried again; he sent some more servants, saying to them, 'Tell those who have been invited, "Here is my banquet all ready, my bullocks and fat cattle have been slaughtered and everything is prepared. Come along to the wedding." ' But they took no notice of this and went off, one to his farm, and another to his business. As for the rest, they got hold of the servants, treated them with insults, and finally killed them. At this the king was very angry and sent his troops and killed those murderers and burned down their city. Then he said to his servants, 'The wedding-feast is all ready, but those who were invited were not good enough for it. So go off now to all the street corners and invite everyone you find there to the feast.' So the servants went out on to the streets and collected together all those whom they found, bad and good alike. And the hall became filled with guests. But when the king came in to inspect the guests, he noticed among them a man not dressed for a wedding. 'How did you come in here, my friend,' he said to him, 'without being properly dressed for the wedding?' And the man had nothing to say. Then the king said to the ushers, 'Tie him up and throw him into the darkness outside, where there will be tears and bitter regret!' For many are invited but few are chosen."

A clever trap—and a penetrating answer

Then the Pharisees went off and discussed how they could trap him in argument. Eventually they sent their disciples with some of the Herod-party to say this, "Master, we know that you are an honest man who teaches the way of God faithfully and that you are not swayed by men's opinion of you. Obviously you don't care for human approval. Now tell us—'Is it right to pay taxes to Caesar or not?' "

But Jesus knowing their evil intention said, "Why try this trick on me, you frauds? Show me the money you pay the tax with." They handed him a silver coin, and he said to them, "Whose head is this and whose name is in the inscription?"

"Caesar's," they said.

"Then give to Caesar," he replied, "what belongs to Caesar and to God what belongs to God!"

This reply astonished them and they went away and let him alone.

Jesus exposes the ignorance of the Sadducees

On the same day some Sadducees (who deny that there is any resurrection) approached Jesus with this question: "Master, Moses said if a man should die without any children, his brother should marry his widow and raise up a family for him. Now, we had a case of seven brothers. The first one married and died, and since he had no family he left his wife to his brother. The same thing happened with the second and the third, right up to the seventh. Last of all the woman herself died. Now in this 'resurrection', whose wife will she be of these seven men—for she belonged to all of them?"

"You are very wide of the mark," replied Jesus to them, "for you are ignorant of both the scriptures and the power of God. For in the resurrection there is no such thing as marrying or being given in marriage—men live like the angels in Heaven. And as for the matter of the resurrection of the dead, haven't you ever read what was said to you by God himself, 'I am the God of Abraham, the God of Isaac and the God of Jacob'? God is not God of the dead but of living men!" When the crowds heard this they were astounded at his teaching.

The greatest commandments in the Law

When the Pharisees heard that he had silenced the Sadducees they came up to him in a body and one of them, an expert in the Law, put this test-question: "Master, which is the Law's greatest commandment?"

Jesus answered him, " 'Thou shalt love the Lord thy God with all thy heart, and with all thy soul, and with all thy mind.' This is the first and great commandment. And there is a second like it: 'Thou shalt love thy neighbour as thyself.' The whole of the Law and the Prophets depends on these two commandments."

Jesus puts an unanswerable question

Then Jesus asked the assembled Pharisees this question: "What is your opinion about Christ? Whose son is he?"

"The Son of David," they answered.

"How then," returned Jesus, "does David when inspired by the Spirit call him Lord? He says—

The Lord said unto my *Lord*,
Sit thou on my right hand,
Till I put thine enemies underneath thy feet?

If David then calls him Lord, how can he be his son?"

Nobody was able to answer this and from that day on no one dared to ask him any further questions.

CHAPTER 23

He publicly warns the people against their religious leaders

THEN Jesus addressed the crowds and his disciples. "The scribes and the Pharisees speak with the authority of Moses," he told them, "so you must do what they tell you and follow their instructions. But you must not imitate their lives! For they preach but do not practise. They pile up back-breaking burdens and lay them on other men's shoulders—yet they themselves will not raise a finger to move them. Their whole lives are planned with an eye to effect. They increase the size of their phylacteries* and lengthen the tassels of their robes; they love seats of honour at dinner parties and front places in the synagogues. They love to be greeted with respect in public places and to have men call them 'rabbi!' Don't you ever be called 'rabbi'—you have only one teacher, and all of you are brothers. And don't call any human being 'father'—for you have one Father and he is in Heaven. And you must not let people call you 'leaders'—you have only one leader, Christ! The only 'superior' among you is the one who serves the others. For every man who promotes himself will be humbled, and every man who learns to be humble will find promotion.

"But alas for you, you scribes and Pharisees, play-actors that you are! You lock the doors of the kingdom of Heaven in men's faces; you will not go in yourselves neither will you allow those at the door to go inside.

* Phylacteries: Strips of parchment inscribed with texts from the Law, worn on the arm or forehead.

"Alas for you, you scribes and Pharisees, play-actors! You scour sea and land to make a single convert, and then you make him twice as ripe for destruction as you are yourselves.

"Alas for you, you blind leaders! You say, 'If anyone swears by the Temple it amounts to nothing, but if he swears by the gold of the Temple he is bound by his oath.' You blind fools, which is the more important, the gold or the Temple which sanctifies the gold? And you say, 'If anyone swears by the altar it doesn't matter, but if he swears by the gift placed on the altar he is bound by his oath.' Have you no eyes—which is more important, the gift, or the altar which sanctifies the gift? Any man who swears by the altar is swearing by the altar and whatever is offered upon it; and anyone who swears by the Temple is swearing by the Temple and by him who dwells in it; and anyone who swears by Heaven is swearing by the throne of God and by the One who sits upon that throne.

"Alas for you, scribes and Pharisees, you utter frauds! For you pay your tithe on mint and dill and cummin, and neglect the things which carry far more weight in the Law—justice, mercy and good faith. These are the things you should have observed—without neglecting the others. You are blind leaders, for you filter out a mosquito yet swallow a camel.

"What miserable frauds you are, you scribes and Pharisees! You clean the outside of the cup and the dish, while the inside is full of greed and self-indulgence. Can't you see, Pharisee? First wash the inside of a cup, and then you can clean the outside.

"Alas for you, you hypocritical scribes and Pharisees! You are like white-washed tombs, which look fine on the outside but inside are full of dead men's bones and all kinds of rottenness. For you appear like good men on the outside—but inside you are a mass of pretence and wickedness.

"What miserable frauds you are, you scribes and Pharisees! You build tombs for the prophets, and decorate monuments for good men of the past, and then say, 'If we had lived in the times of our ancestors we should never have joined in the killing of the prophets.' Yes, 'your ancestors'—*that* shows you to be sons indeed of those who murdered the prophets. Go ahead then, and finish off what your ancestors tried to do! You serpents, you viper's brood, how do you think you are going to avoid being condemned to the fires of destruction? Listen now to the reason why I send you prophets and wise and learned men; some of these you will kill and crucify, others you will flog in your synagogues and hunt from town to town. So that on your hands is all the innocent blood spilt on this earth, from the blood of Abel the good to the blood of Zachariah, Barachiah's son, whom you murdered between the sanctuary and the altar. Yes, I tell you that all this will be laid at the doors of this generation.

Jesus mourns over Jerusalem, and foretells its destruction

"Oh, Jerusalem, Jerusalem! You murder the prophets and stone the messengers that are sent to you. How often have I longed to gather your children round me like a bird gathering her brood together under her wings—and you would never have it. Now all you have left is your house—desolate. I tell you that you will never see me again till the day when you cry, 'Blessed is he who comes in the name of the Lord!' "

CHAPTER 24

THEN Jesus went out of the Temple and was walking away when his disciples came up and drew his attention to its buildings. "You see all these?" replied Jesus. "I tell you every stone will be thrown down till there is not a single one left standing upon another."

And as he was sitting on the slope of the Mount of Olives his disciples came to him privately and said, "Tell us, when will this happen? What will be the signal for your coming and the end of this world?"

"Be careful that no one misleads you," returned Jesus, "for many men will come in my name saying 'I am Christ', and they will mislead many. You will certainly hear of wars and rumours of wars—but don't be alarmed. Such things must indeed happen, but that is not the end. For one nation will rise in arms against another, and one kingdom against another, and there will be famines and earthquakes in different parts of the world. But all that is only the beginning of the birth-pangs. For then comes the time when men will hand you over to persecution, and kill you. And all nations will hate you because you bear my name. Then comes the time when many will lose their faith and will betray and hate each other. Yes, and many false prophets will arise, and will mislead many people. Because of the spread of wickedness the love of most men will grow cold, though the man who holds out to the end will be saved. This good news of the kingdom will be proclaimed to men all over the world as a witness to all the nations, and then the end will come.

Jesus prophesies a future of suffering

"When the time comes, then, that you see the 'abomination of desolation' prophesied by Daniel 'standing in the sacred place'—the reader should note this—then is the time for those in Judaea to take to the hills. A man on his house-top must not waste time going into his house to collect anything; a man at work in the fields must not go back home to fetch his clothes. Alas for the pregnant, alas for those with babes at their breasts at that time! Pray God that you may not have to make your escape in the winter or on the Sabbath day, for then there will be great misery, such as has never happened from the beginning of the world until now, and will never happen again! Yes, if those days had not been cut short no human being would survive. But for the sake of God's people those days are to be shortened.

"If anyone says to you then, 'Look, here is Christ!' or 'There he is!' don't believe it. False christs and false prophets are going to appear and will produce great signs and wonders to mislead, if it were possible, even God's own people. Listen, I am warning you. So that if people say to you, 'There he is, in the desert!' you are not to go out there. If they say, 'Here he is, in this inner room!' don't believe it. For as lightning flashes across from east to west so will the Son of Man's coming be. 'Wherever there is a dead body, there the vultures will flock.'

At the end of time the Son of Man will return

"Immediately after the misery of those days the sun will be darkened, the moon will fail to give her light, the stars will fall from the sky, and the powers of heaven will be shaken. Then the sign of the Son of Man will appear in the sky, and all the nations of the earth will wring their hands as they see the Son of Man coming on the clouds of the sky in power and great splendour. And he will send out his angels with a loud trumpet-call and they will gather together his chosen from the four winds—from one end of the heavens to the other.

"Learn what the fig-tree can teach you. As soon as its branches grow full of sap and produce leaves you know that summer is near. So when you see all these things happening you may know that he is near, at your very door! Believe me, this generation will not disappear till all this has taken place. Heaven and earth will pass away, but my words will never pass away! But about that actual day and time no one knows—not even the angels of Heaven, nor the Son, only the Father. For just as life went on in the days of Noah so will it be at the coming of the Son of Man. In those days before the flood people were eating, drinking, marrying and being given in marriage until the very day that Noah went into the ark, and knew nothing about the flood until it came and destroyed them all. So will it be at the coming of the Son of Man. Two men will be in the field; one is taken and one is left behind. Two women will be grinding at the hand-mill; one is taken and one is left behind. You must be on the alert then, for you do not know on what day your master is coming. You can be sure of this, however, that if the householder had known what time of night the burglar would arrive, he would have been ready for him and would not have allowed his house to be broken into. That is why you must always be ready, for you do not know when to expect the Son of Man to arrive.

Vigilance is essential

"Who then is the faithful and sensible servant, whom his master put in charge of his household to give the others their food at the proper time? Well, he is fortunate if his master finds him doing that duty on his return! Believe me, he will promote him to look after all his property. But if he should be a bad servant who says to himself, 'My master takes his time about returning', and should begin to beat his fellow-servants and eat and drink with drunkards, that servant's master will return on a day which he does not expect and at a time which he does not know, and will punish him severely and send him off to share the penalty of the unfaithful—to the place of tears and bitter regret!

CHAPTER 25

"In those days the kingdom of Heaven will be like ten bridesmaids who took their lamps and went out to meet the bridegroom. Five of them were foolish and five were sensible. The foolish ones took their lamps but did not take any oil with them. But the sensible ones brought their lamps and oil in their flasks as well. Then, as the bridegroom was a very long time, they all grew drowsy and fell asleep. But in the middle of the night there came a shout, 'Wake up, here comes the bridegroom! Out you go to meet him!' Then up got all the bridesmaids and attended to their lamps. The foolish ones said to the sensible ones, 'Please give us some of your oil—our lamps are going out!' 'Oh, no,' returned the sensible ones, 'there might not be enough for all of us. Better go to the oil-shop and buy some for yourselves.' But while they had gone off to buy the oil the bridegroom arrived, and those bridesmaids who were ready went in with him for the festivities and the door was shut behind them. Later on the rest of the bridesmaids came and said, 'Oh, please, sir, open the door for us!' But he replied, 'I tell you I don't know you!' So be on the alert—for you do not know the day or the time.

Life is hard for the faint-hearted

"It is just like a man leaving home who called his household servants together before he went and handed his possessions over to them to manage. He gave one five thousand pounds, another two thousand and another one thousand—according to the man's ability. Then he went away.

"The man who had received five thousand pounds went out at once and by doing business with this sum he made another five thousand. Similarly the man with two thousand pounds made another two thousand. But the man who had received one thousand pounds went off and dug a hole in the ground and hid his master's money.

"Some years later the master of these servants arrived and went into the accounts with them. The one who had the five thousand pounds came in and brought him an additional five thousand with the words, 'You gave me five thousand pounds, sir; look, I've increased it by another five thousand.' 'Well done!' said his master, 'you're a sound, reliable servant. You've been trustworthy over a few things, now I'm going to put you in charge of many more. Come in and share your master's rejoicing.' Then the servant who had received two thousand pounds came in and said, 'You gave me two thousand pounds, sir; look, here's two thousand more that I've managed to make by it.' 'Well done!' said his master, 'you're a sound, reliable servant. You've been trustworthy over a few things, now I'm going to put you in charge of many. Come in and share your master's pleasure.'

"Then the man who had received the one thousand pounds came in and said, 'Sir, I always knew you were a hard man, reaping where you never sowed and collecting where you never laid out—so I was scared and I went off and hid your thousand pounds in the ground. Here is your money, intact.'

" 'You're a wicked, lazy servant!' his master told him. 'You say you knew that I reap where I never sowed and collect where I never laid out? Then you ought to have put my money in the bank, and when I came I should at any rate have received what belongs to me with interest. Take his thousand pounds away from him and give it to the man who now has the ten thousand!' (For the man who has something will have more given to him and will have plenty. But as for the man who has nothing, even his 'nothing' will be taken away.) 'And throw this useless servant into the darkness outside, where there will be tears and bitter regret.'

The final judgment

"But when the Son of Man comes in his splendour with all his angels with him, then he will take his seat on his glorious throne. All the nations will be assembled before him and he will separate men from each other like a shepherd separating sheep from goats. He will place the sheep on his right hand and the goats on his left.

"Then the king will say to those on his right: 'Come, you who have won my Father's blessing! Take your inheritance—the kingdom reserved for you since the foundation of the world! For I was hungry and you gave me food. I was thirsty and you gave me a drink. I was a stranger and you made me welcome. I was naked and you clothed me. I was ill and you came and looked after me. I was in prison and you came to see me there.'

"Then the true men will answer him, 'Lord, when did we see *you* hungry and give you food? When did we see *you* thirsty and give you something to drink? When did we see *you* a stranger and make you welcome, or see *you* naked and clothe you, or see *you* ill or in prison and go to see you?'

"And the king will reply, 'I assure you that whatever you did for the humblest of my brothers you did for me.'

"Then he will say to those on his left, 'Out of my presence, cursed as you are, into the eternal fire prepared for the devil and his angels! For I was hungry and you gave me nothing to eat. I was thirsty and you gave me nothing to drink. I was a stranger and you never made me welcome. When I was naked you did nothing to clothe me; when I was sick and in prison you never cared to visit me.'

"Then they too will answer him, 'Lord, when did we ever see *you* hungry, or thirsty, or a stranger, or naked, or sick or in prison, and fail to look after you?'

"Then the king will answer them with these words, 'I assure you that whatever you failed to do to the humblest of my brothers you failed to do to me.'

"And these will go off to eternal punishment, but the true men to eternal life."

CHAPTER 26

Jesus announces his coming death

WHEN Jesus had finished all this teaching he spoke to his disciples, "Do you realise that the Passover will begin in two days' time; and the Son of Man is going to be betrayed and crucified?"

An evil plot—and an act of love

At that very time the chief priests and elders of the people had assembled in the court of Caiaphas, the High Priest, and were discussing together how they might get hold of Jesus by some trick and kill him. But they kept saying, "It must not be during the festival or there might be a riot."

Back in Bethany, while Jesus was in the house of Simon the leper, a woman came to him with an alabaster flask of most expensive perfume, and poured it on his head as he was at table. The disciples were indignant when they saw this, and said, "What is the point of such wicked waste? Couldn't this perfume have been sold for a lot of money which could be given to the poor?" Jesus knew what they were saying and spoke to them, "Why must you make this woman feel uncomfortable? She has done a beautiful thing for me. You have the poor with you always, but you will not always have me. When she poured this perfume on my body, she was preparing it for my burial. I assure you that wherever the gospel is preached throughout the whole world, what she has done will also be told, as her memorial to me."

The betrayal is arranged

After this, one of the twelve, Judas Iscariot by name, approached the chief priests. "What will you give me," he said to them, "if I hand him over to you?" They settled with him for thirty silver coins, and from then on he looked for a convenient opportunity to betray Jesus.

The last supper

On the first day of unleavened bread the disciples came to Jesus with the question, "Where do you want us to make our preparations for you to eat the Passover?"

"Go into the city," Jesus replied, "to a certain man there and say to him, 'The Master says, "My time is near. I am going to keep the Passover with my disciples at your house." ' " The disciples did as Jesus had instructed them and prepared the Passover. Then late in the evening he took his place at table with the twelve and during the meal he said, "I tell you plainly that one of you is going to betray me." They were deeply distressed at this and each began to say to him in turn, "Surely, Lord, I am not the one?" And his answer was, "A man who has dipped his hand into the dish with me is the man who will betray me. It is true that the Son of Man will follow the road foretold by the scriptures, but alas for the man through whom he is betrayed! It would be better for that man if he had never been born." And Judas, who actually betrayed him, said, "Master, surely I am not the one?"

"You have said it!" replied Jesus.

In the middle of the meal Jesus took a loaf and after blessing it he broke it into pieces and gave it to the disciples. "Take and eat this," he said, "it is my body." Then he took a cup and, after thanking God, he gave it to them with the words, "Drink this, all of you, for it is my blood, the blood of the new agreement shed to set many free from their sins. I tell you I will drink no more wine until I drink it afresh with you in my Father's kingdom." Then they sang a hymn together and went out to the Mount of Olives. There Jesus said to them, "Tonight every one of you will lose his faith in me. For the scripture says, 'I will smite the shepherd, and the sheep of the flock shall be scattered abroad.' But after I am raised I shall go before you into Galilee!"

At this Peter exclaimed, "Even if everyone should lose his faith in you, I never will!"

"I tell you, Peter," replied Jesus, "that tonight, before the cock crows, you will disown me three times."

"Even if it means dying with you I will never disown you," said Peter. And all the disciples made the same protest.

The prayer in Gethsemane

Then Jesus came with the disciples to a place called Gethsemane and said to them, "Sit down here while I go over there and pray." Then he took with him Peter and the two sons of Zebedee and began to be in terrible pain and agony of mind. "My heart is breaking with a death-like grief," he told them, "stay here and keep watch with me." Then he walked on a little way and fell on his face and prayed, "My Father, if it is possible let this cup pass from me—yet it must not be what I want, but what you want."

Then he came back to the disciples and found them fast asleep. He spoke to Peter, "Couldn't you three keep awake with me for a single hour? Watch and pray, all of you, that you may not have to face temptation. Your spirit is willing, but human nature is weak."

Then he went away a second time and prayed, "My Father, if it is not possible for this cup to pass from me without my drinking it, then your will must be done."

And he came and found them asleep again, for they could not keep their eyes open. So he left them and went away again and prayed for the third time using the same words as before. Then he came back to his disciples and spoke to them, "Are you still sleeping and taking your ease? In a moment you will see the Son of Man betrayed into the hands of evil men. Wake up, let us be going! Look, here comes my betrayer!"

The betrayal

And while the words were still on his lips Judas, one of the twelve, appeared with a great crowd armed with swords and staves, sent by the chief priests and Jewish elders. (The traitor himself had given them a sign, "The one I kiss will be the man. Get him!")

Without any hesitation he walked up to Jesus. "Greetings, Master!" he cried and kissed him affectionately. "Judas, my friend," replied Jesus, "why are you here?"

Then the others came up, seized hold of Jesus and held him.

Suddenly one of Jesus' disciples drew his sword, slashed at the High Priest's servant and cut off his ear. At this Jesus said to him, "Put your sword back into its proper place. All those who take the sword die by the sword. Do you imagine that I could not appeal to my Father, and he would at once send more than twelve legions of angels to defend me? But then, how would the scriptures be fulfilled which say that all this must take place?"

And then Jesus spoke to the crowds around him: "So you've come out with your swords and staves to capture me like a bandit, have you? Day after day I sat teaching in the Temple and you never laid a finger on me. But all this is happening as the prophets said it would." And at this point all the disciples deserted him and made their escape.

Jesus before the High Priest

The men who had seized Jesus took him off to Caiaphas the High Priest in whose house the scribes and elders were assembled. Peter followed him at a distance right up to the High Priest's courtyard. Then he went inside and sat down with the servants and waited to see the end.

Meanwhile the chief priests and the whole Council did all they could to find false evidence against Jesus to get him condemned to death. They failed completely, even after a number of perjurers came forward. In the end two men stood up and said, "This man said, 'I can pull down the Temple of God and rebuild it in three days.' " Then the High Priest rose to his feet and addressed Jesus. "Have you no answer? What about the evidence of these men against you?" But Jesus was silent. Then the High Priest said to him, "I command you by the living God, to tell us on your oath if you are Christ, the Son of God." Jesus said to him, "You have said so. Yes, and I tell you that in the future you will see the Son of Man sitting at the right hand of power and coming on the clouds of Heaven."

At this the High Priest tore his robes and cried, "That was blasphemy! Where is the need for further witnesses? Look, you've heard the blasphemy—what's your verdict now?" And they replied, "He deserves to die."

Then they spat in his face and knocked him about, and some slapped him, crying, "Prophesy, you Christ, who was that who hit you?"

Peter disowns his master

All this time Peter was sitting outside in the courtyard, and a maidservant came up to him and said, "Weren't you too with Jesus, the man from Galilee?" But he denied it before them all, saying, "I don't know what you're talking about." Then when he had gone out into the porch, another maid caught sight of him and said to those who were there, "This man was with Jesus of Nazareth." And again he denied it with an oath—"I don't know the man!" A few minutes later those who were standing about came up to Peter and said to him, "You certainly are one of them, it's obvious from your accent." At that he began to curse and swear—"I tell you I don't know the man!" Immediately the cock crew, and the words of Jesus came back into Peter's mind—"Before the cock crows you will disown me three times." And he went outside and wept bitterly.

CHAPTER 27

WHEN the morning came, all the chief priests and elders of the people met in council to decide how they could get Jesus executed. Then they marched him off with his hands tied, and handed him over to Pilate the governor.

The remorse of Judas

When Judas, who had betrayed him, saw that Jesus was condemned, he was overcome with remorse. He returned the thirty silver coins to the chief priests and elders, with the words, "I have done wrong—I have betrayed an innocent man to death."

"And what has that got to do with us?" they replied. "That's your affair."

And Judas flung down the silver in the Temple, left and went away and hanged himself. But the chief priests picked up the money and said, "It is not right to put this into the Temple treasury, for it is the price of a man's life." So, after a further consultation, they purchased with it the Potter's Field to be a burial-ground for foreigners, which is why it is called "the Field of Blood" to this day. And so the words of Jeremiah the prophet came true:

And they took the thirty pieces of silver, the price of him

that was priced, whom certain of the children of Israel did price; and they gave them for the potter's field, as the Lord appointed me.

Jesus before Pilate

Meanwhile Jesus stood in front of the governor, who asked him, "Well, you—*are* you the King of the Jews?"

"That is what you are saying," replied Jesus.

But while the chief priests and elders were making their accusations, he made no reply at all. So Pilate said to him, "Can you not hear the evidence they're bringing against you?" But to the governor's amazement, Jesus did not answer a single one of their accusations.

Now it was the custom at festival-time for the governor to release any one prisoner whom the people chose. And it happened that at this time they had a notorious prisoner called Barabbas. So when they were assembled, Pilate said to them, "Which one do you want me to set free, Barabbas or Jesus called Christ?" For he knew very well that the latter had been handed over to him through sheer malice. And indeed while he was actually sitting on the Bench his wife sent a message to him—"Don't have anything to do with that good man! I had terrible dreams about him last night!" But the chief priests and elders persuaded the mob to ask for Barabbas and demand Jesus' execution. Then the governor asked them directly, "Which of these two are you asking me to release?"

"Barabbas!" they cried.

"Then what am I to do with Jesus who is called Christ?" asked Pilate.

"Have him crucified!" they all cried. At this Pilate said, "Why, what is his crime?" But their voices rose to a roar, "Have him crucified!" When Pilate realised that nothing more could be done but that there would soon be a riot, he took a bowl of water and washed his hands before the crowd, saying, "I take no responsibility for the death of this man. You must see to that yourselves." To this the whole crowd replied, "Let his blood be on us and on our children!" Whereupon Pilate released Barabbas for them, but he had Jesus flogged and handed over for crucifixion.

Then the governor's soldiers took Jesus into the governor's palace and collected the whole guard around him. There they stripped him and put a scarlet cloak upon him. They twisted some thorn-twigs into a crown and put it on his head and put a stick into his right hand. They bowed low before him and jeered at him with the words, "Hail, your majesty, king of the Jews!" Then they spat on him, took the stick and hit him on the head with it. And when they had finished their fun, they stripped the cloak off again, put his own clothes upon him and led him off for crucifixion. On their way out of the city they met a man called Simon, a native of Cyrene in Africa, and they compelled him to carry Jesus' cross.

The crucifixion

Then when they came to a place called Golgotha (which means Skull Hill) they offered him a drink of wine mixed with some bitter drug, but when he had tasted it he refused to drink. And when they had crucified him they shared out his clothes by drawing lots.

Then they sat down to keep guard over him. And over his head they put a placard with the charge against him:

THIS IS JESUS, THE KING OF THE JEWS

Now two bandits were crucified with Jesus at the same time, one on either side of him. The passers-by nodded their heads knowingly and called out to him in mockery, "Hi, you who could pull down the Temple and build it up again in three days—why don't you save yourself? If you are the Son of God, step down from the cross!" The chief priests also joined the scribes and elders in jeering at him, saying, "He saved others, but he can't save himself! If this is the king of Israel, why doesn't he come down from the cross now, and we will believe him! He trusted in God . . . let God rescue him if He wants to. For he said, 'I am God's son'." Even the bandits who were crucified with him hurled the same abuse at him.

Then from midday until three o'clock darkness spread over the whole countryside, and about then Jesus cried with a loud voice, "My God, my God, why did you forsake me?" Some of those who were standing there heard these words which Jesus spoke in Aramaic (*Eli, Eli lama sabachthani?*), and said, "This man is calling for Elijah!" And one of them ran off and fetched a sponge, soaked it in vinegar and put it on a stick and held it up for him to drink. But the others said, "Let him alone! Let's see if Elijah will come and save him." But Jesus uttered one more great cry, and gave up his spirit.

And the sanctuary curtain in the Temple was torn in two from top to bottom. The ground shook, rocks split and graves were opened. (A number of bodies of holy men who were asleep in death rose again. They left their graves after Jesus' resurrection and entered the holy city and appeared to many people.) When the centurion and his company who were keeping guard over Jesus saw the earthquake and all that was happening they were terrified. "Indeed this man was a son of God!" they said.

There were many women at the scene watching from a distance. They had followed Jesus from Galilee to look after his needs. Among them were Mary of Magdala, Mary the mother of James and Joseph, and the mother of Zebedee's sons.

Jesus is buried and the tomb is guarded

When evening fell, Joseph, a wealthy man from Arimathaea, who was himself a disciple of Jesus, went to Pilate and asked for the body of Jesus, and Pilate gave orders for the body to be handed over to him. So Joseph took it, wrapped it in clean linen and placed it in his own new tomb which had been hewn out of the rock. Then he rolled a large stone to the doorway of the tomb and went away. Mary from Magdala and the other Mary were there, sitting in front of the tomb.

Next day, which was the day after the Preparation, the chief priests and the Pharisees went in a body to Pilate and said, "Sir, we have remembered that while this impostor was alive, he said, 'After three days I shall be raised again.' Will you give the order then to have the grave closely guarded until the third day, so that there can be no chance of his disciples' coming and stealing the body and telling people that he has been raised from the dead? We should then be faced with a worse fraud than the first one."

"You have a guard," Pilate told them. "Go and make it as safe as you think necessary." And they went and made the grave secure, putting a seal on the stone and leaving it under guard.

CHAPTER 28

The first Lord's day: Jesus rises

When the Sabbath was over, just as the first day of the week was dawning, Mary from Magdala and the other Mary went to look at the tomb. At that moment there was a great earthquake, for an angel of the Lord came down from Heaven, went forward and rolled back the stone, and sat down upon it. His appearance shone like lightning and his clothes were white as snow. The guards shook with terror at the sight of him and collapsed like dead men. But the angel spoke to the women, "Do not be afraid. I know that you are looking for Jesus who was crucified. He is not here—he has been raised, just as he said. Come and look at the place where he was lying. Then go quickly and tell his disciples that he has been raised from the dead. And, listen, he goes before you into Galilee; you will see him there! Now I have told you my message." Then the women went away quickly from the tomb, their hearts filled with awe and great joy, and ran to give the news to his disciples. But quite suddenly, Jesus stood before them in their path, and said, "Peace be with you!" and they went forward to meet him, and clasping his feet, worshipped him. Then Jesus said to them, "Do not be afraid. Go and tell my brothers to go off now into Galilee and they shall see me there."

And while they were on their way, some of the sentries went into the city and reported to the chief priests everything that had happened. They then joined the elders, and after consultation gave the soldiers a considerable sum of money and told them, "Your story must be that his disciples came after dark, and stole him away while you were asleep. If by any chance this reaches the governor's ears, we will put it right with him and see that you do not suffer for it." So they took the money and obeyed their instructions. The story was spread and is current among the Jews to this day.

Jesus gives his final commission

But the eleven went to the hill-side in Galilee where Jesus had arranged to meet them, and when they had seen him they worshipped him, though some of them were doubtful. But Jesus came and spoke these words to them, "All power in Heaven and on earth has been given to me. You, then, are to go and make disciples of all the nations and baptise them in the name of the Father and of the Son and of the Holy Spirit. Teach them to observe all that I have commanded you and, remember, I am with you always, even to the end of the world."

The Gospel of Mark

It is generally agreed that Mark's Gospel is the earliest. It probably appeared in 65, soon after the Great Fire of Rome which devastated a great part of the city in the winter of 64–65. The Christians were made the scapegoats of this disaster by the Emperor Nero, and it is quite probable that there is a definite connection between the appearance of this first-written Gospel and the monstrously false accusations which were being made against Christians. The original papyrus roll is traditionally supposed to have borne the title—"The Gospel of Jesus Christ the Son of God."

The author is generally thought to have been John Mark, a native of Jerusalem. The house of his mother Mary became one of the meeting places of the early Christians (Acts 12, *12). It has been suggested that perhaps John Mark is the mysterious young man who escaped from the soldiers' hands on the night of Jesus' arrest (Mark* 14, *51). He is also linked with the early growth of the Church, working with Paul, Barnabas and Peter.*

Eusebius, the fourth-century historian, quotes Papias (who wrote about 140*) as saying that Mark was the "interpreter of Peter", and this seems to have been generally accepted by the early Church.*

We may therefore reasonably assume that Mark, drawing on what Peter had told him personally, and being himself convinced of the Divinity of Christ, wrote down this Gospel, probably at Rome, with non-Jewish readers in mind. We notice, for instance, that he hardly quotes at all from the old Testament, that he explains particular Jewish customs and that he translates any Aramaic expression by its Greek equivalent.

His style has no literary polish but it has the forceful vitality of the man who believes what he writes, and it is not without certain vivid flashes of realism. He draws with strong lines the portrait of a man who was thoroughly human but also unmistakably the Son of God.

The manuscript of Mark ends abruptly at 16, 8, *and nearly all scholars regard the subsequent verses as a later addition.*

CHAPTER 1

How it began

THE Gospel of Jesus Christ, the Son of God, begins with the fulfilment of this prophecy of Isaiah—

Behold, I send my messenger before thy face,
Who shall prepare thy way;
The voice of one crying in the wilderness,
Make ye ready the way of the Lord,
Make his paths straight.

For John came and began to baptise men in the desert, proclaiming baptism as the mark of a complete change of heart and of the forgiveness of sins. All the people of the Judaean countryside and everyone in Jerusalem went out to him in the desert and received his baptism in the river Jordan, publicly confessing their sins.

John himself was dressed in camel-hair, with a leather belt round his waist, and he lived on locusts and wild honey. The burden of his preaching was, "There is someone coming after me who is stronger than I—indeed I am not good enough to kneel down and undo his shoes. I have baptised you with water, but he will baptise you with the Holy Spirit."

The arrival of Jesus

It was in those days that Jesus arrived from the Galilean village of Nazareth and was baptised by John in the Jordan. All at once, as he came up out of the water, he saw the heavens split open, and the Spirit coming down upon him like a dove. A voice came out of Heaven, saying,

"You are my dearly-beloved Son, in whom I am well pleased!"

Then the Spirit sent him out at once into the desert, and there he remained for forty days while Satan tempted him. During this time no one was with him but wild animals, and only the angels were there to care for him.

Jesus begins to preach the gospel, and to call men to follow him

It was after John's arrest that Jesus came into Galilee, proclaiming the gospel of God, saying,

"The time has come at last—the kingdom of God has arrived. You must change your hearts and minds and believe the good news."

As he walked along the shore of the Lake of Galilee, he saw two fishermen, Simon and his brother Andrew, casting their nets into the water.

"Come and follow me, and I will teach you to catch men!" he cried.

At once they dropped their nets, and followed him.

Then he went a little further along the shore and saw James the son of Zebedee, aboard a boat with his brother John, overhauling their nets. At once he called them, and they left their father Zebedee in the boat with the hired men, and went off after him.

Jesus begins healing the sick

They arrived at Capernaum, and on the Sabbath day Jesus walked straight into the synagogue and began teaching. They were amazed at his way of teaching, for he taught with the ring of authority—quite unlike the scribes. All at once, a man in the grip of an evil spirit appeared in the synagogue shouting out,

"What have you got to do with us, Jesus from Nazareth? Have you come to kill us? I know who you are—you're God's holy one!"

But Jesus cut him short and spoke sharply,

"Hold your tongue and get out of him!"

At this the evil spirit convulsed the man, let out a loud scream and left him. Everyone present was so astounded that people kept saying to each other,

"What on earth has happened? This new teaching has authority behind it. Why, he even gives his orders to evil spirits and they obey him!"

And his reputation spread like wild-fire through the whole Galilean district.

Then he got up and went straight from the synagogue to the house of Simon and Andrew, accompanied by James and John. Simon's mother-in-law was in bed with a high fever, and they lost no time in telling Jesus about her. He went up to her, took her hand and helped her to her feet. The fever left her, and she began to see to their needs.

Late that evening, after sunset, they kept bringing to him all who were sick or troubled by evil spirits. The whole population of the town gathered round the doorway. And he healed great numbers of people who were suffering from various forms of disease. In many cases he expelled evil spirits; but he would not allow them to say a word, for they knew perfectly well who he was.

He retires for private prayer

Then, in the early morning, while it was still dark, Jesus got up, left the house and went off to a deserted place, and there he prayed. Simon and his companions went in search of him, and when they found him, they said,

"Everyone is looking for you."

"Then we will go somewhere else, to the neighbouring towns," he replied, "so that I may give my message there too—that is why I have come."

So he continued preaching in their synagogues and expelling evil spirits throughout the whole of Galilee.

Jesus cures leprosy

Then a leper came to Jesus, knelt in front of him and appealed to him,

"If you want to, you can make me clean."

Jesus was filled with pity for him, and stretched out his hand and placed it on the leper, saying,

"Of course I want to—*be clean!*"

At once the leprosy left him and he was quite clean. Jesus sent him away there and then with the strict injunction,

"Mind you say nothing at all to anybody. Go straight off and show yourself to the priest, and make the offerings for your cleansing which Moses prescribed, as public proof of your recovery."

But he went off and began to talk a great deal about it in public, spreading his story far and wide. Consequently, it became impossible for Jesus to show his face in the towns and he had to stay outside in lonely places. Yet the people still came to him from all quarters.

CHAPTER 2

Faith at Capernaum

WHEN he re-entered Capernaum some days later, a rumour spread that he was in somebody's house. Such a large crowd collected that while he was giving them his message it was impossible even to get near the doorway. Meanwhile, a group of people arrived to see him, bringing with them a paralytic whom four of them were carrying. And when they found it was impossible to get near him because of the crowd, they removed the tiles from the roof over Jesus' head and let down the paralytic's bed through the opening. And when Jesus saw their faith, he said to the man who was paralysed,

"My son, your sins are forgiven."

But some of the scribes were sitting there silently asking themselves,

"Why does this man talk such blasphemy? Who can forgive sins but God alone?"

Jesus realised instantly what they were thinking, and said to them,

"Why must you argue like this in your minds? Which do you suppose is easier—to say to a paralysed man, 'Your sins are forgiven', or 'Get up, pick up your bed and walk'? But to prove to you that the Son of Man has full authority to forgive sins on earth, I say to you,"—and here he spoke to the paralytic—"Get up, pick up your bed and go home."

At once the man sprang to his feet, picked up his bed and walked off in full view of them all. Everyone was amazed, praised God and said,

"We have never seen anything like this before."

Then Jesus went out again by the lake-side and the whole crowd came to him, and he continued to teach them.

Jesus now calls "a sinner" to follow him

As Jesus went on his way, he saw Levi the son of Alphaeus sitting at his desk in the tax-office, and he said to him,

"Follow me!"

Levi got up and followed him. Later, when Jesus was sitting at dinner in Levi's house, a large number of tax-collectors and disreputable folk came in and joined him and his disciples. For there were many such people among his followers. When the scribes who were Pharisees saw him eating in the company of tax-collectors and outsiders, they remarked to his disciples,

"So he eats with tax-collectors and sinners!"

When Jesus heard this, he said to them,

"It is not the fit and flourishing who need the doctor, but those who are ill. I did not come to invite the 'righteous', but the 'sinners'."

The question of fasting

The disciples of John and the Pharisees were fasting. They came and said to Jesus,

"Why do those who follow John or the Pharisees keep fasts but your disciples do nothing of the kind?"

Jesus told them,

"Can you expect wedding-guests to fast in the bridegroom's presence? Fasting is out of the question as long as they have the bridegroom with them. But the day will come when the bridegroom will be taken away from them—that will be the time for them to fast.

"Nobody," he continued, "sews a patch of unshrunk cloth on to an old coat. If he does, the new patch tears away from the old and the hole is worse than ever. And nobody puts new wine into old wineskins. If he does, the new wine bursts the skins, the wine is spilt and the skins are ruined. No, new wine must go into new wineskins."

Jesus rebukes the sabbatarians

One day he happened to be going through the cornfields on the Sabbath day. And his disciples, as they made their way along, began to pick the ears of corn. The Pharisees said to him,

"Look at that! Why should they do what is forbidden on the Sabbath day?"

Then he spoke to them.

"Have you never read what David did, when there was no food and he and his companions were famished? He went into the house of God when Abiathar was High Priest, and ate the presentation loaves, which nobody is allowed to eat, except the priests—and even gave some of the bread to his companions? The

Sabbath," he continued, "was made for man's sake; man was not made for the sake of the Sabbath. That is why the Son of Man is master even of the Sabbath."

CHAPTER 3

On another occasion when he went into the synagogue, there was a man there whose hand was shrivelled, and they were watching Jesus closely to see whether he would heal him on the Sabbath day, so that they might bring a charge against him. Jesus said to the man with the shrivelled hand,

"Stand up and come out here in front!"

Then he said to them,

"Is it right to do good on the Sabbath day, or to do harm? Is it right to save life or to kill?"

There was a dead silence. Then Jesus, deeply hurt as he sensed their inhumanity, looked round in anger at the faces surrounding him, and said to the man,

"Stretch out your hand!"

And he stretched it out and the hand was restored. The Pharisees walked straight out and discussed with Herod's party how they could get rid of Jesus.

Jesus' enormous popularity

Jesus now retired to the lake-side with his disciples. A huge crowd of people followed him, not only from Galilee, but from Judaea, Jerusalem and Idumaea, some from the district beyond the Jordan and from the neighbourhood of Tyre and Sidon. This vast crowd came to him because they had heard about the sort of things he was doing. So Jesus told his disciples to have a small boat kept in readiness for him, in case the people should crowd him too closely. For he healed so many people that all those who were in pain kept pressing forward to touch him with their hands. Evil spirits, as soon as they saw him, acknowledged his authority and screamed,

"You are the Son of God!"

But he warned them repeatedly that they must not make him known.

Jesus chooses the twelve apostles

Later he went up on to the hill-side and summoned the men whom he wanted, and they went up to him. He appointed a band of twelve to be his companions, whom he could send out to preach, with power to drive out evil spirits. These were the twelve he appointed:

Peter (which was the new name he gave Simon), James the son of Zebedee, and John his brother, (He gave them the name of Boanerges, which means the "Thunderers"); Andrew, Philip, Bartholomew, Matthew, Thomas, James the son of Alphaeus, Thaddaeus, Simon the Patriot, and Judas Iscariot, who betrayed him.

Jesus exposes an absurd accusation

Then he went indoors, but again such a crowd collected that it was impossible for them even to eat a meal. When his relatives heard of this, they set out to take charge of him, for people were saying, "He must be mad!"

The scribes who had come down from Jerusalem were saying that he was possessed by Beelzebub, and that he drove out devils because he was in league with the prince of devils. So Jesus called them to him and spoke to them in parables—

"How can Satan be the one who drives out Satan? If a kingdom is divided against itself, then that kingdom cannot last, and if a household is divided against itself, it cannot last either. And if Satan leads a rebellion against Satan then his ranks are split, he cannot survive and his end is near. No one can break into a strong man's house and steal his property, without first tying up the strong man hand and foot. But if he did that, he could ransack the whole house.

"Believe me, all men's sins can be forgiven and all their blasphemies. But there can never be any forgiveness for blasphemy against the Holy Spirit. That is an eternal sin."

He said this because they were saying, "He is in the power of an evil spirit."

The new relationships in the kingdom

Then his mother and his brothers arrived. They stood outside the house and sent a message asking him to come out to them. There was a crowd sitting round him when the message was brought telling him, "Your mother and your brothers are outside looking for you."

Jesus replied, "And who are really my mother and my brothers?"

And he looked round at the faces of those sitting in a circle about him.

"Look!" he said, "my mother and my brothers are here. Anyone who does the will of God is brother and sister and mother to me."

CHAPTER 4

The story of the sower

THEN once again he began to teach them by the lake-side. A bigger crowd than ever collected around him so that he got into the small boat on the lake and sat down, while the crowd covered the ground right down to the water's edge. He taught them a great deal in parables, and in the course of his teaching he said,

"Listen! A man once went out to sow his seed and as he sowed, some seed fell by the roadside and the birds came and gobbled it up. Some of the seed fell among the rocks where there was not much soil, and sprang up very quickly because there was no depth of earth. But when the sun rose it was scorched, and because it had no root, it withered away. And some of the seed fell among thorn-bushes and the thorns grew up and choked the life out of it, and it bore no crop. And there was some seed which fell on good soil, and when it sprang up and grew, produced a crop which yielded thirty or sixty or even a hundred times as much as the seed."

Then he added,

"Every man who has ears should use them!"

Then when they were by themselves, his close followers and the twelve asked him about the parables, and he told them.

"The secret of the kingdom of God has been given to you. But to those who do not know the secret, everything remains in parables, so that,

> Seeing they may see, and not perceive;
> and hearing they may hear, and not understand;
> lest haply they should turn again, and it should be forgiven them."

Then he continued,

"Do you really not understand this parable? Then how are you going to understand all the other parables? The man who sows, sows the message. As for those who are by the roadside where the message is sown, as soon as they hear it Satan comes at once and takes away what has been sown in their minds. Similarly, the seed sown among the rocks represents those who hear the message without hesitation and accept it joyfully. But they have no real roots and do not last—when trouble or persecution arises because of the message, they give up their faith at once. Then there are the seeds which were sown among thorn-bushes. These are the people who hear the message, but the worries of this world and the false glamour of riches and all sorts of other ambitions creep in and choke the life out of what they have heard, and it produces no crop in their lives. As for the seed sown on good soil, this means the men who hear the message and accept it and do produce a crop—thirty, sixty, even a hundred times as much as they received."

Truth is meant to be used

Then he said to them,

"Is a lamp brought into the room to be put under a bucket or underneath the bed? Surely its place is on the lamp-stand! There is nothing hidden which is not meant to be made perfectly plain one day, and there are no secrets which are not meant one day to be common knowledge. If a man has ears he should use them!

"Pay attention to what you hear," he said to them. "Whatever measure you use will be used towards you, and even more than that. For the man who has something will receive more. As for the man who has nothing, even his 'nothing' will be taken away."

Jesus gives pictures of the kingdom's growth

Then he said,

"The kingdom of God is like a man scattering seed on the ground and then going to bed each night and getting up every morning, while the seed sprouts and grows up, though he has no idea how it happens. The earth produces a crop without any help from anyone: first a blade, then the ear of corn, then the full-grown grain in the ear. And as soon as the crop is ready, he sends the reapers in without delay, for the harvest-time has come."

Then he continued,

"What can we say the kingdom of God is like? How shall we put it in a parable? It is like a tiny grain of mustard-seed which, when it is sown, is smaller than any seed that is ever sown. But after it is sown in the earth, it grows up and becomes bigger than any other plant. It shoots out great branches so that birds can come and nest in its shelter."

So he taught them his message with many parables like these, as far as their minds could understand it. He did not speak to them at all without using parables, although in private he explained everything to his disciples.

Jesus shows himself master of natural forces

On the evening of that day, he said to them,

"Let us cross over to the other side of the lake."

So they sent the crowd home and took him with them in the small boat in which he had been sitting, accompanied by other small craft. Then came a violent squall of wind which drove the waves aboard the boat until it was almost swamped. Jesus was in the stern asleep on the cushion. They awoke him with the words,

"Master, don't you care that we're drowning?"

And he woke up, rebuked the wind, and said to the waves,

"Hush now! be still!"

The wind dropped and there was a dead calm.

"Why are you so frightened? Do you not trust me even yet?" he asked them.

But sheer awe swept over them, and they kept saying to each other,

"Who ever can he be?—even the wind and the waves do what he tells them!"

CHAPTER 5

Jesus meets a violent lunatic

So they arrived on the other side of the lake in the country of the Gerasenes. As Jesus was getting out of the boat, a man in the grip of an evil spirit rushed out to meet him from among the tombs where he was living. It was no longer possible for any human being to restrain him even with a chain. Indeed he had frequently been secured with fetters and lengths of chain, but he had simply snapped the chains and broken the fetters in pieces. No one could do anything with him. All through the night as well as in the day-time he screamed among the tombs and on the hill-side, and cut himself with stones. Now, as soon as he saw Jesus in the distance, he ran and knelt before him, yelling at the top of his voice,

"What have you got to do with me, Jesus, Son of the Most High God? For God's sake, don't torture me!"

For Jesus had already said, "Come out of this man, you evil spirit!"

Then he asked him,

"What is your name?"

"My name is legion," he replied, "for there are many of us."

Then he begged and prayed him not to send "them" out of the country.

A large herd of pigs was grazing there on the hill-side, and the evil spirits implored him, "Send us over to the pigs and we'll get into them!"

So Jesus allowed them to do this, and they came out of the man, and made off and went into the pigs. The whole herd of about two thousand stampeded down the cliff into the lake and was drowned. The swineherds took to their heels and spread their story in the city and all over the countryside. Then the people came to see what had happened. As they approached Jesus, they saw the man who had been devil-possessed sitting there properly clothed and perfectly sane—the same man who had been possessed by "legion"—and they were really frightened. Those who had seen the incident told them what had happened to the devil-possessed man and about the disaster to the pigs. Then they began to implore Jesus to leave their district. As he was embarking on the small boat, the man who had been possessed begged that he might go with him. But Jesus would not allow this.

"Go home to your own people," he told him, "and tell them what the Lord has done for you, and how kind he has been to you!"

So the man went off and began to spread throughout the Ten Towns the story of what Jesus had done for him. And they were all simply amazed.

Faith is followed by healing

When Jesus had crossed again in the boat to the other side of the lake, a great crowd collected around him as he stood on the shore. Then came a man called Jairus, one of the synagogue presidents. And when he saw Jesus, he knelt before him, pleading desperately for his help.

"My little girl is dying," he said. "Will you come and put your hands on her—then she will get better and live."

Jesus went off with him, followed by a large crowd jostling at his elbow. Among them was a woman who had suffered from haemorrhages for twelve years and who had gone through a great deal at the hands of many doctors, spending all her money in the process. She had derived no benefit from them but, on the contrary, was getting worse. This woman had heard about Jesus and came up behind him under cover of the crowd, and touched his cloak,

"For if I can only touch his clothes," she kept saying, "I shall be all right."

The haemorrhage was stopped immediately, and she knew in herself that she was cured of her trouble. At once Jesus knew intuitively that power had gone out of him, and he turned round in the middle of the crowd and said,

"Who touched my clothes?"

His disciples replied,

"You can see this crowd jostling you. How can you ask, 'Who touched me?' "

But he looked all round at their faces to see who had done so. Then the woman, scared and shaking all over because she knew that she was the one to whom this thing had happened, came and flung herself before him and told him the whole story. But he said to her,

"Daughter, it is your faith that has healed you. Go home in peace, and be free from your trouble."

While he was still speaking, messengers arrived from the synagogue president's house, saying,

"Your daughter is dead—there is no need to bother the master any further."

But when Jesus heard this message, he said to the president of the synagogue,

"Now don't be afraid, just go on believing!"

Then he allowed no one to follow him except Peter and James and John, James's brother. They arrived at the president's house and Jesus noticed the hubbub and all the weeping and wailing, and as he went in, he said to the people in the house,

"Why are you making such a noise with your crying? The

child is not dead; she is fast asleep."

They greeted this with a scornful laugh. But Jesus turned them all out, and taking only the father and mother and his own companions with him, went into the room where the child was. Then he took the little girl's hand and said to her in Aramaic,

"Little girl, I tell you to get up!"

At once she jumped to her feet and walked round the room, for she was twelve years old. This sight sent the others nearly out of their minds with joy. But Jesus gave them strict instructions not to let anyone know what had happened—and ordered food to be given to the little girl.

CHAPTER 6

The "prophet without honour"

THEN he left that district and came into his own native town, followed by his disciples. When the Sabbath day came, he began to teach in the synagogue. The congregation were astonished at what they heard, and remarked,

"Where does he get all this? What is this wisdom that he has been given—and what about these marvellous things that he can do? He's only the carpenter, Mary's son, the brother of James, Joses, Judas and Simon; and his sisters are living here with us!"

And they were deeply offended with him. But Jesus said to them,

"No prophet goes unhonoured—except in his native town or with his own relations or in his own home!"

And he could do nothing miraculous there apart from laying his hands on a few sick people and healing them; their lack of faith astonished him.

The twelve are sent out to preach the gospel

Then he made his way round the villages, continuing his teaching. He summoned the twelve, and began to send them out in twos, giving them power over evil spirits. He instructed them to take nothing for the road except a staff—no bread, no satchel and no money in their pockets. They were to wear sandals and not to take more than one coat. And he told them,

"Wherever you are, when you go into a house, stay there until you leave that place. And wherever people will not welcome you or listen to what you have to say, leave them and shake the dust off your feet as a protest against them!"

So they went out and preached publicly that men should change their whole outlook. They expelled many evil spirits and anointed many sick people with oil and healed them.

Herod's guilty conscience

All this came to the ears of king Herod, for Jesus' reputation was spreading, and people were saying that John the Baptist had risen from the dead, and that was why he was showing such miraculous powers. Others maintained that he was Elijah, and others that he was one of the prophets of the old days come back again. But when Herod heard of all this, he said,

"It must be John whom I beheaded, risen from the dead!"

For Herod himself had sent and arrested John and had him bound in prison, all on account of Herodias, wife of his brother Philip. He had married her, though John used to say to Herod, "It is not right for you to possess your own brother's wife." Herodias herself nursed a grudge against John for this and wanted to have him executed, but she could not do it, for Herod had a deep respect for John, knowing that he was a just and holy man, and kept him under his protection. He used to listen to him and be profoundly disturbed, and yet he enjoyed hearing him.

Then a good opportunity came, for Herod gave a birthday party for his courtiers and army commanders and for the leading people in Galilee. Herodias' daughter came in and danced, to the great delight of Herod and his guests. The king said to the girl,

"Ask me anything you like and I will give it to you!"

And he swore to her,

"I will give you whatever you ask me, up to half my kingdom!"

And she went out and spoke to her mother,

"What shall I ask for?"

And she said,

"The head of John the Baptist!"

The girl rushed back to the king's presence, and made her request.

"I want you to give me, this minute, the head of John the Baptist on a dish!" she said.

Herod was aghast, but because of his oath and the presence of his guests, he did not like to refuse her. So he sent the executioner straightaway to bring him John's head. He went off and beheaded him in the prison, brought back his head on the dish, and gave it to the girl who handed it to her mother. When his disciples heard what had happened, they came and took away his body and put it in a tomb.

The apostles return: the huge crowds make rest impossible

The apostles returned to Jesus and reported to him every detail of what they had done and taught.

"Now come along to some quiet place by yourselves, and rest for a little while," said Jesus, for there were people coming and going incessantly so that they had not even time for meals. They went off in the boat to a quiet place by themselves, but a great many saw them go and recognised them, and people from all the towns hurried on foot to get there first. When Jesus disembarked he saw the large crowd and his heart was touched with pity for them because they seemed to him like sheep without a shepherd. And he settled down to teach them about many things. As the day wore on, his disciples came to him and said,

"We are right in the wilds here and it is getting late. Let them go now, so that they can buy themselves something to eat from the farms and villages around here."

But Jesus replied,

"You give them something to eat!"

"You mean we're to go and spend twenty pounds on bread? Is that how you want us to feed them?"

"What bread have you got?" asked Jesus. "Go and have a look."

And when they had found out, they told him,

"We have five loaves and two fish."

Jesus miraculously feeds five thousand people

Then Jesus told them to arrange all the people in parties, sitting on the green grass. And they settled down, looking like flower-beds, in groups of fifty or a hundred. Then Jesus took the five loaves and the two fish, and looking up to Heaven, thanked God, broke the loaves and gave them to the disciples to distribute to the people. And he divided the two fish among them all. Everybody ate and was satisfied. Afterwards they collected twelve baskets full of pieces of bread and fish that were left over. There were five thousand men who ate the loaves.

Jesus' mastery over natural law

Directly after this, Jesus made his disciples get aboard the boat and go on ahead to Bethsaida on the other side of the lake, while he himself sent the crowds home. And when he had sent them all on their way, he went off to the hill-side to pray. When it grew late, the boat was in the middle of the lake, and he was by himself on land. He saw them straining at the oars, for the wind was dead against them, and in the small hours he went towards them, walking on the waters of the lake, intending to come alongside. But when they saw him walking on the water, they thought he was a ghost, and screamed out. For they all saw him and they were absolutely terrified. But Jesus at once spoke quietly to them,

"It's all right, it is I myself; don't be afraid!"

And he climbed aboard the boat with them, and the wind dropped, But they were scared out of their wits. They had not had the sense to learn the lesson of the loaves; their minds were still in the dark.

And when they had crossed over to the other side of the lake, they landed at Gennesaret and tied up there. As soon as they came ashore, the people recognised Jesus and rushed all over the countryside and began to carry the sick around on their beds to wherever they heard that he was. Wherever he went, in villages or towns or hamlets, they laid down their sick right in the market-places and begged him that they might "just touch the edge of his cloak". And all those who touched him were healed.

CHAPTER 7

Jesus exposes the danger of man-made traditions

AND now Jesus was approached by the Pharisees and some of the scribes who had come from Jerusalem. They had noticed that his disciples ate their meals with "common" hands—meaning that they had not gone through a ceremonial washing. (The Pharisees, and indeed all the Jews, will never eat unless they have washed their hands in a particular way, following a traditional rule. And they will not eat anything bought in the market until they have first performed their "sprinkling". And there are many other things which they consider important, concerned with the washing of cups, jugs and basins.) So the Pharisees and the scribes put this question to Jesus,

"Why do your disciples refuse to follow the ancient tradition, and eat their bread with 'common' hands?"

Jesus replied,

"You hypocrites, Isaiah described you beautifully when he wrote—

This people honoureth me with their lips,
But their heart is far from me.
But in vain do they worship me,
Teaching as doctrines the precepts of men.

You are so busy holding on to the traditions of men that you let go the commandment of God!"

Then he went on,

"It is wonderful to see how you can set aside the commandment of God to preserve your own tradition! For Moses said, 'Honour thy father and thy mother' and 'He that speaketh evil of father or mother, let him die the death.' But you say, 'if a man says to his father or his mother, Korban—meaning, I have given God whatever duty I owed to you', then he need not lift a finger any longer for his father or mother, so making the word of God impotent for the sake of the tradition which you hold. And this is typical of much of what you do."

Then he called the crowd close to him again, and spoke to them,

"Listen to me now, all of you, and understand this. There is nothing outside a man which can enter into him and make him 'common'. It is the things which come out of a man that make him 'common'!"

Later, when he had gone indoors away from the crowd, his disciples asked him about this parable.

"Oh, are you as dull as they are?" he said. "Can't you see that anything that goes into a man from outside cannot make him 'common' or unclean? You see, it doesn't go into his heart, but into his stomach, and passes out of the body altogether, so that all food is clean enough. But," he went on, "whatever comes out of a man, that is what makes a man 'common' or unclean. For it is from inside, from men's hearts and minds, that evil thoughts arise —lust, theft, murder, adultery, greed, wickedness, deceit, sensuality, envy, slander, arrogance and folly! All these evil things come from inside a man and make him unclean!"

The faith of a gentile is rewarded

Then he got up and left that place and went off to the

neighbourhood of Tyre. There he went into a house and wanted no one to know where he was. But it proved impossible to remain hidden. For no sooner had he got there, than a woman who had heard about him, and who had a daughter possessed by an evil spirit, arrived and prostrated herself before him. She was a Greek, a Syrophoenician by birth, and she asked him to drive the evil spirit out of her daughter. Jesus said to her,

"You must let the children have all they want first. It is not right, you know, to take the children's food and throw it to the dogs."

But she replied,

"Yes, Lord, I know, but even the dogs under the table eat the scraps the children leave."

"If you can answer like that," Jesus said to her, "you can go home! The evil spirit has left your daughter."

And she went back to her home and found the child lying quietly on her bed, and the evil spirit gone.

Jesus restores speech and hearing

Once more Jesus left the neighbourhood of Tyre and passed through Sidon towards the Lake of Galilee, and crossed the Ten Towns territory. They brought to him a man who was deaf and unable to speak intelligibly, and they implored him to put his hand upon him. Jesus took him away from the crowd by himself. He put his fingers in the man's ears and touched his tongue with his own saliva. Then, looking up to Heaven, he gave a deep sigh and said to him in Aramaic,

"Open!"

And his ears were opened and immediately whatever had tied his tongue came loose and he spoke quite plainly. Jesus gave instructions that they should tell no one about this happening, but the more he told them, the more they broadcast the news. People were absolutely amazed, and kept saying,

"How wonderfully he has done everything! He even makes the deaf hear and the dumb speak."

CHAPTER 8

He again feeds the people miraculously

About this time it happened again that a large crowd collected and had nothing to eat. Jesus called the disciples over to him and said,

"My heart goes out to this crowd; they have been with me three days now and they have no food left. If I send them off home without anything, they will collapse on the way—and some of them have come from a distance."

His disciples replied,

"Where could anyone find the food to feed them here in this deserted spot?"

"How many loaves have you got?" Jesus asked them.

"Seven," they replied.

So Jesus told the crowd to settle themselves on the ground. Then he took the seven loaves into his hands, and with a prayer of thanksgiving broke them, and gave them to the disciples to distribute to the people; and this they did. They had a few small fish as well, and after blessing them, Jesus told his disciples to give these also to the people. They ate and they were satisfied. Moreover, they picked up seven baskets full of pieces left over. The people numbered about four thousand. Jesus sent them home, and then he boarded the boat at once with his disciples and went on to the district of Dalmanutha.

Jesus refuses to give a sign

Now the Pharisees came out and began an argument with him. They were out to test him and wanted a sign from Heaven. Jesus gave a deep sigh, and then said,

"What makes this generation want a sign? I can tell you this, they will certainly not be given one!"

Then he left them and got aboard the boat again, and crossed the lake.

The disciples had forgotten to take any food and had only one loaf with them in the boat. Jesus spoke seriously to them, "Keep your eyes open! Be on your guard against the 'yeast' of the Pharisees and the 'yeast' of Herod!" And this sent them into an earnest consultation among themselves because they had brought no bread. Jesus knew it and said to them,

"Why all this discussion about bringing no bread? Don't you understand or grasp what I say even yet? Are your minds closed? Are you like the people who 'having eyes, do not see, and having ears, do not hear'? Have you forgotten—when I broke five loaves for five thousand people, how many baskets full of pieces did you pick up?"

"Twelve," they replied.

"And when there were seven loaves for four thousand people, how many baskets of pieces did you pick up?"

"Seven," they said.

"And does that still mean nothing to you?" he said.

Jesus restores sight

So they arrived at Bethsaida where a blind man was brought to him, with the earnest request that he should touch him. Jesus took the blind man's hand and led him outside the village. Then he moistened his eyes with saliva and putting his hands on him, asked,

"Can you see at all?"

The man looked up and said,

"I can see people. They look like trees—only they are walking about."

Then Jesus put his hands on his eyes once more and his sight came into focus, and he recovered and saw everything sharp and clear. And Jesus sent him off to his own house with the words,

"Don't even go into the village."

Jesus' question: Peter's inspired answer

Jesus then went away with his disciples to the villages of Caesarea Philippi. On the way he asked them,

"Who are men saying that I am?"

"John the Baptist," they answered. "But others say that you are Elijah or, some say, one of the prophets."

Then he asked them,

"But what about you—who do you say that I am?"

"You are Christ!" answered Peter.

Then Jesus impressed it upon them that they must not mention this to anyone.

Jesus speaks of the future and of the cost of discipleship

And he began to teach them that it was inevitable that the Son of Man should go through much suffering and be utterly repudiated by the elders and chief priests and scribes, and be killed, and after three days rise again. He told them all this quite bluntly.

This made Peter draw him on one side and take him to task about what he had said. But Jesus turned and faced his disciples and rebuked Peter.

"Out of my way, Satan!" he said. "Peter, your thoughts are not God's thoughts, but man's!"

Then he called his disciples and the people around him, and said to them,

"If anyone wants to follow in my footsteps, he must give up all right to himself, take up his cross and follow me. The man who tries to save his life will lose it; it is the man who loses his life for my sake and the gospel's who will save it. What good can it do a man to gain the whole world at the price of his own soul? What can a man offer to buy back his soul once he has lost it? If anyone is ashamed of me and my words in this unfaithful and sinful generation, the Son of Man will be ashamed of him when he comes in the Father's glory with the holy angels around him."

CHAPTER 9

Jesus foretells his glory

THEN he added,

"Believe me, there are some of you standing here who will know nothing of death until you have seen the kingdom of God already come in power!"

Six days later, Jesus took Peter and James and John with him and led them high up on a hill-side where they were entirely alone. His whole appearance changed before their eyes, while his clothes became white, dazzling white—whiter than any earthly bleaching could make them. Elijah and Moses appeared to the disciples and stood there in conversation with Jesus. Peter burst out to Jesus,

"Master, it is wonderful for us to be here! Shall we put up three shelters—one for you, one for Moses and one for Elijah?"

He really did not know what to say, for they were very frightened. Then came a cloud which overshadowed them and a voice spoke out of the cloud,

"This is my dearly-loved Son. Listen to him!"

Then, quite suddenly they looked all round them and saw nobody at all with them but Jesus. And as they came down the hill-side, he warned them not to tell anybody what they had seen till "the Son of Man should have risen again from the dead". They were deeply impressed by this remark and tried to puzzle out among themselves what "rising from the dead" could mean. Then they asked him this question,

"Why do the scribes say that Elijah must come before Christ?"

"It is quite true," he told them, "that Elijah does come first, and begins the restoration of all things. But what does the scripture say about the Son of Man? This: that he must go through much suffering and be treated with contempt! I tell you that not only has Elijah come already but they have done to him exactly what they wanted—just as the scripture says of him."

Jesus heals an epileptic boy

Then as they rejoined the other disciples, they saw that they were surrounded by a large crowd and that some scribes were arguing with them. As soon as the people saw Jesus, they ran forward excitedly to welcome him.

"What is the trouble?" Jesus asked them.

A man from the crowd answered,

"Master, I brought my son to you because he has a dumb spirit. Wherever he is, it gets hold of him, throws him down on the ground and there he foams at the mouth and grinds his teeth. It's simply wearing him out. I did speak to your disciples to get them to drive it out, but they hadn't the power to do it."

Jesus answered them,

"Oh, what a faithless people you are! How long must I be with you, how long must I put up with you? Bring him here to me."

So they brought the boy to him, and as soon as the spirit saw Jesus, it convulsed the boy, who fell to the ground and writhed there, foaming at the mouth.

"How long has he been like this?" Jesus asked the father.

"Ever since he was a child," he replied. "Again and again it has thrown him into the fire or into water to finish him off. But if you can do anything, please take pity on us and help us."

"If *I* can do anything!" retorted Jesus. "Everything is possible to the man who believes."

"I do believe," the boy's father burst out. "Help me to believe more!"

When Jesus noticed that a crowd was rapidly gathering, he spoke sharply to the evil spirit, with the words,

"I command you, deaf and dumb spirit, come out of this boy, and never go into him again!"

The spirit gave a loud scream and after a dreadful convulsion left him. The boy lay there like a corpse, so that most of the bystanders said, "He is dead."

But Jesus grasped his hands and lifted him up, and then he stood on his own feet. When he had gone home, Jesus' disciples asked him privately,

"Why were we unable to drive it out?"

"Nothing can drive out this kind of thing except prayer," replied Jesus.

Jesus privately warns his disciples of his own death

Then they left that district and went straight through Galilee. Jesus kept this journey secret for he was teaching his disciples that the Son of Man would be betrayed into the power of men, that they would kill him and that three days after his death he would rise again. But they were completely mystified by this saying, and were afraid to question him about it.

Jesus defines the new "greatness"

So they came to Capernaum. And when they were indoors he asked them,

"What were you discussing as we came along the road?"

They were silent, for on the way they had been arguing about who should be the greatest. Jesus sat down and called the twelve, and said to them,

"If any man wants to be first, he must be last and servant of all."

Then he took a little child and stood him in front of them all, and putting his arm round him, said to them,

"Anyone who welcomes one little child like this for my sake is welcoming me. And the man who welcomes me is welcoming not only me but the one who sent me!"

Then John said to him,

"Master, we saw somebody driving out evil spirits in your name, and we tried to stop him, for he is not one who follows us."

But Jesus replied,

"You must not stop him. No one who exerts such power in my name would readily say anything against me. For the man who is not against us is on our side. In fact, I assure you that the man who gives you a mere drink of water in my name, because you are followers of mine, will most certainly be rewarded. And I tell you too, that the man who disturbs the faith of one of the humblest of those who believe in me would be better off if he were thrown into the sea with a great mill-stone hung round his neck!

Entering the kingdom may mean painful sacrifice

"Indeed, if it is your own hand that spoils your faith, you must cut it off. It is better for you to enter life maimed than to keep both your hands and go to the rubbish-heap, where the fire never dies. If your foot spoils your faith, you must cut it off. It is better for you to enter life on one foot than to keep both your feet and be thrown on to the rubbish-heap. And if your eye leads you astray, pluck it out. It is better for you to go one-eyed into the kingdom of God than to keep both eyes and be thrown on to the rubbish-heap, where decay never stops and the fire never goes out. For everyone will be salted with fire. Salt is a good thing; but if it should lose its saltiness, what can you do to restore its flavour? You must have salt in yourselves, and live at peace with each other."

CHAPTER 10

The divine purpose in marriage

THEN he got up and left Galilee and went off to the borders of Judaea and beyond the Jordan. Again great crowds assembled to meet him, and again, according to his custom, he taught them. Then some Pharisees arrived to ask him this test-question.

"Is it right for a man to divorce his wife?"

Jesus replied by asking them,

"What has Moses commanded you to do?"

"Moses allows men to write a divorce-notice and then to dismiss her," they said.

"Moses gave you that commandment," returned Jesus, "because you know so little of the meaning of love. But from the beginning of the creation, God made them male and female. 'For this cause shall a man leave his father and mother, and shall cleave to his wife; and the twain shall become one flesh.' So that in body they are no longer two people but one. That is why man must never separate what God has joined together."

On reaching the house, his disciples questioned him again about this matter.

"Any man who divorces his wife and marries another woman," he told them, "commits adultery against his wife. And if she herself divorces her husband and marries someone else, she commits adultery."

He welcomes small children

Then some people came to him bringing little children for him to touch. The disciples tried to discourage them. When Jesus saw this, he was indignant and told them,

"You must let little children come to me—never stop them! For the kingdom of God belongs to such as these. Indeed, I assure you that the man who does not accept the kingdom of God like a little child will never enter it."

Then he took the children in his arms and laid his hands on them and blessed them.

Jesus shows the danger of riches

As he began to take the road again, a man came running up and fell at his feet, and asked him,

"Good Master, tell me, please, what must I do to be sure of eternal life?"

"Why do you call me good?" returned Jesus. "No one is good —only God. You know the commandments, 'Do no murder, Do not commit adultery, Do not steal, Do not bear false witness, Do not cheat, Honour thy father and mother'."

"Master," he replied, "I have carefully kept all these since I was quite young."

Jesus looked steadily at him, and his heart warmed towards him. Then he said,

"There is one thing you still need. Go and sell everything you have, give the money away to the poor—you will have riches in Heaven. And then come back and follow me."

At these words his face fell and he went away in deep distress, for he was very rich. Then Jesus looked round at them all, and said to his disciples,

"How difficult it is for those who have great possessions to enter the kingdom of God!"

The disciples were staggered at these words, but Jesus continued,

"Children, you don't know how hard it is to get into the kingdom of God. Why, a camel could more easily pass through the eye of a needle than a rich man get into the kingdom of God."

At this their astonishment knew no bounds, and they said to each other,

"Then who can possibly be saved?"

Jesus looked straight at them and said,

"Humanly speaking it is impossible, but not with God. Everything is possible with God."

Then Peter burst out,

"But look, we have left everything and followed you!"

"I promise you," returned Jesus, "that nobody has left home or brothers or sisters or mother or father or children or land for my sake and the gospel's without getting back a hundred times over, now in this present life, homes and brothers and sisters, mothers and children and land—though not without persecution—and in the next world eternal life. But many who are first now will then be last, and the last now will then be first."

The last journey to Jerusalem begins

They were now on their way going up to Jerusalem and Jesus walked on ahead. The disciples were dismayed at this, and those who followed were afraid. Then once more he took the twelve aside and began to tell them what was going to happen to him.

"We are now going up to Jerusalem," he said, "as you can see. And the Son of Man will be betrayed into the power of the chief priests and scribes. They are going to condemn him to death and hand him over to pagans who will jeer at him and spit at him and flog him and kill him. But after three days he will rise again."

An ill-timed request

Then Zebedee's two sons James and John approached him, saying,

"Master, we want you to do for us whatever we ask."

"What do you want me to do for you?" answered Jesus.

"Give us permission to sit one on each side of you when you reign in your glory!"

"You don't know what you are asking," Jesus said to them. "Can you drink the cup I have to drink? Can you go through the baptism I have to bear?"

"Yes, we can," they replied.

Then Jesus told them,

"You will indeed drink the cup I am drinking, and you will undergo the baptism which I have to bear! But as for sitting on either side of me, that is not for me to give—such places belong to those for whom they are prepared."

When the other ten heard about this, they began to be highly indignant with James and John; so Jesus called them all to him, and said,

"You know that the so-called rulers of the heathen lord it over them, and their great men have absolute power. But it must not be so among you. No, whoever among you wants to be great must become the servant of you all, and if he wants to be first among you he must be the slave of all men! For the Son of Man himself has not come to be served but to serve, and to give his life to set many others free."

Then they came to Jericho, and as he was leaving it accompanied by his disciples and a large crowd, Bartimaeus (that is, the son of Timaeus), a blind beggar, was sitting by the side of the road. When he heard that it was Jesus of Nazareth he began to call out,

"Jesus, Son of David, have pity on me!"

Many of the people told him sharply to keep quiet, but he shouted all the more,

"Son of David, have pity on me!"

Jesus stood quite still and said,

"Call him here."

So they called the blind man, saying,

"It's all right now, get up, he's calling you!"

At this he threw off his coat, jumped to his feet and came to Jesus.

"What do you want me to do for you?" he asked him. The blind man answered,

"Oh, Master, let me see again!"

"Go on your way then," returned Jesus, "your faith has healed you."

And he recovered his sight at once and followed Jesus along the road.

CHAPTER 11

Jesus arranges for his entry into the city

WHEN they were approaching Jerusalem and had come to Bethphage and Bethany near the Mount of Olives, he sent off two of his disciples with these instructions,

"Go into the village just ahead of you and as soon as you enter it you will find a tethered colt on which no one has yet ridden. Untie it, and bring it here. If anybody asks you, 'Why are you doing this?', just say, 'His master needs him, and will send him back immediately.'"

So they went off and found the colt tethered by a doorway outside in the open street, and they untied it. Some of the bystanders did say, "What are you doing, untying this colt?", but they made the reply Jesus told them to make, and the men raised no objection. So they brought the colt to Jesus, threw their coats on its back, and he took his seat upon it.

Many of the people spread out their coats in his path as he rode along, and others put down rushes which they had cut from the fields. The whole crowd, both those who were in front and those who were behind Jesus, shouted,

"God save him!—God bless the one who comes in the name of the Lord! God bless the coming kingdom of our father David! God save him from on high!"

Jesus entered Jerusalem and went into the Temple and looked round on all that was going on. And then, since it was already late in the day, he went out to Bethany with the twelve.

On the following day, when they had left Bethany, Jesus felt hungry. He noticed a fig-tree in the distance covered with leaves, and he walked up to it to see if he could find any fruit on it. But when he got to it, he could find nothing but leaves, for it was not yet the season for figs. Then Jesus spoke to the tree,

"May nobody ever eat fruit from you!"

And the disciples heard him say it.

Then they came into Jerusalem and Jesus went into the Temple and began to drive out those who were buying and selling there. He over-turned the tables of the money-changers and the benches of the dove-sellers, and he would not allow anyone to make a short cut through the Temple when carrying such things as water-pots. And he began to teach them and said,

"Doesn't the scripture say, 'My house shall be called a house of prayer for all nations'? But you have turned it into a thieves' kitchen!"

The chief priests and scribes heard him say this and tried to find a way of getting rid of him. But they were in fact afraid of him, for his teaching had captured the imagination of the people. And every evening they left the city.

Jesus talks of faith, prayer and forgiveness

One morning as they were walking along, they noticed that the fig-tree had withered away from the roots. Peter remembered it, and said,

"Master, look, the fig-tree that you cursed is all shrivelled up!"

"Have faith in God," replied Jesus to them. "I tell you that if anyone should say to this hill, 'Get up and throw yourself into the sea', and without any doubt in his heart believe that what he says will happen, then it *will* happen! That is why I tell you, whatever you pray about and ask for, believe that you have received it and it will be yours. And whenever you stand praying, you must forgive any grudge that you are holding against anyone else, and your Heavenly Father will forgive you *your* sins."

Jesus' authority is directly challenged

So they came once more to Jerusalem, and while Jesus was walking in the Temple, the chief priests, scribes and elders approached him, and asked,

"What authority have you for what you're doing? And who gave you permission to do these things?"

"I am going to ask you a question," replied Jesus, "and if you answer me, I will tell you what authority I have for what I do. The baptism of John, now—did it come from Heaven or was it purely human? Tell me that."

At this they argued with each other, "If we say from Heaven, he will say, 'then why didn't you believe in him?' but if we say it was purely human, well . . ." For they were frightened of the people, since all of them believed that John was a real prophet. So they answered Jesus,

"We do not know."

"Then I cannot tell you by what authority I do these things," returned Jesus.

CHAPTER 12

Jesus tells a story, with a pointed application

THEN he began to talk to them in parables.

"A man once planted a vineyard," he said, "fenced it round, dug out the hole for the wine-press and built a watch-tower. Then he let it out to some farm-workers and went abroad. At the end of the season he sent a servant to the tenants to receive his share of the vintage. But they got hold of him, knocked him about and sent him off empty-handed. The owner tried again. He sent another servant to them, but this one they knocked on the head and generally insulted. Once again he sent them another servant, but him they murdered. He sent many others and some they beat up and some they murdered. He had one man left—his own son who was very dear to him. He sent him last of all to the tenants, saying to himself, 'They will surely respect my own son.' But they said to each other, 'This fellow is the future owner—come on, let's kill him, and the property will be ours!' So they got hold of him and murdered him, and threw his body out of the vineyard. What do you suppose the owner of the vineyard is going to do? He will come and destroy the men who were working his vineyard and will hand it over to others. Have you never read this scripture—

The stone which the builders rejected,
The same was made the head of the corner;
This was from the Lord,
And it is marvellous in our eyes?"

At this they longed to get their hands on him, for they knew perfectly well that he had aimed this parable at them—but they were afraid of the people. So they left him and went away.

A test question

Later they sent some of the Pharisees and some of the Herod-party to trap him in an argument. They came up and said to him,

"Master, we know that you are an honest man and that you are not swayed by men's opinion of you. Obviously you don't care for human approval but teach the way of God with the strictest regard for truth—is it right to pay tribute to Caesar or not: are we to pay or not to pay?"

But Jesus saw through their hypocrisy and said to them,

"Why try this trick on me? Bring me a coin and let me look at it."

So they brought one to him.

"Whose face is this?" asked Jesus, "and whose name is in the inscription?"

"Caesar's," they replied. And Jesus said,

"Then pay to Caesar what belongs to Caesar, and to God what belongs to God!"—a reply which staggered them.

Jesus reveals the ignorance of the Sadducees

Then some of the Sadducees (a party which maintains that there is no resurrection) approached him, and put this question to him,

"Master, Moses instructed us that if a man's brother dies leaving a widow but no child, then the man should marry the woman and raise children for his brother. Now there were seven brothers, and the first one married and died without leaving issue. Then the second one married the widow and died leaving no issue behind him. The same thing happened with the third, and indeed the whole seven died without leaving any child behind them. Finally the woman herself died. Now in this 'resurrection', when men rise up again, whose wife is she going to be—for she was the wife of all seven of them?"

Jesus replied, "Does not this show where you go wrong—and how you fail to understand both the scriptures and the power of God? When people rise from the dead they neither marry nor are they given in marriage; they live like the angels in Heaven. But as for this matter of the dead being raised, have you never read in the book of Moses, in the passage about the bush, how God spoke to him in these words, 'I am the God of Abraham and the God of Isaac and the God of Jacob'? God is not God of the dead but of living men! That is where you make your great mistake"

The most important commandments

Then one of the scribes approached him. He had been listening to the discussion, and had noticed how well Jesus had answered them, and he put this question to him,

"What are we to consider the greatest commandment of all?"

"The first and most important one is this," Jesus replied—"'Hear, O Israel: The Lord our God, the Lord is one: and thou shalt love the Lord thy God with all thy heart, and with all thy soul, and with all thy mind, and with all thy strength.' The second is this, 'Thou shalt love thy neighbour as thyself.' No other commandment is greater than these."

"I am well answered, master," replied the scribe. "You are absolutely right when you say that there is one God and no other God exists but him; and to love him with the whole of our hearts, the whole of our intelligence and the whole of our strength, and to love our neighbours as ourselves is infinitely more important than all these burnt-offerings and sacrifices."

Then Jesus, noting the wisdom of his reply, said to him, "You are not far from the kingdom of God!"

After this nobody felt they could ask him any more questions.

Jesus criticises the scribes' teaching and behaviour

Later, while Jesus was teaching in the Temple, he remarked, "How can the scribes maintain that Christ is David's *son*, for David himself, inspired by the Holy Spirit, said,

> The Lord said unto my *Lord*,
> Sit thou on my right hand,
> Till I make thine enemies the footstool of thy feet.

David is himself calling Christ 'Lord'—where do they get the idea that he is his son?"

The vast crowd heard this with great delight, and Jesus continued in his teaching,

"Be on your guard against these scribes who love to walk about in long robes and to be greeted respectfully in public and to have the front seats in the synagogue and the best places at dinner-parties! These are the men who grow fat on widows' property and cover up what they are doing by making lengthy prayers. They are only adding to the severity of their punishment!"

Then Jesus sat down opposite the Temple almsbox and watched the people putting their money into it. A great many rich people put in large sums. Then a poor widow came up and dropped in two little coins, worth together about a farthing. Jesus called his disciples to his side and said to them,

"Believe me, this poor widow has put in more than all the others. For they have all put in what they can easily afford, but she in her poverty who needs so much, has given away everything, her whole living!"

CHAPTER 13

Jesus prophesies the ruin of the Temple

THEN as Jesus was leaving the Temple, one of his disciples said to him,

"Look, Master, what wonderful stonework, what a size these buildings are!"

Jesus replied,

"You see these great buildings? Not a single stone will be left standing on another; every one will be thrown down!"

Then, while he was sitting on the slope of the Mount of Olives facing the Temple, Peter, James, John and Andrew asked him privately,

"Tell us, when will these things happen? What sign will there be that all these things are going to come to an end?"

So Jesus began to tell them:

"Be very careful that no one deceives you. Many are going to come in my name and say, 'I am he', and will lead many astray. When you hear of wars and rumours of wars, don't be alarmed. Such things are bound to happen, but the end is not yet. Nation will take up arms against nation and kingdom against kingdom. There will be earthquakes in different places and famines too. But these are only the beginning of birth-pangs. You yourselves must keep your wits about you, for men will hand you over to their councils, and will beat you in their synagogues. You will have to stand in front of rulers and kings for my sake to bear your witness to them. For before the end comes the gospel must be proclaimed to all nations. But when they are taking you off to trial, do not worry beforehand about what you are going to say—simply say the words you are given when the time comes. For it is not really you who will speak, but the Holy Spirit.

Jesus foretells utter misery

"A brother is going to betray his own brother to death, and a father his own child. Children will stand up against their parents and condemn them to death. There will come a time when the whole world will hate you because you are known as my followers. Yet the man who holds out to the end will be saved.

"But when you see 'the abomination of desolation' standing where it ought not—(let the reader take note of this)—then those who are in Judaea must take to the hills! The man on his house-top must not go down nor go into his house to fetch anything out of it, and the man in the field must not turn back to fetch his coat. Alas for the women who are pregnant at that time, and alas for those with babies at their breasts! Pray that it may not be winter when that time comes, for there will be such utter misery in those days as has never been from God's creation until now—and never will be again. Indeed, if the Lord did not shorten those days, no human being would survive. But for the sake of the people whom he has chosen he has shortened those days.

He warns against false christs, and commands vigilance

"If anyone tells you at that time, 'Look, here is Christ', or 'Look, there he is', don't believe it! For false christs and false prophets will arise and will perform signs and wonders, to deceive, if it be possible, even the men of God's choice. You must keep your eyes open! I am giving you this warning before all these things happen.

"But, in those days, when that misery is past, the light of the sun will be darkened and the moon will not give her light; stars will be falling from the sky and the powers of the heaven will rock on their foundations. Then men shall see the Son of Man coming in the clouds with great power and glory. And then shall he send out the angels to gather his chosen together from every quarter, from furthest earth to highest heaven. Let the fig-tree illustrate this for you: when its branches grow tender and produce leaves, you know that summer is near. So when you see these things happening, you may know that he is near, at your very doors! I tell you that this generation will not have passed until all these things have come true. Earth and sky will pass away, but what I have told you will never pass away! But no one knows the day or the hour of this happening, not even the angels in Heaven, no, not even the Son—only the Father. Keep your eyes open, keep on the alert, for you do not know when the time will be. It is as if a man who is travelling abroad had left his house and handed it over to be managed by his servants. He has given each one his work to do and has ordered the doorkeeper to be on the look-out. Just so must you keep a look-out, for you do not know when the master of the house will come—it might be late evening, or midnight, or cock-crow, or early morning—otherwise he might come unexpectedly and find you sound asleep. What I am saying to you I am saying to all; keep on the alert!"

CHAPTER 14

An act of love

In two days' time the festival of the Passover and of unleavened bread was due. Consequently, the chief priests and the scribes were trying to think of some trick by which they could get Jesus into their power and have him executed.

"But it must not be during the festival," they said, "or there will be a riot."

Jesus himself was now in Bethany in the house of Simon the leper. As he was sitting at table, a woman approached him with an alabaster flask of very costly spikenard perfume. She broke the neck of the flask and poured the perfume on Jesus' head. Some of those present were highly indignant and muttered,

"What is the point of such wicked waste of perfume? It could have been sold for over thirty pounds and the money given to the poor." And there was a murmur of resentment against her. But Jesus said,

"Let her alone, why must you make her feel uncomfortable? She has done a beautiful thing for me. You have the poor with you always and you can do good to them whenever you like, but you will not always have me. She has done all she could—for she has anointed my body in preparation for burial. I assure you that wherever the gospel is preached throughout the whole world, this deed of hers will also be recounted, as her memorial to me."

Judas volunteers to betray Jesus

Then Judas Iscariot, who was one of the twelve, went off to the chief priests to betray Jesus to them. And when they heard what he had to say, they were delighted and undertook to pay him money. So he looked for a convenient opportunity to betray him.

The Passover-supper prepared

On the first day of unleavened bread, the day when the Passover was sacrificed, Jesus' disciples said to him,

"Where do you want us to go and make the preparations for you to eat the Passover?"

Jesus sent off two of them with these instructions,

"Go into the town and you will meet a man carrying a pitcher of water. Follow him and say to the owner of the house which he enters, 'The master says, where is the room for me to eat the Passover with my disciples?' And he will show you a large upstairs room, set out and ready. That is where you must make our preparations."

So the disciples set off and went into the town, found everything as he had told them, and prepared for the Passover.

The last supper together: the mysterious bread and wine

Late in the evening he arrived with the twelve. And while they were sitting there, right in the middle of the meal, Jesus remarked,

"Believe me, one of you is going to betray me—someone who is now eating with me."

This deeply distressed them and one after another they began to say to him,

"Surely, I'm not the one?"

"It is one of the twelve," Jesus told them, "a man who is dipping his hand into the dish with me. It is true that the Son of Man will follow the road foretold by the scriptures, but alas for the man through whom he is betrayed! It would be better for that man if he had never been born."

And while they were still eating Jesus took a loaf, blessed it and broke it and gave it to them, with the words,

"Take this, it is my body."

Then he took a cup, and after thanking God, he gave it to them, and they all drank from it, and he said to them,

"This is my blood of the new agreement, and it is shed for many. I tell you truly I will drink no more wine until the day comes when I drink it fresh in the kingdom of God!"

Then they sang a hymn and went out to the Mount of Olives.

"Every one of you will lose your faith in me," Jesus told them, "as the scripture says:

I will smite the shepherd,
And the sheep shall be scattered abroad.

Yet after I have risen, I shall go before you into Galilee!"

Peter's bold words—and Jesus' reply

Then Peter said to him,

"Even if everyone should lose his faith, I never will."

"Believe me, Peter," returned Jesus, "this very night before the cock crows twice, you will disown me three times."

But Peter protested violently,

"Even if it means dying with you, I will never disown you!"

And they all made the same protest.

The last desperate prayer in Gethsemane

Then they arrived at a place called Gethsemane, and Jesus said to his disciples,

"Sit down here while I pray."

He took with him Peter, James and John, and began to be horror-stricken and desperately depressed.

"My heart is breaking with a death-like grief," he told them. "Stay here and keep watch."

Then he walked forward a little way and flung himself on the ground, praying that, if it were possible, the hour might pass him by.

"Dear Father," he said, "all things are possible to you. Let me not have to drink this cup! Yet it is not what I want but what you want."

Then he came and found them fast asleep. He spoke to Peter,

"Are you asleep, Simon? Couldn't you manage to stay awake for a single hour? Stay awake and pray, all of you, that you may not have to face temptation. Your spirit is willing, but human nature is weak."

Then he went away again and prayed in the same words, and once more he came and found them asleep. They could not keep their eyes open and they did not know what to say for themselves. When he came back for the third time, he said,

"Are you still going to sleep and take your ease? All right—the moment has come; now you will see the Son of Man betrayed into the hands of evil men! Get up, let us be going! Look, here comes my betrayer!"

Judas betrays Jesus

And suddenly, while the words were still on his lips, Judas, one of the twelve, arrived with a mob armed with swords and staves, sent by the chief priests and scribes and elders. The betrayer had given them a sign; he had said, "The one I kiss will be the man. Get hold of him and you can take him away without any trouble." So he walked straight up to Jesus, cried, "Master!" and kissed him affectionately. And so they got hold of him and held him. Somebody present drew his sword and struck at the High Priest's servant, slashing off his ear. Then Jesus spoke to them,

"So you've come out with your swords and staves to capture me like a bandit, have you? Day after day I was with you in the Temple, teaching, and you never laid a finger on me. But the scriptures must be fulfilled."

Then all the disciples deserted him and made their escape. There happened to be a young man among Jesus' followers who wore nothing but a linen shirt. They seized him, but he left the shirt in their hands and took to his heels stark naked.

Jesus before the High Priest

So they marched Jesus away to the High Priest in whose presence all the chief priests and elders and scribes had assembled.

(Peter followed him at a distance, right into the High Priest's courtyard. There he sat in the firelight with the servants, keeping himself warm.) Meanwhile, the chief priests and the whole council were trying to find some evidence against Jesus which would warrant the death penalty. But they failed completely. There were plenty of people ready to give false testimony against him, but their evidence was contradictory. Then some more perjurers stood up and said,

"We heard him say, 'I will destroy this Temple that was built by human hands and in three days I will build another made without human aid.' "

But even so their evidence conflicted. So the High Priest himself got up and took the centre of the floor.

"Have you no answer to make?" he asked Jesus. "What about all this evidence against you?"

But Jesus remained silent and offered no reply. Again the High Priest asked him,

"Are you Christ, Son of the blessed one?"

And Jesus said,

"I am! Yes, you will see the Son of Man sitting at the right hand of power, coming in the clouds of heaven."

Then the High Priest tore his robes and cried,

"Why do we still need witnesses? You heard the blasphemy; what is your opinion now?"

Their unanimous verdict was that he deserved to die. Then some of them began to spit at him. They blindfolded him and then smacked him, saying,

"Now prophesy who hit you!"

Even the servants who took him away slapped his face.

Peter, in fear, disowns his master

In the meantime, while Peter was in the courtyard below, one of the High Priest's maids came and saw him warming himself. She looked closely at him, and said,

"You were with the Nazarene too—with Jesus!"

But he denied it, saying,

"I neither know nor understand what you're talking about."

And he walked out into the gateway, and a cock crew.

Then the maid who had noticed him began to say again to the men standing there,

"This man is one of them!"

But he denied it again. A few minutes later the bystanders themselves said to Peter,

"You certainly are one of them. Why, you're a Galilean!"

But he started to curse and swear, saying,

"I tell you I don't know the man you're talking about!"

Immediately the cock crew for the second time, and back into Peter's mind came the words of Jesus, "Before the cock crows twice, you will disown me three times."

And as the truth broke upon him he burst into tears.

CHAPTER 15

Jesus before Pilate

THE moment daylight came the chief priests called together a meeting of elders, scribes and the whole council. They bound Jesus and took him off and handed him over to Pilate. Pilate asked him straight out,

"Well, you—*are* you the king of the Jews?"

"You say that I am," he replied.

The chief priests brought many accusations. So Pilate questioned him again,

"Have you nothing to say? Listen to all their accusations!"

But Jesus made no further answer—to Pilate's astonishment.

Now it was Pilate's custom at festival-time to release a prisoner—anyone they asked for. There was in the prison at the time, with some other rioters who had committed murder in a recent revolt, a man called Barabbas. The crowd surged forward and began to demand that Pilate should do what he usually did for them. So he spoke to them,

"Do you want me to set free the king of the Jews for you?"

For he knew perfectly well that the chief priests had handed Jesus over to him through sheer malice. But the chief priests worked upon the crowd to get them to release Barabbas rather than Jesus. So Pilate addressed them once more,

"Then what am I to do with the man whom you call the king of the Jews?"

They shouted back,

"Crucify him!"

But Pilate replied,

"Why, what crime has he committed?"

But their voices rose to a roar,

"Crucify him!"

And as Pilate wanted to satisfy the crowd, he set Barabbas free for them, and after having Jesus flogged handed him over to be crucified.

Then the soldiers marched him away inside the courtyard of the governor's residence and called their whole company together. They dressed Jesus in a purple robe, and twisting some thorn-twigs into a crown, they put it on his head. Then they began to salute him,

"Hail, your majesty—king of the Jews!"

They hit him on the head with a stick and spat at him, and then bowed low before him on bended knee. And when they had finished their fun with him, they took off the purple cloak and dressed him again in his own clothes. Then they led him outside to crucify him. They compelled Simon, a native of Cyrene in Africa (the father of Alexander and Rufus), who was on his way from the fields at the time, to carry Jesus' cross.

The crucifixion

They took him to a place called Golgotha (which means Skull Hill) and they offered him some drugged wine, but he would not take it. Then they crucified him, and shared out his garments, drawing lots to see what each of them would get. It was nine o'clock in the morning when they nailed him to the cross. Over his head the placard of his crime read, "THE KING OF THE JEWS." They also crucified two bandits at the same time, one on each side of him. And the passers-by jeered at him, shaking their heads in mockery, saying,

"Hi, you! You could destroy the Temple and build it up again in three days, why not come down from the cross and save yourself?"

The chief priests also made fun of him among themselves and the scribes, and said,

"He saved others, he cannot save himself. If only this Christ, the king of Israel, would come down now from the cross, we should see it and believe!"

And even the men who were crucified with him hurled abuse at him.

At midday darkness spread over the whole countryside and lasted until three o'clock in the afternoon, and at three o'clock Jesus cried out in a loud voice,

"My God, my God, why did you forsake me?"

Some of the bystanders heard these words which Jesus spoke in Aramaic (*Eloi, Eloi, lama sabachthani?*), and said,

"Listen, he's calling for Elijah!"

One man ran off and soaked a sponge in vinegar, put it on a stick, and held it up for Jesus to drink, calling out,

"Let him alone! Let's see if Elijah will come and take him down!"

But Jesus let out a great cry, and expired. The curtain of the Temple sanctuary was split in two from the top to the bottom. And when the centurion who stood in front of Jesus saw how he died, he said,

"This man was certainly a son of God!"

There were some women there looking on from a distance, among them Mary of Magdala, Mary the mother of the younger James and Joses, and Salome. These were the women who used to follow Jesus as he went about in Galilee and look after him. And there were many other women there who had come up to Jerusalem with him.

The body of Jesus is reverently laid in a tomb

When the evening came, because it was the day of preparation, that is the day before the Sabbath, Joseph from Arimathaea, a distinguished member of the council, who was himself prepared to accept the kingdom of God, went with great courage into Pilate's presence and asked for the body of Jesus. Pilate was surprised that he could be dead already and he sent for the centurion and asked whether he had been dead long. On hearing the centurion's report, he gave Joseph the body of Jesus. So Joseph brought a linen winding-sheet, took Jesus down and wrapped him in it, and then put him in a tomb which had been hewn out of the solid rock, rolling a stone over the entrance to it. Mary of Magdala and Mary the mother of Joses were looking on and saw where he was laid.

CHAPTER 16

Early on the first Lord's day: the women are amazed

WHEN the Sabbath was over, Mary of Magdala, Mary the mother of James, and Salome bought spices so that they could go and anoint him. And very early in the morning on the first day of the week, they came to the tomb, just as the sun was rising.

"Who is going to roll the stone back from the doorway of the tomb?" they asked each other.

And then as they looked closer, they saw that the stone, which was a very large one, had been rolled back. So they went into the tomb and saw a young man in a white robe sitting on the right-hand side, and they were simply astonished. But he said to them,

"There is no need to be astonished. You are looking for Jesus of Nazareth who was crucified. He has risen; he is not here. Look, here is the place where they laid him. But now go and tell his disciples, and Peter, that he will be in Galilee before you. You will see him there just as he told you."

And they got out of the tomb and ran away from it. They were trembling with excitement. They did not dare to breathe a word to anyone.*

An ancient appendix

When Jesus rose early on that first day of the week, he appeared first of all to Mary of Magdala, from whom he had driven out seven evil spirits. And she went and reported this to his sorrowing and weeping followers. They heard her say that he was alive and that she had seen him, but they did not believe it.

Later, he appeared in a different form to two of them who were out walking, as they were on their way to the country. These two came back and told the others, but they did not believe them either. Still later he appeared to the eleven themselves as they were sitting at table and reproached them for their lack of faith and refusal to believe those who had seen him after he had risen. Then he said to them,

"You must go out to the whole world and proclaim the gospel to every creature. He who believes it and is baptised will be saved, but he who disbelieves it will be condemned. These signs will follow those who do believe: they will drive out evil spirits in my name; they will speak with new tongues; they will pick up snakes, and if they drink any poison it will do them no harm; they will lay their hands upon the sick and they will recover."

Jesus, his mission accomplished, returns to Heaven

After these words to them, the Lord Jesus was taken up into Heaven and was enthroned at the right hand of God. They went out and preached everywhere. The Lord worked with them, confirming their message by the signs that followed.

* *An alternative ending found in certain MSS. following verse 8.* But they gave all these instructions briefly to Peter and his companions. Afterwards Jesus himself sent out through them, from east to west, the proclamation of the holy and incorruptible message of eternal salvation.

The Gospel of Luke

The author of this Gospel is beyond reasonable doubt Luke, "the beloved physician", companion and fellow-worker of Paul. This work is, of course, only the first of his "two volumes", the second being what we know as The Acts of the Apostles. It is generally recognised that he was not a Jew and that he was a doctor by profession.

This Gospel is thought by many to be the most beautiful of the four, both because of its style and of the imaginative sympathy with which Luke paints the portrait of his Master. There is a persistent legend that he was an artist, and while this is a matter of uncertainty, we owe him a definite enrichment and enlargement of the story of Jesus which gives the impression of an artist's sensitivity.

On his own admission Luke has carefully compared and edited existing narratives, but it would seem that he had access to a good deal of additional material, and we can reasonably guess at some of the sources from which he drew it. He would almost certainly know Mark's Gospel; he would be able to draw from the mysterious "Q", which scholars believe to have existed, although there is no trace of it; and he had his own reminiscences and material collected in Caesarea (Acts 24, 27).

Though it is impossible to state accurately how the work was composed, a great many scholars think that there was a first version possibly written during the travels with Paul, and that later material—the birth stories and the preface, for example—was incorporated later. Luke, like Mark, is writing primarily for the non-Jewish reader. A Gentile centurion, for example, is singled out as having more faith than Jesus had found in Israel; more than once, Samaritans, who were anathema to the Jews, are singled out for praise. Jesus' ancestry is traced back, not to Abraham the father of the Jewish race, but to Adam the father of all mankind.

None of the other evangelists shows so clearly the love and sympathy of Jesus for the sinner, the outcast and the unfortunate. And there is a reverence for women as the story unfolds, which shows the writer, through his understanding of his Master, far ahead of his time. Many scholars nowadays would place the writings of Luke's Gospel and of The Acts of the Apostles soon after Paul's death and before the Fall of Jerusalem, i.e. between 65 and 70. The graphic, but always careful and accurate, style conveys a strong impression of veracity.

CHAPTER 1

Prefatory Note

DEAR THEOPHILUS,

Many people have already written an account of the events which have happened among us, basing their work on the evidence of those who, we know, were eye-witnesses as well as teachers of the message. I have therefore decided, since I have traced the course of these happenings carefully from the beginning, to set them down for you myself in their proper order, so that you may have reliable information about the matters in which you have already had instruction.

A vision comes to an old priest of God

The story begins in the days when Herod was king of Judaea with a priest called Zacharias (who belonged to the Abijah section of the priesthood), whose wife Elisabeth was, like him, a descendant of Aaron. They were both truly religious people, blamelessly observing all the Lord's commandments and requirements. They were childless through Elisabeth's infertility, and both of them were getting on in years. One day, while Zacharias was performing his priestly functions (it was the turn of his division to be on duty), it fell to him to go into the sanctuary and burn the incense. The crowded congregation outside was praying at the actual time of the incense-burning, when an angel of the Lord appeared on the right side of the incense-altar. When Zacharias saw him, he was terribly agitated and a sense of awe swept over him. But the angel spoke to him,

"Do not be afraid, Zacharias; your prayers have been heard. Elisabeth your wife will bear you a son, and you are to call him John. This will be joy and delight to you and many more will be glad because he is born. He will be one of God's great men; he will touch neither wine nor strong drink and he will be filled with the Holy Spirit from the moment of his birth. He will turn many of Israel's children to the Lord their God. He will go out before God in the spirit and power of Elijah—to reconcile fathers and children, and bring back the disobedient to the wisdom of good men—and he will make a people fully ready for their Lord."

But Zacharias replied to the angel,

"How can I know that this is true? I am an old man myself and my wife is getting on in years . . ."

"I am Gabriel," the angel answered. "I stand in the presence of God, and I have been sent to speak to you and tell you this good news. Because you do not believe what I have said, you shall live in silence, and you shall be unable to speak a word until the day that it happens. But be sure that everything that I have told you will come true at the proper time."

Meanwhile, the people were waiting for Zacharias, wondering why he stayed so long in the sanctuary. But when he came out and was unable to speak a word to them—for although he kept making signs, not a sound came from his lips—they realised that he had seen a vision in the Temple. Later, when his days of duty were over, he went back home, and soon afterwards his wife Elisabeth became pregnant and kept herself secluded for five months.

"How good the Lord is to me," she would say, "now that he has taken away the shame that I have suffered."

A vision comes to a young woman in Nazareth

Then, in the sixth month, the angel Gabriel was sent from God to a Galilean town, Nazareth by name, to a young woman who was engaged to a man called Joseph (a descendant of David). The girl's name was Mary. The angel entered her room and said,

"Greetings to you, Mary. O favoured one!—the Lord is with you!"

Mary was deeply perturbed at these words and wondered what such a greeting could possibly mean. But the angel said to her,

"Do not be afraid, Mary; God loves you dearly. You are going to be the mother of a son, and you will call him Jesus. He will be great and will be known as the Son of the Most High. The Lord God will give him the throne of his forefather, David, and he will be king over the people of Jacob for ever. His reign shall never end."

Then Mary spoke to the angel,

"How can this be," she said, "I am not married!"

But the angel made this reply to her:

"The Holy Spirit will come upon you, the power of the Most High will overshadow you. Your child will therefore be called holy—the Son of God. Your cousin Elisabeth has also conceived a son, old as she is. Indeed, this is the sixth month for her, a woman who was called barren. For no promise of God can fail to be fulfilled."

"I belong to the Lord, body and soul," replied Mary, "let it happen as you say." And at this the angel left her.

With little delay Mary got ready and hurried off to the hill-side town in Judaea where Zacharias and Elisabeth lived. She went into their house and greeted Elisabeth. When she heard Mary's greeting, the unborn child stirred inside her and she herself was filled with the Holy Spirit, and cried out,

*"Blessed are you among women,/and blessed is your child!/ What an honour it is to have the mother of my Lord/come to see me!/As soon as your greeting reached my ears,/the child within me jumped for joy!/Oh, how happy is the woman who believes in God,/for his promises to her come true."/

Then Mary said,/"My heart is overflowing with praise of my Lord,/my soul is full of joy in God my Saviour./For he has deigned to notice me, his humble servant/and all generations to come/will call me the happiest of women!/The One who can do all things/has done great things for me—/oh, holy is his Name!/ Truly, his mercy rests on those who fear him/in every generation./ He has shown the strength of his arm,/he has swept away the high and mighty./He has set kings down from their thrones/and lifted up the humble./He has satisfied the hungry with good things/ and sent the rich away with empty hands./Yes, he has helped Israel, his child:/he has remembered the mercy/that he promised to our forefathers,/to Abraham and his sons for evermore!"/

The old woman's son, John, is born

So Mary stayed with Elisabeth about three months, and then went back to her own home. Then came the time for Elisabeth's child to be born, and she gave birth to a son. Her neighbours and relations heard of the great mercy the Lord had shown her and shared her joy.

When the eighth day came, they were going to circumcise the child and call him Zacharias, after his father, but his mother said,

"Oh, no! He must be called John."

"But none of your relations is called John," they replied. And they made signs to his father to see what name he wanted the child to have. He beckoned for a writing-tablet and wrote the

* This passage up to verse 55, and vv. 68–79, together with Ch. 2 vv. 29–32, were almost certainly known as hymns in the early Church and a likely verse form is indicated by oblique lines.

words, "His name is John", which greatly surprised everybody. Then his power of speech suddenly came back, and his first words were to thank God. The neighbours were awe-struck at this, and all these incidents were reported everywhere in the hill-country of Judaea. People turned the whole matter over in their hearts, and said,

"What is this child's future going to be? For the Lord's blessing is plainly upon him."

Then Zacharias, his father, filled with the Holy Spirit and speaking like a prophet, said,

"Blessings on the Lord, the God of Israel,/because he has turned his face towards his people/and has set them free!/And he has raised up for us a standard of salvation/in the house of his servant David./Long, long ago, through the words of his holy prophets,/ he promised to do this for us,/so that we should be safe from our enemies/and secure from all who hate us./So does he continue the mercy/he showed to our forefathers./So does he remember the holy agreement/he made with them/and the oath which he swore to our father Abraham,/to make us this gift:/that we should be saved/from the hands of our enemies,/and in his presence should serve him unafraid/in holiness and righteousness all our lives./

"And you, little child, will be called the prophet/of the Most High;/for you will go before the Lord/to prepare the way for his coming./It will be for you to give his people/knowledge of their salvation/through the forgiveness of their sins./Because the heart of our God/is full of mercy towards us,/the first light of Heaven shall come to visit us—/to shine on those who lie in darkness/and under the shadow of death,/and to guide our feet into the path of peace."/

The little child grew up and became strong in spirit. He lived in lonely places until the day came for him to show himself to Israel.

CHAPTER 2

The census brings Mary and Joseph to Bethlehem

At that time a proclamation was made by Caesar Augustus that all the inhabited world should be registered. This was the first census, undertaken while Cyrenius was governor of Syria; and everybody went to the town of his birth to be registered. Joseph went up from the town of Nazareth in Galilee to David's town, Bethlehem, in Judaea, because he was a direct descendant of

David, to be registered with his future wife, Mary, who was pregnant. So it happened that it was while they were there in Bethlehem that she came to the end of her time. She gave birth to her first child, a son. And as there was no place for them inside the inn, she wrapped him up and laid him in a manger.

A vision comes to shepherds on the hill-side

There were some shepherds living in the same part of the country, keeping guard throughout the night over their flock in the open fields. Suddenly an angel of the Lord stood before them, the splendour of the Lord blazed around them, and they were terror-stricken. But the angel said to them,

"Do not be afraid! Listen, I bring you glorious news of great joy which is for all the people. This very day, in David's town, a Saviour has been born for you. He is Christ, the Lord. Let this prove it to you: you will find a baby, wrapped up and lying in a manger."

And in a flash there appeared with the angel a vast host of the armies of Heaven, praising God, saying,

"Glory to God in the highest Heaven! Peace upon earth among men of goodwill!"

When the angels left them and went back into Heaven, the shepherds said to each other,

"Now let us go straight to Bethlehem and see this thing which the Lord has made known to us."

So they went as fast as they could and they found Mary and Joseph—and the baby lying in the manger. And when they had seen this sight, they told everybody what had been said to them about the little child. And all those who heard them were amazed at what the shepherds said. But Mary treasured all these things and turned them over in her mind. The shepherds went back to work, glorifying and praising God for everything that they had heard and seen, which had happened just as they had been told.

Mary and Joseph bring their newly-born son to the Temple

At the end of the eight days, the time came for circumcising the child and he was called Jesus, the name given to him by the angel before his conception.

When the "purification" time, stipulated by the Law of Moses, was completed, they brought Jesus to Jerusalem to present him to the Lord. This was to fulfil a requirement of the law of the Lord—

"Every male that openeth the womb shall be called holy to the Lord."

They also offered the sacrifice prescribed by the Law—

"A pair of turtle doves, or two young pigeons."

In Jerusalem there was at this time a man by the name of Simeon. He was an upright man, devoted to the service of God, living in expectation of the Restoration of Israel. His heart was open to the Holy Spirit, and it had been revealed to him that he would not die before he saw the Lord's Christ. He had been led by the Spirit to go into the Temple, and when Jesus' parents brought the child in to have done to him what the Law required, he took him up in his arms, blessed God and said—

"Now, Lord, you are dismissing your servant/in peace, as you promised!/For with my own eyes I have seen your salvation/which you have made ready for all peoples to see/—a light to show truth to the gentiles/and bring glory to your people Israel."/

The child's father and mother were still amazed at what was said about him, when Simeon gave them his blessing. He said to Mary, the child's mother,

"This child is destined to make many fall and many rise in Israel and to set up a standard which many will attack—for he will expose the secret thoughts of many hearts. And for you . . . your very soul will be pierced by a sword."

There was also present, Anna, the daughter of Phanuel of the tribe of Asher, who was a prophetess. She was a very old woman, having had seven years' married life and was now a widow of eighty-four. She spent her whole life in the Temple and worshipped God night and day with fastings and prayers. She came up at this very moment, praised God and spoke about Jesus to all those in Jerusalem who were expecting redemption.

When they had completed all the requirements of the Law of the Lord, they returned to Galilee, to their own town of Nazareth. The child grew up and became strong and full of wisdom. And God's blessing was upon him.

Twelve years later: the boy Jesus goes with his parents to Jerusalem

Every year at the Passover festival, Jesus' parents used to go to Jerusalem. When he was twelve years old they went up to the city as usual for the festival. When it was over they started back home, but the boy Jesus stayed behind in Jerusalem, without his parents' knowledge. They went a day's journey assuming that he was somewhere in their company, and then they began to look for him among their relations and acquaintances. They failed to find him, however, and turned back to the city, looking for him as they went. Three days later, they found him—in the Temple, sitting among the teachers, listening to them and asking them questions. All those who heard him were astonished at his powers of comprehension and at the answers that he gave. When Joseph and Mary saw him, they could hardly believe their eyes, and his mother said to him,

"Why have you treated us like this, my son? Here have your father and I been worried, looking for you everywhere!"

And Jesus replied,

"But why were you looking for me? Did you not know that I must be in my Father's house?"

But they did not understand his reply. Then he went home with them to Nazareth and was obedient to them. And his mother treasured all these things in her heart. And as Jesus continued to grow in body and mind, he grew also in the love of God and of those who knew him.

CHAPTER 3

Several years later: John prepares the way of Christ

In the fifteenth year of the reign of the Emperor Tiberius (a year when Pontius Pilate was governor of Judaea, Herod tetrarch of Galilee, Philip, his brother, tetrarch of the territory of Ituraea and Trachonitis, and Lysanias tetrarch of Abilene, while Annas and Caiaphas were the High Priests), the word of God came to John, the son of Zacharias, while he was in the desert. He went into the whole country round about the Jordan proclaiming baptism as a mark of a complete change of heart and of the forgiveness of sins, as the book of the prophet Isaiah says—

The voice of one crying in the wilderness,
Make ye ready the way of the Lord,
Make his paths straight.
Every valley shall be filled,
And every mountain and hill shall be brought low:
And the crooked shall become straight,
And the rough ways smooth:
And all flesh shall see the salvation of God.

So John used to say to the crowds who came out to be baptised by him,

"Who warned you, you serpent's brood, to escape from the wrath to come? See that your lives prove that your hearts are really changed! Don't start thinking that you can say to yourselves, 'We are Abraham's children', for I tell you that God could produce children of Abraham out of these stones! The axe already lies at the root of the tree, and the tree that fails to produce good fruit is cut down and thrown into the fire."

Then the crowds would ask him, "Then what shall we do?"

And his answer was, "The man who has two shirts must share with the man who has none, and the man who has food must do the same."

Some of the tax-collectors also came to him to be baptised and they asked him,

"Master, what are we to do?"

"You must not demand more than you are entitled to," he replied.

And the soldiers asked him, "And what are we to do?"

"Don't bully people, don't bring false charges, and be content with your pay," he replied.

The people were in a great state of expectation and were all inwardly debating whether John could possibly be Christ. But John answered them all in these words,

"It is true that I baptise you with water, but the one who follows me is stronger than I am—indeed I am not fit to undo his shoe-laces—he will baptise you with the fire of the Holy Spirit. He will come all ready to separate the wheat from the chaff, and to clear the rubbish from his threshing-floor. The wheat he will gather into his barn and the chaff he will burn with a fire that cannot be put out."

These and many other things John said to the people as he exhorted them and announced the good news. But the tetrarch Herod, who had been condemned by John in the affair of Herodias, his brother's wife, as well as for the other evil things that he had done, crowned his misdeeds by putting John in prison.

Jesus is himself baptised

When all the people had been baptised, and Jesus was praying after his own baptism, Heaven opened and the Holy Spirit came down upon him in the bodily form of a dove. Then there came a voice from Heaven, saying,

"You are my dearly-loved Son, in whom I am well pleased."

Jesus himself was about thirty years old at this time when he began his work.

The ancestry of Jesus traced to Adam

People assumed that Jesus was the son of Joseph, who was the son of Heli, who was the son of Matthat, who was the son of Levi, who was the son of Melchi, who was the son of Jannai, who was the son of Joseph, who was the son of Mattathias, who was the son of Amos, who was the son of Nahum, who was the son of Esli, who was the son of Naggai, who was the son of Maath, who was the son of Mattathias, who was the son of Semein, who was the son of Josech, who was the son of Joda, who was the son of Joanan, who was the son of Rhesa, who was the son of Zerubbabel, who was the son of Shealtiel, who was the son of Neri, who was the son of Melchi, who was the son of Addi, who was the son of Cosam, who was the son of Elmadam, who was the son of Er, who was the son of Jesus, who was the son of Eliezer, who was the son of Jorim, who was the son of Matthat, who was the son of Levi, who was the son of Symeon, who was the son of Judas, who was the son of Joseph, who was the son of Jonam, who was the son of Eliakim, who was the son of Melea, who was the son of Menna, who was the son of Mattatha, who was the son of Nathan, who was the son of David, who was the son of Jesse, who was the son of Obed, who was the son of Boaz, who was the son of Salmon, who was the son of Nahshon, who was the son of Amminadab, who was the son of Arni, who was the son of Hezron, who was the son of Perez, who was the son of Judah, who was the son of Jacob, who was the son of Isaac, who was the son of Abraham, who was the son of Terah, who was the son of Nahor, who was the son of Serug, who was the son of Reu, who was the son of Peleg, who was the son of Eber, who was the son of Shelah, who was the son of Cainan, who was the son of Arphaxad, who was the son of Shem, who was the son of Noah, who was the son of Lamech, who was the son of Methuselah, who was the son of Enoch, who was the son of Jared, who was the son of Mahalaleel, who was the son of Cainan, who was the son of Enos, who was the son of Seth, who was the son of Adam, who was the son of God.

CHAPTER 4

Jesus faces temptation

JESUS returned from the Jordan full of the Holy Spirit and he was led by the Spirit to spend forty days in the desert, where he was tempted by the devil. He ate nothing during that time and afterwards he felt very hungry.

"If you are the Son of God," the devil said to him, "tell this stone to turn into a loaf."

Jesus answered,

"The scripture says, 'Man shall not live by bread alone.'"

Then the devil took him up and showed him all the kingdoms of mankind in a sudden vision, and said to him,

"I will give you all this power and magnificence, for it belongs to me and I can give it to anyone I please. It shall all be yours if you will fall down and worship me."

To this Jesus replied,

"It is written, 'Thou shalt worship the Lord thy God and him only shalt thou serve.'"

Then the devil took him to Jerusalem and set him on the highest pinnacle of the Temple.

"If you are the Son of God," he said, "throw yourself down from here, for the scripture says, 'He shall give his angels charge concerning thee, to guard thee', and 'On their hands they shall bear thee up, lest haply thou dash thy foot against a stone.'"

To which Jesus replied,

"It is also said, 'Thou shalt not tempt the Lord thy God.'"

And when he had exhausted every kind of temptation, the devil withdrew until his next opportunity.

Jesus begins his ministry in Galilee

And now Jesus returned to Galilee in the power of the Spirit, and news of him spread through all the surrounding district. He taught in their synagogues, to everyone's great admiration.

Then he came to Nazareth where he had been brought up and, according to his custom, went to the synagogue on the Sabbath day. He stood up to read the scriptures and the book of the prophet Isaiah was handed to him. He opened the book and found the place where these words are written—

The Spirit of the Lord is upon me,
Because he anointed me to preach good tidings to the poor:
He hath sent me to proclaim release to the captives,
And recovering of sight to the blind,
To set at liberty them that are bruised,
To proclaim the acceptable year of the Lord.

Then he shut the book, handed it back to the attendant and resumed his seat. Every eye in the synagogue was fixed upon him and he began to tell them, "This very day this scripture has been fulfilled, while you have been listening to it!"

Everybody heard what he said. They were amazed at the beautiful words that came from his lips, and they kept saying,

"Isn't this Joseph's son?"

So he said to them,

"I expect you will quote this proverb to me, 'Cure yourself, doctor!' Let us see you do in your own country all that we have heard that you did in Capernaum!" Then he added, "I assure you that no prophet is ever welcomed in his own country. I tell you the plain fact that in Elijah's time, when the heavens were shut up for three and a half years and there was a great famine through the whole country, there were many widows in Israel, but Elijah was not sent to any of them. But he *was* sent to Sarepta, to a widow in the country of Sidon. In the time of Elisha the prophet, there were many lepers in Israel, but not one of them was healed—only Naaman, the Syrian."

But when they heard this, everyone in the synagogue was furiously angry. They sprang to their feet and drove him right out of the town, taking him to the brow of the hill on which it was built, intending to hurl him down headlong. But he walked straight through the whole crowd and went on his way.

Jesus heals in Capernaum

Then he came down to Capernaum, a town in Galilee, and taught them on the Sabbath day. They were astonished at his teaching, for his words had the ring of authority.

There was a man in the synagogue under the influence of some evil spirit and he yelled at the top of his voice, "Hi! What have you got to do with us, Jesus, you Nazarene—have you come to kill us? I know who you are all right, you're God's holy one!"

Jesus cut him short and spoke sharply,

"Be quiet! Get out of him!"

And after throwing the man down in front of them, the devil did come out of him without hurting him in the slightest. At this everybody present was amazed and they kept saying to each other,

"What sort of words are these? He speaks to these evil spirits with authority and power and out they go."

And his reputation spread over the whole surrounding district.

When Jesus got up and left the synagogue he went into Simon's house. Simon's mother-in-law was in the grip of a high fever, and they asked Jesus to help her. He stood over her as she lay in bed, brought the fever under control and it left her. At once she got up and began to see to their needs.

Then, as the sun was setting, all those who had friends suffering from every kind of disease brought them to Jesus and he laid his hands on each one of them separately and healed them. Evil spirits came out of many of these people, shouting, "You are the Son of God!"

But he spoke sharply to them and would not allow them to say any more, for they knew perfectly well that he was Christ.

Jesus attempts to be alone—in vain

At daybreak, he went off to a deserted place, but the crowds tried to find him and when they did discover him, tried to prevent him from leaving them. But he told them, "I must tell the good news of the kingdom of God to other towns as well—that is my mission."

And he continued proclaiming his message in the synagogues of Judaea.

CHAPTER 5

Simon, James and John become Jesus' followers

One day the people were crowding closely round Jesus to hear God's message, as he stood on the shore of Lake Gennesaret. Jesus noticed two boats drawn up on the beach, for the fishermen had left them there while they were cleaning their nets. He went aboard one of the boats, which belonged to Simon, and asked him to push out a little from the shore. Then he sat down and continued his teaching of the crowds from the boat.

When he had finished speaking, he said to Simon, "Push out now into deep water and let down your nets for a catch."

Simon replied, "Master! We've worked all night and never caught a thing, but if you say so, I'll let the nets down."

And when they had done this, they caught an enormous shoal of fish—so big that the nets began to tear. So they signalled to their partners in the other boat to come and help them. They came and filled both the boats to sinking point. When Simon Peter saw this, he fell at Jesus' knees and said,

"Keep away from me, Lord, for I'm only a sinful man!"

For he and his companions (including Zebedee's sons, James and John, Simon's partners) were staggered at the haul of fish they had made.

Jesus said to Simon, "Don't be afraid, Simon. From now on your catch will be *men*."

So they brought the boats ashore, left everything and followed him.

Jesus cures leprosy

While he was in one of the towns, Jesus came upon a man who was a mass of leprosy. When he saw Jesus, he prostrated himself before him and begged,

"If you want to Lord, you can make me clean."

Jesus stretched out his hand, placed it on the leper, saying,

"Certainly I want to. Be clean!"

Immediately the leprosy left him and Jesus warned him not to tell anybody, but to go and show himself to the priest and to make the offerings for his recovery which Moses prescribed, as evidence to the authorities.

Yet the news about him spread all the more, and enormous crowds collected to hear Jesus and to be healed of their complaints. But he slipped quietly away to deserted places for prayer.

Jesus cures a paralytic in soul and body

One day while Jesus was teaching, some Pharisees and experts in the Law were sitting near him. They had come out of every village in Galilee and Judaea as well as from Jerusalem. The Lord's power to heal people was with him. Soon some men arrived carrying a paralytic on a small bed and they kept trying to carry him in to put him down in front of Jesus. When they failed to find a way of getting him in because of the dense crowd, they went up on to the top of the house and let him down, bed and all, through the tiles, into the middle of the crowd in front of Jesus. When Jesus saw their faith, he said to the man,

"My friend, your sins are forgiven."

The scribes and the Pharisees began to argue about this, saying, "Who is this man who talks blasphemy? Who can forgive sins? Only God can do that."

Jesus realised what was going on in their minds and spoke straight to them.

"Why must you argue like this in your minds? Which do you suppose is easier—to say, 'Your sins are forgiven' or to say, 'Get up and walk'? But to make you realise that the Son of Man has full authority on earth to forgive sins—I tell *you*," he said to the man who was paralysed, "get up, pick up your bed and go home!"

Instantly the man sprang to his feet before their eyes, picked up the bedding on which he used to lie, and went off home, praising God. Sheer amazement gripped every man present, and they praised God and said in awed voices, "We have seen incredible things today."

Jesus calls Levi to be his disciple

Later on, Jesus went out and looked straight at a tax-collector called Levi, as he sat in his office.

"Follow me," he said to him.

And he got to his feet, left everything behind and followed him.

Then Levi gave a big reception for Jesus in his own house, and there was a great crowd of tax-collectors and others at table with them. The Pharisees and their companions the scribes kept muttering indignantly about this to Jesus' disciples, saying,

"Why do you have your meals with tax-collectors and sinners?"

Jesus answered them,

"It is not the healthy who need the doctor, but those who are ill. I did not come with an invitation for the 'righteous' but for the 'sinners'—to change their ways."

Jesus hints at who he is

Then people said to him,

"Why is it that John's disciples are always fasting and praying, just like the Pharisees' disciples, but yours both eat and drink?"

Jesus answered,

"Can you expect wedding-guests to fast while they have the bridegroom with them? The day will come when they will lose the bridegroom; that will be the time for them to fast!"

Then he gave them this illustration.

"Nobody tears a piece from a new coat to patch up an old one. If he does, he ruins the new one and the new piece does not match the old.

"Nobody puts new wine into old wineskins. If he does, the new wine will burst the skins—the wine will be spilt and the skins ruined. No, new wine must be put into new wineskins. Of course, nobody who has been drinking old wine will want the new at once. He is sure to say, 'The old is a good sound wine'."

CHAPTER 6

Jesus speaks of the Sabbath—

ONE Sabbath day, as Jesus happened to be passing through the cornfields, his disciples began picking the ears of corn, rubbing them in their hands, and eating them. Some of the Pharisees remarked,

"Why are you doing what the Law forbids men to do on the Sabbath day?"

Jesus answered them and said,

"Have you never read what David and his men did when they were hungry? He went into the house of God, took the presentation loaves, ate some bread himself and gave some to those with him, even though the Law does not permit anyone except the priests to eat it."

Then he added, "The Son of Man is master even of the Sabbath."

—and provokes violent antagonism

On another Sabbath day when he went into a synagogue to teach, there was a man there whose right hand was wasted away. The scribes and the Pharisees were watching Jesus closely to see whether he would heal on the Sabbath day, which would give them grounds for an accusation. But he knew what was going on in their minds, and said to the man with the wasted hand,

"Stand up and come forward."

And he got up and stood there. Then Jesus said to them,

"I am going to ask you a question. Does the Law command us to do good on the Sabbath or do harm—to save life or destroy it?"

He looked round, meeting all their eyes, and said to the man,

"Now stretch out your hand."

He did so, and his hand was restored as sound as the other one. But they were filled with insane fury and kept discussing with each other what they could do to Jesus.

After a night of prayer Jesus selects the twelve

It was in those days that he went up the hill-side to pray, and spent the whole night in prayer to God. When daylight came, he summoned his disciples to him and out of them he chose twelve whom he called apostles. They were—

Simon (whom he called Peter),
Andrew, his brother,
James,
John,
Philip,
Bartholomew,
Matthew,
Thomas,
James, the son of Alphaeus,
Simon, called the nationalist,
Judas, the son of James, and
Judas Iscariot, who later betrayed him.

Then he came down with them and stood on a level piece of ground, surrounded by a large crowd of his disciples and a great number of people from all parts of Judaea and Jerusalem and the coastal district of Tyre and Sidon, who had come to hear him and to be healed of their diseases. (And even those who were troubled with evil spirits were cured.) The whole crowd were trying to touch him with their hands, for power was going out from him and he healed them all.

Jesus declares who is happy and who is to be pitied, and defines a new attitude towards life

Then Jesus looked steadily at his disciples and said,

"How happy are you who own nothing, for the kingdom of God is yours!

"How happy are you who are hungry now, for you will be satisfied!

"How happy are you who weep now, for you are going to laugh!

"How happy you are when men hate you and turn you out of their company; when they slander you and reject all that you stand for because you are loyal to the Son of Man. Be glad when that happens and jump for joy—your reward in Heaven is magnificent. For that is exactly how their fathers treated the prophets.

"But how miserable for you who are rich, for you have had all your comforts!

"How miserable for you who have all you want, for you are going to be hungry!

"How miserable for you who are laughing now, for you will know sorrow and tears!

"How miserable for you when everybody praises you, for that is exactly how their fathers treated the false prophets.

"But I say to all of you who will listen to me: love your enemies, do good to those who hate you, bless those who curse you, and pray for those who treat you spitefully.

"As for the man who hits you on one cheek, offer him the other one as well! And if a man is taking away your coat, do not stop him from taking your shirt as well. Give to everyone who asks you, and when a man has taken what belongs to you, don't demand it back.

"Treat men exactly as you would like them to treat you. If you love only those who love you, what credit is that to you? Even sinners love those who love them! And if you do good only to those who do good to you, what credit is that to you? Even sinners do that much. And if you lend only to those from whom you hope to get your money back, what credit is that to you? Even sinners lend to sinners and expect to get their money back. No, you are to love your *enemies* and do good and lend without hope of return. Your reward will be wonderful and you will be sons of the Most High. For he is kind to the ungrateful and the wicked!

"You must be merciful, as your Father is merciful. Don't judge other people and you will not be judged yourselves. Don't condemn and you will not be condemned. Forgive others and people will forgive you. Give and men will give to you

—yes, good measure, pressed down, shaken together and running over will they pour into your lap. For whatever measure you use with other people, they will use in their dealings with you."

The need for thorough-going sincerity

Then he gave them an illustration—

"Can one blind man be guide to another blind man? Surely they will both fall into the ditch. A disciple is not above his teacher, but when he is fully trained he will be like his teacher.

"Why do you look at the speck of sawdust in your brother's eye and fail to notice the plank in your own? How can you say to your brother, 'Let me take the speck out of your eye' when you cannot see the plank in your own? You fraud, take the plank out of your own eye first and then you can see clearly to remove the speck out of your brother's eye.

"It is impossible for a good tree to produce bad fruit—as impossible as it is for a bad tree to produce good fruit. Do not men know what a tree is by its fruit? You cannot pick figs from briars, or gather a bunch of grapes from a blackberry bush! A good man produces good things from the good stored up in his heart, and a bad man produces evil things from his own stores of evil. For a man's words express what overflows from his heart.

"And what is the point of calling me, 'Lord, Lord', without doing what I tell you to do? Let me show you what the man who comes to me, hears what I have to say, and puts it into practice, is really like. He is like a man building a house, who dug down to rock-bottom and laid the foundation of his house upon it. Then when the flood came and the flood-water swept down upon that house, it could not shift it because it was properly built. But the man who hears me and does not act upon what he hears is like a man who built his house upon soft earth without foundation. When the flood-water swept down upon it, it collapsed and the whole house crashed down in ruins."

CHAPTER 7

A Roman centurion's extraordinary faith in Jesus

When Jesus had finished these talks to the people, he came to Capernaum, where it happened that there was a man very seriously ill and in fact at the point of death. He was the slave of a centurion who thought very highly of him. When the centurion heard about Jesus, he sent some Jewish elders to him with the request that he would come and save his slave's life. When they came to Jesus, they urged him strongly to grant this request, saying that the centurion deserved to have this done for him. "He loves our nation and has built us a synagogue out of his own pocket," they said.

So Jesus went with them, but as he approached the house, the centurion sent some of his friends with the message,

"Don't trouble yourself, sir! I'm not important enough for you to come into my house—I didn't think I was fit to come to you in person. Just give the order, please, and my boy will recover. I am used to working under orders, and I have soldiers under me. I can say to one, 'Go', and he goes, or I can say to another, 'Come here', and he comes; or I can say to my slave, 'Do this job', and he does it."

These words amazed Jesus and he turned to the crowd who were following him and said,

"I have never found faith like this anywhere, even in Israel!"

Then those who had been sent by the centurion returned to the house and found the slave perfectly well.

Jesus brings a dead youth back to life

Not long afterwards, Jesus went into a town called Nain, accompanied by his disciples and a large crowd. As he approached the city gate, it happened that some people were carrying out a dead man, the only son of his widowed mother. The usual crowd of fellow-townsmen was with her. When the Lord saw her, his heart went out to her and he said,

"Don't cry."

Then he walked up and put his hand on the bier while the bearers stood still. Then he said,

"Young man, get up!"

And the dead man sat up and began to talk, and Jesus handed him to his mother. Everybody present was awe-struck and they praised God, saying,

"A great prophet has arisen among us and God has turned his face towards his people."

And this report of him spread through the whole of Judaea and the surrounding countryside.

Jesus sends John a personal message

John's disciples reported all these happenings to him. Then he summoned two of them and sent them to the Lord with this message,

"Are you the one who is to come, or are we to look for someone else?"

When the men came to Jesus, they said,

"John the Baptist has sent us to you with this message, 'Are you the one who is to come, or are we to look for someone else?'"

At that very time Jesus was healing many people of their diseases and ailments and evil spirits, and he restored sight to many who were blind. Then he answered them,

"Go and tell John what you have seen and heard. The blind are recovering their sight, cripples are walking again, lepers being healed, the deaf hearing, dead men are being brought to life again, and the good news is being given to those in need. And happy is the man who never loses his faith in me."

Jesus emphasises the greatness of John—and the greater importance of the kingdom of God

When these messengers had gone back, Jesus began to talk to the crowd about John.

"What did you go out into the desert to look at? Was it a reed waving in the breeze? Well, *what* was it you went out to see? A man dressed in fine clothes? But the men who wear fine clothes live luxuriously in palaces. But what *did* you really go to see? A prophet? Yes, I tell you, a prophet and far more than a prophet! This is the man of whom the scripture says,

Behold, I send my messenger before thy face,
Who shall prepare thy way before thee.

"Believe me, no one greater than John has ever been born, and yet a humble member of the kingdom of God is greater than he.

"All the people, yes, even the tax-collectors, when they heard John, acknowledged God and were baptised by his baptism. But the Pharisees and the experts in the Law frustrated God's purpose for them, for they refused John's baptism.

"What can I say that the men of this generation are like—what sort of men are they? They are like children sitting in the market-place and calling out to each other, 'We played at weddings for you, but you wouldn't dance, and we played at funerals for you, and you wouldn't cry!' For John the Baptist came in the strictest austerity and you say he is crazy. Then the Son of Man came, enjoying food and drink, and you say, 'Look, a drunkard and a glutton, a bosom-friend of the tax-collector and the outsider!' So wisdom is proved right by all her children!"

Jesus contrasts unloving righteousness with loving penitence

Then one of the Pharisees asked Jesus to a meal with him. When Jesus came into the house, he took his place at the table and a woman, known in the town as a bad character, found out that Jesus was there and brought an alabaster flask of perfume and stood behind him crying, letting her tears fall on his feet and then drying them with her hair. Then she kissed them and anointed them with the perfume. When the Pharisee who had invited him saw this, he said to himself, "If this man were really a prophet, he would know who this woman is and what sort of a person is touching him. He would have realised that she is a bad woman." Then Jesus spoke to him,

"Simon, there is something I want to say to you."

"Very well, Master," he returned, "say it."

"Once upon a time, there were two men in debt to the same money-lender. One owed him fifty pounds and the other five. And since they were unable to pay, he generously cancelled both of their debts. Now, which one of them do you suppose will love him more?"

"Well," returned Simon, "I suppose it will be the one who has been more generously treated."

"Exactly," replied Jesus, and then turning to the woman, he said to Simon,

"You see this woman? I came into your house but you provided no water to wash my feet. But she has washed my feet with her tears and dried them with her hair. You gave me no kiss of welcome, but she, from the moment I came in, has not stopped covering my feet with kisses. You gave me no oil for my head, but she has put perfume on my feet. That is why I tell you, Simon, that her sins, many as they are, are forgiven; for she has so much love. But the man who has little to be forgiven has only a little love to give."

Then he said to her,

"Your sins are forgiven."

And the men at table with him began to say to themselves,

"And who is this man, who even forgives sins?"

But Jesus said to the woman,

"It is your faith that has saved you. Go in peace."

CHAPTER 8

NOT long after this incident, Jesus went through every town and village preaching and telling the people the good news of the kingdom of God. He was accompanied by the twelve and some women who had been cured of evil spirits and illnesses—Mary, known as "the woman from Magdala" (who had once been possessed by seven evil spirits), Joanna the wife of Chuza, an agent of Herod, Susanna, and many others who used to look after Jesus' and his companions' comfort from their own resources.

Jesus' parable of the mixed reception given to the truth

When a large crowd had collected and people were coming to him from one town after another, he spoke to them and gave them this parable:

"A sower went out to sow his seed, and while he was sowing, some of the seed fell by the roadside and was trodden down and the birds gobbled it up. Some fell on the rock, and when it sprouted it withered for lack of moisture. Some fell among thornbushes which grew up with the seeds and choked the life out of them. And some seed fell on good soil and grew and produced a crop—a hundred times what had been sown."

And when he had said this, he called out,

"Let the man who has ears to hear use them!"

Then his disciples asked him the meaning of the parable. To which Jesus replied,

"You have been given the privilege of understanding the secrets of the kingdom of God, but the others are given parables so that they may go through life with their eyes open and see nothing, and with their ears open, and understand nothing of what they hear.

"This is what the parable means. The seed is the message of God. The seed sown by the roadside represents those who hear the message, and then the devil comes and takes it away from their hearts so that they cannot believe it and be saved. That sown on the rock represents those who accept the message with great delight when they hear it, but have no real root. They believe for a little while but when the time of temptation comes, they lose faith. And the seed sown among the thorns represents the people who hear the message and go on their way, and with the worries and riches and pleasures of living, the life is choked out of them, and in the end they produce nothing. But the seed sown on good soil means the men who hear the message and grasp it with a good and honest heart, and go on steadily producing a good crop.

Truth is not a secret to be hidden but a gift to be used

"Nobody lights a lamp and covers it with a basin or puts it under the bed. No, a man puts his lamp on a lamp-stand so that those who come in can see the light. For there is nothing hidden now which will not become perfectly plain and there are no secrets now which will not become as clear as daylight. So take care how you listen—more will be given to the man who has something already, but the man who has nothing will lose even what he thinks he has."

Then his mother and his brothers arrived to see him, but could not get near him because of the crowd. So a message was passed to him,

"Your mother and your brothers are standing outside wanting to see you."

To which he replied,

"My mother and my brothers? They are those who listen to God's message and obey it."

Jesus' mastery of wind and water

It happened on one of these days that he got into a boat with his disciples and said to them,

"Let us cross over to the other side of the lake."

So they set sail, and when they were under way he fell asleep. Then a squall of wind swept down upon the lake and they were in grave danger of being swamped. Coming forward, they woke him up, saying,

"Master, master, we're drowning!"

Then he got up and reprimanded the wind and the stormy waters, and they died down, and everything was still. Then he said to them,

"What has happened to your faith?"

But they were frightened and bewildered and kept saying to each other,

"Who ever can this be? He gives orders even to the winds and waters and they obey him."

Jesus encounters and heals a dangerous lunatic

They sailed on to the country of the Gergesenes which is on the opposite side of the lake to Galilee. And as Jesus disembarked, a man from the town who was possessed by evil spirits met him. He had worn no clothes for a long time and did not live inside a house, but among the tombs. When he saw Jesus, he let out a howl and fell down in front of him, yelling,

"What have you got to do with me, you Jesus, Son of the Most High God? Please, please, don't torment me."

For Jesus was commanding the evil spirit to come out of the man. Again and again the evil spirit had taken control of him, and though he was bound with chains and fetters and closely watched, he would snap his bonds and go off into the desert with the devil at his heels. Then Jesus asked him,

"What is your name?"

"Legion!" he replied. For many evil spirits had gone into him, and were now begging Jesus not to order them off to the bottomless pit. It happened that there was a large herd of pigs feeding on the hill-side, so they implored him to allow them to go into the pigs, and he let them go. And when the evil spirits came out of the man and went into the pigs, the whole herd stampeded down the cliff into the lake and was drowned. When the swineherds saw what had happened, they took to their heels, pouring out the story to the people in the town and countryside. These people came out to see what had happened, and approached Jesus. They found the man, whom the evil spirits had left, sitting down at Jesus' feet, properly clothed and quite sane. That frightened them.

Those who had seen it told the others how the man with the evil spirits had been cured. And the whole crowd of people from the district surrounding the Gergesenes' country begged Jesus to go away from them, for they were thoroughly frightened. Then he re-embarked on the boat and turned back. The man who had had the evil spirits kept begging to go with Jesus, but he sent him away with the words,

"Go back home and tell them all that God has done for you."

So the man went away and told the story of what Jesus had done for him, all over the town.

On Jesus' return, the crowd welcomed him back, for they had all been looking for him.

Jesus heals in response to faith

Then up came Jairus (who was president of the synagogue), and fell at Jesus' feet, begging him to come into his house, for his daughter, an only child about twelve years old, was dying.

But as he went, the crowds nearly suffocated him. Among them was a woman, who had had a chronic haemorrhage for twelve years and who had derived no benefit from anybody's treatment. She came up behind Jesus and touched the edge of his cloak, and her haemorrhage stopped at once.

"Who was that who touched me?" said Jesus.

And when everybody denied it, Peter remonstrated,

"Master, the crowds are all round you and are pressing you on all sides. . . ."

But Jesus said,

"Somebody touched me, for I felt that power went out from me."

When the woman realised that she had not escaped notice she came forward trembling, and fell at his feet and admitted before everybody why she had had to touch him, and how she had been instantly cured.

"Daughter," said Jesus, "It is your faith that has healed you—go in peace."

While he was still speaking, somebody came from the synagogue president's house to say,

"Your daughter is dead—there is no need to trouble the master any further."

But when Jesus heard this, he said to him,

"Now don't be afraid, go on believing and she will be all right."

Then when he came to the house, he would not allow anyone to go in with him except Peter, John and James, and the child's parents. All those already there were weeping and wailing over her, but he said,

"Stop crying! She is not dead, she is fast asleep."

This drew a scornful laugh from them, for they were quite certain that she had died. But he took the little girl's hand and called out to her,

"Get up, my child!"

And her spirit came back and she got to her feet at once, and Jesus told them to give her some food. Her parents were nearly out of their minds with joy, but Jesus told them not to tell anyone what had happened.

CHAPTER 9

Jesus commissions the twelve to preach and heal

THEN he called the twelve together and gave them power and authority over all evil spirits and the ability to heal disease. He sent them out to preach the kingdom of God and to heal the sick, with these words,

"Take nothing for your journey—neither a stick nor a purse nor food nor money, nor even extra clothes! When you come to stay at a house, remain there until you go on your way again. And where they will not welcome you, leave that town, and shake the dust off your feet as a protest against them!"

So they set out, and went from village to village preaching the gospel and healing people everywhere.

Herod's uneasy conscience after his execution of John

All these things came to the ears of Herod the tetrarch and caused him acute anxiety, because some people were saying that John had risen from the dead, some maintaining that the prophet Elijah had appeared, and others that one of the old-time prophets had come back.

"I beheaded John," said Herod. "Who can this be that I hear all these things about?"

And he tried to find a way of seeing Jesus.

The twelve return and tell their story

Then the apostles returned, and when they had made their report to Jesus of what they had done, he took them with him privately and retired into a town called Bethsaida.

Jesus welcomes the crowds, teaches, heals and feeds them

But the crowds observed this and followed him. And he welcomed them and talked to them about the kingdom of God, and cured those who were in need of healing. As the day drew to its close the twelve came to him and said,

"Please dismiss the crowd now so that they can go to the villages and farms round about and find some food and shelter, for we're quite in the wilds here."

"You give them something to eat!" returned Jesus.

"But we've nothing here," they replied, "except five loaves and two fish, unless you want us to go and buy food for all this crowd?" (There were approximately five thousand men there.)

Then Jesus said to the disciples,

"Get them to sit down in groups of about fifty."

This they did, making them all sit down. Then he took the five loaves and the two fish and looked up to Heaven, blessed them, broke them into pieces and passed them to his disciples to serve to the crowd. Everybody ate and was satisfied. Afterwards they collected twelve baskets full of broken pieces which were left over.

Jesus asks a question and receives Peter's momentous answer

Then came this incident. While Jesus was praying by himself, having only the disciples near him, he asked them this question:

"Who are the crowd saying that I am?"

"Some say that you are John the Baptist," they replied. "Others that you are Elijah, and others think that one of the old-time prophets has come back to life."

Then he said,

"And who do you say that I am?"

"God's Christ!" said Peter.

Jesus foretells his own suffering: the paradox of losing life to find it

But Jesus expressly told them not to say a word to anybody,

at the same time warning them of the inevitability of the Son of Man's great suffering, of his repudiation by the elders, chief priests and scribes, and of his death and of being raised to life again on the third day. Then he spoke to them all:

"If anyone wants to follow in my footsteps, he must give up all right to himself, carry his cross every day and keep close behind me. For the man who wants to save his life will lose it, but the man who loses his life for my sake will save it. For what is the use of a man gaining the whole world if he loses or forfeits his own soul? If anyone is ashamed of me and my words, the Son of Man will be ashamed of him, when he comes in his glory and the glory of the Father and the holy angels. I tell you the simple truth—there are men standing here today who will not taste death until they have seen the kingdom of God!"

Peter, John and James are allowed to see the glory of Jesus

About eight days after these sayings, Jesus took Peter, James and John and went off with them to the hill-side to pray. And then, while he was praying, the whole appearance of his face changed and his clothes became white and dazzling. Suddenly two men could be seen talking with Jesus. They were Moses and Elijah—revealed in heavenly splendour, and their talk was about the way he must take and the end he must fulfil in Jerusalem. But Peter and his companions had been overcome by sleep and it was as they struggled into wakefulness that they saw the glory of Jesus and the two men standing with him. Just as they were parting from him, Peter said to Jesus,

"Master, it is wonderful for us to be here! Let us put up three shelters—one for you, one for Moses and one for Elijah." But he did not know what he was saying. While he was still talking, a cloud overshadowed them and awe swept over them as it enveloped them. A voice came out of the cloud, saying,

"This is my Son, my chosen! Listen to him!"

But when the voice had spoken, they found no one there but Jesus. The disciples were reduced to silence, and in those days never breathed a word to anyone of what they had seen.

Jesus heals an epileptic boy

Then on the following day, as they came down the hill-side, a great crowd met him. Suddenly a man from the crowd shouted out,

"Master, please come and look at my son! He's my only child, and without any warning some spirit gets hold of him and he calls out suddenly. Then it convulses him until he foams at the mouth, and only after a fearful struggle does it go away and leave him bruised all over. I begged your disciples to get rid of it, but they couldn't."

"You really are an unbelieving and difficult people," replied Jesus. "How long must I be with you, how long must I put up with you? Bring him here to me."

But even while the boy was on his way, the spirit hurled him to the ground in a dreadful convulsion. Then Jesus reprimanded the evil spirit, healed the lad and handed him back to his father. And everybody present was amazed at this demonstration of the power of God.

The realism of Jesus in the midst of enthusiasm

And while everybody was full of wonder at all the things they saw him do, Jesus was saying to the disciples,

"Store up in your minds what I tell you nowadays, for the Son of Man is going to be handed over to the power of men."

But they made no sense of this saying—something made it impossible for them to understand it, and they were afraid to ask him what he meant.

Jesus and "greatness"

Then an argument arose among them as to who should be the greatest. But Jesus, knowing what they were arguing about, picked up a little child and stood him by his side. And then he said to them,

"Anyone who accepts a little child in my name is accepting me, and the man who accepts me is accepting the one who sent me. It is the humblest among you all who is really the greatest."

Then John broke in,

"Master, we saw a man driving out evil spirits in your name, but we stopped him, for he is not one of us who follow you."

But Jesus told him,

"You must not stop him. The man who is not against you is on your side."

He sets off for Jerusalem to meet inevitable death

Now as the days before he should be taken back into Heaven were running out, he set his face firmly towards Jerusalem, and sent messengers ahead of him. They set out and entered a Samaritan village to make preparations for him. But the people there refused to welcome him because he was obviously intending to go to Jerusalem. When the disciples James and John saw this, they said,

"Master, do you want us to call down fire from heaven and burn them all up?"

But Jesus turned and reproved them, and they all went on to another village.

As the little company made its way along the road, a man said to him,

"I'm going to follow you wherever you go."

And Jesus replied,

"Foxes have earths, birds have nests, but the Son of Man has nowhere to lay his head."

But he said to another man,

"Follow me."

And he replied,

"Let me go and bury my father first."

But Jesus told him,

"Leave the dead to bury their own dead. You must come away and preach the kingdom of God."

Another man said to him,

"I am going to follow you, Lord, but first let me bid farewell to my people at home."

But Jesus told him,

"Anyone who puts his hand to the plough and then looks behind him is useless for the kingdom of God."

CHAPTER 10

Jesus now despatches thirty-five couples to preach and heal the sick

LATER on the Lord commissioned seventy other disciples and sent them off in twos as advance-parties into every town and district where he intended to go himself.

"There is a great harvest," he told them, "but only a few are working in it—which means you must pray to the Lord of the harvest that he will send out more reapers to bring in his harvest.

"Now go on your way. I am sending you out like lambs among wolves. Don't carry a purse or a bag or a pair of shoes, and don't stop to greet anyone you meet on the road. When you go into a house, say first of all, 'Peace be to this household!' If there is a lover of peace there, he will accept your words of blessing, and if not, they will come back to you. Stay in the same house and eat and drink whatever they put before you—a workman deserves his wages. But don't move from one house to another.

"Whatever town you go into and the people welcome you, eat the meals they give you and heal the people who are ill there. Tell them, 'The kingdom of God is very near to you now.' But whenever you come into a town and they will not welcome you, you must go into the streets and say, 'We brush off even the dust of your town from our feet as a protest against you. But it is still true that the kingdom of God has arrived!' I assure you that it will be easier for Sodom in 'that day' than for that town.

"Alas for you, Chorazin, and alas for you, Bethsaida! For if Tyre and Sidon had seen the demonstrations of God's power that you have seen, they would have repented long ago and sat in sackcloth and ashes. It will be easier for Tyre and Sidon in the judgment than for you! As for you, Capernaum, do you think you will be exalted to the heavens? I tell you you will go hurtling down among the dead!"

Then he added to the seventy.

"Whoever listens to you is listening to me, and the man who rejects you rejects me too. And the man who rejects me rejects the One who sent me!"

Jesus tells the returned missioners not to be enthusiastic over mere power

Later the seventy came back full of joy.

"Lord," they said, "even evil spirits obey us when we use your name!"

"Yes," returned Jesus, "I was watching and saw Satan fall from heaven like a flash of lightning! It is true that I have given you the power to tread on snakes and scorpions and to overcome all the enemy's power—there is nothing at all that can do you any harm. Yet it is not your power over evil spirits which should give you such joy, but the fact that your names are written in Heaven."

Jesus prays aloud to his Father

At that moment Jesus' heart was filled with joy by the Holy Spirit, and he exclaimed,

"O Father, Lord of Heaven and earth, I thank you for hiding these things from the wise and the clever and for showing them to mere children! Yes, I thank you, Father, that this was your will." Then he went on,

"Everything has been put in my hands by my Father; and nobody knows who the Son is except the Father. Nobody knows who the Father is except the Son—and the man to whom the Son chooses to reveal him!"

Then he turned to his disciples and said to them quietly,

"How fortunate you are to see what you are seeing! I tell you that many prophets and kings have wanted to see what you are seeing but they never saw it, and to hear what you are hearing but they never heard it."

Jesus shows the relevance of the Law to actual living

Once one of the experts in the Law stood up to test him and said,

"Master, what must I do to be sure of eternal life?"

"What does the Law say and what has your reading taught you?" said Jesus.

"The Law says, 'Thou shalt love the Lord thy God with all thy heart and with all thy soul and with all thy strength and with all thy mind—and thy neighbour as thyself'," he replied.

"Quite right," said Jesus. "Do that and you will live."

But the man, wanting to justify himself, continued,

"But who is my 'neighbour'?"

And Jesus gave him the following reply:

"A man was once on his way down from Jerusalem to Jericho. He fell into the hands of bandits who stripped off his clothes, beat him up, and left him half dead. It so happened that a priest was going down that road, and when he saw him, he passed by on the other side. A Levite also came on the scene and when he saw him, he too passed by on the other side. But then a Samaritan traveller came along to the place where the man was lying, and at the sight of him he was touched with pity. He went across to him and bandaged his wounds, pouring on oil and wine. Then he put him on his own mule, brought him to an inn and did what he could for him. Next day he took out two silver coins and gave them to the inn-keeper with the words, 'Look after him, will you? I will pay you back whatever more you spend, when I come through here on my return.' Which of these three seems to you to have been a neighbour to the bandits' victim?"

"The man who gave him practical sympathy," he replied.

"Then you go and give the same," returned Jesus.

Yet emphasises the need for quiet listening to his words

As they continued their journey, Jesus came to a village and a woman called Martha welcomed him to her house. She had a sister by the name of Mary who settled down at the Lord's feet and was listening to what he said. But Martha was very worried about her elaborate preparations and she burst in, saying,

"Lord, don't you mind that my sister has left me to do everything by myself? Tell her to come and help me!"

But the Lord answered her,

"Martha, my dear, you are worried and bothered about providing so many things. Only one thing is really needed. Mary has chosen the best part and it must not be taken away from her!"

CHAPTER 11

Jesus gives a model prayer

ONE day it happened that Jesus was praying in a certain place, and after he had finished, one of his disciples said,

"Lord, teach us how to pray, as John used to teach his disciples."

"When you pray," returned Jesus, "you should say, 'Father, may your name be honoured—may your kingdom come. Give us the bread we need for each day, and forgive us our failures, for we forgive everyone who fails us; and keep us clear of temptation.'"

The willingness of the Father to answer prayer

Then he added,

"If any of you has a friend, and goes to him in the middle of the night and says, 'Lend me three loaves, my dear fellow, for a friend of mine has just arrived after a journey and I have no food to put in front of him'; and then he answers from inside the house, 'Don't bother me with your troubles. The front door is locked and my children and I have gone to bed. I simply cannot get up now and give you anything!' Yet, I tell you, that even if he won't get up and give him what he wants simply because he is his friend, yet if he persists, he will rouse himself and give him everything he needs. And so I tell you, ask and it will be given you, search and you will find, knock and the door will be opened to you. The one who asks will always receive; the one who is searching will always find, and the door is opened to the man who knocks. Some of you are fathers, and if your son asks you for some fish, would you give him a snake instead, or if he asks you for an egg, would you make him a present of a scorpion? So, if you, for all your evil, know how to give good things to your children, how much more likely is it that your Heavenly Father will give the Holy Spirit to those who ask him!"

Jesus shows the absurdity of "his being in league with the devil"

Another time, Jesus was expelling an evil spirit which was preventing a man from speaking, and as soon as the evil spirit left him, the dumb man found his speech, to the amazement of the crowds.

But some of them said,

"He expels these spirits because he is in league with Beelzebub, the chief of the evil spirits."

Others among them, to test him, tried to get a sign from Heaven out of him. But he knew what they were thinking and told them,

"Any kingdom divided against itself is doomed and a disunited household will collapse. And if Satan disagrees with Satan, how does his kingdom continue?—for I know you are saying that I expel evil spirits because I am in league with Beelzebub. But if I do expel devils because I am an ally of Beelzebub, who is your own sons' ally when they do the same thing? They can settle that question for you. But if it is by the finger of God that I am expelling evil spirits, then the kingdom of God has swept over you here and now.

"When a strong man armed to the teeth guards his own house, his property is secure. But when a stronger man comes and conquers him, he removes all the arms on which he pinned his faith and divides the spoil among his friends.

"Anyone who is not with me is against me, and the man who does not gather with me is really scattering.

The danger of a spiritual vacuum in a man's soul

"When the evil spirit comes out of a man, it wanders through waterless places looking for rest, and when it fails to find any, it says, 'I will go back to my house from which I came.' When it arrives, it finds it cleaned and all in order. Then it goes and collects seven other spirits more evil than itself to keep it company, and they all go in and make themselves at home. The last state of that man is worse than the first."

Jesus brings sentimentality down to earth

And while he was still saying this, a woman in the crowd called out and said,

"Oh, what a blessing for a woman to have brought you into the world and nursed you!"

But Jesus replied,

"Yes, but a far greater blessing is to hear the word of God and obey it."

His scathing judgment on his contemporary generation

Then as the people crowded closely around him, he continued,

"This is an evil generation! It looks for a sign and it will be given no sign except that of Jonah. Just as Jonah was a sign to the people of Nineveh, so will the Son of Man be a sign to this generation. When the judgment comes, the Queen of the South will rise up with the men of this generation and she will condemn them. For she came from the ends of the earth to listen to the wisdom of Solomon, and there is more than the wisdom of Solomon with you now. The men of Nineveh will stand up at the judgment with this generation and will condemn it. For they did repent when Jonah preached to them, and there is something more than Jonah's preaching with you now.

The need for complete sincerity

"No one takes a lamp and puts it in a cupboard or under a bucket, but on a lamp-stand, so that those who come in can see the light. The lamp of your body is your eye. When your eye is sound, your whole body is full of light, but when your eye is evil, your whole body is full of darkness. So be very careful that your light never becomes darkness. For if your whole body is full of light, with no part of it in shadow, it will all be radiant—it will be like having a bright lamp to give you light."

While he was talking, a Pharisee invited him to dinner. So he went into his house and sat down at table. The Pharisee noticed with some surprise that he did not wash before the meal. But the Lord said to him,

"You Pharisees are fond of cleaning the outside of your cups and dishes, but inside yourselves you are full of greed and wickedness! Have you no sense? Don't you realise that the one who made the outside is the maker of the inside as well? If you would only make the inside clean by giving the contents to those in need, the outside becomes clean as a matter of course! But alas for you Pharisees, for you pay out your tithe of mint and rue and every little herb, and lose sight of the justice and the love of God. Yet these are the things you ought to have been concerned with—it need not mean leaving the lesser duties undone. Yes, alas for you Pharisees, who love the front seats in the synagogues and having men bow down to you in public! Alas for you, for you are like unmarked graves—men walk over your corruption without ever knowing it is there."

Jesus denounces the learned for obscuring the truth

Then one of the experts in the Law said to him,

"Master, when you say things like this, you are insulting us as well."

And he returned,

"Yes, and I do blame you experts in the Law! For you pile up back-breaking burdens for men to bear, but you yourselves will not raise a finger to lift them. Alas for you, for you build memorial tombs for the prophets—the very men whom your fathers murdered. You show clearly enough how you approve your fathers' actions. They did the killing and you put up the memorials. That is why the Wisdom of God has said, 'I will send them prophets and apostles; some they will kill and some they will persecute!' So that the blood of all the prophets shed from the foundation of the earth, from Abel to Zachariah who died between the altar and the sanctuary, shall be charged to this generation. Yes, I tell you this generation must answer for it all!

"Alas for you experts in the Law, for you have taken away the key of knowledge. You have never gone in yourselves and you have hindered everyone else who was at the door!"

And when he left that place, the scribes and the Pharisees began to nurture a bitter hatred against him, and tried to draw him out on a great many subjects, waiting to pounce on some incriminating remark.

CHAPTER 12

MEANWHILE, the crowds had gathered in thousands, so that they were actually treading on each other's toes, and Jesus, speaking primarily to his disciples, said,

"Be on your guard against yeast—I mean the yeast of the Pharisees, which is sheer pretence. For there is nothing covered up which is not going to be exposed, nor anything private which is not going to be made public. Whatever you may say in the dark will be heard in daylight, and whatever you whisper within four walls will be shouted from the house-tops.

Man need only fear God

"I tell you, as friends of mine, that you are not to be afraid of those who can kill the body, but afterwards cannot do anything more. I will show you the only one you need to fear—the one who, after he has killed, has the power to throw you into destruction! Yes, I tell you, it is right to stand in awe of him. The market-price of five sparrows is two farthings, isn't it? Yet not one of them is forgotten in God's sight. Why, the very hairs of your heads are all numbered! Don't be afraid then; you are worth more than a great many sparrows! I tell you that every man who acknowledges me before men, I, the Son of Man, will acknowledge in the presence of the angels of God. But the man who disowns me before men will find himself disowned before the angels of God!

"Anyone who speaks against the Son of Man will be forgiven, but there is no forgiveness for the man who speaks evil against the Holy Spirit. And when they bring you before the synagogues and magistrates and authorities, don't worry as to what defence you are going to put up or what words you are going to use. For the Holy Spirit will tell you at the time what is the right thing for you to say."

Jesus gives a warning about the love of material security

Then someone out of the crowd said to him,

"Master, tell my brother to share his legacy with me."

But Jesus replied,

"My dear man, who appointed me a judge or arbitrator in your affairs?"

And then, turning to the disciples, he said to them,

"Notice that, and be on your guard against covetousness in any shape or form. For a man's real life in no way depends upon the number of his possessions."

Then he gave them a parable in these words,

"Once upon a time a rich man's farmland produced heavy crops. So he said to himself, 'What shall I do, for I have no room to store this harvest of mine?' Then he said, 'I know what I'll do. I'll pull down my barns and build bigger ones where I can store all my grain and my goods and I can say to my soul, Soul, you have plenty of good things stored up there for years to come. Relax! Eat, drink and have a good time!' But God said to him, 'You fool, this very night you will be asked for *your soul*! Then, who is going to possess all that you have prepared?' That is what happens to the man who hoards things for himself and is not rich in the eyes of God."

And then he added to the disciples,

"That is why I tell you, don't worry about life, wondering what you are going to eat, or what clothes your body will need. Life is much more important than food, and the body more important than clothes. Think of the ravens. They neither sow nor reap, and they have neither store nor barn, but God feeds them. And how much more valuable do you think you are than birds? Can any of you make himself even a few inches taller however much he worries about it? And if you can't manage a little thing like this, why do you worry about anything else? Think of the wild flowers, and how they neither work nor weave. Yet I tell you that Solomon in all his glory was never arrayed like one of these. If God so clothes the grass, which flowers in the field today and is burnt in the stove tomorrow, is he not much more likely to clothe you, you little-faiths? You must not set your heart on what you eat or drink, nor must you live in a state of anxiety. The whole heathen world is busy about getting food and drink, and your Father knows well enough that you need such things. No, set your heart on his kingdom, and your food and drink will come as a matter of course. Don't be afraid, you tiny flock! Your Father plans to give you the kingdom. Sell your possessions and give the money away to those in need. Get yourselves purses that never grow old, inexhaustible treasure in Heaven, where no thief can ever reach it, or moth destroy it. For wherever your treasure is, you may be certain that your heart will be there too!

Jesus' disciples must be on the alert

"You must be ready dressed and have your lamps alight, like men who wait to welcome their lord and master on his return from the wedding-feast, so that when he comes and knocks at the door, they may open it for him at once. Happy are the servants whom their lord finds on the alert when he arrives. I assure you that he will then take off his outer clothes, make them sit down to dinner, and come and wait on them. And if he should come just after midnight or in the very early morning, and find them still on the alert, their happiness is assured. But be certain of this, that if the householder had known the time when the burglar would come, he would not have let his house be broken into. So you must be on the alert, for the Son of Man is coming at a time when you may not expect him."

Then Peter said to him,

"Lord, do you mean this parable for us or for everybody?"

But the Lord continued,

"Well, who will be the faithful, sensible steward whom his master will put in charge of his household to give them their supplies at the proper time? Happy is the servant if his master finds him so doing when he returns. I tell you he will promote him to look after all his property. But suppose the servant says to himself, 'My master takes his time about returning', and then begins to beat the men and women servants and to eat and drink and get drunk, that servant's master will return suddenly and unexpectedly, and he will punish him severely and send him to share the penalty of the unfaithful. The slave who knows his master's plan but does not get ready or act upon it will be severely punished, but the servant who did not know the plan, though he has done wrong, will be let off lightly. Much will be expected from the one who has been given much, and the more a man is trusted, the more people will expect of him.

"It is fire that I have come to bring upon the earth—how I could wish it were already ablaze! There is a baptism that I must undergo and how strained I must be until it is all over!

Jesus declares that his coming is bound to bring division

"Do you think I have come to bring peace on the earth? No, I tell you, not peace, but division! For from now on, there will be five people divided against each other in one house, three against two, and two against three. It is going to be father against son, and son against father, mother against daughter, and daughter against mother; mother-in-law against her daughter-in-law, and daughter-in-law against mother-in-law!"

Intelligence should be used not only about the weather but about the times in which men live

Then he said to the crowds,

"When you see a cloud rising in the west, you say at once that it is going to rain, and so it does. And when you feel the south wind blowing, you say that it is going to be hot, and so it is. You frauds! You know how to interpret the look of the earth and the sky. Why can't you interpret the meaning of the times in which you live?

"And why can't you decide for yourselves what is right? For instance, when you are going before the magistrate with your opponent, do your best to come to terms with him while you have the chance, or he may rush you off to the judge, and the judge hand you over to the police-officer, and the police-officer throw you into prison. I tell you you will never get out again until you have paid your last farthing."

CHAPTER 13

Jesus is asked about the supposed significance of disasters

It was just at this moment that some people came up to tell him the story of the Galileans whose blood Pilate had mixed with that of their own sacrifices. Jesus made this reply to them:

"Are you thinking that these Galileans were worse sinners than any other men of Galilee because this happened to them? I assure you that is not so. You will all die just as miserable a death unless your hearts are changed! You remember those eighteen people who were killed at Siloam when the tower collapsed upon them? Are you imagining that they were worse offenders than any of the other people who lived in Jerusalem? I assure you they were not. You will all die as tragically unless your whole outlook is changed!"

And hints at God's patience with the Jewish nation

Then he gave them this parable:

"Once upon a time a man had a fig-tree growing in his garden, and when he came to look for the figs, he found none at all. So he said to his gardener, 'Look, I have come expecting fruit on this fig-tree for three years running and never found any. Better cut it down. Why should it use up valuable ground?' And the gardener replied, 'Master, don't touch it this year till I have had a chance to dig round it and give it a bit of manure. Then, if it bears after that, it will be all right. But if it doesn't, then you can cut it down.'"

Jesus reduces the sabbatarians to silence

It happened that he was teaching in one of the synagogues on the Sabbath day. In the congregation was a woman who for eighteen years had been ill from some psychological cause; she was bent double and was quite unable to straighten herself up. When Jesus noticed her, he called her and said,

"You are set free from your illness!"

And he put his hands upon her, and at once she stood upright and praised God. But the president of the synagogue, in his annoyance at Jesus' healing on the Sabbath, announced to the congregation,

"There are six days in which men may work. Come on one of them and be healed, and not on the Sabbath day!"

But the Lord answered him, saying,

"You hypocrites, every single one of you unties his ox or his donkey from the stall and leads him away to water on the Sabbath day! This woman, a daughter of Abraham, whom you all know Satan has kept bound for eighteen years—surely she should be released from such bonds on the Sabbath day!"

These words reduced his opponents to shame, but the crowd was thrilled at all the glorious things he did.

Then he went on,

"What is the kingdom of God like? What illustration can I use to make it plain to you? It is like a grain of mustard-seed which a man took and dropped in his own garden. It grew and became a tree and the birds came and nested in its branches."

Then again he said,

"What can I say the kingdom of God is like? It is like the yeast which a woman took and covered up in three measures of flour until the whole had risen."

The kingdom is not entered by drifting but by decision

So he went on his way through towns and villages, teaching as he went and making his way towards Jerusalem. Someone asked him,

"Lord, are only a few men to be saved?"

And Jesus told them,

"You must try your hardest to get in through the narrow door, for many, I assure you, will try to do so and will not succeed. For once the master of the house has got up and shut the door, you will find yourselves standing outside and knocking at the door crying, 'Lord, please open the door for us.' He will reply to you, 'I don't know who you are or where you come from.' 'But', you will protest, 'we have had meals with you, and you taught in our streets!' Yet he will say to you, 'I tell you I do not know where you have come from. Be off, you are all scoundrels!' At that time there will be tears and bitter regret—to see Abraham and Isaac and Jacob and all the prophets inside the kingdom of God, and you yourselves banished outside! Yes, and people will come from the east and the west, and from the north and the south, and take their seats in the kingdom of God. There are some at the back now who will be in front then, and there are some in front now who will then be far behind."

The Pharisees warn Jesus of Herod; he replies

Just then some Pharisees arrived to tell him,

"You must get right away from here, for Herod intends to kill you."

"Go and tell that fox," returned Jesus, "anyone can see that today and tomorrow I am expelling evil spirits and continuing my work of healing, and on the third day my work will be finished. But I must journey on today, tomorrow, and the next day, for it would never do for a prophet to meet his death outside Jerusalem!

"O Jerusalem, Jerusalem, you murder the prophets and stone the messengers that are sent to you! How often have I longed to gather your children round me like a bird gathering her brood together under her wings, but you would never have it. Now all you have left is your house. For I tell you that you will never see me again till the day when you cry, 'Blessed is he who comes in the name of the Lord!' "

CHAPTER 14

Strict sabbatarianism is again rebuked

ONE Sabbath day he went into the house of one of the leading Pharisees for a meal, and they were watching him closely. Right in front of him was a man afflicted with dropsy. So Jesus spoke to the scribes and Pharisees and asked,

"Well, is it right to heal on the Sabbath day or not?"

But there was no reply. So Jesus took the man and healed him and let him go. Then he said to them,

"If a donkey or an ox belonging to one of you fell into a well, wouldn't you rescue it without the slightest hesitation even though it were the Sabbath?"

And this again left them quite unable to reply.

A lesson in humility

Then he gave a pointed word of advice to the guests when he noticed how they were choosing the best seats. He said to them,

"When you are invited to a wedding reception, don't sit down in the best seat. It might happen that a more distinguished man than you has also been invited. Then your host might say, 'I am afraid you must give up your seat for this man.' And then, with considerable embarrassment, you will have to sit in the humblest place. No, when you are invited, go and take your seat in an inconspicuous place, so that when your host comes in he may say to you, 'Come on, my dear fellow, we have a much better seat than this for you.' That is the way to be important in the eyes of all your fellow-guests! For everyone who makes himself important will become insignificant, while the man who makes himself insignificant will find himself important."

Then, addressing his host, Jesus said,

"When you give a luncheon or a dinner party, don't invite your friends or your brothers or relations or wealthy neighbours, for the chances are they will invite you back, and you will be fully repaid. No, when you give a party, invite the poor, the crippled, the lame and the blind. That way lies real happiness for you. They have no means of repaying you, but you will be repaid when good men are rewarded—at the resurrection."

Then, one of the guests, hearing these remarks of Jesus, said, "What happiness for a man to eat a meal in the kingdom of God!"

Men who are "too busy" for the kingdom of God

But Jesus said to him,

"Once upon a time, a man planned a big dinner party and invited a great many people. At dinner-time, he sent his servant out to tell those who were invited, 'Please come, everything is now ready.' But they all, as one man, began to make their excuses. The first one said to him, 'I have bought some land. I must go and look at it. Please excuse me.' Another one said, 'I have bought five yoke of oxen and am on my way to try them out. Please convey my apologies.' And another one said, 'I have just got married and I am sure you will understand I cannot come.' So the servant returned and reported all this to his master. The master of the house was extremely annoyed and said to his servant, 'Hurry out now into the streets and alleys of the town, and bring here the poor and crippled and blind and lame.' Then the servant said, 'I have done what you told me, sir, and there are still empty places.' Then the master replied, 'Now go out to the roads and hedgerows and make them come inside, so that my house may be full. For I tell you that not one of the men I invited shall have a taste of my dinner.' "

Now as Jesus proceeded on his journey, great crowds accompanied him, and he turned and spoke to them,

"If anyone comes to me without 'hating' his father and mother and wife and children and brothers and sisters, and even his own life, he cannot be a disciple of mine. The man who will not take up his cross and follow in my footsteps cannot be my disciple.

"If any of you wanted to build a tower, wouldn't he first sit down and work out the cost of it, to see if he can afford to finish it? Otherwise, when he has laid the foundation and found himself unable to complete the building, everyone who sees it will begin to jeer at him, saying, 'This is the man who started to build a tower but couldn't finish it!' Or, suppose there is a king who is going to war with another king, doesn't he sit down first and consider whether he can engage the twenty thousand of the other king with his own ten thousand? And if he decides he can't, then, while the other king is still a long way off, he sends messengers to him to ask for conditions of peace. So it is with you; only the man who says goodbye to all his possessions can be my disciple.

"Salt is a very good thing, but if salt loses its flavour, what can you use to restore it? It is no good for the ground and no good as manure. People just throw it away. Every man who has ears should use them!"

CHAPTER 15

Jesus speaks of the love of God for "the lost"

Now all the tax-collectors and "outsiders" were crowding around to hear what he had to say. The Pharisees and the scribes complained of this, remarking,

"This man welcomes sinners and even eats his meals with them."

So Jesus spoke to them, using this parable:

"Wouldn't any man among you who owned a hundred sheep, and lost one of them, leave the ninety-nine to themselves in the open, and go after the one which is lost until he finds it? And when he has found it, he will lift it on to his shoulders with great joy, and as soon as he gets home, he will call his friends and neighbours together. 'Rejoice with me,' he will say, 'for I have found that sheep of mine which was lost.' I tell you that it is the same in Heaven—there is more joy over one sinner whose heart is changed than over ninety-nine righteous people who have no need for repentance.

"Or if a woman who has ten silver coins should lose one, won't she take a lamp and sweep and search the house from top to bottom until she finds it? And when she has found it, she calls her friends and neighbours together. 'Rejoice with me,' she says, 'for I have found that coin I lost.' I tell you, it is the same in Heaven—there is rejoicing among the angels of God over one sinner whose heart is changed."

Then he continued,

"Once there was a man who had two sons. The younger one said to his father, 'Father, give me my share of the property that will come to me.' So he divided up his estate between the two of them. Before very long, the younger son collected all his belongings and went off to a distant land, where he squandered his wealth in the wildest extravagance. And when he had run through all his money, a terrible famine arose in that country, and he began to feel the pinch. Then he went and hired himself out to one of the citizens of that country who sent him out into the fields to feed the pigs. He got to the point of longing to stuff himself with the husks the pigs were eating, and not a soul gave him anything. Then he came to his senses and cried aloud, 'Why, dozens of my father's hired men have more food than they can eat and here am I dying of hunger! I will get up and go back to my father, and I will say to him, "Father, I have done wrong in the sight of Heaven and in your eyes. I don't deserve to be called your son any more. Please take me on as one of your hired men." ' So he got up and went to his father. But while he was still some distance off, his father saw him and his heart went out to him, and he ran and fell on his neck and kissed him. But his son said, 'Father, I have done wrong in the sight of Heaven and in your eyes. I don't deserve to be called your son any more. . . .' 'Hurry!' called out his father to the servants, 'fetch the best clothes and put them on him! Put a ring on his finger and shoes on his feet, and get that fatted calf and kill it, and we will have a feast and a celebration! For this is my son—he was dead, and he's alive again. He was lost, and now he's found!' And they began to get the festivities going.

"But his elder son was out in the fields, and as he came near the house, he heard music and dancing. So he called one of the servants across to him and enquired what was the meaning of it all. 'Your brother has arrived, and your father has killed the fatted calf because he has got him home again safe and sound,' was the reply. But he was furious and refused to go inside the house. So his father came outside and pleaded with him. Then he burst out, 'Look, how many years have I slaved for you and never disobeyed a single order of yours, and yet you have never given me so much as a young goat so that I could give my friends a dinner? But when this son of yours arrives, who has spent all your money on prostitutes, for him you kill the fatted calf!' But the father replied, 'My dear son, you have been with me all the time and everything I have is yours. But we had to celebrate and show our joy. For this is your brother; he was dead—and he's alive. He was lost—and now he is found!' "

CHAPTER 16

A clever rogue, and the right use of money

THEN there is this story he told his disciples:

"Once there was a rich man whose agent was reported to him to be mismanaging his property. So he summoned him and said, 'What's this that I hear about you? Give me an account of your stewardship—you're not fit to manage my household any longer.' At this the agent said to himself, 'What am I going to do now that my employer is taking away the management from me? I am not strong enough to dig and I can't sink to begging. Ah, I know what I'll do so that when I lose my position people will welcome me into their homes!' So he sent for each one of his master's debtors. 'How much do you owe my master?' he said to the first. 'A hundred barrels of oil,' he replied. 'Here,' replied the agent, 'take your bill, sit down, hurry up and write in fifty.' Then he said to another, 'And what's the size of your debt?' 'A thousand bushels of wheat,' he replied. 'Take your bill,' said the agent, 'and write in eight hundred.' Now the master praised this rascally agent because he had been so careful for his own future. For the children of this world are considerably more shrewd in dealing with their contemporaries than the children of light. Now my advice to you is to use 'money', tainted as it is, to make yourselves friends, so that when it comes to an end, they may welcome you into the houses of eternity.

"The man who is faithful in the little things will be faithful in the big things, and the man who cheats in the little things will cheat in the big things too. So that if you are not fit to be trusted to deal with the wicked wealth of this world, who will trust you with the true riches? And if you are not trustworthy with someone else's property, who will give you property of your own? No servant can serve two masters. He is bound to hate one and love the other, or give his loyalty to one and despise the other. You cannot serve God and the power of money at the same time."

Now the Pharisees, who were very fond of money, heard all this with a sneer. But he said to them,

"You are the people who advertise your goodness before men, but God knows your hearts. Remember, there are things men consider splendid which are detestable in the sight of God!

Jesus states that the kingdom of God has superseded "the Law and the Prophets"

"The Law and the Prophets were in force until John's day. From then on the good news of the kingdom of God has been proclaimed and everyone is trying to force his way into it.

"Yet it would be easier for Heaven and earth to disappear than for a single point of the Law to become a dead letter.

"Any man who divorces his wife and marries another woman commits adultery. And so does any man who marries the woman who was divorced from her husband.

Jesus shows the fearful consequence of social injustice

"There was once a rich man who used to dress in purple and fine linen and lead a life of daily luxury. And there was a poor man called Lazarus who was put down at his gate. He was covered with sores. He used to long to be fed with the scraps from the rich man's table. Yes, and the dogs used to come and lick his sores. Well, it happened that the poor man died, and was carried by the angels into Abraham's bosom. The rich man also died and was buried. And from the place of the dead he looked up in torment and saw Abraham a long way away, and Lazarus in his arms. 'Father Abraham,' he cried out, 'please pity me! Send Lazarus to dip the tip of his finger in water and cool my tongue, for I am in agony in these flames.' But Abraham replied, 'Remember, my son, that you used to have the good things in your lifetime, just as Lazarus suffered the bad. Now he is being comforted here, while you are in agony. And besides this, a great chasm has been set between you and us, so that those who want to go to you from this side cannot do so, and people cannot come to us from your side.' At this he said, 'Then I beg you, father, to send him to my father's house for I have five brothers. He could warn them and prevent their coming to this place of torture.' But Abraham said, 'They have Moses and the Prophets: they can listen to them.' 'Ah no, father Abraham,' he said, 'if only someone were to go to them from the dead, they would change completely.' But Abraham told him, 'If they will not listen to Moses and the Prophets, they would not be convinced even if somebody were to rise from the dead.' "

CHAPTER 17

Jesus warns his disciples about spoiling the spirit of the new kingdom

THEN Jesus said to his disciples,

"It is inevitable that there should be pitfalls, but alas for the man who is responsible for them! It would be better for that man to have a mill-stone hung round his neck and be thrown into the sea, than that he should trip up one of these little ones. So be careful how you live. If your brother offends you, take him to task about it, and if he is sorry, forgive him. Yes, if he wrongs you seven times in one day and turns to you and says, 'I am sorry' seven times, you must forgive him."

And the apostles said to the Lord,

"Give us more faith."

And he replied,

"If your faith were as big as a grain of mustard-seed, you could say to this mulberry tree, 'Pull yourself up by the roots and plant yourself in the sea', and it would obey you!

Work in the kingdom must be taken as a matter of course

"If any of you has a servant ploughing or looking after the sheep, are you likely to say to him when he comes in from the fields, 'Come straight in and sit down to your meal'? Aren't you more likely to say, 'Get my supper ready: change your coat, and wait on me while I eat and drink: and then, when I've finished, you can have your meal'? Do you feel grateful to your servant for doing what you tell him? I don't think so. It is the same with yourselves—when you have done everything that you are told to do, you can say, 'We are not much good as servants; we have only done what we ought to do.' "

Jesus heals ten men of leprosy: only one shows his gratitude

In the course of his journey to Jerusalem, Jesus crossed the boundary between Samaria and Galilee, and as he was approaching a village, ten lepers met him. They kept their distance but shouted out,

"Jesus, Master, have pity on us!"

When Jesus saw them, he said,
"Go and show yourselves to the priests."
And it happened that as they went on their way they were cured. One of their number, when he saw that he was healed, turned round and praised God at the top of his voice, and then fell on his face before Jesus and thanked him. This man was a Samaritan. And at this Jesus remarked,
"Weren't there ten men cured? Where are the other nine? Is nobody going to turn and praise God, except this stranger?"
And he said to the man,
"Stand up now, and go on your way. It is your faith that has made you well."

Jesus tells the Pharisees that the kingdom is here and now

Later, he was asked by the Pharisees when the kingdom of God was coming, and he gave them this reply:
"The kingdom of God never comes by looking for signs of it. Men cannot say, 'Look, here it is', or 'there it is', for the kingdom of God is inside you."

Jesus tells his disciples about the future

Then he said to the disciples,
"The time will come when you will long to see again a single day of the Son of Man, but you will not see it. People will say to you, 'Look, there it is', or 'Look, here it is.' Stay where you are and don't follow them! For the day of the Son of Man will be like lightning flashing from one end of the sky to the other. But before that happens, he must go through much suffering and be utterly rejected by this generation. In the time of the coming of the Son of Man, life will be as it was in the days of Noah. People ate and drank, married and were given in marriage, right up to the day when Noah entered the ark—and then came the flood and destroyed them all. It will be just the same as it was in the days of Lot. People ate and drank, bought and sold, planted and built, but on the day that Lot left Sodom, it rained fire and brimstone from heaven, and destroyed them all. That is how it will be on the day when the Son of Man is revealed. When that day comes, the man who is on the roof of his house, with his goods inside it, must not come down to get them. And the man

out in the fields must not turn back for anything. Remember what happened to Lot's wife. Whoever tries to keep his life safe will lose it, and the man who is prepared to lose his life will preserve it. I tell you, that night there will be two men in one bed; one man will be taken and the other will be left. Two women will be turning the grinding-mill together; one will be taken and the other left."

"But where, Lord?" they asked him.

"Wherever there is a dead body, there the vultures will flock," he replied.

CHAPTER 18

Jesus urges his disciples to persist in prayer

THEN he gave them an illustration to show that they must always pray and never lose heart.

"Once upon a time," he said, "there was a magistrate in a town who had neither fear of God nor respect for his fellow-men. There was a widow in the town who kept coming to him, saying, 'Please protect me from the man who is trying to ruin me.' And for a long time he refused. But later he said to himself, 'Although I don't fear God and have no respect for men, yet this woman is such a nuisance that I shall give judgment in her favour, or else her continual visits will be the death of me!' "

Then the Lord said,

"Notice how this dishonest magistrate behaved. Do you suppose God, patient as he is, will not see justice done for his chosen, who appeal to him day and night? I assure you he will not delay in seeing justice done. Yet, when the Son of Man comes, will he find men on earth who believe in him?"

Jesus tells a story against the self-righteous

Then he gave this illustration to certain people who were confident of their own goodness and looked down on others:

"Two men went up to the Temple to pray, one was a Pharisee, the other was a tax-collector. The Pharisee stood and prayed like this with himself, 'O God, I do thank thee that I am not like the rest of mankind, greedy, dishonest, impure, or even like that tax-collector over there. I fast twice every week; I give away a tenth-part of all my income.' But the tax-collector stood in a distant corner, scarcely daring to look up to Heaven, and with a gesture of despair, said, 'God, have mercy on a sinner like me.' I assure you that he was the man who went home justified in God's sight, rather than the other one. For everyone who sets himself up as somebody will become a nobody, and the man who makes himself nobody will become somebody."

Jesus welcomes babies

Then people began to bring babies to him so that he could put his hands on them. But when the disciples noticed it, they frowned on them. But Jesus called them to him, and said,

"You must let little children come to me, and you must never prevent their coming. The kingdom of God belongs to little children like these. I tell you, the man who will not accept the kingdom of God like a little child will never get into it at all."

Jesus and riches

Then one of the Jewish rulers put this question to him,

"Master, I know that you are good; tell me, please, what must I do to be sure of eternal life?"

"I wonder why you call me good?" returned Jesus. "No one is good—only the one God. You know the commandments—

"Thou shalt not commit adultery.

"Thou shalt not commit murder.

"Thou shalt not steal.

"Thou shalt not bear false witness.

"Honour thy father and thy mother."

"All these," he replied, "I have carefully kept since I was quite young."

And when Jesus heard that, he said to him,

"There is still one thing you have missed. Sell everything you possess and give the money away to the poor, and you will have riches in Heaven. Then come and follow me."

But when he heard this, he was greatly distressed for he was very rich.

And when Jesus saw how his face fell, he remarked,

"How difficult it is for those who have great possessions to enter the kingdom of God! A camel could squeeze through the eye of a needle more easily than a rich man could get into the kingdom of God."

Those who heard Jesus say this, exclaimed,
"Then who can possibly be saved?"
Jesus replied,
"What men find impossible is possible with God."
"Well," rejoined Peter, "we have left all that we ever had and followed you."
And Jesus told them,
"Believe me, nobody has left his home or wife, or brothers or parents or children for the sake of the kingdom of God, without receiving very much more in this present life—and eternal life in the world to come."

Jesus foretells his death and resurrection

Then Jesus took the twelve on one side and spoke to them,
"Listen to me. We are now going up to Jerusalem and everything that has been written by the prophets about the Son of Man will come true. For he will be handed over to the heathen, and he is going to be jeered at and insulted and spat upon, and then they will flog him and kill him. But he will rise again on the third day."
But they did not understand any of this. His words were quite obscure to them and they had no idea of what he meant.

On the way to Jericho he heals a blind beggar

Then, as he was approaching Jericho, it happened that there was a blind man sitting by the roadside, begging. He heard the crowd passing and enquired what it was all about. And they told him, "Jesus the man from Nazareth is going past you." So he shouted out,
"Jesus, Son of David, have pity on me!"
Those who were in front tried to hush his cries. But that made him call out all the more,
"Son of David, have pity on me!"
So Jesus stood quite still and ordered the man to be brought to him. And when he was quite close, he said to him,
"What do you want me to do for you?"
"Lord, make me see again," he cried.
"You can see again! Your faith has cured you," returned Jesus.
And his sight was restored at once, and he followed Jesus, praising God. All the people who saw it thanked God too.

CHAPTER 19

The chief tax-collector is converted to faith in Jesus

THEN he went into Jericho and was making his way through it. And here we find a wealthy man called Zacchaeus, a chief collector of taxes, wanting to see what sort of person Jesus was. But the crowd prevented him from doing so, for he was very short. So he ran ahead and climbed up into a sycamore tree to get a view of Jesus as he was heading that way. When Jesus reached the spot, he looked up and said to him,

"Zacchaeus, hurry up and come down. I must be your guest today."

So Zacchaeus hurriedly climbed down and gladly welcomed him. But the bystanders muttered their disapproval, saying,

"Now he has gone to stay with a real sinner."

But Zacchaeus himself stood and said to the Lord,

"Look, sir, I will give half my property to the poor. And if I have swindled anybody out of anything I will pay him back four times as much."

Jesus said to him,

"Salvation has come to this house today! Zacchaeus is a descendant of Abraham, and it was the lost that the Son of Man came to seek—and to save."

Life requires courage, and is hard on those who dare not use their gifts

Then as the crowd still listened attentively, Jesus went on to give them this parable. For the fact that he was nearing Jerusalem made them imagine that the kingdom of God was on the point of appearing.

"Once upon a time a man of good family went abroad to accept a kingdom and then return. He summoned ten of his servants and gave them a pound each, with the words, 'Use this money to trade with until I come back.' But the citizens detested him and they sent a delegation after him, to say, 'We will not have this man to be our king.' Then later, when he had received his kingdom, he returned and gave orders for the servants to whom he had given the money to be called to him, so that he could find out what profit they had made. The first came into his presence, and said, 'Sire, your pound has made ten pounds more.' 'Splendid, my good fellow,' he said, 'since you have proved trustworthy over this small amount, I am going to put you in charge of ten towns.' The second came in and said, 'Sire, your pound has made five pounds.' And he said to him, 'Good, you're appointed governor of five towns.' When the last came, he said, 'Sire, here is your pound, which I have been keeping wrapped up in a handkerchief. I have been scared—I know you're a hard man, getting something for nothing and reaping where you never sowed.' To which he replied, 'You scoundrel, your own words condemn you! You knew perfectly well, did you, that I am a hard man who gets something for nothing and reaps where he never sowed? Then why didn't you put my money into the bank, and then when I returned I could have had it back with interest?' Then he said to those who were standing by, 'Take away his pound and give it to the fellow who has ten.'

" 'But, sire, he has ten pounds already,' they said to him. 'Yes,' he replied, 'and I tell you that the man who has something will get more given to him. But as for the man who has nothing, even his "nothing" will be taken away. And as for these enemies of mine who objected to my being their king, bring them here and execute them in my presence.' "

After these words, Jesus walked on ahead of them on his way up to Jerusalem.

Jesus arranges his own entrance into Jerusalem

Then as he was approaching Bethphage and Bethany, near the hill called the Mount of Olives, he sent off two of his disciples, telling them,

"Go into the village just ahead of you, and there you will find a colt tied, on which no one has ever yet ridden. Untie it and bring it here. And if anybody asks you, 'Why are you untying it?' just say, 'The Lord needs it.' "

So the messengers went off and found things just as he had told them. In fact, as they were untying the colt, the owners did say, "Why are you untying it?" and they replied, "The Lord needs it." So they brought it to Jesus and, throwing their cloaks upon the colt, mounted Jesus on its back. Then as he rode along, people spread out their coats in the roadway. And as he approached the city, where the road slopes down from the Mount of Olives, the whole crowd of his disciples joyfully shouted praises to God for all the marvellous things that they had seen done.

"God bless the king who comes in the name of the Lord!" they cried. "There is peace in Heaven and glory on high!"

There were some Pharisees in the crowd who said to Jesus, "Master, restrain your disciples!"

To which he replied,

"I tell you that if they kept quiet, the very stones in the road would burst out cheering!"

The sight of the city moves him to tears

And as he came still nearer to the city, he caught sight of it and wept over it, saying,

"Ah, if you only knew, even at this eleventh hour, on what your peace depends—but you cannot see it. The time is coming when your enemies will encircle you with ramparts, surrounding you and hemming you in on every side. And they will hurl you and all your children to the ground—yes, they will not leave you one stone standing upon another—all because you did not recognise when God Himself was visiting you!"

Then he went into the Temple, and began to throw out the traders there.

"It is written," he told them, " 'My house shall be a house of prayer', but you have turned it into a thieves' kitchen!"

Jesus teaches daily in the Temple

Then day after day he was teaching inside the Temple. The chief priests, the scribes and the national leaders were all the time looking for an opportunity to destroy him, but they could not find any way to do it since all the people hung upon his words.

CHAPTER 20

THEN one day as he was teaching the people in the Temple, and preaching the gospel to them, the chief priests, the scribes and elders confronted him in a body and asked him this direct question,

"Tell us by whose authority you act as you do—who gave you such authority?"

"I have a question for you, too," replied Jesus. "John's baptism, now—tell me, did it come from Heaven or was it purely human?"

At this they began arguing with each other, saying,

"If we say, 'from Heaven,' he will say to us, 'Then why didn't you believe in him?' but if we say it was purely human, this mob will stone us to death, for they are convinced that John was a prophet." So they replied that they did not know where it came from.

"Then," returned Jesus, "neither will I tell you by what authority I do what I am doing."

He tells the people a pointed story

Then he turned to the people and told them this parable:

"There was once a man who planted a vineyard, let it out to farm-workers, and went abroad for some time. Then, when the season arrived, he sent a servant to the farm-workers so that they could give him his share of the crop. But the farm-workers beat him up and sent him back empty-handed. So he sent another servant, and they beat him up as well, manhandling him disgracefully, and sent him back empty-handed. Then he sent a third servant, but after wounding him severely they threw him out. Then the owner of the vineyard said, 'What shall I do now? I will send them my son who is so dear to me. Perhaps they will respect him.' But when the farm-workers saw him, they talked the matter over with each other and said, 'This man is the heir—come on, let's kill him, and the property will be ours!' And they threw him out of the vineyard and killed him. What then do you suppose the owner will do to them? He will come and destroy the men who were working his property, and hand it over to others."

When they heard this, they said,

"God forbid!"

But he looked them straight in the eyes and said,

"Then what is the meaning of this scripture—

The stone which the builders rejected,
The same was made the head of the corner?

The man who falls on that stone will be broken, and the man on whom it falls will be crushed to powder."

The authorities resort to trickery

The scribes and chief priests longed to get their hands on him at that moment, but they were afraid of the people. They knew well enough that his parable referred to them. They watched him, however, and sent some spies into the crowd, pretending that they were honest men, to fasten on something that he might say which could be used to hand him over to the authority and power of the governor.

These men asked him,

"Master, we know that what you say and teach is right, and that you teach the way of God truly without fear or favour. Now, is it right for us to pay taxes to Caesar or not?"

But Jesus saw through their cunning and said to them,

"Show me one of the coins. Whose face is this, and whose name is in the inscription?"

"Caesar's," they said.

"Then give to Caesar," he replied, "what belongs to Caesar, and to God what belongs to God."

So his reply gave them no sort of handle that they could use against him publicly. And in fact they were so taken aback by his answer that they had nothing more to say.

Jesus exposes the ignorance of the Sadducees

Then up came some of the Sadducees (who deny that there is any resurrection) and they asked him,

"Master, Moses told us in the scripture, 'If a man's brother should die leaving a wife but no children, he should marry the widow and raise up a family for his brother.' Now, there were once seven brothers. The first married and died childless, and the second and the third married the woman, and in fact all the seven married her and died without leaving any children. Lastly, the woman herself died. Now in this 'resurrection' whose wife is she of these seven men, for she was wife to all of them?"

"People in this world," Jesus replied, "marry and are given in marriage. But those who are considered worthy of reaching that world, which means rising from the dead, neither marry nor are they given in marriage. They cannot die any more but live like the angels; for being children of the resurrection, they are the sons of God. But that the dead are raised, even Moses showed to be true in the story of the bush, when he calls the Lord the God of Abraham, the God of Isaac and the God of Jacob. For God is not God of the dead, but of the living. For all men are alive to him."

To this some of the scribes replied,

"Master, that was a good answer."

And indeed nobody had the courage to ask him any more questions. But Jesus went on to say,

"How can they say that Christ is David's *son*? For David himself says in the book of psalms—

The Lord said unto my *Lord*.
Sit thou on my right hand,
Till I make thine enemies the footstool of thy feet.

David is plainly calling him 'Lord'. How then can he be his *son*?"

Jesus warns his disciples against religious pretentiousness

Then while everybody was listening, Jesus remarked to his disciples,

"Be on your guard against the scribes, who enjoy walking round in long robes and love having men bow to them in public, getting front seats in the synagogue, and the best places at dinner parties—while all the time they are battening on widows' property and covering it up with long prayers. These men are only heading for deeper damnation."

CHAPTER 21

THEN he looked up and saw the rich people dropping their gifts into the treasury, and he noticed a poor widow drop in two coppers, and he commented,

"I assure you that this poor widow has put in more than all of them, for they have all put in what they can easily spare, but she in her poverty has given away her whole living."

Jesus foretells the destruction of the Temple

Then when some of them were talking about the Temple and pointing out the beauty of its lovely stonework and the various ornaments that people had given, he said,

"Yes, you can gaze on all this today, but the time is coming when not a single stone will be left upon another without being thrown down."

So they asked him,

"Master, when will this happen, and what sign will there be that these things are going to take place?"

"Be careful that you are not deceived," he replied. "There will be many coming in my name, saying 'I am he' and 'The time is very near now.' Never follow men like that. And when you hear about wars and disturbances, don't be alarmed. These things must indeed happen first, but the end will not come immediately."

And prophesies world-wide suffering

Then he continued,

"Nation will rise up against nation, and kingdom against kingdom; there will be great earthquakes and famines and plagues in this place or that. There will be dreadful sights, and great signs from heaven. But before all this happens, men will arrest you and persecute you, handing you over to synagogue or prison, or bringing you before kings and governors, for my name's sake. This will be your chance to witness for me. So make up your minds not to think out your defence beforehand. I will give you such eloquence and wisdom that none of your opponents will be able to resist or contradict it. But you will be betrayed, even by parents and brothers and kinsfolk and friends, and there will be some of you who will be killed and you will be hated everywhere for my name's sake. Yet, not a hair of your head will perish. Hold on, and you will win your souls!

"But when you see Jerusalem surrounded by armed forces, then you will know that the time of her devastation has arrived. Then is the time for those who are in Judaea to fly to the hills. And those who are in the city itself must get out of it, and those who are already in the country must not try to get into the city. For these are the days of vengeance, when all that the scriptures have said will come true. Alas for those who are pregnant and those who have babies at the breast in those days! For there will be bitter misery in the land and great anger against this people. They will die by the sword. They will be taken off as prisoners into all nations. Jerusalem will be trampled under foot by the heathen until the heathen's day is over. There will be signs in the sun and moon and stars, and on the earth there will be dismay among the nations and bewilderment at the roar of the surging sea. Men's courage will fail completely as they realise what is threatening the world, for the very powers of heaven will be shaken. Then men will see the Son of Man coming in a cloud with great power and splendour! But when these things begin to happen, stand up, hold your heads high, for you will soon be free."

Vigilance is essential

Then he gave them a parable.

"Look at a fig-tree, or indeed any tree, when it begins to burst its buds, and you realise without anybody telling you that summer is nearly here. So, when you see these things happening, you can be equally sure that the kingdom of God has nearly come. Believe me, this generation will not disappear until all this has taken place. Heaven and earth will pass away, but my words will never pass away.

"Be on your guard—see to it that your minds are never clouded by dissipation or drunkenness or the worries of this life, or else that day may catch you like the springing of a trap—for it will come upon every inhabitant of the whole earth.

"You must be vigilant at all times, praying that you may be strong enough to come safely through all that is going to happen, and stand in the presence of the Son of Man."

And every day he went on teaching in the Temple, and every evening he went off and spent the night on the hill which is called the Mount of Olives. And all the people used to come early in the morning to listen to him in the Temple.

CHAPTER 22

Judas Iscariot becomes the tool of the authorities

Now as the feast of unleavened bread, called the Passover, was approaching, fear of the people made the chief priests and scribes try desperately to find a way of getting rid of Jesus. Then Satan entered into the mind of Judas Iscariot, who was one of the twelve. He went and discussed with the chief priests and officers a method of getting Jesus into their hands. They were delighted and arranged to pay him cash for it. He agreed, and began to look for a suitable opportunity for betrayal when there was no crowd present.

Jesus makes arrangements for his last Passover with his disciples

Then the day of unleavened bread arrived, on which the Passover lamb had to be sacrificed, and Jesus sent off Peter and John with the words, "Go and make all the preparations for us to eat the Passover."

"Where would you like us to do this?" they asked.

And he replied,

"Listen, just as you're going into the city a man carrying a jug of water will meet you. Follow him to the house he is making for. Then say to the owner of the house, 'The master has this message for you—which is the room where my disciples and I may eat the Passover?' And he will take you upstairs and show you a large room furnished for our needs. Make all the preparations there."

So they went off and found everything exactly as he had told them it would be, and they made the Passover preparations.

Then, when the time came, he took his seat at table with the apostles, and spoke to them,

"With all my heart I have longed to eat this Passover with you before the time comes for me to suffer. Believe me, I shall not eat the Passover again until all that it means is fulfilled in the kingdom of God."

Then taking a cup from them, he thanked God and said,

"Take this and share it amongst yourselves, for I tell you that from this moment I shall drink no more wine until the kingdom of God comes."

The mysterious words which were remembered later

Then he took a loaf and after thanking God he broke it and gave it to them, with these words,

"This is my body which is given for you: do this in remembrance of me."

So too, he gave them a cup after supper with the words,

"This cup is the new agreement made in my own blood which is shed for you. Yet the hand of the man who is betraying me lies with mine on this table. The Son of Man goes on his appointed way: yet alas for the man by whom he is betrayed!"

Jesus again teaches humility

And at this they began to debate among themselves as to which of them would do this thing.

And then a dispute arose among them as to who should be considered the most important.

But Jesus said to them,

"Among the heathen it is their kings who lord it over them, and their rulers are given the title of 'benefactors'. But it must not be so with you! Your greatest man must become like a junior and your leader must be a servant. Who is the greater, the man who sits down to dinner or the man who serves him? Obviously, the man who sits down to dinner—yet I am among you as your servant. But you are the men who have stood by me in all that I have gone through, and as surely as my Father has given me my kingdom, so I give you the right to eat and drink at my table in that kingdom. Yes, you will sit on thrones and judge the twelve tribes of Israel!

The personal warning to Simon

"Oh, Simon, Simon, do you know that Satan has asked to have you all to sift like wheat?—but I have prayed for you that you may not lose your faith. Yes, when you have turned back to me, you must strengthen these brothers of yours."

Peter said to him,

"Lord, I am ready to go to prison, or even to die with you!"

"I tell you, Peter," returned Jesus, "before the cock crows today you will deny three times that you know me!"

Jesus tells his disciples that the crisis has arrived

Then he continued to them all,

"That time when I sent you out without any purse or wallet or shoes—did you find you needed anything?"

"No, not a thing," they replied.

"But now," Jesus continued, "if you have a purse or wallet, take it with you, and if you have no sword, sell your coat and buy one! For I tell you that this scripture must be fulfilled in me—

And he was reckoned with transgressors.

So comes the end of what they wrote about me."

Then the disciples said,

"Lord, look, here are two swords."

And Jesus returned,

"That is enough."

Then he went out of the city and up on to the Mount of Olives, as he had often done before, with the disciples following him. And when he reached his usual place, he said to them,

"Pray that you may not have to face temptation!"

Then he went off by himself, about a stone's throw away, and falling on his knees, prayed in these words—

"Father, if you are willing, take this cup away from me—but it is not my will, but yours, that must be done."

Then he got to his feet from his prayer and walking back to the disciples, he found them sleeping through sheer grief.

"Why are you sleeping?" he said to them. "You must get up and go on praying that you may not have to face temptation."

The mob arrives and Judas betrays

While he was still speaking a crowd of people suddenly appeared led by the man called Judas, one of the twelve. He stepped up to Jesus to kiss him.

"Judas, would you betray the Son of Man with a kiss?" said Jesus to him.

And the disciples, seeing what was going to happen cried,

"Lord, shall we use our swords?"

And one of them did slash at the High Priest's servant, cutting off his right ear. But Jesus retorted,

"That is enough!"

And he touched his ear and healed him. Then he spoke to the chief priests, Temple officers and elders who were there to arrest him,

"So you have come out with your swords and staves as if I were a bandit. Day after day I was with you in the Temple and you never laid a finger on me—but this is your hour and the power of darkness is yours!"

Jesus is arrested: Peter follows but denies his master three times

Then they arrested him and marched him off to the High Priest's house. Peter followed at a distance, and sat down among some people who had lighted a fire in the middle of the courtyard and were sitting round it. A maid-servant saw him sitting there in the firelight, peered into his face and said,

"This man was with him too."

But he denied it and said,

"I don't know him, girl!"

A few minutes later someone else noticed Peter, and said,

"You're one of these men too."

But Peter said,

"Man, I am not!"

Then about an hour later someone else insisted,

"I am convinced this fellow was with him. Why, he is a Galilean!"

"Man," returned Peter, "I don't know what you're talking about."

And immediately, while he was still speaking, the cock crew. The Lord turned his head and looked straight at Peter, and into his mind flashed the words that the Lord had said to him ... "You will disown me three times before the cock crows today." And he went outside and wept bitterly.

Then the men who held Jesus made a great game of knocking him about. And they blindfolded him and asked him,

"Now, prophet, guess who hit you that time!"

And that was only the beginning of the way they insulted him.

In the early morning Jesus is formally interrogated

Then when daylight came, the assembly of the elders of the people, which included both chief priests and scribes, met and marched him off to their own council. There they asked him,

"If you really are Christ, tell us!"

"If I tell you, you will never believe me, and if I ask you a question, you will not answer me. But from now on the Son of Man will take his seat at the right hand of almighty God."

Then they all said,

"So you are the Son of God then?"

"You are right; I am," Jesus told them.

Then they said,

"Why do we need to call any more witnesses, for we ourselves have heard this thing from his own lips?"

CHAPTER 23

Jesus is taken before Pilate and Herod

THEN they rose up in a body and took him off to Pilate, and began their accusation in these words,

"Here is this man whom we have found corrupting our people, and telling them that it is wrong to pay taxes to Caesar, claiming that he himself is Christ, a king."

But Pilate addressed his question to Jesus,

"Are you the king of the Jews?"

"That is what you say," he replied.

Then Pilate spoke to the chief priests and the crowd,

"I find nothing criminal about this man."

But they pressed their charge, saying,

"He's a trouble-maker among the people. He teaches through the whole of Judaea, all the way from Galilee to this place."

When Pilate heard this, he enquired whether the man were a Galilean, and when he discovered that he came under Herod's jurisdiction, he passed him on to Herod who happened to be in Jerusalem at that time. When Herod saw Jesus, he was delighted, for he had been wanting to see him for a long time. He had heard a lot about Jesus and was hoping to see him perform a miracle. He questioned him thoroughly, but Jesus gave him absolutely no reply, though the chief priests and scribes stood there making the most violent accusations. So Herod joined his own soldiers in scoffing and jeering at Jesus. Finally, they dressed him up in a gorgeous cloak, and sent him back to Pilate. On that day Herod and Pilate became firm friends, though previously they had been at daggers drawn.

Pilate declares Jesus' innocence

Then Pilate summoned the chief priests, the officials and the people and addressed them in these words,

"You have brought this man to me as a mischief-maker among the people, and I want you all to realise that, after examining him in your presence, I have found nothing criminal about him, in spite of all your accusations. And neither has Herod, for he has sent him back to us. Obviously, then, he has done nothing to deserve the death penalty. I propose, therefore, to teach him a sharp lesson and let him go."

But they all yelled as one man,

"Take this man away! We want Barabbas set free!"

(Barabbas was a man who had been put in prison for causing a riot in the city and for murder.) But Pilate wanted to set Jesus free and he called out to them again, but they shouted back at him,

"Crucify, crucify him!"

Then he spoke to them, for the third time,

"What is his crime, then? I have found nothing in him that deserves execution; I am going to teach him his lesson and let him go."

But they shouted him down, yelling their demand that he should be crucified.

Their shouting won the day, and Pilate gave the decision that their request should be granted. He released the man for whom they asked, the man who had been imprisoned for rioting and murder, and surrendered Jesus to their demands.

And as they were marching him away, they caught hold of Simon, a native of Cyrene in Africa, who was on his way home from the fields, and put the cross on his back for him to carry behind Jesus.

On the way to the cross

A huge crowd of people followed him, including women who wrung their hands and wept for him. But Jesus turned to them and said,

"Women of Jerusalem, do not shed your tears for me, but for yourselves and for your children! For the days are coming when men will say, 'Lucky are the women who are childless—the bodies which have never borne, and the breasts which have never given nourishment.' Then men will begin to say to the mountains, 'Fall upon us!' and will say to the hills, 'Cover us up!' For if this is what men do when the wood is green, what will they do when it is seasoned?"

Jesus is crucified with two criminals

Two criminals were also led out with him for execution, and when they came to the place called The Skull, they crucified him with the criminals, one on either side of him. But Jesus himself was saying,

"Father, forgive them; they do not know what they are doing."

Then they shared out his clothes by casting lots.

The people stood and stared while their rulers continued to scoff, saying, "He saved other people, let's see him save himself, if he is really God's Christ—his chosen!"

The soldiers also mocked him by coming up and presenting sour wine to him, saying,

"If you are the king of the Jews, why not save yourself?" For there was a placard over his head which read,

THIS IS THE KING OF THE JEWS.

One of the criminals hanging there covered him with abuse, and said,

"Aren't you Christ? Why don't you save yourself—and us?"

But the other one checked him with the words,

"Aren't you afraid of God even when you're getting the same punishment as he is? And it's fair enough for us, for we've only got what we deserve, but this man never did anything wrong."

Then he said,

"Jesus, remember me when you come into your kingdom."

And Jesus answered,

"I tell you truly, this very day you will be with me in paradise."

The darkness, and the death of Jesus

It was now about midday, but darkness came over the whole countryside until three in the afternoon, for the sun's light was eclipsed. The veil in the Temple sanctuary was split in two. Then Jesus gave a great cry and said,

"Father, I commend my spirit into your hands."

And with these words, he expired.

When the centurion saw what had happened, he exclaimed reverently,

"That was indeed a good man!"

And the whole crowd who had collected for the spectacle, when they saw what had happened, went home in deep distress. And all those who had known him, as well as the women who had followed him from Galilee, remained standing at a distance and saw these things happen.

Joseph from Arimathaea lays the body of Jesus in a tomb

Now there was a man called Joseph, a member of the Jewish council. He was a good and just man, and had neither agreed with their plan nor voted for their decision. He came from the Jewish city of Arimathaea and was awaiting the kingdom of God. He went to Pilate and asked for Jesus' body. He took it down and wrapped it in linen and placed it in a rock-hewn tomb which had not been used before.

It was now the day of the preparation and the Sabbath was beginning to dawn, so the women who had accompanied Jesus from Galilee followed Joseph, noted the tomb and the position of the body, and then went home to prepare spices and perfumes. On the Sabbath they rested, in obedience to the commandment.

CHAPTER 24

The first day of the week: the empty tomb

BUT at the first signs of dawn on the first day of the week, they went to the tomb, taking with them the aromatic spices they had prepared. They discovered that the stone had been rolled away from the tomb, but on going inside, the body of the Lord Jesus was not to be found. While they were still puzzling over this, two men suddenly stood at their elbow, dressed in dazzling light. The women were terribly frightened, and turned their eyes away and looked at the ground. But the two men spoke to them,

"Why do you look for the living among the dead? He is not here: he has been raised! Remember what he said to you, while he was still in Galilee—that the Son of Man must be betrayed into the hands of sinful men, and must be crucified, and must rise again on the third day."

Then they did remember what he had said, and they turned their backs on the tomb and went and told all this to the eleven and the others who were with them.

It was Mary of Magdala, Joanna, Mary, the mother of James, and their companions who made this report to the apostles. But it struck them as sheer imagination, and they did not believe the women. Only Peter got up and ran to the tomb. He stooped down and saw nothing but the linen clothes lying there, and he went home wondering at what had happened.

The walk to Emmaus

Then on the same day we find two of them going off to Emmaus, a village about seven miles from Jerusalem. As they went they were deep in conversation about everything that had happened. While they were absorbed in their serious talk and discussion, Jesus himself approached and walked along with them, but something prevented them from recognising him. Then he spoke to them,

"What is all this discussion that you are having on your walk?"

They stopped, their faces drawn with misery, and the one called Cleopas replied,

"You must be the only visitor to Jerusalem who hasn't heard all the things that have happened there recently!"

"What things?" asked Jesus.

"Oh, all about Jesus, from Nazareth. There was a man—a prophet strong in what he did and what he said, in God's eyes as well as the people's. Haven't you heard how our chief priests and rulers handed him over for execution, and had him crucified? But we were hoping he was the one who was to come and set Israel free. . . .

"Yes, and as if that were not enough, it's three days since all this happened; and some of our womenfolk have disturbed us profoundly. For they went to the tomb at dawn, and then when they couldn't find his body they said that they had had a vision of angels who said that he was alive. Some of our people went straight off to the tomb and found things just as the women had described them—but they didn't see *him!*"

Then he himself spoke to them,

"Oh, how foolish you are, how slow to believe in all that the prophets have said! Was it not inevitable that Christ should suffer like that and so find his glory?"

Then, beginning with Moses and all the prophets, he explained to them everything in the scriptures that referred to himself.

They were by now approaching the village to which they were going. He gave the impression that he meant to go on further, but they stopped him with the words,

"Do stay with us. It is nearly evening and the day will soon be over."

So he went indoors to stay with them. Then it happened! While he was sitting at table with them he took the loaf, gave thanks, broke it and passed it to them. Their eyes opened wide and they knew him! But he vanished from their sight. Then they said to each other,

"Weren't our hearts glowing while he was with us on the road when he made the scriptures plain to us?"

And they got to their feet without delay and turned back to Jerusalem. There they found the eleven and their friends all together, full of the news—

"The Lord is really risen—he has appeared to Simon now!"

Then they told the story of their walk, and how they recognised him when he broke the loaf.

Jesus suddenly appears to the disciples

And while they were still talking about these things, Jesus himself stood among them and said,

"Peace be with you all!"

But they shrank back in terror for they thought they were seeing a ghost.

"Why are you so worried?" said Jesus, "and why do doubts arise in your minds? Look at my hands and my feet—it is really I myself! Feel me and see; ghosts have no flesh or bones as you can see that I have."

But while they still could not believe it through sheer joy and were quite bewildered, Jesus said to them,

"Have you anything here to eat?"

They gave him a piece of broiled fish, which he took and ate before their eyes. Then he said,

"Here and now are fulfilled the words that I told you when I was with you: that everything written about me in the Law of Moses and in the prophets and psalms must come true."

Then he opened their minds so that they could understand the scriptures, and added,

"That is how it was written, and that is why it was inevitable that Christ should suffer, and rise from the dead on the third day. So must the change of heart which leads to the forgiveness of sins be proclaimed in his name to all nations, beginning at Jerusalem.

Jesus commissions them with the new message

"You are eye-witnesses of these things. Now I hand over to you the promise of my Father. Stay in the city, then, until you are clothed with power from on high."

Then he led them outside as far as Bethany, where he blessed them with uplifted hands. While he was in the act of blessing them he was parted from them and was carried up to Heaven. They worshipped him, and turned back to Jerusalem with great joy, and spent their days in the Temple, praising God.

The Gospel of John

It is quite plain that in this Gospel we are breathing a very different atmosphere from that of Matthew, Mark and Luke. The story itself shows great differences, almost the whole of the "action" taking place in Jerusalem; while a large amount of both the teaching and the healing ministries described by Mark, for example, find no place in "John" at all. There is also the remarkable difference that in this Gospel Jesus is recognised as the Messiah in the very first chapter by John, Andrew and Philip. Consequently John's version lacks the note of mounting tension which is very strong in the other three. The discourses of Jesus differ remarkably from those in the other three Gospels, where they consist for the most part of parables or short memorable rules of the way in which life is meant to be lived. In John's Gospel the discourses are long and different in style; they deal almost entirely with the great themes of life, light, love, truth and Christ's relationship with the Father. There are many similes and metaphors but no parables at all.

Naturally, this and many other sharp differences have given rise to an enormous amount of study and research. There is a vast body of literature commenting on the situation, and offering widely different explanations. To mention but one basic problem: in view of the difference of style between this and the other three Gospels, are we to suppose that Jesus spoke in different styles on different occasions, or are we to suppose that John is re-writing in his own style of Greek what Jesus spoke in Aramaic? The subject is obviously much too large to be more than introduced here, and the reader in search of further information is referred to the work of scholars writing particularly about St John's Gospel.

Whether this Gospel was written as a conscious supplement (or even a deliberate corrective) to the other three, we simply do not know. But the majority of Christian scholars, for all their disagreements, would not deny the enormous spiritual value of this document. It seems probable that the author knew Jesus personally, and although modern scholarship is mostly against considering him to be the apostle John, there can be no doubt that the author had close spiritual acquaintance with Christ, and had reflected long and deeply on the nature of the divine Word. Here he gives to the world the results of his thoughts, prayers and meditations about the life which is the light of men.

Modern scholarship has gradually set the probable date of the Gospel earlier and earlier, and it is now fairly generally agreed that it was written at Ephesus between 90 *and* 110.

CHAPTER 1

Prologue

At the beginning God expressed himself. That personal expression, that word, was with God, and was God, and he existed with God from the beginning. All creation took place through him, and none took place without him. In him appeared life and this life was the light of mankind. The light still shines in the darkness and the darkness has never put it out.

The gospel's beginning on earth

A man called John was sent by God as a witness to the light, so that all who heard his testimony might believe in the light. This man was not himself the light: he was sent simply as a witness to that light.

That was the true light, which shines upon every man, which was now coming into the world. He came into the world—the world he had created—and the world failed to recognise him. He came into his own world, and his own people would not accept him. Yet wherever men did accept him he gave them the power to become sons of God. These were the men who truly believed in him, and their birth depended not on natural descent nor on any physical impulse or plan of man, but on God.

So the word of God became a human being and lived among us. We saw his glory (the glory like that of a father's only son), full of grace and truth. And it was about him that John stood up and testified, exclaiming: "Here is the one I was speaking about when I said that although he would come after me he would always be in front of me; for he existed before I was born!" Indeed, every one of us has shared in his riches—there is a grace in our lives because of his grace. For while the Law was given by Moses, grace and truth came through Jesus Christ. It is true that no one has ever seen God at any time. Yet the divine and only Son, who lives in the closest intimacy with the Father, has made him known.

John's witness

This then is the testimony of John, when the Jews sent priests and Levites from Jerusalem to ask him who he was. He admitted with complete candour, "I am not Christ."

So they asked him, "Who are you then? Are you Elijah?"

"No, I am not," he replied.

"Are you the Prophet?"

"No," he replied.

"Well then," they asked again, "who are you? We want to give an answer to those who sent us. What would you call yourself?"

"I am a voice shouting in the desert, 'Make straight the way of the Lord!' as Isaiah the prophet said."

Now some of the Pharisees had been sent to John, and they questioned him, "What is the reason, then, for your baptising people if you are not Christ and not Elijah and not the Prophet?"

To which John returned, "I do baptise—with water. But somewhere among you stands a man you do not know. He comes after me, it is true, but I am not fit to undo his shoes!" (All this happened in Bethany on the far side of the Jordan where the baptisms of John took place.)

On the following day, John saw Jesus coming towards him and said, "Look, there is the lamb of God who takes away the sin of the world! This is the man I meant when I said 'A man comes after me who is always in front of me, for he existed before I was born!' It is true I have not known him, yet it was to make him known to Israel that I came and baptised with water."

Then John gave this testimony, "I have seen the Spirit come down like a dove from Heaven and rest upon him. Indeed I did not recognise him, but he who sent me to baptise with water told me this: 'The one on whom you will see the Spirit coming down and resting is the man who baptises with the Holy Spirit!' Now I have seen this and I declare before you all that he is the Son of God!"

Men begin to follow Jesus

On the following day John was again standing with two of his disciples. He looked straight at Jesus as he walked along and said, "There is the lamb of God!" The two disciples heard what he said and followed Jesus. Then Jesus turned round and when he saw them following him, spoke to them. "What do you want?" he said.

"Rabbi, where are you staying?" they replied.

"Come and see," returned Jesus.

So they went and saw where he was staying and remained with him the rest of that day. (It was then about four o'clock in the afternoon.) One of the two men who had heard what John said and had followed Jesus was Andrew, Simon Peter's brother. He went straight off and found his own brother, Simon, and told him, "We have found the Messiah!" (meaning Christ). And he brought him to Jesus.

Jesus looked steadily at him and said, "You are Simon, the son of John. From now on your name is Cephas"—(that is, Peter, meaning "a rock").

The following day Jesus decided to go into Galilee. He found Philip and said to him, "Follow me!" Philip was a man from Bethsaida, the town that Andrew and Peter came from. Now Philip found Nathanael and told him, "We have discovered the man whom Moses wrote about in the Law and about whom the Prophets wrote too. He is Jesus, the son of Joseph and comes from Nazareth."

"Can anything good come out of Nazareth?" retorted Nathanael.

"You come and see," replied Philip.

Jesus saw Nathanael coming towards him and remarked, "Now here is a true man of Israel; there is no deceit in him!"

"How can you know me?" returned Nathanael.

"When you were underneath that fig-tree," replied Jesus, "before Philip called you, I saw you."

At which Nathanael exclaimed, "Rabbi, you are the Son of God, you are the king of Israel!"

"Do you believe in me," replied Jesus, "because I said I had seen you underneath that fig-tree? You are going to see greater things than that! Believe me," he added, "I tell you all that you will see Heaven wide open and God's angels ascending and descending upon the Son of Man!"

CHAPTER 2

The Son of God and a village wedding

Two days later there was a wedding in the Galilean village of Cana. Jesus' mother was there and he and his disciples were invited to the festivities. The supply of wine gave out, and Jesus' mother told him, "They have no more wine."

"Is that your concern, or mine, Mother?" replied Jesus. "My time has not come yet."

So his mother said to the servants, "Do whatever he tells you."

In the room were six stone water-jars (actually for the Jewish ceremonial cleansing), each holding about twenty gallons. Jesus said to them, "Fill the jars with water", and they filled them to the brim. Then he said to them, "Now draw some out and take it to the master of ceremonies", and they did so. When this man tasted the water, which had now become wine, without knowing where it came from (although the servants who had drawn the water knew), he called out to the bridegroom and said to him, "Everybody I know puts his good wine on first and then when men have had plenty to drink, he brings out the poor stuff. But you have kept back your good wine till now!" Jesus gave this, the first of his signs, at Cana in Galilee. So he showed his glory and his disciples believed in him.

Jesus in the Temple

After this incident, Jesus, accompanied by his mother, his brothers and his disciples, went down to Capernaum and stayed there a few days. The Jewish Passover was approaching and Jesus made the journey up to Jerusalem. In the Temple-precincts he discovered cattle and sheep dealers and dove-sellers, as well as money-changers sitting at their tables. So he made a whip out of cords and drove the whole lot of them, sheep and cattle as well, out of the Temple. He sent the coins of the money-changers flying and turned their tables upside down. Then he said to the dove-sellers, "Take those things out of here. Don't you dare turn my Father's house into a market!" His disciples remembered the scripture—

The zeal of thine house shall eat me up.

As a result of this, the Jews said to him, "What sign can you give us to justify what you are doing?"

"Destroy this temple," Jesus retorted, "and I will rebuild it in three days!"

To which the Jews replied, "This Temple took forty-six years to build, and are you going to rebuild it in three days?"

He was, in fact, speaking about the temple of his own body, and when he was raised from the dead the disciples remembered what he had said to them and that made them believe both the scripture and the words that Jesus had spoken.

While he was in Jerusalem at Passover-time, during the festivities many believed in him as they saw the signs that he gave. But Jesus, on his side, did not trust himself to them—for he knew them all. He did not need anyone to tell him what people were like: he understood human nature.

CHAPTER 3

Jesus and a religious leader

ONE night Nicodemus, a leading Jew and a Pharisee, came to see Jesus.

"Rabbi," he began, "we realise that you are a teacher who has come from God. For no one could show the signs that you show unless God were with him."

"Believe me," returned Jesus, "when I assure you that a man cannot see the kingdom of God without being born again."

"And how can a man who has grown old possibly be born?" replied Nicodemus. "Surely he cannot go into his mother's womb a second time to be born?"

"I do assure you," said Jesus, "that unless a man is born from water and from spirit he cannot enter the kingdom of God. Flesh gives birth to flesh and spirit gives birth to spirit: you must not be surprised that I told you that all of you must be born again. The wind blows where it likes, you can hear the sound of it but you have no idea where it comes from or where it goes. Nor can you tell how a man is born by the wind of the Spirit."

"How on earth can things like this happen?" replied Nicodemus.

"So you are the teacher of Israel," said Jesus, "and you do not understand such things? I assure you that we are talking about what we know and we are witnessing to what we have observed, yet you will not accept our evidence. Yet if I have spoken to you about things which happen on this earth and you will not believe me, what chance is there that you will believe me if I tell you about what happens in Heaven? No one has ever been up to Heaven except the Son of Man who came down from Heaven. The Son of Man must be lifted above the heads of men—as Moses lifted up that serpent in the desert—so that any man who believes in him may have eternal life. For God loved the world so much that he gave his only Son, so that everyone who believes in him should not be lost, but should have eternal life. God has not sent his Son into the world to pass sentence upon it, but to save it—through him. Any man who believes in him is not judged at all. It is the one who will not believe who stands already condemned, because he will not believe in the character of God's only Son. This *is* the judgment—that light has entered the world and men have preferred darkness to light because their deeds were evil. Everybody who does wrong hates the light and keeps away from it, for fear his deeds may be exposed. But everybody who is living by the truth will come to the light to make it plain that all he has done has been done through God."

Jesus and John again

After this Jesus went into the country of Judaea with his disciples and stayed there with them while the work of baptism was being carried on. John, too, was in Aenon near Salim, baptising people because there was plenty of water in that district and they were continually coming to him for baptism. (John, of course, had not yet been put in prison.)

This led to a question arising between John's disciples and one of the Jews about the whole matter of being cleansed. They approached John and said to him, "Rabbi, look, the man who was with you on the other side of the Jordan, the one you testified to, is now baptising and everybody is coming to him!"

"A man can receive nothing at all," replied John, "unless it is given him from Heaven. You yourselves can witness that I said, 'I am not Christ but I have been sent as his forerunner.' It is the bridegroom who possesses the bride, yet the bridegroom's friend who merely stands and listens to him can be overjoyed to hear the bridegroom's voice. That is why my happiness is now complete. He must grow greater and greater and I less and less.

"The one who comes from above is naturally above everybody. The one who arises from the earth belongs to the earth and speaks from the earth. The one who comes from Heaven is above all others and he bears witness to what he has seen and heard—yet no one is accepting his testimony. Yet if a man does accept it, he is acknowledging the fact that God is true. For the one whom God sent speaks the authentic words of God—and there can be no measuring of the Spirit given to *him*! The Father loves the Son and has put everything under his control. The man who believes in the Son has eternal life. The man who refuses to believe in the Son will not see life; he lives under the anger of God."

CHAPTER 4

Jesus meets a Samaritan woman

Now, when Jesus learned that the Pharisees had heard that he was making and baptising more disciples than John—although, in fact, it was not Jesus who did the baptising but his disciples—he left Judaea and went off again to Galilee, which meant his passing through Samaria. There he came to a Samaritan town called Sychar, which is near the plot of land that Jacob gave to his son, Joseph, and "Jacob's Spring" was there. Jesus, tired with the journey, sat down beside it, just as he was. The time was about midday. Presently, a Samaritan woman arrived to draw some water.

"Please give me a drink," Jesus said to her, for his disciples had gone away to the town to buy food. The Samaritan woman said to him, "How can you, a Jew, ask for a drink from me, a woman of Samaria?" (For Jews have no dealings with Samaritans.)

"If you knew what God can give," Jesus replied, "and if you knew who it is that said to you, 'Give me a drink', you would have asked him, and he would have given you living water!"

"Sir," said the woman, "you have no bucket and this well is deep—where can you get your living water? Are you a greater man than our ancestor, Jacob, who gave us this well, and drank here himself with his family, and his cattle?"

Jesus said to her, "Everyone who drinks this water will be thirsty again. But whoever drinks the water I will give him will never be thirsty again. For my gift will become a spring in the man himself, welling up into eternal life."

The woman said, "Sir, give me this water, so that I may stop being thirsty—and not have to make this journey to draw water any more!"

"Go and call your husband and then come back here," said Jesus to her.

"I haven't got a husband!" the woman answered.

"You are quite right in saying, 'I haven't got a husband'," replied Jesus, "for you have had five husbands and the man you have now is not your husband at all. Yes, you spoke the truth when you said that."

"Sir," said the woman again, "I can see that you are a prophet! Now our ancestors worshipped on this hill-side, but you Jews say that Jerusalem is the place where men ought to worship——"

"Believe me," returned Jesus, "the time is coming when worshipping the Father will not be a matter of 'on this hill-side' or 'in Jerusalem'. Nowadays you are worshipping what you do not know. We Jews are worshipping what we know, for the salvation of mankind is to come from our race. Yet the time is coming, yes, and has already come, when true worshippers will worship the Father in spirit and in reality. Indeed, the Father looks for men who will worship him like that. God is Spirit, and those who worship him can only worship in spirit and in reality."

"Of course I know that Messiah is coming," returned the woman, "you know, the one who is called Christ. When he comes he will make everything plain to us."

"I am Christ speaking to you now," said Jesus.

At this point his disciples arrived, and were very surprised to find him talking to a woman, but none of them asked, "What do you want with her?" or "Why are you talking to her?" So the woman left her water-pot behind and went into the town and began to say to the people, "Come out and see the man who told me everything I've ever done! Can this be 'Christ'?" So they left the town and started to come to Jesus.

Meanwhile the disciples were begging him, "Master, do eat something."

To which Jesus replied, "I have food to eat that you know nothing about."

This, of course, made the disciples ask each other, "Do you think anyone has brought him any food?"

Jesus said to them, "My food is doing the will of him who sent me and finishing the work he has given me. Don't you say, 'Four months more and then comes the harvest'? But I tell you to open your eyes and look at the fields—they are gleaming white, all ready for the harvest! The reaper is already being rewarded and getting in a harvest for eternal life, so that both sower and reaper may be glad together. For in this harvest the old saying comes true, 'One man sows and another reaps.' I have sent you to reap a harvest for which you never laboured; other men have worked hard and you have reaped the result of their labours."

Many of the Samaritans who came out of that town believed in him through the woman's testimony—"He told me everything I've ever done." And when they arrived they begged him to stay with them. He did stay there two days and far more believed in him because of what he himself said. As they told the woman, "We don't believe any longer now because of what you said. We have heard him with our own ears. We know now that this really is the Saviour of the World!"

Jesus, in Cana again, heals in response to faith

After the two days were over, Jesus left and went away to Galilee. (For Jesus himself testified that a prophet enjoys no honour in his own country.) And on his arrival the people received him with open arms. For they had seen all that he had done in Jerusalem during the festival, since they had themselves been present. So Jesus came again to Cana in Galilee, the place where he had made the water into wine. At Capernaum there was an official whose son was very ill. When he heard that Jesus had left Judaea and had arrived in Galilee, he went off to see him and begged him to come down and heal his son, who was by this time at the point of death.

Jesus said to him, "Will you never believe unless you see signs and wonders?"

"Sir," returned the official, "please come down before my boy dies!"

"You can go home," returned Jesus, "your son is alive."

And the man believed what Jesus had said to him and went on his way.

On the journey back his servants met him with the report: "Your son is alive and well." So he asked them at what time he had begun to recover, and they replied: "The fever left him yesterday at one o'clock in the afternoon." Then the father knew that this must have happened at the very moment when Jesus had said to him, "Your son is alive." And he and his whole household believed in Jesus. This, then, was the second sign that Jesus gave on his return from Judaea to Galilee.

CHAPTER 5

Jesus heals in Jerusalem

SOME time later came one of the Jewish feast-days and Jesus went up to Jerusalem. There is in Jerusalem near the sheep-pens a pool surrounded by five arches, which has the Hebrew name of Bethzatha. Under these arches a great many sick people were in the habit of lying; some of them were blind, some lame, and some had withered limbs. (They used to wait there for the "moving of the water", for at certain times an angel used to come down into the pool and disturb the water, and then the first person who stepped into the water after the disturbance would be healed of whatever he was suffering from.) One particular man had been there ill for thirty-eight years. When Jesus saw him lying there on his back—knowing that he had been like that for a long time, he said to him, "Do you want to get well again?"

"Sir," replied the sick man, "I haven't got anybody to put me into the pool when the water is all stirred up. While I'm trying to get there somebody else gets down into it first."

"Get up," said Jesus, "pick up your bed and walk!"

At once the man recovered, picked up his bed and began to walk.

This happened on a Sabbath day, which made the Jews keep on telling the man who had been healed, "It's the Sabbath; it is not right for you to carry your bed."

"The man who made me well," he replied, "was the one who told me, 'Pick up your bed and walk.'"

Then they asked him, "And who is the man who told you to do that?"

But the one who had been healed had no idea who it was, for Jesus had slipped away in the dense crowd. Later Jesus found him in the Temple and said to him, "Look: you are a fit man now. Do not sin again or something worse might happen to you!"

Then the man went off and informed the Jews that the one who had made him well was Jesus. It was because Jesus did such things on the Sabbath day that the Jews persecuted him. But Jesus' answer to them was this, "My Father is still at work and therefore I work as well."

This remark made the Jews all the more determined to kill him, because not only did he break the Sabbath but he referred to God as his own Father, so putting himself on equal terms with God.

Jesus makes his tremendous claim

Jesus therefore said to them, "I solemnly assure you that the Son can do nothing of his own accord, but only what he sees the Father doing. For whatever the Father does the Son does the same. For the Father loves the Son and shows him everything that he does himself. Yes, and he will show him even greater things than these to fill you with wonder. For just as the Father raises the dead and makes them live, so does the Son give life to any man he chooses. The Father is no man's judge: he has put judgment entirely into the Son's hands, so that all men may honour the Son equally with the Father. The man who does not honour the Son does not honour the Father who sent him. I solemnly assure you that the man who hears what I have to say and believes in the one who has sent me has eternal life. He does not have to face judgment; he has already passed from death into life. Yes, I assure you that a time is coming, in fact has already come, when the dead will hear the voice of the Son of God and those who have heard it will live! For just as the Father has life in himself, so by the Father's gift, the Son also has life in himself. And he has given him authority to judge because he is Son of Man. No, do not be surprised—the time is coming when all those who are dead and buried will hear his voice and out they will come—those who have done right will rise again to life, but those who have done wrong will rise to face judgment!

"By myself I can do nothing. As I hear from God, I judge, and my judgment is true because I do not live to please myself but to do the will of the Father who sent me. You may say that I am bearing witness about myself, that therefore what I say about myself has no value, but I would remind you that there is one who witnesses about me and I know that his witness about me is absolutely true. You sent to John, and he testified to the truth. Not that it is man's testimony that I need—I only tell you this to help you to be saved. John certainly was a lamp that burned and shone, and for a time you were willing to enjoy the light that he gave. But I have a higher testimony than John's. The work that the Father gave me to complete, yes, these very actions which I do are my witness that the Father has sent me. This is how the Father who has sent me has given his own personal testimony to me.

"Now you have never at any time heard what he says or seen what he is like. Nor do you really allow his word to find a home in your hearts, for you refuse to believe the man whom he has sent. You pore over the scriptures for you imagine that you will find eternal life in them. All the time they give their testimony to me, but you are not willing to come to me to have real life! I do not need the praise of men, but I can tell that you have none of the love of God in your hearts. I have come in the name of my Father and you will not accept me. Yet if another man comes simply in his own name, you will accept him. How on earth can you believe while you are for ever looking for each other's approval and not for the glory that comes from the one God? There is no need for you to think that I have come to accuse you before the Father. You already have an accuser—Moses, in whom you put all your confidence! For if you really believed Moses, you would be bound to believe me; for it was about me that he wrote. But if you do not believe what he wrote, how can you believe what I say?"

CHAPTER 6

Jesus shows his power over material things

AFTER this, Jesus crossed the Lake of Galilee (or Tiberias), and a great crowd followed him because they had seen the signs which he gave in his dealings with the sick. But Jesus went up the hill-side and sat down there with his disciples. The Passover, the Jewish festival, was near. So Jesus, raising his eyes and seeing a great crowd on their way towards him, said to Philip, "Where can we buy food for these people to eat?" (He said this to test Philip, for he himself knew what he was going to do.)

"Twenty pounds' worth of bread would not be enough for them," Philip replied, "even if they had only a little each."

Then Andrew, Simon Peter's brother, another disciple, put in, "There is a boy here who has five barley loaves and a couple of fish, but what's the good of that for such a crowd?"

Then Jesus said, "Get the people to sit down."

There was plenty of grass there, and the men, some five thousand of them, sat down. Then Jesus took the loaves, gave thanks for them and distributed them to the people sitting on the grass, and he distributed the fish in the same way, giving them as much as they wanted. When they had eaten enough, Jesus said to his disciples, "Collect the pieces that are left over so that nothing is wasted."

So they did as he suggested and filled twelve baskets with the broken pieces of the five barley loaves, which were left over after the people had eaten. When the men saw this sign of Jesus' power, they kept saying, "This is surely the Prophet who was to come into the world!"

Then Jesus, realising that they were going to carry him off and make him their king by force, retired once more to the hill-side quite alone.

In the evening, his disciples went down to the lake, embarked on the boat and made their way across the lake to Capernaum. Darkness had already fallen and Jesus had not yet returned to them. A strong wind sprang up and the water grew very rough. When they had rowed about three or four miles, they saw Jesus walking on the water and coming towards the boat, and they were terrified. But he spoke to them, "Don't be afraid: it is I myself."

So they gladly took him aboard, and at once the boat reached the shore they were making for.

Jesus teaches about the true bread

The following day, the crowd, who had remained on the other side of the lake, noticed that only the one boat had been there, and that Jesus had not embarked on it with his disciples, but that they had in fact gone off by themselves. Some other small boats from Tiberias had landed near the place where they had eaten the food and the Lord had given thanks. When the crowd realised that neither Jesus nor the disciples were there any longer, they themselves went aboard the boats and went off to Capernaum to look for Jesus. When they had found him on the other side of the lake, they said to him, "Rabbi, when did you come here?"

"Believe me," replied Jesus, "when I tell you that you are looking for me now not because you saw my signs but because you ate that food and had all you wanted. You should not work for the food which does not last but for the food which lasts on into eternal life. This is the food the Son of Man will give you, and he is the one who bears the stamp of God the Father."

This made them ask him, "What must we do to carry out the work of God?"

"The work of God for you," replied Jesus, "is to believe in the one whom he has sent to you."

Then they asked him, "Then what sign can you give us that

will make us believe in you? What work are you doing? Our forefathers ate manna in the desert just as the scripture says,

He gave them bread out of Heaven to eat."

To which Jesus replied, "That is true indeed, but what matters is not that Moses *gave you* bread from Heaven but that my Father is *giving you* the true bread from Heaven. For the bread of God which comes down from Heaven gives life to the world."

This made them say to him, "Lord, please give us this bread, now and always!"

Then Jesus said to them, "I myself am the bread of life. The man who comes to me will never be hungry and the man who believes in me will never be thirsty. Yet I have told you that you have seen me and do not believe. Everything that my Father gives me will come to me and I will never refuse anyone who comes to me. For I have come down from Heaven, not to do what I want, but to do the will of him who sent me. The will of him who sent me is that I should not lose anything of what he has given me, but should raise it up when the last day comes. And this is the will of the One who sent me, that everyone who sees the Son and trusts him should have eternal life, and I will raise him up when the last day comes."

At this, the Jews began grumbling at him because he said, "I am the bread which came down from Heaven", remarking "Is not this Jesus, the son of Joseph, whose parents we know? How can he now say that 'I have come down from Heaven'?"

So Jesus answered them, "Do not grumble among yourselves. Nobody comes to me unless he is drawn to me by the Father who sent me, and I will raise him up when the last day comes. In the Prophets it is written—

'And they shall all be taught of God,'

and this means that everybody who has heard the Father's voice and learned from him will come to me. Not that anyone has ever seen the Father except the one who comes from God—he alone has seen the Father. I solemnly assure you that the man who trusts in him has eternal life already. I myself am the bread of life. Your forefathers ate manna in the desert, *and they died*. This is bread that comes down from Heaven, so that a man may eat it and never die. I myself am the living bread which came down from Heaven, and if anyone eats this bread he will live for ever. The bread which I will give is my own body and I shall give it for the life of the world."

This led to a fierce argument among the Jews, some of them saying, "How can this man give us his body to eat?"

So Jesus said to them, "Unless you do eat the body of the Son of Man and drink his blood, I assure you that you are not really living at all. The man who eats my flesh and drinks my blood has eternal life and I will raise him up when the last day comes. For my body is real food and my blood is real drink. The man who eats my body and drinks my blood shares my life and I share his. Just as the living Father sent me and I am alive because of the Father, so the man who lives on me will live because of me. *This* is the bread which came down from Heaven! It is not like the manna which your forefathers used to eat, *and died.* The man who eats this bread will live for ever."

Jesus said all these things while teaching in the synagogue at Capernaum. Many of his disciples heard him say these things, and commented, "This is hard teaching indeed; who could accept that?"

Then Jesus, knowing intuitively that his disciples were complaining about what he had just said, went on, "Is this too much for you? Then what would happen if you were to see the Son of Man going up to the place where he was before? It is the Spirit which gives life. The flesh will not help you. The things which I have told you are spiritual and are life. But some of you do not believe me."

For Jesus knew from the beginning which of his followers did not trust him and who was the man who would betray him. Then he added, "This is why I said to you, 'No one can come to me unless my Father puts it into his heart to come.'"

As a consequence of this, many of his disciples withdrew and no longer followed him. So Jesus said to the twelve, "And are you too wanting to go away?"

"Lord," answered Simon Peter, "who else should we go to? Your words have the ring of eternal life! And we believe and are convinced that you are the Holy One of God."

Jesus replied, "Did I not choose you twelve—and one of you has the devil in his heart?"

He was speaking of Judas, the son of Simon Iscariot, one of the twelve, who was planning to betray him.

CHAPTER 7

Jesus delays his arrival at the festival

After this, Jesus moved about in Galilee but decided not to do so in Judaea since the Jews were planning to take his life. As the

Jewish festival, "The feast of the tabernacles", was approaching, his brothers said to him, "You ought to leave here and go to Judaea so that your disciples can see what you are doing, for nobody works in secret if he wants to be known publicly. If you are doing things like this, let the world see what you are doing." For not even his brothers had any faith in him. Jesus replied by saying, "It is not yet the right time for me, but any time is right for you. It is impossible for you to arouse the world's hatred, but I provoke hatred because I show the world how evil its deeds really are. No, you go up to the festival; I shall not go up now, for it is not yet time for me to go." And after these words he remained where he was in Galilee.

Later, after his brothers had gone to the festival, he went up himself, not openly but as though he did not want to be seen. Consequently, the Jews kept looking for him at the festival and asking "Where is that man?" And there was an undercurrent of discussion about him among the crowds. Some would say, "He is a good man", others maintained that he was not, but that he was "misleading the people". Nobody, however spoke openly about him for fear of the Jews.

Jesus openly declares his authority

But in the middle of the festival, Jesus went up to the Temple and began teaching. The Jews were amazed and remarked, "How does this man know all this—he has never been taught?"

Jesus replied to them, "My teaching is not really mine but comes from the One who sent me. If anyone wants to do God's will, he will know whether my teaching is from God or whether I merely speak on my own authority. A man who speaks on his own authority has an eye for his own reputation. But the man who is considering the glory of God who sent him is a true man. There can be no dishonesty about him.

"Did not Moses give you the Law? Yet not one of you keeps the Law. Why are you trying to kill me?"

The crowd answered, "You must be mad! Who is trying to kill you?"

Jesus answered them, "I have done one thing and you are all amazed at it. Moses gave you circumcision (not that it came from Moses originally but from your forefathers), and you circumcise a man even on the Sabbath. If a man receives the cutting of circumcision on the Sabbath to avoid breaking the Law of

Moses, why should you be angry with me because I have made a man's body perfectly whole on the Sabbath? You must not judge by the appearance of things but by the reality!"

Some of the people of Jerusalem, hearing him talk like this, were saying, "Isn't this the man whom they are trying to kill? Yet here he is, talking quite openly and they haven't a word to say to him. Surely our rulers haven't decided that this really is Christ! But then, we know this man and where he comes from—when Christ comes, no one will know where he comes from."

Jesus makes more unique claims

Then Jesus, in the middle of his teaching, called out in the Temple, "So you know me and know where I have come from? But I have not come of my own accord; I am sent by One who is true and you do not know him! I do know him, because I come from him and he has sent me here."

Then they attempted to arrest him, but actually no one laid a finger on him because the right moment had not yet come. Yet many of the crowd believed in him and kept on saying, "When Christ comes, is he going to show greater signs than this man?"

The Pharisees heard the crowd whispering these things about him, and they and the chief priests sent officers to arrest him. Then Jesus said, "I shall be with you only a little while longer and then I am going to him who sent me. You will look for me then but you will never find me. You cannot come where I shall be."

This made the Jews say to each other, "Where is he going to go so that we cannot find him? Surely he's not going to our refugees among the Greeks to teach Greeks? What does he mean when he says, 'You will look for me and you will never find me' and 'You cannot come where I shall be'?"

Then, on the last day, the climax of the festival, Jesus stood up and cried out, "If any man is thirsty, he may come to me and drink! The man who believes in me, as the scripture said, will have rivers of living water flowing from his inmost heart." (Here he was speaking about the Spirit which those who believe in him would receive. The Spirit had not yet been given because Jesus had not yet been glorified.) When they heard these words, some of the people were saying, "This really is the Prophet." Others said, "This is Christ!" But some said, "And does Christ come from Galilee? Don't the scriptures say that Christ will be descended from David, and will come from Bethlehem, the village where David lived?"

So the people were in two minds about him—some of them wanted to arrest him, but no one laid hands on him.

Then the officers returned to the Pharisees and chief priests, who said to them, "Why haven't you brought him?"

"No man ever spoke as this man speaks!" they replied.

"Has he pulled the wool over your eyes, too?" retorted the Pharisees. "Have any of the authorities or any of the Pharisees believed in him? But this crowd, who know nothing about the Law, is damned anyway!"

One of their number, Nicodemus (the one who had previously been to see Jesus), said to them, "But surely our Law does not judge the accused without first hearing what he has to say, and finding out what he has done?"

"Are you a Galilean, too?" they retorted. "Look where you will—you won't find that any prophet comes out of Galilee!"

So they broke up their meeting and went home, while Jesus went off to the Mount of Olives.*

CHAPTER 8

Jesus deflates the rigorists

EARLY next morning he returned to the Temple and the entire crowd came to him. So he sat down and began to teach them. But the scribes and Pharisees brought in to him a woman who had been caught in adultery. They made her stand in front, and then said to him, "Now, master, this woman has been caught in adultery, in the very act. According to the Law, Moses commanded us to stone such women to death. Now, what do you say about it?"

They said this to test him, so that they might have some good grounds for an accusation. But Jesus stooped down and began to write with his finger in the dust on the ground. But as they persisted in their questioning, he straightened himself up and said to them, "Let the one among you who has never sinned throw the first stone at her." Then he stooped down again and continued writing with his finger on the ground. And when they heard what he said, they were convicted by their own consciences

* See note 4, page 552.

and went out, one by one, beginning with the eldest.

Jesus was left alone, with the woman still standing where they had put her. So he stood up and said to her, "Where are they all —did no one condemn you?"

And she said, "No one, sir."

"Neither do I condemn you," said Jesus to her. "Go away now and do not sin again."

Jesus' bold claims—about himself—and his Father

Later, Jesus spoke to the people again and said, "I am the light of the world. The man who follows me will never walk in the dark but will live his life in the light."

This made the Pharisees say to him, "You are testifying to yourself—your evidence is not valid."

Jesus answered. "Even if I am testifying to myself, my evidence is valid, for I know where I have come from and I know where I am going. But as for you, you have no idea where I come from or where I am going. You are judging by human standards, but I am not judging anyone. Yet if I should judge, my decision would be just, for I am not alone—the Father who sent me is with me. In your Law, it is stated that the witness of two persons is valid. I am one testifying to myself and the second witness to me is the Father who sent me."

"And where is this father of yours?" they asked.

"You do not know my Father," returned Jesus, "any more than you know me: if you had known me, you would have known him also."

Jesus made these statements while he was teaching in the Temple treasury. Yet no one arrested him, for his time had not yet come.

Later, Jesus spoke to them again and said, "I am going away and you will try to find me, but you will die in your sins. You cannot come where I am going."

This made the Jews say, "Is he going to kill himself, then? Is *that* why he says, 'You cannot come where I am going'?"

"The difference between us," Jesus said to them, "is that you come from below and I am from above. You belong to this world but I do not. That is why I told you you will die in your sins. For unless you believe that I am who I am, you will die in your sins."

Then they said, "*Who are you?*"

"I am what I have told you I was from the beginning," replied

Jesus. "There is much in you that I could speak about and condemn. But he who sent me is true and I am only speaking to this world what I myself have heard from him."

They did not realise that he was talking to them about the Father. So Jesus resumed, "When you have lifted up the Son of Man, then you will realise that I am who I say I am, and that I do nothing on my own authority but speak simply as my Father has taught me. The one who sent me is with me now: the Father has never left me alone for I always do what pleases him." And even while he said these words, many people believed in him.

Jesus speaks of personal freedom

So Jesus said to the Jews who believed in him, "If you are faithful to what I have said, you are truly my disciples. And you will know the truth and the truth will set you free!"

"But we are descendants of Abraham," they replied, "and we have never in our lives been any man's slaves. How can you say to us, 'You will be set free'?"

Jesus returned, "Believe me when I tell you that every man who commits sin is a slave. For a slave is no permanent part of a household, but a son is. If the Son, then, sets you free, you are really free! I know that you are descended from Abraham, but some of you are looking for a way to kill me because you can't bear my words. I am telling you what I have seen in the presence of my Father, and you are doing what you have seen in the presence of your father."

"Our father is Abraham!" they retorted.

"If you were the children of Abraham, you would do the sort of things Abraham did. But in fact you are looking for a way to kill me, simply because I am a man who has told you the truth that I have heard from God. Abraham would never have done that. No, you are doing your father's work."

"We are not illegitimate!" they retorted. "We have one Father —God."

"If God were really your Father," replied Jesus, "you would have loved me. For I came from God; and I am here. I did not come of my own accord—he sent me, and I am here. Why do you not understand my words? It is because you cannot hear what I am really saying. Your father is the devil, and what you are wanting to do is what your father longs to do. He always was a murderer, and has never dealt with the truth, since the truth will have nothing to do with him. Whenever he tells a lie, he speaks in character, for he is a liar and the father of lies. And it is because I speak the truth that you will not believe me. Which of you can prove me guilty of sin? If I am speaking the truth, why is it that you do not believe me? The man who is born of God can hear the words of God and the reason why you cannot hear the words of God is simply this, that you are not the sons of God."

"How right we are," retorted the Jews, "in calling you a Samaritan, and mad at that!"

"No," replied Jesus, "I am not mad. I am honouring my Father and you are dishonouring me. But I am not concerned with my own glory: there is one whose concern it is, and he is the true judge. Believe me when I assure you that if anybody accepts my words, he will never see death at all."

"Now we know that you're mad," replied the Jews. "Why, Abraham died and the prophets, too, and yet you say, 'If a man accepts my words, he will never experience death!' Are you greater than our father, Abraham? He died, and so did the prophets—who are you making yourself out to be?"

"If I were to glorify myself," returned Jesus, "such glory would be worthless. But it is my Father who glorifies me, the very one whom you say is your God—though you have never known him. But I know him, and if I said I did not know him, I should be as much a liar as you are! But I do know him and I am faithful to what he says. As for your Father, Abraham, his great joy was that he would see my coming. Now he has seen it and he is overjoyed."

"Look," said the Jews to him, "you are not fifty yet—and have you seen Abraham?"

"I tell you in solemn truth," returned Jesus, "before there was an Abraham, I AM!"

At this, they picked up stones to hurl at him, but Jesus was nowhere to be seen; and he made his way out of the Temple.

CHAPTER 9

Jesus and blindness, physical and spiritual

LATER, as Jesus walked along he saw a man who had been blind from birth.

"Rabbi, whose sin caused this man's blindness," asked the disciples, "his own or his parents'?"

"He was not born blind because of his own sin or that of his parents," returned Jesus, "but to show the power of God at work in him. We must carry on the work of him who sent me while the daylight lasts. Night is coming, when no one can work. I am the world's light as long as I am in it."

Having said this, he spat on the ground and made a sort of clay with the saliva. This he applied to the man's eyes and said, "Go and wash in the pool of Siloam." (Siloam means "one who has been sent".) So the man went off and washed and came back with his sight restored.

His neighbours and the people who had often seen him before as a beggar remarked, "Isn't this the man who used to sit and beg?"

"Yes, that's the one," said some.

Others said, "No, but he's very like him."

But he himself said, "I'm the man all right!"

"Then how was your blindness cured?" they asked.

"The man called Jesus made some clay and smeared it on my eyes," he replied, "and then he said, 'Go to Siloam and wash.' So off I went and washed—and that's how I got my sight!"

"Where is he now?" they asked.

"I don't know," he returned.

So they brought the man who had been blind before the Pharisees. (It should be noted that Jesus made the clay and restored his sight on a Sabbath day.) The Pharisees asked the question all over again as to how he had become able to see.

"He put clay on my eyes; I washed it off; now I can see—that's all," he replied.

Some of the Pharisees commented, "This man cannot be from God since he does not observe the Sabbath."

"But how can a sinner give such wonderful signs as these?" others demurred. And they were in two minds about him. Finally, they asked the blind man again, "And what do *you* say about him? You're the one whose sight was restored."

"I believe he is a prophet," he replied.

The Jews did not really believe that the man had been blind and then had become able to see, until they had summoned his parents and asked them, "Is this your son who you say was born blind? How does it happen that he can now see?"

"We know that this is our son, and we know that he was born blind," returned his parents, "but how he can see now, or who made him able to see, we have no idea. Why don't you ask him? He is a grown-up man; he can speak for himself."

His parents said this because they were afraid of the Jews who had already agreed that anybody who admitted that the man was Christ should be excommunicated. It was this which made his parents say, "Ask him, he is a grown-up man."

So, once again they summoned the man who had been born blind and said to him, "You should give God the glory for what has happened to you. We know that this man is a sinner."

"Whether he is a sinner or not, I couldn't tell, but one thing I am sure of," the man replied, "I used to be blind, now I can see!"

"But what did he *do* to you—how did he make you see?" they continued.

"I've told you before," he replied. "Weren't you listening? Why do you want to hear it all over again? Are you wanting to be his disciples too?"

At this, they turned on him furiously.

"You're the one who is his disciple! We are disciples of Moses. We know that God spoke to Moses, but as for this man, we don't even know where he came from."

"Now here's the extraordinary thing," he retorted, "you don't know where he came from and yet he gave me the gift of sight. Everybody knows that God does not listen to sinners. It is the man who has a proper respect for God and does what he wants him to do—he's the one God listens to. Why, since the world began, nobody's ever heard of a man who was born blind being given his sight. If this man did not come from God, he couldn't do anything!"

"You misbegotten wretch!" they flung back at him. "Are you trying to teach *us*?" And they threw him out.

Jesus heard that they had expelled him and when he had found him, he said, "Do you believe in the Son of Man?"

"And who is he, sir?" the man replied. "Tell me, so that I can believe in him."

"You have seen him," replied Jesus. "It is the one who is talking to you now."

"Lord, I do believe," he said, and worshipped him.

Then Jesus said, "My coming into this world is itself a judgment—those who cannot see have their eyes opened and those who think they can see become blind."

Some of the Pharisees near him overheard this and said, "So we're blind, too, are we?"

"If you were blind," returned Jesus, "nobody could blame you, but, as you insist 'We can see', your guilt remains."

CHAPTER 10

Jesus declares himself the true shepherd of men

THEN Jesus said, "Believe me when I tell you that anyone who does not enter the sheepfold through the door, but climbs in by some other way, is a thief and a rogue. It is the shepherd of the flock who goes in by the door. It is to him the door-keeper opens the door and it is his voice that the sheep recognise. He calls his own sheep by name and leads them out of the fold, and when he has brought all his own flock outside, he goes in front of them himself, and the sheep follow him because they know his voice. They will never follow a stranger—indeed, they will run away from him, for they do not recognise strange voices."

Jesus gave them this illustration but they did not grasp the point of what he was saying to them. So Jesus said to them once more, "I do assure you that I myself am the door for the sheep. All who have gone before me are like thieves and rogues, but the sheep did not listen to them. I am the door. If a man goes in through me, he will be safe and sound; he can come in and out and find his food. The thief comes only to steal, to kill and to destroy, but I have come to bring them life in its fullness. I am the good shepherd. The good shepherd gives his life for the sake of his sheep. But the hired man, who is not the shepherd, and does not own the sheep, will see the wolf coming, desert the sheep and run away. And the wolf will attack the flock and send them flying. The hired man runs away because he is only a hired man and has no interest in the sheep. I am the good shepherd, and I know those that are mine and my sheep know me, just as the Father knows me and I know the Father. And I give my life for the sake of the sheep.

"And I have other sheep who do not belong to this fold. I must lead these also, and they will hear my voice. So there will be one flock and one shepherd. This is the reason why the Father loves me—that I lay down my life so that I may take it up again! No one is taking it from me, but I lay it down of my own free will. I have the power to lay it down and I have the power to take it up again. This is the command that I have received from my Father."

Jesus plainly declares who he is

Once again, the Jews were in two minds about him because of these words, many of them remarking, "The devil's in him and he's insane. Why do you listen to him?"

But others were saying, "This is not the sort of thing a devil-possessed man would say! Can a devil make a blind man see?"

Then came the dedication festival at Jerusalem. It was winter-time and Jesus was walking about inside the Temple in Solomon's cloisters. So the Jews closed in on him and said, "How much longer are you going to keep us in suspense? If you really are Christ, tell us so straight out!"

"I have told you," replied Jesus, "and you do not believe it. What I have done in my Father's name is sufficient to prove my claim, but you do not believe because you are not my sheep. My sheep recognise my voice and I know who they are. They follow me and I give them eternal life. They will never die and no one can snatch them out of my hand. My Father, who has given them to me, is greater than all. And no one can snatch anything out of the Father's hand. I and the Father are One."

Again the Jews reached for stones to stone him to death, but Jesus answered them, "I have shown you many good things from the Father—for which of these do you intend to stone me?"

"We're not going to stone you for any good things," replied the Jews, "but for blasphemy: because you, who are only a man, are making yourself out to be God."

"Is it not written in your own Law," replied Jesus, " 'I have said ye are gods'? And if he called those men 'gods' to whom the word of God came (and the Scripture cannot be broken), can you say to the one whom the Father has consecrated and sent into the world, 'You are blaspheming' because I said, 'I am the Son of God'? If I fail to do what my Father does, then do not believe me. But if I do, even though you have no faith in me personally, then believe in the things that I do. Then you may come to know and realise that the Father is in me and I am in the Father."

And again they tried to arrest him, but he moved out of their reach.

Then Jesus went off again across the Jordan to the place where John had first baptised and there he stayed. A great many people came to him, and said, "John never gave us any sign but all that he said about this man was true."

And in that place many believed in him.

CHAPTER 11

Jesus shows his power over death

Now there was a man by the name of Lazarus who became seriously ill. He lived in Bethany, the village where Mary and her sister Martha lived. (Lazarus was the brother of the Mary who poured perfume upon the Lord and wiped his feet with her hair.) So the sisters sent word to Jesus: "Lord, your friend is very ill."

When Jesus received the message, he said, "This illness will not end in death; it will bring glory to God—for it will show the glory of the Son of God."

Now Jesus loved Martha and her sister and Lazarus. So when he heard of Lazarus' illness he stayed where he was two days longer. Only then did he say to the disciples, "Let us go back into Judaea."

"Rabbi!" returned the disciples, "only a few days ago, the Jews were trying to stone you to death—are you going there again?"

"There are twelve hours of daylight every day, are there not?" replied Jesus. "If a man walks in the daytime, he does not stumble, for he has the daylight to see by. But if he walks at night he stumbles, because he has no light to see by."

Jesus spoke these words; then after a pause he said to them, "Our friend Lazarus has fallen asleep, but I am going to wake him up."

At this, his disciples said, "Lord, if he has fallen asleep, he will be all right."

Actually Jesus had spoken about his death, but they thought that he was speaking about falling into natural sleep. This made Jesus tell them quite plainly, "Lazarus has died, and I am glad that I was not there—for your sakes, that you may learn to believe. And now, let us go to him."

Thomas (known as the Twin) then said to his fellow-disciples, "Come on, then, let us all go and die with him!"

When Jesus arrived, he found that Lazarus had already been in the grave four days. Now Bethany is quite near Jerusalem, rather less than two miles away, and many of the Jews had come out to see Martha and Mary to offer them sympathy over their brother's death. When Martha heard that Jesus was on his way, she went out and met him, while Mary stayed in the house.

"If only you had been here, Lord," said Martha, "my brother would never have died. And I know that, even now, God will give you whatever you ask from him."

"Your brother will rise again," Jesus replied to her.

"I know," said Martha, "that he will rise again in the resurrection on the last day."

"I myself am the resurrection and the life," Jesus told her. "The man who believes in me will live even though he dies, and anyone who is alive and believes in me will never die at all. Can you believe that?"

"Yes, Lord," replied Martha. "I do believe that you are Christ, the Son of God, the one who was to come into the world." Saying this she went away and called Mary her sister, whispering, "The master's here and is asking for you." When Mary heard this she sprang to her feet and went to him. Now Jesus had not yet arrived at the village itself, but was still where Martha had met him. So when the Jews who had been comforting Mary in the house saw her get up quickly and go out, they followed her, imagining that she was going to the grave to weep there.

When Mary met Jesus, she looked at him, and then fell down at his feet. "If only you had been here, Lord," she said, "my brother would never have died."

When Jesus saw Mary weep and noticed the tears of the Jews who came with her, he was deeply moved and visibly distressed.

"Where have you laid him?" he asked.

"Lord, come and see," they replied, and at this Jesus himself wept.

"Look how much he loved him!" remarked the Jews, though some of them asked, "Could he not have kept this man from dying if he could open that blind man's eyes?"

Jesus was again deeply moved, and went on to the grave. It was a cave, and a stone lay in front of it.

"Take away the stone," said Jesus.

"But Lord," said Martha, the dead man's sister, "he has been dead four days. By this time he will be decaying. . . ."

"Did I not tell you," replied Jesus, "that if you believed, you would see the wonder of what God can do?"

Then they took the stone away and Jesus raised his eyes and said, "Father, I thank you that you have heard me. I know that you always hear me, but I have said this for the sake of these people standing here so that they may believe that you have sent me."

And when he had said this, he called out in a loud voice, "Lazarus, come out!"

And the dead man came out, his hands and feet bound with grave-clothes and his face muffled with a handkerchief.

"Now unbind him," Jesus told them, "and let him go home."

Jesus' miracle leads to deadly hostility

After this many of the Jews who had accompanied Mary and observed what Jesus did, believed in him. But some of them went off to the Pharisees and told them what Jesus had done. Consequently, the chief priests and Pharisees summoned the council and said, "What can we do? This man obviously shows many remarkable signs. If we let him go on doing this sort of thing we shall have everybody believing in him. Then we shall have the Romans coming and that will be the end of our holy place and our very existence as a nation!"

But one of them, Caiaphas, who was High Priest that year, addressed the meeting: "You plainly don't understand what is involved here. You do not realise that it would be a good thing for us if one man should die for the sake of the people—instead of the whole nation being destroyed." (He did not make this remark on his own initiative but, since he was High Priest that year, he was in fact inspired to say that Jesus was going to die for the nation's sake—and in fact not for that nation only, but to bring together into one family all the children of God scattered throughout the world.) From that day then, they planned to kill him. As a consequence Jesus made no further public appearance among the Jews but went away to the countryside on the edge of the desert, and stayed with his disciples in a town called Ephraim. The Jewish Passover was approaching and many people went up from the country to Jerusalem before the actual Passover, to go through a ceremonial cleansing. They were looking for Jesus there and kept saying to one another as they stood in the Temple, "What do you think? Surely he won't come to the festival?"

It should be understood that the chief priests and the Pharisees had issued an order that anyone who knew of Jesus' whereabouts should tell them, so that they could arrest him.

CHAPTER 12

An act of love as the end approaches

SIX days before the Passover, Jesus came to Bethany, the village of Lazarus whom he had raised from the dead. They gave a supper for him there, and Martha waited on the party while Lazarus took his place at table with Jesus. Then Mary took a whole pound of very expensive perfume, pure nard, and anointed Jesus' feet and then wiped them with her hair. The entire house was filled with the fragrance of the perfume. But one of his disciples, Judas Iscariot (the man who was going to betray Jesus), burst out, "Why on earth wasn't this perfume sold? It's worth thirty pounds, which could have been given to the poor!"

He said this, not because he cared about the poor, but because he was dishonest, and when he was in charge of the purse used to help himself from the contents.

But Jesus replied to this outburst. "Let her alone, she has saved this for the day of my burial. You have the poor with you always —you will not always have me!"

The large crowd of Jews discovered that he was there and came to the scene—not only because of Jesus but to catch sight of Lazarus, the man whom he had raised from the dead. Then the chief priests planned to kill Lazarus as well, because he was the reason for many of the Jews' going away and putting their faith in Jesus.

Jesus experiences a temporary triumph

The next day, the great crowd who had come to the festival heard that Jesus was coming into Jerusalem, and went out to meet him with palm branches in their hands, shouting, "God save him! God bless the man who comes in the name of the Lord, God bless the king of Israel!"

For Jesus had found a young donkey and was seated upon it, just as the scripture foretold—

> Fear not, daughter of Zion: behold, thy king cometh, sitting on an ass's colt.

(The disciples did not realise the significance of what was happening at the time, but when Jesus was glorified, then they recollected that these things had been written about him and that they had carried them out for him.)

The people who had been with him, when he had summoned Lazarus from the grave and raised him from the dead, were continually talking about it. This accounts for the crowd who went out to meet him, for they had heard that he had given this sign. Seeing all this, the Pharisees remarked to one another, "You see?—There's nothing one can do! The whole world is running after him."

Among those who had come up to worship at the festival were some Greeks. They approached Philip (whose home town was Bethsaida in Galilee) with the request, "Sir, we want to see Jesus."

Philip went and told Andrew, and Andrew went with Philip and told Jesus.

Jesus told them, "The time has come for the Son of Man to be glorified. I tell you truly that unless a grain of wheat falls into the earth and dies, it remains a single grain of wheat; but if it dies, it brings a good harvest. The man who loves his own life will lose it, and the man who hates his life in this world will preserve it for eternal life. If a man wants to enter my service, he must follow my way; and where I am, my servant will also be. And my Father will honour every man who enters my service.

"Now comes my hour of heart-break, and what can I say, 'Father, save me from this hour'? No, it was for this very purpose that I came to this hour. 'Father, honour your own name!' "

At this there came a voice from Heaven, "I have honoured it and I will honour it again!"

When the crowd of bystanders heard this, they said it thundered, but some of them said, "An angel spoke to him."

Then Jesus said, "That voice came for your sake, not for mine. Now is the time for the judgment of this world to begin, and now will the spirit that rules this world be driven out. As for me, if I am lifted up from the earth, I will draw all men to myself." (He said this to show the kind of death he was going to die.)

Then the crowd said, "We have heard from the Law that Christ lives for ever. How can you say that the Son of Man must be 'lifted up'? Who is this Son of Man?"

At this, Jesus said to them, "You have the light with you only a little while longer. Go on while the light is good, before the darkness comes down upon you. For the man who walks in the dark has no idea where he is going. You must believe in the light while you have the light, that you may become the sons of light."

Jesus said all these things, and then went away, out of their sight. But though he had given so many signs, yet they did not believe in him, so that the prophecy of Isaiah was fulfilled, when he said,

> Lord, who hath believed our report?
> And to whom hath the arm of the Lord been revealed?

Thus, they could not believe, for Isaiah said again—

> He hath blinded their eyes, and he hardened their heart:
> Lest they should see with their eyes, and perceive with their heart,
> And should turn,
> And I should heal them.

Isaiah said these things because he saw the glory of Christ, and spoke about him. Nevertheless, many even of the authorities did believe in him. But they would not admit it for fear of the Pharisees, in case they should be excommunicated. They were more concerned to have the approval of men than to have the approval of God.

But later, Jesus cried aloud, "Every man who believes in me, is believing in the one who sent me rather than in me; and every man who sees me is seeing the one who sent me. I have come into the world as light, so that no one who believes in me need remain in the dark. Yet, if anyone hears my sayings and does not keep them, I do not judge him—for I did not come to judge the world but to save it. Every man who rejects me and will not accept my sayings has a judge—on the last day, the very words that I have spoken will be his judge. For I have not spoken on my own authority: the Father who sent me has commanded me what to say and how to speak. And I know that what he commands means eternal life. All that I say I speak only in accordance with what the Father has told me."

CHAPTER 13

Jesus teaches his disciples humility

BEFORE the festival of the Passover began, Jesus realised that the time had come for him to leave this world and return to the Father. He had loved those who were his own in this world and he loved them to the end. By supper-time, the devil had already put the thought of betraying Jesus into the mind of Judas Iscariot, Simon's son. Jesus, with the full knowledge that the Father had put everything into his hands and that he had come from God and was going to God, rose from the supper-table, took off his outer clothes, picked up a towel and fastened it round his waist. Then he poured water into a basin and began to wash the disciples' feet and to dry them with the towel around his waist.

So he came to Simon Peter, who said to him, "Lord, are you going to wash my feet?"

"You do not realise now what I am doing," replied Jesus, "but later on you will understand."

Then Peter said to him, "You must never wash my feet!"

"Unless you let me wash you, Peter," replied Jesus, "you cannot be my true partner."

"Then Lord," returned Simon Peter, "please—not just my feet but my hands and my face as well!"

"The man who has bathed," returned Jesus, "only needs to wash his feet to be clean all over. And you are clean—though not all of you."

(For Jesus knew his betrayer and that is why he said, "though not all of you".)

When Jesus had washed their feet and put on his clothes, he sat down again and spoke to them, "Do you realise what I have just done to you? You call me 'teacher' and 'Lord' and you are quite right, for I am your teacher and your Lord. But if I, your teacher and Lord, have washed your feet, you must be ready to wash one another's feet. I have given you this as an example so that you may do as I have done. Believe me, the servant is not greater than his master and the messenger is not greater than the man who sent him. Once you have realised these things, you will find your happiness in doing them.

Jesus foretells his betrayal

"I am not speaking about all of you—I know the men I have chosen. But let this scripture be fulfilled—

He that eateth my bread lifted up his heel against me.

From now onwards, I shall tell you about things before they happen, so that when they do happen, you may believe that I am the one I claim to be. I tell you truly that anyone who accepts my messenger will be accepting me, and anyone who accepts me will be accepting the One who sent me."

After Jesus had said this, he was clearly in anguish of soul, and he added, solemnly

"I tell you plainly, one of you is going to betray me."

At this the disciples stared at each other, completely mystified as to whom he could mean. And it happened that one of them, whom Jesus loved, was sitting very close to him. So Simon Peter nodded to this man and said, "Tell us who he means."

He simply leaned forward on Jesus' shoulder, and asked, "Lord, who is it?"

And Jesus answered, "It is the one I am going to give this piece of bread to, after I have dipped it in the dish."

Then he took a piece of bread, dipped it in the dish and gave it to Simon's son, Judas Iscariot. After he had taken the piece of bread, Satan entered his heart. Then Jesus said to him, "Be quick about your business!"

No one else at table knew what he meant in telling him this. Indeed, some of them thought that, since Judas had charge of the purse, Jesus was telling him to buy what they needed for the festival, or that he should give something to the poor. So Judas took the piece of bread and went out quickly—into the night.

When he had gone, Jesus spoke, "Now comes the glory of the Son of Man, and the glory of God in him! If God is glorified through him then God will glorify the Son of Man—and that without delay. Oh, my children, I am with you such a short time! You will look for me and I have to tell you as I told the Jews, 'Where I am going, you cannot follow.' Now I am giving you a new command—love one another. Just as I have loved you, so you must love one another. This is how all men will know that you are my disciples, because you have such love for one another."

Simon Peter said to him, "Lord, where are you going?"

"I am going," replied Jesus, "where you cannot follow me now, though you will follow me later."

"Lord, why can't I follow you now?" said Peter. "I would lay down my life for you!"

"Would you lay down your life for me?" replied Jesus. "Believe me, you will disown me three times before the cock crows!"

CHAPTER 14

Jesus reveals spiritual truths

"You must not let yourselves be distressed—you must hold on to your faith in God and to your faith in me. There are many rooms in my Father's House. If there were not, should I have told you that I am going away to prepare a place for you? It is true that I am going away to prepare a place for you, but it is just as true that I am coming again to welcome you into my own home, so that you may be where I am. You know where I am going and you know the way I am going to take."

"Lord," Thomas remonstrated, "we do not know where you're going, and how can we know what way you're going to take?"

"I myself am the way," replied Jesus, "and the truth and the life. No one approaches the Father except through me. If you had known who I am, you would have known my Father. From now on, you do know him and you have seen him."

Jesus explains his relationship with the Father

Then Philip said to him, "Show us the Father, Lord, and we shall be satisfied."

"Have I been so long with you," returned Jesus, "without your really knowing me, Philip? The man who has seen me has seen the Father. How can you say, 'Show us the Father'? Do you not believe that I am in the Father and the Father is in me? The very words I say to you are not my own. It is the Father who lives in me who carries out his work through me. You must believe me when I say that I am in the Father and the Father is in me. But if you cannot, then believe me because of what you have seen me do. I assure you that the man who believes in me will do the same things that I have done, yes, and he will do even greater things than these, for I am going away to the Father. Whatever you ask the Father in my name, I will do—that the Son may bring glory to the Father. And if you ask me anything in my name, I will grant it.

Jesus promises the Spirit

"If you really love me, you will keep the commandments I have given you and I shall ask the Father to give you Someone else to stand by you, to be with you always. I mean the Spirit of truth, whom the world cannot accept, for it can neither see nor recognise that Spirit. But you recognise him, for he is with you now and is in your hearts. I am not going to leave you alone in the world—I am coming to you. In a very little while, the world will see me no more but you will see me, because I am really alive and you will be alive too. When that day comes, you will realise that I am in my Father, that you are in me, and I am in you.

"Every man who knows my commandments and obeys them is the man who really loves me, and every man who really loves me will himself be loved by my Father, and I too will love him and make myself known to him."

Then Judas (not Iscariot) said, "Lord, how is it that you are going to make yourself known to us but not to the world?"

And to this Jesus replied, "When a man loves me, he follows my teaching. Then my Father will love him, and we will come to that man and make our home within him. The man who does not really love me will not follow my teaching. Indeed, what you are hearing from me now is not really my saying, but comes from the Father who sent me.

"I have said all this while I am still with you. But the one who is coming to stand by you, the Holy Spirit whom the Father will send in my name, will be your teacher and will bring to your minds all that I have said to you.

"I leave behind with you—peace; I give you my own peace and my gift is nothing like the peace of this world. You must not be distressed and you must not be daunted. You have heard me say, 'I am going away and I am coming back to you.' If you really loved me, you would be glad because I am going to my Father, for the Father is greater than I. And I have told you of it now, before it happens, so that when it does happen, your faith in me will not be shaken. I shall not be able to talk much longer to you, for the spirit that rules this world is coming very close. He has no hold over me, but I go on my way to show the world that I love the Father and do what he sent me to do. . . . Get up now! Let us leave this place.

CHAPTER 15

Jesus teaches union with himself

"I AM the real vine, my Father is the vine-dresser. He removes any of my branches which is not bearing fruit and he prunes every branch that does bear fruit to increase its yield. Now, you have already been pruned by my words. You must go on growing in me and I will grow in you. For just as the branch cannot bear any fruit unless it shares the life of the vine, so you can produce nothing unless you go on growing in me. I am the vine itself, you are the branches. It is the man who shares my life and whose life I share who proves fruitful. For apart from me you can do nothing at all. The man who does not share my life is like a branch that is broken off and withers away. He becomes just like the dry sticks that men collect and use for firewood. But if you live your life in me, and my words live in your hearts, you can ask for whatever you like and it will come true for you. This is how my Father will be glorified—in your becoming fruitful and being my disciples.

"I have loved you just as the Father has loved me. You must go on living in my love. If you keep my commandments you will live in my love just as I have kept my Father's commandments and live in his love. I have told you this so that you can share my joy, and that your joy may be complete. This is my commandment: that you love each other as I have loved you. There is no greater love than this—that a man should lay down his life for his friends. You are my friends if you do what I tell you to do. I shall not call you servants any longer, for a servant does not share his master's confidence. No, I call you friends, now, because I have told you everything that I have heard from the Father.

"It is not that you have chosen me; but it is I who have chosen you. I have appointed you to go and bear fruit that will be lasting; so that whatever you ask the Father in my name, he will give it to you.

Jesus speaks of the world's hatred

"This I command you, love one another! If the world hates you, you know that it hated me first. If you belonged to the world, the world would love its own. But because you do not belong to the world and I have chosen you out of it, the world will hate you. Do you remember what I said to you, 'The servant is not greater than his master'? If they have persecuted me, they will persecute you as well, but if they have followed my teaching, they will also follow yours. They will do all these things to you as my disciples because they do not know the One who sent me. If I had not come and spoken to them, they would not have been guilty of sin, but now they have no excuse for their sin. The man who hates me, hates my Father as well. If I had not done among them things that no other man has ever done, they would not have been guilty of sin, but as it is they have seen and they have hated both me and my Father. Yet this only fulfils what is written in their Law—

They hated me without a cause.

But when the Helper comes, that is, the Spirit of truth, who comes from the Father and whom I myself will send to you from the Father, he will speak plainly about me. And you yourselves will also speak plainly about me for you have been with me from the first.

CHAPTER 16

Jesus speaks of the future without his bodily presence

"I HAVE told you this now so that your faith in me may not be shaken. They will excommunicate you from their synagogues. Yes, the time is coming when a man who kills you will think he is thereby serving God! They will act like this because they have never had any true knowledge of the Father or of me, but I have told you all this so that when the time comes for such things to happen you may remember that I told you about them. I have not spoken like this to you before, because I have been with you; but now the time has come for me to go away to the One who sent me. None of you asks me, 'Where are you going?' That is because you are so distressed at what I have told you. Yet I am telling you the simple truth when I assure you that it is a good thing for you that I should go away. For if I did not go away, the divine Helper would not come to you. But if I go, then I will send him to you. When he comes, he will convince the world of the meaning of sin, of true goodness and of judgment. He will expose their sin because they do not believe in me; he will reveal true goodness for I am going away to the Father and you will see me no longer; and he will show them the meaning of judgment, for the spirit which rules this world will have been judged.

"I have much more to tell you but you cannot bear it now. Yet when that one I have spoken to you about comes—the Spirit of truth—he will guide you into everything that is true. For he will not be speaking of his own accord but exactly as he hears, and he will inform you about what is to come. He will bring glory to me for he will draw on my truth and reveal it to you. Whatever the Father possesses is also mine; that is why I tell you that he will draw on my truth and will show it to you.

The disciples are puzzled: Jesus explains

"In a little while you will not see me any longer, and again, in a little while you will see me."

At this some of his disciples remarked to each other, "What is this that he tells us now, 'A little while and you will not see me, and again, in a little while you will see me' and 'for I am going away to the Father'? What is this 'little while' that he talks about?" they were saying. "We simply do not know what he means!"

Jesus knew that they wanted to ask him what he meant, so he said to them, "Are you trying to find out from each other what I meant when I said, 'In a little while you will not see me, and again, in a little while you will see me'? I tell you truly that you are going to be both sad and sorry while the world is glad. Yes, you will be deeply distressed, but your grief will turn into joy. When a woman gives birth to a child, she knows grievous pain when her time comes. Yet as soon as she has given birth to the child, she no longer remembers her agony for joy that a man has been born into the world. Now you are going through pain, but I shall see you again and your hearts will thrill with joy—the joy that no one can take away from you—and on that day you will not ask me any questions.

"I assure you that whatever you ask the Father he will give you in my name. Up to now you have asked nothing in my name; ask, and you will receive, that your joy may be overflowing.

Jesus speaks further of the future

"I have been speaking to you in parables—but the time is coming to give up parables and tell you plainly about the Father. When that day comes, you will make your requests to him in my name, for I need make no promise to plead to the Father for you, for the Father himself loves you, because you have loved me and have believed that I came from God. Yes, I did come from the Father and I came into the world. Now I leave the world behind and return to the Father."

"Now you are speaking plainly," cried the disciples, "and are not using parables. Now we know that everything is known to you—no more questions are needed. This make us sure that you did come from God."

"So you believe in me now?" replied Jesus. "The time is coming, indeed, it has already come, when you will be scattered, every one of you going home and leaving me alone. Yet I am not really alone, for the Father is with me. I have told you all this so that you may find your peace in me. You will find trouble in the world—but, never lose heart, I have conquered the world!"

CHAPTER 17

Jesus' prayer for his disciples—present and future

When Jesus had said these words, he raised his eyes to Heaven and said, "Father, the hour has come. Glorify your Son now so that he may bring glory to you, for you have given him authority over all men to give eternal life to all that you have given to him. And this is eternal life, to know you, the only true God, and him whom you have sent—Jesus Christ.

"I have brought you honour upon earth, I have completed the task which you gave me to do. Now, Father, honour me in your own presence with the glory that I knew with you before the world was made. I have shown your self to the men whom you gave me from the world. They were your men and you gave them to me, and they have accepted your word. Now they realise that all that you have given me comes from you—and that every message which you gave me I have given them. They have accepted it all and have come to know in their hearts that I did come from you—they are convinced that you sent me.

"I am praying to you for them: I am not praying for the world but for the men whom you gave me, for they are yours—everything that is mine is yours and yours mine—and they have done me honour. Now I am no longer in the world, but they are in the world and I am returning to you. Holy Father, keep the men you gave me by your power that they may be one, as we are one. As long as I was with them, I kept them by the power that you gave me; I guarded them, and not one of them has been lost, except the son of destruction—that the scripture might come true.

"And now I come to you and I say these things in the world that these men may find my joy completed in themselves. I have given them your word, and the world has hated them, for they are no more sons of the world than I am. I am not praying that you will take them out of the world but that you will keep them from the evil one. They are no more the sons of the world than I am—make them holy by the truth; for your word is the truth. I have sent them to the world just as you sent me to the world and I consecrated myself for their sakes that they may be made holy by the truth.

"I am not praying only for these men but for all those who will believe in me through their message, that they may all be one.

Just as you, Father, live in me and I live in you, I am asking that they may live in us, and that the world may believe that you did send me. I have given them the honour that you gave me, that they may be one, as we are one—I in them and you in me, that they may grow complete into one, so that the world may realise that you sent me and have loved them as you loved me. Father, I want those whom you have given me to be with me where I am; I want them to see that glory which you have made mine—for you loved me before the world began. Father of all goodness the world has not known you, but I have known you and these men now know that you have sent me. I have made your self known to them and I will continue to do so that the love which you have had for me may be in their hearts—and that I may be there also."

CHAPTER 18

Jesus is arrested in the garden

WHEN Jesus had spoken these words, he went out with his disciples across the Cedron valley to a place where there was a garden, and they went into it together. Judas who betrayed him knew the place, for Jesus often met his disciples there. So Judas fetched the guard and the officers which the chief priests and Pharisees had provided for him, and came to the place with torches and lanterns and weapons. Jesus, fully realising all that was going to happen to him, went forward and said to them, "Who are you looking for?"

"Jesus of Nazareth," they answered.

"I am the man," said Jesus. (Judas who was betraying him was standing there with the others.)

When he said to them, "I am the man", they retreated and fell to the ground. So Jesus asked them again, "Who are you looking for?"

And again they said, "Jesus of Nazareth."

"I have told you that I am the man," replied Jesus. "If I am the man you are looking for, let these others go." (Thus fulfilling his previous words, "I have not lost one of those whom you gave me.")

At this, Simon Peter, who had a sword, drew it and slashed at the High Priest's servant, cutting off his right ear. (The servant's name was Malchus.) But Jesus said to Peter, "Put your sword back into its sheath. Am I not to drink the cup the Father has given me?"

Peter follows Jesus, only to deny him

Then the guard, with their captain and the Jewish Officers, took hold of Jesus and tied his hands together, and led him off first to Annas, for he was father-in-law to Caiaphas, who was High Priest that year. Caiaphas was the man who advised the Jews, "that it would be a good thing that one man should die for the sake of the people". Behind Jesus followed Simon Peter, and one other disciple who was known personally to the High Priest. He went in with Jesus into the High Priest's courtyard, but Peter was left standing at the door outside. So this other disciple, who was acquainted with the High Priest, went out and spoke to the door-keeper, and brought Peter inside. The young woman at the door remarked to Peter, "Are you one of this man's disciples, too?"

"No, I am not," retorted Peter.

In the courtyard, the servants and officers stood around a charcoal fire which they had made, for it was cold. They were warming themselves, and Peter stood there with them, keeping himself warm.

Meanwhile the High Priest interrogated Jesus about his disciples and about his own teaching.

"I have always spoken quite openly to the world," replied Jesus. "I have always taught in the synagogue or in the Temple-precincts where all Jews meet together, and I have said nothing in secret. Why do you question me? Why not question those who have heard me about what I said to them? Obviously they are the ones who know what I actually said."

As he said this, one of those present, an officer, slapped Jesus with his open hand, remarking, "Is that the way for you to answer the High Priest?"

"If I have said anything wrong," Jesus said to him, "you must give evidence about it, but if what I said was true, why do you strike me?"

Then Annas sent him, with his hands still tied, to the High priest Caiaphas.

Peter's denial

In the meantime Simon Peter was still standing, keeping himself warm. Some of them said to him, "Surely you too are one of his disciples, aren't you?"

The body of Jesus is removed

As it was the day of preparation for the Passover, the Jews wanted to avoid the bodies being left on the crosses over the Sabbath (for that was a particularly important Sabbath), and they requested Pilate to have the men's legs broken and the bodies removed. So the soldiers went and broke the legs of the first man and of the other who was crucified with Jesus. But when they came to him, they saw that he was dead already and they did not break his legs. But one of the soldiers pierced his side with a spear, and at once there was an outrush of blood and water. And the man who saw this is our witness: his evidence is true. He is certain that he is speaking the truth, so that you may believe as well. For this happened to fulfil the scripture,

> A bone of him shall not be broken.

And again another scripture says—

> They shall look on him whom they pierced.

After it was all over, Joseph (who came from Arimathaea and was a disciple of Jesus, though secretly for fear of the Jews) requested Pilate that he might take away Jesus' body, and Pilate gave him permission. So he came and took his body down. Nicodemus also, the man who had come to him at the beginning by night, arrived bringing a mixture of myrrh and aloes, weighing about a hundred pounds. So they took his body and wound it round with linen strips with the spices, according to the Jewish custom of preparing a body for burial. In the place where he was crucified, there was a garden containing a new tomb in which nobody had yet been laid. Because it was the preparation day and because the tomb was conveniently near, they laid Jesus in this tomb.

CHAPTER 20

The first day of the week: the risen Lord

But on the first day of the week, Mary of Magdala arrived at the tomb, very early in the morning, while it was still dark, and noticed that the stone had been taken away from the tomb. At this she ran, found Simon Peter and the other disciple whom Jesus loved, and told them, "They have taken the Lord out of the tomb and we don't know where they have laid him."

Peter and the other disciple set off at once for the tomb, the two of them running together. The other disciple ran faster than

And he denied it and said, "No I am not."

Then one of the High Priest's servants, a relation of the man whose ear Peter had cut off, remarked, "Didn't I see you in the garden with him?"

And again Peter denied it. And immediately the cock crew.

Jesus is taken before the Roman authority

Then they led Jesus from Caiaphas' presence into the palace. It was now early morning and the Jews themselves did not go into the palace, for fear that they would be contaminated and would not be able to eat the Passover. So Pilate walked out to them and said, "What is the charge that you are bringing against this man?"

"If he were not an evil-doer, we should not have handed him over to you," they replied.

To which Pilate retorted, "Then take him yourselves and judge him according to your law."

"We are not allowed to put a man to death," replied the Jews (thus fulfilling Christ's prophecy of the method of his own death).

So Pilate went back into the palace and called Jesus to him. "Are you the king of the Jews?" he asked.

"Are you asking this of your own accord," replied Jesus, "or have other people spoken to you about me?"

"Do you think *I* am a Jew?" replied Pilate. "It's your people and your chief priests who handed you over to me. What have you done, anyway?"

"My kingdom is not founded in this world—if it were, my servants would have fought to prevent my being handed over to the Jews. But in fact my kingdom is not founded on all this!"

"So you are a king, are you?" returned Pilate.

"You say that I am a king," Jesus replied; "the reason for my birth and the reason for my coming into the world is to witness to the truth. Every man who loves truth recognises my voice."

To which Pilate retorted, "What is 'truth'?" and went straight out again to the Jews and said:

"I find nothing criminal about him at all. But I have an arrangement with you to set one prisoner free at Passover time. Do you wish me then to set free for you the 'king of the Jews'?"

At this, they shouted at the top of their voices, "No, not this man, but Barabbas!"

Barabbas was a bandit.

CHAPTER 19

Pilate's vain efforts to save Jesus

THEN Pilate took Jesus and had him flogged, and the soldiers twisted thorn-twigs into a crown and put it on his head, threw a purple robe around him and kept coming into his presence, saying, "Hail, king of the Jews!" And then they slapped him with their open hands.

Then Pilate went outside again and said to them, "Look, I bring him out before you here, to show that I find nothing criminal about him at all."

And at this Jesus came outside too, wearing the thorn crown and the purple robe.

"Look," said Pilate, "here's the man!"

The sight of him made the chief priests and Jewish officers shout at the top of their voices, "Crucify! Crucify!"

"You take him and crucify him," retorted Pilate, "He's no criminal as far as I can see!"

The Jews answered him, "we have a Law, and according to that Law, he must die, for he made himself out to be Son of God!"

When Pilate heard them say this, he became much more uneasy, and returned to the palace and again spoke to Jesus, "Where *do* you come from?"

But Jesus gave him no reply. So Pilate said to him, "Won't you speak to me? Don't you realise that I have the power to set you free, and I have the power to have you crucified?"

"You have no power at all against me," replied Jesus, "except what was given to you from above. And for that reason the one who handed me over to you is even more guilty than you are."

From that moment, Pilate tried hard to set him free but the Jews were yelling, "If you set this man free, you are no friend of Caesar! Anyone who makes himself out to be a king is anti-Caesar!"

When Pilate heard this, he led Jesus outside and sat down upon the Judgment-seat in the place called the Pavement (in Hebrew, Gabbatha). It was the preparation day of the Passover and it was now about midday. Pilate now said to the Jews, "Look, here's your king!"

At which they yelled, "Take him away, take him away, crucify him!"

"Am I to crucify your king?" Pilate asked them.

"Caesar is our king and no one else," replied the chief priests. And at this Pilate handed Jesus over to them for crucifixion.

The crucifixion

So they took Jesus and he went out carrying the cross himself, to a place called Skull Hill (in Hebrew, Golgotha). There they crucified him, and two others, one on either side of him with Jesus in the middle. Pilate had a placard written out and put on the cross, reading, JESUS OF NAZARETH, THE KING OF THE JEWS. This placard was read by many of the Jews because the place where Jesus was crucified was quite near Jerusalem, and it was written in Hebrew as well as in Latin and Greek. So the chief priests said to Pilate, "You should not write 'The King of the Jews', but 'This man said, I am King of the Jews.' "

To which Pilate retorted, "What I have written, I have written."

When the soldiers had crucified Jesus, they divided his clothes between them, taking a quarter-share each. There remained his tunic, which was seamless—woven in one piece from the top to the bottom. So they said to each other, "Don't let us tear it; let's draw lots and see who gets it."

This happened to fulfil the scripture which says—

They parted my garments among them,
And upon my vesture did they cast lots.

Jesus provides for his mother from the cross

While the soldiers were doing this, Jesus' mother was standing near his cross with her sister, and with them Mary, the wife of Clopas, and Mary of Magdala. Jesus saw his mother and the disciple whom he loved standing by her side, and said to her, "Mother, there is your son!" And then he said to the disciple, "And there is your mother!"

And from that time the disciple took Mary into his own home.

After this, Jesus realising that everything was now completed, said (fulfilling the saying of scripture), "I am thirsty."

There was a bowl of sour wine standing there. So they soaked a sponge in the wine, put it on a spear, and pushed it up towards his mouth. When Jesus had taken it, he cried, "It is finished!" his head fell forward, and he breathed his last breath.

Peter and was the first to arrive at the tomb. He stooped and looked inside and saw the linen cloths lying there but did not go in himself. Hard on his heels came Simon Peter and went straight into the tomb. He noticed that the linen cloths were lying there, and that the handkerchief, which had been round Jesus' head, was not lying with the linen cloths but was rolled up by itself, a little way apart. Then the other disciple, who was the first to arrive at the tomb, came inside as well, saw what had happened and believed. (They did not yet understand the scripture which said that he must rise from the dead.) So the disciples went back again to their homes.

But Mary stood just outside the tomb, and she was crying. And as she cried, she looked into the tomb and saw two angels in white who sat, one at the head and the other at the foot of the place where the body of Jesus had lain.

The angels spoke to her, "Why are you crying?" they asked.

"Because they have taken away my Lord, and I don't know where they have laid him!" she said.

With these words she turned and noticed Jesus standing there, without realising that it was Jesus.

"Why are you crying?" said Jesus to her. "Who are you looking for?"

She, supposing that he was the gardener, said, "Oh, sir, if you have carried him away, please tell me where you have laid him and I will take him away."

Jesus said to her, "Mary!"

At this she turned right round and said to him, in Hebrew, "Master!"

"No!" said Jesus, "do not hold me now. I have not yet gone up to the Father. Go and tell my brothers that I am going up to my Father and your Father, to my God and your God."

And Mary of Magdala went off to the disciples, with the news, "I have seen the Lord!", and she told them what he had said to her.

In the evening of that first day of the week, the disciples had met together with the doors locked for fear of the Jews. Jesus came and stood right in the middle of them and said, "Peace be with you!"

Then he showed them his hands and his side, and when they saw the Lord the disciples were overjoyed.

Jesus said to them again, "Yes, peace be with you! Just as the Father sent me, so I am now going to send you."

And then he breathed upon them and said, "Receive the Holy Spirit. If you forgive any men's sins, they are forgiven, and if you hold them unforgiven, they are unforgiven."

The risen Jesus and Thomas

But one of the twelve, Thomas (called the Twin), was not with them when Jesus came. The other disciples kept on telling him, "We have seen the Lord," but he replied, "Unless I see in his own hands the mark of the nails, and put my finger where the nails were, and put my hand into his side, I will never believe!"

Just over a week later, the disciples were indoors again and Thomas was with them. The doors were locked, but Jesus came and stood in the middle of them and said, "Peace be with you!"

Then he said to Thomas, "Put your finger here—look, here are my hands. Take your hand and put it in my side. You must not doubt, but believe."

"My Lord and my God!" cried Thomas.

"Is it because you have seen me that you believe?" Jesus said to him. "Happy are those who have never seen me and yet have believed!"

Jesus gave a great many other signs in the presence of his disciples which are not recorded in this book. But these have been written so that you may believe that Jesus is Christ, the Son of God, and that in that faith you may have life through his name.

CHAPTER 21

The risen Jesus and Peter

LATER on, Jesus showed himself again to his disciples on the shore of Lake Tiberias, and he did it in this way. Simon Peter, Thomas (called the Twin), Nathanael from Cana of Galilee, the sons of Zebedee and two other disciples were together, when Simon Peter said,

"I'm going fishing."

"All right," they replied, "we'll go with you."

So they went out and got into the boat and during the night caught nothing at all. But just as dawn began to break, Jesus stood there on the beach, although the disciples had no idea that it was Jesus.

"Have you caught anything, lads?" Jesus called out to them.

"No," they replied.

"Throw the net on the right side of the boat," said Jesus, "and you'll have a catch."

So they threw out the net and found that they were now not strong enough to pull it in because it was so full of fish! At this, the disciple that Jesus loved said to Peter, "It is the Lord!"

Hearing this, Peter slipped on his clothes, for he had been naked, and plunged into the sea. The other disciples followed in the boat, for they were only about a hundred yards from the shore, dragging in the net full of fish. When they had landed, they saw that a charcoal fire was burning, with a fish placed on it, and some bread. Jesus said to them, "Bring me some of the fish you've just caught."

So Simon Peter got into the boat and hauled the net ashore full of large fish, one hundred and fifty-three altogether. But in spite of the large number the net was not torn.

Then Jesus said to them, "Come and have your breakfast."

None of the disciples dared to ask him who he was; they knew it was the Lord.

Jesus went and took the bread and gave it to them and gave them all fish as well. This was now the third time that Jesus showed himself to his disciples after his resurrection from the dead.

When they had finished breakfast Jesus said to Simon Peter, "Simon, son of John, do you love me more than these others?"

"Yes, Lord," he replied, "you know that I am your friend."

"Then feed my lambs," returned Jesus. Then he said for the second time.

"Simon, son of John, do you love me?"

"Yes, Lord," returned Peter. "You know that I am your friend."

"Then care for my sheep," replied Jesus. Then for the third time, Jesus spoke to him and said,

"Simon, son of John, *are* you my friend?"

Peter was deeply hurt because Jesus' third question to him was "Are you my friend?", and he said, "Lord, you know everything. You know that I am your friend!"

"Then feed my sheep," Jesus said to him. "I tell you truly, Peter, that when you were younger, you used to dress yourself and go where you liked, but when you are an old man, you are going to stretch out your hands and someone else will dress you and take you where you do not want to go."

(He said this to show the kind of death by which Peter was going to honour God.)

Then Jesus said to him, "You must follow me."

Then Peter turned round and noticed the disciple whom Jesus loved following behind them. (He was the one who had his head on Jesus' shoulder at supper and had asked, "Lord, who is the one who is going to betray you?") So he said, "Yes, Lord, but what about him?"

"If it is my wish," returned Jesus, "for him to stay until I come, is that your business, Peter? You must follow me."

This gave rise to the saying among the brothers that this disciple would not die. Yet, of course, Jesus did not say, "He will not die", but simply, "If it is my wish for him to stay until I come, is that your business?"

All the above was written by an eye-witness

Now it is this same disciple who is hereby giving his testimony to these things and has written them down. We know that his witness is reliable. Of course, there are many other things which Jesus did, and I suppose that if each one were written down in detail, there would not be room in the whole world for all the books that would have to be written.

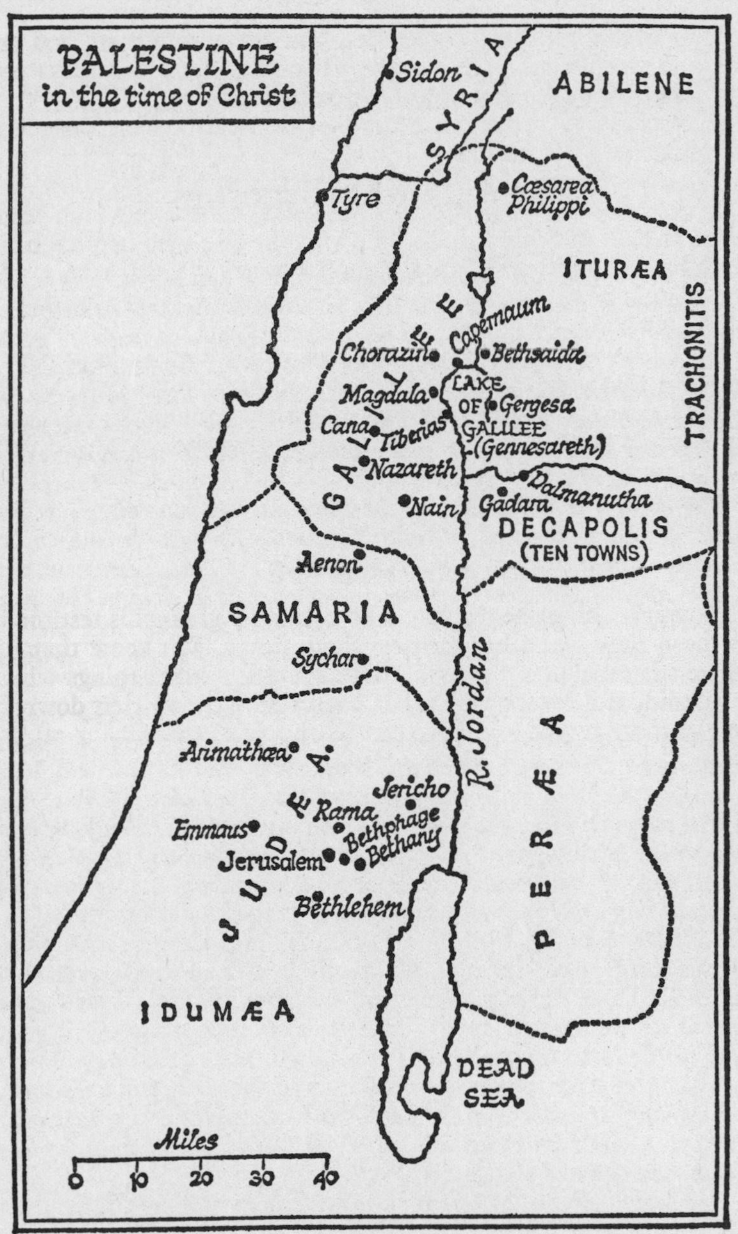
PALESTINE
in the time of Christ
Sidon
SYRIA
ABILENE
Tyre
Cæsarea Philippi
ITURÆA
TRACHONITIS
GALILEE
Capernaum
Chorazin
Bethsaida
Magdala
LAKE OF GALILEE (Gennesareth)
Gergesa
Cana
Tiberias
Nazareth
Dalmanutha
Nain
Gadara
DECAPOLIS
(TEN TOWNS)
Aenon
SAMARIA
Sychar
R. Jordan
Arimathæa
JUDÆA
PERÆA
Jericho
Rama
Bethphage
Emmaus
Bethany
Jerusalem
Bethlehem
IDUMÆA
DEAD SEA
Miles
0
10
20
30
40

THE YOUNG CHURCH IN ACTION

The Acts of the Apostles

The above, which is the conventional title of this remarkable book, is something of a mistranslation. The Greek title, Praxeis Apostolon, *has no definite articles and could be translated more accurately* "Acts of Apostles", *or, quite fairly,* "Some Acts of Some Apostles". *The author, who is unquestionably Luke, makes no attempt to give an exhaustive history of the early days of the Church—much as we may wish he had done so—but he does record with vividness and accuracy* some *actions of* some *Apostles.*

The book is characterised by the same easy-flowing Greek as the third Gospel, its vocabulary containing some fifty words common to these two works, but not found elsewhere in the New Testament. As in his Gospel Luke shows the same deep interest in women, the same sympathy for the sick and poor, and the same concern for the Gentiles. There is also the same doctor's precision in the use of medical language.

Luke's sources of information were probably first-class. The deacon Philip was still living at Caesarea during the two years of Paul's captivity at Rome with which this book closes, and Luke would have been able to obtain much early information from him. There would also be many still living who were present on the day of Pentecost and who would have supplied information about those early days. In the latter part of the book Luke is obviously making use of his own personal diaries. The first person plural is used quite naturally (16, *10–17;* 20, *5 to* 21, *18;* 27, *1 to* 28, *16*) *and the narrative gains in dramatic power through the reader's sudden realisation that the author was actually present at the time. Indeed, Luke's close association with Paul, an association which meant sharing a good deal of the latter's dangers and fatigues, is not the least of Luke's qualifications as an author of a book such as this. It is rash to surmise, but humanly speaking, the Gospel for all men might easily have been confined to Jews and Gentile proselytes if it had not been for the vision, courage and tenacity of Paul.*

The period covered by this book is roughly from 30 *to* 63, *i.e. from the Ascension of Christ to Paul's imprisonment at Rome. It is a fascinating guess, though no more than a guess, that Luke intended to write a third work, for the present book ends on a triumphant but rather unfinished note. Possibly Luke was never able to complete the story, possibly the work never got beyond the notes of events which he almost certainly took, possibly the work is irretrievably lost. Or, of course, the existence of such a work may be a wild guess with no foundation at all. Nevertheless readers of this book may feel, as I do, not only a hunger for more, but a sense that the author had not fully finished the history he set out to write.*

Luke is a careful historian and his geographical as well as his historical accuracy should be noted. He has a sound knowledge of Roman government and procedure. Although it cannot be proved, there is at least a likelihood that he was a Greek-speaking Gentile, converted under the ministry of Paul and Barnabas at Antioch.

It is most difficult to assign a date to this work. Some incline to the belief that it was written shortly after the closing date mentioned in the book, which would put it as early as 65. *Others are convinced that it was written after the fall of Jerusalem* (70), *and others again that Luke must have had access to Josephus' "Jewish Antiquities", which did not appear till* 94. *I myself am inclined to place the date not very long after Paul's two-year imprisonment, possibly in* 65 *or* 66.

CHAPTER 1

Introduction

MY DEAR THEOPHILUS,

In my first book I gave you some account of all that Jesus began to do and teach until the time of his ascension. Before he ascended he gave his instructions, through the Holy Spirit, to the messengers of his choice. For after his suffering he showed himself alive to them in many convincing ways, and appeared to them repeatedly over a period of forty days talking with them about the affairs of the kingdom of God.

Jesus' parting words before his ascension

On one occasion, while he was eating a meal with them, he emphasised that they were not to leave Jerusalem, but to wait for the Father's promise.

"You have already heard me speak about this," he said, "for

John used to baptise with water, but before many days are passed you will be baptised with the Holy Spirit."

This naturally brought them all together, and they asked him,

"Lord, is this the time when you are going to restore the kingdom to Israel?"

To this he replied,

"You cannot know times and dates which have been fixed by the Father's sole authority. But you are to be given power when the Holy Spirit has come to you. You will be witnesses to me, not only in Jerusalem, not only throughout Judaea, not only in Samaria, but to the very ends of the earth."

When he had said these words he was lifted up before their eyes till a cloud hid him from their sight. While they were still gazing up into the sky as he went, suddenly two men dressed in white stood beside them and said,

"Men of Galilee, why are you standing here looking up into the sky? This very Jesus who has been taken up from you into Heaven will come back in just the same way as you have seen him go."

At this they returned to Jerusalem from the Mount of Olives which is near the city, only a sabbath day's journey away. On entering Jerusalem they went straight to the upstairs room where they had been staying. There were Peter, John, James, Andrew, Philip, Thomas, Bartholomew, Matthew, James the son of Alphaeus, Simon the Nationalist, and Judas the son of James. By common consent all these men, together with the women who had followed Jesus, Mary his mother, as well as his brothers, devoted themselves to prayer.

Judas' place is filled

It was during this period that Peter stood up among the brothers —there were about a hundred and twenty present at the time— and said,

"My brothers, the prophecy of scripture given through the Holy Spirit by the lips of David concerning Judas was bound to come true. He was the man who acted as guide to those who arrested Jesus, though he was one of our number and he had a share in this ministry of ours."

(This man had bought a piece of land with the price of his treachery, but his body swelled up and ruptured, so that his intestines poured out. This fact became well known to all the residents of Jerusalem so that the piece of land came to be called in their language Akeldama, which means Field of Blood.) "Now it is written in the book of psalms of such a man:

> Let his habitation be made desolate,
> And let no man dwell therein:

and

> His office let another take.

"It becomes necessary then that whoever joins us must be someone who has been in our company during the whole time that the Lord Jesus lived his life with us, from the beginning when John baptised him until the day when he was taken up from us. This man must be an eye-witness with us to the resurrection of Jesus."

Two men were put forward, Joseph called Barsabas who was also called Justus, and Matthias. Then they prayed,

"Thou Lord, who knowest the hearts of all men, show us which of these two thou hast chosen to accept the ministry of an apostle which Judas forfeited to go where he belonged."

Then they drew lots for these men, and the lot fell to Matthias, and thereafter he was considered equally an apostle with the eleven.

CHAPTER 2

The first Pentecost for the young Church

THEN when the actual day of Pentecost came they were all assembled together. Suddenly there was a sound from heaven like the rushing of a violent wind, and it filled the whole house where they were seated. Before their eyes appeared tongues like flames, which separated off and settled upon each one of them. They were all filled with the Holy Spirit and began to speak in different languages as the Spirit gave them power to proclaim the message.

The Church's first impact on devout Jews

Now there were living in Jerusalem Jews of deep faith from every nation of the world. When they heard this sound a crowd quickly collected and were completely bewildered because each one of them heard these men speaking in his own language. They were absolutely amazed and said in their astonishment,

"Listen, surely all these speakers are Galileans? Then how does it happen that every single one of us can hear the particular language he has known from a child? There are Parthians, Medes and Elamites; there are men whose homes are in Mesopotamia, in Judaea and Cappadocia, Pontus, Asia, Phrygia, Pamphylia, Egypt, and the parts of Libya near Cyrene, as well as visitors from Rome! There are Jews and proselytes, men from Crete and men from Arabia, yet we can all hear these men speaking of the glorious works of God in our native language."

Everyone was utterly amazed and did not know what to make of it. Indeed they kept saying to each other,

"What on earth can this mean?"

But there were others who laughed mockingly and said,

"These fellows have drunk too much sweet wine!"

Peter explains the fulfilment of God's promise

Then Peter, with the eleven standing by him, raised his voice and addressed them:

"Fellow-Jews, and all who are living now in Jerusalem, listen carefully to what I say while I explain to you what has happened! These men are not drunk as you suppose—it is only nine o'clock in the morning of this great feast day. No, this is something which was predicted by the prophet Joel:

And it shall be in the last days, saith God,
I will pour forth of my Spirit upon all flesh:
And your sons and your daughters shall prophesy,
And your young men shall see visions,
And your old men shall dream dreams:
Yea and on my servants and on my handmaidens in those days
Will I pour forth of my Spirit; and they shall prophesy.
And I will shew wonders in the heaven above,
And signs on the earth beneath;
Blood, and fire, and vapour of smoke:
The sun shall be turned into darkness,
And the moon into blood,
Before the day of the Lord come,
That great and notable day:
And it shall be, that whosoever shall call on the name of the Lord shall be saved.

"Men of Israel, I beg you to listen to my words. Jesus of Nazareth was a man proved to you by God himself through the works of power, the miracles and the signs which God showed through him here amongst you—as you very well know. This man, who was put into your power by the predetermined plan and foreknowledge of God, you nailed up and murdered, and you used for your purpose men without the Law! But God would not allow the bitter pains of death to hold him. He raised him to life again—and indeed there was nothing by which death could hold such a man. When David speaks about him he says,

I beheld the Lord always before my face;
For he is on my right hand, that I should not be moved:
Therefore my heart was glad, and my tongue rejoiced;
Moreover my flesh also shall dwell in hope:
Because thou wilt not leave my soul in Hades,
Neither wilt thou give thy holy one to see corruption.
Thou madest known unto me the ways of life;
Thou shalt make me full of gladness with thy countenance.

"Men and brother-Jews, I can surely speak freely to you about the patriarch David. There is no doubt that he died and was buried, and his grave is here among us to this day. But while he was alive he was a prophet. He knew that God had given him a most solemn promise that he would place one of his descendants upon his throne. He foresaw the resurrection of Christ, and it is this of which he is speaking. Christ did not 'leave his soul in Hades' and his body 'did not see corruption'. This man Jesus God raised up—a fact of which all of us are eye-witnesses! He has been raised to the right hand of God; he has received from the Father and poured out upon us the promised Holy Spirit—*that* is what you now see and hear! David never ascended to Heaven, but he certainly said,

The Lord said unto my *Lord*,
Sit thou on my right hand,
Till I make thine enemies the footstool of thy feet.

"Now therefore the whole nation of Israel must know beyond the shadow of a doubt that this Jesus, whom you crucified, God has declared to be both Lord and Christ."

The reaction to Peter's speech

When they heard this they were cut to the quick, and they cried to Peter and the other apostles,

"Men and fellow-Jews, what shall we do now?"

Peter told them,

"You must repent and every one of you must be baptised in the name of Jesus Christ, so that you may have your sins forgiven and receive the gift of the Holy Spirit. For this great promise is for you and your children—yes, and for all who are far away, for as many as the Lord our God shall call to himself!"

Peter said much more than this as he gave his testimony and implored them, saying,

"Save yourselves from this perverse generation!"

The first large-scale conversion

Then those who welcomed this message were baptised, and on that day alone about three thousand souls were added to the number of disciples. They continued steadily learning the teaching of the apostles, and joined in their fellowship, in the breaking of bread, and in prayer.

Everyone felt a deep sense of awe, while many miracles and signs took place through the apostles. All the believers joined together and shared everything in common; they sold their possessions and goods and divided the proceeds among the fellowship according to individual need. Day after day they met by common consent in the Temple; they broke bread together in their homes, sharing meals with simple joy. They praised God continually and all the people respected them. Every day the Lord increased the number of those who were finding salvation.

CHAPTER 3

A public miracle and its explanation

ONE afternoon Peter and John were on their way to the Temple for the three o'clock hour of prayer. A man who had been lame from birth was being carried along in the crowd, for it was the daily practice to put him down at what was known as the Beautiful Gate of the Temple, so that he could beg from the people as they went in. As this man saw Peter and John just about to enter he asked them to give him something. Peter looked intently at the man and so did John. Then Peter said,

"Look straight at us!"

The man looked at them expectantly, hoping for a gift from them.

"I have neither silver nor gold," said Peter, "but what I have

I will certainly give you. In the name of Jesus Christ of Nazareth, *walk!*"

Then he grasped him by the right hand and lifted him up. At once his feet and ankle bones were strengthened, and he sprang to his feet, stood, and then walked. Then he went with them into the Temple, where he walked about, leaping and thanking God. Everyone noticed him as he walked and praised God and recognised him as the beggar who used to sit at the Beautiful Gate, and they were all overcome with wonder and sheer astonishment at what had happened to him. Then while the man himself still clung to Peter and John all the people in their excitement ran together and crowded round them in what is called Solomon's Porch. When Peter saw this he spoke to the crowd.

"Men of Israel, why are you so surprised at this, and why are you staring at us as though we had made this man walk through some power or piety of our own? It is the God of Abraham and Isaac and Jacob, the God of our fathers, who has done this thing to honour his servant Jesus—the man whom you betrayed and denied in the presence of Pilate, even when he had decided to let him go. But you disowned the holy and righteous one, and begged to be granted instead a man who was a murderer! You killed the pioneer of Life, but God raised him from the dead—a fact of which we are eye-witnesses. It is the name of this same Jesus, it is faith in that name, which has cured this man whom you see and recognise. Yes, it was faith in Christ which gave this man perfect health and strength in full view of you all.

Peter explains ancient prophecy

"Now of course I know, my brothers, that you had no idea of what you were doing any more than your leaders had. But God had foretold through all his prophets that his Christ must suffer and this was how his words came true. Now you must repent and turn to God so that your sins may be wiped out, that your souls may know the times of refreshment which come from the presence of the Lord. Then he will send you your long-heralded Christ, that is Jesus. Heaven must receive him until that universal restoration of which God spoke in ancient times through all his holy prophets. For Moses said,

> A prophet shall the Lord God raise up unto you from among your brethren, like unto me; to him shall ye hearken in all things whatsoever he shall speak unto you. And it shall be

that every soul, which shall not hearken to that prophet, shall be utterly destroyed from among the people.

Indeed, all the prophets who have spoken from Samuel onwards have foretold these days. You are the sons of the prophets and heirs of the agreement which God made with your fathers when he said to Abraham, 'Through your children shall all the families of the earth be blessed.' It was to you first that God sent his servant after he had raised him up, to bring you great blessing by turning every one of you away from his evil ways."

CHAPTER 4

The first clash with Jewish authorities

WHILE they were still talking to the people the priests, the captain of the Temple guard and the Sadducees moved towards them, thoroughly incensed that they should be teaching the people and should assure them that the resurrection of the dead had been proved through the rising of Jesus. So they arrested them and, since it was now evening, kept them in custody until the next day. Nevertheless, many of those who had heard what they said believed, and the number of men alone rose to about five thousand.

Peter's boldness at formal questioning

Next day the leading members of the council, the elders and scribes, met in Jerusalem with Annas the High Priest, Caiaphas, John, Alexander, and the whole of the High Priest's family. They had the apostles brought in to stand before them and they asked them formally,

"By what power and in whose name have you done this thing?"

At this Peter, filled with the Holy Spirit, spoke to them,

"Leaders of the people and elders, if we are being called in question today over the matter of a kindness done to a helpless man and as to how he was healed, it is high time that all of you and the whole people of Israel knew that it was done in the name of Jesus Christ of Nazareth! He is the one whom you crucified but whom God raised from the dead, and it is by his power that this man at our side stands in your presence perfectly well. He is the 'stone which you builders rejected, which has now become the head of the corner'. In no one else can salvation be found. For in all the world no other name has been given to men but this, and it is by this name that we must be saved!"

The embarrassment of the authorities

When they saw the complete assurance of Peter and John, who were in their view uneducated and untrained men, they were staggered, recognising them as men who had been with Jesus. Yet since they could see the man who had been cured standing beside them, they could find no effective reply. All they could do was to order them out of the Sanhedrin and hold a conference among themselves.

"What are we going to do with these men?" they said to each other. "It is evident to everyone living in Jerusalem that an extraordinary miracle has taken place through them, and that is something we cannot deny. Nevertheless, to prevent such a thing spreading further among the people, let us warn them that if they say anything more to anyone in this name it will be at their peril."

So they called them in and ordered them bluntly not to speak or teach a single further word to anyone in the name of Jesus. But Peter and John gave them this reply:

"Whether it is right in the eyes of God for us to listen to what you say rather than to what he says, you must decide; for we cannot help speaking about what we have actually seen and heard!"

After further threats they let them go. They could not think of any way of punishing them because of the attitude of the people. Everybody was thanking God for what had happened—that this miracle of healing had taken place in a man who was more than forty years old.

The united prayer of the young Church—

After their release the apostles went back to their friends and reported to them what the chief priests and elders had said to them. When they heard it they raised their voices to God in united prayer and said,

"Almighty Lord, thou art the one who hast made the heaven and the earth, the sea and all that is in them. It was thou who didst speak by the Holy Spirit through the lips of our forefather David thy servant in the words:

Why did the gentiles rage,
And the peoples imagine vain things?
The kings of the earth set themselves in array,
And the rulers were gathered together,
Against the Lord, and against his anointed:

For indeed in this city the rulers have joined together against thy holy servant, Jesus, thine anointed—yes, Herod and Pontius Pilate, the gentiles and the peoples of Israel have gathered together to carry out what thine hand and will had planned to happen. And now, O Lord, observe their threats and give thy servants courage to speak thy word fearlessly, while thou dost stretch out thine hand to heal, and cause signs and wonders to be performed in the name of thy holy servant Jesus."

When they had prayed their meeting-place was shaken; they were all filled with the Holy Spirit and spoke the Word of God fearlessly.

—and their close fellowship

Among the large number who had become believers there was complete agreement of heart and soul. Not one of them claimed any of his possessions as his own but everything was common property. The apostles continued to give their witness to the resurrection of the Lord Jesus with great force, and a wonderful spirit of generosity pervaded the whole fellowship. Indeed, there was not a single person in need among them. For those who owned land or property would sell them and bring the proceeds of the sales and place them at the apostles' feet. They would distribute to each one if he were in need.

Generosity and covetousness

It was at this time that Barnabas (the name, meaning son of comfort, given by the apostles to Joseph, a Levite from Cyprus) sold his farm and put the proceeds at the apostles' disposal.

CHAPTER 5

But there was a man named Ananias who, with his wife Sapphira, had sold a piece of property, but with her full knowledge, reserved part of the price for himself. He brought the remainder to put at the apostles' disposal. But Peter said to him,

"Ananias, why has Satan so filled your mind that you could cheat the Holy Spirit and keep back for yourself part of the price of the land? Before the land was sold it was yours, and after the sale the disposal of the price you received was entirely in your hands, wasn't it? Then whatever made you think of such a thing as this? You have not lied to men, but to God!"

As soon as Ananias heard these words he collapsed and died. All who were within earshot were awe-struck at this incident. The young men got to their feet and after wrapping up his body carried him out and buried him.

About three hours later it happened that his wife came in not knowing what had taken place. Peter spoke directly to her,

"Tell me, did you sell your land for so much?"

"Yes," she replied, "that was it."

Then Peter said to her,

"How could you two have agreed to put the Spirit of the Lord to such a test? Listen, you can hear the footsteps of the men who have just buried your husband coming back through the door, and they will carry you out as well!"

Immediately she collapsed at Peter's feet and died. When the young men came into the room they found her a dead woman, and they carried her out and buried her by the side of her husband. At this happening a deep sense of awe swept over the whole Church and indeed over all those who heard about it.

The young Church takes its stand in the Temple—

By common consent they all used to meet now in Solomon's Porch. But as far as the others were concerned no one dared to associate with them, even though their general popularity was very great. Yet more and more believers in the Lord joined them, both men and women in really large numbers.

—and miraculous power radiates from it

*Many signs and wonders were now being shown among the people through the apostles' ministry. In consequence people would bring out their sick into the streets and lay them down on

* Transposing the first part of v. 12 to the beginning of v. 15, which makes better sense.

beds or stretchers, so that as Peter came by at least his shadow might fall upon some of them. In addition a large crowd collected from the cities round about Jerusalem, bringing with them their sick and all those who were suffering from evil spirits. And they were all cured.

Furious opposition reduced to impotence

All this roused the High Priest and his allies the Sadducean party of the day, and in a fury of jealousy they had the apostles arrested and put into the common jail. But during the night an angel of the Lord opened the prison doors and led them out, saying,

"Go and stand and speak in the Temple. Tell the people all about this new life!"

After receiving these instructions they entered the Temple about daybreak, and began to teach. When the High Priest arrived he and his supporters summoned the Sanhedrin and indeed the whole senate of the people of Israel. Then he sent to the jail to have the apostles brought in. But when the officers arrived at the prison they could not find them there. They came back and reported,

"We found the prison securely locked and the guard standing on duty at the doors, but when we opened up we found no one inside."

When the captain of the Temple guard and the chief priests heard this report they were completely mystified at the apostles' disappearance and wondered what else could happen. However, someone arrived and reported to them,

"Why, the men you put in jail are standing in the Temple teaching the people!"

Then the captain went out with his men and fetched them. They dared not use any violence however, for the people might have stoned them. So they brought them in and made them stand before the Sanhedrin. The High Priest called for an explanation.

"We gave you the strictest possible orders," he said to them, "not to give any teaching in this name. And look what has happened—you have filled Jerusalem with your teaching, and what is more you are determined to fasten the guilt of that man's death upon us!"

The apostles speak the unpalatable truth

Then Peter and the apostles answered him,

"It is our duty to obey the orders of God rather than the orders of men. It was the God of our fathers who raised up Jesus, whom you murdered by hanging him on a cross of wood. God has raised this man to his own right hand as prince and saviour, to bring repentance and the forgiveness of sins to Israel. What is more, we are witnesses to these matters, and so is the Holy Spirit given by God to those who obey his commands."

Calm counsel temporarily prevails

When the members of the council heard these words they were stung to fury and wanted to kill them. But one man stood up in the assembly, a Pharisee by the name of Gamaliel, a teacher of the Law who was held in great respect by the people, and gave orders for the apostles to be taken outside for a few minutes. Then he addressed the assembly:

"Men of Israel, be very careful of what action you intend to take against these men! Remember that some time ago a man called Theudas made himself conspicuous by claiming to be someone or other, and he had a following of four hundred men. He was killed, all his followers were dispersed, and the movement came to nothing. Then later, in the days of the census, that man Judas from Galilee appeared and enticed many of the people to follow him. But he too died and his whole following melted away. My advice to you now therefore is to let these men alone; leave them to themselves. For if this teaching or movement is merely human it will collapse of its own accord. But if it should be from God you cannot defeat them, and you might actually find yourselves to be fighting against God!"

They accepted his advice and called in the apostles. They had them beaten and after commanding them not to speak in the name of Jesus they let them go. So the apostles went out from the presence of the Sanhedrin full of joy that they had been considered worthy to bear humiliation for the sake of the name. Then day after day in the Temple and in people's houses they continued to teach unceasingly and to proclaim the good news of Jesus Christ.

CHAPTER 6

The first deacons are chosen

About this time, when the number of disciples was continually increasing, the Greeks complained that in the daily distribution of food the Hebrew widows were being given preferential treatment. The twelve summoned the whole body of the disciples together, and said,

"It is not right that we should have to neglect preaching the Word of God in order to look after the accounts. You, our brothers, must look round and pick out from your number seven men of good reputation who are both practical and spiritually-minded and we will put them in charge of this matter. Then we shall devote ourselves whole-heartedly to prayer and the ministry of the Word."

This suggestion met with unanimous approval and they chose Stephen a man full of faith and the Holy Spirit, Philip, Prochorus, Nicanor, Timon, Parmenas, and Nicolas of Antioch who had previously been a convert to the Jewish faith. They brought these men before the apostles, and they, after prayer, laid their hands upon them.

So the Word of God gained more and more ground. The number of disciples in Jerusalem greatly increased, while a considerable proportion of the priesthood accepted the faith.

The attack on the new deacon, Stephen

Stephen, full of grace and spiritual power, continued to perform miracles and remarkable signs among the people. However, members of a Jewish synagogue known as that of the Freed Men, together with some from the synagogues of Cyrene and Alexandria, as well as some men from Cilicia and Asia, tried debating with Stephen, but found themselves quite unable to stand up against either his practical wisdom or the spiritual force with which he spoke. In the end they bribed men to allege, "We have heard this man making blasphemous statements against Moses and against God." At the same time they worked upon the feelings of the people, the elders and the scribes. Then they suddenly confronted Stephen, seized him and took him before the Sanhedrin. There they brought forward false witnesses to say, "This man's speeches are one long attack against this holy place and the Law. We have heard him say that Jesus of Nazareth will destroy this place and change the customs which Moses handed down to us." All who sat there in the Sanhedrin looked intently at Stephen, and as they looked his face appeared to them like the face of an angel.

CHAPTER 7

Stephen makes his defence from Israel's history:

i. THE TIME OF ABRAHAM

THEN the High Priest said,

"Is this statement true?"

And Stephen answered,

"My brothers and my fathers, listen to me. Our glorious God appeared to our forefather Abraham while he was in Mesopotamia before he ever came to live in Charran, and said to him, 'Get thee out of thy land and from thy kindred, and come into a land which I shall shew thee.' That was how he came to leave the land of the Chaldeans and settle in Charran. And it was from there after his father's death that God moved him into this very land where you are living today. Yet God gave him no part of it as an inheritance, not a foot that he could call his own, and yet promised that it should eventually belong to him and his descendants—even though at the time he had no descendant at all. And this is the way in which God spoke to him: he told him that his descendants should live as strangers in a foreign land where they would become slaves and be ill-treated for four hundred years, 'And the nation to which they shall be in bondage will I judge, said God: and after that shall they come forth, and serve me in this place.'

"Further, he gave him the agreement of circumcision, so that when Abraham became the father of Isaac he circumcised him on the eighth day.

Stephen's defence:

ii. THE PATRIARCHS

"Isaac became the father of Jacob, and Jacob the father of the twelve patriarchs. Then the patriarchs in their jealousy of Joseph sold him as a slave into Egypt. But God was with him and saved him from all his troubles and gave him favour and wisdom in the eyes of Pharaoh the king of Egypt. Pharaoh made him governor of Egypt and put him in charge of his own entire household.

"Then came the famine over all the land of Egypt and Canaan which caused great suffering, and our forefathers could find no food. But when Jacob heard that there was grain in Egypt he sent our forefathers out of their own country for the first time. It was on their second visit that Joseph was recognised by his brothers, and his ancestry became plain to Pharaoh. Then Joseph sent and invited to come and live with him his father and all his kinsmen, seventy-five people in all. So Jacob came down to Egypt and both he and our fathers ended their days there. After their death they were carried back into Sychem and laid in the tomb which Abraham had bought with silver from the sons of Hemmor in Sychem.

"But as the time drew near for the fulfilment of the promise which God had made to Abraham, our people grew and became more and more numerous in Egypt. But at last another king came to the Egyptian throne who knew nothing of Joseph. This man cleverly victimised our race. He treated our forefathers with cunning cruelty, forcing them to expose their infant children so that they should not survive.

Stephen's defence:

iii. GOD'S PROVIDENCE AND MOSES

"It was at this very time that Moses was born. He was a child of divine beauty, and for three months he was brought up in his father's house, and then when the time came for him to be abandoned Pharaoh's daughter adopted him and brought him up as her own son. So Moses was trained in all the wisdom of the Egyptians, and became not only an excellent speaker but a man of action as well.

Moses' first abortive attempt at rescue

"Now when he was forty years old the thought came into his mind that he should go and look into the condition of his own brothers, the sons of Israel. He saw one of them being unjustly treated, went to the rescue and avenged the man who had been ill-treated by striking down the Egyptian. He fully imagined that his brothers would understand that God was using him to rescue them. But they did not understand. Indeed, on the very next day he came upon two of them who were quarrelling and urged them to make peace, saying, 'Men, you are brothers. What good can come from your injuring each other?' But the man who was wronging his neighbour pushed Moses aside, saying, 'Who made you a ruler and judge over us? Do you want to kill me as you killed that Egyptian yesterday?' At that retort Moses fled and lived as an exile in the land of Midian, where he became the father of two sons.

Moses hears the voice of God

"It was forty years later in the desert of Mount Sinai that an angel appeared to him in the flames of a burning bush, and the sight filled Moses with wonder. As he approached to look at it more closely the voice of the Lord spoke to him, saying, 'I am the God of thy fathers, the God of Abraham, and the God of Isaac, and the God of Jacob.' Then Moses trembled and was afraid to look any more. But the Lord spoke to him and said, 'Loose the shoes from thy feet: for the place whereon thou standest is holy ground. I have surely seen the affliction of my people which is in Egypt, and have heard their groaning, and I am come down to deliver them: and now come, I will send thee into Egypt.'

But Israel rejects Moses

"So this same Moses whom they had rejected in the words, 'Who appointed you a ruler and judge?' God sent to be both ruler and deliverer with the help of the angel who had appeared to him in the bush. This is the man who showed wonders and signs in Egypt and in the Red Sea, the man who led them out of Egypt and was their leader in the desert for forty years. He was Moses, the man who said to the sons of Israel, 'A prophet shall God raise up unto you from among your brethren, like unto me.' In that assembly in the desert this was the man who was the mediator between the angel who spoke to him on Mount Sinai and our fathers. This was the man who received words, living words, which were to be given to us; and this was the man to whom our forefathers turned a deaf ear! They disregarded him, and in their hearts hankered after Egypt. They said to Aaron, 'Make us gods to go before us. For as for this Moses who led us out of Egypt, we do not know what has become of him.' In those days they even made a calf, and offered sacrifices to their idol. They rejoiced in the work of their own hands. So God turned away from them and left them to worship the Host of Heaven, as it is written in the book of the prophets,

Did ye offer unto me slain beasts and sacrifices
Forty years in the wilderness, O house of Israel?
And ye took up the tabernacle of Moloch,
And the star of the god Rephan,
The figures which ye made to worship them:
And I will carry you away beyond Babylon.

God's privileges to Israel

"There in the desert our forefather possessed the Tabernacle of witness made according to the pattern which Moses saw when God instructed him to build it. This Tabernacle was handed down to our forefathers, and they brought it here when the gentiles were defeated under Joshua, for God drove them out as our ancestors advanced. Here it stayed until the time of David. David won the approval of God and prayed that he might find a habitation for the God of Jacob, even though it was not he but Solomon who actually built a house for him. Yet of course the Most High does not live in man-made houses. As the prophet says,

The heaven is my throne,
And the earth the footstool of my feet:
What manner of house will ye build me? saith the Lord:
Or what is the place of my rest?
Did not my hand make all these things?

Yet Israel is blind and disobedient

"You obstinate people, heathen in your thinking, heathen in the way you are listening to me now! It is always the same—you never fail to resist the Holy Spirit! Just as your fathers did so are you doing now. Can you name a single prophet whom your fathers did not persecute? They killed the men who foretold the coming of the just one, and now in our own day you have become his betrayers and his murderers. You are the men who have received the Law of God by the hand of angels, and you are the men who have failed to keep it!"

The truth arouses murderous fury

These words stung them to fury and they ground their teeth at him in rage. Stephen, filled through all his being with the Holy Spirit, looked steadily up into Heaven. He saw the glory of God, and Jesus himself standing at his right hand.

"Look!" he exclaimed, "the heavens are opened and I can see the Son of Man standing at God's right hand!"

At this they put their fingers in their ears. Yelling with fury, as one man they made a rush at him and hustled him out of the city and stoned him. The witnesses* of the execution flung their clothes at the feet of a young man by the name of Saul.

So they stoned Stephen while he called upon God, and said,
"Lord Jesus, receive my spirit!"
Then, on his knees, he cried in ringing tones,
"Lord, forgive them for this sin."

And with these words he fell into the sleep of death, while Saul gave silent assent to his execution.

CHAPTER 8

Widespread persecution follows Stephen's death

On that very day a great storm of persecution burst upon the Church in Jerusalem. All except the apostles were scattered over the countryside of Judaea and Samaria. While reverent men buried Stephen and mourned deeply over him, Saul harassed the Church bitterly. He would go from house to house, drag out both men and women and have them committed to prison. Those who were dispersed went throughout the country, preaching the good news of the message as they went. Philip went down to the city of Samaria and preached Christ to the people there. His words met with a ready and sympathetic response from the large crowds who listened to him and saw the miracles which he performed. With loud cries evil spirits came out of those who had been possessed by them; and many paralysed and lame people were cured. There was great rejoicing in that city.

A magician believes in Christ

But there was a man named Simon in the city who had been practising magic for some time and mystifying the people of Samaria. He pretended that he was somebody great and everyone from the lowest to the highest was fascinated by him. Indeed, they used to say, "This man must be that great power of God." They paid him great attention because he had been astounding

* In Jewish Law the "witnesses" were also the executioners.

them for a long time by his magical practices. But when they had come to believe Philip as he proclaimed to them the good news of the kingdom of God and of the name of Jesus Christ, men and women alike were baptised. Even Simon himself became a believer and after his baptism attached himself closely to Philip. As he saw the signs and remarkable demonstrations of power which took place, he lived in a state of constant wonder.

God confirms Samaria's acceptance of the gospel

When the apostles in Jerusalem heard that Samaria had accepted the Word of God, they sent Peter and John down to them. When these two had arrived they prayed for the Samaritans that they might receive the Holy Spirit for as yet he had not fallen upon any of them. They were living simply as those who had been baptised in the name of the Lord Jesus. So then and there they laid their hands on them and they received the Holy Spirit.

Simon's monstrous suggestion is sternly rebuked

When Simon saw that the Spirit was given through the apostles' laying their hands upon people he offered them money with the words,

"Give me this power too, so that if I were to put my hands on anyone he would receive the Holy Spirit."

But Peter said to him,

"To hell with you and your money!* How dare you think you could buy the gift of God for money! You can have no share or part in this matter, for your heart is not honest before God. All you can do now is to repent of this wickedness of yours and pray earnestly to the Lord that if possible the evil intention of your heart may be forgiven. For I can see inside you, and I see a man bitter with jealousy and bound with his own sin!"

To this Simon answered,

"Please pray to the Lord for me that none of these things that you have spoken about may come upon me!"

When Peter and John had given their clear witness and spoken the Word of the Lord, they returned to Jerusalem, preaching the good news to many Samaritan villages as they went.

* This is really what the Greek says. It is a pity that modern English usage obscures the literal meaning.

Philip is given an unique opportunity

But an angel of the Lord said to Philip,

"Get up and go south down the road which runs from Jerusalem to Gaza, out in the desert."

Philip arose and began his journey. At the same time an Ethiopian eunuch, a minister and in fact the treasurer to Candace, queen of the Ethiopians, was on his way home after going to Jerusalem to worship. He was sitting in his carriage reading the prophet Isaiah. The Spirit said to Philip,

"Approach this carriage, and keep close to it."

Then as Philip ran forward he heard the man reading the prophet Isaiah, and he said,

"Do you understand what you are reading?"

And he replied,

"How can I unless I have someone to guide me?"

And he invited Philip to get up and sit by his side. The passage of scripture he was reading was this:

> He was led as a sheep to the slaughter;
> And as a lamb before his shearer is dumb,
> So he openeth not his mouth:
> In his humiliation his judgment was taken away:
> His generation who shall declare?
> For his life is taken from the earth.

The eunuch turned to Philip and said,

"Tell me, I beg you, about whom is the prophet saying this—is he speaking about himself or about someone else?"

Then Philip began, and using this scripture as a starting point, he told him the good news about Jesus. As they proceeded along the road they came to some water, and the eunuch said,

"Look, here is some water; is there any reason why I should not be baptised?"

And he gave orders for the carriage to stop. Then both of them went down to the water and Philip baptised the eunuch. When they came up out of the water the Spirit of the Lord took Philip away suddenly and the eunuch saw no more of him, but proceeded on his journey with a heart full of joy. Philip found himself at Azotus and as he passed through the countryside he went on telling the good news in all the cities until he came to Caesarea.

CHAPTER 9

The crisis for Saul

BUT Saul, still breathing murderous threats against the disciples of the Lord, went to the High Priest requesting him for letters of authority to the synagogues in Damascus, so that if he should find there any followers of the Way, whether men or women, he could bring them back to Jerusalem as prisoners.

But on his journey, as he neared Damascus, a light from the sky suddenly blazed around him, and he fell to the ground. Then he heard a voice speaking to him,

"Saul, Saul, why are you persecuting me?"

"Who are you, Lord?" he asked.

"I am Jesus whom you are persecuting," was the reply. "But now stand up and go into the city and there you will be told what you must do."

His companions on the journey stood there speechless, for they had heard the voice but could see no one. Saul got up from the ground, but when he opened his eyes he could see nothing. So they took him by the hand and led him into Damascus. There he remained sightless for three days, and during that time he had nothing either to eat or drink.

God's preparation for the converted Saul

Now in Damascus there was a disciple by the name of Ananias. The Lord spoke to this man in a dream, calling him by his name.

"I am here, Lord," he replied.

Then the Lord said to him,

"Get up and go down to the street called Straight and enquire at the house of Judas for a man named Saul from Tarsus. At this moment he is praying and he sees in his mind's eye a man by the name of Ananias coming into the house, and placing his hands upon him to restore his sight."

But Ananias replied,

"Lord, I have heard on all hands about this man and how much harm he has done to your holy people in Jerusalem! Why even now he holds powers from the chief priests to arrest all who call upon your name."

But the Lord said to him,

"Go on your way, for this man is my chosen instrument to bear my name before the gentiles and their kings, as well as to the sons of Israel. Indeed, I myself will show him how much he must suffer for the sake of my name."

Then Ananias set out and went to the house, and there he laid his hands upon Saul, and said,

"Saul, brother, the Lord has sent me—Jesus who appeared to you on your journey here—so that you may recover your sight, and be filled with the Holy Spirit."

Immediately something like scales fell from Saul's eyes, and he could see again. He got to his feet and was baptised. Then he took some food and regained his strength.

Saul's conversion astounds the disciples

Saul stayed with the disciples in Damascus for some time. Without delay he began to proclaim Jesus in the synagogues declaring that he is the Son of God. All his hearers were amazed and kept saying,

"Isn't this the man who so bitterly persecuted those who called on the name in Jerusalem, and came down here with the sole object of taking back all such people as prisoners before the chief priests?"

But Saul went on from strength to strength, reducing to confusion the Jews who lived at Damascus by proving beyond doubt that this man is Christ.

The long revenge on the "renegade" begins

After some time the Jews made a plot to kill Saul, but news of this came to his ears. Although in their murderous scheme the Jews watched the gates day and night for him, his disciples took him one night and let him down through an opening in the wall by lowering him in a basket.

At Jerusalem Saul is suspect: Barnabas conciliates

When Saul reached Jerusalem he tried to join the disciples. But they were all afraid of him, finding it impossible to believe that he was a disciple. Barnabas, however, took him by the hand and introduced him to the apostles, and explained to them how he had seen the Lord on his journey, and how the Lord had spoken to him. He further explained how Saul had spoken in Damascus with the utmost boldness in the name of Jesus. After that Saul joined with them in all their activities in Jerusalem, preaching fearlessly in the name of the Lord. He used to talk and argue with the Greek-speaking Jews, but they made several attempts on his life. When the brothers realised this they took him down to Caesarea and sent him off to Tarsus.

A time of peace

The whole Church throughout Judaea, Galilee and Samaria now enjoyed a period of peace. It became established and as it went forward in reverence for the Lord and in the strengthening presence of the Holy Spirit, continued to grow in numbers.

Peter heals at Lydda

Now it happened that Peter, in the course of travelling about among them all, came down to God's people living at Lydda. There he found a man called Æneas who had been bed-ridden for eight years through paralysis. Peter said to him,

"Æneas, Jesus Christ heals you! Get up and make your bed."

He got to his feet at once. And all those who lived in Lydda and Sharon saw him and turned to the Lord.

And again at Joppa

Then there was a woman in Joppa, a disciple called Tabitha, whose name in Greek was Dorcas (meaning Gazelle). She was a woman whose whole life was full of good and kindly actions, but in those days she became seriously ill and died. So when they had washed her body they laid her in a room upstairs. Now Lydda is quite near Joppa, and when the disciples heard that Peter was in Lydda, they sent two men to him and begged him,

"Please come to us without delay."

Peter got up and went back with them, and when he arrived in Joppa they took him to the room upstairs. All the widows stood around him with tears in their eyes, holding out for him to see the dresses and cloaks which Dorcas used to make for them while she was with them. But Peter put them all outside the room and knelt down and prayed. Then he turned to the body and said,

"Tabitha, get up!"

She opened her eyes, and as soon as she saw Peter she sat up.

He took her by the hand, helped her to her feet, and then called out to the believers and widows and presented her to them alive. This became known throughout the whole of Joppa and many believed in the Lord. Peter himself remained there for some time, staying with a tanner called Simon.

CHAPTER 10

God speaks to a good-living gentile

THERE was a man in Caesarea by the name of Cornelius, a centurion in what was called the Italian regiment. He was a deeply religious man who reverenced God, as did all his household. He made many charitable gifts to the people and was a man of regular prayer. About three o'clock one afternoon he saw perfectly clearly in a vision an angel of God coming into his room, approaching him, and saying,

"Cornelius!"

He stared at the angel in terror, and said,

"What is it, Lord?"

The angel replied,

"Your prayers and your deeds of charity have gone up to Heaven and are remembered before God. Now send men to Joppa for a man called Simon, who is also known as Peter. He is staying as a guest with another Simon, a tanner, whose house is down by the sea."

When the angel who had spoken to him had gone, Cornelius called out for two of his house-servants and a devout soldier, who was one of his personal attendants. He told them the whole story and then sent them off to Joppa.

Peter's startling vision

Next day, while these men were still on their journey and approaching the city, Peter went up about midday on to the flat roof of the house to pray. He became very hungry and longed for something to eat. But while the meal was being prepared he fell into a trance and saw the heavens open and something like a great sheet descending upon the earth, let down by its four corners. In it were all kinds of animals, reptiles and birds. Then came a voice which said to him,

"Get up, Peter, kill and eat!"

But Peter said,

"Never, Lord! For not once in all my life have I ever eaten anything common or unclean."

Then the voice spoke to him a second time,

"You must not call what God has cleansed common."

This happened three times, and then the thing was gone, taken back into heaven.

The meaning of the vision becomes apparent

While Peter was still puzzling about the meaning of the vision which he had just seen, the men sent by Cornelius had arrived asking for the house of Simon. They were in fact standing at the very doorway calling out to enquire if Simon, surnamed Peter, were lodging there. Peter was still thinking deeply about the vision when the Spirit said to him,

"There are some men here looking for you. Get up and go downstairs. Go with them without any misgiving, for I myself have sent them."

So Peter went down to the men and said,

"I am the man you are looking for; what brings you here?"

They replied,

"Cornelius the centurion, a good-living and God-fearing man, whose character can be vouched for by the whole Jewish people, was commanded by a holy angel to send for you to come to his house, and to listen to your message."

Then Peter invited them in and entertained them.

Peter, obeying the Spirit, disobeys Jewish law

On the next day he got up and set out with them, accompanied by some of the brothers from Joppa, arriving at Caesarea on the day after that. Cornelius was expecting them and had invited together his relations and intimate friends. As Peter entered the house Cornelius met him by falling at his feet and worshipping him. But Peter raised him with the words,

"Stand up, I am a human being too!"

Then Peter went right into the house in deep conversation with Cornelius and found that a large number of people had assembled. Then he spoke to them,

"You all know that it is forbidden for a man who is a Jew to associate with, or even visit, a man of another nation. But God has shown me plainly that no man must be called 'common' or 'unclean'. That is why I came here when I was sent for without raising any objection. Now I want to know what made you send for me."

Then Cornelius replied,

"Four days ago, about this time, I was observing the afternoon hour of prayer in my house, when suddenly a man in shining clothes stood before me and said, 'Cornelius, your prayer has been heard and your charitable deeds have been remembered before God. Now you must send to Joppa and invite here a man called Simon whose surname is Peter. He is staying in the house of a tanner by the name of Simon, down by the sea.' So I sent to you without delay and you have been most kind in coming. Now we are all here in the presence of God to listen to everything that the Lord has commanded you to say."

Peter's momentous discovery

Then Peter began to speak,

"In solemn truth I can see now that God does not discriminate between people, but that in every nation the man who reverences him and does what is right is acceptable to him! He has sent his message to the sons of Israel by giving us the good news of peace through Jesus Christ—he is Lord of all. You must know the story of Jesus of Nazareth—why, it has spread through the whole of Judaea, beginning from Galilee after the baptism that John proclaimed. You must have heard how God anointed him with the power of the Holy Spirit, of how he went about doing good and healing all who suffered under the devil's power—because God was with him. Now we are eye-witnesses of everything that he did, both in the Judaean country and in Jerusalem itself, and they murdered him by hanging him on a cross. But on the third day God raised that same Jesus and let him be clearly seen, not indeed by the whole people, but by witnesses whom God had previously chosen. We are those witnesses, we who ate and drank with him after he had risen from the dead! Moreover, we are the men whom he commanded to preach to the people and solemnly witness to the fact that he is the one appointed by God to be the judge of both the living and the dead. It is to him that all the prophets bear witness, so that every man who believes in him may receive forgiveness of sins through his name."

The Holy Spirit confirms Peter's action

While Peter was still speaking these words the Holy Spirit fell upon all who were listening to his message. The Jewish believers who had come with Peter were absolutely amazed that the gift of the Holy Spirit was being poured out even upon gentiles; for they heard them speaking in foreign tongues and glorifying God.

Then Peter exclaimed,

"Could anyone refuse water or object to these men being baptised—men who have received the Holy Spirit just as we did ourselves?"

And he gave orders for them to be baptised in the name of Jesus Christ. Afterwards they asked him to stay with them for some days.

CHAPTER 11

The Church's disquiet at Peter's action

Now the apostles and the brothers who were in Judaea heard that the gentiles also had received God's message. So when Peter next visited Jerusalem the circumcision-party were full of criticism, saying to him, "You actually went in and shared a meal with uncircumcised men!"

Peter's explanation

But Peter began to explain how the situation had actually arisen.

"I was in the city of Joppa praying," he said, "and while completely unconscious of my surroundings I saw a vision—something like a great sheet coming down towards me, let down from heaven by its four corners. It came right down to me and when I looked at it closely I saw animals and wild beasts, reptiles and birds. Then I heard a voice say to me, 'Get up, Peter, kill and eat.' But I said, 'Never, Lord, for nothing common or unclean has ever passed my lips.' But the voice from Heaven spoke a second time and said, 'You must not call what God has cleansed common.' This happened three times, and then the whole thing was drawn up again into heaven. The extraordinary thing is that at that very moment three men arrived at the house where we were staying, sent to me personally from Caesarea. The Spirit told me to go with these men without any misgiving. And these six of our brothers accompanied me and we went into the man's house. He told us how he had seen the angel standing in his house, saying, 'Send to Joppa and bring Simon, surnamed Peter. He will give you a message which will save both you and your whole household.' While I was beginning to tell them this message the Holy Spirit fell upon them just as on us at the beginning. There came into my mind the words of our Lord when he said, 'John indeed baptised with water, but you will be baptised with the Holy Spirit.' If then God gave to them exactly the same gift as he gave to us when we believed on the Lord Jesus Christ, who was I to try to hinder the working of God?"

The flexibility of the young Church

When they heard this they had no further objection to raise. And they praised God, saying,

"Then obviously God has given to the gentiles also the gift of repentance which leads to life."

Persecution has spread the gospel

Now those who had been dispersed by the persecution which arose over Stephen travelled as far as Phoenicia, Cyprus and Antioch, giving the message as they went to Jews only. However, among their number were natives of Cyprus and Cyrene, and these men, on their arrival at Antioch, proclaimed their message to the Greeks as well, telling them the good news of the Lord Jesus. The hand of the Lord was with them, and a great number believed and turned to the Lord. News of these things came to the ears of the Church in Jerusalem and they sent Barnabas to Antioch. When he arrived and saw this working of God's grace, he was delighted. He urged them all to be resolute in their faithfulness to the Lord, for he was a good man, full of the Holy Spirit and of faith. So it happened that a considerable number of people became followers of the Lord.

Believers are called "Christians" for the first time

Then Barnabas went to Tarsus to find Saul. When he found him he brought him to Antioch. Then for a whole year they met together with the Church and taught a large crowd. It was in Antioch that the disciples were first given the name of "Christians".

The young Church and famine relief

During this period some prophets came down from Jerusalem to Antioch. One of them by the name of Agabus stood up and foretold by the Spirit that there was to be a great famine throughout the world. (This actually happened in the days of Claudius.) The disciples determined to send relief to the brothers in Judaea, each contributing as he was able. This they did, sending their contribution to the elders there personally through Barnabas and Saul.

CHAPTER 12

Herod kills James and imprisons Peter

It was at this time that King Herod made a violent attack on some of the Church members. James, John's brother, he executed with the sword, and when he found this action pleased the Jews he went on to arrest Peter as well. It was during the days of unleavened bread that he actually made the arrest. He put Peter in prison with no less than four squads of soldiers to guard him, intending to bring him out to the people after the Passover. So Peter was closely guarded in the prison, while the Church prayed to God earnestly on his behalf.

Peter's miraculous rescue

On the very night that Herod was planning to bring him out, Peter was asleep between two soldiers, secured by double chains, while guards maintained a strict watch at the doorway of the prison. Suddenly an angel of the Lord appeared, and light shone in the cell. He tapped Peter on the side and woke him up, saying, "Get up quickly." His chains fell away from his hands and the angel said to him, "Fasten your belt and put on your sandals." And he did so. Then the angel continued, "Wrap your cloak round you and follow me." So Peter followed him out, not knowing whether what the angel was doing were real—indeed he felt he must be seeing a vision. They passed right through the first and second guard-points and came to the iron gate that led

Miles
0
100
200
300
EUXINE SEA
Antioch
PISIDIA
Iconium
Lystra
LYCAONIA
Derbe
Perga
Attalia
SEA OF PAMPHYLIA
Antioch
Seleucia
CYPRUS
Salamis
Paphos
MEDITERRANEAN SEA
N
PAUL'S JOURNEY №1

out into the city. This opened for them of its own accord, and they went out and had passed along one street when the angel suddenly vanished from Peter's sight. Then Peter came to himself and said, "Now I know for certain that the Lord has sent his angel to rescue me from the power of Herod and from all that the Jewish people were expecting." As the truth broke upon him he went to the house of Mary, the mother of John surnamed Mark, where many were gathered together in prayer. As he knocked at the outer door a young maid called Rhoda came to answer it, but on recognising Peter's voice failed to open the door from sheer joy. Instead she ran inside and reported that Peter was standing outside. At this they said to her,

"You must be mad!"

But she insisted that it was true. Then they said,

"Then it is his angel."

But Peter continued to stand there knocking on the door, and when they opened it they saw him and were simply amazed. Peter, however, made a gesture to them to stop talking while he explained to them how the Lord had brought him out of prison. Then he said,

"Go and tell James and the other brothers what has happened."

After this he left the house and went on to another place.

Peter's escape infuriates Herod

But when morning came there was a great commotion among the soldiers as to what could have happened to Peter. When Herod had had a search put out for him without success, he cross-examined the guards and then ordered their execution. Then he left Judaea and went down to Caesarea and stayed there.

But Herod dies a terrible death

Now Herod was very angry with the people of Tyre and Sidon. They approached him in a body and after winning over Blastus the king's chamberlain, they begged him for peace, for their country's food supply was dependent on the king's lands. So on an appointed day Herod put on his royal robes, took his seat on the public throne and made a speech to them. At this the people kept shouting. "This is a god speaking, not a mere man!" Immediately an angel of the Lord struck him down because he did not give God the glory. And he was eaten by worms and died.

The message continues to spread

But the Word of the Lord continued to gain ground and increase its influence. Barnabas and Saul returned from Jerusalem when they had completed their mission there, bringing with them to Antioch John whose surname was Mark.

CHAPTER 13

Saul and Barnabas are called to a special task

Now there were in the church at Antioch both prophets and teachers—Barnabas, Simeon surnamed Niger, Lucius the Cyrenian, Manaen the foster-brother of the governor Herod, and Saul. While they were worshipping the Lord and fasting, the Holy Spirit spoke to them, saying,

"Set Barnabas and Saul apart for me for a task to which I have called them."

At this, after further fasting and prayer, they laid their hands on them and set them free for this work. So these two, sent out at the Holy Spirit's command, went down to Seleucia and from there they sailed off to Cyprus.* On their arrival at Salamis they began to proclaim God's message in the Jewish synagogues, having John as their assistant. As they made their way through the island as far as Paphos they came across a man named Bar-Jesus, a Jew who was both a false prophet and a magician. This man was attached to Sergius Paulus, the proconsul, who was himself a man of intelligence. He had sent for Barnabas and Saul as he was anxious to hear God's message. But Elymas the magician (for that is the translation of his name) opposed them, doing his best to dissuade the proconsul from accepting the faith. Then Saul (who is also called Paul), filled with the Holy Spirit, eyed him closely and said,

"You son of the devil, you enemy of all true goodness, you monster of trickery and evil, is it not high time you gave up trying to pervert the truth of the Lord? Now listen, the Lord himself will touch you, for some time you will not see the light of the sun—you will be blind!"

Immediately a mist and then an utter blackness came over his eyes, and he went round trying to find someone to lead him by the hand. When the proconsul saw what had happened he believed, for he was shaken to the core at the Lord's teaching.

* See page 261.

Saul (now Paul) comes to Antioch in Pisidia

Then Paul and his companions set sail from Paphos and went to Perga in Pamphylia. There John left them and turned back to Jerusalem, but they continued their journey through Perga and arrived at Antioch in Pisidia. They went to the synagogue on the Sabbath day and took their seats. After the reading of the Law and Prophets, the leaders of the synagogue sent to them with a message,

"Men and brothers, if you have any message of encouragement for the people, by all means speak."

Paul shows the Jews where their history leads

So Paul stood up, and motioning with his hand, began:

"Men of Israel and all of you who fear God, listen to me. The God of this people Israel chose our fathers and made them into a great people while they were exiles in the land of Egypt. Then he lifted up his arm and led them out of that land. Yes, and he sustained them for some forty years in the desert. He destroyed seven nations in the land of Canaan before he gave them that land as their inheritance for some four hundred and fifty years. After that he gave them judges until the time of the prophet Samuel. Then when they begged for a king God gave them Saul the son of Kish, a man of the tribe of Benjamin, to be their king for forty years. After he had deposed him he raised David to the throne, a man of whom God himself bore testimony in the words, 'I have found David, the son of Jesse, a man after my own heart, who shall do all my will.' From the descendants of this man, according to his promise, God has brought Jesus to Israel to be their saviour. John came before him to prepare his way, preaching the baptism of repentance for all the people of Israel. Indeed, as John reached the end of his time he said these words: 'What do you think I am? I am not he. But know this, someone comes after me whose shoelace I am not fit to untie!'

Now the message is urgent and contemporary

"Men and brothers, sons of the race of Abraham, and all among you who fear God, it is to us that this message of salvation has now been sent! For the people of Jerusalem and their rulers refused to recognise him or to understand the voice of the prophets which are read every Sabbath day—even though in condemning him they fulfilled these very prophecies! For though they found no cause for putting him to death, they begged Pilate to have him executed. And when they had completed everything that was written about him, they took him down from the cross and laid him in a tomb. But God raised him from the dead. For many days he was seen by those who had come up from Galilee to Jerusalem with him, and these men are now his witnesses to the people. And as for us we tell you the good news that the promise made to our forefathers has come true—that, in raising up Jesus, God has fulfilled it for us their children. This is endorsed in the second psalm: 'Thou art my son, this day have I begotten thee.' And as for the fact of God's raising him from the dead, never to return to corruption, he has spoken in these words: 'I will give you the sure mercies of David.' And then going further he says in another psalm, 'Thou shalt not suffer thine holy one to see corruption'. For David, remember, after he had served God's purpose in his own generation fell asleep and was laid with his ancestors. He did in fact 'see corruption', but this man whom God raised never saw corruption! It is therefore imperative, men and brothers, that every one of you should realise that forgiveness of sins is now proclaimed to you through this man. And through faith in him a man is absolved from all those things from which the Law of Moses could never set him free. Take care then that this saying of the prophets should never apply to you:

Behold, ye despisers, and wonder, and perish;
For I work a work in your days,
A work which ye shall in no wise believe, if one declare it unto you."

Paul succeeds in arousing deep interest—

As they were going out the people kept on asking them to say all this again on the following Sabbath. After the meeting of the synagogue broke up many of the Jews and devout proselytes followed Paul and Barnabas who spoke personally to them and urged them to put their trust in the grace of God.

—but a week later he meets bitter opposition

On the next Sabbath almost the entire population of the city assembled to hear the message of the Lord, but when the Jews saw the crowds they were filled with jealousy and contradicted what Paul was saying, covering him with abuse. At this Paul and Barnabas did not mince their words but said,

"We felt it our duty to speak the message of God to you first, but since you spurn it and evidently do not think yourselves fit for eternal life, watch us now as we turn to the gentiles! Indeed the Lord has commanded us to do so in the words:

I have set thee for a light of the gentiles,
That thou shouldest be for salvation unto the uttermost part of the earth."

When the gentiles heard this they were delighted and thanked God for his message. All those who were destined for eternal life believed, and the Word of the Lord spread over the whole country. But the Jews worked upon the feelings of devout and reputable women and of the leading citizens, and succeeded in starting a persecution against Paul and Barnabas, and expelled them from the district. But they on their part simply shook off the dust from their feet in protest and went on to Iconium. And the disciples continued to be full of joy and the Holy Spirit.

CHAPTER 14

Jewish behaviour repeats itself

MUCH the same thing happened at Iconium. On their arrival they went to the Jewish synagogue and spoke with such conviction that a very large number of both Jews and Greeks believed. But the unbelieving Jews stirred up the feelings of the gentiles and poisoned their minds against the brothers. So they remained there for a long time and spoke fearlessly about the Lord, who made it plain that they were proclaiming the Word of his grace, by allowing them to perform signs and miracles. But the great mass of the people of the city were divided, some taking the side of the Jews, and some that of the apostles. But when a hostile movement arose from both gentiles and Jews in collaboration with the authorities to insult and stone them, they got to know about it, fled to the Lycaonian cities of Lystra and Derbe, and the surrounding countryside—and from there they continued to proclaim the gospel.

A miracle in a completely pagan city

Now it happened at Lystra that a man was sitting who had

no power in his feet. He had in fact been lame from birth and had never been able to walk. He was listening to Paul as he spoke. and Paul, looking him straight in the eye and seeing that he had the faith to be made well, said in a loud voice,

"Stand straight up on your feet!"

And he sprang to his feet and began to walk about. When the crowd saw what Paul had done they shouted in the Lycaonian language,

"The gods have come down to us in human form!"

They began to call Barnabas Zeus, and Paul Hermes, since he was the chief speaker. What is more, the high priest of Zeus whose temple was at the gateway of the city, brought garlanded oxen to the gates and wanted to offer sacrifice with the people. But when the apostles, Barnabas and Paul, heard of their intention they tore their clothes and rushed into the crowd, crying at the top of their voices,

"Men, why are you doing these things? We are only human beings with feelings just like yours! We are here to tell you good news—that you should turn from these meaningless things to the living God! He is the one who made heaven and earth, the sea and all that is in them. In generations gone by he allowed all nations to go on in their own ways—not that he left men without evidence of himself. For he has shown kindnesses to you; he has sent you rain from heaven and fruitful seasons, giving you food and happiness to your hearts' content."

Yet even with these words they only just succeeded in restraining the crowd from making sacrifices to them.

Paul is dogged by his Jewish enemies

Then some Jews arrived from Antioch and Iconium and after turning the minds of the people against Paul they stoned him and dragged him out of the city thinking he was dead. But while the disciples were gathered in a circle round him, Paul got up and walked back to the city. And the next day he went out with Barnabas to Derbe, and when they had preached the gospel to that city and made many disciples, they turned back to Lystra, then to Iconium and on to Antioch. They put fresh heart into the disciples, urging them to stand firm in the faith, and reminding them that it is "through many tribulations" that we must enter into the kingdom of God. They appointed elders for them in each church, and with prayer and fasting commended these men to the Lord in whom they had believed. They then crossed Pisidia and arrived in Pamphylia. They proclaimed their message in Perga and then went down to Attalia. From there they sailed back to Antioch (in Syria) where they had first been commended to the grace of God for the task which they had now completed. When they arrived there they called the church together and reported to them how greatly God had worked with them and how he had opened the door of faith to the gentiles. And here at Antioch they spent a considerable time with the disciples.

CHAPTER 15

The opposition from reactionaries

THEN some men came down from Judaea and began to teach the brothers, saying, "unless you are circumcised according to the custom of Moses you cannot be saved". Paul and Barnabas sharply disagreed with them and there was a good deal of argument. Finally it was settled that Paul and Barnabas should go up to Jerusalem with some of their own people to confer with the apostles and elders about the whole question.

The church sent them off on their journey and as they went through Phoenicia and Samaria they told the story of the conversion of the gentiles, and all the brothers were overjoyed to hear about it. On their arrival at Jerusalem they were welcomed by the Church, by the apostles and elders, and they reported how greatly God had worked with them. But some members of the Pharisees' party who had become believers stood up and declared that it was essential that these men be circumcised and told to observe the Law of Moses.

Peter declares that God is doing something new

The apostles and elders met to consider this matter. After an exhaustive debate Peter stood up and addressed them in these words:

"Men and brothers, you know that from our earliest days together God chose me as the one from whose lips the gentiles should hear the message of the gospel and should believe it. Moreover, God who knows men's inmost thoughts has plainly shown that this is so, for he gave the Holy Spirit to the gentiles exactly as he did to us. He made no distinction between us and them, once he had cleansed their hearts by faith. Why then must

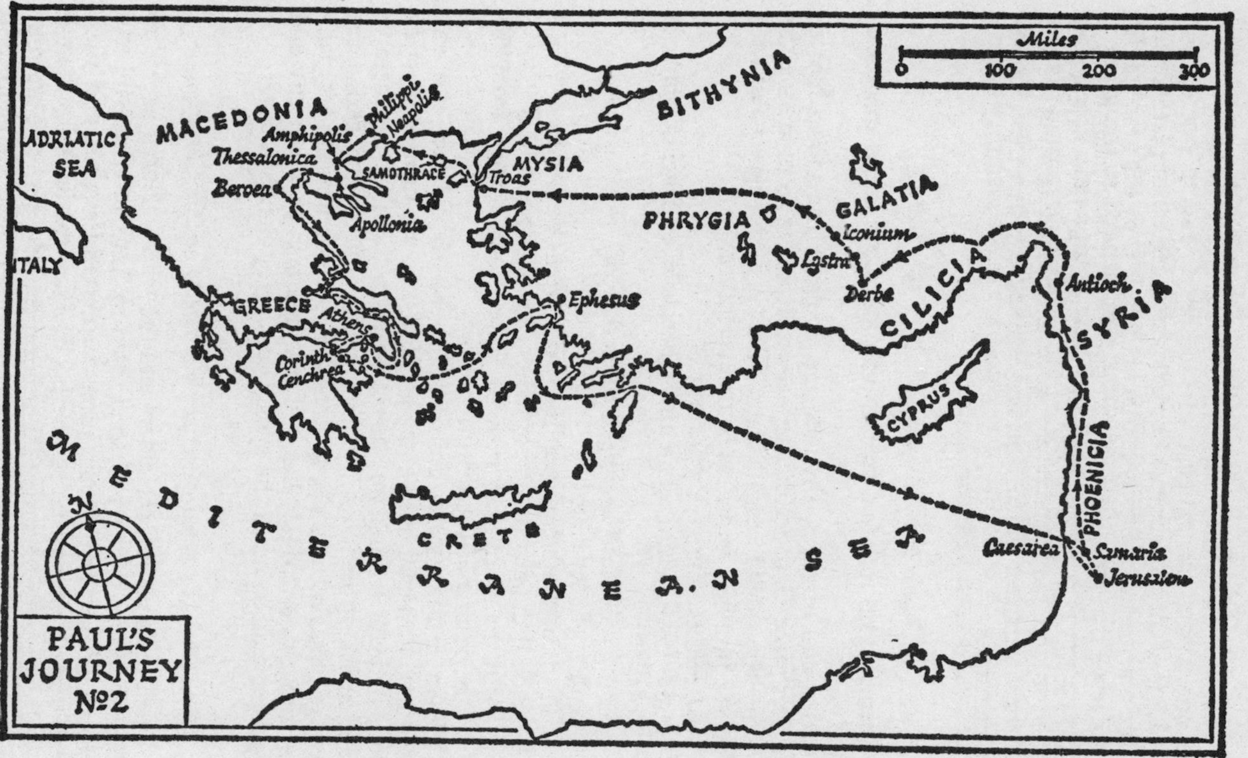

Miles
0
100
200
300
BITHYNIA
MACEDONIA
Philippi
Neapolis
Amphipolis
Thessalonica
ADRIATIC SEA
SAMOTHRACE
MYSIA
Troas
Beroea
Apollonia
GALATIA
PHRYGIA
Iconium
Lystra
ITALY
Derbe
CILICIA
Antioch
SYRIA
GREECE
Ephesus
Athens
Corinth
Cenchrea
CYPRUS
PHOENICIA
MEDITERRANEAN SEA
N
CRETE
Caesarea
Samaria
Jerusalem
PAUL'S JOURNEY No2

you now strain the patience of God by trying to put on the shoulders of these disciples a burden which neither our fathers nor we are able to bear? Surely the fact is that it is by the grace of the Lord Jesus that we are saved through faith, just as they are!"

These words produced absolute silence, and they listened to Barnabas and Paul while they gave a detailed account of the signs and wonders which God had worked through them among the gentiles.

James expresses the feeling of the meeting

Silence again followed their words and then James made this reply:

"Men and brothers, listen to me. Symeon has shown how in the first place God decided to choose a people from among the nations who should bear his name. This is in full agreement with what the prophets wrote, as in this scripture:

> After these things I will return,
> And I will build again the tabernacle of David, which is fallen;
> And I will build again the ruins thereof,
> And I will set it up:
> That the residue of men may seek after the Lord,
> And all the gentiles, upon whom my name is called,
> Saith the Lord who maketh these things known from the beginning of the world.

"I am firmly of the opinion that we should not put any additional obstacles before any gentiles who are turning towards God. Instead, I think we should write to them telling them to avoid anything polluted by idols, sexual immorality, eating the meat of strangled animals, or tasting blood. For after all, for many generations now Moses has had his preachers in every city and has been read aloud in the synagogues every Sabbath day."

The Church's deputation: the message to gentile Christians

Then the apostles, the elders and the whole Church agreed to choose representatives and send them to Antioch with Paul and Barnabas. Their names were Judas, surnamed Barsabas, and Silas, both leading men of the brotherhood. They carried with them a letter bearing this message: "The apostles and elders who are your brothers send their greetings to the brothers who are gentiles in

Antioch, Syria and Cilicia. Since we have heard that some of our number have caused you deep distress and have unsettled your minds by giving you a message which certainly did not originate from us, we are unanimously agreed to send you chosen representatives with our well-loved Barnabas and Paul—men who have risked their lives for the name of our Lord Jesus Christ. So we have sent you Judas and Silas who will give you the same message personally by word of mouth. For it has seemed right to the Holy Spirit and to us to lay no further burden upon you except what is absolutely essential, namely, that you avoid what has been sacrificed to idols, tasting blood, eating the meat of what has been strangled and sexual immorality. Keep yourselves clear of these things and you will make good progress. Farewell."

The message is received with delight

So this party, sent off by the Church, went down to Antioch and after gathering the congregation together, they handed over the letter to them. And they, when they read it, were delighted with the encouragement it gave them. Judas and Silas were themselves both inspired preachers and greatly encouraged and strengthened the brothers by many talks to them. Then, after spending some time there, the brothers sent them back in peace to those who had commissioned them. Paul and Barnabas however stayed on in Antioch teaching and preaching the gospel of the Word of the Lord in company with many others.

Paul and Barnabas flatly disagree, but the work prospers

Some days later Paul spoke to Barnabas,

"Now let us go back and visit the brothers in every city where we have proclaimed the Word of the Lord to see how they are."

Barnabas wanted to take John, surnamed Mark, as their companion. But Paul strongly disapproved of taking with them a man who had deserted them in Pamphylia and was not prepared to go on with them in their work. There was a sharp clash of opinion, so much so that they went their separate ways, Barnabas taking Mark and sailing to Cyprus, while Paul* chose Silas and set out on his journey, commended to the grace of the Lord by the brothers as he did so. He travelled through Syria and Cilicia and strengthened the churches.

* See page 269.

CHAPTER 16

Paul chooses Timothy as companion

HE went to Derbe and on to Lystra. At Lystra there was a disciple by the name of Timothy whose mother was a Jewish Christian, though his father was a Greek. Timothy was held in high regard by the brothers at Lystra and Iconium, and Paul wanted to take him on as his companion. Everybody knew that his father was a Greek, and Paul therefore had him circumcised because of the attitude of the Jews in these places. As they went on their way through the cities they passed on to them for their observance the decisions which had been reached by the apostles and elders in Jerusalem. Consequently the churches grew stronger in the faith and their numbers increased daily.

Paul and Silas find their journey divinely directed

They made their way through Phrygia and the Galatia district, since the Holy Spirit prevented them from speaking God's message in the province of Asia. When they approached Mysia they tried to enter Bithynia, but again the Spirit of Jesus would not allow them. So they passed by Mysia and came down to Troas. One night Paul had a vision of a Macedonian man standing and appealing to him in the words: "Come over to Macedonia and help us!" As soon as Paul had seen this vision we made every effort to get on to Macedonia, convinced that God had called us to give them the good news.

The gospel comes to Europe: a business-woman is converted

So we set sail from Troas and ran a straight course to Samothrace, and on the following day to Neapolis. From there we went to Philippi, a Roman garrison-town and the chief city in that part of Macedonia. We spent some days in Philippi and on the Sabbath day we went out of the city gate to the riverside, where we supposed there was a place for prayer. There we sat down and spoke to the women who had assembled. One of our hearers was a woman named Lydia. (She came from Thyatira and was a dealer in purple-dyed cloth.) She was already a believer in God, who had opened her heart to accept Paul's words. When she and her household had been baptised, she appealed to us, saying,

"If you are satisfied that I am a true believer in the Lord, then come down to my house and stay there."

And she insisted on our doing so.

Conflict with evil spirits and evil men

One day while we were going to the place of prayer we met a young girl who had a spirit of clairvoyance and brought her owners a good deal of profit by foretelling the future. She would follow Paul and the rest of us, crying out, "These men are servants of the Most High God, and they are telling you the way of salvation." She continued this behaviour for many days, and then Paul, in a burst of irritation, turned round and spoke to the spirit in her.

"I command you in the name of Jesus Christ to come out of her!"

And it came out immediately. But when the girl's owners saw that their hope of making money out of her had disappeared, they seized Paul and Silas and dragged them before the authorities in the market-square. There they brought them before the magistrates, and said,

"These men are Jews and are causing a great disturbance in our city. They are proclaiming customs which it is illegal for us as Roman citizens to accept or practise."

At this the crowd joined in the attack, and the magistrates had them stripped and ordered them to be beaten with rods. Then, after giving them a severe beating, they threw them into prison, instructing the jailer to keep them safe. On receiving such strict orders, he hustled them into the inner jail and fastened their feet securely in the stocks.

The midnight deliverance: the jailer becomes a Christian

But about midnight Paul and Silas were praying and singing hymns to God while the other prisoners were listening to them. Suddenly there was a great earthquake, big enough to shake the foundations of the prison. Immediately all the doors flew open and everyone's chains were unfastened. When the jailer woke and saw that the doors of the prison had been opened he drew his sword and was on the point of killing himself, for he imagined that all the prisoners had escaped. But Paul called out to him at the top of his voice,

"Don't hurt yourself—we are all here!"

Then the jailer called for lights, rushed in, and trembling all over, fell at the feet of Paul and Silas. He led them outside, and said,

"Sirs, what must I do to be saved?"

And they replied,

"Believe in the Lord Jesus and then you will be saved, you and your household."

Then they told him and all the members of his household the message of the Lord. There and then in the middle of the night he took them aside and washed their wounds and he himself and all his family were baptised without delay. Then he took them into his house and offered them food, he and his whole household overjoyed at finding faith in God.

Paul, in a strong position, makes the authorities apologise

When morning came, the magistrates sent their constables with the message, "Let those men go." The jailer reported this message to Paul, saying,

"The magistrates have sent to have you released. So now you can leave this place and go on your way in peace."

But Paul said to the constables,

"They beat us publicly without any kind of trial; they threw us into prison despite the fact that we are Roman citizens. And now do they want to get rid of us in this underhand way? Oh no, let them come and take us out themselves!"

The constables reported these words to the magistrates, who were thoroughly alarmed when they heard that they were Romans. So they came in person and apologised to them, and after taking them outside the prison, requested them to leave the city. But on leaving the prison Paul and Silas went to Lydia's house, and when they had seen the brothers and given them fresh courage, they took their leave.

CHAPTER 17

Bitter opposition at Thessalonica—

NEXT they journeyed through Amphipolis and Apollonia and arrived at Thessalonica. Here there was a synagogue of the Jews which Paul entered, following his usual custom. On three Sabbath days he argued with them from the scriptures, explaining and quoting passages to prove the necessity for the death of Christ and his rising again from the dead. "This Jesus whom I am proclaiming to you," he concluded, "is God's Christ!" Some of them were convinced and sided with Paul and Silas, and they were joined by a great many believing Greeks and a considerable number of influential women. But the Jews, in a fury of jealousy, got hold of some of the unprincipled loungers of the market-place to incite a mob together and set the city in an uproar. Then they attacked Jason's house in an attempt to bring Paul and Silas out before the people. When they could not find them they hustled Jason and some of the brothers before the civic authorities, shouting, "These are the men who have turned the world upside down and have now come here, and Jason has taken them into his house. What is more, all these men act against the decrees of Caesar, saying that there is another king called Jesus!" By these words the Jews succeeded in alarming both the people and the authorities, and they only released Jason and the others after binding them over to keep the peace.

—followed by encouragement at Berœa

Without delay the brothers despatched Paul and Silas off to Berœa that night. On their arrival there they went to the Jewish synagogue. The Jews proved more sympathetic than those in Thessalonica, for they accepted the message most eagerly and studied the scriptures every day to see if what they were now being told were true. As a result many of them became believers, and so did a number of Greek women of social standing and quite a number of men. But when the Jews at Thessalonica found out that God's message had been proclaimed by Paul at Berœa as well, they came there too to stir up trouble and spread alarm among the crowds. The brothers at Berœa then sent Paul off at once to make his way to the sea-coast, but Silas and Timothy remained there. The men who escorted Paul took him as far as Athens and returned with instructions for Silas and Timothy to rejoin Paul as soon as possible.

Paul is irritated by the idols of Athens

Paul had some days to wait at Athens for Silas and Timothy to arrive, and while he was there his soul was exasperated at the sight of a city so completely idolatrous. He felt compelled to discuss the matter with the Jews in the synagogue as well as with God-fearing gentiles, and he even argued daily in the open market-place with the passers-by. While he was speaking there some Epicurean and Stoic philosophers came across him, and some of them remarked,

"What is this cock-sparrow trying to say?"

Others said,

"He seems to be trying to proclaim some more gods to us, and foreign ones at that!"

For Paul was actually proclaiming "Jesus" and "the resurrection". So they got hold of him and conducted him to their council, the Areopagus. There they asked him,

"May we know what this new teaching of yours really is? You talk of matters which sound strange to our ears, and we should like to know what they mean." (For all the Athenians, and even foreign visitors to Athens, had an obsession for any novelty and would spend their whole time talking about or listening to anything new.)

Paul's speech to the "gentlemen of Athens"

So Paul got to his feet in the middle of their council, and began,

"Gentlemen of Athens, my own eyes tell me that you are in all respects an extremely religious people. For as I walked through your city looking at your shrines, I even found one altar on which were inscribed the words, TO GOD THE UNKNOWN. It is this God whom you are worshipping in ignorance that I am here to proclaim to you! God who made the world and all that is in it, being Lord of both Heaven and earth, does not live in man-made temples, nor is he ministered to by human hands, as though he had need of anything—seeing that he is the one who gives to all men life and breath and everything else. From one ancestor he has created every race of men to live over the face of the whole earth. He has determined the times of their existence and the limits of their habitation, so that they might search for God, in the hope that they might feel for him and find him—yes, even though he is not far from any one of us. Indeed, it is in him that we live and move and have our being. Some of your own poets have endorsed this in the words, 'For we are indeed his children'. If then we are the children of God, we ought not to think of him in terms of gold or silver or stone, designed by human art and imagination. Now while it is true that God has overlooked the days of ignorance he now commands all men everywhere to repent. For he has fixed a day on which he will judge the whole world in justice by the standard of a man whom he has appointed. That this is so he has guaranteed to all men by raising this man from the dead."

But when his audience heard Paul talk about the resurrection from the dead some of them jeered, but others said,

"We should like to hear you speak again on this subject."

So with this mixed reception Paul retired from their assembly. Yet some did in fact join him and accept the faith, including Dionysius a member of the Areopagus, a woman by the name of Damaris, and some others as well.

CHAPTER 18

At Corinth Paul is yet again rejected by the Jews

BEFORE long Paul left Athens and went on to Corinth where he found a Jew called Aquila, a native of Pontus. This man had recently come from Italy with his wife Priscilla, because Claudius had issued a decree that all Jews should leave Rome. He went to see them in their house and because they practised the same trade as himself he stayed with them. They all worked together, for their trade was tent-making. Every Sabbath Paul used to speak in the synagogue trying to persuade both Jews and Greeks. By the time Silas and Timothy arrived from Macedonia Paul was completely absorbed in preaching the message, showing the Jews as clearly as he could that Jesus is Christ. However, when they turned against him and abused him he shook his garments at them, and said,

"Your blood be on your own heads! From now on I go with a perfectly clear conscience to the gentiles."

Then he left them and went to the house of a man called Titius Justus, a man who reverenced God and whose house was next door to the synagogue. Crispus, the president of the synagogue, became a believer in the Lord, with all his household, and many of the Corinthians who heard the message believed and were baptised. Then one night the Lord spoke to Paul in a vision,

"Do not be afraid, but go on speaking and let no one silence you, for I myself am with you and no man shall lift a finger to harm you. There are many in this city who belong to me."

So Paul settled down there for eighteen months and taught them God's message.

Paul's enemies fail to impress the governor

Then, while Gallio was proconsul of Achaia, the Jews banded together to attack Paul, and took him to court, saying,

"This man is perverting men's minds to make them worship God in a way that is contrary to the Law."

Paul was all ready to speak, but before he could utter a word Gallio said to the Jews,

"Listen, Jews! If this were a matter of some crime or wrongdoing I might reasonably be expected to put up with you. But if it is a question which concerns words and names and your own Law, you must attend to it yourselves. I flatly refuse to be judge in these matters."

And he had them ejected from the court. Then they all seized Sosthenes, the president of the synagogue, and beat him in front of the court-house. But Gallio remained completely unconcerned.

Paul returns, and reports to Jerusalem and Antioch

Paul stayed for some time after this incident and then took leave of the brothers and sailed for Syria, taking Priscilla and Aquila with him. At Cenchrea he had his hair cut short, for he had taken a solemn vow. They all arrived at Ephesus and there Paul left Aquila and Priscilla, but he himself went into the synagogue and debated with the Jews. When they asked him to stay longer he refused, bidding them farewell with the words, "If it is God's will I will come back to you again." Then he set sail from Ephesus and went down to Caesarea. Here he disembarked and after paying his respects to the Church in Jerusalem, he went down to Antioch. He spent some time there before he left and proceeded to visit systematically throughout Galatia and Phrygia, putting new heart into all the disciples as he went.

Apollos speaks powerfully at Ephesus and Corinth

Now a Jew called Apollos, a native of Alexandria and a gifted speaker, well-versed in the scriptures, arrived at Ephesus. He had been instructed in the way of the Lord, and he spoke with burning zeal, teaching the facts about Jesus faithfully even though he only knew the baptism of John. This man began to speak with great boldness in the synagogue. But when Priscilla and Aquila heard him they took him aside and explained the Way of God to him more accurately. Then as he wanted to cross into Achaia, the brothers gave him every encouragement and wrote a letter to the disciples there, asking them to make him welcome. On his arrival he proved a source of great strength to those who had believed through grace, for by his powerful arguments he publicly refuted the Jews, quoting from the scriptures to prove that Jesus is Christ.

CHAPTER 19

Ephesus has its own Pentecost

WHILE Apollos was in Corinth* Paul journeyed through the upper parts of the country and arrived at Ephesus. There he discovered some disciples, and he asked them,

"Did you receive the Holy Spirit when you believed?"

"No," they replied, "we have never even heard that there is a Holy Spirit."

"Well then, how were you baptised?" asked Paul.

"We were baptised with John's baptism," they replied.

"John's baptism was a baptism to show a change of heart," Paul explained, "but he always told the people that they must believe in the one who should come after him, that is, in Jesus."

When these men heard this they were baptised in the name of the Lord Jesus, and then, when Paul had laid his hands on them, the Holy Spirit came upon them and they began to speak with tongues and the inspiration of prophets. (There were about twelve of them in all.)

Paul's two-year ministry at Ephesus

Then Paul made his way into the synagogue there and for three months he spoke with the utmost confidence, using both argument and persuasion as he talked of the kingdom of God. But when some of them hardened in their attitude towards the message and refused to believe it, and, what is more, spoke offensively about the Way in public, Paul left them, and withdrew his disciples, and held daily discussions in the lecture-hall of Tyrannus.

* See page 281.

He continued this practice for two years, so that all who lived in the province of Asia, both Greeks and Jews, could hear the Lord's message. God gave most unusual demonstrations of power through Paul's hands, so much so that people took to the sick any towels or handkerchiefs which had been in contact with his body, and they were cured of their diseases and their evil spirits left them.

The violence of evil and the power of the "name"

But there were some itinerant Jewish exorcists who attempted to invoke the name of the Lord Jesus when dealing with those who had evil spirits. They would say, "I command you in the name of Jesus whom Paul preaches." Seven brothers, sons of a chief priest called Sceva, were engaged in this practice on one occasion, when the evil spirit answered, "Jesus I know, and I know about Paul, but who are you?" And the man in whom the evil sprit was living sprang at them and overpowered them all with such violence that they rushed out of that house wounded, with their clothes torn off their backs. This incident became known to all the Jews and Greeks who were living in Ephesus, and a great sense of awe came over them all, while the name of the Lord Jesus became even more respected. Many of those who had professed their faith began openly to admit their former practices. A number of those who had previously practised magic collected their books and burned them publicly. (They estimated the value of these books and found it to be no less than five thousand pounds.) In this way the Word of the Lord continued to grow in influence and power.

Paul speaks of his plans

After these events Paul was led by the Spirit to plan a journey to Jerusalem, going by way of Macedonia and Achaia, remarking, "After I have been there I must see Rome as well."

Then he despatched to Macedonia two of his assistants, Timothy and Erastus, while he himself stayed for a while in Asia.

The silversmiths' riot at Ephesus

Now it happened about this time that a great commotion arose concerning the Way. A man by the name of Demetrius, a silversmith who made silver shrines of Artemis, provided considerable

ADRIATIC SEA
ITALY
MACEDONIA
Thessalonica
Beroea
Philippi
Neapolis
GREECE
Corinth
Cenchreae
BITHYNIA
ASIA
Troas
Assos
Mitylene
CHIOS
SAMOS
Ephesus
Trogyllium
Miletus
COS
Cnidus
Rhodes
RHODES
Patara
CRETE
MEDITERRANEAN SEA
PISIDIA
Antioch
Lystra
Iconium
Derbe
Tarsus
Antioch
Seleucia
SYRIA
PHOENICIA
CYPRUS
Tyre
Ptolemais
Caesarea
Jerusalem
N
Miles
0
100
200
300
PAUL'S JOURNEY No 3

business for his craftsmen. He gathered these men together with workers in similar trades, and spoke to them,

"Men," he said, "you all realise how our prosperity depends on this particular work. If you use your eyes and ears you also know that not only in Ephesus but practically throughout Asia this man Paul has succeeded in changing the minds of a great number of people by telling them that gods made by human hands are not gods at all. Now the danger is not only that this craft of ours might fall into disrepute, but also that the temple of the great goddess Artemis herself might come to be lightly regarded. There is a further danger, that her actual majesty might be degraded, she whom the whole of Asia, and indeed the whole world, worships!"

When they heard this they were furiously angry, and shouted,

"Great is Artemis of the Ephesians!"

Soon the whole city was in an uproar, and on a common impulse the people rushed into the theatre dragging with them Gaius and Aristarchus, two Macedonians who were Paul's travelling companions. Paul himself wanted to go in among the crowd, but the disciples would not allow him. Moreover, some high-ranking officials who were Paul's friends sent to him begging him not to risk himself in the theatre. Meanwhile some were shouting one thing and some another, and the whole assembly was at sixes and sevens, for most of them had no idea why they had come together at all. A man called Alexander whom the Jews put forward was pushed as spokesman into the forefront of the crowd, and there, after making a gesture with his hand, he tried to make a speech of defence to the people. But as soon as they realised that he was a Jew they shouted as one man for about two hours, "Great is Artemis of the Ephesians!"

Public authority intervenes

But when the town clerk had finally quietened the crowd, he said,

"Gentlemen of Ephesus, who in the world could be ignorant of the fact that our city of Ephesus is temple-guardian of the great Artemis and of the image which fell from the sky? These are undeniable facts and it is your plain duty to remain calm and do nothing which you might afterwards regret. For you have brought these men forward, though they are neither plunderers of the temple, nor have they uttered any blasphemy against our goddess. If Demetrius and his fellow-craftsmen have a charge to bring against anyone, well, the courts are open and there are proconsuls; let them take legal action. But if you require anything beyond that then it must be resolved in the regular assembly. For all of us are in danger of being charged with rioting over today's events particularly as we have no real excuse to offer for this commotion."

And with these words he dismissed the assembly.

CHAPTER 20

Paul departs on his second journey to Europe

*AFTER this disturbance had died down, Paul sent for the disciples and after speaking encouragingly said good-bye to them, and set out on his journey to Macedonia. As he made his journey through these districts he spoke many heartening words to the people and then went on to Greece, where he stayed for three months. Then when he was on the point of setting sail for Syria the Jews made a further plot against him and he decided to make his way back through Macedonia. His companions on the journey were Sopater a Berœan, the son of Pyrrhus, two Thessalonians, Aristarchus and Secundus, Gaius from Derbe, Timothy, and two Asians, Tychicus and Trophimus. This party proceeded to Troas to await us there, while we sailed from Philippi after the days of unleavened bread, and joined them five days later at Troas, where we spent a week.

Paul's enthusiasm leads to an accident

On the Saturday, when we were assembled for the breaking of bread, Paul, since he intended to leave on the following day, began to speak to them and prolonged his address until midnight. There were a great many lamps burning in the upper room where we met, and a young man called Eytychus who was sitting on the window-sill grew more and more sleepy as Paul's address became longer and longer. Finally, completely overcome by sleep, he fell to the ground from the third storey and was picked up as dead. But Paul went down, flung himself beside him and holding him gently in his arms, said,

"Don't be alarmed; he is still alive."

Then he went upstairs again and, when he had broken bread and eaten, continued a long earnest talk with them until daybreak,

* See page 281.

and so finally departed. As for the boy, they took him home alive, feeling immeasurably relieved.

We sail to Miletus

Meanwhile we had gone aboard the ship and sailed on ahead for Assos, intending to pick up Paul there, for that was the arrangement he had made, since he himself had planned to go overland. When he met us on our arrival at Assos we took him aboard and went on to Mitylene. We sailed from there and arrived off the coast of Chios the next day. On the day following we crossed to Samos, and the day after that we reached Miletus. For Paul had decided to sail past Ephesus with the idea of spending as little time as possible in the province of Asia. He hoped, if it should prove possible, to reach Jerusalem in time for the day of Pentecost.

Paul's moving farewell message to the elders of Ephesus

At Miletus he sent to Ephesus to summon the elders of the church. On their arrival he addressed them in these words:

"I am sure you know how I have lived among you ever since I first set foot in Asia. You know how I have served the Lord most humbly and what tears I have shed and what trials have come to me through the plots of the Jews. You know I have never shrunk from telling you anything that was for your good, nor from teaching you in public or in your own homes. On the contrary I have most emphatically urged upon both Jews and Greeks repentance towards God and faith in our Lord Jesus. And now here I am, compelled by the Spirit to go to Jerusalem. I do not know what may happen to me there, except that the Holy Spirit warns me that imprisonment and persecution await me in every city that I visit. But I do not consider my own life important or valuable to me, so long as I can finish my course and complete the ministry which the Lord Jesus has given me in declaring the good news of the grace of God. Now I know well enough that not one of you among whom I have moved as I preached the kingdom of God will ever see my face again. That is why I must tell you solemnly today that my conscience is clear as far as any of you is concerned, for I have never shrunk from declaring to you the whole purpose of God. Now be on your guard for yourselves and for every flock of which the Holy Spirit has made you guardians—you are to be shepherds to the Church of God, which he won at the cost of his own blood. I know that after my departure savage wolves will come in among you without mercy for the flock. Yes, and even from among you men will arise speaking perversions of the truth, trying to draw away the disciples and make them followers of themselves. This is why I tell you to keep on the alert, remembering that for three years I never failed night and day to warn every one of you, even with tears in my eyes. Now I commend you to God and to the message of his grace which can build you up and give you your inheritance among all those who are consecrated to him. I have never coveted anybody's gold or silver or clothing. You know well enough that these hands of mine have provided for my own needs and for those of my companions. In everything I have shown you that by such hard work we must help the weak and must remember the words of the Lord Jesus when he said, 'To give is happier than to receive'."

With these words he knelt down with them all and prayed. All of them were in tears, and throwing their arms round Paul's neck they kissed him affectionately. What saddened them most of all was his saying that they would never see his face again. And they went with him down to the ship.

CHAPTER 21

The brothers of Tyre warn Paul not to go to Jerusalem

WHEN we had finally said farewell to them we set sail, running a straight course to Cos, and the next day we went to Rhodes and from there to Patara. Here we found a ship bound for Phoenicia, and we went aboard her and set sail. After sighting Cyprus and leaving it on our left we sailed to Syria and put in at Tyre, since that was where the ship was to discharge her cargo. We sought out the disciples there and stayed with them for a week. They felt led by the Spirit again and again to warn Paul not to go up to Jerusalem. But when our time was up we left them and continued our journey. They all came out to see us off, bringing their wives and children with them, accompanying us till we were outside the city. Then kneeling down on the beach we prayed and said good-bye to each other. Then we went aboard the ship, while the disciples went back home. We sailed away from Tyre and arrived at Ptolemais. We greeted the brothers there and stayed with them for just one day. On the following day we left and came to Caesarea and there we went to stay at the house of Philip the evangelist, one of the seven deacons. He had four unmarried daughters, all of whom spoke by the Spirit of God. During our stay there of several days a prophet by the name of Agabus came down from Judaea. When he came to see us he took Paul's girdle and used it to tie his own hands and feet together, saying, "The Holy Spirit says this: the man to whom this girdle belongs will be bound like this by the Jews in Jerusalem and handed over to the gentiles!"

We all warn Paul, but he is immovable

When we heard him say this, we and the people there begged Paul not to go up to Jerusalem. Then Paul answered us,

"What do you mean by unnerving me with all your tears? I am perfectly prepared not only to be bound but to die in Jerusalem for the sake of the name of the Lord Jesus."

Since he could not be dissuaded all we could do was to say, "May the Lord's will be done," and no more.

Paul is warmly welcomed at first

After this we made our preparations and went up to Jerusalem. Some of the disciples from Caesarea accompanied us and they took us to Mnason, a native of Cyprus and one of the earliest disciples, with whom we were going to stay. On our arrival at Jerusalem the brothers gave us a very warm welcome. On the following day Paul went with us to visit James, and all the elders were present. When he had greeted them he gave them a detailed account of all that God had done among the gentiles through his ministry, and they, on hearing this account, glorified God. Then they said to him,

"You know, brother, how many thousands there are among the Jews who have become believers, and that every one of these is a staunch upholder of the Law. They have been informed about you—that you teach all Jews who live among the gentiles to disregard the Law of Moses, and tell them not to circumcise their children nor observe the old customs. What will happen now, for they are bound to hear that you have arrived? Now why not follow this suggestion of ours? We have four men here under a vow. Suppose you join them and be purified with them, pay their expenses so that they may have their hair cut short, and then everyone will know there is no truth in the stories about you, but that you yourself observe the Law. As for those gentiles who have believed, we have sent them a letter with our decision that they should abstain from what has been offered to idols, from blood and from what has been strangled, and from sexual immorality."

But his enemies attempt to murder him

So Paul joined the four men and on the following day, after being purified with them, went into the Temple to give notice of the time when the period of purification would be finished and an offering would be made on behalf of each one of them. The seven days were almost over when the Jews from the province of Asia caught sight of Paul in the Temple. They stirred up the whole crowd and seized him, shouting, "Men of Israel, help! This is the man who is teaching everybody everywhere to despise our people, our Law and this place. Why, he has even brought Greeks into the Temple and he has defiled this holy place!" For they had previously seen Trophimus the Ephesian with Paul in the city and the had concluded that Paul had brought him into the Temple. The whole city was stirred by this speech and a mob collected who seized Paul and dragged him outside the Temple, and the doors were slammed behind him.

Paul is rescued by Roman soldiers

They were trying to kill him when a report reached the ears of the colonel of the regiment that the whole of Jerusalem was in an uproar. Without a moment's delay he took soldiers and centurions and ran down to them. When they saw the colonel and the soldiers they stopped beating Paul. The colonel came up to Paul and arrested him and ordered him to be shackled with two chains. Then he enquired who the man was and what he had been doing. Some of the crowd shouted one thing and some another, and since he could not be certain of the facts because of the shouting that was going on, the colonel ordered him to be brought to the barracks. When Paul got to the steps he was actually carried by the soldiers because of the violence of the mob. For the mass of the people followed, shouting, "Kill him!" Just as they were going to take him into the barracks Paul asked the colonel,

"May I say something to you?"

"So you know Greek, do you?" the colonel replied. "Aren't you that Egyptian who not long ago raised a riot and led those four thousand assassins into the desert?"

"I am a Jew," replied Paul. "I am a man of Tarsus in Cilicia, a citizen of that not insignificant city. I ask you to let me speak to the people."

Paul attempts to defend himself

On being given permission Paul stood on the steps and made a gesture with his hand to the people. There was a deep hush as he began to speak to them in Hebrew.

CHAPTER 22

"MY brothers and my fathers, listen to what I have to say in my own defence."

As soon as they heard him addressing them in Hebrew the silence became intense.

"I myself am a Jew," Paul went on. "I was born in Tarsus in Cilicia, but I was brought up here in this city, I received my training at the feet of Gamaliel, and I was schooled in the strictest observance of our fathers' Law. I was as much on fire with zeal for God as you all are today. I am also the man who persecuted this Way to the death, arresting both men and women and throwing them into prison, as the High Priest and the whole council can readily testify. Indeed, it was after receiving letters from them to their brothers in Damascus that I set out for that city, intending to arrest any followers of the Way I could find there and bring them back to Jerusalem as prisoners for punishment. Then this happened to me. As I was on my journey and getting near to Damascus, about midday a great light from the sky suddenly blazed around me. I fell to the ground, and I heard a voice saying to me, 'Saul, Saul, why are you persecuting me?' I replied, 'Who are you, Lord?' He said to me, 'I am Jesus of Nazareth whom you are persecuting.' My companions naturally saw the light, but they did not hear the voice of the one who was talking to me. 'What am I to do, Lord?' I asked. And the Lord told me, 'Get up and go on to Damascus and there you will be told of all that has been determined for you to do.' I was blinded by the brightness of that light and my companions had to take me by the hand and so

I came to Damascus. There, there was a man called Ananias, a reverent observer of the Law and a man highly respected by all the Jews who lived there. He came to visit me and as he stood by my side said, 'Saul, brother, you may see again!' At once I regained my sight and looked at him. 'The God of our fathers,' he went on, 'has chosen you to know his will, to see the Righteous One, to hear words from his own lips, for you will be his witness before all men of what you have seen and heard. And now what are you waiting for? Get up and be baptised! Be clean from your sins as you call on his name.'

Paul claims that God sent him to the gentiles

"Then it happened that after my return to Jerusalem, while I was at prayer in the Temple, I fell into a trance and saw Jesus, and he said to me, 'Make haste and leave Jerusalem at once, for they will not accept your testimony about me.' And I said, 'Lord, they know how I have been through the synagogues imprisoning and beating all those who believe in you. They know also that when the blood of your martyr Stephen was shed I stood by, giving my approval—why, I was even in charge of the outer garments of those who killed him.' But he said to me, 'Go, for I will send you far away to the gentiles'."

The consequence of Paul's speech

They had listened to him until he said this, but now they raised a great shout,

"Away with him, rid the earth of such a man! He is not fit to live!"

As they were yelling and flapping their clothes and hurling dust into the air, the colonel gave orders to bring Paul into the barracks and directed that he should be examined by scourging, so that he might discover the reason for such an uproar against him. But when they had strapped him up, Paul spoke to the centurion standing by,

"Is it legal for you to flog a man who is a Roman citizen, and untried at that?"

On hearing this the centurion went in to the colonel and reported to him, saying.

"Do you realise what you were about to do? This man is a Roman citizen!"

Then the colonel himself came up to Paul, and said,
"Tell me, are you a Roman citizen?"
And he said,
"Yes."
Whereupon the colonel replied,
"It cost me a good deal to get my citizenship."
"Ah," replied Paul, "but I was born a citizen."
Then those who had been about to examine him left hurriedly, while even the colonel himself was alarmed at discovering that Paul was a Roman and that he had had him bound.

Roman fair-mindedness

Next day the colonel, determined to get to the bottom of Paul's accusation by the Jews, released him and ordered the assembly of the chief priests and the whole Sanhedrin. Then he took Paul down and placed him in front of them.

CHAPTER 23

Paul again attempts defence

PAUL looked steadily at the Sanhedrin and spoke to them,

"Men and brothers, I have lived my life with a perfectly clear conscience before God up to the present day——" Then Ananias the High Priest ordered those who were standing near to strike him on the mouth. At this Paul said to him,

"God will strike you, you white-washed wall! How dare you sit there judging me by the Law and give orders for me to be struck, which is clean contrary to the Law?"

Those who stood by said,

"Do you mean to insult God's High Priest?"

But Paul said,

"My brothers, I did not know that he was the High Priest, for it is written:

Thou shalt not speak evil of a ruler of thy people."

Paul seizes his opportunity

Then Paul, realising that part of the council were Sadducees and the other part Pharisees, raised his voice and said to them,

"I am a Pharisee, the son of Pharisees. It is for my hope in the resurrection of the dead that I am on trial!"

At these words an immediate tension arose between the Pharisees and the Sadducees, and the meeting was divided. For the Sadducees claim that there is no resurrection and that there is neither angel nor spirit, while the Pharisees believe in all three. A great uproar ensued and some of the scribes of the Pharisees' party jumped to their feet and protested violently.

"We find nothing wrong with this man! Suppose some angel or spirit has really spoken to him?"

As the tension mounted the colonel began to fear that Paul would be torn to pieces between them. He therefore ordered his soldiers to come down and rescue him from them and bring him back to the barracks.

God's direct encouragement to Paul

That night the Lord stood by Paul, and said,

"Take heart!—for as you have witnessed boldly for me in Jerusalem so you must give your witness for me in Rome."

Paul's acute danger

Early in the morning the Jews formed a conspiracy and bound themselves by a solemn oath that they would neither eat nor drink until they had killed Paul. Over forty of them were involved in this plot, and they approached the chief priests and elders, and said,

"We have bound ourselves by a solemn oath to let nothing pass our lips until we have killed Paul. Now you and the council must make it plain to the colonel that you want him to bring Paul down to you, suggesting that you want to examine his case more closely. We shall be standing by ready to kill him before he gets here."

Leakage of information leads to Paul's protection

However, Paul's nephew got wind of this plot and he came and found his way into the barracks and told Paul about it. Paul called one of the centurions and said,

"Take this young man to the colonel for he has something to report to him."

So the centurion took him and brought him into the colonel's presence, and said,

"The prisoner Paul called for me and requested that this young man should be brought to you as he has something to tell you."

The colonel took his hand, and drew him aside (where they could not be overheard), and asked,

"What have you got to report to me?"

And he replied,

"The Jews have agreed to ask you to bring Paul down to the Sanhedrin tomorrow as though they were going to enquire more carefully into his case. But I beg you not to let them persuade you. For more than forty of them are waiting for him—they have sworn a solemn oath that they will neither eat nor drink until they have killed him. They are all ready at this moment—all they want is for you to give the order."

At this the colonel dismissed the young man with the caution,

"Don't let anyone know that you have given me this information."

Then he summoned two of his centurions, and said,

"Get two hundred men ready to proceed to Caesarea, with seventy horsemen and two hundred spearmen, by nine o'clock tonight. Mounts must also be provided to carry Paul safely to Felix the governor."

The Roman view of Paul's position

He further wrote a letter to Felix in these terms:

"Claudius Lysias sends greeting to his excellency the governor Felix.

"This man had been seized by the Jews and was on the point of being murdered by them when I arrived with my troops and rescued him, since I had discovered that he was a Roman citizen. Wishing to find out what the accusation was that they were making against him, I had him brought down to their Sanhedrin. There I discovered he was being accused over questions of their laws, and that there was no charge against him which deserved either death or imprisonment. Now, however, that I have received private information of a plot against his life, I have sent him to you without delay. At the same time I have notified his accusers that they must make their charges against him in your presence."

Paul is taken into protective custody

The soldiers, acting on their orders, took Paul and, moving by night, brought him down to Antipatris. Next day they returned to the barracks, leaving the horsemen to accompany him further. They went into Caesarea and after delivering the letter to the governor, they handed Paul over to him. When the governor had read the letter he asked Paul what province he came from, and on learning that he came from Cilicia, he said,

"I will hear your case as soon as your accusers arrive."

Then he ordered him to be kept under guard in Herod's palace.

CHAPTER 24

The "professional" puts the case against Paul

FIVE days later Ananias the High Priest came down himself with some of the elders and a barrister by the name of Tertullus. They presented their case against Paul before the governor, and when Paul had been summoned, Tertullus began the prosecution in these words:

"We owe it to you personally, your excellency, that we enjoy lasting peace, and we know that it is due to your foresight that the nation enjoys improved conditions of living. At all times, and indeed everywhere, we acknowledge these things with the deepest gratitude. However—for I must not detain you too long—I beg you to give us a brief hearing with your customary kindness. The simple fact is that we have found this man a pestilential disturber of the peace among the Jews all over the world. He is a ringleader of the Nazarene sect, and he was on the point of desecrating the Temple when we overcame him. But you yourself will soon discover from the man himself all the facts about which we are accusing him."

Paul is given the chance to defend himself

The Jews joined in, asserting that these were the facts. Then Paul, at a nod from the governor, made his reply:

"I am well aware that you have been governor of this nation for many years, and I can therefore make my defence with every confidence. You can easily verify the fact that it is not more than twelve days ago that I went up to worship at Jerusalem. I was never found either arguing with anyone in the temple or gathering a crowd, either in the synagogues or anywhere in the city. These men are quite unable to prove the charges they are now making against me. I will freely admit to you, however, that I do worship the God of our fathers according to the Way which they call a sect, although in fact I believe in the scriptural authority of both the Law and the Prophets. I have the same hope in God which they themselves hold, that there is to be a resurrection of both good men and bad. With this hope before me I also do my utmost to live my whole life with a clear conscience before God and man.

Paul has nothing to hide

"It was after several years' absence from Jerusalem that I came back to make charitable gifts to my own nation and to make my offerings. It was in the middle of these duties that they found me, a man purified in the Temple. There was no mob and there was no disturbance until these Jews from Asia came, who should in my opinion have come before you and made their accusation, if they had anything against me. Or else, let these men themselves speak out now and say what crime they found me guilty of when I stood before the Sanhedrin—unless it was that one sentence that I shouted as I stood among them. All I said was this, 'It is about the resurrection of the dead that I am on trial before you this day'."

Felix defers decision

Then Felix, who was better acquainted with the Way than most people, adjourned the case and said,

"As soon as Colonel Lysias arrives I will give you my decision."

Then he gave orders to the centurion to keep Paul in custody, but to grant him reasonable liberty and allow any of his personal friends to look after his needs.

Felix plays for safety—and hopes for personal gain

Some days later Felix arrived with his wife Drusilla, herself a Jewess, and sent for Paul, and heard what he had to say about faith in Christ Jesus. But while Paul was talking about goodness, self-control and the judgment that is to come, Felix became alarmed, and said,

"You may go for the present. When I find a convenient moment I will send for you again."

At the same time he nursed a secret hope that Paul would pay him money—which is why Paul was frequently summoned to come and talk with him. However, when two full years had passed, Felix was succeeded by Porcius Festus and, as he wanted to remain in favour with the Jews, he left Paul still a prisoner.

CHAPTER 25

Felix's successor begins his duties with vigour—

THREE days after Festus had taken over his province he went up from Caesarea to Jerusalem. The chief priests and leaders of the Jews informed him of the case against Paul and begged him as a special favour to have Paul sent to Jerusalem. They themselves had already made a plot to kill him on the way. But Festus replied that Paul was in custody in Caesarea, and that he himself was going there shortly.

"What you must do," he told them, "is to provide some competent men of your own to go down with me and if there is anything wrong with the man they can present their charges against him."

Festus spent not more than eight or ten days among them at Jerusalem and then went down to Caesarea. On the day after his arrival he took his seat on the bench and ordered Paul to be brought in. As soon as he arrived the Jews from Jerusalem stood up on all sides of him, bringing forward many serious accusations which they were quite unable to substantiate. Paul, in his defence, maintained,

"I have committed no offence in any way against the Jewish Law, or against the Temple or against Caesar."

—but is afraid of antagonising the Jews

But Festus, wishing to show goodwill to the Jews, spoke directly to Paul,

"Are you prepared to go up to Jerusalem and stand your trial over these matters in my presence there?"

But Paul replied,

"I am now standing in Caesar's court and that is where I should be judged. I have done the Jews no harm, as you very well know. It comes to this: if I were a criminal and had committed some crime which deserved the death penalty, I do not object to dying. But as in fact there is no truth in the accusations these men have made, no one can use me as a gift to the Jews—*I appeal to Caesar!*"

Then Festus, after a conference with his advisers, replied, "You have appealed to Caesar—then to Caesar you shall go!"

Festus outlines Paul's case to Agrippa

Some days later King Agrippa and Bernice arrived at Caesarea on a state visit to Festus. They prolonged their stay for some days, and this gave Festus an opportunity of laying Paul's case before the king.

"I have a man here," he said, "who was left a prisoner by Felix. When I was in Jerusalem the chief priests and Jewish elders made allegations against him and demanded his conviction. I told them that the Romans were not in the habit of giving anybody up to please anyone, until the accused had had the chance of facing his accusers personally and been given the opportunity of defending himself on the charges made against him. Since these Jews came back here with me, I wasted no time but on the very next day I took my seat on the bench and ordered the man to be brought in. But when his accusers got up to speak they did not charge him with any such crimes as I had anticipated. Their differences with him were about their own religion and concerning a certain Jesus who had died, but whom Paul claimed to be still alive. I did not feel qualified to investigate such matters and so I asked the man if he were willing to go to Jerusalem and stand his trial over these matters there. But when Paul appealed to be kept in custody for the decision of the Emperor himself, I ordered him to be detained until such time as I could send him to Caesar."

Then Agrippa said to Festus,

"I have been wanting to hear this man myself."

"Then you shall hear him tomorrow," replied Festus.

Festus formally explains the difficulty of Paul's case

When the next day came, Agrippa and Bernice proceeded to the audience chamber with great pomp and ceremony, with an escort of military officers and prominent townsmen. Festus ordered Paul to be brought in and then he spoke:

"King Agrippa and all of you who are present, you see here the man about whom the whole Jewish people both at Jerusalem and in this city have petitioned me. They din it into my ears that he ought not to live any longer, but I for my part discovered nothing that he has done which deserves the death penalty. And since he has appealed to Caesar, I have decided to send him to Rome. But I have nothing specific to write to the emperor about him, and I have therefore brought him forward before you all, and especially before you, King Agrippa, so that from your examination of him there may emerge some charge which I may put in writing. For it seems senseless to me to send a prisoner before the emperor without indicating the charges against him."

CHAPTER 26

THEN Agrippa said to Paul,

"You have our permission to speak for yourself."

Paul repeats his story on a state occasion

So Paul, with a gesture of the hand, began his defence:

"King Agrippa, in answering all the charges that the Jews have made against me, I must say how fortunate I consider myself to be in making my defence before you personally today. For I know that you are thoroughly familiar with all the customs and disputes that exist among the Jews. I therefore ask you to listen to me patiently.

"The fact that I lived from my youth upwards among my own people in Jerusalem is well known to all Jews. They have known all the time, and could witness to the fact if they wished, that I lived as a Pharisee according to the strictest sect of our religion. Even today I stand here on trial because of a hope that I hold in a promise that God made to our forefathers—a promise for which our twelve tribes serve God zealously day and night, hoping to see it fulfilled. It is about this hope, your majesty, that I am being accused by Jews! Why does it seem incredible to you all that God should raise the dead? I once thought it my duty to oppose with the utmost vigour the name of Jesus of Nazareth. Yes, that is what I did in Jerusalem, and I had many of God's people imprisoned on the authority of the chief priests, and when they were condemned to death I gave my vote against them. Many and many a time in all the synagogues I had them punished and I used to try and force them to deny their Lord. I was mad with fury against them, and I hounded them even to distant cities. Once, your majesty, on my way to Damascus on this business, armed with the full authority and commission of the chief priests, at midday I saw a light from the sky, far brighter than the sun, blazing about me and my fellow-travellers. We all fell to the ground and I heard a voice saying to me in Hebrew, 'Saul, Saul, why are you persecuting me? It is hard for you to kick against your own conscience.' 'Who are you, Lord?' I said. And the Lord said to me, 'I am Jesus whom you are persecuting. Now get up and stand on your feet for I have shown myself to you for a reason—you are chosen to be my servant and a witness of what you have seen of me today, and of visions of me which you will see. I will rescue you both from your own people and from the gentiles to whom I now send you. I send you to open their eyes, to turn them from darkness to light, from the power of Satan to God, so that they may know forgiveness of their sins and take their place with all those who are made holy by their faith in me.'

"After that, King Agrippa, I could not disobey the heavenly vision. But first in Damascus and then in Jerusalem, through the whole of Judaea, and to the gentiles, I preached that men should repent and turn to God and live lives to prove their change of heart. This is why the Jews seized me in the Temple and tried to murder me. To this day I have received help from God himself, and I stand here as a witness to high and low, adding nothing to what the prophets and Moses foretold should take place, that is, that Christ should suffer, that he should be the first to rise from the dead, and so proclaim the message of light both to our people and to the gentiles!"

Festus concludes that Paul's enthusiasm is insanity

While he was thus defending himself Festus burst out,

"You are raving, Paul! All your learning has driven you mad!"

But Paul replied,

"I am not mad, your excellency. I speak nothing but the sober truth. The king knows of these matters, and I can speak freely before him. I cannot believe that any of these matters has escaped his notice, for it has been no hole-and-corner business. King

Agrippa, do you believe the prophets? But I know that you believe them."

"Much more of this, Paul," returned Agrippa, "and you will be making me a Christian!"

"Ah," returned Paul, "whether it means 'much more' or only a little, I would to God that both you and all who can hear me this day might become as I am—but without these chains!"

The Roman officials consider Paul innocent

Then the king rose to his feet and so did the governor and Bernice and those sitting with them, and when they had retired from the assembly they discussed the matter among themselves and agreed, "This man is doing nothing to deserve either death or imprisonment."

Agrippa said to Festus,

"This man might easily have been discharged if he had not appealed to Caesar."

CHAPTER 27

The last journey begins

As soon as it was decided that we should sail to Italy, Paul and some other prisoners were put under the charge of a centurion named Julius, of the emperor's own regiment.* We embarked on a ship hailing from Adramyttium, bound for the Asian ports, and set sail. Among our company was Aristarchus, a Macedonian from Thessalonica. On the following day we put in at Sidon, where Julius treated Paul most considerately by allowing him to visit his friends and accept their hospitality. From Sidon we put to sea again and sailed to leeward of Cyprus, since the winds were against us. Then, when we had crossed the gulf that lies off the coasts of Cilicia and Pamphylia, we arrived at Myra in Lycia. There the centurion found an Alexandrian ship bound for Italy and put us aboard her. For several days we beat slowly up to windward and only just succeeded in arriving off Cnidus. Then, since the wind was still blowing against us, we sailed under the lee of Crete, and rounded Cape Salmone. Coasting along with difficulty we came to a place called Fair Havens, near which is the city of Lasea. We had by now lost a great deal of time and sailing had already become dangerous as it was so late in the year. (The time of the autumn Fast was over.)

* See page 301.

Paul's warning is disregarded

So Paul warned them, and said,

"Men, I can see that this voyage is likely to result in damage and considerable loss—not only to ship and cargo, but even of our own lives as well."

But Julius paid more attention to the helmsman and the captain than to Paul's words of warning. Moreover, since the harbour is unsuitable for a ship to winter in, the majority were in favour of setting sail again in the hope of reaching Phoenix and wintering there. Phoenix is a harbour in Crete, facing south-west and north-west. So, when a moderate breeze sprang up, thinking they had obtained just what they wanted, they weighed anchor, and coasted along, hugging the shores of Crete. But before long a terrific gale, which they called a north-easter, swept down upon us. The ship was caught by it and since she could not be brought up into the wind we had to let her fall off and run before it. Then, running under the lee of a small island called Clauda, we managed with some difficulty to secure the ship's boat. After hoisting it aboard they used cables to undergird the ship. To add to the difficulties they were afraid all the time of drifting on to the Syrtis banks, so they shortened sail and let her drift. The next day, as we were still at the mercy of the violent storm, they began to throw cargo overboard. On the third day with their own hands they threw the ship's tackle over the side. Then, when for many days there was no glimpse of sun or stars and we were still in the grip of the gale, all hope of our being saved was given up.

Paul's practical courage and faith

Nobody had eaten for some time, when Paul came forward among the men and said,

"Men, you should have listened to me and not have set sail from Crete and suffered this damage and loss. However, now I beg you to keep up your spirits for no one's life is going to be lost, though we shall lose the ship. I know this because last night, the angel of God to whom I belong, and whom I serve, stood by me and said, 'Have no fear, Paul! You must stand before Caesar, and God has granted you the lives of those who are sailing with you.' Take courage then, men, for I believe God, and I am certain that everything will happen exactly as I have been told. But we shall have to run the ship ashore on some island."

ITALY
ADRIATIC SEA
EUXINE SEA
BITHYNIA
MACEDONIA
Rome
Three Taverns
Forum Apii
Puteoli
SICILY
Rhegium
Syracuse
GREECE
CILICIA
LYCIA
Cnidus
Myra
SEAS OF PAMPHYLIA & CILICIA
CYPRUS
CRETE
Phoenix
Lasea
C. Salmone
CLAUDA
FAIR HAVENS
MELITA
Sidon
Caesarea
Jerusalem
MEDITERRANEAN SEA
CYRENAICA
N
PAUL'S JOURNEY TO ROME
Miles
0
100
200
300
400
500

At last we near land

On the fourteenth night of the storm, as we were drifting in the Adriatic, about midnight the sailors sensed that we were nearing land. Indeed, when they sounded they found twenty fathoms, and then after sailing on only a little way they sounded again and found fifteen. So, for fear that we might be hurled on the rocks, they threw out four anchors from the stern and prayed for daylight. The sailors wanted to desert the ship and they got as far as letting a boat down into the sea, pretending that they were going to run out anchors from the bows. But Paul said to the centurion and the soldiers,

"Unless these men stay aboard the ship there is no hope of your being saved."

At this the soldiers cut the ropes of the boat and let her fall away.

Paul's sturdy commonsense

Then while everyone waited for the day to break Paul urged them to take some food, saying,

"For fourteen days now you've had no food—you haven't had a bite while you've been on watch. Now take some food, I beg of you—you need it for your survival. I assure you that not a hair of anyone's head will be lost."

When he had said this he took some bread and, after thanking God before them all, he broke it and began to eat. This raised everybody's spirits and they began to take food themselves. There were about two hundred and seventy-six of us all told aboard that ship. When they had eaten enough they lightened the ship by throwing the grain into the sea.

Land at last—but we lose the ship

When daylight came no one recognised the land. But they made out a bay with a sandy shore where they planned to beach the ship if they could. So they cut away the anchors and left them in the sea, and at the same time unlashed the ropes which held the steering-oars. Then they hoisted the foresail to catch the wind and made for the beach. But they struck a shoal and the ship ran aground. The bow stuck fast, while the stern began to break up under the pounding of the waves. The soldiers' plan had been to kill the prisoners in case any of them should try to swim to shore and escape. But the centurion, in his desire to save Paul, put a stop to this, and gave orders that all those who could swim should jump overboard first and get to land, while the rest should follow, some on planks and others on the wreckage of the ship. So it came true that everyone reached the shore in safety.

CHAPTER 28

A small incident establishes Paul's reputation

AFTER our escape we discovered that the island was called Melita. The natives treated us with exceptional kindness. Because of the driving rain and cold they lit a fire and made us all welcome. Then when Paul had collected a large bundle of sticks and was about to put it on the fire, a viper driven out by the heat fastened itself on his hand. When the natives saw the creature hanging from his hand they said to each other, "This man is obviously a murderer. He has escaped from the sea but justice will not let him live." But Paul shook off the viper into the fire without suffering any ill effect. Naturally they expected him to swell up or suddenly fall down dead, but after waiting a long time and seeing nothing out of the ordinary happen to him, they changed their minds and kept saying that he was a god.

Paul's acts of healing: the islanders' gratitude

In that part of the island were estates belonging to the governor, whose name was Publius. This man welcomed us and entertained us most kindly for three days. Now it happened that Publius' father was lying ill with attacks of fever and dysentery. Paul visited him and after prayer laid his hands on him and healed him. After that all the other sick people on the island came forward and were cured. Consequently they honoured us with many presents, and when the time came for us to sail they provided us with everything we needed.

Spring returns and we resume our journey

It was no less than three months later that we set sail in an Alexandrian ship which had wintered in the island, a ship that had the heavenly twins as her figurehead. We put in at Syracuse and stayed there three days, and from there we tacked round to

Rhegium. A day later the south wind sprang up and we sailed to Puteoli, reaching it in only two days. There we found some of the brothers and they begged us to stay a week with them, and so we came to Rome.

A Christian welcome awaits us in the capital

The brothers there had heard about us and came out from the city to meet us, as far as the Market of Appius and the Three Taverns. When Paul saw them he thanked God and his spirits rose. When we reached Rome Paul was given permission to live alone with the soldier who was guarding him.

Paul explains himself frankly to the Jews in Rome

Three days later Paul invited the leading Jews to meet him, and when they arrived he spoke to them,

"Men and brothers, although I have done nothing against our people or the customs of our forefathers, I was handed over to the Romans as a prisoner in Jerusalem. They examined me and were prepared to release me, since they found me guilty of nothing deserving the death penalty. But the attacks of the Jews there forced me to appeal to Caesar—not that I had any charge to make against my own nation. But it is because of this accusation of the Jews that I have asked to see you and talk matters over with you. In actual fact it is on account of the hope of Israel that I am here in chains."

But they replied,

"We have received no letters about you from Judaea, nor have any of the brothers who have arrived here said anything, officially or unofficially, against you. We want to hear you state your views, although as far as this sect is concerned we do know that serious objections have been raised to it everywhere."

Paul's earnest and prolonged effort to win his own people for Christ

When they had arranged a day for him they came to his lodging in great numbers. From morning till evening he explained the kingdom of God to them, giving his personal testimony, trying to persuade them about Jesus from the Law of Moses and the Prophets. As a result several of them were won over by his words, but others would not believe. When they could not reach any agreement among themselves and began to go away, Paul added as a parting shot, "How rightly did the Holy Spirit speak to your forefathers through the prophet Isaiah when he said,

Go thou unto this people, and say,
By hearing ye shall hear, and shall in no wise understand;
And seeing ye shall see, and shall in no wise perceive:
For this people's heart is waxed gross,
And their ears are dull of hearing,
And their eyes they have closed;
Lest haply they should perceive with their eyes,
And hear with their ears,
And understand with their heart,
And should turn again,
And I should heal them.

"Let it be plainly understood then that this salvation of our God has been sent to the gentiles, and they at least will listen to it!"

The last glimpse of Paul . . .

So Paul stayed for two full years in his own rented apartment welcoming all who came to see him. He proclaimed to them all the kingdom of God and gave them the teaching of the Lord Jesus Christ with the utmost freedom and without hindrance from anyone.

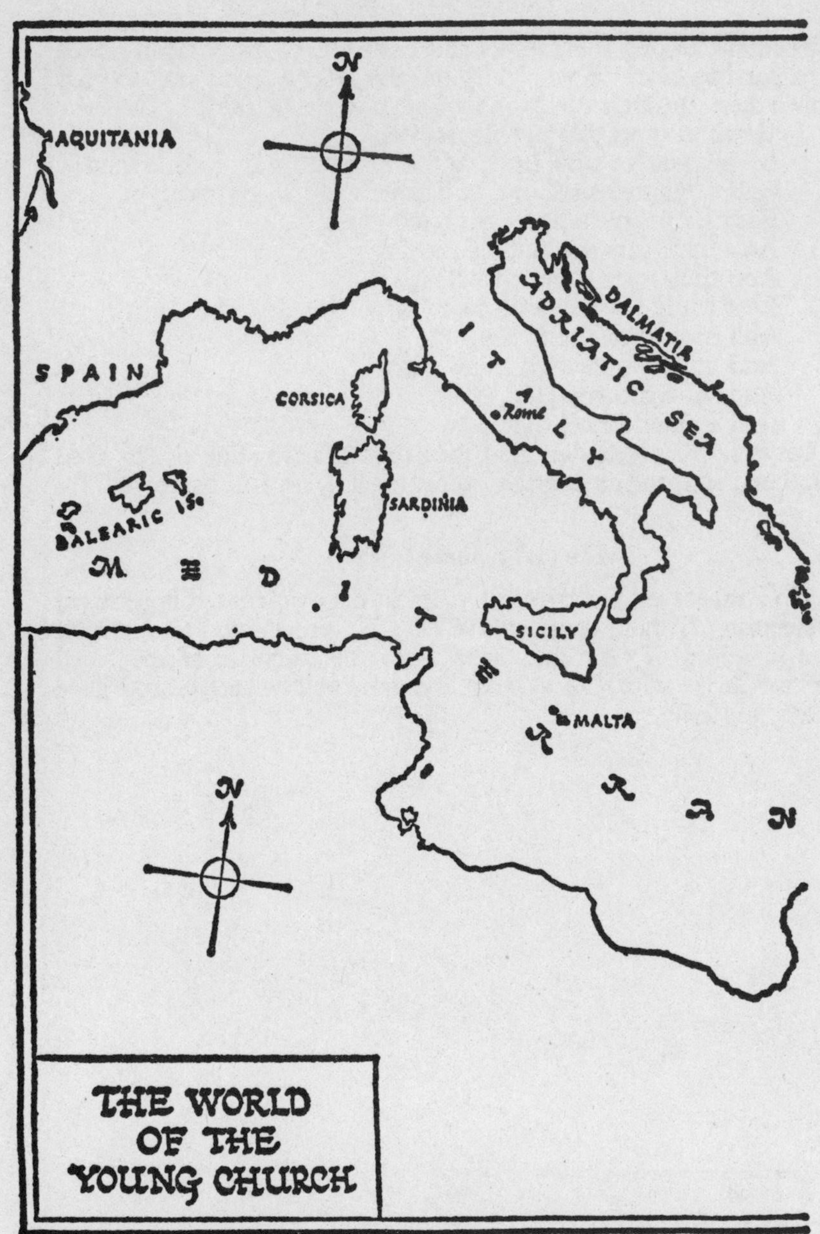
N
AQUITANIA
SPAIN
CORSICA
SARDINIA
BALEARIC Is.
DALMATIA
ADRIATIC SEA
ITALY
Rome
SICILY
MALTA
MEDITERRAN
N
THE WORLD
OF THE
YOUNG CHURCH

DACIA
EUXINE SEA
GREATER
ARMENIA
PONTUS
MACEDONIA
THRACE
Thessalonica
Philippi
BITHYNIA
GALATIA
CAPPADOCIA
Beroea
Troas
PHRYGIA
Antioch of Pisidia
Lystra
Tarsus
Derbe
Athens
Corinth
Cenchrea
Ephesus
Laodicea
Colossae
CILICIA
LYCIA
Antioch
SYRIA
PARTHIAN
KINGDOM
PHOENICIA
CYPRUS
Damascus
Sidon
Tyre
GALILEE
CRETE
Caesarea
Joppa
Jerusalem
Gaza
JUDAEA
SEA
IDUMAEA
Cyrene
CYRENAICA
Alexandria
ARABIA
MT. SINAI
EGYPT
RED SEA
Miles
0
100
200
300
400
500
600
700
800
900

LETTERS TO YOUNG CHURCHES

(THE EPISTLES)

The Letter to the Christians at Rome

AUTHOR. *Paul, probably written from Corinth (Acts 20, 3).*
DATE. *About 57.*
DESTINATION. *The Christians at Rome. No one knows how the church at Rome was founded, though it is perfectly possible that some Romans present on the day of Pentecost in Jerusalem (Acts 2, 10) carried back with them the Christian faith. The Roman Catholic tradition that Peter founded the Church in Rome is without reliable evidence.*

Paul is evidently writing to both converted Jews and converted pagans, which is what one would expect to find in the metropolitan city of the Roman Empire.

THEME. *This letter, with the possible exception of the "Letter to Jewish Christians", is the only one that appears to be written deliberately as a religious treatise and not merely in the ordinary way of correspondence. It is possible that Paul, naturally impressed that he was writing to the heart of the Empire, would take extra pains to "polish" this exposition of the faith.*

The theme is almost entirely that of God's "salvation" and needs a little explanation to the modern mind.

To Paul, brought up under the rigid Jewish Law, God was pre-eminently the God of Righteousness, i.e. moral perfection. In these days when the majority of people assume God to be a vague easy-going Benevolence it is difficult to appreciate the force of Paul's problem, or the wonder of its solution.

If we are prepared to grant the absolute moral perfection of God, eternally aflame with positive goodness, truth and beauty, we can perhaps understand that any form of sin or evil cannot approach God without instant dissolution. This is as inevitable as, for example, the destruction of certain germs by the light of the sun.

How then, asks Paul, can man who has failed and, moreover, sinned deliberately, ever approach God or hope to share in his timeless existence?

The Law offers the first method. If men will themselves fully obey the law of God they will be free from moral taint and able to approach God in safety. Unhappily, as Paul points out at some length, men have signally failed to keep either the Law revealed to the Jews or the universal moral law of human conscience. If they have broken all the laws or only a few they have all failed and are all guilty. They can, moreover, do nothing to remove their guilt. The Law which ought to be a finger-post to God becomes to them nothing but a warning-notice. This is the crux of Paul's problem.

The heart of the Gospel is that God himself meets this deadlock by a personal visit to this world. God, as Jesus Christ, became representative man, and as such deliberately accepted the eventual consequence of evil, namely, suffering and death. Any man therefore who sincerely entrusts his life to Christ can now be accepted by God by virtue of God's personal act of atonement. Salvation, i.e. being safe from the horrible long-term consequences of sin and safe in the presence of God's utter holiness, now becomes a matter of "believing" and not "achieving".

The theme is worked out in this letter, with a parenthetical passage about God's chosen people, the Jews, and is closely followed by advice as to the sort of life that the "justified" and "saved" man should now live.

The letter closes with personal news and greetings.

CHAPTER 1

THIS letter comes to you from Paul, a servant of Christ Jesus, called as a messenger and appointed for the service of that gospel of God which was long ago promised by the prophets in the holy scriptures.

The gospel is centred in God's Son, a descendant of David by human genealogy and patently marked out as the Son of God by the power of that Spirit of holiness which raised him to life again from the dead. He is our Lord, Jesus Christ, from whom we received grace and our commission in his name to forward obedience to the faith in all nations. And of this great number you are also called to belong to him.

To you all in Rome then, loved of God and called to be Christ's men and women, grace and peace from God our Father and from the Lord Jesus Christ.

A personal message

I must begin by telling you how I thank God through Jesus Christ for you all, since the news of your faith has become known everywhere. Before God, whom I serve with my spirit in the gospel of his Son, I assure you that you are always in my prayers. I am constantly asking him that he will somehow make it possible for me now, at long last, to come to see you. I am longing to see you: I want to bring you some spiritual gift to deepen your faith; and that will mean that I shall be encouraged by you, each of us cheered by the other's faith.

Then I should like you to know, my brothers, that I have long intended to come to you (but something has always prevented me), for I should like to see some results among you, as I have among other gentiles. I feel myself under a sort of universal obligation, I owe something to all men, from cultured Greek to ignorant savage. That is why I want, as far as my ability will carry me, to preach the gospel to you who live in Rome as well. For I am not ashamed of the gospel. I see it as the very power of God working for the salvation of everyone who believes it, for the Jew first but also for the Greek. I see in it God's plan for making men right in his sight, a process begun and continued by their faith. For, as the scripture says:

The righteous shall live by faith.

The righteousness of God and the sin of man

Now the holy anger of God is disclosed from Heaven against the godlessness and evil of those men who render truth dumb and impotent by their wickedness. It is not that they do not know the truth about God; indeed he has made it quite plain to them. For since the beginning of the world the invisible attributes of God, e.g. his eternal power and deity, have been plainly discernible through things which he has made and which are commonly seen and known, thus leaving these men without a rag of excuse. They knew all the time that there is a God, yet they refused to acknowledge him as such, or to thank him for what he is or does. Thus they became fatuous in their argumentations, and plunged their silly minds still further into the dark. Behind a façade of "wisdom" they became just fools, fools who would exchange the glory of the immortal God for an image of a mortal man, or of creatures that run or fly or crawl. They gave up

God: and therefore God gave them up—to be the playthings of their own foul desires in dishonouring their own bodies.

The fearful consequence of deliberate atheism

These men deliberately forfeited the truth of God and accepted a lie, paying homage and giving service to the creature instead of to the Creator, who alone is worthy to be worshipped for ever and ever, amen. God therefore handed them over to disgraceful passions. Their women exchanged the normal practices of sexual intercourse for something which is abnormal and unnatural. Similarly the men, turning from natural intercourse with women, were swept into lustful passions for one another. Men with men performed these shameful horrors, receiving in their own personalities the consequences of their perversity.

Moreover, since they considered themselves too high and mighty to acknowledge God, he allowed them to become the slaves of their degenerate minds, and to perform unmentionable deeds. They became filled with wickedness, rottenness, greed and malice; their minds became steeped in envy, murder, quarrelsomeness, deceitfulness and spite. They became whisperers-behind-doors, stabbers-in-the-back, God-haters; they overflowed with insolent pride and boastfulness, and their minds teemed with diabolical invention. They scoffed at duty to parents, they mocked at conscience, recognised no obligations of honour, lost all natural affection, and had no use for mercy. More than this—being well aware of God's pronouncement that all who do these things deserve to die, they not only continued their own practices, but did not hesitate to give their thorough approval to others who did the same.

CHAPTER 2

Yet we cannot judge them, for we also are sinners: God is the only judge

Now if you feel inclined to set yourself up as a judge of those who sin, let me assure you, whoever you are, that you are in no position to do so. For at whatever point you condemn others you automatically condemn yourself, since you, the judge, commit the same sins. God's judgment, we know, is utterly impartial in its action against such evil-doers. What makes you think that you, who so readily judge the sins of others, can consider yourself beyond the judgment of God? Are you, perhaps, misinterpreting God's generosity and patient mercy towards you as weakness on his part? Don't you realise that God's kindness is meant to lead you to repentance? Or are you by your obstinate refusal to repent simply storing up for yourself an experience of the wrath of God in the day of his anger when he shows his hand in righteous judgment?

He will "render to every man according to his works", and that means eternal life to those who, in patiently doing good, aim at the unseen glory and honour of the eternal world. It also means anger and wrath for those who rebel against God's plan of life, and refuse to obey his rules, and who, in so doing, make themselves the very servants of evil. Yes, it means bitter pain and agony for every human soul who works on the side of evil, for the Jew first and then the Greek. But there is glory and honour and peace for every worker on the side of good, for the Jew first and also for the Greek. For there is no preferential treatment with God.

God's judgment is absolutely just

All who have sinned without knowledge of the Law will die without reference to the Law; and all who have sinned knowing the Law shall be judged according to the Law. It is not familiarity with the Law that justifies a man in the sight of God, but obedience to it.

When the gentiles, who have no knowledge of the Law, act in accordance with it by the light of nature, they show that they have a law in themselves, for they demonstrate the effect of a law operating in their own hearts. Their own consciences endorse the existence of such a law, for there is something which condemns or excuses their actions.

We may be sure that all this will be taken into account in the day of true judgment, when God will judge men's secret lives by Christ Jesus, as my gospel plainly states.

You Jews are privileged—do you live up to your privileges?

Now you, my reader, who bear the name of Jew, take your stand upon the Law, and are, so to speak, proud of your God. You know his plan, and are able through your knowledge of the Law truly to appreciate moral values. You can, therefore, confidently look upon yourself as a guide to those who do not know the way, and as a light to those who are groping in the dark. You can instruct those who have no spiritual wisdom: you can teach those who, spiritually speaking, are only just out of the cradle. You have in the Law a certain grasp of the basis of true knowledge. But, prepared as you are to instruct others, do you ever teach yourself anything? You preach against stealing, for example, but are you sure of your own honesty? You denounce the practice of adultery, but are you sure of your own purity? You loathe idolatry, but how honest are you towards the property of heathen temples? Everyone knows how proud you are of the Law, but that means a proportionate dishonour to God when men know that you break it! Don't you know that the very name of God is cursed among the gentiles because of the behaviour of Jews? There is a verse of scripture to that effect.

Being a true "Jew" is an inward not an outward matter

That most intimate sign of belonging to God that we call circumcision does indeed mean something if you keep the Law. But if you flout the Law you are to all intents and purposes uncircumcising yourself! Conversely, if an uncircumcised man keep the Law's commandments, does he not thereby "circumcise" himself? Moreover, is it not plain to you that those who are physically uncircumcised, and yet keep the Law, are a continual judgment upon you who, for all your circumcision and knowledge of the Law, break it?

I have come to the conclusion that a true Jew is not the man who is merely a Jew outwardly, and real circumcision is not just a matter of the body. The true Jew is one who belongs to God in heart, a man whose circumcision is not just an outward physical affair but is a God-made sign upon the heart and soul, and results not in the approval of man, but in the approval of God.

CHAPTER 3

Jews are privileged, but even they have failed

Is there any advantage then in being a Jew? Does circumcision mean anything? Yes, of course, a great deal in every way. You have only to think of one thing to begin with—it was the Jews to whom God's messages were entrusted. Some of them were undoubtedly faithless, but what then? Can you imagine that their faithlessness could disturb the faithfulness of God? Of course not! God must be true, even if every living man be proved a liar. Remember the scripture?

> That thou mightest be justified in thy words,
> And mightest prevail when thou comest into judgment.

But if our wickedness advertises the goodness of God, do we feel that God is being unfair to punish us in return? (I'm using a human tit-for-tat argument.) Not a bit of it! How then could God judge the world? It is like saying that if my lying throws into sharp relief the truth of God and increases his glory, then why should he still judge me a sinner? Why not do evil that good may come? As a matter of fact, I am reported as urging this very thing, by some slanderously and others quite seriously! But, of course, such an argument is quite properly condemned.

Are we Jews then a march ahead of other men? By no means. For I have shown above that all men from Jews to Greeks are under the condemnation of sin. The scriptures endorse this fact plainly enough.

> There is none righteous, no, not one.
> There is none that understandeth,
> There is none that seeketh after God;
> They have all turned aside, they are together become unprofitable;
> There is none that doeth good, no, not so much as one:
> Their throat is an open sepulchre;
> With their tongues they have used deceit;
> The poison of asps is under their lips:
> Whose mouth is full of cursing and bitterness:
> Their feet are swift to shed blood;
> Destruction and misery are in their ways:
> And the way of peace have they not known;
> There is no fear of God before their eyes.

We know what the message of the Law is, to those who live under it—that every excuse may die on the lips of him who makes it and no living man can be beyond the judgment of God. No man can justify himself before God by a perfect performance of the Law's demands—indeed it is the straight-edge of the Law that shows us how crooked we are.

God's new plan—righteousness by faith, not through the Law

But now we are seeing the righteousness of God declared quite apart from the Law (though amply testified to by both Law and Prophets)—it is a right relationship given to, and operating in, all who have faith in Jesus Christ. For there is no distinction to be made anywhere: everyone has sinned, everyone falls short of the beauty of God's plan. A man who has faith is now freely acquitted in the eyes of God by his generous dealing in the redemptive act of Christ Jesus. God has appointed him as the means of propitiation, a propitiation accomplished by the shedding of his blood, to be received and made effective in ourselves by faith. God has done this to demonstrate his righteousness both by the wiping out of the sins of the past (the time when he withheld his hand), and by showing in the present time that he is a just God and that he justifies every man who has faith in Jesus.

Faith, not pride of achievement

What happens now to human pride of achievement? There is no more room for it. Why, because failure to keep the Law has killed it? Not at all, but because the whole matter is now on a different plane—believing instead of achieving. We see now that a man is justified before God by the fact of his faith in God's appointed Saviour and not by what he has managed to achieve under the Law.

Do you think that God is only God for the Jews and not for the gentiles? Certainly not! God is God of the gentiles as well. The one God is ready to justify the circumcised by faith and the uncircumcised by faith also.

Are we then undermining the Law by this insistence on faith? Not a bit of it! We put the Law in its proper place.

CHAPTER 4

Let us go back and consider our father Abraham

Now how does all this affect the position of our human ancestor Abraham? Well, if justification were by achievement he could quite fairly be proud of what he achieved—but not, I am sure, proud before God. For what does the scripture say about him?

And Abraham believed God, and it was reckoned unto him
for righteousness.

Now if a man *works* his wages are not counted as a gift but as a fair reward. But if a man, irrespective of his work, has faith in him who justifies the sinful, then that man's *faith* is counted as righteousness. This is the happy state of the man whom God accounts righteous, apart from his achievements, as David expresses it:

Blessed are they whose iniquities are forgiven
And whose sins are covered.
Blessed is the man to whom the Lord will not reckon sin.

It is a matter of faith, not circumcision

Now the question arises: is this happiness for the circumcised only, or for the uncircumcised as well?

Note this carefully. We began by saying that Abraham's faith was counted unto him for righteousness. When this happened, was he a circumcised man? He was not, he was still uncircumcised. It was *afterwards* that the sign of circumcision was given to him, as a seal upon that righteousness which God was accounting to him *as yet an uncircumcised man!* God's purpose here was that Abraham might be the spiritual father of all who since that time, despite their uncircumcision, show the faith that is counted as righteousness, and that he might be the circumcised father of all those who are not only circumcised, but are living by the same sort of faith which he himself had before he was circumcised.

The promise, from the beginning, was made to faith

The ancient promise made to Abraham and his descendants, that they should eventually possess the world, was given not because of any achievements made through obedience to the Law, but because of the righteousness which had its root in faith. For if, after all, they who pin their faith to keeping the Law were to inherit God's world, it would make faith meaningless and destroy the whole point of the promise. For the Law can produce no promise, only the threat of wrath to come. And, indeed, if there were no Law the question of sin would not arise.

The whole thing, then, is a matter of faith on man's part and generosity on God's. He gives the security of his own promise to all men who can be called "children of Abraham", i.e. both those who have lived in faith by the Law, and those who have exhibited a faith like that of Abraham. To whichever group we belong, Abraham is in a real sense our father, as the scripture says:

A father of many nations have I made thee.

This promise was valid because of his faith in God himself, who can make the dead live, and summon those who are in existence as though they were not yet born.

Abraham was a shining example of faith

Abraham, when hope was dead within him, went on hoping in faith, believing that he would become "the father of many nations". He relied on the word of God which definitely referred to "thy seed". With undaunted faith he looked at the facts—his own impotence (he was practically a hundred years old at the time) and his wife Sarah's apparent barrenness. Yet he refused to allow any distrust of a definite pronouncement of God to make him waver. He drew strength from his faith, and, while giving the glory to God, remained absolutely convinced that God was able to implement his own promise. This was the "faith" which was counted unto him for righteousness.

Now this counting of faith for righteousness was not recorded simply for Abraham's credit, but as a divine principle which should apply to us as well. Faith is to be reckoned as righteousness to us also, who believe in him who raised from the dead Jesus our Lord, who was delivered to death for our sins and raised again to secure our justification.

CHAPTER 5

Faith means the certainty of God's love, now and hereafter

SINCE then it is by faith that we are justified, let us grasp the fact that we *have* peace with God through our Lord Jesus Christ. Through him we have confidently entered into this new relationship of grace, and here we take our stand, in happy certainty of the glorious things he has for us in the future.

This doesn't mean, of course, that we have only a hope of

future joys—we can be full of joy here and now even in our trials and troubles. These very things will give us patient endurance; this in turn will develop a mature character, and a character of this sort produces a steady hope, a hope that will never disappoint us. Already we have the love of God flooding through our hearts by the Holy Spirit given to us. And we can see that it was at the very time that we were powerless to help ourselves that Christ died for sinful men. In human experience it is a rare thing for one man to give his life for another, even if the latter be a good man, though there have been a few who have had the courage to do it. Yet the proof of God's amazing love is this: that it was while we were sinners that Christ died for us. Moreover, if he did that for us while we were sinners, now that we are men justified by the shedding of his blood, what reason have we to fear the wrath of God? If, while we were his enemies, Christ reconciled us to God by dying for us, surely now that we are reconciled we may be perfectly certain of our salvation through his living in us. Nor, I am sure, is this a matter of bare salvation—we may hold our heads high in the light of God's love because of the reconciliation which Christ has made.

A brief résumé—the consequence of sin and the gift of God

This, then, is what has happened. Sin made its entry into the world through one man, and through sin, death. The entail of sin and death passed on to the whole human race, and no one could break it for no one was himself free from sin.

Sin, you see, was in the world long before the Law, though I suppose, technically speaking, it was not "sin" where there was no law to define it. Nevertheless death, the complement of sin, held sway over mankind from Adam to Moses, even over those whose sin was quite unlike Adam's.

Adam, the first man, foreshadows in some degree the man who has to come. But the gift of God through Christ is a very different matter from the "account rendered" through the sin of Adam. For while as a result of one man's sin death by natural consequence became the common lot of men, it was by the generosity of God, the free giving of the grace of the one man Jesus Christ, that the love of God overflowed for the benefit of all men.

Nor is the effect of God's gift the same as the effect of that one man's sin. For in the one case one man's sin brought its inevitable judgment, and the result was condemnation. But, in the other, countless men's sins are met with the free gift of grace, and the result is justification before God.

For if one man's offence meant that men should be slaves to death all their lives, it is a far greater thing that through another man, Jesus Christ, men by their acceptance of his more than sufficient grace and righteousness, should live their lives victoriously.

We see, then, that as one act of sin exposed the whole race of men to God's judgment and condemnation, so one act of perfect righteousness presents all men freely acquitted in the sight of God. One man's disobedience placed all men under the threat of condemnation, but one man's obedience has the power to present all men righteous before God.

Grace is a bigger thing than the Law

Now we find that the Law keeps slipping into the picture to point the vast extent of sin. Yet, though sin is shown to be wide and deep, thank God his grace is wider and deeper still! The whole outlook changes—sin used to be the master of men and in the end handed them over to death; now grace is the ruling factor, with its purpose making men right with God and its end the bringing of them to eternal life through Jesus Christ our Lord.

CHAPTER 6

Righteousness by faith, in practice

Now what is our response to be? Shall we sin to our heart's content and see how far we can exploit the grace of God? What a terrible thought! We, who have died to sin—how could we live in sin a moment longer? Have you forgotten that all of us who were baptised into Jesus Christ were, by that very action, sharing in his death? We were dead and buried with him in baptism, so that just as he was raised from the dead by that splendid revelation of the Father's power so we too might rise to life on a new plane altogether. If we have, as it were, shared his death, we shall also share in his resurrection. Let us never forget that our old selves died with him on the cross that the tyranny of sin over us might be broken—for a dead man can safely be said to be free from the power of sin. And if we were dead men with Christ we can believe that we shall also be men alive with him. We can be sure that the risen Christ never dies again—death's power to master him is finished. He died, because of sin, once: he lives for God for ever. In the same way look upon yourselves as dead to the appeal and power of sin but alive to God through Christ Jesus our Lord.

Do not, then, allow sin to establish any power over your mortal bodies in making you give way to its lusts. Nor hand over your bodily parts to be, as it were, weapons of evil for the devil's purposes. But, like men rescued from certain death, put yourselves in God's hands as weapons of good for his own purposes. For sin can never be your master—you are no longer living under the Law, but under grace.

The new service completely ousts the old

Now, what shall we do? Shall we go on sinning because we have no Law to condemn us any more, but are living under grace? Never! Just think what it would mean. You *belong* to the power which you choose to obey, whether you choose sin, whose reward is death, or God, obedience to whom means the reward of righteousness. Thank God that you, who were at one time the servants of sin, honestly responded to the impact of Christ's teaching when you came under its influence. Then, released from the service of sin, you entered the service of righteousness. (I use an everyday illustration because human nature grasps truth more readily that way.) In the past you voluntarily gave your bodies to the service of vice and wickedness—for the purposes of evil. So, now, give yourselves to the service of righteousness—for the purpose of becoming truly good. For when you were employed by sin you owed no duty to righteousness. Yet what sort of a harvest did you reap from those things that today you blush to remember? In the long run those things mean one thing only—death.

But now that you are freed from sin and employed by God, you owe no duty to sin, and you reap the fruit of being made righteous, while at the end of the road there is life for evermore.

Sin *pays* its servants: the wage is death. But God *gives* to those who serve him: his free gift is eternal life through Jesus Christ our Lord.

CHAPTER 7

How to be free from the Law

You know very well, my brothers (for I am speaking to those well acquainted with the subject), that the Law can only exercise authority over a man so long as he is alive. A married woman, for example, is bound by law to her husband so long as he is alive. But if he dies, then his legal claim over her disappears. This means that, if she should give herself to another man while her husband is alive, she incurs the stigma of adultery. But if, after her husband's death, she does exactly the same thing, no one could call her an adulteress, for the legal hold over her has been dissolved by her husband's death.

So, my brothers, the death of Christ on the cross has made you "dead" to the claims of the Law, and you are free to give yourselves in marriage, so to speak, to another, the one who was raised from the dead, that we may be productive for God.

While we were "in the flesh" the Law stimulated our sinful passions and so worked in our nature that we became productive —for death! But now that we stand clear of the Law, the claims which existed are dissolved by our "death", and we are free to serve God not in the old obedience to the letter of the Law, but in a new way, in the Spirit.

Sin and the Law

It now begins to look as if sin and the Law were the same thing—can this be a fact? Of course it cannot. But it must be admitted that I should never have had sin brought home to me but for the Law. For example, I should never have felt guilty of the sin of coveting if I had not heard the Law saying "Thou shalt not covet". But the sin in me, finding in the commandment an opportunity to express itself, stimulated all my desires. For sin, in the absence of the Law, has no life of its own. As long, then as I was without the Law I was alive. But when the commandment arrived, sin sprang to life and I "died". The commandment, which was meant to be a direction to life, I found was a sentence to death. The commandment gave sin its opportunity, and without my realising what it was doing, it "killed" me.

The Law is itself good

It can scarcely be doubted that the Law itself is holy, and the commandment is holy, fair and good. Can it be that something that is intrinsically good could mean death to me? No, what happened was this. Sin, at the touch of the Law, was forced to show itself as sin, and *that* meant death for me. The contact of the Law showed the utterly sinful nature of sin.

But it cannot make men good

For we know that the Law itself is concerned with the spiritual —it is I who am carnal, and have sold my soul to sin. My own behaviour baffles me. For I find myself doing what I really loathe but not doing what I really want to do. Yet surely if I do things that I really don't want to do, I am admitting that I really agree that the Law is good. But it cannot be said that "I" am doing them at all—it must be sin that has made its home in my nature. And, indeed, I know from experience that the carnal side of my being can scarcely be called the home of good! I often find that I have the will to do good, but not the power. That is, I don't accomplish the good I set out to do, and the evil I don't really want to do I find I am always doing. Yet if I do things that I don't really want to do then it is not, I repeat, "I" who do them, but the sin which has made its home within me. My experience of the Law is that when I want to do good, only evil is within my reach. For I am in hearty agreement with God's Law so far as my inner self is concerned. But then I find another law in my bodily members, which is in continual conflict with the Law which my mind approves, and makes me a prisoner to the law of sin which is inherent in my mortal body. For left to myself, I serve the Law of God with my mind, but in my unspiritual nature I serve the law of sin. It is an agonising situation, and who can set me free from the prison of this mortal body? I thank God there is a way out through Jesus Christ our Lord.

CHAPTER 8

The way out—new life in Christ

The truth is that no condemnation now hangs over the head of those who are "in" Christ Jesus. For the new spiritual principle of life "in" Christ Jesus lifts me out of the old vicious circle of sin and death.

The Law never succeeded in producing righteousness—the failure was always the weakness of human nature. But God has met this by sending his own Son to live in sinful human nature like ours. And, while Christ was dealing with sin, God condemned that sinful nature. Therefore we are able to meet the Law's requirements, for we are living no longer by the dictates of our sinful nature, but in obedience to the promptings of the Spirit. The carnal man sees no further than carnal things. But the spiritual man is concerned with the things of the spirit. The former attitude means, bluntly, death: the latter means life and inward peace. And this is only to be expected, for the carnal attitude is inevitably opposed to the purpose of God, and neither can nor will follow his Law. Men who hold this attitude cannot possibly please God.

What the presence of Christ within means

But you are not carnal but spiritual if the Spirit of God finds a home within you. You cannot, indeed, be a Christian at all unless you have something of his Spirit in you. Now if Christ does live within you his presence means that your sinful nature is dead, but your spirit becomes alive because of the righteousness he brings with him. Once the Spirit of him who raised Christ Jesus from the dead lives within you he will, by that same Spirit, bring to your whole being, yes even your mortal bodies, new strength and vitality. For he now lives in you.

So then, my brothers, you can see that we owe no duty to our sensual nature, or to live life on the level of the instincts. Indeed that way of living leads to certain spiritual death. But if on the other hand you cut the nerve of your instinctive actions by obeying the Spirit, you will live.

Christ is within—follow the lead of his Spirit

All who follow the leading of God's Spirit are God's own sons. Nor are you meant to relapse into the old slavish attitude of fear—you have been adopted into the very family circle of God and you can say with a full heart, "Father, my Father". The Spirit himself endorses our inward conviction that we really are the children of God. Think what that means. If we are his children then we are God's heirs, and all that Christ inherits will belong to all of us as well! Yes, if we share in his sufferings we shall certainly share in his glory.

Present distress is temporary and negligible

In my opinion whatever we may have to go through now is less than nothing compared with the magnificent future God has in store for us. The whole creation is on tiptoe to see the wonderful sight of the sons of God coming into their own. The world of creation cannot as yet see reality, not because it chooses to be blind, but because in God's purpose it has been so limited—yet it has been given hope. And the hope is that in the end the whole of created life will be rescued from the tyranny of change and decay, and have its share in that magnificent liberty which can only belong to the children of God!

It is plain to anyone with eyes to see that at the present time all created life groans in a sort of universal travail. And it is plain, too, that we who have a foretaste of the Spirit are in a state of painful tension, while we wait for that redemption of our bodies which will mean that we have realised our full sonship in him. We were saved by this hope, and let us remember that hope always means waiting for something that we do not yet see. For whoever hopes when he can *see*? But if we hope for something we cannot see, then we must settle down to wait for it in patience.

This is not mere theory—the Spirit helps us to find it true

The Spirit also helps us in our present limitations. For example, we do not know how to pray worthily, but his Spirit within us is actually praying for us in those agonising longings which cannot find words. He who knows the heart's secrets understands the Spirit's intention as he prays according to God's will for those who love him.

Moreover we know that to those who love God, who are called according to his plan, everything that happens fits into a pattern for good. For God, in his foreknowledge, chose them to bear the family likeness of his Son, that he might be the eldest of a family of many brothers. He chose them long ago; when the time came he called them, he made them righteous in his sight, and then lifted them to the splendour of life as his own sons.

We hold, in Christ, an impregnable position

In face of all this, what is there left to say? If God is for us, who can be against us? He who did not grudge his own Son but gave him up for us all—can we not trust such a God to give us, with him, everything else that we can need?

Who would dare to accuse us, whom God has chosen? God himself has declared us free from sin. Who is in a position to condemn? Only Christ Jesus, and Christ died for us, Christ also rose for us, Christ reigns in power for us, Christ prays for us!

Who can separate us from the love of Christ? Can trouble, pain or persecution? Can lack of clothes and food, danger to life and limb, the threat of force of arms? Indeed some of us know the truth of that ancient text:

For thy sake we are killed all the day long;
We were accounted as sheep for the slaughter.

No, in all these things we win an overwhelming victory through him who has proved his love for us.

I have become absolutely convinced that neither death nor life, neither messenger of Heaven nor monarch of earth, neither what happens today nor what may happen tomorrow, neither a power from on high nor a power from below, nor anything else in God's whole world has any power to separate us from the love of God in Christ Jesus our Lord!

CHAPTER 9

The fly in the ointment—the infidelity of my own race

Before Christ and my own conscience in the Holy Spirit I assure you that I am speaking the plain truth when I say that there is something that makes me feel very depressed, like a pain that never leaves me. It is the condition of my brothers and fellow-Israelites, and I have actually reached the pitch of wishing myself cut off from Christ if it meant that they could be won for God.

Just think what the Israelites have had given to them. The privilege of being adopted as sons of God, the experience of the glory of God, the agreements made with God, the gift of the Law, true ways of worship, God's own promises—all these are theirs. The patriarchs are theirs, and so too, as far as human descent goes, is Christ himself, Christ who is over all. May God be blessed for ever. Amen.

God's purpose is not utterly defeated by this infidelity

Now this does not mean that God's word to Israel has failed. For you cannot count all "Israelites" as the true Israel of God. Nor can all Abraham's descendants be considered truly children of Abraham. The promise was that "in Isaac shall thy children be called". That means that it is not the natural descendants who are children of God, but that the children of the promise are to be considered truly Abraham's children. For this was the promise: "About this time I will come and Sarah shall have a son." And then, again, a word of promise came to Rebecca, at the time when she was pregnant with two children by the one man, Isaac our forefather. It came before the children were born or had done anything good or bad, plainly showing that God's act of choice has nothing to do with achievements, but is entirely a matter of his will. She was told:

> The elder shall serve the younger.

And we get a later endorsement of this in the words:

> Jacob I loved, but Esau I hated.

We must not jump to conclusions about God

Now do we conclude that God is unjust? Never! For God says long ago to Moses:

> I will have mercy on whom I have mercy, and I will have compassion on whom I have compassion.

It is obviously not a question of human will or human effort, but of divine mercy. The scripture says to Pharaoh:

> For this very purpose did I raise thee up, that I might show in thee my power, and that my name might be published abroad in all the earth.

It seems plain, then, that God chooses on whom he will have mercy, and whom he will harden in their sin.

I can almost hear your retort: "If this is so, and God's will is irresistible, why does God blame men for what they do?" But the question really is this: "Who are you, a man, to make any such reply to God?" When a craftsman makes anything he doesn't expect it to turn round and say, "Why did you make me like this?" The potter, for instance, has complete control over the clay, making with one part of the lump a lovely vase, and with another a pipe for sewage. May it not be that God, though he must sooner or later expose his wrath against sin and show his controlling hand, has yet most patiently endured the presence in his world of things that cry out to be destroyed? Can we not see, in this, his purpose in demonstrating the boundless resources of his glory upon those whom he considers fit to receive his mercy, and whom he long ago planned to raise to glorious life? And by these chosen people I mean you and me, whom he has called out from both Jews and gentiles. He says in Hosea:

> I will call that my people, which was not my people;
> And her beloved, which was not beloved.
> And it shall be, that in the place where it was said unto them, Ye are not my people,
> There shall they be called sons of the living God.

And Isaiah, speaking about Israel, proclaims:

> If the number of the children of Israel be as the sand of the sea, it is the remnant that shall be saved:
> For the Lord will execute his word upon the earth, finishing it and cutting it short.

And previously, Isaiah said:

> Except the Lord of Sabaoth had left us a seed,
> We had become as Sodom and had been made like unto Gomorrah.

At present the gentiles have gone further than the Jews

Now, what do we conclude? That the gentiles who never seriously pursued righteousness, have attained righteousness, righteousness-by-faith. But Israel, earnestly following the Law of righteousness, failed to reach their goal. And why? Because their minds were fixed on what they achieved instead of on what they believed. They tripped over that very stone the scripture mentions:

> Behold, I lay in Zion a stone of stumbling and a rock of offence:
> And he that believeth on him shall not be put to shame.

CHAPTER 10

How Israel has missed the way

MY brothers, from the bottom of my heart I long and pray to God that Israel may be saved! I know from experience what a passion for God they have, but alas, it is not a passion based on knowledge. They do not know God's righteousness, and all the time they are trying to prove their own righteousness they have the wrong attitude to receive his. For Christ means the end of the struggle for righteousness-by-the-Law for everyone who believes in him.

Moses writes of righteousness-by-the-Law when he says that the man who perfectly obeys the Law shall find life in it. But righteousness-by-faith speaks like this:

"You need not say in your heart, 'Who could go up to Heaven to bring Christ down to us, or who could descend into the depths to bring him up from the dead?' No, the word is very near you, *on your own lips* and in *your own heart*!" It is this word, which is the burden of our preaching, and it says, in effect, "If you openly admit by your own lips that Jesus is the Lord, and if you believe in *your own heart* that God raised him from the dead, you will be saved." For it is believing *in the heart* that makes a man righteous before God, and it is stating his belief by *his own lips* that confirms his salvation. And the scripture says: "Whosoever believes in him shall not be disappointed." And that "whosoever" means anyone, without distinction between Jew or Greek. For all have the same Lord, whose boundless resources are sufficient for all who turn to him in faith. For:

> Whosoever shall call upon the name of the Lord shall be saved.

Can we offer the excuse of ignorance on Israel's behalf?

Now how can they call on one in whom they have never believed? How can they believe in one of whom they have never heard? And how can they hear unless someone proclaims him? And who will go to tell them unless he is sent? As the scripture puts it:

> How beautiful are the feet of them that bring glad tidings of good things!

Yet not all have responded to the gospel. Isaiah asks, you remember,

Lord, who hath believed our report?

Faith, you see, can only come from hearing the message, and the message is the word of Christ.

But when I ask myself: "Did they never hear?" I have to answer that they *have* heard, for

Their sound went out into all the earth,
And their words unto the ends of the world.

Then I say to myself: "Did Israel not know?" And my answer must be that they did. For Moses says:

I will provoke you to jealousy with that which is no nation,
With a nation void of understanding will I anger you.

And Isaiah, more daring still, puts these words into the mouth of God:

I was found of them that sought me not.
I became manifest unto them that asked not of me.

And then, speaking to Israel:

All the day long did I spread out my hands unto a disobedient and gainsaying people.

CHAPTER 11

Israel's failure—yet remember the faithful few

THIS leads me to the question, "Has God then totally repudiated his people?" Certainly not! For I myself am an Israelite, a descendant of Abraham and of the tribe of Benjamin. It is unthinkable that God should have repudiated his own people, the people whose destiny he himself appointed. Don't you remember what the scripture says in the story of Elijah? How he pleaded with God on Israel's behalf:

Lord, they have killed thy prophets
They have digged down thine altars:
And I am left alone, and they seek my life.

And do you remember God's reply?

I have left for myself seven thousand men
Who have not bowed the knee to Baal.

In just the same way, there is at the present time a minority, chosen by the grace of God. And if it is a matter of the grace of God, it cannot be a question of their actions especially deserving God's favour, for that would make grace meaningless.

What conclusion do we reach now? That Israel did not, as a whole, obtain the object of his striving, but a chosen few achieved it. The remainder became more and more insensitive to the righteousness of God. This is borne out by the scripture:

God gave them a spirit of stupor,
Eyes that they should not see,
And ears that they should not hear,
Unto this very day.

And David says of them:

Let their table be made a snare, and a trap,
And a stumbling-block, and a recompense unto them:
Let their eyes be darkened, that they may not see,
And bow thou down their back alway.

In the providence of God disaster has been turned to good account

Now I ask myself, "Was this fall of theirs an utter disaster?" It was not! For through their failure the benefit of salvation has passed to the gentiles, with the result that Israel is made to see and feel what they have missed. For if their failure has so enriched the world, and their defection proved such a benefit to the gentiles, think what tremendous advantages their fulfilling of God's plan could mean!

Now a word to you who are gentiles. I should like you to know that I make as much as I can of my ministry as "God's messenger to the gentiles" so as to make my kinsfolk jealous and thus save some of them. For if their exclusion from the pale of salvation has meant the reconciliation of the rest of mankind to God, what would their inclusion mean? It would be nothing less than life from the dead! If the flour is consecrated to God so is the whole loaf, and if the roots of a tree are dedicated to God every branch will belong to him also.

A word of warning

But if some of the branches of the tree have been lopped off, while you, a shoot of wild-olive, have been grafted in, and share like a natural branch the rich nourishment of the root, don't let yourself feel superior to the former branches. If you feel inclined that way, remind yourself that you do not support the root, the root supports you. You may make the natural retort, "But the branches were lopped off to make room for my grafting!" Very well, then. They lost their position because they failed to believe; you only maintain yours because you do believe. The situation does not call for conceit but for a certain wholesome fear. If God removed the natural branches for a good reason, take care that you don't give him the same reason for removing you. You must try to appreciate both the kindness and the strict justice of God. Those who fell experienced his justice, while you are experiencing his kindness, and will continue to do so as long as you do not abuse that kindness. Otherwise you too will be cut off from the tree. And as for the fallen branches, unless they are obstinate in their unbelief, they will be grafted in again. Such a restoration is by no means beyond the power of God. And, in any case, if you who were, so to speak, a cutting from a wild-olive, were grafted in against the natural order, is it not a far simpler matter for the natural branches to be grafted back into the parent stem?

God still has a plan for Israel

Now I don't want you, my brothers, to be totally ignorant of God's secret plan. And I should not wish you to have ideas of your own which may be false. No, the partial insensibility which has come to Israel is only to last until the full number of the gentiles has been called in. Once this has happened, all Israel will be saved, as the scripture says:

> There shall come out of Zion the deliverer;
> He shall turn away ungodliness from Jacob:
> And this is my covenant unto them,
> When I shall take away their sins.

As far as the gospel goes, they are at present God's enemies—which is to your advantage. But as far as God's purpose in choosing is concerned, they are still beloved for their fathers' sakes. For once they are made, God does not withdraw his gifts or his calling.

The whole scheme looks topsy-turvy, until we see the amazing wisdom of God!

Just as in the past you were disobedient to God but have found that mercy which might have been theirs but for their disobedience, so they, who at the present moment are disobedient, will eventually share the mercy which has been extended to you. God has all men penned together in the prison of disobedience, that he may have mercy upon them all.

I stand amazed at the fathomless wealth of God's wisdom and God's knowledge. How could man ever understand his reasons for action, or explain his methods of working? For:

Who hath known the mind of the Lord?
Or who hath been his counsellor?
Or who hath first given to him, and it shall be recompensed unto him again?

For everything began with him, continues its existence because of him, and ends in him.
To him be the glory for ever, amen.

CHAPTER 12

We have seen God's mercy and wisdom: how shall we respond?

WITH eyes wide open to the mercies of God, I beg you, my brothers, as an act of intelligent worship, to give him your bodies, as a living sacrifice, consecrated to him and acceptable by him. Don't let the world around you squeeze you into its own mould, but let God re-make you so that your whole attitude of mind is changed. Thus you will prove in practice that the will of God is good, acceptable to him and perfect.

As your spiritual teacher I, by the grace God gave me, give this advice to each one of you. Don't cherish exaggerated ideas of yourself or your importance, but try to have a sane estimate of your capabilities by the light of the faith that God has given to you all. For just as you have many members in one physical body and those members differ in their functions, so we, though many in number, compose one body in Christ and are all members to one another. Through the grace of God we have different gifts. If our gift is preaching, let us preach to the limit of our vision. If it is serving others let us concentrate on our service; if it is teaching let us give all we have to our teaching; and if our gift be the stimulating of the faith of others let us set ourselves to it. Let the man who is called to give, give freely; let the man in authority work with enthusiasm; and let the man who feels sympathy for his fellows in distress help them cheerfully.

Let us have real Christian behaviour

Let us have no imitation Christian love. Let us have a genuine hatred for evil and a real devotion to good. Let us have real warm affection for one another as between brothers, and a willingness to let the other man have the credit. Let us not allow slackness to spoil our work and let us keep the fires of the spirit burning, as we do our work for the Lord. Base your happiness on your hope in Christ. When trials come endure them patiently; steadfastly maintain the habit of prayer. Give freely to fellow-Christians in want, never grudging a meal or a bed to those who need them. And as for those who try to make your life a misery, bless them. Don't curse, bless. Share the happiness of those who are happy, and the sorrow of those who are sad. Live in harmony with each other. Don't become snobbish but take a real interest in ordinary people. Don't become set in your own opinions. Don't pay back a bad turn by a bad turn, to anyone. See that your public behaviour is above criticism. As far as your responsibility goes, live at peace with everyone. Never take vengeance into your own hands, my dear friends: stand back and let God punish if he will. For it is written:

> Vengeance belongeth unto me: I will recompense, saith the Lord.

And it is also written:

> If thine enemy hunger, feed him;
> If he thirst, give him to drink:
> For in so doing thou shalt heap coals of fire upon his head.

Don't allow yourself to be overpowered by evil. Take the offensive —overpower evil with good!

CHAPTER 13

The Christian and the civil law

EVERYONE ought to obey the civil authorities, for all legitimate authority is derived from God's authority, and the existing authority is appointed under God. To oppose authority then is to oppose God, and such opposition is bound to be punished.

The honest citizen has no need to fear the keepers of law and order, but the dishonest man will always be afraid of them. If you want to avoid this anxiety just lead a law-abiding life, and all that can come your way is a word of approval. The officer is God's servant for your protection. But if you are leading a wicked life you have reason to be alarmed. The "power of the law" which is vested in every legitimate officer, is no empty phrase.

He is, in fact, divinely appointed to inflict God's punishment upon evil-doers.

You must, therefore, obey the authorities, not simply because it is the safest, but because it is the right thing to do. It is right, too, for you to pay taxes for the civil authorities are appointed by God for the constant maintenance of public order. Give everyone his legitimate due, whether it be toll, or taxes, or reverence, or honour.

To love others is the highest conduct

Keep out of debt altogether, except that perpetual debt of love which we owe one another. The man who loves his neighbour has obeyed the whole Law in regard to his neighbour. For the commandments, "Thou shalt not commit adultery", "Thou shalt not kill", "Thou shalt not steal", "Thou shalt not covet" and all other commandments are summed up in this one rule: "Thou shalt love thy neighbour as thyself." Love hurts nobody: therefore love is the answer to the Law's commands.

Wake up and live!

Why all this stress on behaviour? Because, as I think you have realised the present time is of the highest importance—it is time to wake up to reality. Every day brings God's salvation nearer than the day in which we took the first step of faith.

The night is nearly over, the day has almost dawned. Let us therefore fling away the things that men do in the dark, let us arm ourselves for the fight of the day! Let us live cleanly, as in the daylight, not in the delights of getting drunk or playing with sex, nor yet in quarrelling or jealousies. Let us be Christ's men from head to foot, and give no chances to the flesh to have its fling.

CHAPTER 14

Don't criticise each other's convictions

WELCOME a man whose faith is weak, but not with the idea of arguing over his scruples. One man believes that he may eat anything, another man, without this strong conviction, is a vegetarian. The meat-eater should not despise the vegetarian, nor should the vegetarian condemn the meat-eater—they should reflect that God has accepted them both. After all, who are you to criticise the servant of somebody else? It is to his own master that he stands or falls. And he will stand for the Lord is well able to make him do so.

People are different—make allowances

Again, one man thinks one day of more importance than others. Another man considers them all alike. Let every one be definite in his own convictions. If a man specially observes one particular day, he does so for the Lord's sake. The man who eats, eats for the Lord's sake, for he thanks God for the food. The man who fasts also does it for the Lord's sake, for he thanks God for the benefits of fasting. The truth is that we neither live nor die as self-contained units. At every turn life links us to the Lord and when we die we come face to face with him. In life or death we are in the hands of the Lord. Christ lived and died that he might be the Lord in both life and death.

Why, then, do you criticise your brother's actions, why do you try to make him look small? We shall all be judged one day, not by each other's standards or even by our own, but by the judgment of God. It is written:

> As I live, saith the Lord, to me every knee shall bow,
> And every tongue shall confess to God.

It is to God alone that we shall have to answer for our actions.

This should be our attitude

Let us therefore stop turning critical eyes on one another. Let us rather be critical of our own conduct and see that we do nothing to make a brother stumble or fall.

I am convinced, and I say this as in the presence of the Lord Jesus, that nothing is intrinsically unholy. But none the less it is unholy to the man who thinks it is. If your habit of unrestricted diet seriously upsets your brother, you are no longer living in love towards him. And surely you wouldn't let food mean ruin to a man for whom Christ died. You mustn't let something that is all right for you look like an evil practice to somebody else. After all, the kingdom of Heaven is not a matter of whether you get what you like to eat and drink, but of righteousness and peace and joy in the Holy Spirit. If you put these things first in serving Christ you will please God and are not likely to offend men. So let us concentrate on the things which make for harmony, and on the growth of our fellowship together. Surely we shouldn't wish to undo God's work for the sake of a plate of meat!

I freely admit that all food is, in itself, harmless, but it can be harmful for the man who eats it and so upsets the faith of others. We should be willing to be both vegetarians and teetotallers or abstain from anything else if by doing otherwise we should impede a brother's progress in the faith. Your personal convictions are a matter of faith between yourself and God, and you are happy if you have no qualms about what you allow yourself to eat. Yet if a man eats meat with an uneasy conscience, you may be sure he is wrong to do so. For his action does not spring from his faith, and when we act apart from our faith we sin.

CHAPTER 15

Christian behaviour to one another

We who have strong faith ought to shoulder the burden of the doubts and qualms of the weak and not just go our own sweet way. We should consider the good of our neighbour and help to build up his character. For even Christ did not choose his own pleasure, but as it is written:

The reproaches of them that reproached thee fell upon me.

For all those words which were written long ago are meant to teach us today; so that we may be encouraged to endure and to go on hoping in our own time. May the God who inspires men to endure, and gives them constant encouragement, give you a mind united with one another in your common loyalty to Christ Jesus. And then, as one man, you will sing from the heart the praises of God the Father of our Lord Jesus Christ. So open your hearts to one another as Christ has opened his heart to you, and God will be glorified.

A reminder—Christ the universal saviour

Christ was made a servant of the Jews to prove God's trustworthiness, since he implemented the promises made long ago to the fathers, and also that the gentiles might bring glory to God for his mercy to them. It is written:

Therefore will I give praise unto thee among the gentiles
And sing unto thy name.

And again:

Rejoice, ye gentiles, with his people.

And yet again:

Praise the Lord, all ye gentiles;
And let all the peoples praise him.

And then Isaiah says:

There shall be the root of Jesse,
And he that ariseth to rule over the gentiles:
On him shall the gentiles hope.

May the God of hope fill you with all joy and peace in your faith, that by the power of the Holy Spirit, your whole life and outlook may be radiant with hope.

What I have tried to do

For myself I feel certain that you, my brothers, have real Christian character and experience, and that you are capable of keeping each other on the right road. Nevertheless I have in some places written to you with a greater frankness, to refresh your minds with truths that you already know. It is by virtue of the commission given to me by God that I am the minister of Christ to the gentiles. This makes it my priestly duty to tell them the gospel of God, and thus to present them as an offering which he can accept, because they are sanctified by the Holy Spirit. And I think I have something to be proud of through Jesus Christ in my work for God. I am not competent to speak of the work Christ has done through others, but I do know that through me he has secured the obedience of gentiles in word and deed, working by sign and miracle and all the power of the Holy Spirit. Thus I have been able to complete the preaching of the gospel of Christ from Jerusalem as far round as Illyricum. My constant ambition has been to preach the gospel where the name of Christ was previously unknown, and to avoid building on another man's foundation, as Scripture says:

They shall see, to whom no tidings of him came,
And they who have not heard shall understand.

My future plans

Perhaps this will explain why I have so frequently been prevented from coming to see you. But now, since my work in these places no longer needs my presence, and since for many years I have had a great desire to see you, I hope to visit you on my way to Spain. I hope to see you on my way through, and I hope also that you will speed me on my journey, after I have had the satisfaction of seeing you all. At the moment my next call is to Jerusalem, to look after the welfare of the Christians there. The churches in Macedonia and Achaia, you see, have thought it a good thing to make a contribution towards the poor Christians in Jerusalem. They have decided to do this, and indeed they owe it to them. For if the gentiles have had a share in the Jews' spiritual good things it is only fair that they should look after the Jews as far as the good things of this world are concerned.

When I have completed this task, then, and put this gift safely into their hands, I shall come to you *en route* for Spain. I feel sure that in this visit I shall bring with me the full blessing of Christ.

Now, my brothers, I am going to ask you, for the sake of our Lord Jesus Christ and for the love we bear each other in the Spirit, to stand behind me in earnest prayer to God on my behalf—that I may not fall into the hands of the unbelievers in Judaea, and that the Jerusalem Christians may welcome the gift I am taking to them. Then I shall come to you, in the purpose of God, with a happy heart, and may even enjoy with you a little holiday.

The God of peace be with you all, amen.

CHAPTER 16

Personal greetings and messages

I WANT this letter to introduce to you Phoebe, our sister, a deaconess of the church at Cenchrea. Please give her a Christian welcome, and any assistance with her work that she may need. She has herself been of great assistance to many, not excluding myself.

Give my good wishes to Prisca and Aquila. They have not only worked with me for Christ Jesus, but have risked their necks to save my life. Not only I, but all the gentile churches, owe them a great debt. Give my love to the church that meets in their house.

My good wishes also to dear Epaenetus, Asia's first man to be won for Christ, and of course greet Mary who has worked so hard for you. A warm greeting, too, for Andronicus and Junias my fellow-countrymen and fellow-prisoners; they are outstanding men among the messengers and were Christians before I was.

Another warm greeting for Ampliatus, dear Christian that he is, and also for Urbanus, who has worked with me for Christ, and dear Stachys, too.

More greetings from me, please, to:
Apelles, the man who has proved his faith,
The household of Aristobulus,
Herodion, my fellow-countryman,
Narcissus' household, who are Christians.

Remember me to Tryphena and Tryphosa, who work so hard for the Lord, and to my dear Persis who has also done great work for him.

My greetings also to Rufus—that splendid Christian, and greet his mother, who has been a mother to me too. Greetings to Asyncritus, Phlegon, Hermes, Patrobas, Hermas and their Christian group: also to Philologus and Julia, Nereus and his sister, and Olympas and the Christians who are with them.

Give each other a hearty handshake all round in Christian love. The greetings of all the churches come to you with this letter.

A final warning

And now I implore you, my brothers, to keep a watchful eye on those who cause trouble and make difficulties among you, in plain opposition to the teaching you have been given, and steer clear of them. Such men do not really serve our Lord Christ at all but their own ambitions. Yet with their plausible and attractive arguments they deceive those who are too simple-hearted to see through them.

Your loyalty to the gospel is known everywhere, and that gives me great joy. I want to see you experts in good, and not even beginners in evil. It will not be long before the God of peace will crush Satan under your feet. May the grace of our Lord Jesus be with you.

Timothy, who works with me, sends his greetings, and so do Lucius and Jason and Sosipater my fellow-countrymen. I, Tertius, who have been taking down this epistle from Paul's dictation, send you my Christian greetings too. Gaius, my host (and the host as a matter of fact of the whole church here), sends you his greetings. Erastus, our city treasurer, and Quartus, another Christian brother, send greetings too.

Now to him who is able to set you firmly on your feet—according to my gospel, according to the preaching of Jesus Christ himself, and in accordance with the disclosing of that secret purpose which, after long ages of silence, has now been made known (in full agreement with the writings of the prophets long ago), by the command of the everlasting God to all the gentiles, that they might turn to him in the obedience of faith—to him, I say, the God who alone is wise, be glory for ever through Jesus Christ, amen!

The First Letter to the Christians at Corinth

AUTHOR. *Paul, writing from Ephesus, where he stayed for more than two years. He had evidently written at least one previous letter to the church at Corinth.*

DATE. *About* 56.

DESTINATION. *The Christian church at Corinth, which was then the largest town in Greece. Acts* 18 *gives some account of the beginnings of the church there. It is worth remembering that Corinth was a most important seaport, a garrison town, and a strategic road-junction. It was the capital of the Roman province of Achaia. It would have been full of a cosmopolitan crowd, and even in those days was a byword for immorality, idolatry and loose-living of all kinds.*

THEME. *The beginning of the letter is an impassioned indictment of the "party-spirit", which can have no place in a church where all men belong to Christ. Paul then proceeds to deal sternly with a particularly revolting case of sexual immorality, which the Corinthian Christians appear to treat with complacency. The litigiousness of the Corinthian church is next censured. Paul's somewhat ascetic views on marriage follow, and modern readers need to remind themselves of the shameless sexual promiscuity existing in Corinth, against which Paul is obviously violently reacting.*

Butcher's meat in a city like Corinth had often been exposed before heathen idols before being offered for sale. This meant a practical difficulty for Christians and Paul advises upon it.

He then lays down some rules about public worship, particularly on the reverent conduct of what we now call the Holy Communion.

The question of the diversity of the gifts of God's Spirit is dealt with patiently and logically, and then follows the famous passage about the highest gift of all—Christian love.

Then comes the almost equally famous passage on the "resurrection of the body", by no means irrelevant to modern ears.

The matter of the Jerusalem Sick and Poor Fund and some interesting personal messages close the letter.

CHAPTER 1

PAUL, commissioned by the will of God as a messenger of Christ Jesus, and Sosthenes, a Christian brother, to the church of God at Corinth—to those whom Christ Jesus has made holy, who are called to be God's men and women, to all true believers in Jesus Christ, their Lord and ours—grace and peace be to you from God the Father and the Lord, Jesus Christ!

I am thankful for your faith

I am always thankful to God for what the gift of his grace in Christ Jesus has meant to you. For, as the Christian message has become established among you, he has enriched your whole lives, from the words on your lips to the understanding in your hearts. And you have been eager to receive his gifts during this time of waiting for his final appearance. He will keep you steadfast in the faith to the end, so that when his day comes you need fear no condemnation. God is utterly dependable, and it is he who has called you into fellowship with his Son Jesus Christ, our Lord.

But I am anxious over your "divisions"

Now I do beg you, my brothers, by all that our Lord Jesus Christ means to you, to speak with one voice, and not allow yourselves to be split up into parties. All together you should be achieving a unity in thought and judgment. For I know, from what some of Chloe's people have told me, that you are each making different claims—"I am one of Paul's men," says one; "I am one of Apollos'," says another; or "I am one of Cephas'"; while someone else says, "I owe my faith to Christ alone."

Do consider how serious these divisions are!

What *are* you saying? Is there more than one Christ? Was it Paul who died on the cross for you? Were you baptised in the name of Paul? It makes me thankful that I didn't actually baptise any of you (except Crispus and Gaius), or perhaps someone would be saying I did it in my own name. (Oh yes, I did baptise Stephanas' family, but I can't remember anyone else.) For Christ did not send me primarily to baptise, but to proclaim the gospel. And I have not done this by the persuasiveness of clever words, for I have no desire to rob the cross of its power. The preaching of the cross is, I know, nonsense to those who are involved in this dying world, but to us who are being saved from that death it is nothing less than the power of God.

The cross shows that God's wisdom is not man's wisdom by any means

It is written:

I will destroy the wisdom of the wise,
And the prudence of the prudent will I reject.

For consider, what have the philosopher, the writer and the critic of this world to show for all their wisdom? Has not God made the wisdom of this world look foolish? For it was after the world in its wisdom had failed to know God, that he in his wisdom chose to save all who would believe by the "simple-mindedness" of the gospel message. For the Jews ask for miraculous proofs and the Greeks an intellectual panacea, but all we preach is Christ crucified—a stumbling-block to the Jews and sheer nonsense to the gentiles, but for those who are called, whether Jews or Greeks, Christ the power of God and the wisdom of God. And this is really only natural, for God's "foolishness" is wiser than men, and his "weakness" is stronger than men.

Nor are God's values the same as man's

For look at your own calling as Christians, my brothers. You don't see among you many of the wise (according to this world's judgment) nor many of the ruling class, nor many from the noblest families. But God has chosen what the world calls foolish to shame the wise; he has chosen what the world calls weak to shame the strong. He has chosen things of little strength and small repute, yes and even things which have no real existence, to explode the pretensions of the things that are—that no man may boast in the presence of God. Yet from this same God you have received your standing in Jesus Christ, and he has become for us the true wisdom, a matter, in practice, of being made righteous and holy, in fact, of being redeemed. And this makes us see the truth of the scripture:

He that glorieth, let him glory in the Lord.

CHAPTER 2

I came to you in God's strength not my own

In the same way, my brothers, when I came to proclaim to you God's secret purpose, I did not come equipped with any brilliance of speech or intellect. You may as well know now that it was my secret determination to concentrate entirely on Jesus Christ himself and the fact of his death upon the cross. As a matter of fact, in myself I was feeling far from strong; I was nervous and rather shaky. What I said and preached had none of the attractiveness of the clever mind, but it was a demonstration of the power of the Spirit! Plainly God's purpose was that your faith should rest not upon man's cleverness but upon the power of God.

There is, of course, a real wisdom, which God allows us to share with him

We do, of course, speak "wisdom" among those who are spiritually mature, but it is not what is called wisdom by this world, nor by the powers-that-be, who soon will be only the powers that have been. The wisdom we speak of is that mysterious secret wisdom of God which he planned before the creation for our glory today. None of the powers of this world have known this wisdom—if they had they would never have crucified the Lord of glory! But, as it is written:

Things which eye saw not, and ear heard not,
And which entered not into the heart of man,
Whatsoever things God prepared for them that love him.

Thus God has, through the Spirit, let us share his secret. For nothing is hidden from the Spirit, not even the deep wisdom of God. For who could really understand a man's inmost thoughts except the spirit of the man himself? How much less could anyone understand the thoughts of God except the very Spirit of God? We have now received not the spirit of the world but the Spirit of God himself, so that we can understand something of God's generosity towards us.

This wisdom is only understood by the spiritual

It is these things that we talk about, not using the expressions of the human intellect but those which the Holy Spirit teaches us, explaining spiritual things to those who are spiritual.

But the unspiritual man simply cannot accept the matters which the Spirit deals with—they just don't make sense to him, for, after all, you must be spiritual to see spiritual things. The spiritual man, on the other hand, has an insight into the meaning of everything, though his insight may baffle the man of the world. This is because the former is sharing in God's wisdom, and

Who hath known the mind of the Lord,
That he should instruct him?

Nevertheless, we who are spiritual have the very thoughts of Christ!

CHAPTER 3

But I cannot yet call you spiritual

I, MY brothers, was unable to talk to you as spiritual men: I had to talk to you as unspiritual, as yet babies in the Christian life. And my practice has been to feed you, as it were, with "milk" and not with "meat". You were unable to digest "meat" in those days, and I don't believe you can do it now. For you are still unspiritual; all the time that there is jealousy and squabbling among you you show that you are—you are living just like men of the world. While one of you says, "I am one of Paul's converts" and another says, "I am one of Apollos' ", are you not plainly unspiritual?

After all, who is Apollos? Who is Paul? No more than servants through whom you came to believe as the Lord gave each man his opportunity. I may have done the planting and Apollos the watering, but it was God who made the seed grow! The planter and the waterer are nothing compared with him who gives life to the seed. Planter and waterer are alike insignificant, though each shall be rewarded according to his particular work.

We work on God's foundation

In this work, we work with God, and that means that you are a field under God's cultivation, or, if you like, a house being built to his plan. I, like a master-builder who knows his job, by the grace God has given me, lay the foundation; someone else builds upon it. I only say this, let the builder be careful how he builds! The foundation is laid already, and no one can lay another, for it is Jesus Christ himself. But any man who builds on the foundation using as his material gold, silver, precious stones, wood, hay or straw, must know that each man's work will one day be shown for what it is. The day will show it plainly enough, for the day will arise in a blaze of fire, and that fire will prove the value of each man's work. If the work which a man has built upon the foundation stands this test, he will be rewarded. But if his work is burnt down, he loses it all. He personally will be safe, though rather like a man rescued from a fire.

Make no mistake: you are God's holy building

Don't you realise that you yourselves are the temple of God, and that God's Spirit lives in you? God will destroy anyone who defiles his temple, for his temple is holy—*and that is exactly what you are!*

Let no one be under any illusion over this. If any man among you thinks himself one of the world's clever ones, let him discard his cleverness that he may learn to be truly wise. For this world's cleverness is stupidity to God. It is written:

> He that taketh the wise in their craftiness.

And again:

> The Lord knoweth the reasonings of the wise, that they are vain.

So let no one boast of men. Everything belongs to you! Paul, Apollos or Cephas; the world, life, death, the present or the future, everything is yours! For you belong to Christ, and Christ belongs to God.

CHAPTER 4

Trust us, but make no hasty judgments

You should look upon us as ministers of Christ, as trustees of the secrets of God. And it is a prime requisite in a trustee that he should prove worthy of his trust. But, as a matter of fact, it matters very little to me what you, or any man, thinks of me—I don't even value my opinion of myself. For I might be quite ignorant of any fault in myself—but that doesn't justify me before God. My only true judge is the Lord.

The moral of this is that we should make no hasty or premature judgments. When the Lord comes he will bring into the light of day all that at present is hidden in darkness, and he will expose the secret motives of men's hearts. Then shall God himself give each man his share of praise.

Having your favourite teacher is not only silly but wrong

I have used myself and Apollos above as an illustration, so that you might learn from what I have said about us not to assess man above his value in God's sight, and may thus avoid the pride which comes from making one teacher more important than another. For who makes you different from anybody else, and what have you got that was not given to you? And if anything has been given to you, why boast of it as if you had achieved it yourself?

Think sometimes of what your happiness has cost us!

Oh, I know you are rich and flourishing! You've been living like kings, haven't you, while we've been away? I would to God you were really kings in God's sight so that we might reign with you!

I sometimes think that God means us, the messengers, to appear last in the procession of mankind, like the men who are to die in the arena. For indeed we are made a public spectacle before the angels of Heaven and the eyes of men. We are looked upon as fools, for Christ's sake, but you are wise in the Christian faith. We are considered weak, but you have become strong: you have found honour, we little but contempt. Up to this very hour we are hungry and thirsty, ill-clad, knocked about and practically homeless. We still have to work for our living by manual labour. Men curse us, but we return a blessing: they make our lives miserable but we take it patiently. They ruin our reputations but we go on trying to win them for God. We are the world's rubbish, the scum of the earth, yes, up to this very day.

A personal plea

I don't write these things merely to make you feel uncomfortable, but that you may realise facts, as my dear children. After all, you may have ten thousand teachers in the Christian faith, but you cannot have many fathers! For in Christ Jesus I am your spiritual father through the gospel; that is why I implore you to follow the footsteps of me your father. I have sent Timothy to you to help you in this. For he himself is my much-loved and faithful son in the Lord, and he will remind you of those ways of living in Christ which I teach in every church to which I go.

Some of you have apparently grown conceited since I did not visit you. But please God it will not be long before I do come to you in person. Then I shall be able to see what power, apart from their words, these pretentious ones among you really possess. For the kingdom of God is not a matter of a spate of words but of the power of Christian living.

Now it's up to you to choose! Shall I come to you ready to chastise you, or in love and gentleness?

CHAPTER 5

A horrible sin and a stern remedy

It is actually reported that there is sexual immorality among you, and immorality of a kind that even pagans condemn—a man has apparently taken his father's wife! Are you still proud of yourselves? Shouldn't you be overwhelmed with sorrow? The man who has done such a thing should certainly be expelled from your fellowship!

I know I am not with you physically but I am with you in spirit, and I assure you as though I were actually with you that I have already pronounced judgment in the name of the Lord Jesus on the man who has done this thing. As one present in spirit when you are assembled, I say by the power of the Lord Jesus that the man should be left to the mercy of Satan so that while his body will experience the destructive powers of sin his spirit may yet be saved in the day of the Lord.

Your pride in yourselves is lamentably out of place. Don't you know how a little yeast can permeate the whole lump? Clear out every bit of the old yeast that you may be new unleavened bread! We Christians have had a Passover lamb sacrificed for us—none other than Christ himself! So let us "keep the feast" with no trace of the yeast of the old life, nor the yeast of vice and wickedness, but with the unleavened bread of unadulterated truth!

In my previous letter I said, "Don't mix with the immoral." I didn't mean, of course, that you were to have no contact at all with the immoral of this world, nor with any cheats or thieves or idolaters—for that would mean going out of the world altogether! But in this letter I tell you not to associate with any professing Christian who is known to be an impure man or a swindler, an idolater, a man with a foul tongue, a drunkard or a thief. My instruction is: "Don't even eat with such a man." Those outside the church it is not my business to judge. But surely it is your business to judge those who are inside the church—God alone can judge those who are outside. It is your plain duty to expel this wicked man from your fellowship!

CHAPTER 6

Don't go to law in pagan courts

WHEN any of you has a grievance against another, aren't you ashamed to bring the matter to be settled before a pagan court instead of before the church? Don't you know that Christians will one day judge the world? And if you are to judge the world do you consider yourselves incapable of settling such infinitely smaller matters? Don't you also know that we shall judge the very angels themselves—how much more then matters of this world only! In any case, if you find you have to judge matters of this world, why choose as judges those who count for nothing in the church? I say this deliberately to rouse your sense of shame. Are you really unable to find among your number one man with enough sense to decide a dispute between one and another of you, or must one brother resort to law against another and that before those who have no faith in Christ! It is surely obvious that something must be seriously wrong in your church for you to be having lawsuits at all. Why not *let* yourself be wronged or cheated? Instead of that you cheat and wrong your own brothers.

Have you forgotten that the kingdom of God will never belong to the wicked? Don't be under any illusion—neither the impure, the idolater or the adulterer; neither the effeminate, the pervert or the thief; neither the swindler, the drunkard, the foul-mouthed or the rapacious shall have any share in the kingdom of God. *And such were some of you!* But you have cleansed yourselves from all that, you have been made whole in spirit, you have been justified in the name of the Lord Jesus and in the Spirit of our God.

Christian liberty does not mean moral licence

As a Christian I *may* do anything, but that does not mean that everything is good for me. I may do everything, but I must not be a slave of anything. Food was meant for the stomach and the stomach for food; but God has no permanent purpose for either. But you cannot say that our physical body was made for sexual promiscuity; it was made for the Lord, and in the Lord is the answer to its needs. The God who raised the Lord from the dead will also raise us mortal men by his power. Have you not realised that your bodies are integral parts of Christ himself? Am I then to take parts of Christ and join them to a prostitute? Never! Don't you realise that when a man joins himself to a prostitute he makes with her a physical unity? For, God says, "the two shall be one flesh". On the other hand the man who joins himself to the Lord is one with him in spirit.

Avoid sexual looseness like the plague! Every other sin that a man commits is done outside his own body, but this is an offence against his own body. Have you forgotten that your body is the temple of the Holy Spirit, who lives in you and is God's gift to you, and that you are not the owner of your own body? You have been bought, and at a price! Therefore bring glory to God in your body.

CHAPTER 7

The question of marriage in present circumstances

Now let me deal with the questions raised in your letter.

It is a good principle for a man to have no physical contact with women. Nevertheless, because casual liaisons are so prevalent, let every man have his own wife and every woman her own husband. The husband should give his wife what is due to her as his wife, and the wife should be as fair to her husband. The wife has no longer full rights over her own person, but shares them with her husband. In the same way the husband shares his personal rights with his wife. Do not cheat each other of normal sexual intercourse, unless of course you both decide to abstain temporarily to make special opportunity for prayer. But afterwards you should resume relations as before, or you will expose yourselves to the obvious temptation of Satan.

I give the advice above more as a concession than as a command. I wish that all men were like myself, but I realise that everyone has his own particular gift from God, some one thing and some another. Yet to those who are unmarried or widowed, I say definitely that it is a good thing to remain unattached, as I am. But if they have not the gift of self-control in such matters, by all means let them get married. It is better for them to be married than to be tortured by unsatisfied desire.

To those who are already married my command, or rather, the Lord's command, is that the wife should not be separated from her husband. But if she is separated from him she should either remain unattached or else be reconciled to her husband. A husband must not desert his wife.

Advice over marriage between Christian and pagan

To other people my advice (though this is not a divine command) is this. If a brother has a non-Christian wife who is willing to live with him he should not leave her. A wife in a similar position should not leave her husband. For the unbelieving husband is consecrated by being joined to the person of his wife; the unbelieving wife is similarly consecrated by the Christian brother she has married. If this were not so then your children would bear the stains of paganism, whereas they are actually consecrated to God.

But if the unbelieving partner decides to separate, then let there be a separation. The Christian partner need not consider himself bound in such cases. Yet God has called us to live in peace, and after all how can you, who are a wife, know whether you will be able to save your husband or not? And the same applies to you who are a husband.

I merely add to the above that each man should live his life with the gifts that the Lord has given him and in the condition in which God has called him. This is the rule I lay down in all the churches.

For example, if a man was circumcised when God called him he should not attempt to remove the signs of his circumcision. If on the other hand he was uncircumcised he should not become circumcised. Being circumcised or not being circumcised, what do they matter? The great thing is to obey the orders of God. Everyone should continue in the state in which he heard the call of God. Were you a slave when you heard the call? Don't let that worry you, though if you find an opportunity to become free you had better take it. But a slave who is called to life in Christ is set free in the eyes of the Lord. Similarly a man who was free when God called him becomes a slave—to Christ himself! You have been redeemed, at tremendous cost; don't therefore sell yourselves as slaves to men! My brothers, let every one of us continue to live his life with God in the state in which he was when he was called.

In present circumstances it is really better not to marry

Now as far as young unmarried women are concerned, I must confess that I have no direct commands from the Lord. Nevertheless, I give you my considered opinion as of one who is, I think, to be trusted after all his experience of God's mercy.

My opinion is this, that amid all the difficulties of the present time you would do best to remain just as you are. Are you married? Well, don't try to be separated. Are you separated? Then don't try to get married. But if you, a man, should marry, don't think that you have done anything sinful. And the same applies to a young woman. Yet I do believe that those who take this step are bound to find the married state an extra burden in these critical days, and I should like to spare you that. All our futures are so foreshortened, indeed, that those who have wives should live, so to speak, as though they had none! There is no time to indulge in sorrow, no time for enjoying our joys; those who buy have no time to enjoy their possessions, and indeed their every contact with the world must be as light as possible, for the present scheme of things is rapidly passing away. That is why I should like you to be free from worldly anxieties. The unmarried man is free to concern himself with the Lord's affairs, and how he may please him. But the married man is sure to be concerned also with matters of this world, that he may please his wife—his interests are divided. You find the same difference in the case of the unmarried and the married woman. The unmarried concerns herself with the Lord's affairs, and her aim in life is to make herself holy, in body and in spirit. But the married woman must concern herself with the things of this world, and her aim will be please her husband.

I tell you these things to help you; I am not putting difficulties in your path but setting before you an ideal, so that your service of God may be as far as possible free from worldly distractions.

But marriage is not wrong

But if any man feels he is not behaving honourably towards the woman he loves, especially as she is beginning to lose her first youth and the emotional strain is considerable, let him do what his heart tells him to do—let them be married, there is no sin in that. Yet for the man of steadfast purpose who is able to bear the strain and has his own desires well under control, if he decides not to marry the young woman, he too will be doing the right thing. Both of them are right, one in choosing marriage and the other in refraining from marriage, but the latter has chosen the better of two right courses.

A woman is bound to her husband while he is alive, but if he dies she is free to marry whom she likes—but let her be guided by the Lord. In my opinion she would be happier to remain as she is, unmarried. And I think I am here expressing not only my opinion, but the will of the Spirit as well.

CHAPTER 8

A practical problem: shall we be guided by superior knowledge or love?

Now to deal with the matter of food which has been sacrificed to idols. It is easy to think that we "know" over problems like this, but we should remember that while this "knowing" may make a man look big, it is only love that can make him grow to his full stature. For if a man thinks he "knows" he may still be quite ignorant of what he ought to know. But if he loves God he is the man who is known to God.

In this matter, then, of eating food which has been offered to idols, we are sure that no idol has any real existence, and that there is no God but one. For though there are so-called gods both in heaven and earth, gods and lords galore in fact, for us there is only one God, the Father, from whom everything comes, and for whom we live. And there is one Lord, Jesus Christ, through whom everything exists, and through whom we ourselves are alive. But this knowledge of ours is not shared by all men. For some, who until now have been used to idols, eat the food as food really sacrificed to a god, and their delicate conscience is thereby injured. Now our acceptance by God is not a matter of food. If we eat it, that does not make us better men, nor are we the worse if we do not eat it. You must be careful that your freedom to eat food does not in any way hinder anyone whose faith is not as robust as yours. For suppose you with your knowledge of God should be observed eating food in an idol's temple, are you not encouraging the man with a delicate conscience to do the same? Surely you would not want your superior knowledge to bring spiritual disaster to a weaker brother for whom Christ died? And when you sin like this and damage the weak consciences of your brethren you really sin against Christ. This makes me determined that, if there is any possibility of food injuring my brother, I will never eat food as long as I live, for fear I might do him harm.

CHAPTER 9

A word of personal defence to my critics

Is there any doubt that I am a free man, any doubt that I am a genuine messenger? Have I not seen Jesus our Lord with my own eyes? Are not you yourselves samples of my work for the Lord? Even if other people should refuse to recognise my divine commission, yet to you at any rate I shall always be a true messenger, for you are a living proof of the Lord's call to me. This is my real ground of defence to those who cross-examine me.

Aren't we allowed to eat and drink? May we not travel with a Christian wife like the other messengers, like other Christian brothers, and like Cephas? Are Barnabas and I the only ones not allowed to leave their ordinary work to give time to the ministry?

Even a preacher of the gospel has some rights!

Just think for a moment. Does any soldier ever go to war at his own expense? Does any man plant a vineyard and have no share in its fruits? Does the shepherd who tends the flock never taste the milk? This is, I know an argument from everyday life, but it is a principle endorsed by the Law. For is it not written in the Law of Moses:

Thou shalt not muzzle the ox when he treadeth out the corn? Now does this imply merely God's care for oxen, or does it include his care for us too? Surely we are included! You might even say that the words were written for us. For both the ploughman as he ploughs, and the thresher as he threshes should have some hope of an ultimate share in the harvest. If we have sown for you the seed of spiritual things need you be greatly perturbed because we reap some of your material things? And if there are others with the right to have these things from you, have not we an even greater right? Yet we have never exercised this right and have put up with all sorts of things, so that we might not hinder the spread of the gospel.

I am entitled to a reward, yet I have not taken it

Are you ignorant of the fact that those who minister sacred things take part of the sacred food of the Temple for their own use, and those who attend the altar have their share of what is placed on the altar? On the same principle the Lord has ordered that those who proclaim the gospel should receive their livelihood from those who accept the gospel.

But I have never used any of these privileges, nor am I writing now to suggest that I should be given them. Indeed I would rather die than have anyone make this boast of mine an empty one!

My reward is to make the gospel free to all men

For I take no special pride in the fact that I preach the gospel. I feel compelled to do so; I should be utterly miserable if I failed to preach it. If I do this work because I choose to do so then I am entitled to a reward. But if it is no choice of mine, but a sacred responsibility put upon me, what can I expect in the way of reward? This, that when I preach the gospel, I can make it absolutely free of charge, and need not claim what is my rightful due as a preacher. For though I am no man's slave, yet I have made myself everyone's slave, that I might win more men to Christ. To the Jews I was a Jew that I might win the Jews. To those who were under the Law I put myself in the position of being under the

Law (although in fact I stand free of it), that I might win those who are under the Law. To those who had no Law I myself became like a man without the Law (even though in fact I cannot be a lawless man for I am bound by the law of Christ), so that I might win the men who have no Law. To the weak I became a weak man, that I might win the weak. I have, in short, been all things to all sorts of men that by every possible means I might win some to God. I do all this for the sake of the gospel; I want to play my part properly.

To preach the gospel faithfully is my set purpose

Do you remember how, on a racing-track, every competitor runs, but only one wins the prize? Well, you ought to run with your minds fixed on winning the prize! Every competitor in athletic events goes into serious training. Athletes will take tremendous pains—for a fading crown of leaves. But our contest is for a crown that will never fade.

I run the race then with determination. I am no shadow-boxer, I really fight! I am my body's sternest master, for fear that when I have preached to others I should myself be disqualified.

CHAPTER 10

Spiritual experience does not guarantee infallibility

For I should like to remind you, my brothers, that our ancestors all had the experience of being guided by the cloud in the desert and of crossing the sea dry-shod. They were all, so to speak, "baptised" into Moses by these experiences. They all shared the same spiritual food and drank the same spiritual drink (for they drank from the spiritual rock which followed them, and that rock was Christ). Yet in spite of all these experiences most of them failed to please God, and left their bones in the desert. Now in these events our ancestors stand as examples to us, warning us not to crave after evil things as they did. Nor are you to worship false gods as they did. The scripture says—

The people sat down to eat and drink, and rose up to play.

Neither should we give way to sexual immorality as did some of them, for we read that twenty-three thousand fell in a single day! Nor should we dare to exploit the goodness of God as some of them did, and fell victims to poisonous snakes. Nor yet must you curse the lot that God has appointed to you as some of them did, and met their end at the hand of the angel of death.

Now these things which happened to our ancestors are illustrations of the way in which God works, and they were written down to be a warning to us who are living in the final days of the present order.

So let the man who feels sure of his standing today be careful that he does not fall tomorrow.

God still governs human experience

No temptation has come your way that is too hard for flesh and blood to bear. But God can be trusted not to allow you to suffer any temptation beyond your powers of endurance. He will see to it that every temptation has its way out, so that it will be possible for you to bear it.

We have great spiritual privileges: let us live up to them

The lesson we must learn, my brothers, is at all costs to avoid worshipping a false god. I am speaking to you as intelligent men: use your judgment over what I am saying.

The cup of blessing which we bless, is it not a very sharing in the blood of Christ? When we break the bread do we not actually share in the body of Christ? The very fact that we, many as we are, share one bread makes us all one body. Look at the Jewish people. Isn't there a fellowship between all those who eat the altar sacrifices?

Now am I implying that a false god really exists, or that sacrifices made to any god have some value? Not at all! I say emphatically that gentile sacrifices are made to evil spiritual powers and not to God at all. I don't want you to have any fellowship with such powers. You cannot drink both the cup of the Lord and the cup of devils. You cannot be a guest at the Lord's table and at the table of devils. Are we trying to arouse the wrath of the Lord? Do we think we are stronger than he?

The Christian's guiding principle is love not knowledge

As I have said before, the Christian position is this: I may do anything, but everything is not useful. Yes, I may do anything, but everything is not constructive. Let no man, then, set his own advantage as his objective, but rather the good of his neighbour.

Eat whatever is sold in the meat-market without any question of conscience. The whole earth and all that is in it belongs to the Lord.

If a pagan asks you to dinner and you want to go, feel free to eat whatever is set before you, without asking any questions through conscientious scruples. But if someone should say straight out, "This has been offered to an idol", then don't eat it, for his sake—I mean for the sake of conscience, not yours but his.

Now why should my freedom to eat be at the mercy of someone else's conscience? Or why should any evil be said of me when I have eaten food with gratitude, and have thanked God for it? Because, whatever you do, eating or drinking or anything else, everything should be done to bring glory to God.

Do nothing that might make men stumble, whether they are Jews or Greeks or members of the church of God. I myself try to be agreeable to all men without considering my own advantage but that of the majority, that if possible they may be saved.

CHAPTER 11

COPY me, my brothers, as I copy Christ himself.

The reasons that lie behind some of the traditions

I must give you credit for remembering what I taught you and adhering to the traditions I passed on to you. But I want you to know that Christ is the head of every individual man, just as a man is the "head" of the woman and God is the head of Christ. If a man prays or preaches with his head covered, he is dishonouring his own head. But in the case of a woman, if she prays or preaches with her head uncovered it is just as much a disgrace as if she had had it closely shaved. For if a woman does not cover her head she might just as well have her hair cropped. And if to be cropped or closely shaven is a sign of disgrace to women, then that is all the more reason for her to cover her head. A man ought not to cover his head, for he represents the very person and glory of God, while the woman reflects the glory of the man. For man does not exist because woman exists, but vice versa.

Man was not created originally for the sake of woman, but woman was created for the sake of man. For this reason a woman ought to bear on her head an outward sign of man's authority for all the angels to see.

Of course, in the sight of the Lord neither "man" nor "woman" has any separate existence. For if woman was made originally from man, no man is now born except by a woman, and both man and woman, like everything else, owe their existence to God. But use your own judgment: do you think it right and proper for a woman to pray to God bare-headed? Isn't there a natural principle here, that makes us feel that long hair is disgraceful to a man, but of glorious beauty to a woman? We feel this because the long hair is the cover provided by nature for the woman's head. But if anyone wants to be argumentative about it, I can only say that we and the churches of God generally hold this ruling on the matter.

I must mention serious faults in your Church

But in giving you the following rules, I cannot commend your conduct, for it seems that your church meetings do you more harm than good! For first, when you meet for worship I hear that you split up into small groups, and I think there must be truth in what I hear. (I grant that you must be able to make choices or your best men might go unrecognised.) But, as it is, when you are assembled in one place you do not eat the *Lord's* supper. For everyone tries to grab his food before anyone else, with the result that one goes hungry and another has too much to drink! Haven't you houses of your own to have your meals in, or are you showing contempt for the church of God and causing acute embarrassment to those who have no other home?

What do you expect from me? Compliments? Certainly not on this!

To partake of the Lord's supper is a supremely serious thing

The teaching I gave you was given me personally by the Lord himself, and it was this: the Lord Jesus, in the same night in which he was betrayed, took bread and when he had given thanks he broke it and said, "This is my body—and it is for you. Do this in remembrance of me." Similarly, when supper was ended, he took the cup saying, "This cup is the new agreement made by my blood: do this, whenever you drink it, in remembrance of me."

This can only mean that whenever you eat this bread and drink this cup, you are proclaiming the Lord's death until he comes again. So that, whoever eats the bread or drinks the cup of the Lord without proper reverence is sinning against the body and blood of the Lord.

No, a man should thoroughly examine himself, and only then should he eat the bread or drink of the cup. He that eats and drinks carelessly is eating and drinking a condemnation of himself, for he is blind to the presence of the Body.

Careless communion means spiritual weakness: let us take due care

It is this careless participation which is the reason for the many feeble and sickly Christians in your church, and the explanation of the fact that many of you are spiritually asleep.

If we were closely to examine ourselves beforehand, we should avoid the judgment of God. But when God does judge us, he disciplines us as his own sons, that we may not be involved in the general condemnation of the world.

Now, my brothers, when you come together to eat this bread, wait your proper turn. If a man is really hungry let him satisfy his appetite at home. Don't let your communions be God's judgment upon you!

The other matters I will settle in person, when I come.

CHAPTER 12

The Holy Spirit inspires men's faith and imparts spiritual gifts

Now, my brothers, I want to give you some further information in spiritual matters. You have not forgotten that you are gentiles, following dumb idols just as your impulses led you. Now I want you to understand, as Christians, that no one speaking by the Spirit of God could say, "a curse on Jesus", and no one could say, "Jesus is Lord", except by the Holy Spirit.

Men have different gifts, but it is the same Spirit who gives them. There are different ways of serving God, but it is the same

Lord who is served. God works through different men in different ways, but it is the same God who achieves his purposes through them all. The Spirit openly makes his gift to each man, so that he may use it for the common good.

One man's gift by the Spirit is to speak with wisdom, another's to speak with knowledge. The same Spirit gives to another man faith, to another the ability to heal, to another the use of spiritual powers. The same Spirit gives to another man the gift of preaching the word of God, to another the ability to discriminate in spiritual matters, to another speech in different tongues and to yet another the power to interpret the tongues. Behind all these gifts is the operation of the same Spirit, who distributes to each individual man, as he wills.

The human body is an example of organic unity

As the human body, which has many parts, is a unity, and those parts, despite their multiplicity, constitute one single body, so it is with Christ. For we were all baptised by the one Spirit into one body, whether we were Jews, Greeks, slaves or free men, and we have all had experience of the same Spirit.

Now the body is not one part but many. If the foot should say, "Because I am not a hand I don't belong to the body," does that alter the fact that the foot *is* a part of the body? Or if the ear should say, "Because I am not an eye I don't belong to the body," does that mean that the ear really is no part of the body? After all, if the body were all one eye, for example, where would be the sense of hearing? Or if it were all one ear, where would be the sense of smell? But God has arranged all the parts in the one body according to his design. For if everything were concentrated in one part, how could there be a body at all? The fact is there are many parts, but only one body. So that the eye cannot say to the hand, "I don't need you!" nor, again, can the head say to the feet, "I don't need you!" On the contrary, those parts of the body which seem to have less strength are more essential to health: and to those parts of the body which seem to us to be less admirable we have to allow the highest honour of function. The parts which do not look beautiful have a deeper beauty in the work they do, while the parts which look beautiful may not be at all essential to life! But God has harmonised the whole body by giving importance of function to the parts which lack apparent importance, that the body should work together as a whole with all the members in sympathetic relationship with one another. So it happens that if one member suffers all the other members suffer with it, and if one member is honoured all the members share a common joy.

Now you are together the body of Christ, and each of you is a part of it. And in the Church God has appointed first some to be his messengers, secondly, some to be preachers of power, thirdly teachers. After them he has appointed workers of spiritual power, men with the gift of healing, helpers, counsellors and those with the gift of speaking various "tongues".

As we look at the body of Christ do we find all are his messengers, all are preachers, or all teachers? Do we find all wielders of spiritual power, all able to heal, all able to speak with tongues, or all able to interpret the tongues?

You should set your hearts on the best spiritual gifts, but I will show you a way which surpasses them all.

CHAPTER 13

Christian love—the highest and best gift

If I speak with the eloquence of men and of angels, but have no love, I become no more than blaring brass or crashing cymbal. If I have the gift of foretelling the future and hold in my mind not only all human knowledge but the very secrets of God, and if I also have that absolute faith which can move mountains, but have no love, I amount to nothing at all. If I dispose of all that I possess, yes, even if I give my own body to be burned, but have no love, I achieve precisely nothing.

This love of which I speak is slow to lose patience—it looks for a way of being constructive. It is not possessive: it is neither anxious to impress nor does it cherish inflated ideas of its own importance.

Love has good manners and does not pursue selfish advantage. It is not touchy. It does not keep account of evil or gloat over the wickedness of other people. On the contrary, it shares the joy of those who live by the truth.

Love knows no limit to its endurance, no end to its trust, no fading of its hope; it can outlast anything. Love never fails.

All gifts except love will be superseded one day

For if there are prophecies they will be fulfilled and done with, if there are "tongues" the need for them will disappear, if there is knowledge it will be swallowed up in truth. For our knowledge is always incomplete and our prophecy is always incomplete, and when the complete comes, that is the end of the incomplete.

When I was a little child I talked and felt and thought like a little child. Now that I am a man I have finished with childish things.

At present we are men looking at puzzling reflections in a mirror. The time will come when we shall see reality whole and face to face! At present all I know is a little fraction of the truth, but the time will come when I shall know it as fully as God has known me!

In this life we have three lasting qualities—faith, hope and love. But the greatest of them is love.

CHAPTER 14

"Tongues" are not the greatest gift

FOLLOW, then, the way of love, while you set your heart on the gifts of the Spirit. The highest gift you can wish for is to be able to speak the messages of God. The man who speaks in a "tongue" addresses not men (for no one understands a word he says) but God: and only in his spirit is he speaking spiritual secrets. But he who preaches the word of God is using his speech for the building up of the faith of one man, the encouragement of another or the consolation of another. The speaker in a "tongue" builds up his own soul, but the preacher builds up the Church.

I should indeed like you all to speak with "tongues", but I would much rather that you all preached the word of God. For the preacher of the word does a greater work than the speaker with "tongues", unless of course the latter interprets his words for the benefit of the Church.

Unless "tongues" are interpreted do they help the Church?

For suppose I came to you, my brothers, speaking with "tongues", what good could I do you unless I could give you some revelation of truth, some knowledge in spiritual things, some message from God, or some teaching about the Christian life?

Even in the case of inanimate objects which are capable of making sound, such as a flute or harp, unless their notes have the proper intervals, who can tell what tune is being played on them? Unless the bugle-notes are clear who will be called to arms? So, in your case, unless you make intelligible sounds with your "tongue" how can anyone know what you are talking about? You might just as well be addressing an empty room!

There may be in the world a great variety of spoken sounds and none is without meaning. But if the sounds of the speaker's voice mean nothing to me I am bound to sound like a foreigner to him, and he like a foreigner to me.

So, with yourselves, since you are so eager to possess spiritual gifts, concentrate your ambition upon receiving those which make for the real growth of your church. And that means if one of your number speaks with a "tongue", he should pray that he may be able to interpret what he says.

If I pray in a "tongue" my spirit is praying but my mind is inactive. I am therefore determined to pray with my spirit *and* my mind, and if I sing I will sing with both spirit and mind. Otherwise, if you are praising God with your spirit, how can the uninstructed man say amen to your thanksgiving, since he does not know what you are talking about? You may be thanking God splendidly, but it doesn't help the other man at all. I thank God that I have a greater gift of "tongues" than any of you, yet when I am in church I would rather speak five words with my mind (which might teach something to other people) than ten thousand words in a "tongue" which nobody understands.

You must use your minds in this matter of tongues

My brothers, don't be children but use your intelligence! By all means be innocent as babes as far as evil is concerned, but where your minds are concerned be full-grown men! In the Law it is written:

> By men of strange tongues and by the lips of strangers will I speak unto this people: and not even thus will they hear me, saith the Lord.

That means that tongues are a sign of God's power, not for those who are unbelievers but for those who already believe.*

* See note 5, page 552.

Preaching the word of God, on the other hand, is a sign of God's power to those who do not believe rather than to believers. So that, if at a full church meeting you are all speaking with tongues and men come in who are uninstructed or without faith, will they not say that you are insane? But if you are preaching God's word and such a man should come in to your meeting, he is convicted and challenged by your united speaking of the truth. His secrets are exposed and he will fall on his knees acknowledging God and saying that God is truly among you!

Some practical regulations for the exercise of spiritual gifts

Well then, my brothers, whenever you meet let everyone be ready to contribute a psalm, a piece of teaching, a spiritual truth, or a "tongue" with an interpreter. Everything should be done to make your church strong in the faith.

If the question of speaking with a "tongue" arises, confine the speaking to two or three at the most. They must speak in turn and have someone to interpret what is said. If you have no interpreter then let the speaker with a "tongue" keep silent in the church and speak only to himself and God. Don't have more than two or three preachers either, while the others think over what has been said. But should a message of truth come to one who is seated, then the original speaker should stop talking. For in this way you can all have the opportunity to give a message, one after the other, and everyone will learn something and everyone will have his faith stimulated. The spirit of a true preacher is under that preacher's control, for God is not a God of disorder but of harmony, as is plain in all the churches.

The speaking of women in church is forbidden

Let women be silent in church; they are not to be allowed to speak. They must submit to this regulation, as the Law itself instructs. If they have questions to ask they must ask their husbands at home, for there is something improper about a woman's speaking in church.

You must accept the rules I have given by authority

Are you beginning to imagine that the Word of God originated in your church, or that you have a monopoly of God's truth?

If any of your number think himself a true preacher and a spiritually-minded man, let him realise that what I have written is by divine command! If a man does not recognise this he himself should not be recognised.

In conclusion then, my brothers, set your heart on preaching the word of God, while not forbidding the use of "tongues". Let everything be done decently and in order.

CHAPTER 15

A reminder of the gospel message: the resurrection is an integral part of our faith

Now, my brothers, I want to remind you of the gospel which I have previously preached to you, which you accepted, on which you have taken your stand and by which, if you remain faithful to the message I gave you, your salvation is being worked out—unless, of course, your faith had no meaning behind it at all.

For I passed on to you,—as essential, the message I had myself received—that Christ died for our sins, as the scriptures said he would; that he was buried and rose again on the third day, again as the scriptures foretold. He was seen by Cephas, then by the twelve, and subsequently he was seen simultaneously by over five hundred Christians, of whom the majority are still alive, though some have since died. He was then seen by James, then by all the messengers. And last of all, as to one born abnormally late, he appeared even to me! I am the least of the messengers, and indeed I do not deserve that title at all, because I persecuted the Church of God. But what I am now I am by the grace of God. The grace he gave me has not proved a barren gift. I have worked harder than any of the others—and yet it was not I but this same grace of God within me. In any event, whoever has done the work, whether I or they, this has been our message and this has been your faith.

If the resurrection is the heart of the gospel how can any Christian deny life after death?

Now if the rising of Christ from the dead is the very heart of our message, how can some of you deny that there is any resurrection? For if there is no such thing as the resurrection of the dead, then Christ was never raised. And if Christ was not raised then neither our preaching nor your faith has any meaning at all. Further it would mean that we are lying in our witness for God, for we have given our solemn testimony that he did raise up Christ—and that is utterly false if it should be true that the dead do not, in fact, rise again! For if the dead do not rise neither did Christ rise, and if Christ did not rise your faith is futile and your sins have never been forgiven. Moreover those who have died believing in Christ are utterly dead and gone. Truly, if our hope in Christ were limited to this life only we should, of all mankind, be the most to be pitied!

But Christianity rests on a fact—Christ did rise

But the glorious fact is that Christ was raised from the dead: he has become the very first to rise of all who sleep the sleep of death. As death entered the world through a man, so has rising from the dead come to us through a man! As members of a sinful race all men die; as members of Christ all men shall be raised to life, each in his proper order, with Christ the very first and after him all who belong to him when he comes.

Then, and not till then, comes the end when Christ, having abolished all other rule, authority and power, hands over the kingdom to God the Father. Christ's reign will and must continue until every enemy has been conquered. The last enemy of all to be destroyed is death itself. The scripture says:

> He hath put all things in subjection under his feet.

But in the term "all things" it is quite obvious that God, who brings them all under subjection to Christ, is himself excepted. Nevertheless, when everything has been made subject to God, then shall the Son himself be subject to God, who gave him power over all things. Thus, in the end, shall God be wholly and absolutely God.

To refuse to believe in the resurrection is both foolish and wicked

Further, you should consider this, that if there is to be no resurrection what is the point of some of you being baptised for the dead by proxy? Why should you be baptised for *dead bodies*? And why should we live a life of such hourly danger? I assure you, by the proud certainty which we share in Christ Jesus our Lord, that I face death every day of my life! And if, to use the popular expression, I have "fought with wild beasts" here in Ephesus, what is the good of an ordeal like that if there is no life after this one? Let us rather eat, drink and be merry, for tomorrow we die!

Don't let yourselves be deceived. It is true that "evil communications corrupt good manners".* Come back to your right senses, and stop sinning like this! Remember that there are men who have no knowledge of God. You should be ashamed that I have to write like this!

Parallels in nature help us to grasp the truths of the resurrection

But perhaps someone will ask, "How is the resurrection achieved? With what sort of body do the dead arrive?" Now that is a silly question! In your own experience you know that a seed does not germinate without itself "dying". When you sow a seed you do not sow the "body" that will eventually be produced, but bare grain, of wheat, for example, or one of the other seeds. God gives the seed a "body" according to his laws—a different "body" to each kind of seed.

Then again, all flesh is not identical. There is a difference in the flesh of human beings, animals, birds and fish.

There are bodies which exist in the heavens, and bodies which exist in this world. The splendour of an earthly body is quite a different thing from the splendour of a heavenly body. The sun, the moon and the stars all have their own particular splendour; and one star differs from another in splendour.

There are illustrations here of the raising of the dead. The body is "sown" in corruption; it is raised beyond the reach of corruption. It is "sown" in dishonour; it is raised in splendour. It is sown in weakness; it is raised in power. It is sown a natural body; it is raised a spiritual body. As there is a natural body so will there be a spiritual body.

It is written, moreover, that:

> The first man Adam became a living soul.

So the last Adam is a life-giving Spirit. But we should notice that the "spiritual" does not come first: the order is "natural" first and then "spiritual". The first man came out of the earth, a material creature; the second man came from heaven. For the life of this world men are made like the material man; but for the life that is to come they are made like the one from heaven. So that just as we have been made like the material pattern, so we shall

* This is a direct quotation from the Greek dramatist Menander (c. 342-291 B.C.). It must have been a proverbial saying throughout the Greek-speaking Mediterranean countries, and it is still a proverb in English.

be made like the heavenly pattern. For I assure you, my brothers, it is utterly impossible for flesh and blood to possess the kingdom of God. The transitory could never possess the everlasting.

The dead and the living will be fitted for immortality

Listen, and I will tell you a secret. We shall not all die, but suddenly, in the twinkling of an eye, every one of us will be changed as the last trumpet sounds! For the trumpet will sound and the dead shall be raised beyond the reach of corruption, and we shall be changed. For this perishable nature of ours must be wrapped in imperishability, these bodies which are mortal must be wrapped in immortality. So when the perishable is lost in the imperishable, the mortal lost in the immortal, this scripture will come true:

Death is swallowed up in victory.

Where now, O death, is your victory; where now is your stinging power? It is sin which gives death its sting, and it is the Law which gives sin its power. All thanks to God, then, who gives us the victory over these things through our Lord Jesus Christ!

And so, brothers of mine, stand firm! Let nothing move you as you busy yourselves in the Lord's work. Be sure that nothing you do for him is ever lost or ever wasted.

CHAPTER 16

The matter of the fund: my own immediate plans

Now as far as the fund for Christians in need is concerned, I should like you to follow the same rule that I gave to the Galatian church.

On the first day of the week let everyone put so much by him, according to his financial prosperity, so that there will be no need for collections when I come. Then, on my arrival, I will send whomever you approve to take your gift, with my written recommendation, to Jerusalem. If it seems right for me to go as well, we will make up a party together. I shall come to you after my intended journey through Macedonia and I may stay with you awhile or even spend the winter with you. Then you can see me on my way—wherever it is that I go next. I don't wish to see you now, for it would merely be in passing, and I hope to spend some time with you, if it is the Lord's will. I shall stay here in Ephesus until the feast of Pentecost, for I have been given a great opportunity of doing useful work, and there are many against me.

News of Timothy and Apollos

If Timothy comes to you, put him at his ease. He is as genuine a worker for the Lord as I am, and there is therefore no reason to look down on him. Send him on his way in peace, for I am expecting him to come to me here with the other Christian brothers. As for our brother Apollos I pressed him strongly to go to you with the rest, but it was definitely not God's will for him to do so then. However, he will come to you as soon as an opportunity occurs.

A little sermon in a nutshell!

Be on your guard, stand firm in the faith, live like men, be strong! Let everything that you do be done in love.

A request, and final greetings

Now I have a request to make of you, my brothers.

You remember the household of Stephanas, the first men of Achaia to be won for Christ? Well, they have made up their minds to devote their lives to looking after Christian brothers. I do beg you to recognise such men, and to extend your recognition to anyone who works and labours with them.

I am very glad that Stephanas, Fortunatus and Achaicus have arrived. They have made up for what you were unable to do. They have relieved my anxiety and yours. You should appreciate having men like that!

Greetings from the churches of Asia. Aquila and Prisca send you their warmest Christian greetings and so does the church that meets in their house. All the Christians here send greetings. I should like you to shake hands all round as a sign of Christian love.

Here is my own greeting, written by me, Paul.

"If any man does not love the Lord, a curse be on him; may the Lord soon come!"

The grace of the Lord Jesus be with you and my love be with you all in Christ Jesus.

The Second Letter to the Christians at Corinth

AUTHOR. *Paul, writing in Macedonia, probably as soon as Titus had arrived back from Corinth, bringing news of the reception of the "first letter". (Some think that Paul had paid a hurried personal visit to Corinth between the writing of these two letters.)*

DATE. *Possibly* 57.

DESTINATION. *The church at Corinth, as in the "first letter".*

THEME. *There is a good deal of Paul's personal circumstances, feelings, activities, and attitude to his own ministry in this highly interesting letter. The Corinthian church appears to have disciplined the guilty member referred to in the first letter, and Paul recommends his restoration to the fellowship of the church.*

Again in this letter Paul has to defend his own divine commission as messenger, and even has to threaten strong action against his traducers in a personal visit.

Throughout this letter the reader cannot help feeling how "human" was Paul, and how genuine in his concern for the young and struggling churches under his care.

NOTE. *Many scholars believe that this letter contains parts of other "lost" letters in the passages:* 6, *14 to* 7, *1, and chapters* 10–13, *which seem out of key with the rest. The first-named passage may form part of the letter referred to by Paul in I Corinthians* 5, *9.*

CHAPTER 1

THIS letter comes to you from Paul, God's messenger for Christ Jesus by the will of God, and from brother Timothy, and is addressed to the church of God in Corinth and all Christians throughout Achaia.

May grace and peace come to you from God our Father and from the Lord Jesus Christ.

THE SECOND LETTER TO THE CHRISTIANS AT CORINTH 1

God's encouragements are adequate for all life's troubles

Thank God, the Father of our Lord Jesus Christ, that he is our Father and the source of all mercy and comfort. For he gives us comfort in all our trials so that we in turn may be able to give the same sort of strong sympathy to others in their troubles that we receive from God. Indeed, experience shows that the more we share in Christ's immeasurable suffering the more we are able to give of his encouragement. This means that if we experience trouble it is for your comfort and spiritual protection; for if we ourselves have been comforted we know how to encourage you to endure patiently the same sort of troubles that we ourselves endure. We are quite confident that if you have to suffer troubles as we have done, then, like us, you will find the comfort and encouragement of God.

Man's extremity is God's opportunity

We should like you, our brothers, to know something of the trouble we went through in Asia. At that time we were completely overwhelmed, the burden was more than we could bear, in fact we told ourselves that this was the end. Yet we believe now that we had this sense of impending disaster so that we might learn to trust, not in ourselves, but in God who can raise the dead. It was God who preserved us from such deadly perils, and it is he who still preserves us. We put our full trust in him and he will keep us safe in the future. Here you can co-operate by praying for us, so that the help that is given to us in answer to many prayers will mean that many will thank God for our preservation.

Our dealings with you have always been straightforward

Now it is a matter of pride to us—endorsed by our conscience—that our activities in this world, particularly our dealings with you, have been absolutely above-board and sincere before God. They have not been marked by any worldly wisdom, but by the grace of God. Our letters to you have no double meaning—they mean just what you understand them to mean when you read them. I hope you will always understand these letters. Just as I believe that you have partially understood me, so you will come to realise that you can be as honestly proud of us, as we are of you, on the day of the Lord Jesus.

Change of plan does not necessarily mean fickleness of heart

Trusting you, and believing that you trusted us, our original plan was to pay you a visit first, and give you a double "treat". We meant to come here to Macedonia after first visiting you, and then to visit you again on leaving here. You could thus have helped us on our way towards Judaea. Because we had to change this plan, does it mean that we are fickle? Do you think I plan with my tongue in my cheek, saying "yes" and "no" to suit my own wishes? We solemnly assure you that as certainly as God is faithful so we have never given you a message meaning "yes" and "no". Jesus Christ, the Son of God, whom Silvanus, Timothy and I have preached to you, was himself no doubtful quantity, he is the divine "yes". Every promise of God finds its affirmative in him, and through him can be said the final amen, to the glory of God. Both you and we owe our position in Christ to this God of positive promise: it is he who has consecrated us to this special work, he who has given us the living guarantee of the Spirit in our hearts.

I have never wanted to hurt you

No, I declare before God—and I would stake my life on it—that it was to avoid hurting you that I did not come to Corinth. We are not trying to dominate you and your faith—your faith is firm enough—but we can work with you to increase your joy.

CHAPTER 2

AND I made up my mind that I would not pay you another painful visit. For what point is there in my depressing the very people who can give me such joy? The real purpose of my previous letter was in fact to save myself from being saddened by those whom I might reasonably expect to bring me joy. I felt sure that my happiness was also yours! I wrote to you in deep distress and out of a most unhappy heart (I don't mind telling you I shed tears over that letter), not, believe me, to cause you pain, but to show you how very deep is my love for you.

A word of explanation

If the behaviour of a certain person has caused distress, it does not mean so much that he has injured me, but that to some extent (I do not wish to exaggerate), he has injured all of you. But now I think that the punishment which most of you inflicted on such a man has been sufficient. Now is the time to offer him forgiveness and comfort, so that a man in his position is not completely overwhelmed by remorse. I ask you to assure him now that you love him. My previous letter was something of a test—I wanted to make sure that you would follow my orders implicitly. If you forgive a certain person for anything, I forgive him too. Insofar as I had anything personally to forgive, I do forgive him for your sake, as before Christ. We don't want Satan to win any victory here, and well we know his methods!

And a further confidence

Well, when I came to Troas to preach the gospel of Christ, although there was an obvious God-given opportunity, I must confess I was on edge the whole time because there was no sign of brother Titus. So I said good-bye and went from there to Macedonia. Thanks be to God who leads us, wherever we are, on Christ's triumphant way and makes our knowledge of him spread throughout the world like a lovely perfume! We Christians have the unmistakable "scent" of Christ, discernible alike to those who are being saved and to those who are heading for death. To the latter it seems like the deathly smell of doom, to the former it has the refreshing fragrance of life itself.

Who is fit for such a task! We are not like that large number who corrupt the Word of God. No, we speak in utter sincerity as men sent by God, Christ's ministers under the eyes of God.

CHAPTER 3

You yourselves are the proof of our ministry

DOES this mean yet another production of credentials? Do we need, as some apparently do, to exchange testimonials before we can be friends? You yourselves are our testimonial, written in our hearts and yet open for anyone to inspect and read. You are an open letter about Christ delivered by us and written, not with pen and ink but with the Spirit of the living God, engraved not on stone, but on human hearts.

We dare to say such things because of the confidence we have in God through Christ. Not that we are in any way confident of doing anything by our own resources—our ability comes from God. It is he who makes us competent administrators of the new agreement, concerned not with the letter but with the Spirit. The letter of the Law leads to the death of the soul; the Spirit alone can give it life.

The splendour of our ministry outshines that of Moses

The administration of the Law which was engraved in stone (and which led in fact to spiritual death) was so magnificent that the Israelites were unable to look unflinchingly at Moses' face, for it was alight with heavenly splendour. Now if the old administration held such heavenly, even though transitory, splendour, can we not see what a much more glorious thing is the new administration of the Spirit of life? If to administer a system which is to end in condemning men had its glory, how infinitely more splendid is it to administer a system which ends in making men right with God! And while it is true that the former glory has been eclipsed by the latter, we do well to remember that it is eclipsed because the present and permanent is so much more glorious than the old and transient.

Our ministry is an open and splendid thing

With this hope in our hearts we are quite frank and open in our ministry. We are not like Moses, who veiled his face to prevent the Israelites from seeing its fading glory. But it was their minds really which were blinded, for even today when the old agreement is read to them there is still a veil over their minds—though the veil has actually been lifted by Christ. Yes even to this day there is still a veil over their hearts when the writings of Moses are read. Yet if they "turned to the Lord" the veil would disappear. For the Lord to whom they could turn is the Spirit, and wherever the Spirit of the Lord is, men's souls are set free.

But all of us who are Christians have no veils on our faces, but reflect like mirrors the glory of the Lord. We are transformed in ever-increasing splendour into his own image, and this is the work of the Lord who is the Spirit.

CHAPTER 4

Ours is a straightforward ministry bringing light into darkness

THIS is the ministry which God in his mercy has given us and nothing can daunt us. We have set our faces against all shameful secret practices; we use no clever tricks, no dishonest manipulation of the Word of God. We speak the plain truth and so commend ourselves to every man's conscience in the sight of God. If our gospel is "veiled", the veil must be in the minds of those who are spiritually dying. The god of this world has blinded the minds of those who do not believe, and prevents the light of the glorious gospel of Christ, the image of God, from shining on them. For it is Christ Jesus as Lord whom we preach, not ourselves; we are your servants for Jesus' sake. God, who first ordered light to shine in darkness, has flooded our hearts with his light, so that we can enlighten men with the knowledge of the glory of God, as we see it in the face of Christ.

We experience death—we give life, by the power of God

This priceless treasure we hold, so to speak, in common earthenware—to show that the splendid power of it belongs to God and not to us. We are hard-pressed on all sides, but we are never frustrated; we are puzzled, but never in despair. We are persecuted, but are never deserted: we may be knocked down but we are never knocked out! Every day we experience something of the death of Jesus, so that we may also show the power of the life of Jesus in these bodies of ours. Yes, we who are living are always being exposed to death for Jesus' sake, so that the life of Jesus may be plainly seen in our mortal lives. We are always facing physical death, so that you may know spiritual life. Our faith is like that mentioned in the scripture:

I believed and therefore did I speak.

For we too speak because we believe, and we know for certain that he who raised the Lord Jesus from death shall also raise us with Jesus. We shall all stand together before him.

We live a transitory life with our eyes on the life eternal

All this is indeed working out for your benefit, for as more grace is given to more and more people so will the thanksgiving to the glory of God be increased. This is the reason why we never lose heart. The outward man does indeed suffer wear and tear, but every day the inward man receives fresh strength. These little troubles (which are really so transitory) are winning for us a permanent, glorious and solid reward out of all proportion to our pain. For we are looking all the time not at the visible things but at the invisible. The visible things are transitory: it is the invisible things that are really permanent.

CHAPTER 5

We know, for instance, that if our earthly dwelling were taken down, like a tent, we have a permanent house in Heaven, made, not by man, but by God. In this present frame we sigh with deep longing for our heavenly house, for we do not want to face utter nakedness. So long as we are clothed in this temporary dwelling we have a painful longing, not because we want just to get rid of these "clothes" but because we want to know the full cover of the permanent. We want our transitory life to be absorbed into the life that is eternal.

Death can have no terrors, for it means being with God

Now the power that has planned this experience for us is God, and he has given us the Spirit as a guarantee of its truth. This makes us confident, whatever happens. We realise that being "at home" in the body means that to some extent we are "away" from the Lord, for we have to live by trusting him without seeing him. We are so sure of this that we would really rather be "away" from the body and be "at home" with the Lord.

It is our aim, therefore, to please him, whether we are "at home" or "away". For every one of us will have to stand without pretence before Christ our judge, and we shall each receive our due for what we did when we lived in our bodies, whether it was good or bad.

Our ministry is based on solemn convictions

All our persuading of men, then, is with this solemn fear of God in our minds. What we are is utterly plain to God—and I hope to your consciences as well. No, we are not recommending ourselves to you again, but we can give you grounds for legitimate pride in us—if that is what you need to meet those who are so proud of the outward rather than the inward qualification. If we are "mad" it is for God's glory; if we are perfectly sane it is for your benefit. The very spring of our actions is the love of Christ. We look at it like this: if one died for all men, then, in a sense, they all died, and his purpose in dying for them is that their lives should now be no longer lived for themselves but for him who died and was raised to life for them. This means that our knowledge of men can no longer be based on their outward lives (indeed, even though we knew Christ as a man we do not know him like that any longer). For if a man is in Christ he becomes a new person altogether—the past is finished and gone, everything has become fresh and new. All this is God's doing, for he has reconciled us to himself through Christ; and he has made us agents of the reconciliation. God was in Christ personally reconciling the world to himself—not counting their sins against them—and has commissioned us with the message of reconciliation. We are now Christ's ambassadors, as though God were appealing direct to you through us. For Christ's sake we beg you, "Make your peace with God." For God caused Christ, who himself knew nothing of sin, actually to *be* sin for our sakes, so that in Christ we might be made good with the goodness of God.

CHAPTER 6

The hard but glorious life of God's ministers

As co-operators with God himself we beg you, then, not to fail to use the grace of God which you have received. For God's word is—

At an acceptable time I hearkened unto thee,
And in a day of salvation did I succour thee.

Now *is* the "acceptable time", and this very day *is* the "day of salvation".

As far as we are concerned we do not wish to stand in anyone's way, nor do we wish to bring discredit on the ministry God has given us. Indeed we want to prove ourselves genuine ministers of God whatever we have to go through—patient endurance of troubles, hardship, desperate situations, being flogged or imprisoned; being mobbed, overworked, sleepless and starving;

with sincerity, with insight and patience; by sheer kindness and the Holy Spirit; with genuine love, speaking the plain truth, and living by the power of God. Our sole defence, our only weapon, is a life of integrity, whether we meet honour or dishonour, praise or blame. Called "impostors" we must be true, called "nobodies" we must be in the public eye. Never far from death, yet here we are alive, always "going through it" yet never "going under". We know sorrow, yet our joy is inextinguishable. We have "nothing to bless ourselves with" yet we bless many others with true riches. We are penniless, and yet we possess everything.

We have used utter frankness, won't you do the same?

Dear friends in Corinth, we are hiding nothing from you and our hearts are absolutely open to you. Any restraint between us must be on your side, for we assure you there is none on ours. Do reward me (I talk to you as though you were my own children) with the same complete candour!

We must warn you against entanglement with pagans

Don't link up with unbelievers and try to work with them. What common interest can there be between goodness and evil? How can light and darkness share life together? How can there be harmony between Christ and the devil? What can a believer have in common with an unbeliever? What common ground can idols hold with the temple of God? For we, remember, are ourselves temples of the living God, as God has said:

> I will dwell in them and walk in them:
> And I will be their God, and they shall be my people.
> Therefore
> Come ye out from among them and be ye separate, saith the Lord,
> And touch no unclean thing;
> And I will receive you,
> And will be to you a Father,
> And ye shall be to me sons and daughters,
> Saith the Lord Almighty.

CHAPTER 7

WITH these promises ringing in our ears, dear friends, let us cleanse ourselves from anything that pollutes body or soul. Let us prove our reverence for God by consecrating ourselves to him completely.

Does "that letter" still rankle? Hear my explanation

Do make room in your hearts for us! Not one of you has ever been wronged or ruined or cheated by us. I don't say this to condemn your attitude, but simply because, as I said before, whether we meet death or life together you live in our hearts. I talk to you with utter frankness; I think of you with deepest pride. Whatever troubles I have gone through, the thought of you has filled me with comfort and deep happiness.

For even when we arrived in Macedonia we found no rest but trouble all round us—wrangling outside and anxiety within. Not but what God, who cheers the depressed, gave us the comfort of the arrival of Titus. And it wasn't merely his coming that cheered us, but the comfort you had given him, for he could tell us of your eagerness to see me, your deep sorrow and keen interest on my behalf. All that made me doubly glad to see him. For although my letter had hurt you I don't regret it now (even if I did at one time). I can see that the letter did upset you, though only for a time, and now I am glad I sent it, not because I want to hurt you but because it made you grieve for things that were wrong. In other words, the result was to make you sorry as God would have had you sorry, and not to make you feel injured by what we said. The sorrow which God uses means a change of heart and leads to salvation without regret—it is the world's sorrow that is such a deadly thing. You can look back now and see how the hand of God was in that sorrow. Look how seriously it made you think, how eager it made you to prove your innocence, how indignant it made you and how afraid! Look how it made you long for my presence, how it stirred up your keenness for the faith, how ready it made you to punish the offender! You have completely cleared yourselves in this matter.

Now I did not write that letter really for the sake of the man who sinned, or even for the sake of the one who was sinned against, but to let you see for yourselves, in the sight of God, how deeply you really do care for us. That is why we now feel so encouraged, and, in addition, our sense of joy was greatly enhanced by knowing what happiness you all gave to Titus by setting his mind at rest. You see, I had told him of my pride in you, and you have not let me down. I have always spoken the truth *to* you, and this proves that my proud words *about* you were true as well. Titus himself has a much greater love for you, now that he has seen for himself the obedience you gave him, and the respect and reverence with which you treated him. I am profoundly glad to have my confidence in you so fully proved.

CHAPTER 8

The Macedonian churches have given magnificently: will you not do so too?

Now, my brothers, we must tell you about the grace that God has given to the Macedonian churches. Somehow, in most difficult circumstances, their overflowing joy and the fact of being down to their last penny themselves, produced a magnificent concern for other people. I can guarantee that they were willing to give to the limit of their means, yes and beyond their means, without the slightest urging from me or anyone else. In fact they simply begged us to accept their gifts and so let them share the honour of supporting their brothers in Christ. Nor was their gift, as I must confess I had expected, a mere cash payment. Instead they made a complete dedication of themselves first to the Lord and then to us, because God willed it.

Now this has made us ask Titus, who began this task, to complete it by arranging for you to share in this work of generosity. Already you are well to the fore in every good quality—you have faith, you can express that faith in words; you have knowledge, enthusiasm and your love for us. Could you not add generosity to your virtues? I don't give you this as an order. It is only my suggestion, prompted by what I have seen in others of eagerness to help, that here is a way to prove the reality of your love. Do you remember the generosity of Jesus Christ, the Lord of us all? He was rich, yet he became poor for your sakes so that his poverty might make you rich.

I merely suggest that you finish your original generous gesture

Here is my opinion in the matter. I think it would be a good thing for you, who were the first a year ago to think of helping, as well as the first to give, to carry through what you then intended to do. Finish it, then, as well as your means allow, and show that you can complete what you set out to do with as much readiness as you showed eagerness to begin. The important thing is to be willing to give as much as we can—that is what God accepts, and no one is asked to give what he has not got. Of course, I don't mean that others should be relieved to an extent that leaves you in distress. It is a matter of share and share alike. At present your plenty should supply their need, and then at some future date their plenty may supply your need. In that way we share with each other, as the scripture says,

He that gathered much had nothing over,
And he that gathered little had no lack.

Titus is bringing you this letter personally

Thank God Titus feels the same deep concern for you as we do! He accepts the suggestion outlined above, and in his enthusiasm comes to you personally at his own request. We are sending with him that brother whose services to the gospel are universally praised in the churches. He has moreover been chosen to travel with us in this work of administering this generous gift. It is a task that brings glory to God and demonstrates also our willingness to help. Naturally we want to avoid the slightest breath of criticism in the distribution of their gifts, and to be absolutely above-board not only in the sight of God but in the eyes of men.

With these two we are also sending our brother, of whose keenness we have ample proof and whose interest is especially aroused on this occasion as he has such confidence in you. As for Titus, he is my partner and colleague in your affairs, and both the brothers are official messengers of the churches, a credit to Christ. So do let them see how genuine is your love, and justify my pride in you, so that all the churches may see it.

CHAPTER 9

A word in confidence about this gift of yours

Of course I know it is really quite superfluous for me to be writing to you about this matter of giving to fellow Christians, for I know how willing you are. Indeed I have told the Macedonians with some pride that "Achaia was ready to undertake this service twelve months ago". Your enthusiasm has consequently stimulated most of them. I am, however, sending the brothers just to make sure that our pride in you is not unjustified and that you are ready, as I said you were. For it would never do if some of the Macedonians were to accompany me on my visit to you and find you unprepared! We (not to speak of you) should be acutely embarrassed, just because we had been so confident in you. This is my reason, then, for urging the brothers to visit you before I come myself, so that they can get your promised gift ready in good time. For I should like it to be a spontaneous gift, and not money squeezed out of you. All I will say is that poor sowing means a poor harvest, and generous sowing means a generous harvest.

Giving does not only help the one who receives

Let everyone give as his heart tells him, neither grudgingly nor under compulsion, for God loves the man who gives cheerfully. God can give you more than you can ever need, so that you may always have sufficient for yourselves and enough left over to give to every good cause. As the scripture says:

> He hath scattered abroad, he hath given to the poor;
> His righteousness abideth for ever.

He who gives the seed to the sower and bread to eat, will give you the seed of generosity to sow and will make it grow into a harvest of good deeds done. The more you are enriched the more scope will there be for generous giving, and your gifts, administered through us, will mean that many will thank God. For your giving does not end in meeting the wants of your fellow-Christians. It also results in an overflowing tide of thanksgiving to God. Moreover, your very giving proves the reality of your faith, and that means that men thank God that you practise the gospel of Christ that you profess to believe in, as well as for the actual gifts your fellowship makes to them and to others. And yet further, men will pray for you and feel drawn to you because you have obviously received a generous measure of the grace of God.

Thank God, then, for his indescribable generosity to you!

CHAPTER 10

We are not merely human agents but God-appointed ministers

Now I am going to appeal to you personally, by the gentleness and kindness of Christ himself. Yes, I, Paul, the one who is "humble enough in our presence but outspoken when away from us", am begging you to make it unnecessary for me to be outspoken and stern in your presence. For I am afraid otherwise that I think I shall have to do some plain speaking to those of you who will persist in reckoning that our activities are on the purely human level. The truth is that, although we lead normal human lives, the battle we are fighting is on the spiritual level. The very weapons we use are not human but powerful in God's warfare for the destruction of the enemy's strongholds. Our battle is to break down every deceptive argument and every imposing defence that men erect against the true knowledge of God. We fight to capture every thought until it acknowledges the authority of Christ. Once we are sure of your obedience we are ready to punish every disobedience.

I really am a Christian, you know!

Do look at things which stare you in the face! So-and-so considers himself to belong to Christ. All right; but let him think again about himself, for we belong to Christ every bit as much as he. You may think that I have boasted unduly of my authority (which the Lord gave me, remember, to build you up not to break you down), but I don't think I have done anything which will make me ashamed. Yet I don't want you to think of me merely as the man who writes you terrifying letters. I know my critics say, "His letters are impressive and moving, but his actual presence is feeble and his speaking beneath contempt." Let them realise that we can be just as "impressive and moving" in person as we are in our letters.

God's appointment means more than self-recommendation

Of course we shouldn't dare include ourselves in the same class as those who write their own testimonials, or even to compare ourselves with them! All they are doing, of course, is to measure themselves by their own standards or by comparisons within their own circle, and that doesn't make for accurate estimation, you may be sure. No, we shall not make any wild claims, but simply judge ourselves by that line of duty which God has marked out for us, and that line includes our work on your behalf. We do not exceed our duty when we embrace your interests, for it was our preaching of the gospel which brought us into contact with you. Our pride is not in matters beyond our proper sphere nor in the labours of other men. No, our hope is that your growing faith will mean the expansion of our proper sphere of action, so that before long we shall be preaching the gospel in districts beyond you, instead of being proud of work that has already been done in someone else's province.

But,

He that glorieth let him glory in the Lord.

It is not self-commendation that matters, it is winning the approval of God.

CHAPTER 11

Why do you so readily accept the false and reject the true?

I WISH you could put up with a little of my foolishness—please try! My jealousy over you is the right sort of jealousy, for in my eyes you are like a fresh unspoiled girl whom I am presenting as fiancée to your only husband, Christ himself. I am afraid that your minds may be seduced from a single-hearted devotion to him by the same subtle means that the serpent used towards Eve. For apparently you cheerfully accept a man who comes to you preaching a different Jesus from the one we told you about, and you readily receive a spirit and a gospel quite different from the ones you originally accepted. Yet I cannot believe I am in the least inferior to these extra-special messengers. Perhaps I am not a polished speaker, but I do know what I am talking about, and both what I am and what I say is well known to you. Perhaps I made a mistake in lowering myself (though I did it to raise you up) by preaching the gospel of God without a fee? As a matter of fact I was only able to do this by "robbing" other churches, for it was what they paid me that made it possible to minister to you. Even when I was with you and was hard up, I did not bother any of you. It was the brothers who came from Macedonia who brought me all that I needed. Yes, I kept myself from being a burden to you then, and so I intend to do in the future. By the truth of Christ within me, no one shall stop my being proud of this independence through all Achaia!

Does this mean that I do not love you? God knows it doesn't, but I am determined to go on doing as I am doing, so as to cut the ground from under the feet of those who would dearly love to be thought of as God's messengers on the same terms as I am. *God's* messengers? They are counterfeits of the real thing, dishonest practitioners masquerading as the messengers of Christ. Nor do their tactics surprise me when I consider how Satan himself masquerades as an angel of light. It is only to be expected that his agents shall have the appearance of ministers of righteousness —but they will get what they deserve in the end.

If you like self-commendations, listen to mine!

Once more, let me advise you not to look upon me as a fool. Yet if you do, then listen to what this "fool" has to make his little boast about.

I am not now speaking as the Lord commands me but as a fool in this business of boasting. Since all the others are so proud of themselves, let me do a little boasting as well. From your heights of wisdom I am sure you can smile tolerantly on a fool. Oh, you're tolerant all right! You don't mind, do you, if a man takes away your liberty, spends your money, takes advantage of you, puts on airs or even smacks your face? I am almost ashamed to say that I never did brave strong things like that to you. Yet in whatever particular they parade such confidence I (speaking as a fool, remember) can do the same.

Are they Hebrews? So am I.
Are they Israelites? So am I.
Are they descendants of Abraham? So am I.
Are they ministers of Christ? I have more claim to this title than they. This is a silly game but look at this list:
I have worked harder than any of them.
I have served more prison sentences!
I have been beaten times without number.
I have faced death again and again.

I have been beaten the regulation thirty-nine stripes by the Jews five times.

I have been beaten with rods three times.

I have been stoned once.

I have been shipwrecked three times.

I have been twenty-four hours in the open sea.

In my travels I have been in constant danger from rivers, from bandits, from my own countrymen, and from pagans. I have faced danger in city streets, danger in the desert, danger on the high seas, danger among false Christians. I have known drudgery, exhaustion, many sleepless nights, hunger and thirst, fasting, cold and exposure.

Apart from all external trials I have the daily burden of responsibility for all the churches. Do you think anyone is weak without my feeling his weakness? Does anyone have his faith upset without my burning with indignation?

Oh, if I am going to boast, let me boast of the things which have shown up my weakness! The God and Father of the Lord Jesus, he who is blessed for ever, knows that I speak the simple truth.

In Damascus, the town governor, acting by King Aretas' order, had his patrols out to arrest me. I escaped through a window and was let down the wall in a basket.

CHAPTER 12

I have real grounds for "boasting", but I will only hint at them

I DON'T think it's really a good thing for me to boast at all, but if I must I will go on to visions and revelations of the Lord himself. I know a man in Christ who, fourteen years ago, had the experience of being caught up into the third Heaven. I don't know whether it was an actual physical experience, only God knows that. All I know is that this man was caught up into paradise. (I repeat, I do not know whether this was a physical happening or not, God alone knows.) This man heard words that cannot, and indeed must not, be put into human speech. I am proud of an experience like that, but I have made up my mind not to boast of anything personal, except of my weaknesses. If I should want to boast I should certainly be no fool, for I should be speaking nothing but the truth. Yet I am not going to do so, for I don't want anyone to think more highly of me than is warranted by what he sees of me and hears from me. So tremendous, however, were the revelations that God gave me that, in order to prevent my becoming absurdly conceited, I was given a stabbing pain—one of Satan's angels— to plague me and effectually stop any conceit. Three times I begged the Lord for it to leave me, but his reply has been, "My grace is enough for you: for where there is weakness, my power is shown the more completely." Therefore, I have cheerfully made up my mind to be proud of my weaknesses, because they mean a deeper experience of the power of Christ. I can even enjoy weaknesses, insults, privations, persecutions and difficulties for Christ's sake. For my very weakness makes me strong in him.

This boasting is silly, but you made it necessary

I have made a fool of myself in this "boasting" business, but you forced me to do it. If only you had had a better opinion of me it would have been quite unnecessary. For I am not really in the least inferior, nobody as I am, to these extra-special messengers. You have had a demonstration of the power God gives to a genuine messenger by his sheer endurance as well as the miracles, signs and works of spiritual power that you saw with your own eyes. What makes you feel so inferior to other churches? Is it because I have not allowed you to support me financially? My humblest apologies for this great wrong!

What can be your grounds for suspicion of me?

Now I am all ready to visit you for the third time, and I am still not going to be a burden to you. It is you I want—not your money. Children don't have to put by their savings for their parents; parents do that for their children. Consequently I will most gladly spend and be spent for your good utterly. Does that mean that the more I love you the less you love me?

"All right then," I hear you say, "we agree that he himself had none of our money." But are you thinking that I nevertheless was rogue enough to catch you by some trick? Just think. Did I make any profit out of the messengers I sent you? I asked Titus to go, and sent the brother with him. You don't think Titus made anything out of you, do you? Yet didn't I act in the same spirit as he, and take the same line as he did?

Remember what I really am, and whose authority I have

Are you thinking all this time that I am trying to justify myself in your eyes? Actually I am speaking in Christ before God himself, and my only reason for so doing, my dear friends, is to help you in your spiritual life.

For I must confess that I am afraid that when I come I shall not perhaps find you as I should like to find you, and that you will not find me quite as you would like me to be. I am afraid of finding arguments, jealousy, ill-feeling, divided loyalties, slander, whispering, pride and disharmony. When I come again, will God make me feel ashamed of you as I stand among you? Shall I have to grieve over many who have sinned already and are not yet sorry for the impurity, the immorality and the lustfulness of which they are guilty?

CHAPTER 13

THIS will be my third visit to you. Remember the ancient Law: "In the mouth of two or three witnesses shall every word be established." My previous warning, given on my second visit, still stands and, though absent, I repeat it now as though I were present to those who had sinned before and to all the others, that my coming will not mean leniency. That will be the proof you seek that I speak by the power of Christ. The Christ you have to deal with is not a weak person outside you, but a tremendous power inside you. He was "weak" enough to be crucified, yes, but he lives now by the power of God. We are weak as he was weak, but we are strong enough to deal with you for we share his life by the power of God.

Why not test yourselves instead of me?

You should be looking at yourselves to make sure that you are really Christ's. It is yourselves that you should be testing. You ought to know by this time that Christ Jesus is in you, unless you are not real Christians at all. And when you have applied your test, I am confident that you will find that I myself am a genuine Christian. I pray God that you may make no mistake, not because I have any need of your approval, but because I earnestly want you to find the right answer, even if that should make me no real Christian. For we can make no progress against the truth; we can only work for it.

We are always quite happy to be weak if it means that you are strong. Our prayer for you is true Christian maturity. Hence the tone of this letter, so that when I do come I shall not be obliged to use with severity that power which the Lord has given me—though even that is not meant to break you down but to build you up.

Finally, Farewell

Finally, then, my brothers, cheer up! Aim at perfection and accept my encouragement, agree with one another and live at peace. So shall the God of love and peace be ever with you.

A handshake all round, please! All the Christians here send greeting.

The grace of the Lord Jesus Christ, the love of God, and the fellowship that is ours in the Holy Spirit be with you all!

The Letter to the Christians in Galatia

AUTHOR. *Paul probably writing from Corinth, or possibly from Macedonia just before Titus returned from Corinth.*

DATE. 56 *or* 57 *or earlier.*

DESTINATION. *The meaning of "Galatia", to which this letter is addressed, has aroused some controversy, for it could mean the ancient district known by that name or the Roman province also called "Galatia", which included several other districts.*

THEME. *The Galatians appear to have been seduced from their first faith by teachers who insisted that they must still keep the old Jewish Law, including the rite of circumcision. In so doing they impugned Paul's authority, which he feels called upon to justify in this letter. Paul warns the Galatians that although they are free, as Christians, from the Law, yet their lives must exhibit the fruits of the inner law of love implanted by God's Spirit.*

CHAPTER 1

I, PAUL, who am appointed and commissioned a messenger not by man but by Jesus Christ and God the Father (who raised him from the dead), I and all the brothers with me send greetings to the churches in Galatia. Grace and peace to you from God our Father and the Lord Jesus Christ, who according to the will of our God and Father gave himself for our sins and thereby rescued us from the present evil world-order. To him be glory for ever and ever. Amen.

The gospel is God's truth: men must not dare to pervert it

I am amazed that you have so quickly transferred your allegiance from him who called you by the grace of Christ to another "gospel"! Not that it is another gospel, but there are men who are upsetting your faith with a travesty of the gospel of Christ. Yet I say that if I, or an angel from Heaven, were to preach to you any other gospel than the one you have heard, may he be damned! You have heard me say it before and now I say it again —may anybody who preaches any other gospel than the one you have already heard be a damned soul! (Does that make you think now that I am seeking man's approval or God's? Am I trying to please men? If I were trying to win human approval I should never be Christ's servant.)

The gospel was given to me by Christ himself, and not by any human agency, as my story will show

I do assure you, my brothers, that the gospel I preached to you is no human invention. No man gave it to me, no man taught it to me; it came to me as a direct revelation from Jesus Christ. For you have heard of my past career in the Jewish religion, how I persecuted the Church of God with fanatical zeal and, in fact, did my best to destroy it. I was ahead of most of my contemporaries in the Jewish religion, and had a boundless enthusiasm for the old traditions. But when it pleased God (who had chosen me from the moment of my birth, and called me by his grace) to reveal his Son to me so that I might proclaim him to the non-Jewish world, I did not at once talk over the matter with any human being. I did not even go to Jerusalem to meet those who

were God's messengers before me—no, I went away to Arabia and later came back to Damascus. It was not until three years later that I went up to Jerusalem to see Cephas, and I stayed with him just over two weeks. I did not see any of the other messengers, except James, the Lord's brother.

All this that I am telling you is, I assure you before God, the plain truth. Later, I visited districts in Syria and Cilicia, but I was still unknown by sight to the churches of Judaea. All they knew of me, in fact, was the saying: "The man who used to persecute us is now preaching the faith he once tried to destroy." And they thanked God for what had happened to me.

CHAPTER 2

Years later I met church leaders in Jerusalem: no criticism of my gospel was made

FOURTEEN years later, I went up to Jerusalem again, this time with Barnabas, and we took Titus with us. My visit on this occasion was by divine command, and I gave a full exposition of the gospel which I preach among the gentiles. I did this in private conference with the Church leaders, to make sure that what I had done and proposed doing was sound. But no one insisted that my companion Titus, though he was a Greek, should be circumcised. In fact, the suggestion would never have arisen but for the presence of some pseudo-Christians, who wormed their way into our meeting to spy on the liberty we enjoy in Christ Jesus, and then attempted to tie us up with rules and regulations. We did not give in to those men for a moment, for the truth of the gospel for you and all gentiles was at stake. And as far as their reputed leaders were concerned (I neither know nor care what their exact position was: God is not impressed with a man's office), they had nothing to add to my gospel. In fact they recognised that the gospel for the uncircumcised was as much my commission as the gospel for the circumcised was Peter's. For the God who had done such great work in Peter's ministry for the Jews was plainly doing the same in my ministry for the gentiles. When, therefore, James, Cephas and John (who were the recognised "pillars" of the Church there) saw how God had given me his grace, they held out to Barnabas and me the right hand of fellowship, in full agreement that our mission was to the gentiles and theirs to the Jews. The only suggestion they made

was that we should not forget the poor—and with this I was, of course, only too ready to agree.

I had once to defend the truth of the gospel even against a church leader

Later, however, when Cephas came to Antioch I had to oppose him publicly, for he was then plainly in the wrong. It happened like this. Until the arrival of some of James' men, he, Cephas was in the habit of eating his meals with the gentiles. After they came, however, he withdrew and began to separate himself from them—out of sheer fear of the Jews. The other Jewish Christians carried out a similar piece of discrimination, and the force of their bad example was so great that even Barnabas was infected by it. But when I saw that this behaviour was a contradiction of the truth of the gospel, I said to Cephas so that everyone could hear, "If you, who are a Jew, do not live like a Jew but like a gentile, why do you try to make gentiles live like Jews?" And then I went on to explain that we, who are Jews by birth and not gentile sinners, know that a man is justified not by performing what the Law commands but only by faith in Jesus Christ. We ourselves have believed in Christ Jesus, so that we may be made right with God by faith in Christ and not by obeying the Law's commands. For we have recognised that no one can achieve justification by doing the "works of Law". Now if, as we seek justification in Christ, we find that we are ourselves as much sinners as the gentiles, does that mean that Christ is a producer of sin? Of course not! But if I attempt to build again the whole structure of justification by the Law which I have demolished then I do, in earnest, prove myself a sinner. For under the Law I "died", and I am dead to the Law's demands so that I may live for God. I died on the cross with Christ. And my present life is not that of the old "I", but the living Christ within me. The bodily life I now live, I live believing in the Son of God who loved me and sacrificed himself for me. I refuse to make nonsense of the grace of God! For if righteousness were possible under the Law then Christ died for nothing.

CHAPTER 3

What has happened to your life of faith?

O YOU dear idiots of Galatia, who saw Jesus Christ the crucified so plainly, who has been casting a spell over you? I will ask you one simple question: did you receive the Spirit by trying to keep the Law or by believing the message of the gospel? Surely you can't be so stupid as to think that you begin your spiritual life in the Spirit and then complete it by reverting to physical observances? Has all your painful experience brought you nowhere? I simply cannot believe it! Does God, who gives you his Spirit and works miracles among you, do these things because you have obeyed the Law or because you have believed the gospel?

The futility of trying to be justified by the Law: the promises to men of faith

You can go right back to Abraham to see the principle of faith in God. He, we are told, "believed God and it was counted unto him for righteousness." You may be certain, then, that all those who "believe God" are the real "sons of Abraham". The scripture, foreseeing that God would justify the gentiles "by faith", proclaimed the gospel in the words spoken to Abraham, "In thee shall all nations be blessed." All men of faith share the blessing of Abraham who "believed God".

Everyone, however, who is involved in trying to keep the Law's demands falls under a curse, for it is written:

> Cursed is everyone which continueth not
> In *all things* which are written in the book of the Law,
> To do them.

It is clear that no one is justified in God's sight by obeying the Law, for:

> The righteous shall live by *faith*.

And the Law is not a matter of faith at all but of doing, as, for example, in the scripture:

> He that *doeth* them shall live in them.

Now Christ has redeemed us from the curse of the Law by himself becoming a curse for us. For the scripture is plain:

> Cursed is every one that hangeth on a tree.

God's purpose is therefore plain: that the blessing given to Abraham might reach the gentiles through Christ Jesus, and the promise of the Spirit might become ours by faith.

The Law cannot interfere with the original promise

Let me give you an everyday illustration, my brothers. Once a contract has been properly drawn up and signed, it is honoured by both parties, and can neither be disregarded nor modified by a third party.

Now the promises were made to Abraham and his seed. (Note in passing that the scripture says not "seeds" but uses the singular "seed", meaning Christ.) I say then that the Law, which came into existence four hundred and thirty years later, cannot render null and void the original "contract" which God had made, and thus rob the promise of its value. For if the receiving of the inheritance were to depend on the Law, then it does not depend on promise. But God gave it to Abraham by promise.

Where then lies the point of the Law? It was an addition made to underline the existence and extent of sin but only until the arrival of the "seed" to whom the promise referred. The Law was appointed by means of angels, by the hand of an intermediary. The very fact that there was an intermediary is enough to show that this was not the fulfilling of the promise. For the promise of God needs neither angelic witness nor any intermediary but depends on him alone.

Is the Law then to be looked upon as a contradiction of the promises? Certainly not, for if there could have been a law which gave men spiritual life then that law would have produced righteousness. But, as things are, the scripture has all men "imprisoned" under the power of sin, so that to men in such condition the promise might be given to all who believe in Jesus Christ.

By faith we are rescued from the Law and become sons of God

Before the coming of this faith we were all imprisoned under the power of the Law, with our only hope of deliverance the faith that was to be shown to us. The Law was like a strict tutor in charge of us until we went to the school of Christ and learned to be justified by faith in him. Once we have that faith we are completely free from the tutor's authority. For now that you have faith in Christ Jesus you are all sons of God. All of you who were baptised "into" Christ have put on the family likeness of Christ. Gone is the distinction between Jew and Greek, slave and free man, male and female—you are all one in Christ Jesus. And if you belong to Christ, you are true descendants of Abraham, you are true heirs of his promise.

CHAPTER 4

WHAT I am saying is that so long as an heir is a child, though he is destined to be master of everything, he is, in practice, no different from a servant. He has to obey guardians or trustees until the time which his father has chosen for him to receive his inheritance. So is it with us: while we were "children" we lived under the authority of basic moral principles. But when the proper time came God sent his own Son, born of a human mother and born under the jurisdiction of the Law, that he might redeem those who were under the authority of the Law, so that we might become sons of God. It is because you really are his sons that God has sent the Spirit of his Son into our hearts to cry "Father, dear Father". You are not a servant any longer; through God you are a *son*; and, if you are a son, then you are certainly an heir.

Consider your own progress: do you want to go backwards?

At one time when you had no knowledge of God, you were under the authority of gods who had no real existence. But now that you have come to know God, or rather are known by him, how can you revert to the weakness and poverty of such principles and consent to be under their power all over again? Your religion is beginning to be a matter of observing special days and months and seasons and years. You make me wonder if all my efforts over you have been wasted!

I appeal to you by our past friendship, don't be misled

I do beg you to put yourselves in my place, my brothers, as I have put myself in yours. I have nothing against you personally.

You know that it was physical illness which was the cause of my first preaching the gospel to you. You didn't despise me or let yourself be revolted by my disease. No, you welcomed me as though I were an angel of God, or even as though I were Christ Jesus himself! What has happened to that fine spirit of yours? I guarantee that in those days you would, if you could, have plucked out your eyes and given them to me. Have I now become your enemy because I continue to tell you the truth? Oh, I know how keen these men are to win you over, but their motives are all wrong. They would like to see you and me separated altogether, and have you all to themselves. It is always a fine thing that men should take an interest in you, whether I'm there or not, provided their motives are good. Oh, my dear children, I feel the pangs of childbirth all over again till Christ be formed within you, and how I long to be with you now! Perhaps I could then alter my tone. As it is, I honestly don't know how to deal with you.

Let us see what the Law itself has to say

Now tell me, you who want to be under the Law, have you heard what the Law says?

It is written that Abraham had two sons, one by the slave and one by the free woman. The child of the slave was born in the ordinary course of nature, but the child of the free woman was born in accordance with God's promise. This can be regarded as an allegory. Here are the two agreements represented by the two women: the one from Mount Sinai bearing children into slavery, typified by Hagar (Mount Sinai being in Arabia, the land of the descendants of Ishmael, Hagar's son), and corresponding to present-day Jerusalem—for the Jews are still, spiritually speaking, "slaves". But the free woman typifies the heavenly Jerusalem, who is the mother of us all, and is spiritually "free". It is written:

Rejoice, thou barren that bearest not;
Break forth and cry, thou that travailest not:
For more are the children of the desolate
Than of her which hath the husband.

Now you, my brothers, are like Isaac, children born "by promise". But just as in those far-off days the natural son persecuted the "spiritual" son, so it is today. Yet what is the scriptural instruction?

Cast out the handmaid and her son:
For the son of the handmaid shall not inherit
With the son of the free woman.

So then, my brothers, we are not to look upon ourselves as the sons of the slave woman but of the free, not sons of slavery under the Law but sons of freedom under grace.

CHAPTER 5

Do not lose your freedom by giving in to those who urge circumcision

PLANT your feet firmly therefore within the freedom that Christ has won for us, and do not let yourselves be caught again in the shackles of slavery. Listen! I, Paul, say this to you: if you consent to be circumcised then Christ will be of no use to you at all. I say this solemnly again to every one of you: every man who consents to be circumcised is bound to obey all the rest of the Law! If you try to be justified by the Law you automatically cut yourself off from the power of Christ, you put yourself outside the range of his grace. For it is *by faith* that we await in his Spirit the righteousness we hope to see. In Christ Jesus there is no validity in either circumcision or uncircumcision; it is a matter of faith, faith which expresses itself in love.

You were making splendid progress; who stopped you from obeying the truth? That sort of persuasion does not come from the One who is calling you. Alas, it takes only a little leaven to affect the whole lump! I feel confident in the Lord that you will not take any fatal step. But whoever it is who is worrying you will have a serious charge to answer.

And as for me, my brothers, if I were still advocating circumcision, why am I still suffering persecution? I suppose if only I would recommend this little rite all the hostility which the preaching of the cross provokes would disappear! I wish those who are unsettling you would cut themselves off from you altogether!

It is to freedom that you have been called, my brothers. Only be careful that freedom does not become mere opportunity for your lower nature. You should be free to serve each other in love. For after all, the whole Law toward others is summed up by this one command, "Thou shalt love thy neighbour as thyself."

But if freedom means merely that you are free to attack and tear each other to pieces, be careful that it doesn't mean that between you you destroy your fellowship altogether!

The way to live in freedom is by the Spirit

Here is my advice. Live your whole life in the Spirit and you will not satisfy the desires of your lower nature. For the whole energy of the lower nature is set against the Spirit, while the whole power of the Spirit is contrary to the lower nature. Here is the conflict, and that is why you are not able to do what you want to do. But if you follow the leading of the Spirit, you stand clear of the Law.

The activities of the lower nature are obvious. Here is a list: sexual immorality, impurity of mind, sensuality, worship of false gods, witchcraft, hatred, strife, jealousy, bad temper, rivalry, factions, party-spirit, envy, drunkenness, orgies and things like that. I solemnly assure you, as I did before, that those who indulge in such things will never inherit God's kingdom. The Spirit, however, produces in human life fruits such as these: love, joy, peace, patience, kindness, generosity, fidelity, tolerance and self-control—and no law exists against any of them.

Those who belong to Christ Jesus have crucified their lower nature with all that it loved and lusted for. If our lives are centred in the Spirit, let us be guided by the Spirit. Let us not be ambitious for our own reputations, for that only means making each other jealous.

CHAPTER 6

Some practical wisdom

EVEN if a man should be detected in some sin, my brothers, the spiritual ones among you should quietly set him back on the right path, not with any feeling of superiority but being yourselves on guard against temptation. Carry each other's burdens and so live out the law of Christ.

If a man thinks he is "somebody" when he is nobody, he is deceiving himself. Let every man learn to assess properly the value of his own work and he can then be rightly proud when he has done something worth doing, without depending on the approval of others. For every man must "shoulder his own pack".

The man under Christian instruction should be willing to share the good things of life with his teacher.

The inevitability of life's harvest

Don't be under any illusion: you cannot make a fool of God! A man's harvest in life will depend entirely on what he sows. If he sows for his own lower nature his harvest will be the decay and death of his own nature. But if he sows for the Spirit he will reap the harvest of everlasting life from that Spirit. Let us not grow tired of doing good, for, unless we throw in our hand, the ultimate harvest is assured. Let us then do good to all men as opportunity offers, especially to those who belong to the Christian household.

A final appeal, in my own hand-writing

Look at these huge letters I am making in writing these words to you with my own hand!*

These men who are always urging you to be circumcised—what are they after? They want to present a pleasing front to the world and they want to avoid being persecuted for the cross of Christ. For even those who have been circumcised do not themselves keep the Law. But they want you circumcised so that they may be able to boast about your submission to their ruling. Yet God forbid that I should boast about anything or anybody except the cross of our Lord Jesus Christ, which means that the world is a dead thing to me and I am a dead man to the world. But in Christ it is not circumcision or uncircumcision that counts but the power of new birth. To all who live by this principle, to the true Israel of God, may there be peace and mercy!

Let no one interfere with me after this. I carry on my scarred body the marks of Jesus.

The grace of our Lord Jesus Christ, my brothers, be with your spirit. Amen.

* According to centuries-old Eastern usage, this could easily mean, "Note how heavily I have pressed upon the pen in writing this." Thus it could be translated, "Notice how heavily I have underlined these words to you."

The Letter to the Christians at Ephesus

(and in other places)

AUTHOR. *This letter was almost certainly written by Paul, although some argue from the style that it was drafted by another hand, possibly Timothy's, and then corrected and signed by Paul. It is widely accepted that the letter was issued by him, during the same period as the letters to Colossae and Philippi and the personal note to Philemon, while he was in prison. Almost certainly his imprisonment while he despatched these letters was at Rome* (*Acts* 28, *30*).

DATE. *About* 62.

DESTINATION. *Probably not only Ephesus, for although Paul had spent two years there* (*Acts* 19, *9, 10*), *there are no personal references. For this and other good reasons it is generally believed that this is a circular letter meant to reach the churches in Asia. Tychicus, who took the letter in person, would probably reach Ephesus first. The letter would then be copied and taken on to the other churches. It is quite possible that the letter to Laodicaea, mentioned in Colossians* 4, *16, was this particular letter.*

THEME. *Paul is concerned first to establish in his readers' minds as great and wide and deep a conception of Christ as he can. He points out that he is not only the Saviour of the world, but also the divinely appointed focal point of all activity and all knowledge, whether it is physical, mental or spiritual. Race distinctions cannot matter therefore for those who are "in Christ".*

He follows this by stressing the resultant responsibility of the Christian, and his own proper authority as the messenger commissioned to deliver such news.

Then, as usual, Paul points out the practical outcome of being "members of Christ's body", "new men", "children of God", etc., and begs his readers to see that their lives are lived on a level worthy of the staggering privileges that God has given them.

CHAPTER 1

PAUL, messenger of Christ Jesus by God's will, to all faithful Christians at Ephesus: grace and peace be to you from God our Father and the Lord Jesus Christ.

Praise God for what he has done for us Christians!

Praised be the God and Father of our Lord Jesus Christ for giving us through Christ every spiritual benefit as citizens of Heaven! For consider what he has done—before the foundation of the world he chose us to be, in Christ, his children, holy and blameless in his sight. He planned, in his love, that we should be adopted as his own children through Jesus Christ—this was his will and pleasure that we might praise that glorious generosity of his which he granted to us in his Beloved. It is through him, at the cost of his own blood, that we are redeemed, freely forgiven through that free and generous grace which has overflowed into our lives and given us wisdom and insight. For God has allowed us to know the secret of his plan, and it is this: he purposed long ago in his sovereign will that all human history should be consummated in Christ, that everything that exists in Heaven or earth should find its perfection and fulfilment in him. In Christ we have been given an inheritance, since we were destined for this, by the One who works out all his purposes according to the design of his own will. So that we, in due time, as the first to put our hope in Christ, may bring praise to his glory! And you too trusted him, when you had heard the message of truth, the gospel of your salvation. And after you gave your confidence to him you were, so to speak, stamped with the promised Holy Spirit as a pledge of our inheritance, until the day when God completes the redemption of what is his own; and that will again be to the praise of his glory.

I thank God for you, and pray for you

This is why since I heard of this faith of yours in the Lord Jesus and the love which you bear towards fellow-Christians, I thank God continually for you and I never give up praying for you; and this is my prayer. That the God of our Lord Jesus Christ, the all-glorious Father, will give you spiritual wisdom and the insight to know more of him: that you may receive that inner illumination of the spirit which will make you realise how great is the hope to which he is calling you—the magnificence and splendour of the inheritance promised to Christians—and how tremendous is the power available to us who believe in God. That power is the same divine energy which was demonstrated in Christ when he raised him from the dead and gave him the place of highest honour in Heaven—a place that is infinitely superior to any command, authority, power or control, and which carries with it a name far beyond any name that could ever be used in this world or the world to come.

God has placed everything under the power of Christ and has set him up as supreme head to the Church. For the Church is his body, and in that body lives fully the One who fills the whole wide universe.

CHAPTER 2

We were all dead: God gave us life through Christ

You were spiritually dead through your sins and failures, all the time that you followed this world's ideas of living, and obeyed the evil ruler of the spiritual realm—who is indeed fully operative today in those who disobey God. We all lived like that in the past, and followed the desires and imaginings of our lower nature, being in fact under the wrath of God by nature, like everyone else. But even though we were dead in our sins God, who is rich in mercy, because of the great love he had for us, gave us life together with Christ—it is, remember, by grace that you are saved—and has lifted us to take our place with him in Christ Jesus in the Heavens. Thus he shows for all the ages to come the tremendous generosity of the grace and kindness he has expressed towards us in Christ Jesus. For it is by grace that you are saved, through faith. This does not depend on anything you have achieved, it is the free gift of God; and because it is not earned no man can boast about it. For God has made us what we are, created in Christ Jesus to do those good deeds which he planned for us to do.

You were gentiles: we were Jews. God has made us fellow-Christians

Do not lose sight of the fact that you were born "gentiles", known by those whose bodies were circumcised by the hand of man as "the uncircumcised". You were then without Christ, you were utter strangers to God's chosen community, Israel, and you had no knowledge of, or right to, the promised agreements. You had nothing to look forward to and no God to whom you could turn. But now, in Christ Jesus, you who were once far off are brought near through the shedding of Christ's blood. For Christ is our living peace. He has made us both one by breaking down the barrier and enmity which lay between us. By his sacrifice he removed the hostility of the Law, with all its commandments and rules, and made in himself out of the two, Jew and gentile, one new man, thus producing peace. For he reconciled both to God by the sacrifice of one body on the cross, and by his act killed the enmity between them. Then he came and brought the good news of peace to you who were far from God and to us who were near. And it is through him that both of us now can approach the Father in the one Spirit.

So you are no longer outsiders or aliens, but fellow-citizens with every other Christian—you belong now to the household of God. Firmly beneath you is the foundation, God's messengers and prophets, the corner-stone being Christ Jesus himself. In him each separate piece of building, properly fitting into its neighbour, grows together into a temple consecrated to the Lord. You are all part of this building in which God himself lives by his Spirit.

CHAPTER 3

God has made me minister to you gentiles

It is in this great cause that I, Paul, have become a prisoner of Christ Jesus for you gentiles. For you must have heard how God gave me grace to become your minister, and how he allowed me to understand his secret by giving me a direct revelation. What I have written briefly of this above will explain to you my knowledge of the mystery of Christ. This secret was hidden to past generations of mankind, but it has now, by the Spirit, been made plain to God's consecrated messengers and prophets. It is simply this: that the gentiles are to be equal heirs with his chosen people, equal members and equal partners in God's promise given by Christ Jesus through the gospel. And I was made a minister of that gospel by the grace he freely gave me, and by the action within me of his own power. Yes, to me, less than the least of all Christians, has God given this grace, to enable me to proclaim to the gentiles the gospel of the incalculable riches of Christ, and to make plain to all men the meaning of that divine secret which he who created everything has kept hidden from the creation until now. The purpose is that all the angelic powers should now see the complex wisdom of God's plan being worked out through the Church, in conformity to that timeless purpose which he centred in Christ Jesus, our Lord. It is in this same Jesus, because we have faith in him, that we dare, even with confidence, to approach God. So then I beg you not to lose heart because I am now suffering on your behalf. Indeed, you should be honoured.

I pray that you may know God's power in practice

As I think of this great plan I fall on my knees before the Father (from whom all fatherhood, earthly or heavenly, derives its name), and I pray that out of the glorious richness of his resources he will enable you to know the strength of the Spirit's inner re-inforcement—that Christ may actually live in your hearts by your faith. And I pray that you, rooted and founded in love yourselves, may be able to grasp (with all Christians) how wide and long and deep and high is the love of Christ—and to know for yourselves that love so far above our understanding. So will you be filled through all your being with God himself!

Now to him who by his power within us is able to do infinitely more than we ever dare to ask or imagine—to him be glory in the Church and in Christ Jesus for ever and ever, amen!

CHAPTER 4

Christians should be at one, as God is one

As the Lord's prisoner, then, I beg you to live lives worthy of your high calling. Accept life with humility and patience, generously making allowances for each other because you love each other. Make it your aim to be at one in the Spirit, and you will be bound together in peace. There is one Body and one Spirit, just as it was to one hope that you were called. There is one Lord, one faith, one baptism, one God and Father of all, who is the one over all, the one working through all and the one living in all.

God's gifts vary, but it is the same God who gives

To each one of us is given his measure of grace from the richness of Christ's gift. Thus the scripture says:

When he ascended on high, he led captivity captive,
And gave gifts unto men.

Note the implication here—to say that Christ "ascended" means that he must previously have "descended", that is to the depth of this world. The one who made this descent is the same person as he who has now ascended high above the very Heavens —that he might fill the whole universe.

His "gifts unto men" were varied. Some he made his messengers, some prophets, some preachers of the gospel; to some he gave the power to guide and teach his people. His gifts were made that Christians might be properly equipped for their service, that the whole body might be built up until the time comes when, in the unity of common faith and common knowledge of the Son of God, we arrive at real maturity—that measure of development which is meant by "the fulness of Christ".

True maturity means growing up "into" Christ

We are not meant to remain as children at the mercy of every chance wind of teaching, and of the jockeying of men who are expert in the crafty presentation of lies. But we are meant to speak the truth in love, and to grow up in every way into Christ, the head. For it is from the head that the whole body, as a harmonious structure knit together by the joints with which it is provided, grows by the proper functioning of individual parts, and so builds itself up in love.

Have no more to do with the old life! Learn the new

This is my instruction, then, which I give you in the Lord's name. Do not live any longer the futile lives of gentiles. For they live in a world of shadows, and are cut off from the life of God through their deliberate ignorance of mind and sheer hardness of heart. They have lost all decent feelings and abandoned themselves to sensuality, practising any form of impurity which lust can suggest. But you have learned nothing like that from Christ, if you have really heard his voice and understood the truth that Jesus has taught you. No, what you learned was to fling off the dirty clothes of the old way of living, which were rotted through and through with lust's illusions, and, with yourselves mentally and spiritually re-made, to put on the clean fresh clothes of the new life which was made by God's design for righteousness and the holiness which is no illusion.

Finish, then, with lying and let each man tell his neighbour the truth, for we are all parts of the same body. If you are angry, be sure that it is not a sinful anger. Never go to bed angry—don't give the devil that sort of foothold.

The new life means positive good

The man who used to be a thief must give up stealing, and do an honest day's work with his own hands, so that he may be able to give to those in need.

Let there be no more foul language, but good words instead—words suitable for the occasion, which God can use to help other people. Never wound the Holy Spirit. He is, remember, the seal upon you of your eventual full redemption.

Let there be no more bitter resentment or anger, no more shouting or slander, and let there be no bad feeling of any kind among you. Be kind to each other, be compassionate. Be as ready to forgive others as God for Christ's sake has forgiven you.

CHAPTER 5

So then you should try to become like God, for you are his children and he loves you. Live your lives in love—the same sort of love which Christ gave us and which he perfectly expressed when he gave himself up for us as an offering and a sacrifice well-pleasing to God. But as for sexual immorality in all its forms, and the itch to get your hands on what belongs to other people—don't even talk about such things; they are no fit subjects for Christians to talk about. The key-note of your conversation should not be coarseness or silliness or flippancy—which are quite out of place, but a sense of all that we owe to God.

Evil is as utterly different from good as light from darkness

For of this you can be quite certain: that neither the immoral nor the dirty-minded nor the covetous man (whose greed makes him worship gain) has any inheritance in the kingdom of Christ and of God. Don't let anyone fool you with empty words. It is these very things which bring down the wrath of God upon the disobedient. Have nothing to do with men like that—once you were "darkness" but now as Christians you are "light". Live then as children of the light. The light produces in men all that is good and right and true. Let your lives be living proofs of the things which please God. Steer clear of the fruitless activities of darkness; let your lives expose their futility. (You know the sort of things I mean—to detail their secret doings is too shameful to mention.) For light is capable of showing up everything for what it really is. It is even possible for light to turn the thing it shines upon into light also. Thus it is said:

Awake thou that sleepest, and arise from the dead,
And Christ shall shine upon thee.

You know the truth—let your life show it!

Live life, then, with a due sense of responsibility, not as men who do not know the meaning of life but as *those who do*. Make the best use of your time, despite all the evils of these days. Don't be vague but grasp firmly what you know to be the will of the Lord. Don't get your stimulus from wine (for there is always the danger of excessive drinking), but let the Spirit stimulate your souls. Sing among yourselves psalms and hymns and spiritual songs, your voices making music in your hearts for the ears of the Lord! Thank God the Father at all times for everything, in the name of our Lord Jesus Christ. And "fit in with" each other, because of your common reverence for Christ.

Christ and the Church the pattern relationship for husband and wife

You wives must learn to adapt yourselves to your husbands, as you submit yourselves to the Lord, for the husband is the "head" of the wife in the same way that Christ is head of the

Church and saviour of the Body. The willing subjection of the Church to Christ should be reproduced in the submission of wives to their husbands in everything. The husband must give his wife the same sort of love that Christ gave to the Church, when he sacrificed himself for her. Christ gave himself to make her holy, having cleansed her through the baptism of his Word—to make her an altogether glorious Church in his eyes. She is to be free from spots, wrinkles or any other disfigurement—a Church holy and perfect.

So men ought to give their wives the love they naturally have for their own bodies. The love a man gives his wife is the extending of his love for himself to enfold her. Nobody ever hated his own body; he feeds it and looks after it. And that is what Christ does for his Body, the Church. And we are all members of that Body.

For this cause shall a man leave his father and mother,
And shall cleave to his wife; and the twain shall become one flesh.

The marriage relationship is a great mystery, but I see it as a symbol of the marriage of Christ and his Church.

In practice what I have said amounts to this: let every one of you who is a husband love his wife as he loves himself, and let every wife respect her husband.

CHAPTER 6

Children and parents: servants and masters

CHILDREN, the right thing for you to do is to obey your parents as those whom the Lord has set over you. The first commandment to contain a promise was:

Honour thy father and thy mother
That it may be well with thee, and that thou mayest live long on the earth.

Fathers, don't over-correct your children or make it difficult for them to obey the commandment. Bring them up with Christian teaching in Christian discipline.

Slaves, obey your human masters loyally with a proper sense of respect and responsibility, as service rendered to Christ; not only working when you are being watched, as if looking for human approval, but as servants of Christ conscientiously doing what you believe to be the will of God. Work cheerfully as if it were for the Lord and not for a man. You may be sure that the Lord will reward each man for good work irrespectively of whether he be slave or free. And as for you employers, act towards those who serve you in the same way. Do not threaten them, but remember that both you and they have the same Lord in Heaven, who makes no distinction between master and man.

Be forewarned and forearmed in your spiritual conflict

In conclusion be strong—not in yourselves but in the Lord, in the power of his boundless strength. Put on God's complete armour so that you can successfully resist all the devil's craftiness. For our fight is not against any physical enemy: it is against organisations and powers that are spiritual. We are up against the unseen power that controls this dark world, and spiritual agents from the very headquarters of evil. Therefore you must wear the whole armour of God that you may be able to resist evil in its day of power, and that even when you have fought to a standstill you may still stand your ground. Take your stand then with truth as your belt, integrity your breastplate, the gospel of peace firmly on your feet, salvation as your helmet and in your hand the sword of the Spirit, the Word of God. Above all be sure you take faith as your shield, for it can quench every burning missile the enemy hurls at you. In all your petitions pray at all times with every kind of spiritual prayer, keeping alert and persistent as you pray for all Christ's men and women. And pray for me, too, that I may be able to speak the message here boldly, to make known the secret of that gospel for which I am an ambassador in chains. Pray that I may speak out about it as is my plain and obvious duty.

Tychicus, beloved brother and faithful Christian minister, will tell you personally about my affairs and how I am getting on. I am sending him to you bringing this letter for that purpose, so that you will know exactly how we are and may take fresh heart.

Peace be to all Christian brothers, and love with faith from God the Father and the Lord Jesus Christ!

Grace be with all those who love our Lord Jesus Christ with unfailing love.

The Letter to the Christians at Philippi

AUTHOR. *Paul, writing from prison, probably in Rome (Acts 28, 30).*
DATE. *About* 62.
DESTINATION. *The church at Philippi, where Paul had been beaten and imprisoned but had seen his gaoler converted (Acts* 16, *25–34). It was also at Philippi that Lydia, a business woman selling purple-dyed cloth, became one of the first Christians.*
THEME. *The first purpose of the letter is to acknowledge a gift sent to Paul in prison by Epaphroditus from the Christians at Philippi. Possibly this letter was delayed by the serious illness of Epaphroditus while with Paul* (2, *27) and Paul is evidently by now himself expecting early release from prison* (2, *24). Except possibly for the letter to Philemon, this is the most personal example of Paul's correspondence, and he is obviously very fond of the young church at Philippi. It expresses his high hopes for their unity, faithfulness and progress in the faith. It also contains a warning, like that in the letter to the Galatians, against false teachers who wanted to bring these inexperienced Christians under the Jewish Law.*

CHAPTER 1

PAUL and Timothy, servants of Jesus Christ, to all true Christians at Philippi and to their bishops and deacons, grace and peace from God our Father and Jesus Christ the Lord!

I have the most pleasant memories of you all

I thank my God for you whenever I think of you. My constant prayers for you are a real joy, because we have worked together for the gospel from the first day until the present. I am confident of this: that the One who has begun his good work in you will go on developing it until the day of Jesus Christ.

It is only natural that I should feel like this about you all—you are very dear to me. For during the time I was in prison as well as when I was defending and proving the authority of the gospel we shared together the grace of God. God knows how much I long, with the deep love and affection of Christ Jesus, for your companionship. My prayer for you is that you may have still more love—a love that is full of knowledge and every wise insight. I want you to be able always to recognise the highest and the best, and to live sincere and blameless lives until the day of Christ. I want to see your lives full of true goodness, produced by the power that Jesus Christ gives you to the glory and praise of God.

My imprisonment has turned out to be no bad thing

Now I want you to know, my brothers, that what has happened to me has, in effect, turned out to the advantage of the gospel. For, first of all, my imprisonment means a personal witness for Christ before the palace guards, not to mention others who come and go. Then, it means that most of our brothers, taking fresh heart in the Lord from the very fact that I am a prisoner for Christ's sake, have shown far more courage in boldly proclaiming the Word of God. I know that some are preaching Christ out of jealousy, in order to annoy me, but some are preaching him in good faith. These latter are preaching out of their love for me. For they know that I am here to defend the gospel. The motive of the former is questionable—they preach in a partisan spirit, hoping to make my chains even more galling than they are. But what does it matter? However they may look at it, the fact remains that Christ *is* being preached, whether sincerely or not, and that fact makes me very happy. Yes, and I shall go on being happy, for I know that what is happening will result in my release, thanks to your prayers and the resources of the Spirit of Jesus Christ. It all accords with my own earnest wishes and hopes, which are that I should never be in any way ashamed, but that now, as always, I should honour Christ with the utmost boldness by the way I live, whether that means I am to face death or to go on living. For living to me means simply "Christ", and if I die I should merely gain more of him. For me to go on living in this world may serve some good purpose. I should find it very hard to make a choice. I am torn in two directions—on the one hand I long to leave this world and live with Christ, and that is obviously the best thing for me. Yet, on the other hand, it is probably more necessary for you that I should stay here on earth. Because I am sure of this, I know that I shall remain and continue to stand by you all, to help you forward in Christian living and to find increasing joy in your faith. So that you may feel great pride in me as your minister in Christ when I come and see you again!

But whatever happens, make sure that your everyday life is worthy of the gospel of Christ. So that whether I do come and see you, or merely hear about you from a distance, I may know that you are standing fast in a united spirit, battling with a single mind for the faith of the gospel and not caring two straws for your enemies. The fact that they are your enemies is plain proof that they are lost to God, while the fact that you have such men as enemies is plain proof that you yourselves are being saved by God. You are given the privilege not merely of believing in Christ but also of suffering for his sake. Now you are taking part in that battle you once saw me fight, and which, as you hear, I am still fighting.

CHAPTER 2

Above all things be loving, humble, united

Now if you have known anything of Christ's encouragement and of his reassuring love; if you have known something of the fellowship of his Spirit, and of compassion and deep sympathy, do make my joy complete—live together in harmony, live together in love, as though you had only one mind and one spirit between you. Never act from motives of rivalry or personal vanity, but in humility think more of each other than you do of yourselves. None of you should think only of his own affairs, but consider other people's interests also.

Let Christ be your example of humility

Let your attitude to life be that of Christ Jesus himself. For he, who had always been God by nature, did not cling to his privileges as God's equal, but stripped himself of every advantage by consenting to be a slave by nature and being born a man. And, plainly seen as a human being, he humbled himself by living a life of utter obedience, to the point of death, and the death he died was the death of a common criminal. That is why God has now lifted him to the heights, and has given him the name beyond all names, so that at the name of Jesus "every knee shall bow", whether in Heaven or earth or under the earth. And that is why "every tongue shall confess" that Jesus Christ is Lord, to the glory of God the Father.

God is himself at work within you

So then, my dear friends, as you have always obeyed me—and that not only when I was with you—now, even more in my absence, complete the salvation that God has given you with a proper sense of awe and responsibility. For it is God who is at work within you, giving you the will and the power to achieve his purpose.

Do all you have to do without grumbling or arguing, so that you may be blameless and harmless, faultless children of God, living in a warped and diseased age, and shining like lights in a dark world. For you hold up in your hands the very word of life. Thus can you give me something to be proud of in the day of Christ, for I shall know then that I did not spend my energy in vain. Yes, and if it should happen that my life-blood is, so to speak, poured out upon the sacrifice and offering which your faith means to God, then I can still be very happy, and I can share my happiness with you all. You should be glad about this too, and share this happiness with me.

I am sending Epaphroditus with this letter, and Timothy later

But I hope in the Lord Jesus that it will not be long before I send Timothy to you, and then I shall be cheered by news of you and your doings. I have nobody else here who shares my genuine concern for you. They are all wrapped up in their own affairs and do not really care for the cause of Jesus Christ. But you know Timothy's worth, how he has worked with me for the gospel like a son with his father. This is the man I hope to send to you as soon as I can tell how things will work out for me, but God gives me hope that it will not be long before I am able to come myself. I have considered it desirable, however, to send you Epaphroditus. He has been to me brother, fellow-worker and comrade-in-arms, as well as being the messenger you sent to see to my wants. He has been home-sick for you all, and was worried because he knew that you had heard that he was ill. Indeed he was ill, dangerously ill, but God had mercy on him—and incidentally on me as well, so that I did not have the sorrow of losing him to add to my sufferings. I am particularly anxious, therefore, to send him to you so that when you see him again you may be glad, and this will lighten my own sorrows. Welcome him in the Lord with great joy! You should hold men like him in highest honour, for his loyalty to Christ brought him very near death—he risked his life to do for me in person what distance prevented you from doing.

CHAPTER 3

FINALLY, my brothers, delight yourselves in the Lord! It doesn't bore me to repeat a piece of advice like this, and you will find it a safeguard to your souls.

The "circumcision" party are the enemies of your faith and freedom

Be on your guard against these curs, these wicked workmen, these would-be mutilators of your bodies! We are truly circumcised when we worship God by the Spirit; we pride ourselves in Jesus Christ and put no confidence in the flesh.

I was even more of a Jew than these Jews, yet knowing Christ has changed my whole life

If it were right to have such confidence, I could certainly have it, and if any of these men thinks he has grounds for such confidence I can assure him I have more. I was born from the people of Israel, I was circumcised on the eighth day, I was a member of the tribe of Benjamin. I was in fact a full-blooded Jew. As far as keeping the Law is concerned I was a Pharisee, and you can judge my enthusiasm for the Jewish faith by my active persecution of the Church. As far as the Law's righteousness is concerned, I don't think anyone could have found fault with me. Yet every advantage that I had gained I considered lost for Christ's sake. Yes, and I look upon everything as loss compared with the overwhelming gain of knowing Christ Jesus my Lord. For his sake I did in fact suffer the loss of everything, but I considered it mere garbage compared with being able to win Christ. For now my place is in him, and I am not dependent upon any of the self-achieved righteousness of the Law; God has given me that genuine righteousness which comes from faith in Christ. Now I long to know Christ and the power shown by his resurrection; now I long

to share his sufferings, even to die as he died, so that I may somehow attain the resurrection from the dead. Not that I claim to have achieved all this, nor to have reached perfection already. But I keep going on, trying to grasp that purpose for which Christ Jesus grasped me. My brothers, I do not consider myself to have grasped it fully even now. But I do concentrate on this: I forget all that lies behind me and with hands outstretched to whatever lies ahead I go straight for the goal—my reward the honour of my high calling by God in Christ Jesus.

My ambition is the true goal of the spiritually adult: make it yours too

All of us who are spiritually adult should think like this, and if at present you think otherwise, yet you will find that God will make even this clear to you. It is important that we go forward in the light of such truth as we have already learned.

My brothers I should like you all to imitate me and observe those whose lives are based on the pattern that we give you. For there are many, of whom I have told you before and tell you again now, even with tears, whose lives make them the enemies of the cross of Christ. These men are heading for utter destruction—their god is their own appetite, they glory in their shame, and this world is the limit of their horizon. But we are citizens of Heaven; we eagerly wait for the saviour who will come from Heaven, the Lord Jesus Christ. He will change these wretched bodies of ours so that they resemble his own glorious body, by that power of his which makes him in command of everything.

CHAPTER 4

So, my brothers whom I love and long for, my joy and my crown, do stand firmly in the Lord, and remember how much I love you.

Be united, be joyful, be at peace

Euodia and Syntyche, I beg you by name to make up your differences as Christians should! And you, my true fellow-worker, I ask you to help these women. They both worked hard with me for the gospel, as did Clement and all my other fellow-workers whose names are in the book of life.

Delight yourselves in the Lord, yes, find your joy in him at all times. Have a reputation for being reasonable, and never forget the nearness of your Lord.

Don't worry over anything whatever; whenever you pray tell God every detail of your needs in thankful prayer, and the peace of God, which surpasses human understanding, will keep constant guard over your hearts and minds as they rest in Christ Jesus.

My brothers I need only add this. If you believe in goodness and if you value the approval of God, fix your minds on whatever is true and honourable and just and pure and lovely and admirable. Put into practice what you have learned from me and what I passed on to you, both what you heard from me and what you saw in me, and the God of peace will be with you.

The memory of your generosity is an abiding joy to me

It is a great and truly Christian joy to me that after all this time you have shown such renewed interest in my welfare. I don't mean that you had forgotten me, but up till now you had no opportunity of expressing your concern. Nor do I mean that I have been in actual need, for I have learned to be content, whatever the circumstances may be. I know now how to live when things are difficult and I know how to live when things are prosperous. In general and in particular I have learned the secret of eating well or going hungry—of facing either plenty or poverty. I am ready for anything through the strength of the One who lives within me. Nevertheless I am very grateful for the way in which you were willing to share my troubles. You Philippians will

remember that in the early days of the gospel when I left Macedonia, you were the only church who shared with me the fellowship of giving and receiving. Even in Thessalonica you sent me help when I was in need, not once but twice. It isn't the value of the gift that I am keen on, it is the reward that will be credited to you.

Now I have everything I want—in fact I am rich. Yes, I am quite content, thanks to your gifts received through Epaphroditus. Such generosity is like a lovely fragrance, a sacrifice that pleases the very heart of God. My God will supply all that you need from his glorious resources in Christ Jesus. And may glory be to our God and our Father for ever and ever, amen!

Farewell messages

Give my greetings in Christian fellowship to every one of God's people. The brothers here with me also send greetings. All the Christians here would like to send their best wishes, particularly those who belong to the emperor's household.

The grace of the Lord Jesus Christ be with your spirit.

The Letter to the Christians at Colossae

AUTHOR. *Paul, writing probably at the same time as he wrote the letters to Ephesus, Philippi and Philemon while a prisoner in Rome.*

DATE. *About* 62.

DESTINATION. *The church at Colossae, a town in Asia Minor about a hundred miles inland from Ephesus. Paul had never himself been there, and it appears that the church was founded by Epaphras. The latter was apparently imprisoned in Rome after his arrival from Colossae, and this letter was sent back by the hand of Tychicus.*

THEME. *This letter is plainly written to refute the false teaching which was poisoning the church life at Colossae. This false teaching was propagating two errors: first, that the universe contained a number of beings of various degrees of power and importance ranging from man to God, and that Christ was to be thought of as merely one of the superior powers. Paul combats this by his unequivocal declaration that Christ is God's "Son", the first principle and the upholding principle of the whole creation. The second false tendency was the attempt to force on the Colossian Christians a system of purely arbitrary observances and angel-worship, coupled with an extreme asceticism. Paul meets this by pointing out that the Christian's position in God is far beyond the petty observances of man-made rules. The true asceticism, moreover, is to abstain from evil passions and evil thoughts, not to cut oneself off from the normal use of God's good gifts.*

Although writing to those he had never seen, Paul writes with obvious love and interest and is sincerely pleased with the genuine Christianity which has taken root at Colossae.

CHAPTER 1

PAUL, a messenger of Christ Jesus by God's will, and our brother Timothy send this greeting to all faithful Christian brothers at Colossae: grace and peace be to you from God our Father!

We thank God for you and pray constantly for you

We here are constantly praying for you, and whenever we do we thank God the Father of our Lord Jesus Christ for you because we have heard that you believe in Christ Jesus and because you are showing true Christian love towards other Christians. We know that you are showing these qualities because you have grasped the hope reserved for you in Heaven—that hope which first became yours when you heard the message of truth. This is the gospel itself, which has reached you as it spreads all over the world. Wherever that gospel goes, it produces Christian character, and develops it, as it has done in your own case from the time you first heard and realised the truth of God's grace.

You learned these things, we understand, from Epaphras, who is in the same service as we are. He is a faithful and well-loved minister of Christ, and has your well-being at heart. It was from him that we heard about your growth in Christian love, so you will understand that since we heard about you we have never missed you in our prayers. We are asking God that you may be filled with such wisdom and that you may understand his purpose. We also pray that your outward lives, which men see, may bring credit to your master's name, and that you may bring joy to his heart by bearing genuine Christian fruit in all that you do, and that your knowledge of God may grow yet deeper.

We pray for you to have real Christian experience

We pray that you will be strengthened from God's glorious power, so that you may be able to pass through any experience and endure it with joy. You will be able to thank the Father because you are privileged to share the lot of the saints who are living in the light. For he rescued us from the power of darkness, and re-established us in the kingdom of his beloved Son. For it is by him that we have been redeemed and have had our sins forgiven.

Who Christ is, and what he has done

Now Christ is the visible expression of the invisible God. He was born before creation began, for it was through him that everything was made, whether heavenly or earthly, seen or unseen. Through him, and for him, also, were created power and dominion, ownership and authority. In fact, all things were created through, and for, him. He is both the first principle and the upholding principle of the whole scheme of creation. And now he is the head of the Body which is the Church. He is the Beginning, the first to be born from the dead, which gives him pre-eminence over all things. It was in him that the full nature of God chose to live, and through him God planned to reconcile to his own person everything on earth and everything in Heaven, making peace by virtue of Christ's death on the cross.

And you yourselves, who were strangers to God, and, in fact, through the evil things you had done, his spiritual enemies, he has now reconciled through the death of Christ's body on the cross, so that he might welcome you to his presence clean and pure, without blame or reproach. This reconciliation assumes that you maintain a firm position in the faith, and do not allow yourselves to be shifted away from the hope of the gospel, which you have heard, and which, indeed, has been proclaimed to the whole created world under heaven. I, Paul, have become a minister of this same gospel.

My divine commission

It is true at this moment that I am suffering on behalf of you who have heard the gospel, yet I am glad, because it gives me a chance to contribute my own sufferings something to the uncompleted pains which Christ suffers on behalf of his Body, the Church. For I am a minister of the Church by divine commission, a commission granted to me for your benefit, and for a special purpose: that I might fully declare God's Word—that sacred mystery which up till now has been hidden in every age and every generation, but which is now as clear as daylight to those who love God. They are those to whom God has planned to give a vision of the wonder and splendour of his secret plan for the nations. And the secret is simply this: Christ *in you*! Yes, Christ *in you* bringing with him the hope of all the glorious things to come.

To preach and teach Christ is everything to us

So, naturally, we proclaim Christ! We warn everyone we meet, and we teach everyone we can, all that we know about him, so that we may bring every man up to his full maturity in Christ. This is what I am working and struggling at, with all the strength that God puts into me.

CHAPTER 2

I WISH you could understand how deep is my anxiety for you, and for those at Laodicea, and for all who have never met me personally. How I long that they may be encouraged, and find out more and more how strong are the bonds of Christian love. How I long for them to experience the wealth of conviction which is brought by understanding—that they may come to know more fully God's great secret, Christ himself! For it is *in him*, and in him alone, that all the treasures of wisdom and knowledge lie hidden.

Let me warn you against "intellectuals"

I write like this to prevent you from being led astray by someone or other's attractive arguments. For though I am a long way away from you in body, in spirit I am by your side, rejoicing as I see the solid steadfastness of your faith in Christ. Just as you received Christ Jesus the Lord, so go on living in him—in simple faith. Yes, be rooted in him and founded upon him, continually strengthened by the faith as you were taught it and your lives will overflow with joy and thankfulness.

Be careful that nobody spoils your faith through intellectualism or high-sounding nonsense. Such stuff is at best founded on men's ideas of the nature of the world and disregards Christ! Yet it is in him that God gives a full and complete expression of himself in bodily form. Moreover, your own completeness is realised in him, who is the ruler over all authorities, and the supreme head over all powers.

The old Law can't condemn you now

In Christ, you were circumcised, not by any physical act, but by being set free from the sins of the flesh by virtue of Christ's circumcision. You shared in that, just as in baptism you shared in his death, and in him shared the rising again to life—and all this because you have faith in the tremendous power of God, who raised Christ from the dead. You, who were spiritually dead because of your sins and your uncircumcision, God has now made to share in the very life of Christ! He has forgiven you all your sins: he has utterly wiped out the written evidence of broken commandments which always hung over our heads, and has completely annulled it by nailing it to the cross. And then, having drawn the sting of all the powers and authorities ranged against us, he exposed them, shattered, empty and defeated, in his own triumphant victory!

It is the spiritual, not the material, attitude which matters

In view of these tremendous facts, don't let anyone worry you by criticising what you eat or drink, or what holy days you ought to observe, or bothering you over new moons or sabbaths. All these things are no more than foreshadowings: the reality belongs to Christ. Let no man cheat you out of your joy by wanting you to join him in his false humility and worship of angels. Such a man, presuming on the little he has seen, by using an unspiritual imagination, entirely forgets the head. It is from the head alone that the body, through its joints and ligaments, is nourished and built up and grows as God meant it to grow.

So if, through your faith in Christ, you are dead to the principles of this world's life, why, as if you were still part and parcel of this world-wide system, do you take the slightest notice of these purely human prohibitions—"Don't touch this," "Don't taste that" and "Don't handle the other"? "This", "that" and "the other" will all pass away after use! I know that these regulations look wise with their self-inspired efforts at piety, their policy of self-humbling, and their studied neglect of the body. But in actual practice they are of no moral value, but simply pamper the flesh.

CHAPTER 3

Live a new life by the power of the risen Christ

IF you are then raised up with Christ, reach out for the highest gifts of Heaven, where Christ reigns in power. Be concerned with the heavenly things, not with the passing things of earth. For, as far as this world is concerned, you are already dead, and your true life is a hidden one in God, through Christ. One day, Christ, who is your life, will show himself openly, and you will all share in that magnificent revelation.

Consider yourselves dead to worldly contacts: have nothing to do with sexual immorality, dirty-mindedness, uncontrolled passion, evil desire, and the lust for other people's goods, which amounts to idolatry. It is because of these very things that the holy anger of God falls upon those who refuse to obey him. And never forget that you had your part in those dreadful things when you lived that old life.

But now you must put away all these things: evil temper, furious rage, malice, insults and shouted abuse! Don't deceive each other with lies any more, for you have discarded the old nature and all that it did, and you have put on the new nature which, by constant renewal in the likeness of its Creator, leads to a fuller knowledge of God. In this new man there is no distinction between Greek and Jew, circumcised or uncircumcised, foreigner or savage, slave or free man. Christ is all that matters for Christ lives in all.

The expression of the new life (i)

As, therefore, God's picked representatives, purified and beloved, put on that nature which is merciful in action, kindly in heart, and humble in mind. Accept life, and be most patient and tolerant with one another, always ready to forgive if you have a difference with anyone. Forgive as freely as the Lord has forgiven you. And, above everything else, be truly loving, for love binds all the virtues together in perfection.

Let the peace of Christ guide all your decisions, for you were called to live as one united body; and always be thankful. Let the full richness of Christ's teaching find its home among you. Teach and advise one another wisely. Use psalms and hymns and Christian songs, singing God's praises from joyful hearts. And whatever work you have to do, either in speech or action, do everything in the name of the Lord Jesus, thanking God the Father through him.

The expression of the new life (ii)

Wives, adapt yourselves to your husbands; that is your Christian duty. Husbands, give your wives much love; never treat them harshly. As for you children, obey your parents in everything, for this is the right and Christian thing to do. Fathers, don't over-correct your children, or you will take all the heart out of them. Slaves, your job is to obey your human masters, not with the idea of catching their eye or currying favour, but as a sincere expression of your devotion to the Lord. Whatever your task is, put your whole heart and soul into it, as into work done for the Lord and not merely for men—knowing that your real reward will come from him. You are actually slaves of the Lord Christ Jesus.

But the dishonest man will be paid back for his dishonesty, and no favouritism will be shown.

CHAPTER 4

REMEMBER, then, you employers, to be just and fair to those whom you employ, never forgetting that you yourselves have a heavenly Employer.

Some simple, practical advice

Always maintain the habit of prayer: be both alert and thankful as you pray. Include us in your prayers, please, that God may open for us a door for the entrance of the gospel. Pray that we may speak of the mystery of Christ (for which speaking I am at present in chains), and that I may make that mystery plain to men, which I know is my duty.

Be wise in your behaviour towards non-Christians, and make the best possible use of your time. Speak pleasantly to them, but never sentimentally, and learn how to give the proper answer to every questioner.

Greetings and farewell

Tychicus (a well-loved brother, a faithful minister and a fellow-servant of the Lord) will tell you all about my present circumstances. I am sending him to you so that you may find out how we are all getting on, and that he may put new heart into you. With him is Onesimus, one of your own congregation (well-loved and faithful, too). Between them they will tell you of all that goes on here.

Aristarchus, who is also in prison here, sends greetings, and so does Barnabas' cousin, Mark. I gave you instructions before about him; if he comes to you, make him welcome. Jesus Justus is here too. Only these few fellow-Jews are working with me for the kingdom, but what a help they have been!

Epaphras, another member of your Church, and a real servant of Christ Jesus, sends his greeting. He works hard for you even here, for he prays constantly and earnestly for you, that you may become mature Christians, and may fulfil God's will for you. From my own observation I can tell you that he has a real passion for your welfare, and for that of the churches at Laodicea and Hierapolis.

Luke, our beloved doctor, and Demas send their best wishes. My own greetings to the Christians in Laodicea, and to Nympha and the congregation who meet in her house.

When you have had this letter read in your church, see that the Laodiceans have it read in their church too; and see that you in turn read the letter to Laodicea.

A brief message to Archippus: remember the Lord ordained you to your ministry—see that you carry it out!

My personal greeting to you written by myself, Paul.

Don't forget I'm in prison. Grace be with you.

The First Letter to the Christians in Thessalonica

AUTHOR. *Paul, writing from Corinth.*
DATE. *About* 50. *Possibly the earliest Pauline letter in our possession.*
DESTINATION. *The Christian church in Thessalonica (now Salonika) which was founded by Paul (Acts* 17, *1–10). There were evidently many Jews in the town, many of whom were bitterly opposed to the Christian message.*
THEME. *This letter is an encouragement to the young church to stand firm under persecution. It contains a defence of Paul's own position as divinely appointed messenger, in view of the bitter and malicious attacks that were being made upon him. Then follows a plea for sexual purity on the grounds that the sex instinct is part of God's design and is not meant to be despised or exploited.*

The closing section gives some definite teaching about the second coming of Christ, which the Thessalonian Christians were expecting at any moment.

CHAPTER 1

To the church of the Thessalonians, founded on God the Father and the Lord Jesus Christ, grace and peace from Paul, Silvanus and Timothy.

Your faith cheers us and encourages many others

We are always thankful to God as we pray for you all, for we never forget that your faith has meant solid achievement, your love has meant hard work, and the hope that you have in our Lord Jesus Christ means sheer dogged endurance in the life that you live before God, the Father of us all.

We know, brothers, that God not only loves you but has selected you for a special purpose. For we remember how our gospel came to you not as mere words, but as a message with power behind it—the convincing power of the Holy Spirit. You know what sort of men we were when we lived among you. You set yourselves to copy us, and indeed, the Lord himself. You remember how, although accepting the message meant serious trouble, yet you experienced the joy of the Holy Spirit. You thus became an example to all who believe in Macedonia and Achaia. You have become a sort of sounding-board from which the Word of the Lord has rung out, not only in Macedonia and Achaia but everywhere where the story of your faith in God has become known. We find we don't have to tell people about it. They tell *us* the story of our coming to you: how you turned from idols to serve the true living God, and how your whole lives now look forward to the coming of his Son from Heaven—the Son Jesus, whom God raised from the dead, and who delivered us from the judgment which hung over our heads.

CHAPTER 2

The spirit of our visit to you is well known to you all

My brothers, you know from your own experience that our visit to you was no failure. We had, as you also know, suffered and been treated with insults at Philippi, and we came on to you only because God gave us courage. Whatever the strain we came to tell you the gospel of God.

Our message to you is true, our motives are pure, our conduct is absolutely above board. We speak under the solemn sense of being entrusted by God with the gospel. We do not aim to please men, but to please God who knows us through and through. No one could say, as again you know, that we used flattery to conceal greed, and God himself is our witness. We made no attempt to win honour from men, either from you or from anybody else, though I suppose as Christ's own messengers we might have used the weight of our authority. Our attitude among you was one of tenderness, rather like a nurse caring for her babies. Because we loved you, it was a joy to us to give you not only the gospel of God but our very hearts—so dear had you become to us. Our struggles and hard work, my brothers, must be still fresh in your minds. Day and night we worked so that our preaching of the gospel to you might not be a burden to any of you. You are witnesses, as is God himself, that our life among you believers was devoted, straightforward and above criticism. You will remember how we dealt with each one of you personally, like a father with his own children, comforting and encouraging. We told you from our own experience how to live lives worthy of the God who is calling you to share the splendour of his own kingdom.

And so we are continually thankful to God that when you heard the Word of God from us you accepted it, not as a mere human message, but as it really is, God's Word, a power in the lives of you who believe.

You have experienced persecution like your Jewish brothers

For you, my brothers, followed the example of the churches of God which have come into being through Christ Jesus in Judaea. For when you suffered at the hands of your fellow-countrymen you were sharing the experience of the Judaean Christian churches, who suffered persecution by the Jews. It was the Jews who killed their own prophets, the Jews who killed the Lord Jesus, and the Jews who drove us out. They do not please God, and are in opposition to all mankind. They refused to let us speak to the gentiles to tell them the message by which they could be saved. All these years they have been adding to the full record of their sins and finally the wrath of God has fallen upon them.

Absence has indeed made our hearts grow fonder

Since we have been physically separated from you, my brothers (though never for a moment separated in heart), we have longed all the more to see you face to face. Yes, I, Paul, have longed to come and see you more than once—but somehow Satan prevented our coming.

For who could take your place as our hope and joy and pride when our Lord Jesus comes? Who but you, as you will stand before him at his coming? Yes, you are indeed our pride and our joy!

CHAPTER 3

AND so, when the separation became intolerable, we thought the best plan was for us to stay at Athens alone, while we sent Timothy, our brother and God's fellow-worker in the gospel of Christ, to strengthen and encourage you in your faith. We did not want any of you to lose heart at the troubles you were going through, but to realise that we must expect such things. Actually we did warn you what to expect, when we were with you, and our words have come true, as you know. You will understand that, when the suspense became unbearable, I sent to find out how your faith was standing the strain, and to make sure that the tempter's activities had not destroyed our work.

The good news about you is a tonic to us

Timothy has just come straight from you to us, with a glowing account of your faith and love, and definite news that you cherish happy memories of us and long to see us as much as we to see you. This has cheered us, my brothers, in all the miseries and troubles we ourselves are going through. To know that you are standing fast in the Lord is indeed a breath of life to us. How can we thank our God enough for you, and for all the joy you have brought in the presence of our God, as we pray earnestly day and night to see you face to face again, and to complete whatever is imperfect in your faith?

This is our prayer for you

So may God our Father himself and our Lord Jesus guide our steps to you. May the Lord give you the same increasing and overflowing love for each other and towards all men as we have towards you. May he establish you, holy and blameless in heart and soul, before God, the Father of us all, when our Lord Jesus comes with all who belong to him.

CHAPTER 4

Purity, love and hard work are good rules for life

To sum up, my brothers, we beg and pray you by the Lord Jesus, that as you have learned from us the way of life that pleases God, you may continue in it, as indeed you are doing, and deepen your experience of it. You will remember the instructions we gave you then in the name of the Lord Jesus. God's plan is to make you holy, and that means a clean cut with sexual immorality. Every one of you should learn to control his body, keeping it pure and treating it with respect, and never allowing it to fall victim to lust, as do pagans with no knowledge of God. You cannot break this rule without cheating and exploiting your fellow-men. Indeed God will punish all who do offend in this matter, as we have plainly told you and warned you. The calling of God is not to impurity but to the most thorough purity, and anyone who makes light of the matter is not making light of a man's ruling but of God's command. It is not for nothing that the Spirit God gives us is called the *Holy* Spirit.

Next, as regards brotherly love, you don't need any written instructions. God himself is teaching you to love each other, and you are already extending your love to all the Macedonians. Yet we urge you to have more and more of this love, and to make it your ambition to have, in a sense, no ambition! Be busy with your own affairs and do your work yourselves, as we instructed you. Then the world outside will respect your life, and you will never be in want.

God's message regarding those who have died

Now we don't want you, my brothers, to be in any doubt about those who "fall asleep" in death, or to grieve over them like the rest of men who have no hope. If we believe that Jesus died and rose again, then we can believe that God will just as surely bring with Jesus all who are "asleep" in him. Here we have a definite message from the Lord. It is that those who are still living when he comes will not in any way precede those who have previously fallen asleep. One word of command, one shout from the archangel, one blast from the trumpet of God and the Lord himself will come down from Heaven! Those who have died in Christ will be the first to rise, and then we who are still living will be swept up with them into the clouds to meet the Lord in the air. And after that we shall be with him for ever. So by all means use this message to encourage one another.

CHAPTER 5

We must keep awake for his sudden coming

BUT as far as times and seasons go, my brothers, you don't need written instructions. You are well aware that the day of the Lord will come unexpectedly, like a thief in the night. When men are saying "Peace and security", catastrophe will sweep down upon them as suddenly and inescapably as birth-pangs to a pregnant woman.

But because you, my brothers, are not living in darkness the day cannot take you by surprise, like a burglar! You are all sons of light, sons of the day, and none of us belongs to darkness or the night. Let us then never fall asleep, like the rest of the world: let us keep awake, with our wits about us. Night is the time for sleep and the time when men get drunk, but we men of the daylight should be sober, with faith and love as our breastplate and the hope of our salvation as our helmet. For God did not choose us to condemn us, but that we might secure his salvation through Jesus Christ our Lord. He died for us, so that whether we are "awake" or "asleep" we share our life with him. So go on cheering and strengthening each other, as I have no doubt you are doing.

Reverence your ministers: regulate the conduct of church members

We ask you too, my brothers, to recognise those who work so hard among you. They are your leaders in the Lord, to give you good advice. Because of this task of theirs, hold them in respect and affection.

Live together in peace, brothers, and we appeal to you to warn the unruly, encourage the timid, help the weak and be very patient with all men. Be sure that no one repays a bad turn with a bad turn; good should be your objective always, among yourselves and in the world at large.

Be happy in your faith at all times. Never stop praying. Be thankful, whatever the circumstances may be.

For this is the will of God for you in Christ Jesus.

Final advice and farewell

Never damp the fire of the Spirit, and never despise what is spoken in the name of the Lord. By all means use your judgment, and hold on to whatever is good. Steer clear of evil in any form.

May the God of peace make you holy through and through. May you be kept sound in spirit, mind and body, blameless until the coming of our Lord Jesus Christ. He who calls you is utterly faithful and he will finish what he has set out to do.

Pray for us, my brothers. Give a handshake all round among the brotherhood. The Lord's command, which I give you now, is that this letter should be read to all the brothers.

The grace of our Lord Jesus Christ be with you.

The Second Letter to the Christians in Thessalonica

AUTHOR. *Paul, writing from Corinth.*
DATE. *Possibly* 51.
DESTINATION. *The Christian church in Thessalonica.*
THEME. *Since the first letter was written to this church, Paul had evidently heard that the idea of Christ's second coming had become such an obsession with the Thessalonians that some of them had given up working for their living and were thereby bringing the faith into disrepute. He tells them quite plainly that the coming is not to be immediate; and in the meantime it is part of a Christian's duty to work hard and conscientiously.*

CHAPTER 1

To the church of the Thessalonians, founded on God our Father and Jesus Christ the Lord, from Paul, Silvanus and Timothy; grace to you and peace from God the Father and the Lord Jesus Christ.

Your sufferings are a guarantee of great joy one day

My brothers, nowadays I always thank God for you not only in common fairness but as a moral obligation! Your faith has made such strides, and your love, each for all and all for each, has reached such proportions that we actually boast about you in the churches of God, because you have shown such endurance and faith in all the persecutions and troubles which you are now enduring.

See how justly the judgment of God works out! He intends to use your suffering to prove you worthy of his kingdom. For God's justice will repay trouble to those who have troubled you, and give relief to all of us who, like you, have suffered. This judgment will issue in the final appearance of the Lord Jesus from

Heaven with the angels of his power. He will bring full justice in dazzling flame upon those who have refused to recognise God or to obey the gospel of our Lord Jesus. Their punishment will be eternal loss—exclusion from the radiance of the face of the Lord, and the glorious majesty of his power. But to those whom he has made holy his coming will mean splendour unimaginable. It will be a breath-taking wonder to all who believe—including you, for you have believed the message that we have given you.

In view of this we pray for you constantly, that God will count you worthy of his calling, and by his power may fulfil all your good intentions and every effort of faith. We pray that the name of our Lord Jesus may become more glorious through you, and that you may thus share something of his glory—all through the grace of our God and the Lord Jesus Christ.

CHAPTER 2

Before Christ's coming there will be certain signs

Now we implore you, brothers, by the certainty of the coming of our Lord Jesus Christ and of our meeting him together, to keep your heads and not be thrown off your balance by any prediction or message or letter purporting to come from us, and saying that the day of the Lord has already come. Don't let anyone deceive you by any means whatever. That day will not come before there first arises a definite rejection of God and the appearance of the lawless man. He is the product of all that leads to death, and he sets himself up in opposition to every religion. He even takes his seat in the Sanctuary of God, to show that he really claims to be God.

You must surely remember how I talked about this when I was with you. You now know about the "restraining power" which prevents him from being revealed until the proper time. Evil is already insidiously at work but its activities are secret until what I have called the "restraining power" is removed. When that happens the lawless man will be plainly seen—though the words from the mouth of the Lord Jesus spell his doom, and the radiance of his coming will be his utter destruction. The lawless man is produced by the power of Satan and armed with all the force, wonders and signs that falsehood can devise. To those doomed to perish he will come with evil's undiluted power to deceive, for they have refused to love the truth which could have saved them. God sends upon them, therefore, the full force of evil's delusion, so that they put their faith in an utter fraud and meet the inevitable judgment of all who have refused to believe the truth and who have made evil their pleasure.

You, thank God, belong to those who believe the truth

But we must thank God continually for you, brothers, whom the Lord loves. He has chosen you as the first to be saved, to make you holy by the work of his Spirit and your own belief in the truth. It was for this that he called you when we preached the gospel to you, and he wanted you to possess the glory of our Lord Jesus Christ. So stand firm, and hold fast to the teachings we passed on to you, whether by word of mouth or by letter.

May our Lord Jesus Christ himself and God our Father (who has loved us and given us unending encouragement and unfailing hope by his grace) inspire you with courage and confidence in every good thing you say or do.

CHAPTER 3

We ask your prayers for God's work here

FINALLY, my brothers, do pray for us, that the Lord's message may go forward unhindered and may bring him glory, as it has with you. Pray, too, that we may be rescued from bigoted and wicked men; for all men, alas, have not faith. Yet the Lord is utterly to be depended upon and he will give you stability and protection against the evil one. It is he who makes us feel confident about you, that you are acting and will act in accordance with our commands. May the Lord guide your hearts into deeper understanding of God's love and of the patient suffering of Christ.

Remember our example: everyone should do his fair share of work

One order, brothers, we must give you in the name of our Lord Jesus Christ: don't associate with the brother whose life is undisciplined, and not in accordance with the tradition which you received from us. You know well that we ourselves are your examples here, and that our lives among you were never undisciplined. We did not eat anyone's food without paying for it. In fact we toiled and laboured night and day to avoid being the slightest expense to any of you. This was not because we had no right to ask our necessities of you, but because we wanted to set you an example to imitate. When we were actually with you we gave you this principle to work on: "If a man will not work, he shall not eat." Now we hear that you have some among you living quite undisciplined lives, never doing a stroke of work, and busy only in other people's affairs. Our order to such men, indeed our appeal by the Lord Jesus Christ, is to settle down to work and eat the food they have earned themselves.

And the rest of you, my brothers—don't get tired of honest work! If anyone refuses to obey the command given in this letter, mark that man, do not associate with him until he is ashamed of himself. I don't mean, of course, treat him as an enemy, but reprimand him as a brother.

My blessing on you all!

Now may the Lord of peace personally give you peace at all times and in all ways. The Lord be with you all.

This is the greeting of PAUL, written by my own hand—my "mark" on all my letters. This is how I write.

The grace of our Lord Jesus Christ be with you all.

The First Letter to Timothy

AUTHOR. *Probably Paul, writing from Rome during a second term of imprisonment which ended in his martyrdom. Many scholars do not accept the Pauline authorship of the two letters to Timothy or the letter to Titus.*

DATE. *About* 66, *but some hold that it was written by someone other than Paul between the years of* 90 *and* 115.

DESTINATION. *This is a personal letter to Timothy, son of a Greek father and a Jewish mother. He was converted during Paul's visit, to Lystra (Acts* 16, *1). He became Paul's special protégé, and, though evidently diffident and nervous in temperament, was his loyal assistant. He accompanied Paul on various missions and has now been left in charge of the church at Ephesus.*

THE FIRST LETTER TO TIMOTHY 1

THEME. *Paul reminds Timothy of his responsibility as a minister ordained for the preaching of the Gospel and warns him of the dangers of false teaching. He then gives him some interesting details for the ordering of the life of the church, the choosing of church officers and the administration of charitable funds. The letter closes with an earnest plea to Timothy to remain loyal to the true Gospel.*

CHAPTER 1

PAUL, Jesus Christ's messenger by command of God our saviour and Christ Jesus our hope, to Timothy my true son in the faith: grace, mercy and peace be to you from God the Father and Christ Jesus our Lord.

A reminder

I am repeating in this letter the advice I gave you just before I went to Macedonia and urged you to stay at Ephesus. I wanted you to do this so that you could order certain persons to stop inventing new doctrines and to leave hoary old myths and interminable genealogies alone. Such things lead men to speculation rather than to the ordered living which results from faith in God. The ultimate aim of the Christian ministry, after all, is to produce the love which springs from a pure heart, a good conscience and a genuine faith. Some seem to have forgotten this and to have lost themselves in endless words. They want a reputation as teachers of the Law, yet they fail to realise the meaning of their own words still less of the subject they are so dogmatic about. We know, of course, that the Law is good in itself and has a legitimate function. Yet we also know that the Law is not really meant for the good man, but for the man who has neither principles nor self-control; for the man who is really wicked, who has neither scruples nor reverence. Yes, the Law is directed against the sort of people who attack their own parents, who kill their fellows, who are sexually uncontrolled or perverted, or who traffic in the bodies of others. It is against liars and perjurers—in fact it is against any and every action which contradicts the wholesome teaching of the glorious gospel which the blessed God has given and entrusted to me.

My debt to Jesus Christ

I am deeply grateful to Christ Jesus our Lord (to whom I owe all that I have accomplished) for trusting me enough to appoint me his minister, despite the fact that I had previously blasphemed his name, persecuted and insulted him. I believe he was merciful to me because what I did was done in the ignorance of a man without faith. Our Lord poured out his grace upon me, giving me faith in, and love for, Christ Jesus himself. This statement is completely reliable and should be universally accepted:—"Christ Jesus entered the world to rescue sinners". I realise that I was the worst of them all, and that because of this very fact God was particularly merciful to me. It was a demonstration of the extent of Christ's patience towards the worst of men, to serve as an example to all who in the future should trust him for eternal life.

So to the king of all the ages, the immortal, invisible, and only God, be honour and glory for ever and ever, amen!

My personal charge to you

Timothy my son, I give you the following charge. It is in full accord with those prophecies made about you, which sent you out to battle for the right armed only with your faith and a clear conscience. Some have laid these simple weapons contemptuously aside and, as far as their faith is concerned, have run their ships on the rocks. Hymenaeus and Alexander are men of this sort, and as a matter of fact I had to hand them over to Satan to teach them not to blaspheme.

CHAPTER 2

HERE then is my charge:

First, supplications, prayers, intercessions and thanksgivings should be made on behalf of all men: for kings and rulers in positions of responsibility, so that our common life may be lived in peace and quiet, with a proper sense of God and of our responsibility to him for what we do with our lives. In the sight of God our saviour this is undoubtedly the right way to pray; for his purpose is that all men should be saved and come to know the truth. For there is only one God, and only one intermediary between God and men, the Man Christ Jesus. He gave himself as a ransom for all men—an act of redemption which stands at all times as a witness to what he is. I was appointed proclaimer and messenger of this to teach (I speak the sober truth; I do not lie) the gentile world to believe and know the truth.

My views on men and women in the Church

Therefore, I want the men to pray in all the churches with sincerity, without resentment or doubt in their minds. Similarly, the women should be dressed neatly, their adornment being modesty and serious-mindedness. It is not for them to have an elaborate hair-style, jewellery of gold or pearls, or expensive clothes, but, as becomes women who profess to believe in God, it is for them to show their faith by the way they live. A woman should learn quietly and humbly. Personally, I don't allow women to teach, nor do I ever put them in authority over men—I believe they should be quiet. (My reasons are that man was created before woman. Further, it was Eve and not Adam who was first deceived and fell into sin. Nevertheless I believe that women will come safely through child-birth if they maintain a life of faith, love, holiness and modesty.)

CHAPTER 3

The sort of men to bear office: bishops

It is quite true to say that a man who sets his heart on leadership has laudable ambition. Well, for the office of a bishop a man must be of blameless reputation, he must be married to one wife only, and be a man of self-control and discretion. He must be a man of disciplined life; he must be hospitable and have the gift of teaching. He must be neither intemperate nor violent, but gentle. He must not be a controversialist nor must he be greedy for money. He must have proper authority in his own household, and be able to control and command the respect of his children. (For if a man cannot rule in his own house how can he look after a church of God?) He must not be a beginner in the faith, for fear of his becoming conceited and sharing the devil's downfall. He should, in addition to the above qualifications, have a good reputation with the outside world, in case his good name is attacked and he is caught by the devil that way.

Deacons

Deacons, similarly, should be men of serious outlook and sincere conviction. They too should be temperate and not sordidly greedy for profit. They should hold the mystery of the faith with complete sincerity.

Let them serve a period of probation first, and only serve as deacons if they prove satisfactory. Their wives should share their serious outlook, and must be women of discretion and self-control —women who can be thoroughly trusted. Deacons should be men with only one wife, able to control their children and manage their own households properly. Those who do well as deacons earn for themselves a proper standing, as well as the ability to speak freely on matters of the Christian faith.

The tremendous responsibility of being God's minister

At the moment of writing I hope to be with you soon, but if there should be any delay then what I have written will show you the sort of character men of God's household ought to have. It is, remember, the Church of the living God, the pillar and the foundation of the truth. No one would deny that this religion of ours is a tremendous mystery, resting as it does on the one who appeared in human flesh, was vindicated in the spirit, seen by angels; proclaimed among the nations, believed in throughout the world, taken back to Heaven in glory.

CHAPTER 4

Beware of false teachers: warn your people

God's Spirit specifically tells us that in later days there will be men who abandon the true faith and allow themselves to be spiritually seduced by teachings of demons, teachings given by men who are lying hypocrites, whose consciences are as dead as seared flesh. These men forbid marriage and command abstinence from foods—good things which God created to be thankfully enjoyed by those who believe in him and know the truth. Everything God made is good, and is meant to be gratefully used, not despised. The holiness or otherwise of a certain food, for instance, depends not on its nature but on whether it is eaten thankfully or not. It is consecrated by the word of God and by prayer.

You will be a faithful minister of Christ Jesus if you remind your church members of these things. You will show yourself as a man nourished by the message of the true faith and by the sound teaching he has followed. But steer clear of all these heathen old-wives' tales.

Take time and trouble to keep yourself spiritually fit. Bodily fitness has a limited value, but spiritual fitness is of unlimited value, for it holds promise both for this present life and for the life to come. There is no doubt about this at all; it is a truth that you can accept completely. It is because we realise the paramount importance of the spiritual that we labour and struggle. We place all our hopes upon the living God, the Saviour of all men, and especially of those who believe in him. These convictions should be the basis of your instruction and teaching.

A little personal advice

Don't let anyone look down on you because you are young: see that they look up to you because you are an example to believers in your speech and behaviour, in your love and faith and sincerity. Concentrate until my arrival on your reading and on your preaching and teaching. Do not neglect the special gift that was given to you through prophecy at the time when the assembled elders laid their hands on you. Give your whole attention, all your energies, to these things, so that your progress is plain for all to see. Keep a critical eye both upon your own life and on the teaching you give, and if you continue to follow the line I have indicated you will not only save your own soul but the souls of your hearers as well.

CHAPTER 5

DON'T reprimand a senior member of your church, appeal to him as a father. Treat the young men as brothers, and the older women as mothers. Treat the younger women as sisters, and no more.

How to deal with widows in the church

You should treat with great consideration widows who are really alone in the world. But remember that if a widow has children or grandchildren it is primarily their duty to show the genuineness of their religion in their own homes by repaying their parents for what has been done for them, and God readily accepts such service.

But the widow who is really alone and desolate can only hope in God, and she will pray earnestly to him night and day. The widow who plunges into all the pleasure that the world can give her is killing her own soul.

You should therefore make the following rules for the widows, to avoid abuses:

1. You should make it clear that for a man to refuse to look after his own relations, especially those actually living in his house, is a denial of the faith he professes. He is worse than a man who makes no profession.

2. Widows for your church list should be at least sixty years of age, should have had only one husband and have a well-founded reputation for having lived a good life. Some such questions as these should be asked:—has she brought up her children well, has she been hospitable to strangers, has she been willing to serve fellow-Christians in menial ways, has she relieved those in distress, has she, in a word, conscientiously done all the good she can?

3. Don't put the younger widows on your list. My experience is that when their natural desires grow stronger than their spiritual devotion to Christ they want to marry again, thus proving themselves unfaithful to their first loyalty. Moreover, they get into habits of slackness by being so much in and out of other people's houses. In fact they easily become worse than lazy, and degenerate into gossips and busybodies with dangerous tongues.

4. My advice is that the younger widows should, normally, marry again, bear children and run their own households. They should certainly not provide the means for lowering the reputation of the church in the sight of our enemies. Some have already played into their hands.

5. As a general rule it should be taken for granted that any Christians who have widows in the family circle should do everything possible for them and not allow them to become the

church's responsibility. The church will then be free to look after those widows who are alone in the world.

You and your elders

Elders with a gift of leadership should be considered worthy of respect, and of adequate salary, particularly if they work hard at their preaching and teaching. Remember the scriptural principle:

Thou shalt not muzzle the ox when he treadeth out the corn,

and

The labourer is worthy of his hire.

Take no notice of charges brought against an elder unless they can be substantiated by proper witnesses. If sin is actually proved, then the offenders should be publicly rebuked as a salutary warning to others.

I solemnly charge you in the sight of God and Christ Jesus and the holy angels to follow these orders with the strictest impartiality and to have no favourites.

Never be in a hurry to ordain a man by laying your hands upon him, or you may be making yourself responsible for the sins of others. Be careful that your own life is pure. (By the way, I should advise you to drink wine in moderation, instead of water. It will do your stomach good and help you to get over your frequent spells of illness.) Remember that some men's sins are obvious, and are equally obviously bringing them to judgment. The sins of other men are not apparent, but are dogging them, nevertheless, under the surface. Similarly some virtues are plain to see, while others, though not at all conspicuous, will eventually become known.

CHAPTER 6

The behaviour of slaves in the church

CHRISTIAN slaves should treat their masters with respect, and avoid causing dishonour to the name of God and our teaching. If they have Christian masters they should not despise them because they work for brothers in the faith. Indeed they should serve them all the better because they are thereby benefiting those who have the same faith and love as themselves.

The dangers of false doctrine and the love of money

This is the sort of thing you should teach and preach, and if anyone tries to teach some doctrinal novelty and does not follow sound teaching (which we base on our Lord Jesus Christ's own words and which leads to Christ-like living), then he is a conceited idiot! His mind is a morbid jumble of disputation and argument, things which lead to nothing but jealousy, quarrelling, insults and malicious innuendoes—continual wrangling, in fact, among men of warped minds who have lost their real hold on the truth but hope to make some profit out of the Christian religion. There is a real profit, of course. It is peace of heart for those who live as God would have them live. We brought nothing with us when we entered this world and we can be sure we shall take nothing with us when we leave it. Surely then, as far as physical things are concerned, it is sufficient for us to keep our bodies fed and clothed. For men who set their hearts on being wealthy expose themselves to temptation. They fall into a trap and lay themselves open to all sorts of silly and wicked desires, which are quite capable of utterly ruining and destroying their souls. For loving money leads to all kinds of evil, and some men in the struggle to be rich have lost their faith and caused themselves untold agonies of mind.

Maintain a fearless witness until the last day

But you, the man of God, keep clear of such things. Set your heart on integrity, true piety, faithfulness, love, endurance and gentleness. Fight the worthwhile battle of the faith, keep your grip on that life eternal to which you have been called, and to which you boldly professed your loyalty before many witnesses. I charge you in the sight of God who gives life to all things and Christ Jesus who fearlessly witnessed to the truth before Pontius Pilate, to keep your commission clean and above reproach until the final coming of Christ. This will be, in his own time, the final dénouement of God, who is the blessed controller of all things, the king over all kings and the master of all masters, the only source of immortality, the One who lives in unapproachable light, the One whom no mortal eye has even seen or ever can see. To him be acknowledged all honour and power for ever, amen!

Have a word for the rich

Tell those who are rich in this present world not to be contemptuous of others, and not to rest the weight of their confidence on the transitory power of wealth but on the living God, who generously gives us everything for our enjoyment. Tell them to do good, to be rich in kindly actions, to be ready to give to others and to sympathise with those in distress. Their security should be invested in the life to come, so that they may be sure of holding a share in the life which is real and permanent.

My final appeal

Timothy, guard most carefully your divine commission. Avoid the Godless mixture of contradictory notions which is falsely known as "knowledge"—some have followed it *and lost their faith.*

Grace be with you all.

The Second Letter to Timothy

AUTHOR. *Paul, almost certainly writing from Rome, where he is awaiting sentence of death. (But see note on I Timothy.)*

DATE. *About* 67.

DESTINATION. *Timothy, still at Ephesus.*

THEME. *This second letter also aims at stimulating Timothy's faith and courage, and renews its plea for faithfulness to sound teaching and loyalty to what he, Timothy, knows to be true.*

The personal requests which end this letter are peculiarly touching since we realise that Paul knew that it was only a question of time before he was executed.

CHAPTER 1

PAUL, messenger by God's appointment in the promised life of Christ Jesus, to Timothy, my own dearly loved son: grace, mercy and peace be to you from God the Father and Christ Jesus, our Lord.

I thank God for your faith: guard it well

I thank the God of my forefathers, whom I also serve with a clear conscience, as I remember you constantly in my prayers night and day. I am longing to see you, for I can't forget how moved you were when I left you, and to have you with me again would be the greatest possible joy. I often think of that genuine faith of yours—a faith that first appeared in your grandmother Lois, then in Eunice your mother, and is now, I am convinced, in you as well. Because of this faith, I now remind you to stir up that inner fire which God gave you at your ordination through my hands. For God has not given us a spirit of cowardice, but a spirit of power and love and a sound mind. So never be ashamed of bearing witness to our Lord, nor of me, his prisoner. Accept your share of the hardship that faithfulness to the gospel entails in the strength that God gives you. For he has saved us from all that is evil and called us to a life of holiness—not because of any of our achievements but for his own purpose. Before time began he planned to give us in Christ Jesus the grace to achieve this purpose, but it is only since our saviour Christ Jesus has been revealed that the method has become apparent. For Christ has completely abolished death, and has now, through the gospel, opened to us men the shining possibilities of the life that is eternal. It is this gospel that I am commissioned to proclaim; it is of this gospel that I am appointed both messenger and teacher, and it is for this gospel that I am now suffering these things. Yet I am not in the least ashamed. For I know the one in whom I have placed my confidence, and I am perfectly certain that the work he has committed to me is safe in his hands until that day.

So keep my words in your mind as the pattern of sound teaching, given to you in the faith and love of Christ Jesus. Take the greatest care of the treasures which were entrusted to you by the Holy Spirit who lives within us.

Deserters—and a friend

You will know, I expect, that all those who are in Asia have deserted me, Phygelus and Hermogenes among them. But may the Lord have mercy on the household of Onesiphorus. Many times did that man put fresh heart into me, and he was not in the least ashamed of my being a prisoner in chains. Indeed, when he was in Rome he went to a great deal of trouble to find me—may the Lord grant he finds his mercy in that day!—and you well know in how many ways he helped me at Ephesus as well.

CHAPTER 2

Above all things be faithful

So, my son, be strong in the grace that Chrsit Jesus gives. Everything that you have heard me teach in public you should in turn entrust to reliable men, who will be able to pass it on to others.

Put up with your share of hardship as a loyal soldier in Christ's army. Remember: 1. That no soldier on active service gets himself entangled in business, or he will not please his commanding officer. 2. A man who enters an athletic contest wins no prize unless he keeps the rules laid down. 3. Only the man who works on the land has the right to the first share of its produce. Consider these three illustrations of mine and the Lord will help you to understand all that I mean.

Remember always, as the centre of everything, Jesus Christ, a descendant of David, yet raised by God from the dead according to my gospel. For preaching this I am having to endure being chained in prison as if I were some sort of a criminal. But they cannot chain the Word of God, and I can endure all these things for the sake of those whom God is calling, so that they too may receive the salvation of Christ Jesus, and its complement of glory after the world of time. I rely on this saying: *If we died with him we shall also live with him: if we endure we shall also reign with him. If we deny him he will also deny us: yet if we are faithless he always remains faithful. He cannot deny his own nature.*

Hold fast to the true: avoid dangerous error

Remind your people of things like this, and tell them as before God not to fight wordy battles, which help no one and may undermine the faith of those who hear them.

For yourself, concentrate on winning God's approval, on being a workman with nothing to be ashamed of, and who knows kow to use the word of truth to the best advantage. But steer clear of these unchristian babblings, which in practice lead further and further away from Christian living. For their teachings are as dangerous as blood-poisoning to the body, and spread like sepsis from a wound. Hymenaeus and Philetus are responsible for this sort of thing, and they are men who are palpable traitors to the truth, for they say that the resurrection has already happened and, of course, badly upset some people's faith.

God's solid foundation still stands, however, with this double inscription: *The Lord knows those who belong to him*, and *Let every true Christian have no dealings with evil.*

In any big household there are naturally not only gold and silver vessels but wooden and earthenware utensils as well. Some are used for the highest purposes and some for the lowest. If a man keeps himself clean from the contaminations of evil he will be a vessel used for honourable purposes, dedicated and serviceable for the use of the master of the household, all ready, in fact, for any good purpose.

Be positively good—and patient

Turn your back on the turbulent desires of youth and give your positive attention to goodness, integrity, love and peace in company with all those who approach the Lord in sincerity. But have nothing to do with silly and ill-informed controversies which lead inevitably, as you know, to strife. And the Lord's servant must not be a man of strife: he must be kind to all, ready and able to teach: he must be tolerant and have the ability gently to correct those who oppose his message. For God may give them a different outlook, and they may come to know the truth. They may come to their senses and be rescued from the snare of the devil and caught by God for his purposes.

CHAPTER 3

A warning of what to expect

But you must realise that in the last days the times will be full of danger. Men will become utterly self-centred, greedy for money, full of big words. They will be proud and abusive, without any regard for what their parents taught them. They will be utterly lacking in gratitude, reverence and normal human affections. They will be remorseless, scandal-mongers, uncontrolled and violent and haters of all that is good. They will be treacherous, reckless and arrogant, loving what gives them pleasure instead of loving God. They will maintain a façade of "religion" but their life denies its truth. Keep clear of people like that.

From their number come those creatures who worm their way into people's houses, and find easy prey in silly women with an exaggerated sense of sin and assorted desires—who are always anxious to learn and yet never able to grasp the truth. These men are as much enemies to the truth as Jannes and Jambres were to Moses. Their minds are distorted, and they are traitors to the faith. But in the long run they won't get very far. Their folly will become as obvious to everybody as did that of Moses' opponents.

Your knowledge of the truth should be your safeguard

But you, Timothy, have closely followed my teaching and my way of life, my purpose, my faith, my endurance; my love and courage in all those persecutions and difficulties at Antioch, Iconium and Lystra. And you know how the Lord brought me safely through them all. Persecution is inevitable for those who are determined to live really Christian lives, while wicked and deceitful men will go from bad to worse, deluding others and deluding themselves.

Yet you must go on steadily in those things that you have learned and which you know are true. Remember from whom your knowledge has come, and how from early childhood your mind has been familiar with the holy scriptures, which can open the mind to the salvation which comes through believing in Christ Jesus. All scripture is inspired by God and is useful for teaching the faith and correcting error, for re-setting the direction of a man's life and training him in good living. The scriptures are the comprehensive equipment of the man of God, and fit him fully for all branches of his work.

CHAPTER 4

My time is nearly over: you must carry on

I SOLEMNLY charge you, Timothy, in the presence of God and of Christ Jesus who will judge the living and the dead, by his appearing and his kingdom, to preach the Word. Never lose your sense of urgency, in season or out of season. Reprove, correct, and encourage, using the utmost patience in your teaching. For the time is coming when men will not tolerate wholesome teaching. They will want something to tickle their own fancies, and they will collect teachers who will speak what they want to hear. They will no longer listen to the truth, but will wander off after man-made myths.

For yourself, keep your mind sane and balanced, meeting whatever suffering this may involve. Go on steadily preaching the gospel and carry out to the full the commission that God gave you.

As for me, I feel that the last drops of my life are being poured out for God. The time for my departure has arrived. The glorious fight that God gave me I have fought, the course that I was set I have finished, and I have kept the faith. The future for me holds the crown of righteousness which the Lord, the true judge, will give to me in that day—and not, of course, only to me but to all those who have loved what they have seen of him.

Personal messages

Do your best to come to me as soon as you can. Demas, loving this present world, I fear, has left me and gone to Thessalonica. Crescens has gone to Galatia, and Titus is away in Dalmatia. Only Luke is with me now.

When you come, pick up Mark and bring him with you. I can certainly find a ministry for him here. (I had to send Tychicus off to Ephesus.) And please bring with you the cloak I left with Carpus at Troas, and the books, especially the manuscripts. Alexander the coppersmith did me a great deal of harm—the Lord will reward him for what he did—and I should be very careful of him if I were you. He has been a bitter opponent of our teaching.

The first time I had to defend myself no one was on my side —they all deserted me, God forgive them! Yet the Lord himself stood by me and gave me the strength to proclaim the message clearly and fully, so that the gentiles could hear it, and I was rescued "from the lion's mouth". I am sure the Lord will rescue me from every evil plot, and will keep me safe until I reach his heavenly kingdom. Glory be to him for ever and ever, amen!

Closing greetings

Give my love to Prisca and Aquila and Onesiphorus and his family. Erastus is still staying on at Corinth, and Trophimus I had to leave sick at Miletus.

Do your best to get here before the winter. Eubulus, Pudens, Linus, Claudia and all here send their greetings to you. The Lord be with your spirit. Grace be with you all.

The Letter to Titus

AUTHOR. *Paul wrote this letter towards the end of his life, possibly from Rome at roughly the same time as his second letter to Timothy, if as seems likely he was released from his first imprisonment mentioned in Acts,* 28, 30, *and was imprisoned again later.*

DATE. *About* 67.

DESTINATION. *This is a letter of guidance and instruction to Titus, a pagan convert, and plainly now a man whom Paul completely trusts. He is believed by some to have been Luke's brother. He apparently helped Paul to found a church in Crete, where he now receives this letter.*

THEME. *This letter contains directions as to the type of church officer Titus should appoint in Crete, and the sort of Christian character he should try to develop in the Cretan church.*

CHAPTER 1

FROM Paul, a servant of God and messenger of Jesus Christ in the faith God gives to his chosen, in the knowledge of the truth that comes from a God-fearing life, and in the hope of the everlasting life which God, who cannot lie, promised before the beginning of time. At the moment of his choice he made his Word known in the declaration which has been entrusted to me by the command of the God who saves us. To Titus, my true son in our common faith, be grace and peace from God the Father and Christ Jesus our saviour.

Men who are appointed to the ministry must be of the highest character

I left you in Crete to set right matters which needed attention, and told you to appoint elders in every city according to my direction. They were to be men of unquestioned integrity with only one wife, and with children brought up as Christians and not likely to be accused of loose living or law-breaking. To exercise spiritual oversight a man must be of unimpeachable virtue, for he is God's agent in the affairs of his household. He must not be aggressive or hot-tempered or over-fond of wine; nor must he be violent or greedy for financial gain. On the contrary, he must be hospitable, a genuine lover of what is good, a man who is discreet, fair-minded, holy and self-controlled: a man who takes his stand on the true faith, so that he can by sound teaching both stimulate faith and confute opposition.

Be on your guard against counterfeit Christians

For there are many, especially among the Jews, who will not recognise authority, who talk nonsense and yet in so doing have managed to deceive men's minds. They must be silenced, for they upset the faith of whole households, teaching what they have no business to teach for the sake of what they can get. One of them, yes, one of their own prophets, has said: "Men of Crete were always liars, evil and beastly, lazy and greedy." There is truth in this testimonial! Don't hesitate therefore to reprimand them sharply, for you want them to be sound and healthy Christians, with a proper contempt for Jewish fairy tales and orders issued by men who have forsaken the path of truth. Everything is clean to those who have clean minds. But nothing is wholesome to to those who are themselves corrupt and who have no faith in God—their very minds and consciences are diseased. They profess to know God, but their behaviour contradicts their profession. They are vile and disobedient and when it comes to doing any real good they are palpable frauds.

CHAPTER 2

Good character should follow good teaching

Now you must tell them the sort of character which should spring from sound teaching. The old men should be temperate, serious, wise—spiritually healthy through their faith and love and patience. Similarly the old women should be reverent in their behaviour, should not make unfounded complaints and should not be addicted to wine. They should be examples of the good life, so that the younger women may learn to love their husbands and their children, to be sensible and chaste, home-lovers, kind-hearted and willing to adapt themselves to their husbands—a good advertisement for the Christian faith. The young men, too, you should urge to take life seriously, letting your own life stand as a pattern of good living. In all your teaching show the strictest regard for truth, and show that you appreciate the seriousness of the matters you are dealing with. Your speech should be unaffected and above criticism, so that your opponent may feel ashamed at finding nothing with which to discredit us.

The duty of slaves—and of us all

Slaves should be told that it is their duty as Christians to obey their masters and to give them satisfactory service in every way. They are not to answer back or to be light-fingered, but they are to show themselves utterly trustworthy, a shining testimonial to the teaching of God our saviour. For the grace of God, which can save every man, has now been shown for all men, and it teaches us to have no more to do with godlessness or the desires of this world but to live, here and now, responsible, honourable and God-fearing lives. And while we live this life we hope and wait for the glorious dénouement of the great God and of Christ Jesus our saviour. For he gave himself for us, that he might set us free from all our evil ways and make for himself a people of his own, clean and pure, with our hearts set upon living a life that is good.

Tell men of these things. Plead with them, prove the truth to them with full authority—and let no one treat you with contempt.

CHAPTER 3

Instructions for the Christians of Crete

REMIND your people to recognise the power of those who rule and bear authority. They must obey them and be prepared to render whatever good service they can. They are not to speak evil of any man, they must not be quarrelsome but reasonable, showing every consideration to all men. For we ourselves have known what it is to be ignorant, disobedient and deceived, the slaves of various desires and pleasures, while our lives were spent in malice and jealousy—we were hateful and we hated each other. But when the kindness and love of God our saviour dawned upon us, he saved us in his mercy—not by virtue of any moral achievement of ours, but by the cleansing power of a new birth and the renewal of the Holy Spirit, which he poured upon us

through Jesus Christ our Saviour. The result is that we are acquitted by his grace, and can look forward in hope to inheriting life eternal. This is solid truth: I want you to speak about these matters with absolute certainty, so that those who have believed in God may concentrate upon a life of goodness. Good work is good in itself and is also useful to mankind.
But steer clear of stupid speculations, genealogies, controversies and quarrels over the Law. They settle nothing and lead nowhere. If a man is self-opinionated, warn him. But after the second warning you should reject him. You can be sure that he has a moral twist, and he is self-condemned.

Final messages

As soon as I send Artemas to you (or perhaps it will be Tychicus), do your best to come to me at Nicopolis, for I have made up my mind to spend the winter there. See that Zenas the lawyer and Apollos have what they require and give them a good send-off. And our people should learn to earn what they need by honest work and so be self-supporting.

All those here with me send you greetings. Please give our greetings to all who love us in the faith. Grace be with you all.

The Letter to Philemon

AUTHOR. *Paul, who wrote this letter when in prison at the same time as those to Ephesus, Colossae and Philippi, probably in Rome.*

DATE. *About* 62.

DESTINATION. *This is a personal letter to Philemon, a rich leading member of the church at Colossae.*

THEME. *Here we have a charming intimate letter written by Paul to a dear friend. Philemon's slave Onesimus (which means "useful" and explains the untranslatable pun in verse 11!), had run away from him and come under Paul's influence in Rome. He not only became a Christian but became very dear to Paul. They both realise, however, that he must return to his master and Paul sends him back with this "covering" letter.*

THE LETTER TO PHILEMON

PAUL, a prisoner of Christ Jesus, and brother Timothy to Philemon our much-loved fellow-worker, to Apphia our sister and Archippus who is with us in the fight; to the church that meets in your house—grace and peace be to you from God our Father and from the Lord Jesus Christ.

A personal appeal

I always thank God for you, Philemon, in my constant prayers for you, for I have heard how you love and trust both the Lord Jesus himself and those who believe in him. And I pray that those who share your faith may be led into the knowledge of all the good things that believing in Christ Jesus means to us. It is your love, my brother, that gives us such comfort and happiness, and it cheers the hearts of your fellow-Christians. And although I could rely on my authority in Christ and dare to *order* you to do what I consider right, I am not doing that. No, I am appealing in love, a simple personal appeal from Paul the old man, in prison for Christ Jesus' sake. I am appealing for my child. Yes I have become a father though I have been under lock and key, and the child's name is—Onesimus! Oh, I know you have found him useless in the past but he is going to be useful now, to both of us. I am sending him back to you—part of my very heart. I should have dearly loved to have kept him with me: he could have done what you would have done—looked after me here in prison for the gospel's sake. But I would do nothing without consulting you first, for if you have a favour to give me, let it be spontaneous and not forced from you by circumstances!

It occurs to me that there has been a purpose in your losing him. You lost him, a slave for a time; now you are having him back for good, not merely as a slave, but as a beloved brother. He is already especially dear to me—how much more will you be able to love him, both as a man and as a fellow-Christian! You and I have been true friends, haven't we? Then do welcome him as you would welcome me. If he has wronged or cheated you put it down to my account. I've written this with my own hand: I, Paul, hereby promise to repay you. (Of course I'm not stressing the fact that you might be said to owe me your very soul!) Now do grant me this favour, my brother—such a Christian act would set my heart at rest. As I send you this letter I know you'll do what I ask—I believe, in fact, you'll do more.

Will you do something else? Get the guest-room ready for me, for I have great hopes that through your prayers I myself will be returned to you as well!

Epaphras, here in prison with me for Christ Jesus' sake, sends his greetings; so do Mark, Aristarchus, Demas and Luke, all fellow-workers of mine.

The grace of our Lord Jesus Christ be with your spirit, amen.

The Letter to Jewish Christians

(THE EPISTLE TO THE HEBREWS)

AUTHOR. *Although the Authorised Version calls this letter "the Epistle of Paul the Apostle to the Hebrews" it is almost universally agreed that he did not write it. The style is very unlike Paul's, and every other letter of his is plainly stated to be by him. Various fascinating speculations have been made as to its authorship, including the names of Barnabas, Luke, Silas, Apollos and Priscilla.*

DATE. *Probably before the fall of Jerusalem. Possibly* 67.

DESTINATION. *Christian Jews probably living in some large towns. Rome is favoured by some scholars.*

THEME. *The general idea of this letter is to demonstrate that Jesus amply fulfils all the highest conceptions of the Jewish religion, and is infinitely superior to any predecessors. Christian Jews must realise that Christ has fulfilled and surpassed all their old ideas, and they must not therefore relapse into the old Jewish religion. Because the new agreement was established by God's visiting the earth in person, it is infinitely more important than the old agreement of the Law. There is, therefore, for those who belong to Christ far greater privilege in knowing God, but far greater responsibility in serving him loyally.*

THE LETTER TO JEWISH CHRISTIANS 1

CHAPTER 1

GOD, who gave to our forefathers many different glimpses of the truth in the words of the prophets, has now, at the end of the present age, given us the truth in the Son. Through the Son God made the whole universe, and to the Son he has ordained that all creation shall ultimately belong. This Son, radiance of the glory of God, flawless expression of the nature of God, himself the upholding power of all that is, having effected in person the cleansing of men's sin, took his seat at the right hand of the majesty on high—thus proving himself, by the more glorious name that he had been given, far greater than all the angels of God.

Scripture endorses this superiority

For to which of the angels did he ever say such words as these:
Thou art my Son,
This day have I begotten thee?
Or, again:
I will be to him a Father,
And he shall be to me a Son?
Further, when he brings his first-born into this world of men, he says:
Let all the angels of God worship him.
This is what he says of the angels:
Who maketh his angels winds
And his ministers a flame of fire.
But when he speaks of the Son, he says:
Thy throne, O God, is for ever and ever;
And the sceptre of uprightness is the sceptre of thy kingdom.
Thou hast loved righteousness and hated iniquity;
Therefore God, thy God, hath anointed thee
With the oil of gladness above thy fellows.
He also says:
Thou, *Lord*, in the beginning hast laid the foundation of the earth,
And the heavens are the work of thy hands:
They shall perish, but thou continuest:
And they all shall wax old as doth a garment;
And as a mantle shalt thou roll them up,

As a garment, and they shall be changed:
But thou art the same,
And thy years shall not fail.
But does he ever say this to any of the angels:
Sit thou on my right hand,
Till I make thine enemies the footstool of thy feet?
Surely the angels are no more than spirits in the service of God, commissioned to serve the heirs of God's salvation.

CHAPTER 2

The angels had authority in past ages: today the Son is the authority

WE ought, therefore, to pay the greatest attention to the truth that we have heard and not allow ourselves to drift away from it. For if the message given through angels proved authentic, so that defiance of it and disobedience to it received appropriate retribution, how shall we escape if we refuse to pay proper attention to that greater salvation which is offered us? For this salvation came first through the words of the Lord himself: it was confirmed for us by men who had heard him speak, and God moreover has plainly endorsed their witness by signs and miracles, by all kinds of spiritual power, and by gifts of the Holy Spirit, distributed as he pleased.

For God did not put the future world of men under the control of angels, and it is this world that we are now talking about.

But someone has truly said:
What is man, that thou art mindful of him?
Or the son of man, that thou visitest him?
Thou madest him a little lower than the angels;
Thou crownedst him with glory and honour,
And didst set him over the works of thy hands;
Thou didst put all things in subjection under his feet.

Notice that the writer puts "all things" under the sovereignty of man: he left nothing outside his control. But we do not yet see "all things" under his control.

Christ became man, not angel, to save mankind

What we see is Jesus, after being made temporarily inferior

to the angels and so subject to death, in order that he should, by God's grace, taste death for every man, now crowned with glory and honour. It was right and proper that in bringing many sons to glory, God (from whom and by whom everything exists) should make the leader of their salvation perfect through his sufferings. For the one who makes men holy and the men who are made holy share a common humanity. So that he is not ashamed to call them his brothers, for he says:

> I will declare thy name unto my brethren,
> In the midst of the congregation will I sing thy praise.

And again, speaking as a man, he says:

> I will put my trust in him.

And, one more instance, in these words:

> Behold, I and the children which God hath given me.

Since, then, "the children" have a common physical nature as human beings, he also became a human being, so that by going through death as a man he might destroy him who had the power of death, that is, the devil; and might also set free those who lived their whole lives a prey to the fear of death. It is plain that for this purpose his concern is not for angels but for men, the sons of Abraham. It was imperative that he should be made like his brothers in every respect, if he were to become a High Priest both compassionate and faithful in the things of God, and at the same time able to make atonement for the sins of the people. For by virtue of his own suffering under temptation he is able to help those who are exposed to temptation.

CHAPTER 3

Moses was a faithful servant: Christ a faithful son

So then, my brothers in holiness who share a heavenly calling, I want you to think of Christ Jesus the Apostle and High Priest of the faith we hold. See him as faithful to the charge God gave him, and compare him with Moses who also faithfully discharged his duty in the household of God. For this man Jesus has been considered worthy of greater honour than Moses, just as the founder of a house may be truly said to have more honour than the house itself. Every house is founded by someone, but the founder of everything is God himself. Moses was certainly faithful in all his duties in God's household, but he was faithful as a servant and his work was only a foreshadowing of the truth that would be known later. But Christ was faithful as a son in the household of his own Father. And we are members of this household if we hold on to the end, with confidence and pride in our hope.

Let us be on our guard that unbelief does not creep in

We ought to take note of these words in which the Holy Spirit says:

Today if ye shall hear his voice,
Harden not your hearts, as in the provocation,
Like as in the day of the temptation in the wilderness,
Wherewith your fathers tempted me by proving me,
And saw my works forty years.
Wherefore I was displeased with this generation,
And said, they do alway err in their heart:
But they did not know my ways;
As I sware in my wrath,
They shall not enter into my rest.

You should therefore be most careful, my brothers, that there should not be in any of you that wickedness of heart which refuses to trust, and deserts the cause of the living God. Encourage each other every day, while it is still called "today", and beware that none of you becomes deaf and blind to God through the delusive glamour of sin. For we continue to share in all that Christ has for us so long as we steadily maintain until the end the trust with which we began. These words are still being said for our ears to hear:

Today if ye shall hear his voice,
Harden not your hearts, as in the provocation.

For who was it who heard the Word of God and yet provoked his indignation? Was it not all who left Egypt under the leadership of Moses? And who was it with whom God was displeased for forty long years? Was it not those who, after all their hearing of God's Word, fell into sin, and left their bones in the desert? And to whom did God swear that they should never enter into his rest? Was it not these very men who refused to trust him?

Yes, it is all too plain that it was refusal to trust God that prevented these men from entering his rest.

CHAPTER 4

Men failed in the past to find God's rest: let us not fail!

Now since the same promise of rest is offered to us today, let us be continually on our guard that none of us even looks like failing to attain it. For we too have had a gospel preached to us, as those men had. Yet the message proclaimed to them did them no good, because they only heard and did not believe as well. It is only as a result of our faith and trust that we experience that rest. For he said:

As I sware in my wrath,
They shall not enter into my rest:

not because the rest was not prepared—it had been ready since the work of creation was completed, as he says elsewhere in the scriptures, speaking of the seventh day of creation,

And God rested on the seventh day from all his works.

In the passage above he says, "They shall not enter into my rest." It is clear that some were intended to experience this rest and, since the previous hearers of the message failed to attain to it because they would not believe God, he proclaims a further opportunity when he says through David, many years later, "today", just as he had said "today" before.

Today if ye shall hear his voice,
Harden not your hearts.

For if Joshua had given them the rest, we should not find God saying, at a much later date, "today". There still exists, therefore, a full and complete rest for the people of God. And he who experiences his rest is resting from his own work as fully as God from his.

Let us then be eager to know this rest for ourselves, and let us beware that no one misses it through falling into the same kind of unbelief as those we have mentioned. For the Word that God speaks is alive and active; it cuts more keenly than any two-edged sword: it strikes through to the place where soul and spirit meet, to the innermost intimacies of a man's being: it examines the very thoughts and motives of a man's heart. No creature has any cover from the sight of God; everything lies naked and exposed before the eyes of him with whom we have to deal.

For our help and comfort—Jesus the great High Priest

Seeing that we have a great High Priest who has passed through the heavens, Jesus the Son of God, let us hold firmly to our faith. For ours is no High Priest who cannot sympathise with our weaknesses—he himself has shared fully in all our experience of temptation, except that he never sinned.

Let us therefore approach the throne of grace with fullest confidence, that we may receive mercy for our failures and grace to help in the hour of need.

CHAPTER 5

A High Priest must be duly qualified and divinely appointed

NOTE that when a man is chosen as High Priest he is appointed on men's behalf as their representative in the things of God—he offers gifts to God and makes the necessary sacrifices for sins on behalf of his fellow-men. He must be able to deal sympathetically with the ignorant and foolish because he realises that he is himself prone to human weakness. This means that the offering which he makes for sin is made on his own behalf as well as on behalf of those whom he represents.

Note also that nobody chooses for himself the honour of being a High Priest, but he is called by God to the work, as was Aaron, the first High Priest in ancient times.

Thus we see that the Christ did not choose for himself the glory of being High Priest, but he was honoured by the one who said:

Thou art my Son,
This day have I begotten thee.

And he says in another passage:

Thou art a priest for ever
After the order of Melchizedek.

Christ, the perfect High Priest, was the perfect Son

Christ, in the days when he was a man on earth, appealed to the One who could save him from death in desperate prayer and the agony of tears. His prayers were heard because of his willingness to obey. But, Son though he was, he had to prove the meaning of obedience through all that he suffered. Then, when he had been proved the perfect Son, he became the source of eternal salvation to all who should obey him, being designated by God himself as High Priest "after the order of Melchizedek".

There is much food for thought here—but only for the mature Christian

There is a great deal that we should like to say about this high priesthood, but it is not easy to explain to you since you seem so slow to grasp spiritual truth. At a time when you should be teaching others, you need teachers yourselves to repeat to you the ABC of God's revelation to men. You have become people who need a milk diet and cannot face solid food! For anyone who continues to live on "milk" is unable to digest what is right—he simply has not grown up. "Solid food" is only for the adult, that is, for the man who has developed by experience his power to discriminate between what is good and what is evil.

CHAPTER 6

Can we not leave spiritual babyhood behind—and go on to maturity?

Let us leave behind the elementary teaching about Christ and go forward to adult understanding. Let us not lay over and over again the foundation truths—repentance from the deeds which led to death, believing in God, the teaching of baptism and laying-on of hands, belief in the resurrection of the dead and the final judgment. No, if God allows, let us go on.

Going back to the foundations will not help those who have deliberately turned away from God

When you find men who have been enlightened, who have tasted the heavenly gift and received the Holy Spirit, who have known the wholesome nourishment of the Word of God and touched the spiritual resources of the eternal world and who then fall away, it proves impossible to make them repent as they did at first. For they are re-crucifying the Son of God in their own souls, and exposing him to contempt. Ground which absorbs the rain that often falls on it and produces plants which are useful to those who cultivate it, is ground which has the blessing of God. But ground which produces nothing but thorns and thistles is of no value and is bound sooner or later to be condemned—the only thing to do is to burn it.

We want you to make God's promise real through your faith, hope and patience

But although we give these words of warning we feel sure that you, whom we love, are capable of better things and will enjoy the full experience of salvation. God is not unfair: he will not lose sight of all that you have done nor of the loving labour which you have shown for his sake in looking after fellow-Christians (as you are still doing). It is our earnest wish that every one of you should show a similar keenness in fully grasping the hope that is within you, until the end. We do not want any of you to grow slack, but to follow the example of those who through sheer patient faith came to possess the promises.

When God made his promise to Abraham he swore by himself, for there was no one greater by whom he could swear, and he said:

> Surely blessing I will bless thee
> And multiplying I will multiply thee.

And then Abraham, after patient endurance, found the promise true.

Among men it is customary to swear by something greater than themselves. And if a statement is confirmed by an oath, that is the end of all quibbling. So in this matter, God, wishing to show the heirs of his promise even more clearly that his plan was unchangeable, confirmed it with an oath. So that by two utterly immutable things, the word of God and the oath of God, who cannot lie, we who are refugees from this dying world might have a powerful source of strength, and might grasp the hope that he holds out to us. This hope we hold as an utterly reliable anchor for our souls, fixed in the innermost shrine of Heaven, where Jesus has already entered on our behalf, having become, as we have seen, "High Priest for ever after the order of Melchizedek".

CHAPTER 7

The mysterious Melchizedek: his superiority to Abraham and the Levites

Now this Melchizedek was king of Salem and priest of God Most High. He met Abraham when the latter was returning from the defeat of the kings, and blessed him. Abraham gave him a tribute of a tenth part of all the spoils of battle.

Melchizedek means first "king of righteousness," and his other title is "king of peace", for Salem means peace. He had no father or mother and no family tree. He was not born nor did he die, but, being like the Son of God, is a perpetual priest.

Now notice the greatness of this man. Even Abraham the patriarch pays him a tribute of a tenth part of the spoils. Further, we know that, according to the Law, the descendants of Levi who accept the office of priest have the right to demand a "tenth" from the people, that is from their brothers, despite the fact that the latter are descendants of Abraham. But here we have one who is quite independent of Levitic ancestry taking a "tenth" from Abraham, and giving a blessing to Abraham, the holder of God's promises! And no one can deny that the receiver of a blessing is inferior to the one who gives it. Again, in the one case it is mortal men who receive the "tenths", and in the other it is one who, we are assured, is alive. One might say that even Levi, the proper receiver of "tenths", has paid his tenth to this man, for in a sense he already existed in the body of his father Abraham when Melchizedek met him.

The revival of the Melchizedek priesthood means that the Levitical priesthood is superseded

We may go further. It if were possible to bring men to spiritual maturity through the Levitical priestly system (for that is the system under which the people were given the Law), why does the necessity arise for another priest to make his appearance *after the order of Melchizedek*, instead of following the normal priestly calling of Aaron? For if there is a transference of priestly powers, there will necessarily follow an alteration of the Law regarding priesthood. He who is described as our High Priest belongs to another tribe, no member of which had ever attended the altar! For it is a matter of history that our Lord was a descendant of Judah, and Moses made no mention of priesthood in connection with that tribe.

How fundamental is this change becomes all the more apparent when we see this other priest appearing according to the Melchizedek pattern, and deriving his priesthood not by virtue of a command imposed from outside, but from the power of indestructible life within. For the witness to him, as we have seen, is:

Thou are a priest for ever
After the order of Melchizedek.

Quite plainly, then, there is a definite cancellation of the previous commandment because of its ineffectiveness and uselessness—the Law was incapable of bringing anyone to real maturity—followed by the introduction of a better hope, through which we approach God.

The High Priesthood of Christ rests upon the oath of God

This means a far better hope for us because Jesus has become our priest by the oath of God. Other men have been priests without any sworn guarantee, but Jesus has the oath of him that said of him:

The Lord sware and will not repent himself,
Thou art a priest for ever.

And he is, by virtue of this fact, himself the living guarantee of a better agreement. Human High Priests have always been changing, for death made a permanent appointment impossible. But Christ, because he lives for ever, possesses a priesthood that needs no successor. This means that he can save fully and completely those who approach God through him, for he is always living to intercede on their behalf.

Christ the perfect High Priest, who meets our need

Here is the High Priest we need. A man who is holy, faultless, unstained, separated from sinners and lifted above the very Heavens. There is no need for him, like the High Priests we know, to offer up daily sacrifices, first for his own sins and then for the people's. He made one sacrifice, once for all, when he offered up himself.

The Law makes for its High Priests men of human weakness. But the word of the oath, which came after the Law, makes for High Priest the Son, who is perfect for ever!

CHAPTER 8

Christ our High Priest in Heaven is High Priest of a new agreement

Now to sum up—we have an ideal High Priest such as has been described above. He has taken his seat at the right hand of the throne of Heavenly majesty. He is the minister of the sanctuary and of the real tabernacle—that is the one which the Lord has set up and not man. Every High Priest is appointed to offer gifts and make sacrifices. It follows, therefore, that in these holy places this man must have something to offer.

Now if he were still living on earth he would not be a priest at all, for there are already priests offering the gifts prescribed by the Law. These men are serving what is only a pattern or reproduction of things that exist in Heaven. Moses, you will remember, when he was going to construct the tabernacle, was cautioned by God in these words:

See that thou make all things
According to the pattern that was showed thee in the mount.

But our High Priest has been given a far higher ministry for he mediates a higher agreement, which in turn rests upon higher promises. If the first agreement had proved satisfactory there would have been no need to look for a second.

Actually, however, God does show himself dissatisfied for he says:

Behold the days come, saith the Lord,
That I will make a new covenant with the house of Israel and with the house of Judah;
Not according to the covenant that I made with their fathers
In the day that I took them by the hand to lead them forth out of the land of Egypt;
For they continued not in my covenant,
And I regarded them not, saith the Lord.
For this is the covenant that I will make with the house of Israel
After those days, saith the Lord;
I will put my laws into their mind,
And on their heart also will I write them:
And I will be to them a God,
And they shall be to me a people:
And they shall not teach every man his fellow-citizen,
And every man his brother, saying, Know the Lord:
For all shall know me,
From the least to the greatest of them.
For I will be merciful to their iniquities.
And their sins will I remember no more.

The mere fact that God speaks of a new covenant or agreement makes the old one out of date. And when a thing grows weak and out of date it is obviously soon going to disappear.

CHAPTER 9

The sanctuary under the old agreement

Now the first agreement had certain rules for the service of God, and it had a sanctuary, a holy place in this world for the eternal God. A tent was erected: in the outer compartment were placed the lamp-standard, the table and the sacred loaves. Inside, beyond the curtain, was the inner tent called the holy place, in which were the golden incense-altar and the gold-covered ark of the agreement, containing the golden jar of manna. Aaron's budding staff and the stone tablets inscribed with the words of the actual agreement. Above these things were fixed representations of the cherubim of glory, casting their shadow over the mercy seat. (All this is full of meaning but we cannot enter now into a detailed explanation.)

Under this arrangement the outer tent was habitually used by the priests in the regular discharge of their religious duties. But the inner tent was entered once a year only, by the High Priest, alone, bearing a sacrifice of shed blood to be offered for himself and for the sins of the people which they had committed unwittingly.

The old arrangements stood as symbols until Christ, the truth, came

By these things the Holy Spirit means us to understand that the way to the holy place was not yet open, that is, so long as the first tent and all that it stands for still exist. For in this outer tent we see a picture of the present time, in which both gifts and sacrifices are offered and yet are incapable of cleansing the soul of the worshipper. The ceremonies are concerned with food and drink, various washings and rules for bodily conduct, and were only intended to be valid until the time when the new order should be established. For now Christ has come among us, the High Priest of the good things which were to come, and has passed through a greater and more perfect tent which no human hand had made (for it was no part of this world of ours). It was not with goats' or calves' blood but with his own blood that he entered once and for all into the holy place, having won for us men eternal reconciliation with God. For if the blood of bulls and goats and the ashes of a burnt heifer were, when sprinkled on the unholy, sufficient to make the body pure, then how much more will the blood of Christ himself, who in the eternal spirit offered himself to God as the perfect sacrifice, purify our conscience from the deeds of death, that we may serve the living God!

The death of Christ gives him power to administer the new agreement

Christ is consequently the administrator of an entirely new agreement, having the power, by virtue of his death, to redeem transgressions committed under the first agreement: to enable those who obey God's call to enjoy the promises of the eternal inheritance. For, as in the case of a will, the agreement is only valid after death. While the testator lives, a will has no legal power. And indeed we find that even the first agreement of God's will was not put into force without the shedding of blood. For when Moses had told the people every command of the Law he took calves' and goats' blood with water and scarlet wool, and sprinkled both the book and all the people with a sprig of hyssop, saying: "This is the blood of the agreement God makes with you." Moses also sprinkled with blood the tent itself and all the sacred vessels. And you will find that in the Law almost all cleansing is made by means of blood—it implies again and again: "No shedding of blood, no remission of sin."

Christ has achieved the real appearance before God for us

It was necessary for the earthly reproductions of heavenly realities to be purified by such methods, but the actual heavenly things could only be made pure in God's sight by higher sacrifices than these. Christ did not therefore enter into any holy places made by human hands (however truly these may represent heavenly realities), but he entered Heaven itself to make his appearance before God on our behalf. There is no intention that he should offer himself over and over again, like the High Priest entering the holy place year after year with the blood of another creature. For that would mean that he would have to suffer death every time he entered Heaven from the beginning of the world! No, the fact is that now, at this point in time, the end of the present age, he has appeared once and for all to abolish sin by the sacrifice of himself. And just as surely as it is appointed for all men to die once, and after that pass to their judgment, so it is certain that Christ was offered once to bear the sins of many and after that, to those who look for him, he will appear a second time, not this time to deal with sin, but to bring to full salvation those who eagerly await him.

CHAPTER 10

Sacrifices under the Law were "typical" not final

THE Law possessed only a dim outline of the benefits Christ would bring and did not actually reproduce them. Consequently it was incapable of perfecting the souls of those who offered their regular annual sacrifices. For if it had, surely the sacrifices would have been discontinued—on the grounds that the worshippers, having been really cleansed, would have had no further consciousness of sin. In practice, however, the sacrifices amounted to an annual reminder of sins; for the blood of bulls and goats cannot really remove the guilt of sin.

Christ, however, makes the old order obsolete and makes the perfect sacrifice

Therefore, when Christ enters the world, he says:

Sacrifice and offering thou wouldest not,
But a body didst thou prepare for me;
In whole burnt offerings and sacrifices for sin thou hadst no pleasure:
Then said I, Lo, I am come
(In the roll of the book it is written of me)
To do thy will, O God.

After saying that God has "no pleasure in sacrifice, offering and burnt-offering" (which are made according to the Law), Christ then says, "Lo, I am come to do thy will." That means that he is dispensing with the old order of sacrifices, and establishing a new order of obedience to the will of God, and in that will we have been made holy by the single unique offering of the body of Jesus Christ.

Every human priest stands day by day performing his religious duties and offering time after time the same sacrifices—which can never actually remove sins. But this man, after offering one sacrifice for sins for ever, took his seat at God's right hand, from that time offering no more sacrifice, but waiting until "his enemies be made his footstool". For by virtue of that one offering he has perfected for all time every one whom he makes holy. The Holy Spirit himself endorses this truth for us, when he says, first:

This is the covenant that I will make with them
After those days, saith the Lord;

I will put my laws on their heart,
And upon their mind also will I write them.

And then, he adds:

And their sins and their iniquities will I remember no more.

Where God grants remission of sin there can be no question of making further atonement.

Through Christ we can confidently approach God

So, by virtue of the blood of Jesus, you and I, my brothers, may now have confidence to enter the holy place by a fresh and living way, which he has opened up for us by himself passing through the curtain, that is, his own human nature. Further, since we have a great High Priest set over the household of God, let us draw near with true hearts and fullest confidence, knowing that our inmost souls have been purified by the sprinkling of his blood just as our bodies are cleansed by the washing of clean water. In this confidence let us hold on to the hope that we profess without the slightest hesitation—for he is utterly dependable—and let us think of one another and how we can encourage each other to love and do good deeds. And let us not hold aloof from our church meetings, as some do. Let us do all we can to help one another's faith, and this the more earnestly as we see the final day drawing nearer.

A warning: let us not abuse the great sacrifice

Now if we sin deliberately after we have known and accepted the truth, there can be no further sacrifice for sin for us but only a terrifying expectation of judgment and the fire of God's indignation, which will consume all that sets itself against him. The man who showed contempt for Moses' Law died without hope of appeal on the evidence of two or three witnesses. How much more dreadful a punishment will he be thought to deserve who has poured scorn on the Son of God, treated like dirt the blood of the agreement which had once made him holy, and insulted the very Spirit of grace? For we know the one who said:

Vengeance belongeth unto me, I will recompense.

And, again:

The Lord shall judge his people.

Truly it is a terrible thing for a man who has done this to fall into the hands of the living God!

Recollect your former faith, and stand firm today!

You must never forget those past days when you had received the light and endured such a great and painful struggle. It was partly because everyone's eye was on you as you suffered harsh words and hard experiences, partly because you threw in your lot with those who suffered much the same. You sympathised with those who were put in prison and you were cheerful when your own goods were confiscated, for you knew that you had a much more solid and lasting treasure. Don't throw away your trust now—it carries with it a rich reward. Patient endurance is what you need if, after doing God's will, you are to receive what he has promised.

For yet a very little while,
He that cometh shall come, and shall not tarry.
But my righteous one shall live by faith;
And if he shrink back, my soul hath no pleasure in him.

Surely we are not going to be men who cower back and are lost, but men who maintain their faith for the salvation of their souls!

CHAPTER 11

Now faith means that we have full confidence in the things we hope for, it means being certain of things we cannot see. It was this faith that won their reputation for the saints of old. And it is only by faith that our minds accept as fact that the whole universe was formed by God's command—that the world which we can see has come into being through what is invisible.

Faith is the distinctive mark of the saints of the old agreement

ABEL

It was because of his faith that Abel made a better sacrifice to God than Cain, and he had evidence that God looked upon him as a righteous man, whose gifts he could accept. And though Cain killed him, yet by his faith he still speaks to us today.

ENOCH

It was because of his faith that Enoch was taken tc the eternal world without experiencing death. He disappeared from this world because God had taken him, and before that happened his reputation was that "he pleased God". And without faith it is impossible to please him. The man who approaches God must have faith in two things, first that God exists and secondly that God rewards those who search for him.

NOAH

It was through his faith that Noah, on receiving God's warning of impending disaster with reverence, constructed an ark to save his household. This action of faith condemned the unbelief of the rest of the world, and won for Noah the righteousness before God which follows such a faith.

ABRAHAM

It was by faith that Abraham obeyed the summons to go out to a place which he would eventually possess, and he set out in complete ignorance of his destination. It was faith that kept him journeying like a foreigner through the land of promise, with no more home than the tents which he shared with Isaac and Jacob, co-heirs with him of the promise. For Abraham's eyes were looking forward to that city with solid foundations of which God himself is both architect and builder.

SARAH

It was by faith that even Sarah gained the physical vitality to conceive despite her great age, and she gave birth to a child when far beyond the normal years of child-bearing. She did this because she believed that the One who had given the promise was utterly trustworthy. So it happened that from one man, who as a potential father was already considered dead, there arose a race "as numerous as the stars", as "countless as the sands of the sea-shore".

All the heroes of faith looked forward to their true country

All these whom we have mentioned maintained their faith but died without actually receiving God's promises, though they had seen them in the distance, had hailed them as true. They freely admitted that they lived on this earth as exiles and foreigners. Men who say that mean, of course, that their eyes are fixed upon their true home-land. If they had meant the particular country they had left behind, they had ample opportunity to return. No, the fact is that they longed for a better country altogether, nothing less than a heavenly one. And because of this faith of theirs, God is not ashamed to be called their God for he has prepared for them a city.

Abraham's faith once more

It was by faith that Abraham, when put to the test, offered Isaac for sacrifice. Yes, the man who had heard God's promises was prepared to offer up his only son of whom it had been said "In Isaac shall thy seed be called." He believed that God could raise his son up, even if he were dead. And he did, in a manner of speaking, receive him back from death.

The faith of Isaac, Jacob and Joseph

It was by faith that Isaac gave Jacob and Esau his blessing, for his words dealt with what should happen in the future. It was by faith that the dying Jacob blessed each of Joseph's sons as he bowed in prayer over his staff. It was by faith that Joseph on his death-bed spoke of the exodus of the Israelites, and gave orders about the disposal of his own mortal remains.

Moses

It was by faith that Moses was hidden by his parents for three months after his birth, for they saw that he was a beautiful child and refused to be daunted by the king's decree. It was also by faith that Moses himself when grown up refused to be called the son of Pharaoh's daughter. He preferred sharing the burden of God's people to enjoying the temporary advantages of sin. He considered the "reproach of Christ" more precious than all the wealth of Egypt, for he looked steadily at the ultimate reward.

By faith he left Egypt; he defied the king's anger with the strength that came from obedience to the invisible king.

By faith Moses kept the first Passover and made the blood-sprinkling, so that the angel of death which killed the first-born should not touch those of his people.

By faith the people walked through the Red Sea as though it

were dry land, and the Egyptians who tried to do the same thing were drowned.

Rahab

It was by faith that the walls of Jericho collapsed, for the people had obeyed God's command to encircle them for seven days. It was because of her faith that Rahab the prostitute did not share the fate of the disobedient, for she welcomed the Israelites sent out to reconnoitre.

The Old Testament is full of examples of faith

And what other examples shall I give? There is not time to continue by telling the stories of Gideon, Barak, Samson and Jeptha; of David, Samuel and the prophets. Through their faith these men conquered kingdoms, ruled in justice and proved the truth of God's promises. They shut the mouths of lions, they quenched the furious blaze of fire, they escaped death by the sword. From being weaklings they became strong men and mighty warriors; they routed whole armies of foreigners. Women received their dead raised to life again, while others were tortured to death and refused to be ransomed, because they wanted a more honourable resurrection. Others were exposed to the test of public mockery and flogging, and to being left bound in prison. They were killed by stoning, by being sawn in two; they were murdered by the sword. They went about with nothing but sheepskins or goatskins to cover them. They lost everything and yet were spurned and ill-treated by a world too evil to see their worth. They lived as vagrants in the desert, on the mountains, or in caves or holes in the ground.

All these won a glowing testimony to their faith, but they did not then and there receive the fulfilment of the promise. God had something better planned for our day, and it was not his plan that they should reach perfection without us.

CHAPTER 12

We should consider these examples and Christ the perfect example

SURROUNDED then as we are by these serried ranks of witnesses, let us strip off everything that hinders us, as well as the sin which dogs our feet, and let us run the race that we have to run with patience, our eyes fixed on Jesus the source and the goal of our faith. For he himself endured a cross and thought nothing of its shame because of the joy he knew would follow his suffering; and he is now seated at the right hand of God's throne. Think constantly of him enduring all that sinful men could say against him and you will not lose your purpose or your courage.

Look upon suffering as heavenly discipline

After all, your fight against sin has not yet meant the shedding of blood, and you have perhaps lost sight of that piece of advice which reminds you of your sonship in God:

My son, regard not lightly the chastening of the Lord,
Nor faint when thou art reproved of him;
For whom the Lord loveth he chasteneth,
And scourgeth every son whom he receiveth.

Bear what you have to bear as "chastening"—as God's dealing with you as sons. No true son ever grows up uncorrected by his father. For if you had no experience of the correction which all sons have to bear you might well doubt the legitimacy of your sonship. After all, when we were children we had fathers who corrected us, and we respected them for it. Can we not much more readily submit to the discipline of the Father of men's souls, and learn how to live?

For our fathers used to correct us according to their own ideas during the brief days of childhood. But God corrects us for our own benefit, so that we may share in his holiness. Now obviously no "chastening" seems pleasant at the time: it is in fact most unpleasant. Yet when it is all over we can see that it has quietly produced the fruit of real goodness in the characters of those who have accepted it. So tighten your loosening grip and steady your trembling knees. Keep your feet on a steady path, so that the limping foot does not collapse but recovers strength.

In times of testing be especially on your guard against certain sins

Let it be your ambition to live at peace with all men and to achieve holiness "without which no man shall see the Lord". Be careful that none of you fails to respond to the grace of God, for if he does there can spring up in him a bitter spirit which can poison the lives of many others. Be careful, too, that none of you falls into impurity or loses his reverence for the things of God like Esau, who sold his birthright for a single meal. Remember how afterwards, when he wanted to have the blessing which was his birthright, he was refused. He never afterwards found the way of repentance though he sought it desperately and with tears.

Your experience is not that of the old agreement but of the new

You have not had to approach things which your senses could experience as they did in the old days—flaming fire, black darkness, rushing wind and out of it a trumpet-blast, a voice speaking human words. So terrible was that voice that those who heard it begged and prayed that it might say no more. For what it had already commanded was more than they could bear—that "if even a beast touch this mountain it must be stoned". So fearful was the spectacle that Moses cried out, "I am terrified and tremble!"

No, you have been allowed to approach the true Mount Zion, the city of the living God, the heavenly Jerusalem. You have drawn near to the countless angelic army, the assembly of the Church of the first-born whose names are written in Heaven. You have drawn near to God, the judge of all, to the souls of good men made perfect, and to Jesus, mediator of a new agreement, to that cleansing blood which tells a better story than the blood of Abel.

So be sure you do not refuse to hear the voice that speaks. For if they who refused to hear those who spoke to them on earth did not escape, how little chance of escape is there for us if we refuse to hear the One who speaks from Heaven. Then his voice shook, the earth, but now he promises:

Yet once more will I make to tremble
Not the earth only, but also the heaven.

This means that in this final "shaking" all that is impermanent will be removed, that is, everything that is merely "made", and only the unshakable things will remain. Since then we have been given a kingdom that is "unshakable", let us serve God with thankfulness in the ways which please him, but always with reverence and holy fear. For it is perfectly true that our God is a burning fire.

CHAPTER 13

Some practical instructions for Christian living

NEVER let your brotherly love fail, nor refuse to extend your hospitality to strangers—sometimes men have entertained angels unawares. Think constantly of those in prison as if you were prisoners at their side. Think too of all who suffer for you still live in this world.

Marriage is honourable and faithfulness should be respected by you all. God himself will judge those who traffic in the bodies of others or defile the relationship of marriage. Keep your lives free from the lust for money: be content with what you have.

God has said:

I will in no wise fail thee,
Neither will I in any wise forsake thee.

We, therefore, can confidently say:

The Lord is my helper; I will not fear:
What shall man do unto me?

Be loyal to your leaders and, above all, to Christ

Never forget your leaders, who first spoke to you the Word of God. Remember the result of their lives, and imitate their faith.

Jesus Christ is always the same, yesterday, today and for ever. Do not be carried away by various peculiar teachings. It is good to depend on the grace of God for inward strength, and not on rules of diet—which have not spiritually benefited those who followed them. We have an Altar from which those who still serve the tabernacle have no right to eat.

When the blood of animals was presented as a sin-offering by the High Priest in the sanctuary, their bodies were burned outside the precincts of the camp. That is why Jesus, when he sanctified men by the shedding of his own blood, suffered and died outside the city gates. Let us go out to him, then, beyond the boundaries of the camp, proudly bearing his "disgrace". For we have no permanent city here on earth, we are looking for one in the world to come. Through him, therefore, let us offer a constant sacrifice of praise to God—the tribute of lips which openly acknowledge his name. Yet we should not forget to do good and to share our good things with others, for these too are the sort of sacrifices God will accept.

Obey your rulers and recognise their authority. They keep constant watch over your welfare, and they have great responsibility. Try to make their work a pleasure and not a painful burden —that would be no advantage to you.

Personal: our blessing and our greetings

Pray for us. Our conscience is clear before God, and our great desire is to lead a life that is good in every way. Please pray earnestly that I may be restored to you the sooner.

Now the God of peace, who brought back from the dead that great shepherd of the sheep, our Lord Jesus, by the blood of the everlasting agreement, equip you thoroughly for the doing of his will! May he effect in us everything that pleases him through Jesus Christ, to whom be glory for ever and ever. Amen.

My brothers, I ask you to bear with this message of encouragement, for I have indeed compressed it into this short letter!

You will be glad to know that brother Timothy is now at liberty. If he comes here in time, he and I will see you together.

Greetings to all your leaders and all your church members. The Christians of Italy send their greetings.

Grace be with you all.

The Letter of James

AUTHOR. *Quite probably James, brother or step-brother of Jesus. He had a high reputation and was known as "the Just". Paul calls him a messenger (Galatians* 1, *19). Some think he was the first bishop of Jerusalem, and he was certainly the head of the church there at Paul's last visit (Acts* 21, *18).*

DATE. *Possibly early, about* 50, *making it the earliest letter of the New Testament. Some suggest a date as late as "after* 100*". If this is so it cannot be the work of James, who died about* 62.

DESTINATION. *The displaced Jews, or the "Dispersion", i.e. Christian Jews who had been scattered by persecution or force of circumstance.*

THEME. *The teaching closely follows that of Jesus' Sermon on the Mount and reads like a collection of short homilies. It deals particularly with the dangers of an uncontrolled tongue, snobbery, belief in God unaccompanied by Christian conduct, and trusting in material prosperity. The emphasis in this letter on behaviour has sometimes been supposed to contradict Paul's teaching on "justification by faith". In fact it does not contradict but complement. Paul says that a man is "justified" before God not by achievement but by a real faith: James says that the test of a real faith is whether it issues in appropriate behaviour.*

CHAPTER 1

JAMES, a servant of God and of the Lord Jesus Christ, sends greeting to the twelve dispersed tribes.

The Christian can even welcome trouble

When all kinds of trials and temptations crowd into your lives, my brothers, don't resent them as intruders, but welcome them as friends! Realise that they come to test your faith and to produce in you the quality of endurance. But let the process go on until that endurance is fully developed, and you will find you have become men of mature character, men of integrity with no weak spots. And if, in the process, any of you does not know how to meet any particular problem he has only to ask God—who gives generously to all men without making them feel guilty—and he may be quite sure that the necessary wisdom will be given him. But he must ask in sincere faith without secret doubts. For the man who doubts is like a wave of the sea, carried forward by the wind one moment and driven back the next. That sort of man cannot hope to receive anything from the Lord, and the life of a man of divided loyalty will reveal instability at every turn.

Rich and poor can be glad—for different reasons!

The brother who is poor may be proud because God has raised him to the true riches. The rich may be proud that God has shown him his spiritual poverty. For the rich man will wither away like summer flowers. One day the sunrise brings a scorching wind; the grass withers at once and so do all the flowers—

all that lovely sight is destroyed. Just as surely will the rich man and all his ways fall into the blight of decay.

No temptation comes from God, only highest good

The man who patiently endures the temptations and trials that come to him is the truly happy man. For once his testing is complete he will receive the crown of life which the Lord has promised to all who love him.

A man must not say when he is tempted, "God is tempting me." For God cannot be tempted by evil, and does not himself tempt anyone. No, a man's temptation is due to the pull of his own inward desires, which greatly attract him. It is his own desire which conceives and gives birth to sin. And sin when fully grown produces death—make no mistake about that, brothers of mine! But every good endowment and every complete gift must come from above, from the Father of all lights, with whom there is never the slightest variation or shadow of inconsistency. By his own wish he made us his own sons through the Word of truth, that we might be, so to speak, the first specimens of his new creation.

Hear God's Word and put it into practice: that is real religion

Knowing this, then, dear brothers, let every man be quick to listen but slow to use his tongue, and slow to lose his temper. For man's temper is never the means of achieving God's true goodness.

Have done, then, with impurity and every other evil which overflows into the lives of others, and humbly accept the message that God has planted in your hearts, and which can save your souls. Don't only hear the message, but put it into practice; otherwise you are merely deluding yourselves. The man who simply hears and does nothing about it is like a man catching the reflection of his natural face in a mirror. He sees himself, it is true, but he goes off without the slightest recollection of what sort of person he saw in the mirror. But the man who looks into the perfect law, the law of liberty, and makes a habit of so doing, is not the man who hears and forgets. He puts that law into practice and he wins true happiness.

If anyone appears to be "religious" but cannot control his

tongue, he deceives himself and we may be sure that his religion is useless. Religion that is pure and genuine in the sight of God the Father will show itself by such things as visiting orphans and widows in their distress and keeping oneself uncontaminated by the world.

CHAPTER 2

Avoid snobbery: keep the royal law

DON'T ever attempt, my brothers, to combine snobbery with faith in our glorious Lord Jesus Christ! Suppose one man comes into your meeting well-dressed and with a gold ring on his finger, and another man, obviously poor, arrives in shabby clothes. If you pay special attention to the well-dressed man by saying, "Please sit here—it's an excellent seat", and say to the poor man, "You stand over there, or if you must sit, sit on the floor by my feet", doesn't that prove that you are making class-distinctions in your mind, and setting yourselves up to assess a man's quality from wrong motives? For do notice, my dear brothers, that God chose poor men, whose only wealth was their faith, and made them heirs to the kingdom promised to those who love him. And if you behave as I have suggested, it is the poor man that you are insulting. Look around you. Isn't it the rich who are always trying to rule your lives, isn't it the rich who drag you into litigation? Isn't it usually the rich who blaspheme the glorious name by which you are known?

If you obey the royal Law, expressed by the scripture, "Thou shalt love thy neighbour as thyself", all is well. But once you allow any invidious distinctions to creep in, you are sinning, you stand condemned by that Law. Remember that a man who keeps the whole Law but for a single exception is none the less a law-breaker. The one who said, "Thou shalt not commit adultery" also said, "Thou shalt do no murder". If you were to keep clear of adultery but were to murder a man you would have become a breaker of the whole Law.

Anyway, you should speak and act as men who will be judged by the law of freedom. The man who makes no allowances for others will find none made for him. Mercy may laugh in the face of judgment.

The relation between faith and action

Now what use is it, my brothers, for a man to say he "has faith"?

if his actions do not correspond with it? Could that sort of faith save anyone's soul? If a fellow man or woman has no clothes to wear and nothing to eat, and one of you say, "Good luck to you I hope you'll keep warm and find enough to eat", and yet give them nothing to meet their physical needs, what on earth is the good of that? Yet that is exactly what a bare faith without a corresponding life is like—quite dead. A man could challenge us by saying, "You have faith and I have merely good actions. Well, all you can do is to show me a faith without corresponding actions, but I can show you by my actions that I have faith as well."

So you believe that there is one God? That's fine. So do all the devils in hell, and shudder in terror! For, my dear short-sighted man, can't you see far enough to realise that faith without the right actions is dead and useless? Think of Abraham, our ancestor. Wasn't it his action which really justified him in God's sight when his faith led him to offer his son Isaac on the altar? Can't you see that his faith and his actions were, so to speak, partners—that his faith was implemented by his deed? That is what the scripture means when it says:

> And Abraham believed God,
> And it was reckoned unto him for righteousness;
> And he was called the friend of God.

A man is justified before God by what he does as well as by what he believes. Rahab, who was a prostitute, has been quoted as an example of faith, yet surely it was her action that pleased God, when she welcomed Joshua's reconnoitring party and sent them safely back by a different route.

Yes, faith without action is as dead as a body without a soul.

CHAPTER 3

The responsibility of a teacher's position

DON'T aim at adding to the number of teachers, my brothers, I beg you! Remember that we who are teachers will be judged by a much higher standard.

The danger of the tongue

We all make mistakes in all kinds of ways, but the man who

can claim that he never says the wrong thing can consider himself perfect, for if he can control his tongue he can control every other part of his personality! Men control the movements of a large animal like the horse with a tiny bit placed in its mouth. Ships too, for all their size and the momentum they have with a strong wind behind them, are controlled by a very small rudder according to the course chosen by the helmsman. The human tongue is physically small, but what tremendous effects it can boast of! A whole forest can be set ablaze by a tiny spark of fire, and the tongue is a fire, a whole world of evil. It is set within our bodily members but it can poison the whole body, it can set the whole of life ablaze, fed with the fires of hell.

Beasts, birds, reptiles and all kinds of sea-creatures can be, and in fact are, tamed by man, but no one can tame the human tongue. It is an evil always liable to break out, and the poison it spreads is deadly. We use the tongue to bless our Lord and Father and we use the same tongue to curse our fellow-men, who are all created in God's likeness. Blessing and curses come out of the same mouth—surely, my brothers, this is the sort of thing that never ought to happen! Have you ever known a spring to give sweet and bitter water from the same source? Have you ever seen a fig-tree with a crop of olives, or seen figs growing on a vine? It is just as impossible for salt water to produce fresh.

Real, spiritual, wisdom means humility, not rivalry

Is there some wise and understanding man among you? Then let his life be a shining example of the humility that is born of true wisdom. But if your heart is full of bitter jealousy and rivalry, then do not boast and do not deny the truth. You may acquire a certain wisdom, but it does not come from above—it comes from this world, from your own lower nature, even from the devil. For wherever you find jealousy and rivalry you also find disharmony and all other kinds of evil. The wisdom that comes from above is first pure, then peace-loving, gentle, approachable, full of merciful thoughts and kindly actions, straightforward, with no hint of hypocrisy. And the peacemakers go on quietly sowing for a harvest of righteousness.

CHAPTER 4

Your jealousies spring from love of what the world can give

BUT what about the feuds and struggles that exist among you —where do you suppose they come from? Can't you see that they arise from conflicting desires for pleasure within yourselves? You crave for something and don't get it; you are murderously jealous of what you can't possess yourselves; you struggle and fight with one another. You don't get what you want because you don't ask God for it. And when you do ask he doesn't give it to you, for you ask in quite the wrong spirit—you only want to satisfy your own desires.

You are like unfaithful wives, never realising that to be the world's lover means becoming the enemy of God! Anyone who chooses to be the world's friend is thereby making himself God's enemy. Or do you think what the scriptures have to say about this is a mere formality? Do you imagine that this spirit of passionate jealousy is the Spirit he has caused to live in us? Yet he gives us grace which is stronger. That is why he says:

God resisteth the proud,
But giveth grace to the humble.

You should be humble, not proud

Be humble then before God. But resist the devil and you'll find he'll run away from you. Come close to God and he will come close to you. You are sinners: get your hands clean again. Your loyalty is divided: get your hearts made true once more. You should be deeply sorry, you should be grieved, you should even be in tears. Your laughter will have to become mourning, your high spirits will have to become dejection. You must humble yourselves in the sight of the Lord before he will lift you up.

It is for God to judge, not for us

Never pull each other to pieces, my brothers. If you criticise your brother and judge your brother you have become in fact a critic and judge of the Law. Yet if you start to criticise the Law instead of obeying it you are setting yourself up as judge. There is only one judge, the One who gave the Law, to whom belongs absolute power of life and death. How can you then be your neighbour's judge?

It is still true that man proposes, but God disposes

Just a moment, now, you who say, "We are going to such-and-such a city today or tomorrow. We shall stay there a year doing business and make a profit"! How do you know what will happen tomorrow? What, after all, is your life? It is like a puff or smoke visible for a little while and then dissolving into thin air. Your remarks should be prefaced with, "If it is the Lord's will, we shall still be alive and will do so-and-so." As it is, you take a certain pride in planning with such confidence. That sort of pride is all wrong.

Well then, if a man knows what is right and fails to do it, his failure is a real sin.

CHAPTER 5

Riches are going to prove a liability, not an asset, to the selfish

AND now, you men of affluence, is the time for you to weep and wail because of the miseries in store for you! Your riches are ruined, your fine clothes are moth-eaten, your gold and silver are tarnished. Yes, their very tarnish will be evidence against you, and they will burn your flesh like fire. You have made a fine pile in these last days, haven't you? But look, here is the pay of the reaper you hired and whom you never paid, and it cries out against you! And the cries of the harvesters have reached the ears of the Lord of Hosts himself. Yes, you have had a magnificent time on this earth, and have indulged yourselves to the full. You have picked out just what you wanted like soldiers looting after battle. You have condemned and ruined innocent men, and they are powerless to stop you.

Ultimate justice will surely come: be patient meanwhile

But be patient, my brothers, as you wait for the Lord to come. Look at the farmer quietly awaiting the precious harvest of his land. See how he has to possess his soul in patience till the early and late rains have fallen. So must you be patient, resting your hearts on the ultimate certainty. The Lord's coming is very near.

Don't make complaints against each other in the meantime, my brothers—you may be the one at fault yourself. The judge himself is already at the door.

For our example of the patient endurance of suffering we can take the prophets who have spoken in the Lord's name. Remember that it is those who have patiently endured to whom we accord the word "blessed". You have heard of Job's patient endurance and how the Lord dealt with him in the end, and therefore you have seen that the Lord is merciful and full of understanding pity.

Don't emphasise with oaths: speak the plain truth

It is of the highest importance, my brothers, that your speech should be free from oaths (whether they are "by" heaven or earth or anything else). Your yes should be a plain yes, and your no a plain no, and then you cannot go wrong in the matter.

Prayer is a great weapon

If any of you is in trouble let him pray. If anyone is flourishing let him sing praises to God. If anyone is ill he should send for the church elders. They should pray over him, anointing him with oil in the Lord's name. Believing prayer will save the sick man; the Lord will restore him and any sins that he has committed will be forgiven. You should get into the habit of admitting your sins to each other, and praying for each other, so that you may be healed.

Tremendous power is made available through a good man's earnest prayer. Do you remember Elijah? He was a man as human as we are but he prayed earnestly that it should not rain. In fact, not a drop fell on the land for three and a half years. Then he prayed again, the heavens gave the rain and the earth sprouted with vegetation again.

A concluding hint

My brothers, if any of you should wander away from the truth and another should turn him back on to the right path, then the latter may be sure that in turning a man back from his wandering course he has rescued a soul from death, and in so doing will "cover a multitude of sins".

The First Letter of Peter

AUTHOR. *Peter, one of the original Twelve, writing probably from Rome, symbolically described as "Babylon". It is thought that Silvanus, or Silas, did the actual writing of the letter.*

DATE. *Almost certainly* 64.

DESTINATION. *This letter, like that of James, is addressed to the Christian Jews scattered, by persecution or force of circumstance, to various parts of Asia Minor.*

THEME. *We are here largely concerned with the Christian's attitude towards undeserved suffering, possibly because persecution of Christians was becoming common. It also contains advice to Christian husbands and wives and direction for Christian servants and Christian citizens.*

The passage in 3, *18–21, about Christ preaching to "imprisoned spirits", is obscure, and many speculations have arisen from it.*

CHAPTER 1

PETER, a messenger of Jesus Christ, sends this letter to God's people now dispersed in Pontus, Galatia, Cappadocia, Asia and Bithynia, whom God the Father knew and chose long ago to be made holy by his Spirit, that they might obey Jesus Christ and be cleansed by his blood: may you know more and more of God's grace and peace.

THE FIRST LETTER OF PETER 1

Your faith is being tested, but your future is magnificent

Thank God, the God and Father of our Lord Jesus Christ, that in his great mercy we have been born again into a life full of hope, through Christ's rising again from the dead! You can now hope for a perfect inheritance beyond the reach of change and decay, reserved in Heaven for you. And in the meantime you are guarded by the power of God operating through your faith, till you enter fully into the salvation which is all ready to be revealed at the last. This means tremendous joy to you, even though at present you may be temporarily harassed by all kinds of trials. This is no accident—it happens to prove your faith, which is infinitely more valuable than gold, and gold, as you know, even though it is ultimately perishable, must be purified by fire. This proving of your faith is planned to result in praise and glory and honour in the day when Jesus Christ reveals himself. And though you have never seen him, yet you love him. At present you trust him without being able to see him, and even now he brings you a joy that words cannot express and which has in it a hint of the glories of Heaven; and all the time you are receiving the result of your faith in him—the salvation of your own souls. The prophets of old did their utmost to discover and obtain this salvation. They prophesied of this grace that has now come to you. They tried hard to discover to what time and to what sort of circumstances the Spirit of Christ working in them was referring. For he foretold the sufferings of Christ and the glories that should follow them. It was then made clear to them that they were dealing with matters not meant for themselves, but for you. It is these very matters which have been made plain to you by those who preached the gospel to you by the Holy Spirit sent from Heaven—and these are facts to command the interest of the very angels!

Consider soberly what God has done for you

So brace up your minds, and, as men who know what they are doing, rest the full weight of your hopes on the grace that will be yours when Jesus Christ reveals himself. Live as obedient children before God. Don't let your character be moulded by the desires of your ignorant days, but be holy in every part of your lives, for the one who has called you is himself holy. The scripture says:

Ye shall be holy; for I am holy

If you pray to a Father who judges men by their actions without the slightest favouritism, then you should spend the time of your stay here on earth with reverent fear. For you must realise that you have been ransomed from the futile way of living passed on to you by your traditions, but not by any money payment of this passing world. No, the price was in fact the life-blood of Christ, the unblemished and unstained lamb of sacrifice. It is true that he was destined for this purpose before the world was founded, but it was for your benefit that he was revealed in these last days—for you who found your faith in God through him. And God raised him from the dead and gave him heavenly splendour, so that all your faith and hope might be centred in God.

Let your life match your high calling

Now that you have, by obeying the truth, made your souls clean enough for a genuine love of your fellows, see that you do love each other, fervently and from the heart. For you are not just mortals now but sons of God; the live, permanent Word of the living God has given you his own indestructible heredity. It is true that:

All flesh is as grass,
And all the glory thereof as the flower of grass.
The grass withereth, and the flower falleth:
But the word of the Lord abideth for ever.

The Word referred to is the message of the gospel that was preached to you.

CHAPTER 2

HAVE done, then, with all evil and deceit, all pretence and jealousy and slander. You are babies, new-born in God's family, and you should be crying out for unadulterated spiritual milk to make you grow up to salvation! And so you will, if you have already tasted the goodness of the Lord.

You have come to the living Stone despised indeed by men but chosen and greatly honoured by God. So you yourselves, as living stones, must be built up into a spiritual House of God, in which you become a holy priesthood, able to offer those spiritual sacrifices which are acceptable to God by Jesus Christ. There is a passage to this effect in scripture, and it runs like this:

Behold I lay in Zion a chief corner stone, elect, precious:
And he that believeth on him shall not be put to shame.

It is to you who believe in him that he is "precious", but to those who disobey God, it is true that:

The stone which the builders rejected,
The same was made the head of the corner.

And he is, to them,

A stone of stumbling and a rock of offence.

Yes, they stumble at the Word of God for in their hearts they are unwilling to obey it—which makes stumbling a foregone conclusion. But you are God's "chosen generation", his "royal priesthood", his "holy nation", his "peculiar people"—all the old titles of God's people now belong to you. It is for you now to demonstrate the goodness of him who has called you out of darkness into his amazing light. In the past you were not "a people" at all: now you are the people of God. In the past you had no experience of his mercy, but now it is intimately yours.

Your behaviour to the outside world

I beg you, as those whom I love, to live in this world as strangers and "temporary residents", to keep clear of the desires of your lower natures, for they are always at war with your souls. Your conduct among the surrounding peoples in your different countries should always be good and right, so that although they may slander you as evil-doers yet when troubles come, they may glorify God when they see how well you conduct yourselves.

Obey every man-made authority for the Lord's sake—whether it is the emperor, as the supreme ruler, or the governors whom he has appointed to punish evil-doers and reward those who do good service. It is the will of God that you may thus silence the ill-informed criticisms of the foolish. As free men you should never use your freedom as a screen for doing wrong, but live as servants of God. You should have respect for everyone, you should love our brotherhood, fear God and honour the emperor.

A word to household servants

You who are servants should submit to your masters with

proper respect—not only to the good and kind, but also to the difficult. A man does a fine thing when he endures pain, with a clear conscience towards God, though he knows he is suffering unjustly. After all, it is no credit to you if you are patient in bearing a punishment which you have richly deserved! But if you do your duty and are punished for it and can still accept it patiently, you are doing something worthwhile in God's sight. Indeed this is your calling. For Christ suffered for you and left you a personal example, so that you might follow in his footsteps. He was guilty of no sin nor of the slightest prevarication. Yet when he was insulted he offered no insult in return. When he suffered he made no threats of revenge. He simply committed his cause to the One who judges fairly. And he personally bore our sins in his own body on the cross, so that we might be dead to sin and be alive to all that is good. It was the suffering that he bore which has healed you. You had wandered away like so many sheep, but now you have returned to the shepherd and guardian of your souls.

CHAPTER 3

A word to married Christians

In the same spirit you married women should adapt yourselves to your husbands, so that even if they do not obey the Word of God they may be won to God without any word being spoken, simply by seeing the pure and reverent conduct of you, their wives. Your beauty should not be dependent on an elaborate coiffure, or on the wearing of jewellery or fine clothes, but on the inner personality—the unfading loveliness of a calm and gentle spirit, a thing very precious in the eyes of God. This was the beauty of the holy women of ancient times who trusted in God and were submissive to their husbands. Sarah, you will remember, obeyed Abraham and called him her lord. And you have become her true descendants today as long as you too live good lives and do not give way to hysterical fears.

Similarly, you husbands should try to understand the wives you live with, honouring them as physically weaker yet equally heirs with you of the grace of life. If you don't do this, you will find it impossible to pray together properly.

Be good to each other—and to all men

To sum up, you should all be of one mind living like brothers with true love and sympathy for each other, compassionate and humble. Never pay back a bad turn with a bad turn or an insult with another insult, but on the contrary pay back with good. For this is your calling—to do good and to inherit the goodness of God. For:

He that would love life,
And see good days,
Let him refrain his tongue from evil,
And his lips that they speak no guile:
And let him turn away from evil, and do good;
Let him seek peace and pursue it.
For the eyes of the Lord are upon the righteous,
And his ears unto their supplication:
But the face of the Lord is against them that do evil.

Do good, even if you suffer for it

After all, who is likely to injure you for being devoted to what is good? And if it should happen that you suffer for living a good life you are fortunate. You need neither fear men's threats nor worry about them; simply concentrate on being completely devoted to Christ in your hearts. Be ready at any time to give a quiet and reverent answer to any man who wants a reason for the hope that you have within you. Make sure that your conscience is perfectly clear, so that if men should speak slanderously of you as rogues they may come to feel ashamed of themselves for abusing you for your good Christian behaviour.

If it is the will of God that you should suffer it is better to suffer for doing good than for doing wrong. Remember that Christ the just suffered for us the unjust, to bring us to God. That meant the death of his body, but he was brought to life again in the spirit. It was in the spirit that he went and preached to the imprisoned souls of those who had been disobedient in the days of Noah—the days of God's great patience during the period of the building of the ark, in which eventually only eight souls were saved from the water. That water was a kind of prophetic parable of the water of baptism which now saves you. Baptism does not merely mean the washing of a dirty body; it is the appeal of a clear conscience towards God—a thing made possible by the power of Christ's resurrection. For he has now entered Heaven and sits at God's right hand, with all angels, authorities and powers made subject to him.

CHAPTER 4

Following Christ will mean pain

SINCE Christ suffered physical pain you must arm yourselves with the same inner conviction that he had. To be free from sin means bodily suffering, and the man who accepts this will spend the rest of his time here on earth, not in being led by human desires, but in doing the will of God. Your past life may have been good enough for pagan purposes, though it meant sensuality, lust, drunkenness, orgies, carousals and worshipping forbidden gods. Indeed your former companions may think it very strange that you no longer join with them in their riotous excesses, and accordingly say all sorts of abusive things about you. They are the ones who will have to answer for their behaviour before the One who is prepared to judge all men, living or dead. That is why the dead also had the gospel preached to them. For although they must be condemned for the life they lived in the body of men, they might find life in the spirit by obeying God's will.

Your attitude in these last days

We are near the end of all things now, and you should therefore be calm, self-controlled men of prayer. Above everything else be sure that you have real deep love for each other, remembering how love can cover a multitude of sins. Be hospitable to each other without secretly wishing you hadn't got to be! Serve one another with the particular gifts God has given each of you, as faithful dispensers of the wonderfully varied grace of God. If any of you is a preacher then he should preach his message as from God. And in whatever way a man serves the Church he should do it recognising the fact that God gives him his ability, so that God may be glorified in everything through Jesus Christ. To him belong glory and power for ever, amen!

Your attitude to persecution

And now, dear friends of mine. I beg you not to be unduly alarmed at the fiery ordeals which come to test your faith, as though this were some abnormal experience. You should be glad, because it means that you are sharing in Christ's sufferings. One day, when he shows himself in full splendour, you will be filled with the most tremendous joy. If you are reproached for being Christ's followers, that is a cause for joy, for you can be sure that God's Spirit of glory is resting upon you. But take care that none of your number suffers as a murderer, or a thief, a rogue or a busy-body! If he suffers as a Christian he has nothing to be ashamed of and may glorify God by confessing Christ's name.

The time has evidently arrived for God's judgment to begin, and it is beginning at his own household. And if it starts with us, what is it going to mean to those who refuse to obey the gospel of God? If even the good man is only just saved, what will be the fate of the wicked and the sinner? Therefore those who suffer according to God's will can safely commit their souls to their faithful Creator, and go on doing all the good they can.

CHAPTER 5

A word to your leaders

Now may I who am myself an elder say a word to you my fellow-elders? I speak as one who actually saw Christ suffer, and as one who will share with you the glories that are to be unfolded. Shepherd your flock of God, looking after them not because you feel compelled to, but willingly, as God would wish. Never do this work thinking of your personal gain but with true compassion. You should aim not at being dictators but examples of Christian living in the eyes of the flock committed to your charge. And then, when the Chief Shepherd reveals himself, you will receive that crown of glory which cannot fade.

Learn to be humble and to trust

You younger members must also accept the authority of the elders. Indeed all of you should defer to one another and wear the "overall" of humility in serving each other. God is always against the proud, but he is always ready to give grace to the humble. So, humble yourselves under God's strong hand, and in his own good time he will lift you up. You can throw the whole weight of your anxieties upon him, for you are his personal concern.

Resist the devil: you are in God's hands

Be self-controlled and vigilant always, for your enemy the devil is always about, prowling like a lion roaring for its prey. Resist him, standing firm in your faith, remembering that the strain is the same for all your fellow-Christians in other parts of the world. And after you have borne these sufferings a very little while, the God of all grace, who has called you to share his eternal splendour through Christ, will himself make you whole and secure and strong. All power is his for ever and ever, amen!

Final greetings

I am sending this short letter by Silvanus, whom I know to be a faithful brother, to stimulate your faith and assure you that the above words represent the true grace of God. See that you stand fast in that grace!

Your sister-church here in "Babylon" sends you greetings, and so does my son Mark. Give each other a handshake all round as a sign of love.

Peace be to all true Christians.

The Second Letter of Peter

AUTHOR. *The authenticity of this letter was sharply disputed by the early Church, and it is still viewed with suspicion by many. This is partly because one section appears to be copied from the letter of Jude, partly because the general character is different from the first letter of Peter, and partly because competent scholars consider there are references in it to events which happened after Peter's death in approximately* 64. *It is, of course, possible that we have here parts of a genuine letter of Peter with considerable later additions.*

DATE. *About* 130? (*very uncertain*).

DESTINATION. *A particular, but unknown, church.*

THEME. *The letter stresses the observed facts upon which the Christian faith rests. It contains a stern warning and violent attack against false teachers, and a reminder that Christ will certainly return in person, even though his coming appears to men to be long delayed.*

CHAPTER 1

SIMON PETER, a servant and messenger of Jesus Christ, sends this letter to those who have been given a faith as valuable as ours in the righteousness of our God, and saviour Jesus Christ. May you know more and more of grace and peace as your knowledge of God and Jesus our Lord grows deeper.

God has done his part: see that you do yours

He has by his own action given us everything that is necessary for living the truly good life, in allowing us to know the one who has called us to him, through his own glorious goodness. It is through this generosity that God's greatest and most precious promises have become available to us men, making it possible for you to escape the inevitable disintegration that lust produces in the world and to share in God's essential nature. For this very reason you must do your utmost from your side, and see that your faith carries with it real goodness of life. Your goodness must be accompanied by knowledge, your knowledge by self-control, your self-control by the ability to endure. Your endurance too must always be accompanied by devotion to God; that in turn must have in it the quality of brotherliness, and your brotherliness must lead on to Christian love. If you have these qualities existing and growing in you then it means that knowing our Lord Jesus Christ has not made your lives either complacent or unproductive. The man whose life fails to exhibit these qualities is blind—his eyes so closed that he has forgotten that he was cleansed from his former sins.

Set your minds, then, on endorsing by your conduct the fact that God has called and chosen you. If you go along these lines there is no reason why you should stumble. Indeed if you live this sort of life a rich welcome awaits you as you enter the eternal kingdom of our Lord and saviour Jesus Christ.

Truth will bear repetition

Therefore I shall not fail to remind you again and again of things like this although you know them and are already established in the truth which has come to you. I consider it my duty, as long as I live in the temporary dwelling of this body, to stimulate you by these reminders. I know that I shall have to leave this body at very short notice, as our Lord Jesus Christ made clear to me. Consequently I shall make the most of every opportunity, so that after I am gone you will remember these things.

We were not following a cleverly written-up story when we told you about the power and presence of our Lord Jesus Christ—we actually saw his majesty with our own eyes. He received honour and glory from God the Father himself when that voice said to him, out of the sublime glory of Heaven, "This is my beloved Son, in whom I am well pleased." We actually heard that voice speaking from Heaven while we were with him on the sacred mountain. Thus we hold the word of prophecy to be more certain than ever. You should give that word your closest attention, for it shines like a lamp amidst the darkness of the world, until the day dawns, and the morning star rises in your hearts.

False prophets will flourish, but only for a time

But you must understand that this is of the highest importance: no prophecy of scripture can be interpreted by a single human mind. No prophecy came because a man wanted it to: men of God spoke because they were inspired by the Holy Spirit.

CHAPTER 2

But even in those days there were false prophets among the people, just as there will be false teachers among you today. They will be men who will subtly introduce dangerous heresies. They will thereby deny the Lord who redeemed them, and it will not be long before they bring on themselves their own downfall. Many will follow their flagrant immorality and thereby bring discredit on the way of truth. In their lust to make converts these men will try to exploit you too with their bogus arguments. But judgment has been for some time hard on their heels and their downfall is inevitable. For if God did not spare angels who sinned against him, but banished them to the dark imprisonment of hell till judgment day; if he did not spare the ancient world but only saved Noah, the solitary voice that cried out for righteousness, and his seven companions when he brought the flood upon the world in its wickedness; and if God reduced the entire cities of Sodom and Gomorrah to ashes, when he sentenced them to destruction as a fearful example to those who wanted to live in defiance of his laws, and yet saved Lot the righteous man, in acute mental distress at the filthy lives of the godless—Lot, remember, was a good man suffering spiritual agonies day after day at what he saw and heard of their lawlessness—then you may be absolutely certain that the Lord knows how to rescue good men surrounded by temptation, and how to reserve his punishment for the wicked until their day comes.

Let me show you what these men are really like

His judgment is chiefly reserved for those who have indulged all the foulness of their lower natures, and have nothing but contempt for authority. These men are arrogant and presumptuous—they think nothing of scoffing at the glories of the unseen world. Yet even angels, who are their superiors in strength and power, do not bring insulting criticisms of such things before the Lord.

But these men, with no more sense than the unreasoning brute beasts which are born to be caught and killed, scoff at things outside their own experience, and will most certainly be destroyed in their own corruption. Their wickedness has earned them an evil end and they will be paid in full.

These are the men who delight in daylight self-indulgence; they are foul spots and blots, playing their tricks at your very dinner-tables. Their eyes cannot look at a woman without lust, and they miss no opportunity for sin. They captivate the unstable ones, and their technique of getting what they want is, through long practice, highly developed. They are born under a curse, for they have abandoned the right road and wandered off to follow the old trail of Balaam, son of Beor, the man who had no objection to wickedness as long as he was paid for it. But he, you remember, was sharply reprimanded for his wickedness—by a donkey, of all things, speaking with a human voice to check the prophet's wicked infatuation!

These men are like wells without a drop of water in them, like the changing shapes of whirling storm-clouds, and their fate will be the black night of utter darkness. With their high-sounding nonsense they use the sensual pull of the lower passions to attract those who were just on the point of cutting loose from their companions in evil. They promise them liberty. Liberty!—when they themselves are bound hand and foot to utter depravity. For a man is the slave of whatever masters him. If men have escaped from the world's contaminations through knowing our Lord and saviour Jesus Christ, and then become entangled and defeated by them all over again, their last position is worse than their first. For it would be better for them not to have known the way of goodness at all, than after knowing it to turn their backs on the sacred commandments given to them. For them, the old proverbs have come true about the "dog returning to his vomit", and "the sow that had been washed going back to wallow in the muck".

CHAPTER 3

God delays the last day, in his mercy

THIS is the second letter I have written to you, dear friends of mine, and in both of them I have tried to stimulate you, as men with minds uncontaminated by error, by reminding you of what you really know already. This means recalling the words spoken of old by the holy prophets as well as the commands of our Lord and saviour given to you through his messengers.

First of all you must realise that in the last days cynical mockers will undoubtedly come—men whose only guide in life is what they want for themselves—and they will say, "Where is his promised coming? Since our fathers fell asleep, everything remains exactly as it was since the beginning of creation!" They are deliberately shutting their eyes to the fact that there were heavens in the old days and an earth formed by God's command out of water and by water. It was by water that the world of those days was deluged and destroyed, but the present heavens and earth are, also by God's command, being carefully kept and maintained for the fire of the day of judgment and the destruction of wicked men.

But you should never lose sight of this fact, dear friends, that with the Lord a day may be a thousand years, and a thousand years only a day. It is not that he is dilatory about keeping his own promise as some men seem to think; the fact is that he is very patient with you. He has no wish that any man should be destroyed; he wishes that all men should find the way to repentance. Yet the day of the Lord will come as unexpectedly as a thief. In that day the heavens will vanish in a tearing blast, the very elements will disintegrate in heat and the earth and all its works will disappear.

Never lose sight of the eternal world

In view of the fact that all these things are to be dissolved, what sort of people ought you to be? Surely men of good and holy character, who live expecting and working for the coming of the day of God. This day will mean that the heavens will disintegrate in fire and the burning elements will melt, but our hopes are set on new heavens and a new earth which he has promised us, in which justice will make its home.

Because, my dear friends, you have a hope like this before you, I urge you to make certain that the day will find you at peace with God, flawless and blameless in his sight. Meanwhile, consider that our Lord's patience for man's salvation, as our dear brother Paul pointed out in his letter to you, written out of the wisdom God gave him. This is how he writes in all his letters when he refers to these things. There are some points in his letters which are difficult to understand, and which ill-informed and unbalanced people distort (as they do the other scriptures), and bring disaster on their own heads.

But you, my friends whom I love, are forewarned, and should therefore be very careful not to be carried away by the errors of unprincipled men and so lose your proper foothold. On the contrary, you should grow in grace and in knowledge of our Lord and saviour Jesus Christ—to him be glory now and until the day of eternity!

The First Letter of John

AUTHOR. *John, one of the original Twelve, or John the Elder, a close companion of his. It is believed that he wrote it from Ephesus, when a very old man.*

DATE. *Uncertain, possibly about* 90.

DESTINATION. *Augustine refers to this letter as "The Epistle of John to the Parthians", but there is no other evidence of a church in what would now be called Persia or Iran. Many scholars think that this letter is addressed to the local churches round about Ephesus.*

THEME. *This letter emphasises the fact that Christ really did become man, and did not merely "appear" to be human as the heresy of "docetism" maintained. It speaks in the strongest possible language of men being able to live "in" God, and of the fact of God being "in" those who believe in him. God is light and love and life.*

CHAPTER 1

WE are writing to you about something which has always existed yet which we ourselves actually heard and saw with our own eyes: something which we had opportunity to observe closely and even to hold in our hands, something of the Word of life! For it was *life* which appeared before us: we saw it, we are eye-witnesses of it, and are now writing to you about it. It was the very life of all ages, the life that has always existed with the Father, which actually became visible in person to us. We repeat, we really saw and heard what we are now writing to you about. We want you to be with us in this—in this fellowship with the Father, and Jesus Christ his Son. We write and tell you about it, so that our joy may be complete.

Experience of living "in the light"

Here, then, is the message which we heard from him, and now proclaim to you: GOD IS LIGHT and no shadow of darkness can exist in him. Consequently, if we were to say that we enjoyed fellowship with him and still went on living in darkness, we should be both telling and living a lie. But if we really are living in the same light in which he eternally exists, then we have true fellowship with each other, and the blood which his son Jesus shed for us keeps us clean from all sin. If we refuse to admit that we are sinners, then we live in a world of illusion and truth becomes a stranger to us. But if we freely admit that we have sinned, we find him reliable and just—he forgives our sins and makes us thoroughly clean from all that is evil. For if we say "we have not sinned", we are making him a liar and cut outselves off from what he has to say to us.

CHAPTER 2

Love and obedience are essentials for living in the light

I WRITE these things to you, my children, to help you to avoid sin. But if a man should sin, remember that our advocate before the Father is Jesus Christ and he is just, the one who made personal atonement for our sins (and for those of the rest of the world as well). It is only when we obey God's laws that we can be quite sure that we really know him. The man who claims to know God but does not obey his laws is not only a liar but lives in self-delusion. But the more a man obeys God's laws the more truly and fully does he show his love for him. Obedience is the test of whether we really live "in God" or not. The life of a man who professes to be living in him must live as Christ lived.

I am not writing to tell you of any new command, brothers of mine. It is the old command which you had at the beginning; it is the old message which you have heard before. And yet as I write it to you again I know that it is true—in your life as it was in his. For the darkness is beginning to lift and the true light is already shining. Anyone who claims to be "in the light" and hates his brother is, in fact, still in complete darkness. The man who loves his brother lives in the light, and has no reason to stumble. But the man who hates his brother is shut off from the light and gropes his way in the dark without knowing where he is going. For the darkness has made him blind.

As I write I visualise you, my children

I write this letter to you all, as my dear children, because your sins are forgiven for his name's sake. I write to you, fathers, because you have known him who has always existed. And to you young men I am writing because you have defeated the evil one. I have written to you, dear children, because you have known the Father; to you fathers because you have known the one who has always existed, and to you young men because you have all the vigour of youth, because God's truth is at home in you and because you have defeated the evil one.

See "the world" for what it is

Never give your hearts to this world or to any of the things in it. A man cannot love the Father and love the world at the same time. For the whole world-system, based as it is on men's desires, their greedy ambitions and the glamour of all that they think splendid, is not derived from the Father at all, but from the world itself. The world and all its passionate desires will one day disappear. But the man who is following God's will is part of the permanent and cannot die.

Little anti-christs are abroad already

Even now, dear children, we are getting near the last hour. You have heard about the coming of anti-Christ. Believe me, there are anti-christs about already, which confirms my belief that we are near the last hour. These men went out from our company, it is true, but they never really belonged to it. If they had really belonged to us they would have stayed. In fact, their going proves beyond doubt that men like that were not "our men" at all.

Be on your guard against error

God has given you all a certain amount of spiritual insight, and indeed I have not written this warning as if I were writing to men who don't know what error is. I write because your eyes are clear enough to discern a lie when you come across it. And who, I ask you, is the real liar? Surely the one who denies that Jesus is the Christ. I say, therefore, that any man who refuses to acknowledge the Father and the Son is the anti-christ. The man who will not recognise the Son cannot possibly know the Father; yet the man who believes in the Son knows the Father as well.

For yourselves keep faithful to what you heard at the beginning. If you do, you will be living in fellowship with both the Father and the Son. And that means sharing his own life for ever, as he has promised.

I had to write to you about these men who try to lead you astray. Yet I know that the touch of his Spirit never leaves you, and you don't really need a human teacher. You know that his Spirit teaches you about all things, always telling you the truth and never telling you a lie. So, as he has taught you, live continually in him. Yes, now, little children remember to live continually in him. So that if he were to reveal himself we should have confidence, and not have to shrink away from his presence in shame.

What it means to be sons of God

You all know that God is really good. You may be just as sure that the man who leads a really good life is a true child of God.

CHAPTER 3

CONSIDER the incredible love that the Father has shown us in allowing us to be called "children of God"—and that is not just what we are called, but what we *are*. This explains why the world will no more recognise us than it recognised Christ.

Here and now, my dear friends, we *are* God's children. We don't know what we shall become in the future. We only know that when he appears we shall be like him, for we shall see him as he is!

Everyone who has at heart a hope like that keeps himself pure, as Christ is pure.

Conduct will show who is a man's spiritual father

Everyone who commits sin breaks God's law, for that is what sin is—a breaking of God's law. You know, moreover, that Christ became man to take away sin, and that he himself was free from sin. The man who lives "in Christ" does not habitually sin. The regular sinner has never seen or known him. You, my children, should not let anyone deceive you. The man who lives a good life is a good man, as surely as Christ is good. But the man whose life is habitually sinful is spiritually a son of the devil, for the devil has been a sinner from the beginning. Now the Son of God came to earth with the express purpose of undoing the devil's work. The man who is really God's son does not practise sin, for God's nature is in him, for good, and such a heredity is incapable of sin.

Here we have a clear indication as to who are the children of God and who are the children of the devil. The man who does not lead a good life is no son of God, nor is the man who fails to love his brother. For the original command, as you know, is that we should love one another. We are none of us to have the spirit of Cain, who was a son of the evil one and murdered his brother. Have you realised his motive? It was because he realised the goodness of his brother's life and the evil of his own. Don't be surprised, my brothers, if the world hates you.

Love and life are inter-connected

We know that we have crossed the frontier from death to life because we do love our brothers. The man without love for his brother is still living in death. The man who hates his brother is at heart a murderer, and you know that the eternal life of God cannot live in the heart of a murderer.

We know what love is because Christ laid down his life for us. We must in turn lay down our lives for our brothers. But as for the well-to-do man who sees his brother in want but shuts his heart against him, how could anyone believe that the love of God lives in him? My children, let us love not merely in theory or in words—let us love in sincerity and in practice!

Living in love means confidence in God

This is how we shall know that we are children of the truth and can reassure ourselves in the sight of God, even if our own conscience makes us feel guilty. For God is greater than our conscience, and he knows everything. And if, dear friends of mine, our conscience no longer accuses us, we may have the utmost confidence in God's presence. We receive whatever we ask for, because we are obeying his orders and following his wishes. His orders are that we should put our trust in the name of his Son, Jesus Christ, and love one another—as he commanded us to do.

The man who does obey God's commands lives in God and God lives in him, and the guarantee of his presence within us is the Spirit he has given us.

CHAPTER 4

I repeat my warning against false teaching

DON'T trust every spirit, dear friends of mine, but test them to discover whether they come from God or not. For the world is full of false prophets. You can test whether they come from God in this simple way: every spirit that acknowledges the fact that Jesus Christ actually became man, comes from God, but the spirit which denies this fact does not come from God. The latter comes from the anti-Christ, which you were warned would come and which is already in the world.

You, my children, who belong to God have already defeated them, because the one who lives in you is stronger than the anti-Christ in the world. The agents of the anti-Christ are children of the world, they speak the world's language and the world pays attention to what they say. We are God's children and the man who knows God hears our message; what we say means nothing to the man who is not himself a child of God.

This gives us a ready means of distinguishing the spirit of truth from the spirit of falsehood.

Let us love: God has shown us love at its highest

To you whom I love I say, let us go on loving one another, for love comes from God. Every man who truly loves is God's son and knows him. But the man who does not love cannot know him at all, for God is love.

To us, the greatest demonstration of God's love for us has been his sending his only Son into the world to give us life through him. We see real love, not in the fact that we loved God, but that he loved us and sent his Son to make personal atonement for our sins. If God loved us as much as that, surely we, in our turn, should love each other!

It is true that no human being has ever had a direct vision of God. Yet if we love each other God does actually live within us, and his love grows in us towards perfection. And the guarantee of our living in him and his living in us is the share of his own Spirit which he gives us.

Knowing Christ means more love and confidence, less and less fear

We ourselves are eye-witnesses able and willing to testify to the fact that the Father did send the Son to save the world. Everyone who acknowledges that Jesus is the Son of God finds that God lives in him, and he lives in God. So have we come to know and trust the love God has for us. God *is* love, and the man whose life is lived in love does, in fact, live in God, and God does, in fact, live in him. So our love for him grows more and more, filling us with complete confidence for the day when he shall judge all men—for we realise that our life in this world is actually his life lived in us. Love contains no fear—indeed fully-developed love expels every particle of fear, for fear always contains some of the torture of feeling guilty. The man who lives in fear has not yet had his love perfected.

Yes, we love because he first loved us. If a man says, "I love God" and hates his brother, he is a liar. For if he does not love the brother before his eyes how can he love the one beyond his sight? And in any case it is his explicit command that the one who loves God must love his brother too.

CHAPTER 5

Only real faith in Christ as God's son can make a man confident, obedient and loving

EVERYONE who really believes that Jesus is the Christ is himself one of God's family. The man who loves the Father cannot help loving the Father's sons.

The test of our love for God's family lies in this question—do we love God himself and do we obey his commands? For loving God means obeying his commands, and these commands of his are not burdensome. In fact, this faith of ours is the only way in which the world can be conquered. For who could ever be said to conquer the world but the man who really believes that Jesus is God's Son? Jesus Christ himself is the one who came by water and by blood—not by the water only, but by the water and the blood. The Spirit bears witness to this, for the Spirit is the truth. The witness therefore is a triple one—the Spirit, the water of baptism and the blood of atonement—and they all say the same thing. If we accept human testimony, God's own testimony concerning his own Son carries far more weight. The man who really believes in the Son of God will find God's testimony in his own heart. The man who will not believe God is making him out to be a liar, because he is refusing to accept the testimony that God has given concerning his own Son. This is, that God has given men eternal life and this real life is to be found only in his Son. It follows naturally that any man who has Christ has this life; and if he has not, then he does not possess this life at all.

I have written like this to you who already believe in the name of God's Son so that you may be quite sure that, here and now, you possess eternal life. We have such confidence in him that we are certain that he hears every request that is made in accord with his own plan. And since we know that he invariably gives his attention to our prayers, whatever they are, we can be quite sure that what we have asked for is already ours.

Help each other to live without sin

If any of you should see his brother committing a sin—not a deadly sin—he should pray and God will give him life, provided the sin was not a deadly sin. I am not saying that you should pray about that; every act of wrong-doing is a sin, but not all sin is deadly.

Our certain knowledge

We know that the true child of God does not sin, he is in the charge of God's own Son and the evil one cannot touch him.

We know that we ourselves are children of God, and we also know that the world around us is under the power of the evil one. We know too that the Son of God has come, and has given us understanding to know the One who is true. We know that our life is in the true One—in his Son Jesus Christ. This is the real God and this is eternal life.

But be on your guard, my dear children, against every false god!

The Second Letter of John

AUTHOR. *Although the author calls himself simply "the Elder" there is no real reason to suppose that he is not the same person as the author of the first letter. An old "retired apostle" might in his humility call himself by such a title.*

DATE. *Uncertain, possibly* 90.

DESTINATION. *Either a Christian lady and her family, or a church and its members. Nobody knows which.*

THEME. *This brief letter expresses the writer's joy at the true faith exhibited by some members of the family he has met. He urges them to continue in Christian love and to set their faces sternly against teachers of a false Christianity.*

THIS letter comes from the Elder to a lady chosen by God and her children, held in the highest affection not only by me but by all who know the truth. For that truth's sake (which even now we know and which will be our companion for ever) I wish you, in all love and sincerity, grace, mercy and peace from God the Father and the Lord Jesus Christ, the Father's Son.

Let us love, but have no dealings with lies

I was overjoyed to find some of your children living the life of truth, as the Father himself instructed us. I beg you now, dear lady, not as though I were issuing any new order but simply reminding you of the original one, to see that we continue to love one another. Real love means obeying the Father's orders, and you have known from the beginning that you must live in obedience to him. For the world is becoming full of impostors—men who will not admit that Jesus the Christ really became man. Now this is the very spirit of deceit and is anti-Christ. Take care of yourselves; don't throw away all the labour that has been spent on you, but persevere till you receive your full reward.

Have nothing to do with false teachers

The man who is so "advanced" that he is not content with what

Christ taught, has in fact no God. The man who bases his life on Christ's teaching, however, has both the Father and the Son. If any teacher comes to you who is disloyal to what Christ taught, don't have him inside your house; don't even greet him. For to greet such a man is to share in the evil that he is doing.

Personal

I have a lot that I could write to you, but I find it hard to put down on paper. I hope to come and see you personally, and we will have a heart-to-heart talk together—and how we shall enjoy that! The children of your sister, chosen by God, send their love.

The Third Letter of John

AUTHOR. *The same author as the Second Letter of John.*
DATE. *Uncertain, possibly about* 90.
DESTINATION. *The letter is addressed personally to Gaius, possibly the leader of a small church in Asia Minor. Gaius was such a common name that it is impossible to say whether the reference is to any of those of that name mentioned elsewhere in the New Testament.*
THEME. *The letter deals with the Christian duty and privilege of entertaining those who are busy carrying the Gospel from place to place. It roundly condemns the conceited behaviour of Diotrephes and commends the excellent character of Demetrius.*

THE elder sends this letter to my very dear friend Gaius whom I love sincerely.

I thank God for you and pray for you

My prayer for you, my very dear friend, is that you may be as healthy and prosperous in every way as you are in soul. I was delighted when the brothers arrived and spoke so highly of the sincerity of your life—obviously you are living in the truth. Nothing brings me greater joy than hearing that my children are living in the truth.

Your actions have been just right

You are doing a fine faithful piece of work, dear friend, in looking after the brothers who come your way, especially when you have never seen them before. They have testified to your love before the church here. It is a fine thing to help them on their way—you realise the importance of what they are doing for God. They set out on this work for the sake of "the name" and they accept no help from non-Christians. We ought to give such men every support and prove that we too are co-operating with the truth.

I know about Diotrephes

I did write a letter to the church, but Diotrephes, who wants to be head of everything, does not recognise us! If I do come to you, I shall not forget his actions nor the slanderous things he has said in spite against us. And it doesn't stop there, for he refuses to welcome the brothers himself, and stops those who would like to do so—he even excommunicates them!

A little piece of advice: and I shall soon be seeing you personally

Never let evil be your example, dear friend of mine, but good. The man who does good is God's man, but the man who does evil has never seen God.

Everyone has a good word to say for Demetrius, and the very truth speaks well of him. He has our warm recommendation also, and you know you can trust what we say about anyone.

There is a great deal I want to say to you but I can't put it down in black and white. I hope to see you before long, and we will have a heart-to-heart talk. Peace be with you. All our friends here send love: please give ours personally to all our friends.

The Letter of Jude

AUTHOR. *It may still reasonably be held that this letter was written by Jude (Judas), the brother or step-brother of Jesus. Like his brother James, he did not believe in the divinity of Jesus until after the Resurrection.*

DATE. *Between* 70 *and* 80, *or, if not written by Jude, possibly as late as 2nd century.*

DESTINATION. *Some unknown church, where false teaching was prevalent, or possibly for general circulation.*

THEME. *This letter is almost entirely a terrific condemnation of false teachers, with scathing comparisons with evil characters in the Old Testament. It concludes with an exhortation to loyalty to the truth, and with the well-known "doxology".*

JUDE, a servant of Jesus Christ and brother of James, to those who have obeyed the call, who are loved by God the Father and kept in the faith by Jesus Christ—may you ever experience more and more of mercy, peace and love!

The reason for this letter

While I was fully engaged, dear friends, in writing to you about our common salvation, I felt compelled to make my letter to you an earnest appeal to put up a real fight for the faith which has been once and for all handed on to those who are committed to God. For there are men who have surreptitiously entered the Church but who have long ago been marked out for condemnation. They have no reverence for God, and they abuse his grace as an opportunity for immorality. They will not recognise the only master, Jesus Christ our Lord.

Past history warns us that the unfaithful have mingled with the faithful

I want to remind you of something that you really know already: that although the Lord saved all the people from the land of

Egypt, yet afterwards he brought to their downfall those who would not trust him. And the very angels who failed in their high duties and abandoned their proper sphere have been deprived by God of both light and liberty until the judgment of the great day. Sodom and Gomorrah and the adjacent cities who, in the same way as these men today, gave themselves up to sexual immorality and perversion, stand in their punishment as a permanent warning of the fire of judgment. Yet these men are defiling their bodies by their filthy fantasies in just the same way; they show utter contempt for authority and make a jest of the heavenly glories. But I would remind you that even the archangel Michael when he was contending with the devil in the dispute over the body of Moses did not dare to condemn him with mockery. He simply said, the Lord rebuke you!

These fellows, however, are ready to mock at anything that is beyond their knowledge, while in the things that they know by instinct like unreasoning beasts they are utterly depraved. I say, Woe to them! For they have taken the road of Cain; for what they could get they have rushed into the same error as Balaam; they have destroyed themselves by rebelling against God as did Korah long ago.

Be on your guard against these wicked men

These men are blots on the good-fellowship of your feasts, for they eat in your company without reverence, looking after no one but themselves. They are like clouds driven up by the wind, but they bring no rain. They are like trees in autumn without a single fruit—doubly dead for they have been pulled up by the roots. They are like raging waves of the sea producing only the spume of their own shameful deeds. They are like stars which follow no orbit, and their proper place is the everlasting blackness of the regions beyond the light. It was of these men that Enoch (seventh descendant from Adam) prophesied when he said:

> Behold, the Lord came with ten thousands of his holy ones, to execute judgment upon all, and to convict all the ungodly of all their works of ungodliness which they have ungodly wrought, and of all the hard things which ungodly sinners have spoken against him.

These are the men who complain and curse their fate while trying all the time to mould life according to their own desires. They "talk big" but will pay men great respect if it is to their own advantage.

Forewarned is forearmed

Now do remember, dear friends, the words that the messengers of Jesus Christ gave us beforehand when they said "there will come in the last days mockers who live according to their own godless desires". These are the men who split communities, for they are led by human emotions and never by the Spirit of God.

Look after your own faith: save whom you can

But you, dear friends of mine, build yourselves up on the foundation of your most holy faith and by praying through the Holy Spirit keep yourselves within the love of God. Wait patiently for the mercy of our Lord Jesus Christ which will bring you to the life eternal. There are some whom you must pity because of their doubts; some you must save by snatching them out of the fire. But there are others for whom your pity must be mixed with caution, hating the very clothes which their deeds have soiled.

Ascription

Now to him who is able to keep you from falling and to present you before his glory without fault and with unspeakable joy, to the only God, our saviour, be glory and majesty, power and authority, through Jesus Christ our Lord, before time was, now, and in all ages to come, amen.

THE YOUNG CHURCHES
DALMATIA
MACEDONIA
ROME
A.D.57
THESSALONICA
A.D. 50-51
PHILIPPI
A.D.62
Troas
Nicopolis
CORINTH A.D.56,57
ACHAIA
Cenchrea
CRETE
(To Titus)
A.D.66

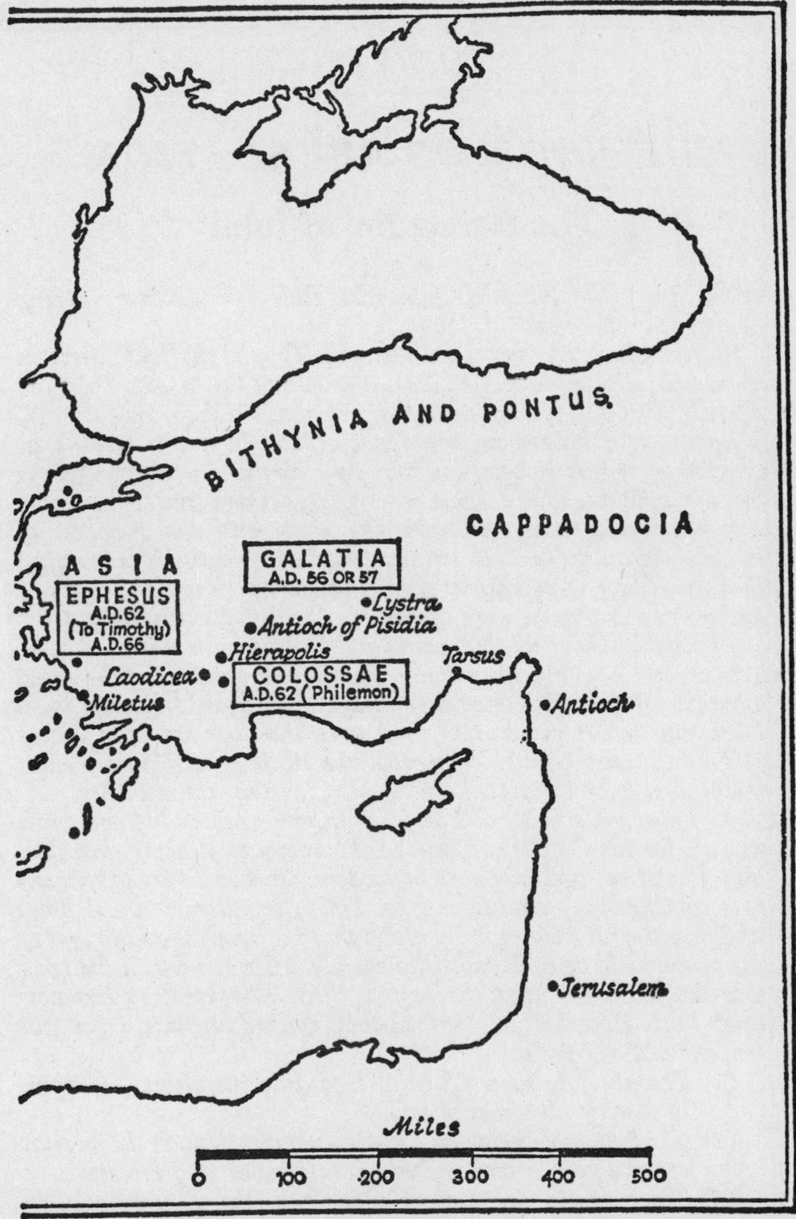
BITHYNIA AND PONTUS
CAPPADOCIA
ASIA
EPHESUS
A.D. 62
(To Timothy)
A.D. 66
GALATIA
A.D. 56 OR 57
Lystra
Antioch of Pisidia
Hierapolis
Laodicea
COLOSSAE
A.D. 62 (Philemon)
Miletus
Tarsus
Antioch
Jerusalem
Miles
0
100
200
300
400
500

THE BOOK OF REVELATION

The Revelation of John

AUTHOR. *John the Apostle, John the Elder or another leading Christian by the name of John.*

(Justin Martyr in his "Dialogue with Trypho the Jew", written about 140, *appears to ascribe the authorship of this book to John the Apostle. But Dionysius, Bishop of Alexandria from* 249 *to* 265, *a learned and holy man, could not accept John the Apostle as the author of this Revelation, and gave almost conclusive reasons for his opinion. Since those early days there has been much argument, and much research has gone into the problem of establishing authorship but without conclusive result. It is essential that the reader should study a good commentary on the subject of authorship, so that he may appreciate the difficulties involved.)*

DATE. *Probably about* 95, *but some hold to an earlier date.*

DESTINATION. *This book is plainly intended primarily for the seven Churches of Asia. But since the message of the book is relevant to all Christians under persecution, and since the book treats of divine judgments upon the whole world, the author must surely have intended it to be circulated among all Christian communities.*

THEME. *This book consists of a series of visions granted to John while in exile for his Christian witness. The language is highly symbolic and figurative, and attempts in modern days to fit its prophecies into contemporary situations have led interpreters into all kinds of difficulties. It is thought by many that the symbols and figures of the book would be understood by the Christians to whom the book was first sent, but that the key to their interpretation has now been lost. However, certain themes emerge distinctly for the modern reader's profit:*

(1) *The absolute sovereignty of God, and his ultimate purpose to destroy all forms of evil.*

(2) *The inevitable judgments of God upon evil, upon the worship of false gods, which include riches, power and success.*

(3) *The necessity for patient endurance, the ultimate security being the knowledge that God is in control of history.*

(4) *The existence of reality, represented here under such symbols as the New Jerusalem, apart and secure from the battles and tribulations of earthly life, promises complete spiritual security to those who are faithful to God and his Christ.*

(5) *The glimpses of worship and adoration, constantly offered to God and the Lamb, are a kind of pattern of man's ultimate acknowledgment of the character of God when he sees him as he is.*

But for any proper appreciation of the themes of this mysterious book it is imperative that the reader should make use of one or more commentaries.

CHAPTER 1

Concerning this book

THIS is a Revelation from Jesus Christ, which God gave him so that he might show his servants what must very soon take place. He made it known by sending his angel to his servant John, who is the witness of all that he saw—the message of God, and the testimony of Jesus Christ.

Happy is the man who reads this prophecy and happy are those who hear it read and pay attention to its message; for the time is near.

John's greeting and ascription

John, to the seven Churches in Asia:

Grace and peace be to you from him who is and who was and who is coming, from the seven Spirits before his throne, and from Jesus Christ the faithful witness, first-born of the dead, and ruler of kings upon earth. To him who loves us and has set us free from our sins through his own blood, who has made us a kingdom of priests to his God and Father, to him be glory and power for timeless ages, amen!

See, he is coming in the clouds and every eye shall see him, even those who pierced him, and his coming will mean bitter sorrow to every tribe upon the earth. So let it be!

"I am Alpha and Omega," says the Lord God, "who is and who was and who is coming, the Almighty."

The message to the seven Churches

I, John, who am your brother and your companion in distress, and in the kingdom and faithful endurance to which Jesus calls us, was on the island called Patmos because I had spoken God's message and borne witness to Jesus. On the Lord's day I knew myself inspired by the Spirit, and I heard from behind me a voice loud as a trumpet-call, saying,

"Write down in a book what you see, and send it to the seven Churches—to Ephesus, Smyrna, Pergamum, Thyatira, Sardis, Philadelphia and Laodicea!"

I turned to see whose voice it was that was speaking to me and when I had turned I saw seven golden lampstands, and among these lampstands I saw someone like a Son of Man. He was dressed in a long robe with a golden girdle around his breast; his head and his hair were white as snow-white wool, his eyes blazed like fire, and his feet shone as the finest bronze glows in the furnace. His voice had the sound of a great waterfall, and I saw that in his right hand he held seven stars. A sharp two-edged sword came out of his mouth, and his face was ablaze like the sun at its height.

When my eyes took in this sight I fell at his feet like a dead man. And then he placed his right hand upon me and said,

"Do not be afraid. I am the first and the last, the living one. I am he who was dead, and now you see me alive for timeless ages! I hold in my hand the keys of death and the grave. Therefore, write down what you have seen, both the things which are now, and the things which are to be hereafter. The secret meaning of the seven stars which you saw in my right hand, and of the seven golden lampstands is this: the seven stars are the angels of the seven Churches and the seven lampstands are the Churches themselves."

CHAPTER 2

(*i*) *To the loveless Church*

"WRITE this to the angel of the Church in Ephesus:

These words are spoken by the one who holds the seven stars safe in his right hand, and who walks among the seven golden lampstands. I know what you have done; I know how hard you have worked and what you have endured. I know that you will not tolerate wicked men, that you have put to the test self-styled 'apostles', who are nothing of the sort, and have found them to be liars. I know your powers of endurance—how you have suffered for the sake of my name and have not grown weary. But I hold this against you, that you do not love as you did at first. Remember then how far you have fallen. Repent and live as you lived at first. Otherwise, if your heart remains unchanged, I shall come to you and remove your lampstand from its place.

Yet you have this to your credit, that you hate the practices of the Nicolaitans, which I myself detest. Let every listener hear what the Spirit says to the Churches:

To the victorious I will give the right to eat from the tree of life which grows in the paradise of God.

(ii) To the persecuted Church

"Write this to the angel of the Church in Smyrna:

These words are spoken by the first and the last, who died and came to life again. I know of your tribulation and of your poverty—though in fact you are rich! I know how you are slandered by those who call themselves Jews, but in fact are no Jews but a synagogue of Satan. Have no fear of what you will suffer. I tell you now that the devil is going to cast some of your number into prison where your faith will be tested and your distress will last for ten days. Be faithful in the face of death and I will give you the crown of life. Let every listener hear what the Spirit says to the Churches:

The victorious cannot suffer the slightest hurt from the second death.

(iii) To the over-tolerant Church

"Write this to the angel of the Church in Pergamum:

These words are spoken by him who has the sharp two-edged sword. I know where you live—where Satan sits enthroned. I know that you hold fast to my name and that you never denied your faith in me even in the days when Antipas, my faithful witness, was killed before your eyes in the very house of Satan.

Yet I have a few things against you—some of your number cling to the teaching of Balaam, the man who taught Balak how to entice the children of Israel into eating meat sacrificed to idols and into sexual immorality. I have also against you the fact that among your number are some who hold just as closely to the teaching of the Nicolaitans. Repent then, or else I shall come to you quickly and make war upon them with the sword of my mouth. Let the listener hear what the Spirit says to the Churches:

I will give the victorious some of the hidden manna, and I will also give him a white stone with a new name written upon it which no man knows except the man who receives it.

(iv) *To the compromising Church*

"Write this to the angel of the Church in Thyatira:

These are the words of the Son of God whose eyes blaze like fire and whose feet shine like the finest bronze:

I know what you have done. I know of your love and your loyalty, your service and your endurance. Moreover, I know that you are doing more than you did at first. But I have this against you, that you tolerate that woman Jezebel who calls herself a prophetess, but who by her teaching deceives my servants into sexual immorality and eating idols'-meat. I have given her time to repent but she has shown no desire to repent of her immorality. See, now, how I throw her into bed and her lovers with her, and I will send them terrible suffering unless they repent of what she has done. As for her children, I shall strike them dead. Then all the Churches will know that I am the one who searches men's hearts and minds, and that I will reward each one of you according to your deeds.

But for the rest of you at Thyatira, who do not hold this teaching, and have not learned what they call 'the deep things of Satan', I will lay no further burden upon you, except that you hold on to what you have until I come!

To the one who is victorious, who carries out my work to the end, I will give authority over the nations, just as I myself have received authority from my Father, and I will give him the morning star. He shall 'shepherd them with a rod of iron'; he shall 'dash them in pieces like a potter's vessel'. Let the listener hear what the Spirit says to the Churches.

CHAPTER 3

(v) *To the sleeping Church*

"Write this to the angel of the Church in Sardis:

These are the words of him who holds in his hand the seven Spirits of God and the seven stars:

I know what you have done, that you have a reputation for being alive, but that in fact you are dead. Now wake up! Strengthen what you still have before it dies! For I have not found any of your deeds complete in the sight of my God. Remember then what you were given and what you were taught. Hold to those things and repent. If you refuse to wake up, then I will come to you like a thief, and you will have no idea of the hour of my coming.

Yet you still have a few names in Sardis of people who have not soiled their garments. They shall walk with me in white, for they have deserved to do so. The victorious shall wear such white garments, and never will I erase his name from the book of life. Indeed, I will speak his name openly in the presence of my Father and of his angels. Let the listener hear what the Spirit says to the Churches.

(*vi*) *To the Church with opportunity*

"Then write this to the angel of the Church in Philadelphia:

These are the words of the Holy One and the true, who holds the key of David, who opens and no man shall shut, and who shuts and no man shall open. I know what you have done. See, I have given you a door flung wide open, which no man can close! For you have some little power and have been faithful to my message and have not denied my name. See how I deal with those of Satan's synagogue, who claim to be Jews, yet are no Jews but liars! Watch how I make them come and bow down before your feet and acknowledge that I have loved you. Because you have obeyed my call to patient endurance I will keep you safe from the hour of trial which is to come upon the whole world, to test all who live upon the earth. I am coming soon; hold fast to what you have—let no one deprive you of your crown. As for the victorious, I will make him a pillar in the Temple of my God, and he will never leave it. I will write upon him the name of my God, and the name of the city of my God, the new Jerusalem which comes down out of Heaven from my God. And I will write upon him my own new name. Let the listener hear what the Spirit says to the Churches.

(*vii*) *To the complacent Church*

"Then write this to the angel of the Church in Laodicea:

These are the words of the Amen, the faithful and true witness, the beginning of God's creation:

I know what you have done, and that you are neither cold nor hot. I could wish that you were either cold or hot! But since you are lukewarm and neither hot nor cold, I intend to spit you out of my mouth! While you say, 'I am rich, I have prospered, and there is nothing that I need', you have no eyes to see that you are wretched, pitiable, poverty-stricken, blind and naked. My advice to you is to buy from me that gold which is refined in the furnace so that you may be rich, and white garments to wear so that you may hide the shame of your nakedness, and salve to put on your eyes to make you see. All those whom I love I correct and discipline. Therefore, shake off your complacency and repent. See, I stand knocking at the door. If anyone listens to my voice and opens the door, I will go into his house and dine with him, and he with me. As for the victorious, I will give him the honour of sitting beside me on my throne, just as I myself have won the victory and have taken my seat beside my Father on his throne. Let the listener hear what the Spirit says to the Churches."

CHAPTER 4

The vision of Heaven

LATER I looked again, and before my eyes a door stood open in Heaven, and in my ears was the voice with the ring of a trumpet, which I had heard at first, speaking to me and saying,

"Come up here, and I will show you what must happen in the future."

Immediately I knew myself to be inspired by the Spirit, and in my vision I saw that a throne had been set up in Heaven, and there was someone seated upon the throne. His appearance blazed like jasper and cornelian, and all around the throne shone a halo like an emerald rainbow. In a circle around the throne there were twenty-four thrones and seated upon them twenty-four elders dressed in white with golden crowns upon their heads. From the central throne come flashes of lightning, noises and peals of thunder. Seven lamps are burning before the throne, and they are the seven Spirits of God. In front of the throne there appears a sea of glass as clear as crystal. On each side, encircling the throne, are four living creatures covered with eyes in front and behind. The first living creature is like a lion, the second is like a calf, the third has a face like a man, and the fourth living creature appears like an eagle in flight. These four creatures have each of them six wings and are covered with eyes, all around them, and even within them. Day and night they never cease to say,

"Holy, holy, holy is the Lord God, the Almighty, who was and who is and who is coming."

The ceaseless worship of Heaven

And whenever the living creatures give glory and honour and thanksgiving to the one who sits upon the throne, who lives for timeless ages, the twenty-four elders prostrate themselves before him who is seated upon the throne and worship the One who lives for timeless ages. They cast their crowns before the throne and say,

"Thou art worthy, O Lord our God, to receive glory and honour and power, for thou didst create all things; by thy will they existed and were created."

CHAPTER 5

The sealed book of future events

THEN I noticed in the right hand of the One seated upon the throne a book filled with writing both inside and on its back, and it was sealed with seven seals. And I saw a mighty angel who called out in a loud voice,

"Who is fit to open the book and break its seals?"

And no one in Heaven or upon earth or under the earth was able to open the book, or even to look at it. I began to weep bitterly because no one could be found fit to open the book, or even to look at it, when one of the elders said to me,

"Do not weep. See, the lion from the tribe of Judah, the root of David, has won the victory and is able to open the book and break its seven seals."

Then, standing in the very centre of the throne and of the four living creatures and of the elders, I saw a Lamb that seemed to have been slaughtered. He had seven horns and seven eyes, which are the seven Spirits of God and are sent out into every corner of the earth. Then he came and took the book from the right hand of him who was seated upon the throne.

The new hymn of the created and of the redeemed

When he had taken the book, the four living creatures and the twenty-four elders prostrated themselves before the Lamb. Each of them had a harp, and they had golden bowls full of incense, which are the prayers of the saints. They sang a new song and these are the words they sang,

"Worthy art thou to take the book and break its seals, for thou hast been slain and by thy blood hast purchased for God men from every tribe, and tongue, and people, and nation! Thou hast made them a kingdom of priests for our God, and they shall reign as kings upon the earth."

The hymn of the whole company of Heaven

Then in my vision I heard the voices of many angels encircling the throne, the living creatures and the elders. There were myriads of myriads and thousands of thousands, crying in a great voice,

"Worthy is the Lamb who was slain, to receive power and riches and wisdom, and strength and honour and glory and blessing!"

Then I heard the voice of everything created in Heaven, upon earth, under the earth and upon the sea, and all that are in them saying,

"Blessing and honour and glory and power be given to him who sits upon the throne, and to the Lamb, for timeless ages!"

The four living creatures said, "Amen", while the elders fell down and worshipped.

CHAPTER 6

THE LAMB BREAKS THE SEALS

The first rider: Conquest

Then I watched while the Lamb broke one of the seven seals, and I heard one of the four living creatures say in a voice of thunder,

"Come out!"

I looked, and before my eyes was a white horse. Its rider carried a bow, and he was given a crown. He rode out conquering and bent on conquest.

The second rider: War

Then, when the Lamb broke the second seal, I heard the second living creature cry,

"Come out!"

And another horse came forth, red in colour. Its rider was given power to deprive the earth of peace, so that men should kill each other. A huge sword was put into his hand.

The third rider: Famine

When the Lamb broke the third seal, I heard the third living creature say,

"Come out!"

I looked again and there before my eyes was a black horse. Its rider had a pair of scales in his hand, and I heard a voice which seemed to come from the four living creatures, saying,

"A quart of wheat for a shilling, and three quarts of barley for a shilling—but no tampering with the oil or the wine!"

The fourth rider: Death

Then, when he broke the fourth seal I heard the voice of the fourth living creature cry,

"Come out!"

Again I looked, and there appeared a horse sickly green in colour. The name of its rider was death, and the grave followed close behind him. A quarter of the earth was put into their power, to kill with the sword, by famine, by violence, and through the wild beasts of the earth.

The cry of the martyrs in Heaven

When the Lamb broke the fifth seal, I could see, beneath the altar, the souls of those who had been killed for the sake of the Word of God and because of the faithfulness of their witness. They cried out in a loud voice, saying,

"How long shall it be, O Lord of all, holy and true, before thou shalt judge and avenge our blood upon the inhabitants of the earth?"

Then each of them was given a white robe, and they were told to be patient a little longer, until the number of their fellow-servants and of their brethren, who were to die as they had died, should be complete.

The awe-full wrath of God

Then I watched while he broke the sixth seal. There was a tremendous earthquake, the sun turned dark like coarse black cloth, and the full moon was red as blood. The stars of the sky fell upon the earth, just as a fig-tree sheds unripe figs when shaken in a gale. The sky vanished as though it were a scroll being rolled up, and every mountain and island was jolted out of its place. Then the kings of the earth, and the great men, the captains, the wealthy, the powerful, and every man, whether slave or free, hid themselves in caves and among mountain rocks. They called out to the mountains and the rocks,

"Fall down upon us and hide us from the face of him who sits upon the throne, and from the wrath of the Lamb! For the great day of their wrath has come, and who can stand against it?"

CHAPTER 7

Judgment stayed for the sealing of God's people

LATER I saw four angels standing at the four corners of the earth holding in check the four winds of the earth that none should blow upon the earth or upon the sea or upon any tree. Then I saw another angel ascending out of the east, holding the seal of the living God. He cried out in a loud voice to the four angels who had the power to harm the earth and the sea:

"Do no harm to the earth, nor to the sea, nor to the trees until we have sealed the servants of our God upon their foreheads."

I heard the number of those who were thus sealed and it was 144,000, from every tribe of the sons of Israel. Twelve thousand were sealed from the tribe of Judah; twelve thousand from the tribe of Reuben; twelve thousand from the tribe of Gad; twelve thousand from the tribe of Asher; twelve thousand from the tribe of Naphtali; twelve thousand from the tribe of Manasseh; twelve thousand from the tribe of Simeon; twelve thousand from the tribe of Levi; twelve thousand from the tribe of Issachar; twelve thousand from the tribe of Zebulun; twelve thousand from the tribe of Joseph; and twelve thousand were sealed from the tribe of Benjamin.

The countless host of the redeemed

When this was done I looked again, and before my eyes appeared a vast crowd beyond man's power to number. They came from every nation and tribe and people and language, and they stood before the throne of the Lamb, dressed in white robes with palm-branches in their hands. With a great voice they shouted these words:

'Salvation belongs to our God who sits upon the throne and to the Lamb!"

Then all the angels stood encircling the throne, the elders and the four living creatures, and prostrated themselves with heads bowed before the throne and worshipped God, saying,

"Amen! Blessing and glory and wisdom and thanksgiving and honour and power and strength be given to our God for timeless ages!"

The countless host explained

Then one of the elders addressed me and asked,

"These who are dressed in white robes—who are they, and where do they come from?"

"You know, my lord," I answered him.

Then he told me,

"These are those who have come through the great oppression: they have washed their robes and made them white in the blood of the Lamb. That is why they now have their place before the throne of God, and serve him day and night in his Temple. He who sits upon the throne will be their shelter. They will never again know hunger or thirst. The sun shall never beat upon them, neither shall there be any scorching heat, for the Lamb who is in the centre of the throne will be their shepherd and will lead them to springs of living water. And God will wipe away every tear from their eyes."

CHAPTER 8

The seventh seal: Complete silence

THEN, when he had broken the seventh seal, there was utter silence in Heaven for what seemed to me half-an-hour.

The vision of the seven trumpeters

Then I saw the seven angels who stand in the presence of God, and seven trumpets were put into their hands.

Then another angel came and stood by the altar holding a golden censer. He was given a great quantity of incense to add to the prayers of all the saints, to be laid upon the golden altar before the throne. And the smoke of the incense rose up before God from the angel's hand, mingled with the prayers of the saints. Then the angel took the censer, filled it with fire from the altar, and hurled it upon the earth. And at that there were thunderings and noises, flashes of lightning and an earthquake.

Then the seven angels who were holding the seven trumpets prepared to blow them.

The first trumpet: Hail and fire

The first angel blew his trumpet. Hail and fire mingled with blood appeared, and were hurled upon the earth. One-third of the earth was burnt up, one-third of all the trees was burnt up, and every blade of green grass was burnt up.

The second trumpet: The blazing mountain

The second angel blew his trumpet, and something like a vast mountain blazing with fire was thrown into the sea. A third-part of the sea turned into blood, a third of all live creatures in the sea died, and a third-part of all shipping was destroyed.

The third trumpet: The poisonous star

Then the third angel blew his trumpet and there fell from the sky a huge star blazing like a torch. It fell upon a third of the rivers and springs of water. The name of the star is said to be Apsinthus (Wormwood). A third of all the waters turned into wormwood, and many people died because the waters had become so bitter.

The fourth trumpet: Light from the sky diminishes

The fourth angel blew his trumpet, and a third-part of the sun, a third-part of the moon and a third of the stars were struck. A third-part of the light of each of them was darkened, so that light by day and light by night were both diminished by a third-part.

The cry of pity from mid-heaven

Then in my vision I heard a solitary eagle flying in mid-heaven, crying in a loud voice,

"Alas, alas, alas for the inhabitants of the earth for there are three more trumpet blasts which the three angels shall sound!"

CHAPTER 9

The fifth trumpet: The fathomless pit

THE fifth angel blew his trumpet. I saw a star that had fallen down from Heaven to earth, and to him was given the key to the shaft of the abyss. Then he opened the shaft and smoke like the smoke of a vast furnace rose out of it, so that the light of the sun and the air itself grew dark from the smoke of the shaft.

Then out of the smoke emerged locusts to descend upon the earth. They were given powers like those of earthly scorpions. They had orders to do no harm to any grass, green thing or tree upon the earth, but to injure only those human beings who did not bear the seal of God upon their foreheads. They were given no power to kill men, but only to torture them for five months. The torture they could inflict was like the pain of a scorpion's sting.

In those days men will seek death but they will never find it; they will long to die but death will elude them. These locusts looked to me in my vision like horses prepared for battle. On their heads were what appeared to be crowns like gold; their faces were like human faces, and they had long hair like women. Their teeth were like lion's teeth, their breasts were like iron-breastplates, and the noise of their wings was like the noise of a host of chariots and horses charging into battle. They have tails and stings like scorpions, and it is in their tails that they possess the power to injure men for five months. They have as their king the angel of the pit, whose name in Hebrew is Abaddon and in Greek Apollyon, (meaning the destroyer).

The first disaster is now past, but I see two more approaching.

The sixth trumpet: The destroying angels

Then the sixth angel blew his trumpet, and I heard a solitary voice speaking from the four corners of the golden altar that stands in the presence of God. And it said to the sixth angel who held the trumpet,

"Release the four angels who are bound at the great river Euphrates!"

Then these four angels who had been held ready for the hour, the day, the month and the year, were set free to kill a third-part of all mankind. The number of their horsemen was two hundred million—I heard what their number was. In my vision I saw these horses and their riders, and their breastplates were fiery-red, blue and yellow. The horses' heads looked to me like the heads of lions, and out of their mouths poured fire and smoke and sulphur. A third of all mankind died from the fearful effects of these three, the fire, the smoke and the sulphur which pours out of their mouths. For the power of these horses lies in their mouths and in their tails. Indeed their tails are like serpents with heads, and with these they inflict injury.

The rest of mankind, who did not die in this fearful destruction, neither repented of the works of their own hands nor ceased to worship evil powers and idols of gold, silver, brass, stone or wood, which can neither see nor hear nor move. Neither did they repent of their murders, their sorceries, their sexual sins, nor of their thieving.

CHAPTER 10

The angel with the little book

THEN I saw another mighty angel descending from Heaven. He was clothed in a cloud, and there was a rainbow around his head. His face blazed like the sun, his legs like pillars of fire, and he had a little book lying open in his hand. He planted his right foot on the sea and his left foot on the land, and then shouted with a loud voice like the roar of a lion. And when he shouted the seven thunders lifted their voices. When the seven thunders had rolled I was on the point of writing but I heard a voice from Heaven, saying,

"Seal up what the seven thunders said, but do not write it down!"

Then the angel whom I had seen bestriding the sea and the land raised his right hand to Heaven and swore by the living one of the timeless ages, who created Heaven, earth and sea and all that is in them:

"There shall be no more delay! In the days which shall soon be announced by the trumpet-blast of the seventh angel the mysterious purpose of God shall be completed, as he assured his servants the prophets."

Then the voice which I had heard from Heaven was again in my ears, saying,

"Go and take the little book which lies open in the hand of the angel whose feet are planted on both sea and land."

So I went off towards the angel, asking him to give me the little book.

"Take it," he said to me, "and eat it up. It will be bitter to your stomach, but sweet as honey in your mouth."

Then I took the little book from the angel's hand and swallowed it. It was as sweet as honey to the taste but when I had eaten it up it was bitter to my stomach.

John is instructed to prophesy

Then they said to me, "It is again your duty to prophesy about peoples, nations, languages and many kings."

CHAPTER 11

AND I was given a measuring rod like a staff, and was I told, "Get up and measure the Sanctuary of God, and the altar, and count those who worship there. But leave out of your measurement the courtyard outside the Sanctuary—do not measure that at all. For it has been given over to the nations, and they will trample over the holy city for forty-two months."

God's two witnesses

"And I will give authority to my two witnesses to proclaim the message, clothed in sackcloth for twelve hundred and sixty days."

These are the two olive trees and the two lampstands which stand before the Lord of the earth. If anyone tries to harm them, fire issues from their mouths and consumes their enemies. Indeed, if anyone should try to hurt them, this is the way in which he will certainly meet his death. These witnesses have power to shut up the sky and stop any rain from falling during the time of their preaching. Moreover, they have power to turn the waters into blood, and to strike the earth with any plague as often as they wish.

The emergence of the animal

Then, when their work of witness is complete, the animal will come up out of the pit and go to war with them. It will conquer and kill them, and their bodies will lie in the street of the great city, which is called by those with spiritual understanding, "Sodom" and "Egypt"—the very place where their Lord himself was crucified. For three and a half days men from all peoples and tribes and languages and nations will gaze upon their bodies and will not allow them to be buried. The inhabitants of the earth will gloat over them and will hold celebrations and send one another presents, because these two prophets had brought such misery to the inhabitants of the earth.

The resurrection and ascension of the two witnesses

But after three and a half days the Spirit of life from God entered them and they stood upright on their feet. This struck terror into the hearts of those who were watching them, and they heard a tremendous voice speaking to these two from Heaven, saying,

"Come up here!"

And they went up to Heaven in a cloud in full view of their enemies. And at that moment there was a great earthquake, a tenth-part of the city fell in ruins and seven thousand people were known to have been killed in the earthquake. The rest were terrified and acknowledged the glory of the God of Heaven.

The seventh trumpet: (i) The worship of Heaven

The second disaster is now past, and I see the third disaster following hard upon the heels of the second. The seventh angel blew his trumpet. There arose loud voices in Heaven and they were saying,

"The kingship of the world now belongs to our Lord and to his Christ, and he shall be king for timeless ages!"

Then the twenty-four elders, who sit upon their thrones in the presence of God, prostrated themselves and, with bowed heads, worshipped God, saying:

"We thank thee, O Lord who art God the Almighty, who art and who wast, that thou hast assumed thy great power and hast become king. The nations were full of fury, but now thy wrath has come and with it the time for the dead to be judged and for reward to be given to thy servants, the prophets and the saints, and all who fear thy name, both small and great. Now is the time for destroying the destroyers of the earth!"

Then the Sanctuary of God in Heaven was thrown open and the

ark of his agreement within his Sanctuary could be clearly seen. Accompanying this sight were flashes of lightning, loud noises, peals of thunder, an earthquake and a violent storm of hail.

CHAPTER 12

The seventh trumpet: (ii) The sign of the woman

THEN a huge sign became visible in the sky—the figure of a woman clothed with the sun, with the moon under her feet, and a crown of twelve stars upon her head. She was pregnant, and cried out in her labour and in the pains of bringing forth her child.

The seventh trumpet: (iii) The dragon, the enemy of the woman

Then another sign became visible in the sky, and I saw that it was a huge red dragon with seven heads and ten horns, with a diadem upon each of his heads. His tail swept down a third of the stars in the sky and hurled them upon the earth. The dragon took his place in front of the woman who was about to give birth to a child, so that as soon as she did so he might devour it. She gave birth to a male child who is to shepherd all the nations "with a rod of iron". Her child was snatched up to God and to his throne, while the woman fled into the desert where she has a place prepared for her by God's command. There they will take care of her for twelve hundred and sixty days.

War in Heaven

Then war broke out in Heaven. Michael and his angels battled with the dragon. The dragon and his angels fought back, but they did not prevail and they were expelled from Heaven. So the huge dragon, the serpent of ancient times, who is called the devil and Satan, the deceiver of the whole world, was hurled down upon the earth, and his angels were hurled down with him.

The victory of Heaven proclaimed

Then I heard a great voice in Heaven cry:

"Now the salvation and the power and kingdom of our God, and the authority of his Christ have come! For the accuser of our brethren has been thrown down from this place, where he stood before our God accusing them day and night. Now they have conquered him through the blood of the Lamb, and through the Word to which they bore witness. They did not cherish life even in the face of death!

"Therefore, rejoice, O Heavens, and all you who live in the Heavens! But alas for the earth and the sea, for the devil has come down to you in great fury, knowing that his time is short!"

The dragon's enmity against the woman

And when the dragon saw that he had been cast down upon the earth, he began to pursue the woman who had given birth to the male child. But she was given two great eagle's wings so that she could fly to her place in the desert, where she is kept safe from the serpent for a time and times and half a time. Then the serpent ejected water from his mouth, streaming like a river in pursuit of the woman, to drown her in its flood. But the earth came to the woman's rescue, opened its mouth and swallowed up the river which the dragon had emitted from his mouth. Then the dragon raged with fury against the woman and went off to make war against the rest of her children—those who keep the commandments of God and bear their witness to Jesus.

CHAPTER 13

The animal from the sea

THEN, as I stood on the sand of the sea-shore, there rose out of the sea before my eyes an animal with seven heads and ten horns. There were diadems upon its horns and blasphemous names upon its heads. The animal which I saw had the appearance of a leopard, though it had the feet of a bear and a mouth like the mouth of a lion. Then the dragon gave it his own power and throne and great authority. One of its heads appeared to have been wounded to death but the mortal wound had healed.

The whole earth followed the animal with wonder, and they worshipped the dragon because he had given authority to the animal. Then they worshipped the animal, too, saying,

"Who is like the animal? Who could make war against it?"

It was allowed to speak monstrous blasphemies and to exert its authority for forty-two months.

So it poured out blasphemies against God, blaspheming his

name and his dwelling-place and those who live in Heaven. Moreover, it was permitted to make war upon the saints and to conquer them; the authority given to it extended over every tribe and people and language and nation. All the inhabitants of the earth will worship it—all those whose names have not been written in the book of life which belongs to the Lamb slain from the foundation of the world.

Parenthetical: a word to the reader

Let the listener hear this:

If any man is destined for captivity he will go into captivity. If any man kills with the sword he must himself be killed with the sword. Amid all this stands the endurance and faith of the saints.

The animal from the earth

Then I saw another animal rising out of the earth, and it had two horns like a lamb but it spoke in the voice of a dragon. It uses the full authority of the first animal in its presence. It compels the earth and all its inhabitants to worship the first animal—the one with the mortal wound which had healed. It performs great signs: before men's eyes it makes fire fall down from heaven to earth. It deceives the inhabitants of the earth by the signs which it is allowed to perform in the presence of the animal, and it tells them to make a statue in honour of the animal which received the sword-thrust and yet survived. Further, it was allowed to give the breath of life to the statue of the animal so that the statue could speak and condemn to death all those who do not worship its statue. Then it compels all, small and great, rich and poor, free men and slaves, to receive a mark on their right hands or on their foreheads. The purpose of this is that no one should be able to buy or sell unless he bears the mark of the name of the animal or the number of its name. Understanding is needed here: let every thinking man calculate the number of the animal. It is the number of a man, and its number is six hundred and sixty-six.

CHAPTER 14

The vision of the Lamb and the first of the redeemed

THEN I looked again and before my eyes the Lamb was standing on Mount Sion, and with him were a hundred and forty-four thousand who had his name and his Father's name written upon their foreheads. Then I heard a sound coming from Heaven like the roar of a great waterfall and the heavy rolling of thunder. Yet the sound which I heard was also like the music of harpists sweeping their strings. And they are singing a new song of praise before the throne, and before the four living creatures and the elders. No one could learn that song except the one hundred and forty-four thousand who had been redeemed from the earth. These are the men who have never defiled themselves with women, for they are celibate. These are the men who follow the Lamb wherever he may go; these men have been redeemed from among mankind as first-fruits to God and to the Lamb. They have never been guilty of any falsehood; they are beyond reproach.

The angel with the gospel

Then I saw another angel flying in mid-heaven, holding the everlasting gospel to proclaim to the inhabitants of the earth—to every nation and tribe and language and people. He was crying in a loud voice,

"Reverence God, and give glory to him; for the hour of his judgment has come! Worship him who made Heaven and earth, the sea and the springs of water."

The angel of doom

Then another, a second angel, followed him crying,

"Fallen, fallen is Babylon the great! She who made all nations drink the wine of her passionate unfaithfulness!"

The angel of judgment

Then a third angel followed these two, crying in a loud voice,

"If any man worships the animal and its statue and bears its mark upon his forehead or upon his hand, then that man shall drink the wine of God's passion, poured undiluted into the cup of his wrath. He shall be tortured by fire and sulphur in the presence of the holy angels and of the Lamb. The smoke of such men's torture ascends for timeless ages, and there is no respite from it day or night. Such are the worshippers of the animal and its statue and among their number are all who bear the mark of its name."

The call to stand fast

In all this stands the endurance of the saints—those who keep the commandments of God and their faith in Jesus.

The security of the saints

Then I heard a voice from Heaven, saying,
"Write this! From henceforth happy are the dead who die in the Lord!"
"Happy indeed," says the Spirit, "for they rest from their labours and their deeds go with them!"

The harvest of God's wrath

Once again I looked, and a white cloud appeared before me with someone sitting upon the cloud with the appearance of a man. He had a golden crown on his head, and held a sharp sickle in his hand. Then another angel came out from the Sanctuary, calling in a loud voice to the one sitting on the cloud,
"Thrust in your sickle and reap, for the time of reaping has come and the harvest of the earth is fully ripe!"
Then the one sitting upon the cloud swung his sickle upon the earth, and the reaping of the earth was done.
Then another angel came out from the Sanctuary in Heaven, and he also had a sharp sickle. Yet another angel came out from the altar where he has command over the fire, and called out in a loud voice to the angel with the sharp sickle,
"Thrust in your sharp sickle and harvest the clusters from the vineyard of the earth for the grapes are fully ripe!"
Then the angel swung his sickle upon the earth and gathered the harvest of the earth's vineyard, and threw it into the great winepress of the wrath of God. The grapes were trodden outside the city, and out of the winepress flowed blood for two hundred miles in a stream as high as the horses' bridles.

CHAPTER 15

The seven last plagues prepared

THEN I saw another sign in Heaven, vast and awe-inspiring: seven angels are holding the seven last plagues, and with these the wrath of God is brought to an end.

The hymn of the redeemed

And I saw what appeared to be a sea of glass shot through with fire, and upon this glassy sea were standing those who had emerged victorious from the fight with the animal, its statue and the number which denotes its name. In their hands they hold harps which God has given them, and they are singing the song of Moses the servant of God, and the song of the Lamb, and these are the words they sing:

"Great and wonderful are thy works, O Lord God, the Almighty! Just and true are thy ways, thou king of the nations! Who should not reverence thee, O Lord, and glorify thy name? For thou alone art holy; therefore all nations shall come and worship before thee, for thy just judgments have been made plain!"

The angels leave the Sanctuary of God—

Later in my vision I saw the Sanctuary of the tabernacle of testimony in Heaven wide open, and out of the Sanctuary came forth the seven angels who hold the seven plagues. They were dressed in spotless shining linen, and they were girded round their breasts with golden girdles.

Then one of the four living creatures gave to the seven angels seven golden bowls filled with the wrath of God who lives for timeless ages. The Sanctuary was filled with smoke from the glory and power of God, and no one could enter the Sanctuary until the seven plagues of the seven angels were past and over.

CHAPTER 16

—and are ordered to pour out the bowls of his wrath

THEN I heard a loud voice from the Sanctuary saying to the seven angels,

"Go and pour out upon the earth the seven bowls of the wrath of God!"

The first bowl: Ulcers

The first angel went off and emptied his bowl upon the earth. Whereupon loathsome and malignant ulcers attacked all those who bore the mark of the animal and worshipped its statue.

The second bowl: Death in the sea

The second angel emptied his bowl into the sea, which turned into a fluid like the blood of a corpse, and every living thing in it died.

The third bowl: Water becomes blood

Then the third angel emptied his bowl into the rivers and springs of water, and they turned into blood. And I heard the angel of the waters say,

"Just art thou in these thy judgments, thou who art and wast the Holy One! For they have spilled the blood of saints and prophets, and now thou hast given them blood to drink. They have what they deserve."

And I heard the altar say,

"Yes, O Lord, God Almighty, thy judgments are true and right."

The fourth bowl: Scorching heat

The fourth angel emptied his bowl over the sun, and the sun was given power to scorch men in its fiery blaze. Then men were terribly burned in the heat, and they blasphemed the name of God who has power over these afflictions; but they neither repented nor gave him glory.

The fifth bowl: The plague of darkness

Then the fifth angel emptied his bowl upon the throne of the animal. Its kingdom was plunged into darkness; men gnawed their tongues in agony, cursed the God of Heaven for their pain and their ulcers, but refused to repent of what they had done.

The sixth bowl: The great river dried up

Then the sixth angel emptied his bowl upon the great river Euphrates. The waters of that river were dried up to prepare a road for the kings from the east. And then I noticed three foul spirits, looking like frogs, emerging from the mouths of the dragon, the animal and the false prophet. They are diabolical spirits performing wonders and they set out to muster all the kings of the world for battle on the great day of God, the Almighty.

The words in the background

"See I am coming like a thief! Happy is the man who stays

awake and keeps his clothes at his side, so that he will not have to walk naked and men see his shame."

So they brought them together to the place called, in Hebrew, Armageddon.

The seventh bowl: Devastation from the air

The seventh angel emptied his bowl into the air. A loud voice came out of the Sanctuary, from the throne, saying,

"The end has come!"

Then followed flashes of lightning, noises and peals of thunder. There was a terrific earthquake, the like of which no man has ever seen since mankind began to live upon the earth—so great and tremendous was this earthquake. The great city was split into three parts, and the cities of all the nations fell in ruins. And God called to mind Babylon the great and made her drink the cup of the wine of his furious wrath. Every island fled and the mountains vanished. Great hailstones like heavy weights fell from the sky, and men blasphemed God for the curse of the hail, for it fell upon them with savage and fearful blows.

CHAPTER 17

The judgment of the evil woman announced

THEN came one of the seven angels who held the seven bowls, and said to me,

"Come, and I will show you the judgment passed upon the great harlot who is seated upon many waters. It is with her that the kings of the earth have debauched themselves and the inhabitants of the earth have become drunk on the wine of her filthiness."

The gorgeous mother of evil

Then he carried me away in spirit into the desert. There I saw a woman riding upon a scarlet animal, covered with blasphemous titles and having seven heads and ten horns. The woman herself was dressed in purple and scarlet, glittering with gold, jewels and pearls. In her hand she held a golden cup full of the earth's filthiness and her own foul impurity. On her forehead is written a name with a secret meaning—BABYLON THE GREAT, MOTHER OF ALL HARLOTS AND OF THE EARTH'S ABOMINATIONS.

The vision explained

Then I noticed that the woman was drunk with the blood of the saints and of the martyrs for Jesus. As I watched her, I was filled with utter amazement, but the angel said to me,

"Why are you amazed? I will explain to you the mystery of the woman and of the animal with seven heads and ten horns which carries her. The animal, which you saw, once lived but now is no more—it will come up out of the abyss only to meet with destruction. The inhabitants of the earth, whose names have not been written in the book of life from the foundation of the world, will be utterly astonished when they see that the animal was, and is not, and yet is to come. (Here we need a mind with understanding.)

"The seven heads are seven hills on which the woman takes her seat. There are also seven kings; five have been dethroned, one reigns and the other has not yet appeared—when he comes he must remain only for a short time. As for the animal which once lived but now lives no longer, it is an eighth king which belongs to the seven, but it goes to utter destruction. The ten horns which you saw are ten kings who have not yet received their power to reign, but they will receive authority to be kings for one hour in company with the animal. They are of one mind, and they will hand over their power and authority to the animal. They will all go to war with the Lamb, and the Lamb, with his called, chosen and faithful followers, will conquer them. For he is Lord of lords and King of kings."

Then he said to me,

"As for the waters which you saw, on which the woman took her seat, they are peoples and vast crowds, nations and languages. The ten horns and the animal which you saw will loathe the harlot, and leave her deserted and naked. Moreover, they will devour her flesh, and then consume her with fire. For God has put it into their hearts to carry out his purpose by making them of one mind, and by handing over their authority to the animal, until the words of God have been fulfilled.

"The woman that you saw is the great city which dominates the kings of the earth."

CHAPTER 18

The final overthrow of Babylon

LATER I saw another angel coming down from Heaven, armed with great authority. The earth shone with the splendour of his presence, and he cried in a mighty voice,

"Fallen, fallen is Babylon* the great! She has become a haunt of devils, a prison for every unclean spirit, and a cage for every foul and hateful bird. For all nations have drunk the wine of her passionate unfaithfulness and have fallen thereby. The kings of the earth have debauched themselves with her, and the merchants of the earth have grown rich from the extravagance of her dissipation!"

Then I heard another voice from Heaven, crying,

"Come out from her, O my people, lest you become accomplices in her sins and must share in her punishment. For her sins have mounted up to the sky, and God has remembered the tale of her wickedness. Pay her back in her own coin—yes, pay her back double for all that she has done! Mix her a drink of double strength in the cup which she mixed for others! For the pride in which she flaunted herself give her torture and misery! Because she says to herself, 'Here I sit a queen on a throne; I am no woman who lacks a man and I shall never know sorrow!' So in a single day her punishments shall strike her—death, sorrow and famine and she shall be burned in the fire. For mighty is the Lord God who judges her!"

The lament over the city

Then the kings of the earth, who debauched and indulged themselves with her, will wail and lament over her. Standing at a safe distance through very fear of her torment, they will watch the smoke of her burning and cry,

"Alas, alas for the great city, Babylon the mighty city, that your judgment should come in a single hour."

The merchants of the earth shall also wail and lament over her, for there is no one left to buy their goods—cargoes of gold and silver, jewels and pearls, fine linen, purple, silk and scarlet, all kinds of scented wood, every sort of ivory vessel, every kind of

* Referring to Rome, but prophetically to any great prosperous but Godless city.

vessel of precious wood, of bronze, iron and marble; cinnamon, spice, incense, myrrh, frankincense, wine, oil, fine flour and corn; cattle, sheep and horses; chariots, slaves, the very souls of men.

Those who bought and sold these things, who had gained their wealth from her, will stand afar off through fear of her punishment, weeping and lamenting and saying,

"Alas, alas for the great city that was dressed in fine linen, purple and scarlet, and was bedecked with gold and jewels and pearls—alas that in a single hour all that wealth should be destroyed!"

Then every shipmaster and seafarer—sailors and all whose business is upon the sea—stood and watched the smoke of her burning from afar, and cried out,

"What city was ever like the great city?"

They even threw dust on their heads and cried aloud as they wept, saying,

"Alas, alas for the great city where all who had ships on the sea grew wealthy through the richness of her treasure! Alas that in a single hour she should be ruined!"

A comment in the background

"Rejoice over her fate, O Heaven, and all you saints, apostles and prophets! For God has pronounced his judgment for you against her!"

The words of Babylon's doom

Then a mighty angel lifted up a stone like a huge mill-stone and hurled it into the sea, saying,

"So shall Babylon the great city be sent hurtling down to disappear for ever! Never more shall the sound of harpists and musicians, flute-players and trumpeters be heard in you again! Never again shall a craftsman of any craft be found in you; never again will the sound of the mill-stone's grinding be heard in you! No light of a lamp shall ever shine in you again, and the voices of bridegroom and bride shall be heard in you no more! The fruit of your soul's desire is lost to you for ever. All your luxuries and brilliance are lost to you and men will never find them in you again!

"For your merchants were the great ones of the earth, and all nations were seduced by your witchery!"

* Verse 14 has been incorporated with verse 23, which seems to be its natural place.

For in her was discovered the blood of prophets and saints, indeed the blood of all who were ever slaughtered upon the earth.

CHAPTER 19

Rejoicing in Heaven

AFTERWARDS I heard what sounded like the mighty roar of a vast crowd in Heaven, crying,

"Alleluia! Salvation and glory and power belong to our God, for his judgments are true and just. He has judged the great harlot who corrupted the earth with her wickedness, and he has avenged upon her the blood of his servants!"

Then they cried a second time,

"Alleluia! The smoke of her destruction ascends for timeless ages!"

Then the twenty-four elders and the four living creatures prostrated themselves and worshipped God who is seated upon the throne, saying,

"Amen, alleluia!"

Then out of the throne came a voice, saying,

"Praise our God, all you who serve him, all you who reverence him, both small and great!"

And then I heard a sound like the voices of a vast crowd, the roar of a great waterfall and the rolling of heavy thunder, and they were saying,

"Alleluia! For the Lord our God, the Almighty, has come into his kingdom! Let us rejoice, let us be glad with all our hearts. Let us give him the glory, for the wedding-day of the Lamb has come, and his bride has made herself ready. She may be seen dressed in linen, gleaming and spotless—for such linen is the righteous living of the saints!"

Instruction to John

Then he said to me,

"Write this down: Happy are those who are invited to the wedding-feast of the Lamb!"

Then he added,

"These are true words of God."

At that I fell at his feet to worship him, but he said to me,

"No! I am your fellow-servant and fellow-servant with your brothers who are holding fast their witness to Jesus. Give your worship to God!"

(This witness to Jesus inspires all prophecy.)

The Word of God on the white horse

Then I saw Heaven wide open, and before my eyes appeared a white horse, whose rider is called faithful and true, for his judgment and his warfare are just. His eyes are a flame of fire and there are many diadems upon his head. There is a name written upon him, known only to himself. He is dressed in a cloak dipped in blood, and the name by which he is known is the Word of God.

The armies of Heaven follow him, riding upon white horses and clad in white and spotless linen. Out of his mouth there comes a sharp sword with which to strike the nations. He will shepherd them "with a rod of iron", and alone he will tread the winepress of the furious wrath of God the Almighty. Written upon his cloak and upon his thigh is the name, KING OF KINGS AND LORD OF LORDS.

The feast of death after battle

Then I saw an angel standing alone in the blazing light of the sun, and he shouted in a loud voice, calling to all the birds flying in mid-air,

"Come, flock together to God's great feast! Here you may eat the flesh of kings and captains, the flesh of strong men, of horses and their riders—the flesh of all men, free men and slaves, small and great!"

And I saw the animal with the kings of the earth and their armies massed together for battle against the rider upon the horse and his army. The animal was captured and with it the false prophet who had performed marvels in its presence, which he had used to deceive those who accepted the mark of the animal and worshipped its statue. These two were thrown alive into the lake of fire which burns with sulphur.

The rest were killed by the sword which issues from the mouth of the rider upon the horse; and all the birds gorged themselves on their flesh.

CHAPTER 20

Satan bound for a thousand years

THEN I saw an angel coming down from Heaven with the key of the pit and a huge chain in his hand. He seized the dragon, the serpent of ancient days, who is both the devil and Satan, and bound him fast for a thousand years. Then he hurled him into the pit, and locked and sealed it over his head, so that he could deceive the nations no more until the thousand years were past. But then he must be set free for a little while.

The first resurrection

And I saw thrones, with appointed judges seated upon them. Then I saw the souls of those who had been executed for their witness to Jesus and for proclaiming the Word of God—those who never worshipped the animal or its statue, and had not accepted its mark upon their foreheads or their hands. They came to life and reigned with Christ for a thousand years. (The rest of the dead did not come to life until the thousand years were over.) This is the first resurrection. Happy and holy is the one who shares in the first resurrection! The second death cannot touch such men; they shall be priests of God and of Christ, and shall reign with him for the thousand years.

Satan finally destroyed

Then, when the thousand years are over, Satan will be released from his prison, and will set out to deceive the nations in the four corners of the earth, Gog and Magog, and to lead them into battle. They will be as numerous as the sand of the seashore.

They came up and spread over the breadth of the earth; they encircled the army of the saints defending the beloved city. But fire came down from the sky and consumed them. The devil who deceived them was hurled into the lake of fire and sulphur to join the animal and the false prophet. And there they shall be tortured day and night for timeless ages.

The final judgment

And then I saw a great white throne, and One seated upon it from whose presence both earth and sky fled and vanished.

Then I saw the dead, great and small, standing before the throne and the books were opened. And another book was opened, which is the book of life. And the dead were judged by what was written in the books concerning what they had done. The sea gave up its dead, and death and the grave gave up the dead which were in them. And men were judged, each according to what he had done.

Then death and the grave were themselves hurled into the lake of fire, which is the second death. If anyone's name was not found written in the book of life he was thrown into the lake of fire.

CHAPTER 21

All things made new

THEN I saw a new Heaven and a new earth, for the first Heaven and the first earth had disappeared and the sea was no more. I saw the holy city, the new Jerusalem, descending from God out of Heaven, prepared as a bride dressed in beauty for her husband. Then I heard a great voice from the throne crying,

"See! The home of God is with men, and he will live among them. They shall be his people, and God himself shall be with them, and will wipe away every tear from their eyes. Death shall be no more, and never again shall there be sorrow or crying or pain. For all those former things are past and gone."

Then he who is seated upon the throne said,

"See, I am making all things new!"

And he added,

"Write this down for my words are true and to be trusted."

Then he said to me,

"It is done! I am Alpha and Omega, the beginning and the end. I will give to the thirsty water without price from the fountain of life. The victorious shall inherit these things, and I will be God to him and he will be son to me. But as for the cowards, the faithless and the corrupt, the murderers, the traffickers in sex and sorcery, the worshippers of idols and all liars—their inheritance is in the lake which burns with fire and sulphur, which is the second death."

The vision of the new Jerusalem

Then one of the seven angels who hold the seven bowls which were filled with the seven last plagues, came to me and said,

"Come, and I will show you the bride, the wife of the Lamb."
Then he carried me away in spirit to the top of a vast mountain, and pointed out to me the city, the holy Jerusalem, descending from God out of Heaven, radiant with the glory of God. Her brilliance sparkled like a very precious jewel with the clear light of crystal. Around her she had a vast and lofty wall in which were twelve gateways with twelve angels at the gates. There were twelve names inscribed over the twelve gateways, and they are the names of the twelve tribes of the sons of Israel. On the east there were three gateways, on the north three gateways, on the south three gateways and on the west three gateways. The wall of the city had twelve foundation-stones, and on these were the names of the twelve apostles of the Lamb.

The measurement of the city

The one who was talking to me had a golden rod in his hand with which to measure the city, its gateways and its wall. The city lies foursquare, its length equal to its breadth. He measured the city with his rod and it was twelve thousand furlongs in each direction, for its length, breadth and height are all equal. Then he measured its wall, and found that to be one hundred and forty-four half-yards high by human measurement, (which the angel was using).

The splendour of the city's building

The wall itself was built of translucent stone, while the city was of purest gold, with the brilliance of glass. The foundation stones of the wall of the city were fashioned out of every kind of precious stone. The first foundation-stone was jasper, the second sapphire, the third chalcedony, the fourth emerald, the fifth onyx, the sixth cornelian, the seventh goldstone, the eighth beryl, the ninth topaz, the tenth green goldstone, the eleventh turquoise, and the twelfth amethyst. The twelve gates were twelve pearls, each gate made of a single pearl. The street of the city was purest gold gleaming like glass.

The splendour within the city

I could see no Sanctuary in the city, for the Lord, the Almighty God, and the Lamb are themselves its Sanctuary. The city has no need for the light of sun or moon, for the splendour of God fills it with light and its radiance is the Lamb. The nations will walk by its light, and the kings of the earth will bring their glory into it. The city's gates shall stand open day after day—and there will be no night there. Into the city they will bring the splendours and honours of the nations.

But nothing unclean, no one who deals in filthiness and lies, shall ever at any time enter it—only those whose names are written in the Lamb's book of life.

CHAPTER 22

A further glimpse of the city

THEN he showed me the river of the water of life, sparkling like crystal as it flowed from the throne of God and of the Lamb. In the middle of the street of the city and on either bank of the river grew the tree of life, bearing twelve fruits, a different kind for each month. The leaves of the tree were for the healing of the nations.

Nothing that has cursed mankind shall exist any longer; the throne of God and of the Lamb shall be within the city. His servants shall worship him; they shall see his face, and his name will be upon their foreheads. Night shall be no more; they have no more need for either lamplight or sunlight, for the Lord God will shed his light upon them and they shall reign as kings for timeless ages.

The angel endorses the revelation

Then the angel said to me,

"These words are true and to be trusted, for the Lord God, who inspired the prophets, has sent his angel to show his servants what must shortly happen."

"See, I come quickly! Happy is the man who pays heed to the words of the prophecy in this book."

John's personal endorsement

It is I, John, who have heard and seen these things. At the time when I heard and saw them I fell at the feet of the angel who showed them to me and I was about to worship him. But he said to me,

"No! I am fellow-servant to you and to your brothers, to the prophets and to those who keep the words of this book. Give your worship to God!"

Then he added,

"Do not seal up the words of the prophecy in this book, for the time of their fulfilment is near. Let the wicked man continue in his wickedness and the filthy man in his filthiness; let the good man continue his good deeds, and the holy man continue in holiness."

The interjected words of Christ

"See, I come quickly! I carry my reward with me, and repay every man according to his deeds. I am Alpha and Omega, the first and the last, the Beginning and the End. Happy are those who wash their robes, for they have the right to the tree of life and the freedom of the gates of the city. Shut out from the city shall be the depraved, the sorcerers, the impure, the murderers and the idolaters, and everyone who loves and practises a lie!

"I, Jesus, have sent my angel to you with this testimony for the Churches. I am both the root and stock of David, and the bright star of the morning!"

The invitation of the Church and the Spirit

The Spirit and the bride say, "Come!"

Let everyone who hears this also say, "Come!"

Let the thirsty man come, and let everyone who wishes take the water of life as a gift.

John's testimony to this book

Now I bear solemn witness to every man who hears the words of prophecy in this book:

If anyone adds to these words God will add to him the disasters described in this book; if anyone takes away from the words of prophecy in this book, God will take away from him his share in the tree of life and in the holy city which are described in this book.

He, who is witness to all this, says,

"Yes, I am coming very quickly!"

"Amen, come, Lord Jesus!"

The grace of the Lord Jesus be with all his people.

Notes

Note 1.

"Scribes."

There is no modern English word by which "scribes" can be fairly translated. It is therefore necessary to explain that the "scribes" of the Gospels were the interpreters of the Divine Law (or Torah), for the people of Israel. The Torah was a kind of textbook for both the religious and civil functions of the community. Since in process of time this had become a highly complex matter, the scribes had to be expert both in knowledge, interpretation and administration. Consequently their position was one of considerable authority and, though there were doubtless noble exceptions, they tended to become both legalist and theological in outlook, and were therefore unprepared to accept the revolutionary teaching of Jesus.

"Pharisees."

The Pharisees were a class of zealous Jews whose chief characteristic lay in their separation from the heathen and from all that they considered evil. They were the Puritans of their day, and emphasised the spiritual rather than the nationalistic side of Judaism. We might fairly say that they were Churchmen rather than statesmen. And, again, though there were good men among them, they tended to concentrate upon rigid outward observances, to the exclusion of human sympathy and understanding. It was this tendency, and the conviction that they alone were right, which brought them into conflict with Jesus.

"Sadducees."

The Sadducees represented the aristocratic conservative element in the Jewish priesthood. Their conservatism, with its desire to maintain things as they were, led them to compromise politically with the Roman occupying power, and thus their moral authority became weakened. Moreover, in clinging to the tenets of the past, they failed to develop in their religion and did not, for example, believe, as the Pharisees did, in the coming Kingdom of God, and only in a very shadowy way did they believe in the immortality of the human soul.

Note 2.

Matthew 5, *22*—Raca.

"Raca" means a fool or empty-headed fellow, but the Greek word used in the previous sentence means much the same thing.

If however it is, as some suggest, a transliteration of the Hebrew "moreh", then we have a further stage of uncharitable condemnation, for this word means "a persistent rebel against God", and thus makes much better sense.

Note 3.

Matthew 16, *19* and 18, *18*—"forbidding" and "permitting".

There is a very curious Greek construction here, viz. a simple future followed by the perfect participle passive. If Jesus had meant to say quite simply, "Whatever you forbid on earth will be forbidden in Heaven", can anyone explain why the simple future passive is not used? It seems to me that if the words of Jesus are accurately reported here, and I have no reason to doubt it, then the force of these sayings is that Jesus' true disciples will be so led by the Spirit that they will be following the heavenly pattern. In other words what they "forbid" or "permit" on earth will be consonant with the Divine rules.

If a simple future passive had been used it would mean an automatic heavenly endorsement of the Church's actions, which to me, at least, is a very different thing.

In the pertinent verses of John's Gospel (chapter 20, *22*, *23*), it is quite plain that "holy spirit", of which Christ is giving his disciples a first breath, so to speak, (for the Holy Spirit in person was not given until Pentecost), would be the factor by which alone human beings could perform the Divine function of forgiving or not forgiving sins. There is again no ground for supposing that celestial endorsement automatically follows human action, however exalted.

Note 4.

John 7, *53* to 8, *11*—The Woman taken in Adultery.

This passage has no place in the oldest manuscripts of John, and is considered by most scholars to be an interpolation from some other source. Almost all scholars would agree that, although the story is out of place here, it is part of a genuine apostolic tradition.

Note 5.

1 Corinthians 14, *22*

This is the sole instance of the translator's departing from the accepted text. He felt bound to conclude, from the sense of the next three verses, that we have here either a slip of the pen on the part of Paul, or, more probably, a copyist's error.

SHORT INDEX OF NAMES, PLACES AND EVENTS

NOTE: *This index is in no sense a substitute for a New Testament concordance. It is simply designed to help the reader to find quickly a significant incident, a person who plays some part in the New Testament story, or a place which is important because of events which happened there. In addition this index will make it easy to find the many parables of Jesus, for example, or the passages which refer to the journeys of St. Paul.*

It is obvious that some words such as "God", "Christ", "Law", as well as the proper names of some important people and places, occur too frequently for inclusion in a simple index. Such words are therefore omitted altogether.

The New Testament student who wants to make a detailed study of particular themes or the growth of certain doctrines will find himself bound to consult a comprehensive concordance.

J. B. P.

INDEX